LOS ANGELES

Thirteenth Edition © 2008 by **ACCESS**®Press. All rights reserved. No portion of this publication may be reproduced or transmitted in any form or manner by any means, including, but not limited to, graphic, electronic, and mechanical methods, photocopying, recording, taping, or any informational storage and retrieval systems without explicit permiss from the publisher. **AC** is a registered tradema HarperCollins Publishe

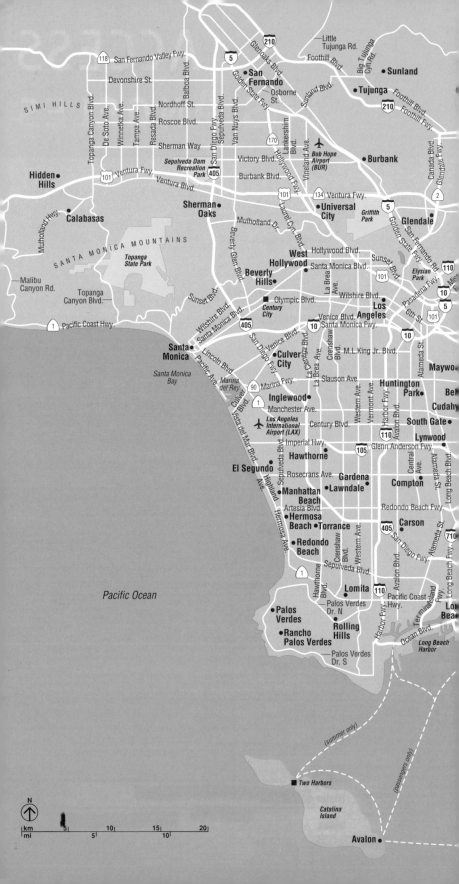

Welcome to LA!

Los Angeles is a peerless puzzle. From fashion to food, it dons a unique style defined mostly by whims. There's a youthful, energetic spirit and a no-rules attitude. It's okay to wear white after Labor Day. Flip-flops are acceptable footwear just about anywhere. You're cool if you're pierced, tattooed, hip, and under 25. This is a mythical city where big breaks happen every day—a fairy-tale metropolis of dreams, schemes, and fortunes, where hordes of wannabe stars flock by plane, train, and bus hoping to someday see their names in the proverbial "lights." Fueled by pie-in-the-sky optimism, they act out their life stories like ideas for screenplays scribbled by aspiring writers on cocktail napkins. But of course, not everybody who comes to LA wants to be in pictures—many just hope to get a shot on a TV game show, and others are simply chasing their own versions of the American Dream.

Los Angeles is a city where anything can happen—and almost everything does, from the sublime to the ridiculous and the tragic. In this picture-postcard setting, snow dusts the mountaintops while sandy-haired, suntanned surfers battle the waves just a few miles away. It is here youngsters can take fantasy trips through some of the most technically advanced theme parks, such as amusement parks **Disneyland Resort** (in neighboring Anaheim), **Universal City, Knott's Berry Farm,** and **Magic Mountain.** It's where TV game-show contestants spin wheels for fortunes, try to become survivors, idols, or rock stars, or smarter than a fifth grader. This is a town fixated by devastating earthquakes, riots, and world-famous murders, and mishaps. But it's also one that weathers all storms with flying colors and continues to enchant, entertain, and endure.

Part movie and entertainment capital, part social experiment, LA is a vast megalopolis where infinite lifestyles and cultures converge in a kaleidoscope of head-spinning contrasts. From cutting-edge architecture like the **Walt Disney Concert Hall** to warm sandy beaches, LA delivers. Contrary to what's normally considered a "city," Los Angeles is actually composed of nine distinct areas or neighborhoods—downtown LA, midtown LA, Hollywood, West Hollywood, Beverly Hills, West LA, Bel Air, Brentwood, and Santa Monica. To sample this City of Angels, cruise the storied boulevards—**Wilshire, Sunset, Santa Monica,** and **Olympic**—that snake like tributaries to the **Pacific Ocean** and its legendary beaches. Heading west on Olympic, stop for crab soup in **Koreatown,** and spy the Beverly Hills High School's oil rig as you approach the striking twin towers of **Century City.** On Sunset, pull over for a drink at the **Sky Bar** at Mondrian, the **Key Club,** or the Art Deco **Tower** hotel, check out the scene at comedian Dan Aykroyd's **House of Blues** nightclub, pick up a movie-star map for a tour of the estates of the rich and famous, or turn off at **Will Rogers State Historic Park** to tour the Rogers home and hike the chaparral-covered hills. You can also ponder the beasts of millennia past at the **La Brea Tar Pits** along Wilshire, browse through the **Los Angeles County Museum of Art's** gallery of German Expressionism, or inspect the latest in haute couture at the exclusive boutiques on **Rodeo Drive** in Beverly Hills. Head over to Santa Monica, where life's a beach by day and a playground by night. Pedal, rollerblade, or skate along the strand, but don't miss a stroll on the pier or the **Third Street Promenade,** with its movie theaters, trendy restaurants, and bookstores.

Los Angeles boasts a thriving restaurant scene that has turned the area into a gastronomic delight as exciting new eateries blaze a culinary trail from downtown LA and beyond. For starters, there's **Patina** at the Walt Disney Concert Hall catering to the theater crowd, **A.O.C., Spago Beverly Hills, Wolfgang Puck's Cut, Wilshire Restaurant, The Penthouse** at the Huntley Hotel in Santa Monica, **The Dive!, Eleven, Privilege,** the **Bar at the Four Seasons Beverly Hills,** the **Bar at the Peninsula Hotel** Beverly Hills, **Dakota, boe, Tower Bar, Luna Park, Falcon,** and **OPUS**— where most of the action is over trendy drinks at the bar. You'll find them all ranked and listed in this guide. Dining in LA has never been this delicious, and it's only just begun. The emergence of a pulsating after-hours club scene has sculpted LA into a lean-and-mean metropolis. No one can ever kick sand in its face again. (And they know whom we're talking about.)

Of course you still have to tackle LA's notoriously congested freeway system with its unending on-ramps and 528 miles of clogged tarmac. But burning fuel

How To Read This Guide

ACCESS® LOS ANGELES is arranged so you can see at a glance where you are and what is around you. The numbers next to the entries in the following chapters correspond to the numbers on the maps.

The text is color-coded according to the kind of place described:

Restaurants/Clubs: Red

Hotels: Purple | Shops: Orange

⊕ Parks/Outdoors: Green | Sights/Culture: Blue

WHEELCHAIR ACCESSIBILITY

An establishment (except a restaurant) is considered wheelchair accessible when a person in a wheelchair can easily enter a building (i.e., no steps, a ramp, a wide-enough door) without assistance. Restaurants are deemed wheelchair accessible *only* if the above applies, *and* if the rest rooms are on the same floor as the dining area and their entrances and stalls are wide enough to accommodate a wheelchair.

RATING THE RESTAURANTS AND HOTELS

The restaurant star ratings take into account the quality, service, atmosphere, and uniqueness of the restaurant. An expensive restaurant doesn't necessarily ensure an enjoyable evening; a small, relatively unknown spot could have good food, professional service, and a lovely atmosphere. Therefore, on a purely subjective basis, stars are used to judge the overall dining value (see the star ratings at right). Keep in mind that chefs and owners often change, which sometimes drastically affects the quality of a restaurant, and menus often change at the tip of a chef's toque. Our ratings are based on information available at press time.

The price ratings, as categorized below, apply to restaurants and hotels. These figures describe general price-range relationships among other restaurants and hotels in the area. The restaurant price ratings are based on the average cost of dinner for one person, excluding tax and tip. Hotel price ratings reflect the base price of a standard room for two people for one night during the peak season.

RESTAURANTS

★	Good
★★	Very Good
★★★	Excellent
★★★★	An Extraordinary Experience
$	The Price Is Right (less than $35)
$$	Reasonable ($40–$70)
$$$	Expensive ($75–$100)
$$$$	Big Bucks ($105 and up)

HOTELS

$	The Price Is Right (less than $125)
$$	Reasonable ($130–$248)
$$$	Expensive ($250–$495)
$$$$	Big Bucks ($500 and up)

MAP KEY

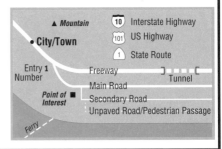

▲ Mountain	🔟 Interstate Highway
● City/Town	🔟1 US Highway
	① State Route
Entry 1 Number	Freeway Tunnel
	Main Road
Point of ■ Interest	Secondary Road
	Unpaved Road/Pedestrian Passage
Ferry	

personifies the Southern California experience, so when you're ready to venture beyond the city limits, fill up your tank, grab a road map, and buckle up for a fascinating tour of the most motorized region in the world. Drive north up the coastal highway and sink your feet into the gilt-edged sands of **Malibu**, home of the rich and beautiful. Or, for a complete contrast to such a privileged lifestyle, head back south to **Venice Beach** with its New Age hippies, bikini-clad roller skaters, well-oiled bodybuilders, and chain-saw jugglers who spend their days by the sea. Wherever you go, you'll enjoy ideal weather (it's practically perfect year-round) and a few surprises along the way.

As you read through this guide you'll notice some major trends and changes. Most notably, many major hotels now boast noteworthy restaurants manned by celebrity chefs, super spas poised to pamper, de-stress, de-tox, and max out your credit card, and youth-obsessed amenities. It's urban renewal gone wild between Hollywood and downtown Los Angeles. Head over to **Long Beach**, which has blossomed into a major player on the tourist front. And for you Internet junkies, Wi-Fi hookups are available on nearly every street corner (along with Starbucks). Okay, now sit back and read about all the nifty things available in and around this wild and wacky town. Just remember things happen.

Getting to Los Angeles

Airports

Los Angeles International Airport (LAX)

The principal hub of the Western Pacific Rim, the world's fifth-busiest airport hosts more than 100 air carriers in 10 terminals, each equipped with hotel/motel information boards, restaurants, cafeterias, snack bars, cocktail lounges, newsstands, rest rooms, gift shops, and lockers. LAX also greets more than 65 million travelers a year. The central complex houses eight terminals (including the five-level, million-square-foot **Tom Bradley International Terminal**) around the perimeter of a two-level loop, which encircles parking, a restaurant, heliport, and control tower. Airlines frequently change terminals; call 310/646.5252 for up-to-date information. You can also get information at www.Lawa.org.

The **Imperial Terminal,** just south of the central complex, handles charter flights and supplemental carriers. A free bus connects with the main terminal every half-hour until 12:30AM. Catch the bus from the center island at each baggage-claim area.

In each terminal, departures, ticketing, and check-in are on the upper level, and arrivals, baggage claim, car-rental booths, hotel information desks, and ground transportation are on the lower level. Blue, green, and white **Airline Connections** shuttles link each terminal at both levels, and buses take passengers to satellite parking lots.

Handicapped Connections is a free minibus with extra-wide doors and a ramp for wheelchairs. For additional airport information, pick up the yellow courtesy telephones inside the terminal to contact the **Airport Information Aides.**

AIRPORT SERVICES

Airport Police	310/646.6253
Business Service Centers are in all terminals.	
Currency Exchange	310/417.0366
Customs and Immigration	310/215.2414
First Aid Station	310/215.6000
Ground Transportation	310/646.5252
Information	310/646.5252
Interpreters	See information desk at Tom Bradley International Terminal.
Lost and Found	310/417.0440
Parking	310/646.2911, 310/646.5252
Traveler's Aid	310/646.2270
TSA	310/655.7382
Wheelchair/Disabled Services	310/646.5252

AIRLINES

Air New Zealand	800/237.6639, www.airnewzealand.co.nz
Alaska	800/426.0333, www.alaskaair.com
Aloha Airlines	800/367.5250, www.alohaairlines.com
American	800/433.7300, www.aa.com
Continental	800/525.0280, www.continental.com
Delta	800/221.1212, www.delta-air.com
Hawaiian Air	800/367.5320, www.hawaiianair.com
Jet Blue	800/538.2583, www.jetblue.com
Mexicana Airlines	800/531.7921, www.mexicana.com
Northwest	800/447.4747, www.nwa.com

Singapore Airlines ....800/741.3333, ...www.singaporeair.com

Southwest..................800/241.6522, www.flyswa.com

United..............................800/241.6522, www.ual.com

USAirways...............800/428.4322, www.usairways.com

Virgin America...877/FLY.VIRGIN, www.virginamerica.com

Getting to and from LAX

By Bus

To help travelers avoid the hassle of driving and parking, door-to-door shuttles offer 24-hour service from the airports to most Los Angeles area destinations. A bewildering array of buses and vans circle the airport loop, stopping at the center island outside each baggage-claim area. Be sure to stand at the correct pickup site. One of the most popular services is **Super Shuttle,** whose bright-blue vans offer door-to-door service from LAX to most destinations in Los Angeles and Orange Counties, including the other major airports. Prices vary, depending on your destination. For pickup at the airport, go outside your terminal to the designated stop or call 310/222.5500 after you have collected your baggage; for service from your home or hotel, call 800/554.3146 24 hours in advance. For more information, check out www.supershuttle.com. Other shuttle services include **Xpress Shuttle** (800/427.7483, www.expressshuttle.com), **All-American Shuttle** (310/641.4090), **Best Shuttle** (310/670.7080), and **Prime Time** (800/733.8267).

In addition, regular public bus service links many parts of town with the bus terminal at **Lot C.** A free connector bus stops at each of the airline terminals every 10 to 20 minutes, 24 hours a day.

By Car

The easiest way to reach downtown Los Angeles from the airport is to take **Century Blvd** east to the **Harbor Fwy (I-110)** north. To get to LAX from downtown Los Angeles, take the **Santa Monica Fwy (I-10)** west to the **San Diego Fwy (I-405)** south and exit at either **La Tijera** or Century Blvd. Alternatively, take the Harbor Freeway (I-110) south to the **Glenn M. Anderson Fwy (I-105)** west, which will funnel drivers into LAX, connecting the 605, 710, 110, and 405 Fwys between Norwalk to the east and the airport. In light traffic, the trip from LAX to downtown can be made in about 20 minutes, but always allow at least an hour.

Rental Cars

More than 30 national and local car-rental agencies are located at and around LAX, and all major hotels have car-rental counters. Options run the gamut—everything from your basic Ford to a Rolls-Royce, Ferrari, or a classic two-seater T-Bird. Weekly (a minimum of five days) or three-day weekend rates are usually the best deals, but you should always shop around. Contact the following major companies for their current rates:

Alamo..........................800/327.9633, www.alamo.com

Avis .... 800/331.1212, www.avis.com

Budget....................... 800/527.0700, 800/221.1203, ...www.drivebudget.com

Dollar.........................800/800.0044, www.dollar.com

Enterprise .... 800/RENT-a-CAR, www.enterprise.com

Hertz.............................800/654.3131, www.hertz.com

National................800/CAR-RENT, www.nationalcar.com

Thrifty............................310/645.1880, www.thrifty.com

Or, for the extremely budget-conscious:

Bob Leech's Auto Rental–LAX .... 800/635.1240, ... www.bnm.com

Rent-a-Wreck... 800/535.1391, ... www.rent-a-wreck.com

And, for the extremely status-conscious:

Beverly Hills Rent a Car......................... 310/337.1400, ...800/479.5996, www.bhrentacar.com

Budget Rent A Car Beverly Hills .... 310/821.1700, ...800/729.7350, www.budgetbeverlyhills.com

Airport Parking

Short-term parking options include the seven **Central Terminal** lots and the **West Imperial Terminal** lot (a total of 8,309 spaces). Rates are reasonable, but these lots are often full on holidays and during peak periods. Metered parking is available throughout the airport (for a two-hour maximum). Long-term and short-term parking is available at two major satellite lots (16,400 spaces): **Lot C** (at Sepulveda Blvd and 96th St) and **Lot B** (at La Cienega Blvd and 111th St). Both of these lots have 24-hour bus service running every 10 to 20 minutes to each of the eight terminals. For greater convenience (but higher cost), leave your car at one of the privately owned lots scattered around the airport such as **The Parking Spot,** a one-of-a-kind facility that caters to commuters with covered parking, courteous shuttle drivers who load and unload your bags, and valet or self-parking, and even throws in a bottle of water, a newspaper, and emergency battery service when needed. Probably the best bang for your buck, at two convenient locations: 5701 W Century Blvd (between Bellanca and Airport Blvds), 800/745.2276; 9101 Sepulveda Blvd (at 92nd St), 866/826.2509. www.TheParkingSpot.com. For more information about airport parking, call 310/646.2911 or 310/646.5252. E-mail: infoline@airports.ci.la.ca.us.

By Limousine

Thanks to astronomical gas prices, limo service between LAX and downtown now runs between $155 and $170 (not including tip), depending on the size of the car. Limousine companies include **Axis Limousine** (800/378.7873), **DAV EL** (800/922.0343, www.davel.com), **elimos** (310/559.5164, www.elimos.com), **Fantasy Limousine** (888/424.8488), and **Mercedes Limousine** (310/271.8559, www.mlslimo.com).

By Taxi

Believe it or not, it is unlawful in LA to hail a cab. At airports, taxis wait for passengers at the authorized ranks located outside each terminal; the fare to downtown averages about $45 and up (plus tip). Outside airports cabs can be found at various designated areas and within whistling distance (by valets only) at hotel entrances.

For other ground-transportation services, check with the ticket/information booths on the sidewalk outside each baggage-claim area.

Other Airports Serving Southern California

Bob Hope Airport .... 818/840.8847, ...www.burbankairport.com

John Wayne Airport............................... 949/252.5200, ... www.ocair.com

Long Beach Municipal Airport............... 562/570.2640, ...800/U-FLY-LGB, www.lgb.org

Ontario International Airport.................. 909/937.2700, ... www.lawa.org

Santa Monica Municipal Airport (small aircraft only)....... ....310/390.7606

Getting Around Los Angeles

BICYCLES

Los Angeles County has more than 200 miles of bicycle trails. The most popular is the **South Bay Bicycle Trail,** which runs along 18 miles of shoreline from Santa Monica to Torrance Beach. Long Beach's three-mile **Oceanside Bike Path** offers a picturesque ride from Shoreline Village to Belmont Shore. The **San Gabriel River Trail** follows a 37-mile course from Santa Fe Dam in Azusa to Shoreline Village. And the eight-mile **Griffith Park Trail** takes in the Los Angeles Zoo, Travel Town, and the Autry Western Heritage Museum.

BOATS

You can charter a boat for **whale watching,** cruising to **Catalina Island,** or **fishing** for barracuda; boats depart from **Long Beach** and **San Pedro Harbors.**

There are a variety of **brunch and dinner tours of Los Angeles Harbor** from Seaport Village in Long Beach (for information, call **Spirit Cruises** at 562/495.5884). **Fishing charters** usually leave at 7AM, but check with the tour operator for specific departure time. A nonstop trip to Catalina takes about an hour, and a more leisurely trip lasts twice as long.

For more information, contact the following companies:

Belmont Pier Sportfishing...................... 310/434.6781

Catalina Express .... 800/429.4601, ...www.catalinaexpress.com

Fantasea Yachts ....310/827.2220, ...www.fantaseayachts.com

The Gondola Getaway............................ 310/433.9595

Hornblower Dining Yachts 800/950.1920

Spirit Cruises and Yacht Parties 562/495.5884

BUSES

Even some locals don't know this, but public transportation *does* exist in Los Angeles. More than 1.3 million people commute on public buses and subway lines daily. The **Metro** operates 208 bus routes in the greater metropolitan area. The fare is $1.35 and each transfer is 25 cents; senior fares are half-price; day passes are $13. From **Spring Street** downtown, bus No. 27 takes you nonstop into **Century City,** and bus No. 439 will take you direct to **LAX,** as well as to **Manhattan, Hermosa,** and **Redondo Beaches.** For trips to and from the beaches along **Santa Monica's coast,** take bus No. 20 on Wilshire Blvd or bus No. 4 on Santa Monica Blvd. Both buses provide 24-hour service (213/626.4455). To obtain a copy of the Metro's *Self-Guided Tours* publication, write to Metro, 1 Gateway Plaza, Los Angeles, CA 90012. Municipal bus information is available through each city's chamber of commerce, www.metro.net.

DASH

The Downtown Area Short Hop (DASH) operates 50 clean-fuel minibuses that shuttle between various spots in the Los Angeles area, including **downtown, Crenshaw, Pacific Palisades, Watts, Fairfax, Hollywood, southeast LA, Van Nuys/Studio City,** and **Warner Center**. There are three special DASH weekend routes: **Shoppers Paradise, Expo Direct,** and **Downtown Discovery.** Buses run every 15 minutes from 10AM to 5PM; call 800/COMMUTE or 213/580.5444. The fare's a mere 25 cents.

DRIVING

If you haven't heard already, you'll quickly learn that the traffic in LA is *always* unpredictable. **So always allow plenty of time to get anywhere in LA.** Tune in to local radio stations in the morning and late afternoon for minute-by-minute traffic reports. The state transportation department often publishes schedules of upcoming road construction in local newspapers, or you can call 213/628.7623 for information on highway conditions. Driving in downtown LA is a particular headache, thanks to the confusing one-way street system and expensive parking. Opt for walking or taking the DASH shuttle.

Distances

From downtown Los Angeles to:

Anaheim (Disneyland)..26 miles

Beverly Hills .... 10 miles

Big Bear Lake ....100 miles

Bob Hope Airport .... 13 miles

Griffith Park.. 6 miles

Hollywood .... 6 miles

Los Angeles International Airport .... 17 miles

Pasadena .... 9 miles

Santa Clarita (Six Flags Magic Mountain)..........30 miles

Santa Monica .... 15 miles

Universal City (Universal Studios)........................ 9 miles

Venice Beach.. 16 miles

Travel time varies widely depending on traffic.

Freeways

#	Name(s)
2	Glendale Freeway
5	Santa Ana Freeway/Golden State Freeway
10	Santa Monica Freeway/San Bernardino Freeway
22	Garden Grove Freeway
55	Costa Mesa Freeway
57	Orange Freeway
60	Pomona Freeway
90	Marina Freeway
91	Artesia Freeway/Riverside Freeway
101	Ventura Freeway/Hollywood Freeway
105	Glenn M. Anderson Freeway
110	Pasadena Freeway/Harbor Freeway
118	Simi Valley–San Fernando Valley Freeway
210	Foothill Freeway
405	San Diego Freeway
605	San Gabriel River Freeway
710	Long Beach Freeway

METRO RAIL

The **Metro Rail system** (213/626.4455; 800/COMMUTE, www.metro.net) includes a light rail line, commuter trains, and even a subway. The **Red Line,** the city's only underground rail, runs from Union Station in downtown LA to Wilshire Boulevard and Vermont, Hollywood and Western, Highland, Universal City, and North Hollywood. The **Blue Line** travels between downtown and Long Beach, and the **Green Line** runs from Norwalk to Redondo Beach, connecting to the Blue Line at the Rosa Parks (Imperial/Wilmington) Station. The Blue Line also connects to the Red Line at the Seventh St/Metro Center Station in downtown Los Angeles. The **Gold Line** links Pasadena to downtown Los Angeles. The 13.7-mile train ride starts in Sierra Madre with stops at Old Pasadena, the Southwest Museum, and Chinatown. www.la.pasblueline.org.

TAXIS

You can find taxis in front of hotels and at **LAX, Union Station,** and other major ports of entry. In addition, downtown LA offers an inexpensive option of getting around with its **One Fare Zone,** which reaches to the 110 Fwy to the west, Main Street to the east, the Convention Center to the south, and the Hollywood Fwy to the north. Wait at the One Fare Zone taxi stand. You also can call one of these major companies for a ride: **Independent Taxi Company** (323/666.0040, 800/521.8294), **LA Taxi** (310/715.1968), **United Independent Taxi Drivers, Inc.** (323/462.1088), and **Yellow Cab Company** (888/793.5569).

TRAINS

Thousands of passengers arrive daily in Los Angeles via the historic **Union Station** depot (800 N Alameda St, between the Santa Ana Fwy and E Macy St), an elegant hybrid of Art Deco and Spanish Mission architectural traditions, located downtown. **Amtrak** provides frequent service from LA to San Diego on its Pacific Surfliner—eight sleek double-decker trains fitted with special business-class compartments, stopping in several cities along the way. Great **day trips by rail** are the coastal routes to Santa Barbara, San Luis Obispo, San Francisco, **San Juan Capistrano,** and the **Del Mar Racetrack.** The best way to ride is in Pacific Business class, where reclinable seats are equipped with laptop outlets, footrests, and audio/video devices. You get a free newspaper, soft drinks, wine (at special times), and snacks. There's also service to **Disneyland** in Anaheim. For information and reservations, call 800/872.7245, 800/USA-RAIL, or go online at www.amtrak.com.

FYI

ACCOMMODATIONS

It is not uncommon to check into an LA hotel and discover that the person checking in alongside you is a movie, television, or rock star. Celeb-style hotels will cost you dearly, however—and you'll need to make your reservations well in advance. But don't despair: If you're just looking for someplace to shower and sleep, sans megastars, you'll do well at one of the smaller hotels or motels throughout the area, and you probably won't need an advance reservation unless there's a convention in town. Generally speaking, accommodations are less expensive in the **San Fernando** and **San Gabriel Valleys** than in Hollywood, Beverly Hills, West LA, or downtown. For assistance in getting a room, call the **Los Angeles Convention and Visitors Bureau** hotel hotline (800/CATCH.LA).

CLIMATE

Raincoats are rarely needed in LA: Rain falls an average of only 35 days a year, usually between the months of November and April. Typically, the sun shines 186 days a year in the city and 137 days at the beach. The average temperature is 74 degrees, with summer highs typically in the mid-80s and winter lows in the low 60s. In the desert, winter temperatures hover in the 70s, and summer highs range between 103 and 110 degrees.

MONTHS	AVERAGE TEMPERATURE (°F)
January–March	69-60
April–June	77-59
July–September	83-63
October–December	77-49

HOURS

Opening and closing times for shops and attractions in this book are listed by day(s) only, as long as they open between 8 and 11AM and close between 4 and 7PM. In all other cases, specific hours are given (e.g., 6AM-2PM; daily, 24 hours; noon-5PM, and so forth).

MONEY

Most banks are open Monday through Friday from 9AM to 3 or 6PM and Saturday mornings. If you need to exchange money, check with the major banks. Most banks have Automatic Teller Machines (ATMs), from which you can withdraw cash instantly.

FESTIVALS AND EVENTS

Los Angeles, always abuzz with activity, hosts a wide variety of special events and festivals throughout the year. The following is just a sampler of the many seasonal treats available in and around the city. For up-to-the-minute information, call the **Greater Los Angeles Convention and Visitors Bureau** multilingual events hot line (213/689.8822) or visit the website at www.LACVB.com.

January

What would **New Year's Day** be without the pomp and pageantry of the **Tournament of Roses Parade**? The promenade of floats down Colorado Blvd in Pasadena starts at 8AM, but to get a good view, spectators start arriving in the wee hours of the morning. For a close-up look at the petal-bedecked floats, stop by Victory Park after the parade. Note: Due to the ne w College Football Playoff rules, the annual **Rose Bowl**, which for years has been the eagerly anticipated culmination of the parade festivities on New Year's Day, is subject to change. This showpiece of collegiate football could occur anytime from 1 January to the middle of the month. True football fans will no doubt be aware of the actual game day. Rose Bowl, 626/419.ROSE. www.tournamentofroses.com

Also on 1 January is the annual swim of **Cabrillo Beach Polar Bears**—hale and hearty souls who dive into the cold Pacific Ocean. Spectators may watch or join in the frigid fun. Free.

During the first week of the month, the **Greater LA Auto Show** takes place at the LA Convention Center, with more than 1,000 hot model cars, trucks, vans, SUVs, and futuristic vehicles on exhibit. Admission. 213/741.1151.

Memorabilia collectors will enjoy the **Vintage Poster Fair** at Santa Monica Civic Auditorium, where over 10,000 vintage posters from around the world are offered for sale. Admission. 415/546.9608.

February

Downtown merchants mark the beginning of Lent each year on the day before Ash Wednesday with an exuberant, Mexican-style **Mardi Gras** in historic El Pueblo de Los Angeles Plaza. Visitors are encouraged to wear costumes to enjoy the music, fun, and costume parade down Olvera Street.

The Annual **LA Bach Festival** is still going strong after more than 60 years. The tribute to Johann Sebastian Bach, held at the First Congregational Church (540 S Commonwealth Ave, at W Sixth St), features not only the music of its venerable namesake but also that of Corelli, Vivaldi, and Handel.

LA's Chinatown celebrates its own **Chinese New Year** anywhere from late January to February. The festivities include the colorful Golden Dragon Parade, a carnival, and a firecracker run. 213/617.0396. www.lachinesechamber.org

March

Running mania reaches a fever pitch on the third Sunday in March with the **City of Los Angeles Marathon and Bike Tour.** The event, which attracts top-flight competitors from around the world, starts at Figueroa and Sixth and ends in front of the library on Fifth St. Free. 310/444.5544.

The Oscars, Hollywood's biggest gala of the year, takes place on cue on the last Monday of the month, attracting tourists and lookie-loos who camp out just for the chance to spot their favorite stars. But alas, no more bleachers at the new Kodak Theater in the heart of Hollywood.

April

People gather at El Pueblo de Los Angeles Historic Park on Holy Saturday, the day before Easter, for the **Blessing of the Animals.** The faithful dress up their pets—dogs, cats, birds, even pigs and chickens. Free. 213/896.1700.

Go back in time at the **Renaissance Pleasure Faire,** where foods of ye olde England, battling knights on horseback, medieval games, theater, and country dancing are celebrated at Glen Helen Regional Park near San Bernardino. 800/52.FAIRE. www.renfaire.com

May

The city's Mexican-American population commemorates **Cinco de Mayo** with colorful festivities featuring mariachi music, shows, folkloric dancing, and many other activities. The gala begins on the last Sunday in April with **LA Fiesta Broadway,** a big street party featuring ethnic food stands and international stars of Latin music.

June

For two days, the Hollywood Bowl hosts some of the biggest names in jazz, big band, fusion, and blues for the annual **Playboy Jazz Festival.**

PARKING

Fines for parking illegally can be high, so read all parking signs carefully before you enter into an agreement with the curb. Be particularly cautious in **West Hollywood,** where parking signs are among the most confusing in the country, listing all sorts of regulations and restrictions.

Most meters in high-traffic commercial areas have a one-hour limit. For periods longer than 60 minutes, a parking garage is less painful on the pocketbook than a parking ticket. A **red curb** means no parking, a **green curb** permits parking for 20 minutes, and a **white curb** means loading and unloading only.

Gay and Lesbian Pride Celebration is a gala West Hollywood event that attracts thousands of onlookers, marchers, and participants. There's fun, food, dancing, and more. 323/658.8700.

July

We love a parade! Especially the **Fourth of July** march of people, floats, and bands who attend what some say is the largest of its kind west of the Mississippi. The event is over 100 years old. 714/374.1535. www.surfcity-hb.org

Stock up on breath mints and don't miss the **Garlic Festival** on the grounds of the Federal Building. Dozens of LA's best chefs apply their talents to the aromatic root and create garlic-laced dishes ranging from appetizers to, yes, even desserts.

August

Downtown LA's Little Tokyo pulls out all the stops for its **Nisei Week Japanese Festival.** The celebration of Japanese culture features folk dancing, music, exhibits, carnivals, art shows, and parades.

September

Celebrate the 1781 founding of LA at **Los Angeles's Birthday Party** in El Pueblo de Los Angeles Plaza. Festivities feature live entertainment, games, and a huge birthday cake.

The huge **LA County Fair,** held at the County Fair Grounds in Pomona, features exhibits of some of the most luscious produce in America, plus carnival rides and entertainment ranging from rodeos to big-name concerts.

October

The Annual **Grand Avenue Festival** promotes LA's cultural scene with music, arts, crafts, and food presentations along a four-block area between First and Fourth Sts on Grand Ave. Free. 213/624.2146.

The **International Festival of the Masks** is among the city's more unusual events. The "mask-e-raid" is held in Hancock Park and features more than 40 booths exhibiting (and sometimes selling) beautiful-to-bizarre masks from around the world.

This is also when the gay community of West Hollywood rocks with their **Halloween Carnival** along Santa Monica Blvd. Open to the public regardless of persuasion, the event's a hoot, with booths, comedians, live music, and, as one might imagine, outrageous costumes. More than 400,000 revelers attend this event, and we mean 400,000. Free. 323/848.6547.

ArchiFest II celebrates Los Angeles's diverse style during this month-long celebration that kicks off with an AIA/LA reception and includes an Architours LA Architectural Scavenger Hunt, the Art Deco Society's Cemetery Tour, and more. For info, go to www.cantructionala.com.

November

Día de los Muertos (Day of the Dead), held in El Pueblo de Los Angeles Plaza at the beginning of the month, is a festival unique to Latino culture. It begins with the celebration of life procession, which leads to ornately decorated altars. 213/485.9777. Free.

The **Doo Dah Parade** is Old Pasadena's parody of the Tournament of Roses parade, with more than 1,200 participants marching and stomping their way through the streets. It's a satirical riot with political pundits, midget gospel singers, dogs in drag, a flying toilet dirigible, the Doo Dah Lama, and more. Free. 626/440.7379.

December

As Christmas nears, the city goes up in lights and decorations (including plenty of artificial snow) and parades liven up the streets and waterways in and around LA. **Las Posadas,** held in El Pueblo de Los Angeles Plaza, is a weeklong celebration with a reenactment of Mary and Joseph's journey to Bethlehem as its centerpiece. From 16 December until Christmas Eve, nightly entertainment begins at 7PM; the procession starts at 8PM.

Colorful **nautical celebrations** of the holiday are held in Marina del Rey, Long Beach, San Pedro, and Redondo Beach.

New Year's Eve celebrations also overtake the town with events such as an annual **Shipwalk Party,** held on the *Queen Mary* in Long Beach, with music, entertainment, food, and fireworks. Admission. 562/435.3511. Similar action takes place at **Two Harbors,** 310/510.2800; **Gladstone's** at the beach, 310/GLA4-FISH; and on **Catalina Island** in the Casino ballroom. All admission. 310/510.1520.

PERSONAL SAFETY

It is generally safe to walk around downtown LA, Beverly Hills, Hollywood, West Hollywood, Brentwood, and Westwood Village during the day. At night, however, parts of the city are more dangerous, particularly **downtown, Hollywood,** and **South Central.** As with any large city, visitors to Los Angeles should exercise some commonsense precautions: Do not carry large amounts of cash or flash expensive jewelry. Know where your handbag and wallet are at all times. Try to blend in with your surroundings so it's not obvious you're a tourist. If you see trouble coming, get out of its way.

Phone Book

EMERGENCIES

AAA Motor Club (road service) 800/222.4357
AIDS Hot Line 800/367.2437
Ambulance/Fire/Police 911
Earthquake Emergency Services.............510/893.0818,
818/304.8383
Missing Children 800/826.4743, 800/843.5200
Poison Control Center.............................. 800/876.4766
USC Medical Center and Women's Hospital.....................
.... 800/872.2273

VISITORS' INFORMATION

Amtrak... 800/872.7245
Beach Information 310/305.3547
Better Business Bureau........................ 213/251.9696
Disabled Riders Hot Line...................... 800/626.4455
Greyhound 800/231.2222, 213/629.8401
LA INC. (Convention and Visitors Bureau) ....
....213/689.8822
LA Convention and Visitors Bureau Hotel Hotline ....
....800/CATCH.LA
Surf Report 213/976.7873
Time 213/853.1212
Transit Authority.................................. 818/888.7549
Weather 805/988.6610
Women's Health Information 888/232.3299

PUBLICATIONS

The *Los Angeles Times*, the only major metropolitan daily in the area, offers in-depth coverage of international and business news, along with suburban zone editions for local news. The Sunday "Calendar" section provides extensive entertainment listings. The *Daily News of Los Angeles* is a suburban daily based in the San Fernando Valley and offering local coverage; its "Weekend" section on Fridays has entertainment information. *Los Angeles Magazine* is published monthly and covers everything from politics to places to go, the best of LA, and, of course, celebrities and fashion. For the most thorough arts and entertainment information, pick up the free *LA Weekly*, distributed on Thursdays at restaurants and book, record, and convenience stores. Los Angeles's daily *La Opinión* is the largest Spanish-language newspaper in the country. And if you're looking for bargains, from used cars to computers, pick up the *Recycler* at liquor stores and corner markets.

RADIO STATIONS

Nowhere does radio boast a more captive audience than in LA, where the average commuter is trapped in his or her car for an hour a day. Listeners get a jump start with the hilarious madcap humor of the legendary Rick Dees in the morning and his team of zany sidekicks on Movin **93.9 FM,** while afternoon commuters get their mojos moving with testosterone-pumping shock-jock host Tom Leykis on **KLSX 97.1FM.** The major LA stations include the following:

AM:
98 .... KFWB 24 Hours of News
570 ....KLAC Big Band Music
690 .... XTRA Talk
790 .... KABC Talk Radio
1260 .... KJAZ Jazz
1540 .... KMPC Sports

FM:
88.9 .... KXLU Electronic Synthesized Music
89.9 .... KCRW Public Radio
93.9 ....KMVN Contemporary Mix
94.7 .... KTWV New Age
97.1 .... KLSX Talk
101.1 .... KRTH Oldies
102.7 .... KIIS Top 40
103.1 ....KACD Spanish
103.5... KOST Light Rock/Pop
104.3 .... KBIG Urban Contemporary
105.1 ....KMZT Classical

RESTAURANTS

Make your reservations weeks in advance whenever possible to avoid being forced to eat dinner at 6PM or 10PM. Except at funky little spots or fast-food joints, don't expect to just walk in and sit down without a reservation. At the trendiest and most expensive restaurants, reservations are essential, and sometimes even if you have one—say, at Spago or the Ivy—still expect a "wait at the bar." In LA even the most stylish establishments (like L'Orangerie) don't require ties for the gentlemen, but they do expect diners to show some dress decorum, and sports jackets are always welcome at the fine dining spots.

SHOPPING

For young, hip, cutting-edge designs, browse the boutiques along **La Brea Avenue** in midtown LA, **Old Pasadena, Melrose Avenue,** Santa Monica's chic **Third Street Promenade,** hip **Montana Avenue,** or groovy **Main Street.**

If you prefer shopping centers, your choices are plentiful, and include the behemoth 350-store **Del Amo Fashion Center** in Torrance; the stylish open-air **Westfield Century City**; the indoor **Beverly Center** in midtown LA; the 200-

store **South Coast Plaza** in Costa Mesa; and the upscale **Fashion Island** shopping complex in Newport Beach. Wholesale shopping outlets can be found in the **Garment District** south of Seventh and Los Angeles Streets in downtown or at the **Citadel** complex in **City of Commerce**. For haute couture, head for **Rodeo Drive** in Beverly Hills.

SMOKING

California won the war against smoking with a strictly enforced statewide ban on smoking in all indoor public places as well as some outdoor venues. (The feud is so fierce that anti-smokers have been known to turn in those who insist on lighting up anyway.)

TAXES

There is a sales tax of 8.25 percent. Hotel-room transient occupancy room tax is 14 percent for the city of Los Angeles; for other areas of the county, the levy varies from 11.5 to 14 percent.

TELEPHONES

Los Angeles and its surroundings have a head-spinning number of area codes—more than any other comparable region in the US. And there are more changes on the horizon. Overloaded circuits have prompted officials to add a 424 area-code overlay to phones in the 310 regions. Translated, this means that folks who now have a 310 prefix can keep it, but newcomers to the same district will be issued a telephone number preceded by 424. Other parts of Southern California will be issued new area codes by the end of the decade. Numbers in downtown LA have the **213** code; Hollywood and Griffith Park have the **323** code; Beverly Hills, Santa Monica, the Westside, and LAX have the **310** code (along with **424**); **714** is for most of northern Orange County, while **949** covers most of the southern portion. The **951** code is for Riverside, **909** for San Bernardino Counties and much of the San Gabriel Valley; **818** is for the San Fernando Valley from Agoura Hills to Glendale. **Los Angeles County** numbers have the 213, 310, 323, 626, 818, or 909 codes. Most of **Long Beach** is now **562**, while most of the **Desert Areas** (e.g., Palm Springs) are **760**. The latest change to be implemented summer of 2008 is the addition of area code 657, which will cover the **Anaheim** resort district along with some northern and central **Orange County** communities, replacing the existing 714 area code in those sections. Throughout OC, callers will be required to dial a 1 before all calls. What will they think up next? Area codes precede all phone numbers in this book.

Public phone booths are scarce in LA, where everybody and their grandmother has a cell phone. And user beware: Independent public phone companies can charge as much as they want, and often do, so be careful or a local call could wind up setting you back several dollars instead of a few cents. For directory assistance, dial 411.

TICKETS

Besides at the individual box offices, you can get tickets to cultural and sporting events through **Ticketmaster** (213/480.3232, www.ticketmaster.com) and **VIP Tickets** (818/907.1548, www.viptickets.com).

TIME ZONE

Los Angeles is in the Pacific Time zone, three hours earlier than New York City.

TIPPING

While tipping is always at your discretion, it's a good idea to grease the palms of the people who assist you if you want to be treated well. Airport baggage handlers and hotel bellhops (at luxury hotels) get at least $2 per bag. Leave the hotel maid $2 to $5 per day (more at luxury properties). Valet parking attendants expect at least $1 or $2, paid upon return of the car; this is in addition to the stiff fee, which can be $18 or higher at some restaurants and hotels. Leave a 15- to 20-percent gratuity in restaurants. Taxi drivers prefer a 15- to 20-percent tip, but 10 percent usually is adequate.

VISITORS' INFORMATION

In LA's downtown financial district, **LA INC. The Convention and Visitors Bureau** (M-Sa; 685 S Figueroa St, at W Seventh St, 213/689.8822) provides maps, information on lodging, and discount tickets to amusement parks and cultural attractions. The bureau also offers a 24-hour multilingual **events hotline** (reached via the general number) that provides information in Spanish, French, Japanese, German, and English. Contact the following visitor information centers for more information:

Anaheim/Orange County ....714/765.8888, www.anaheimoc.org

Beverly Hills .... 310/248.101 or 310/271.8174, www.itinet.com/beverlyhillscc

Long Beach ....562/436.3645, www.visitlongbeach.com

Palm Springs (hotel reservations)...........760/346.8800, 760/770.9000, 800/41.RELAX

Pasadena ....800/307.7977, 626/795.9311, e-mail: cvb@pasadenacal.com

Santa Monica ....310/393.7593, 800/771.2322, e-mail: smcvb@santamonica.com

West Hollywood.......................................310/289.2525, e-mail: info@visitwesthollywood.com; www.visitwesthollywood.com

Chambers of commerce in these surrounding communities also provide free information:

Catalina Island (in Avalon) ....310/510.1520, e-mail: chamber@Catalina.net

Century City ....310/553.2222, e-mail: mkcccc@worldnet.att.net

Hermosa Beach ....310/376.0951, e-mail: donsouzxa@gte.net; www.hbchamber.net

Hollywood ....323/469.8311, www.hollywoodchamber.net

Marina del Rey..310/305.9546, e-mail: bgbruin@aol.com

Santa Barbara ....805/966.9222, e-mail: sbcvb@silcom.com; www.santabarbaraca.com

Torrance.. 310/792.2341

Venice...........310/827.2366, www.venice.net/chamber

DOWNTOWN DISTRICTS

Los Angeles finally has a downtown. It hardly happened over night, but now it's become a mini Manhattan, a cheeky Chicago, a modest Miami, flavored by assorted ethnic influences, burgeoning growth, and an absorbing history. And, much of it can be explored by foot. For easier access we've divided downtown LA into the following three regions (see the map at right):

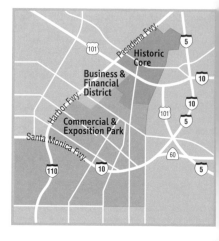

Historic Core: including **El Pueblo de Los Angeles** (site of the first settlement), **City Hall**, **Chinatown**, and **Little Tokyo**; **Business and Financial District:** a corridor of high-rise offices to the east of the **Harbor Freeway** (see page 23); and **Commercial and Exposition Park:** an area that encompasses LA's classic commercial buildings, movie palaces, and markets, extending south to the **University of Southern California** (see page 32).

Downtown took a dramatic turn after the opening of **Staples Center** in 1999. Billions of dollars funded the building of 8,000 residential units, massive improvements, and new entertainment venues. Oddly enough, one of the most anticipated and revered additions was the opening of a gigantic upscale **Ralphs Fresh Fare** grocery store in 2007 on the north side of West Ninth Street between South Flower and South Hope Streets. Part of a chain of supermarkets founded in 1873, this 50,000-square-foot yuppie food emporium attracts downtown denizens who wait in line until midnight at the popular deli counter to order take-out fare. The facility also houses a dry cleaner's and pharmacy and sponsors regular wine-tasting seminars.

The biggest catalyst to downtown's boom was the opening of the **Walt Disney Concert Hall** in 2003, which inspired an influx of visitors and second-nighters to downtown by night. All this added to the startling zeitgeist that transformed a once lifeless area into a vibrant cosmopolitan city. To help you find your way around, there at least 1,300 signs with easy-to-read directions and maps to districts and local landmarks (www.downtownlawalks.com).

HISTORIC CORE

The actual birthplace of Los Angeles, this area was founded in 1781 by a handful of Spanish settlers. Today it remains close to its origins throughout **El Pueblo de Los Angeles.** In 1822, Los Angeles became part of Mexico, after winning independence from Spain. Twenty-five years later, the Stars and Stripes was raised, and local boosters roamed the nation singing the praises of a promised land. Yankee immigrants slowly began streaming in, sleeping in tents and bathtubs, but in 1887, when two competing railroads briefly dropped the fare to a dollar, the trickle turned into a flood.

The land boom quickly went bust, however, leaving downtown LA with twice as many permanent residents as before. The more affluent relocated to the west of downtown, leaving the center and east of the city to new arrivals. Over the years the influx took its toll, and the area around **City Hall** became a civic embarrassment. Urban renewal began in the 1930s, with the institution of **Olvera Street** as a symbol of the original Spanish pueblo. In the late 1940s, the city created the Community Redevelopment Agency (CRA), which acquired properties for renovation and renewal, notably in **Little Tokyo, Chinatown,** and El Pueblo de Los Angeles.

Today, ethnic traditions flourish stronger than ever, and you can enjoy the culture and cuisine of almost every country of Latin America and the Pacific Rim here and in surrounding neighborhoods. Los Angeles's Hispanic population now accounts for an estimated 47% of the entire populace, making it one of the largest Spanish-speaking cities in the United States. There are two centers of Latino activity downtown: Olvera Street for tourists, and **Broadway** (in the "Commercial and Exposition Park" section of this chapter) for locals.

1 EMPRESS PAVILION

★$$ Arguably the most popular Cantonese and Szechuan restaurant in Chinatown, this is the place to go for great dim sum and then some, but expect long lines on weekends. Specialties are served in this spacious second-story restaurant in the **Bamboo Plaza**. Take-out food is available. ♦ Chinese ♦ Daily, breakfast, lunch, and dinner. 988 N Hill St (at Bernard St). 213/617.9898

2 PHOENIX BAKERY

Locals line up, sometimes for hours, to purchase delicious sweets from this popular bakery. The strawberry cake is legendary. ♦ Daily. 969 N Broadway (at Bamboo La). 213/628.4642

3 PLUM TREE INN

★$$ Peking duck and kung pao chicken are specialties at this stylish restaurant. ♦ Chinese ♦ Daily, lunch and dinner. Reservations recommended. 914 N Broadway (between W College St and Bamboo La). 213/613.1819 &

4 SAN ANTONIO WINERY

LA's best-kept secret, this historic winery in the heart of downtown Los Angeles houses tasting rooms, aging cellars, a legendary restaurant, and a wine shop stocked with private-label wines and imported and domestic varieties. Founded in 1917 by Italian winemaker Santo Cambianica, who named it after his patron saint, Anthony, San Antonio is the last working winery in the city. Now operated by the Riboli family, who grow grapes in vineyards estates in Monterey, Santa Barbara, and Napa, the winery has garnered more than 1,000 awards for its private labels. Located just five minutes north of the Music Center, it is well worth a visit. Reservations are necessary for tours. ♦ Plaza San Antonio, 737 Lamar St (at N Main St). 323/223.1401. www.sanantoniowinery.com

Within the San Antonio Winery:

MADDALENA RESTAURANT

★★$$ Named after a family member, this restaurant reflects the charm and graciousness of its owners. As you enter the large room you are greeted by tables of the day's signature dishes—the real thing, not plastic—from which to make your pick. The chicken Caesar salad is tangy, crispy, and one of the best in town; fish and chips is the fresh catch of the day, served with perfectly fried spuds. There's also a variety of Italian dishes, yummy chocolate biscotti, and a fantastic flan made from Mama Riboli's personal recipe. Of course, great wines are available to accompany it all. ♦ Daily, 10AM-7PM. 323/223.1401

5 HOP LI

★$$ A savvy seafood spot to grab some inexpensive authentic-tasting grub. ♦ Chinese/Seafood ♦ Daily, lunch and dinner. Reservations recommended for six or more. 526 Alpine St (between N Hill and Yale Sts). 213/680.3939 &

6 DRAGON GATE INN

$ This Best Western–affiliated lodge (with 50 rooms) is strategically located in the heart of Chinatown. ♦ 818 N Hill St (between Alpine and W College Sts). 213/617.3077, 800/528.1234 &

7 YANG CHOW

★$$ Don't be turned off by the tacky décor. The Szechuan dishes that draw crowds here more than make up for the lack of ambience. Special kudos go to pan-fried dumplings, kung pao chicken, spicy Szechuan beef, and slippery shrimp. ♦ Szechuan ♦ Daily, lunch and dinner. Reservations recommended. 819 N Broadway (between Alpine and W College Sts). 818/625.0811 &

8 SAIGON PLAZA

This marketplace offers a good selection of merchandise, from color-splashed T-shirts to gold jewelry. ♦ Daily. 828 N Broadway (between Alpine and W College Sts). 213/972.1914

9 CHINATOWN

As early as 1852, a Chinese settlement was recorded near the site of today's Union Station. The community resettled a few streets over in 1938 with the dedication of **Central Plaza**, becoming the first modern American Chinatown, owned and planned from the ground up by Chinese. Today the area has turned into a thriving center for an avant-garde westside crowd that comes for the contemporary galleries, boutiques, and restaurants.

The best way to explore Chinatown is to start with a visit to Central Plaza (947 N Broadway), where you will be enchanted by

---

Restaurants/Clubs: Red | **Hotels: Purple** | **Shops: Orange** | **Outdoors/Parks: Green** | **Sights/Culture: Blue**

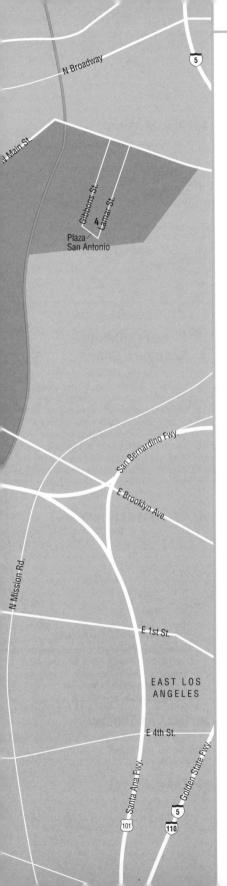

wind chimes and aromatic incense as you stroll through the quaint walkways and tiny shops. The sound of clicking mahjong tiles can be heard through upstairs windows from the halls where many of Chinatown's family associations hold their social meetings. Central Plaza is a popular place for filming, with its distinctive "Gate of Filial Piety," and also boasts a statue of Dr. Sun Yat Sen (founder of the Republic of China), a wishing well dating to 1939, and a five-tiered pagoda. A step outside and to the left of Central Plaza brings you to the doorstep of **Phoenix Bakery** (969 N Broadway; 213/628.4642), the oldest and largest bakery in Chinatown, with a citywide reputation for its strawberry whipped-cream cakes. Turn back and walk south along N Broadway. As you pass the curio shops and jewelry stores, stop to take in the beautiful tile murals on the wall at 913 N Broadway. Across the street, note **Little Joe's Restaurant,** a reminder of the large Italian population that also once lived here. Continue south and you'll come to **Saigon Plaza, Chinatown Plaza,** and **Dynasty Center** (800 block of N Broadway). Chinatown's newest immigrants, from Laos, Vietnam, and Cambodia, own most of the shops and stalls in these bazaars, where you can find bargains on clothing, toys, and assorted knicknacks. As you walk on the west side of the street, your eyes will be caught by a number of jewelry stores sparkling with 18K and 22K gold and exquisite jade creations. On the corner of Alpine and Broadway is **Cathay Bank** (777 N Broadway), the first Chinese-American-owned bank in Chinatown. Also on this block is **Far East Plaza,** considered the first modern ethnic shopping mall in America. Originally constructed as a food center featuring 25 different dining establishments, Far East Plaza still houses Sam Woo BBQ, Sam Woo Seafood, Pho 79, and Kim Chuy Restaurant, serving styles of regional cuisine that can be found here and nowhere else in Chinatown. The plaza is also home to **Wing Hop Fung Ginseng and China Products Center** (727 N Broadway; 213/626.7200; www.winghopfung.com), the largest store of its kind in Chinatown, fragrant with herbs and tea, and overflowing with chinaware, garments, and arts and crafts. A pharmacy and acupuncturist are located within. A little detour will take you into another world: an ornately decorated, incense-filled Taoist temple (750 Yale Street, open daily) that serves as a focal point of the immigrant community and is one of the most beautiful of its kind. As within any religious institution, please be respectful of worshippers and staff on the premises.

North along Hill Street you'll find the **Chinese United Methodist Church** (825 N Hill Street), which exemplifies a unique blending of Chinese and American architecture dating to the 1940s. The **Pacific Alliance Medical Center** at the corner of Hill and College Streets is one of the first hospitals in Los Angeles, built in 1868—originally named the French Hospital—to serve the city's French population. It still boasts a statue of Joan of Arc on its front lawn. Today, the hospital is run by enterprising Chinese doctors and serves the local Chinatown community. A little farther down is **West Plaza**, built in the late 1940s and mentioned in Lisa See's novel *On Gold Mountain*. The **F. See On** shop at the corner of the courtyard is actually run by See family members. West Plaza houses businesses on the ground floor and residences upstairs, and is also home to a burgeoning new art community whose avant-garde galleries and clothing boutiques are interspersed among the curio shops. At the end of N Hill Street, a right turn onto Bernard Street takes you to the headquarters of the **Chinese Historical Society of Southern California,** housed in two historic homes at 411 and 415 Bernard Street. French immigrants built both houses in the late 1880s. The visitor center showcases artifacts and historical photos recounting the history of the Chinese in Southern California. The center is open Sundays from noon to 4PM. Call 323/222.1918 for additional information.

For more details, call the **Chinese Chamber of Commerce** (777 N Broadway; 213/617.0396) or check out these web sites: www.camla.org (The Chinese American Museum), www.chssc.com (the Chinese Historical Society of Southern California), and www.chinatown.com (The Chinatown Business Improvement District).

10 OK SEAFOOD

★$$ Unusually cheerful waiters serve delicious, original renditions of standard and exotic Cantonese dishes (don't miss the crab in garlicky black bean sauce) in a spare room decorated with fish tanks. ◆ Cantonese/Seafood ◆ Daily, lunch and dinner until 1AM. 750 N Hill St (between Ord and Alpine Sts). 213/680.0640 &

11 WON KOK

★$ This busy, boisterous Cantonese restaurant stays open until the wee hours. Particularly satisfying after a night of carousing are their noodle dishes or a bowl of *jook*, a bland but wonderfully soothing thick rice porridge. ◆ Cantonese ◆ Daily, lunch and dinner until 3:30AM. 210 Alpine St (between N Spring and New High Sts). 213/613.0700

12 THANH-VI

★★$ Some of the best Vietnamese food in LA comes out of this raffish noodle bar,

which might have been imported from Saigon. ◆ Vietnamese ◆ Daily, breakfast, lunch, and dinner. 422 Ord St (at N Hill St). 213/687.3522

13 ABC SEAFOOD

★★$$ Cantonese seafood is served in a bustling dining room. Lunch offers a wide assortment of dim sum, but dinner brings the best choices: fresh crab, calamari, or your favorite fish in season. ◆ Cantonese/Seafood ◆ Daily, breakfast, lunch, and dinner. 205 Ord St (between N Spring and New High Sts). 213/680.2887

14 CBS SEAFOOD

★$ Prawns with lobster sauce and wok-charred oysters are favorites in this popular restaurant. ◆ Chinese/Seafood ◆ Daily, breakfast, lunch, and dinner. 700 N Spring St (at Ord St). 213/617.2323 &

15 PHILLIPE'S ORIGINAL SANDWICH SHOP

★$ Legend has it that the French dip sandwich was invented here in 1908. Since then, loyal patrons have been coming here for the simple, honest food and the 10¢ coffee. The crowd is a cross section of LA society, from ballplayers to stockbrokers, and the décor consists of linoleum-topped tables on a sawdust floor. Be sure to have your sandwich double-dipped. ◆ American ◆ Daily, breakfast, lunch, and dinner. 1001 N Alameda St (at Ord St). 213/628.3781

16 PELANCONI HOUSE

Constructed in 1855, this was one of the first brick buildings in Los Angeles. The two-story balconied structure was named for its second owner, Antonio Pelanconi; the second floor is still a private residence. ◆ W-17 Olvera St (southwest of E Macy St)

Within the Pelanconi House:

CASA LA GOLONDRINA

★$$ Mariachis and dancers entertain while you enjoy Mexican food. ◆ Mexican ◆ Daily, breakfast, lunch, and dinner. Reservations recommended for four or more. 213/628.4349

16 CASA DE SOUSA

This shop carries Mexican and Central American folk art. ◆ Daily. W-19 Olvera St (southwest of E Macy St). 213/626.7076

17 ZANJA MADRE

A fragment of the city's original irrigation ditch, it was built in 1781 to carry water from the Los Angeles River near **Elysian Park** into the city. ◆ Olvera St (just southwest of E Macy St)

18 BAZAAR DE MEXICO

Brighten your wardrobe with Taxco silver jewelry and Mexican clothing and costumes. ♦ Daily. W-7 Olvera St (southwest of E Macy St). 213/620.9782

18 SEPULVEDA HOUSE

This redbrick building, a former boardinghouse built in 1887 by Eliosa Martinez de Sepulveda, houses a **Visitor Information Center.** An 18-minute film (available on request) chronicles the history of El Pueblo, and a walking-tour pamphlet is available in a variety of languages. ♦ M-Sa, 10AM-3PM. W-12 Olvera St (southwest of E Macy St). For a walking tour of Olvera Street, call 213/628.1274

19 PLAZA CHURCH (CHURCH OF OUR LADY THE QUEEN OF THE ANGELS)

The oldest religious structure in Los Angeles, this church was originally a simple adobe, built between 1818 and 1822 by Franciscan padres and local Indians. ♦ 535 N Main St (between Arcadia and W Macy Sts). 213/629.3101

20 EL PUEBLO DE LOS ANGELES HISTORIC MONUMENT AND OLVERA STREET

The founding site of the city of Los Angeles encompasses **El Pueblo de Los Angeles Plaza,** Olvera Street, a park, and 27 historic or architecturally significant buildings. The entire area has undergone major urban renewal over the years. Olvera Street, named for a Los Angeles County judge and supervisor, was rebuilt in 1930 in the style of a Mexican marketplace. The brick-paved block is lined with shops and stalls selling Mexican handicrafts and confections. A number of stands and cafés along the street offer food, but for dessert go to the plaza, where peeled mangoes, papayas, and other tropical fruit is available. The confectioners at the center of Olvera Street tempt passersby with Mexican sweets such as candied squash or brown sugar cones, while delicious *churros* (doughnuts) can be found at the bakery near the center of the north side of the street. There are free docent-led tours Tuesday through Saturday (call 213/628.1274 for group reservations). ♦ Bounded by N Alameda and N Spring Sts, and Arcadia and Macy Sts

20 LA LUZ DEL DIA

At this shop, you can watch women skilled in the fast-disappearing art of making tortillas by hand. ♦ Tu-Su. W-1 Olvera St (southwest of E Macy St). 213/628.7495

21 AVILA ADOBE

LA's oldest adobe was built in 1818 by Don Francisco Avila, one-time mayor of the pueblo. Parts of the original two-foot-thick walls survive. The simple one-story structure is characteristic of Mexican design, with a garden patio in the rear. ♦ Free. Tu-Sa. 10 Olvera St (southwest of E Macy St). 213/680.2525

22 EL PUEBLO DE LOS ANGELES PLAZA (OLD PLAZA)

The center of **El Pueblo Historic Monument** and the hub of community life through the 1870s, the plaza now serves as the setting for public festivals that bring back the spirit of the Mexican era. Most notable are Cinco de Mayo (5 May), a Mexican Independence holiday; Día de los Muertos (Day of the Dead; early November), a religious festival in which the souls of the dead return to visit their living relatives; and Las Posadas (the nine consecutive days before Christmas), a parade that commemorates the birth of Christ with different nativity scenes. At the center of the plaza is the **Kiosko,** a hexagonal bandstand with filigree ironwork. ♦ Olvera St (southwest of E Macy St)

23 PICO HOUSE

This Italian palazzo was built by **Ezra F. Kysor** in 1870 for **Pio Pico,** the last Mexican governor of California. During its later heyday, the building was the finest hotel in California south of San Francisco. ♦ Closed to the public. 430 N Main St (between Arcadia and E Macy Sts)

24 MERCED THEATRE

Ezra F. Kysor also designed this three-story 1870 Italianate masonry building with a theater that's no longer in use today. At press time, the interior was being restored. ♦ 420 N Main St (between Arcadia and E Macy Sts)

24 MASONIC HALL

Designed in 1858, this was the city's first lodge, a two-story Italian Renaissance structure with a cast-iron balcony and three arched openings on each floor. ♦ 416 N Main St (between Arcadia and E Macy Sts). No tours or phone number at this time

25 OLD PLAZA FIREHOUSE

A castellated brick structure, this 1884 firehouse is now a museum containing

---

Restaurants/Clubs: Red | Hotels: Purple | Shops: Orange | Outdoors/Parks: Green | Sights/Culture: Blue

firefighting equipment and photographs of 19th-century fire stations. Guided tours available. ♦ Free. Tu-Sa. 501 N Los Angeles St (between Arcadia and N Alameda Sts). 213/625.3741

26 GARNIER BLOCK

Philippe Garnier built this block in 1890 as commercial stores and apartments for the city's Chinese business population. It is constructed of buff brick with sandstone trim and has an unusual cornice of Victorian Romanesque design. ♦ 415 N Los Angeles St (between Arcadia and N Alameda Sts)

27 UNION STATION

One of LA's greatest—yet least appreci-ated—architectural treasures, and one of the last of the country's grand railroad passenger terminals, Union Station was designed by **John** and **Donald Parkinson** in 1939 and built jointly by the **Southern Pacific, Union Pacific, and Santa Fe railroad companies.** It is a free interpreta-tion of Spanish Mission architecture, combining enormous scale with Moderne and Moorish details. The wood-beamed ceiling of the waiting room stands 52 feet high, the floors are made of marble, and deep scalloped archways lead to two patios. A food court offers Mexican food, bagels, and hot dogs. **Amtrak** (800/USA-RAIL, www.amtrak.com) offers comfortable daily service to just about anywhere in the country. Many local commuters forgo freeways to ride the rails to Santa Barbara and the Pacific Northwest and south to San Diego. And for you statisticians, nearly a million passengers go through the depot annually. ♦ 800 N Alameda St (between the Santa Ana Fwy and E Macy St). General information 213/683.6875, schedule and ticket information 800/872.7245

Within Union Station:

TRAXX

★★$$ What could be more fitting than an Art Deco dining room in an Art Deco train station? This narrow little (100-seat) eatery has tables outside near the concourse and on the north patio, and a separate bar in the depot's old telephone room. An open kitchen, headed by chef Tara Thomas, produces such menu items as red chile–dusted shrimp with mizuna and mango, wild striped bass, venison carpaccio, and an irresistible pecan pie. ♦ California ♦ M-F, lunch and dinner; Sa, dinner. 213/625.1999. www.traxxrestaurant.com

28 CITY ARCHIVES

Few people other than city officials know about these archives, but anyone can make an appointment to dig through the treasury of maps, papers, photos, and council records, which document LA since 1827. ♦ M-F. 555 Ramirez St (between Center and Lyon Sts), No. 320. 213/485.3512

29 LOS ANGELES COUNTY COURTHOUSE

Scene of the O.J. Simpson trial, this is where Marcia Clark and the "Dream Team" battled it out while TV crews and T-shirt vendors lined the street. Today it's business as usual—as one high-profile case (Heidi Fleiss, Paris Hilton, Phil Spector, you name them) after another goes before the judge. ♦ W Temple St (between N Spring St and N Broadway)

30 CIVIC CENTER

LA has the second-largest governmental center in the US outside of Washington, DC. Look for a sign that reads, "Abandon hope all ye who enter here." ♦ Bounded by N San Pedro St and N Grand Ave, and First and Aliso Sts

30 UNITED STATES FEDERAL COURTHOUSE BUILDING

The United States District Court occupies this handsome WPA-style structure designed by **Louis Simon & Gilbert Stanley Underwood.** ♦ M-F. 312 N Spring St (between W Temple and W Aliso Sts). 213/894.3650

31 LOS ANGELES CHILDREN'S MUSEUM

Children and adults alike enjoy this touch-and-play experience, where a kids' television station and changing exhibitions covering the city's streets and African-American roots encourage participation. Classes and workshops are scheduled regularly; call for current availability. Labels in Spanish and English explain the exhibitions. Weekday parking is available in the Los Angeles Mall garage. ♦ Admission; children under two free. Tu-Su. 310 N Main St (between E Temple and E Aliso Sts). General information 213/687.8801; recording 213/687.8800

32 CITY HALL

Designed by **John C. Austin, John Parkinson,** and **Albert C. Martin** in 1928, this classic monument underwent a restoration in 2001 thanks to Project Restore, a nonprofit that raised funds through corporations, individuals, and such organizations as the National Endowment for the Arts, the State Office of Historic Preservation, the City of Los Angeles, the Ahmanson Foundation, and the Community Redevelopment Agency. The restoration, which was guided by the architectural firm of Hardy Holzman Pfeiffer Associates, included the Main Street lobby and garage entrance, Spring Street forecourt, rotunda, third-floor lobbies, City Council chambers, Board of Public Works session room, main and secondary corridors, and the bridge to City Hall East. The project cleverly maintained the original design. Until 1957, City Hall with its pyramid-crowned tower was the only exception to the city's 150-foot building height limit. One of the most photographed buildings in LA, it has been featured in countless movies and television shows—most memorably as the *Daily Planet* building in the popular 1950s television series *Superman*. Inside, luxurious marble columns and an inlaid-tile dome give the public areas the feel of a cathedral. On a clear day, you can see forever from the 27th-floor observation deck. ◆ M-F. 200 N Spring St (between W First and W Temple Sts). 213/485.2121; www.cityofla.org

33 LOS ANGELES TIMES

Gordon Kaufman designed this stodgy Moderne block in 1935; the 1973 steel-and-glass addition is by **William Pereira Associates**. A free tour takes you through the making of the newspaper, from newsroom to printing. Children must be 10 or older. Meet the guide at the First Street entrance. Also available (by reservation) is a tour of the **Olympic Plant,** the paper's production facility. ◆ Free. M-F. 202 W First St (at S Spring St). 213/237.5757

34 PARKER CENTER

Named after a former chief of police, this is the headquarters of the Los Angeles Police Department. ◆ 150 N Los Angeles St (between E First and E Temple Sts). Tours are available by appointment only: 213/485.3205

35 VIBIANA PLACE/ST. VIBIANA'S CATHEDRAL

This Baroque-style cathedral was restored by Gilmore Associates of Los Angeles into a magnificent nonprofit performing arts center for Cal State Los Angeles. Originally designed in 1876 by **Ezra F. Kysor,** St. Vibiana is distinguished by a façade of pilasters and volutes crowned with a tower and cupola. Inside, relics of the early Christian martyr St. Vibiana are preserved in a marble sarcophagus. The site also contains 300 loft apartments, two Cal State LA performing arts and continuing higher education centers, a Little Tokyo Branch library, a restaurant, a small boutique hotel, and a rectory. ◆ 114 E Second St (at S Main St). 213/624.3941

36 KYOTO GRAND HOTEL & GARDENS (FORMERLY NEW OTANI HOTEL)

$$$ Far from the maddening crowd, this 434-room Zen-like hotel offers an authentic Japanese flavor enhanced by gracious gardens and specially appointed rooms and suites. Feel like you're in Japan without leaving the country by booking the "Japanese Experience" package for two. You'll bed down in a garden suite complete with futon, hot tub, and a sitting room with shoji screens, then enjoy an amazing Shiatsu massage, hot tub, and sauna followed by dinner at **A Thousand Cranes/ Sen Bazuru** (see below). Worth a stop is the peaceful **Rendezvous Lounge** in the main lobby. Nearby is a three-level shopping courtyard. Don't miss the fourth-story Japanese garden, a haven of tranquility. On the same level, the **Genji Bar** is a lovely place to watch twilight deepen. There is also a spa and a super fitness center. At press time, the New Otani was purchased by Crestline Hotels & Resorts, and the name was changed to Kyoto Grand Hotel & Gardens. ◆ 120 S Los Angeles St (between E Second and E First Sts). 213/629.1200, 800/273.2294 in California, 800/421.8795 in the US and Canada; fax 213/622.0980; www.crestlinehotels.com &

Within the Kyoto Grand Hotel & Gardens:

A THOUSAND CRANES/ SEN BAZURU

★★$$$ This stylish restaurant overlooking the roof garden has separate rooms for sushi, tempura, and the *teppan* grill. The service is excellent. The Sunday buffet brunch is a spectacular offering of Asian and American food accompanied by Champagne and/or tea. ◆ Japanese ◆ Daily, lunch and dinner; Su, brunch. Reservations required. 213/629.1200

37 ASTRONAUT ELLISON S. ONIZUKA STREET

Formerly **Weller Court** but renamed to commemorate an astronaut who died in the *Challenger* explosion, this is a handsome pedestrian precinct. The major tenant is **Matsuzakaya,** a branch of Japan's oldest department store. ◆ Between E Second and E First Sts

38 GEFFEN CONTEMPORARY AT THE MUSEUM OF CONTEMPORARY ART (MOCA)

The transformation of two city-owned warehouses by architect **Frank Gehry** in 1983 was intended as a stopgap while a new building was being readied a few blocks away, but the 55,000-square-foot loft became a permanent facility. Exhibitions have included "Blueprints for Modern Living," "The Automobile and Culture," and "Tokyo: Form and Spirit." But the building would be worth seeing without the art: Gehry has preserved the raw character of the interior, adding a steel-and-chain-link canopy to create an outdoor lobby. A Barbara Kruger mural enlivens the south front. There's low-cost parking and easy access from the DASH shuttle. ◆ Admission (covers the MOCA and the Geffen Center); free for members, children under 12, and Th, 5-8PM. Tu, W, F-Su; Th until 8PM. 152 N Central Ave (just north of E First St). 213/626.6222

39 JAPANESE AMERICAN NATIONAL MUSEUM

Housed in the historic **Nishi Hongwanji Buddhist Temple,** this private museum was designed in 1925 by **Edgar Cline** in a mix of styles, including Japanese and Middle Eastern. Exhibits preserve the Japanese experience as part of US history. A new $22 million pavilion by architect **Gyo Obata** increased the space by 300 percent. ◆ Admission. Tu-Su; F until 8PM. 369 E First St (at N Central Ave). 213/625.0414

40 LITTLE TOKYO

Bounded by **South Alameda, South Main, East Third,** and **East First Streets,** the heart of Southern California's Japanese-American community is home to more than 200,000 people. First settled more than 100 years ago, Little Tokyo began to flourish after World War I but was devastated by the forced evacuation of Japanese-Americans from the Pacific Coast during World War II. It has emerged in the past decade as an active and cohesive area, a mix of late-19th-century commercial buildings and modern structures. **Nisei Week,** held in August, is a major event, with a parade, street dancing, festival food, and demonstrations of flower arranging, *sumi* brush painting, the traditional tea ceremony, and other Japanese arts. If you're a bit skittish about dining here, many of the restaurants display their food in the windows so you can see what you're getting. Those in the know, however, keep local woks sizzling. After dark, karaoke bars abound. Walking

tours of Little Tokyo are available from the **Business Association** (213/620.0570); reservations are required.

41 JAPANESE VILLAGE PLAZA MALL

White stucco with exposed wood framing, blue tile roofs, and a traditional lookout tower distinguish this Japanese minimall, where you can pick up anything from a kimono to herbs and elixirs. At press time, the mall had been acquired by a private Beverly Hills real estate firm. No details were available, but major developmental changes appear imminent. Park on Central Ave. ◆ 385 E Second St (between S Central Ave and S San Pedro St). 213/620.8861

42 RAFU BUSSAN

An unusually large selection of lacquerware and ceramics is sold here. ◆ Daily, except Wednesdays. 326 E Second St (between S Central Ave and S San Pedro St). 213/614.1181

43 PETE'S CAFÉ & BAR

★★$$ Local loft dwellers, scribes from the *Los Angeles Times*, members of City Hall, and visitors stop by this chic New York–style eatery for a bite or a nip, or both, and some good conversation. The food's good, the drinks are strong, and the room is attractively appointed with stunning 1906 mosaic tile flooring, a mahogany-framed vestibule, dark wood paneling, and floor-to-ceiling windows. This place is a madhouse at lunchtime with the power lunch crowd. There's great live music on weekends. ◆ Reservations suggested for dinner. ◆ American. ◆ Daily, lunch and dinner. 400 S Main St (corner of Fourth and Main Sts), 213/617.1000. www.petescafe.com

44 JAPANESE AMERICAN CULTURAL AND COMMUNITY CENTER

The center houses many cultural groups and activities and is a major resource for the entire city. Special events and displays are organized in conjunction with annual community festivals, including Hanamatsuri (birth of the Buddha) in April, Children's Day in May, Obon (Festival of the Dead) in June and July, Nisei Week in August, and Oshogatsu (New Year's festivities). The Center's shop sells posters and distinctive crafts. ◆ 244 S San Pedro St (between E Third and E Second Sts). 213/628.2725

Within the Japanese American Cultural and Community Center:

GEORGE J. DOIZAKI GALLERY

This gallery features regular exhibitions of historical treasures and new art and graphics. ◆ Tu-Su. 213/628.2725

Franklin D. Murphy Library

Japanese magazines and books on Japan and Japanese-Americans are available here; an appointment is necessary to visit. ♦ Open Sa only. 213/628.2725

Japan America Theater

The best in traditional and contemporary performing arts from Japan, including the Grand Kabuki, Bugaku, and Noh dramas, are presented here, along with Bunraku puppet theater and Western dance and chamber music. ♦ Box office: daily, noon–5PM. 213/680.3700

JACCC Plaza

Designed by **Isamu Noguchi,** the monumental rock sculpture in the plaza is dedicated to the Issei (first generation of Japanese immigrants).

James Irvine Garden

A fusion of Eastern and Western cultures, this garden is a sunken oasis for strolling and meditation. It is also known as **Seiryu-en,** or "Garden of the Clear Stream." ♦ Call ahead for hours. 213/628.2725

45 R-23

★★$$ Located in the hip Warehouse District of downtown LA, on the site of a former railroad loading dock, this lofty Japanese eatery attracts a large neighborhood crowd along with foodies who come from far and wide for the authentic cuisine. The airy room is simple, with exposed brick walls and Frank Gehry–designed corrugated cardboard chairs. Go with a group of friends and order lots of courses to share family-style. Start with the sushi or sashimi platter (or have pieces à la carte) and continue on with pine tree mushroom soup or yellowtail carpaccio, followed by fresh fish, beef, or one of the specials of the day. Desserts, such as red-bean or green-tea ice cream, are an acquired taste. The waitstaff is friendly but service can be slow, so allow time for your meal. ♦ Japanese. ♦ M-F, lunch; M-Sa, dinner. Reservations suggested. 923 E Second St (between S Santa Fe Ave and S Alameda St). 213/687.7178. www.r23.com

46 Higashi Hongwangji Buddhist Temple

This traditional structure by **Kajima Associates** was designed in 1976 for the Jodo Shinshu sect. A broad flight of stairs leads to the entrance; the blue tile roof is protected by two golden dragons. ♦ 505 E Third St (at S Central Ave). 213/626.4200

47 Hana Ichimonme

★$ If you saw the movie *Tampopo,* you know how seriously the Japanese take ramen. Here the noodles are fresh, the broth rich and delicately spiced. ♦ Japanese ♦ Daily, lunch and dinner (closed for dinner on Wednesdays). Little Tokyo Square, 333 S Alameda St (between E Fourth and E Third Sts). 213/626.3514 &

Business & Financial District

Wall Street goes west, young man . . .

Guess what folks, LA finally found its own downtown, an urbane core highlighted by **Bunker Hill**, a short, narrow corridor between the Harbor Freeway and Third Street. The seed was planted in 1999 with the opening of **Staples Center**, the catalyst for $17 billion in expenditures that has transformed the area into a desirable center of commerce and leisure living.

At the turn of the century, Bunker Hill ranked as the most desirable residential neighborhood in the city, with Victorian gingerbread mansions looking down on what was even then the city's business district. And now thanks to the ongoing gentrification/urbanization, it is once again an ideal place to live or work, especially with the glut of new chic housing facilities, carved out of old commercial buildings, designed to attract high-salaried downtown workers tired of commuting.

Flower Street, the main avenue of this burgeoning financial district, has boomed with the widespread popularity of branch banking in Southern California and the emergence of Los Angeles as the American capital of the Pacific Rim. Of the six largest banks in California, four have built high-rise headquarters in LA, while the other two maintain their Southern California headquarters here. The 73-story **US Bank Tower** located at 633 W Fifth Street is the tallest office building between Chicago and Taipei. Overseas companies have invested heavily in downtown, too, since real estate in this area is a fraction of the cost of similar districts in Tokyo and Hong Kong. Learn more about downtown online at www.downtownla.com or www.downtownnews.com.

1 Pacific Stock Exchange

The exchange relocated to this bland, modern structure from its landmark building on Spring Street. ♦ Free. Viewing gallery: M-F, 8AM-1PM. 233 S Beaudry Ave (between W Third and W Second Sts). 323/977.4500

2 Bunker Hill Towers

These three high-rise blocks, designed by **Robert Alexander** in 1968, were the first residential structures on redeveloped Bunker

---

Restaurants/Clubs: Red | Hotels: Purple | Shops: Orange | Outdoors/Parks: Green | Sights/Culture: Blue

Hill. ♦ 800 W First St (between S Hope and S Figueroa Sts)

3 DEPARTMENT OF WATER AND POWER BUILDING

West of the Music Center (see below) is the headquarters of the largest utility company in the US. The glass-and-steel building, designed by **AC Martin Partners** in 1964, is an elegant stack of horizontal planes that looks its best when lit up at night. ♦ 111 N Hope St (between W First and W Temple Sts)

4 MUSIC CENTER

The addition of the Walt Disney Concert Hall, home of the LA Philharmonic—possibly the most spectacular auditorium ever conceived—ushered in a phenomenal new era for the city's major performing arts venue and quickly became the shining star of the four-theater facility. One of the three largest performing arts centers in the nation and one of Southern California's premier cultural attractions, The Center is home to four internationally acclaimed resident companies: **The Los Angeles Philharmonic**, **Center Theater Group**, **LA Opera**, and the **Los Angeles Master Chorale.** ♦ 111 S Grand Ave (at the intersection of First St and Grand Ave in Bunker Hill)

Within the Music Center:

WALT DISNEY CONCERT HALL

No structure ever built has received more accolades, oohs, aahs, and other distin-guishable sounds than this mega-masterpiece. Fifteen years in the making with a cast of dream-team architects, designers, and acoustical designers led by **Frank Gehry,** this eagerly anticipated $274 million architectural wonder elevated Los Angeles to new cultural heights when it opened in October 2003. Wrapped in 9,000 panes of stainless steel sheathing, the extraordinary structure sits on a 3.6-acre site across from the Dorothy Chandler Pavilion. The phenomenal acoustical design provides a spectacular showcase home of the LA Philharmonic with a 360-degree wraparound stage offering fantastic viewing from any of its 2,265 seats.

The project began in 1987 with a $50 million endowment by Lillian Disney to construct a world-class performing arts venue. Other members of the famed family later donated additional funds. In 1988, Frank Gehry was chosen to head the design team, with construction commencing in 1992. The result is a study in stainless steel—a metallic sculpture, almost, that curves and flaps around 293,000 square feet. The obvious centerpiece is the auditorium designed by Nagata Acoustics

and Gehry Partners with its vineyard shape and curved wood ceiling, staggered seating, and unique intimacy. Even the entrance waxes grand, with an **Atrium Reception Hall** enclosed by glass windows that fold up, providing an indoor/outdoor venue. There's also the **BP Hall,** a pre-concert foyer set on travertine floors, where lectures and programs are staged. The **Founders Room,** anchoring the northern-most side, offers special amenities for the Center's major donors and guests, while the **W.M. Keck Foundation Children's Amphitheater** sits farthest south. There are two restaurants run by the Patina Group: **Patina** and **Patina Café,** a moderately priced self-serve snack bar. In keeping with the late Lillian Disney's wishes, a lavish garden, landscaped by Melinda Taylor, provides a pleasant place to relax before or after concerts. Even if you don't go for a concert, you should at least head downtown for a glimpse and/or a tour of this magical/majestic music venue. The best way to fully appreciate this amazing auditorium is by taking a free tour. You can explore the hall with a 45-minute self-guided tour through the one-acre gardens, where 45 trees surround a 150-ton Delftware rose-shaped fountain. ♦ 213/972.7211. www.LAPhil.com; www.musiccenter.org; www.lamc.org

Within the Walt Disney Concert Hall:

THE CAFÉ AT WALT DISNEY CONCERT HALL

At this casual café, you hand-pick dishes from a marketplace menu of sandwiches, salads and soups, and daily entrée specials.

PATINA

★★★$$$ This shining star of the Joachim Splichal empire provides a perfect place for pre- or post-theater dining. The romantic, casually elegant mood suits its predomi-nantly urbane clientele, many of whom are heading to or from a play or concert. The seasonally changing cuisine is typically exceptional and you can't go wrong with any dish you order, from foie gras or caviar to scrumptious dessert. Unabashed fans of Splichal, we love it all. We're talking grilled *cote de beouf* for two with wild mushroom ragout, asparagus tips, and black truffle *pomme mousseline* in an outrageous Bordelaise sauce, or cold poached lobster tail with vanilla-marinated pineapple hearts, mango in ginger oil, and toasted coconut broth. And desserts like vanilla panna cotta, Chocolate Tuile Macadamia Nut Decadence, and homemade ice cream and sorbets. There's also a late-night, après-theater supper menu. ♦ Continental

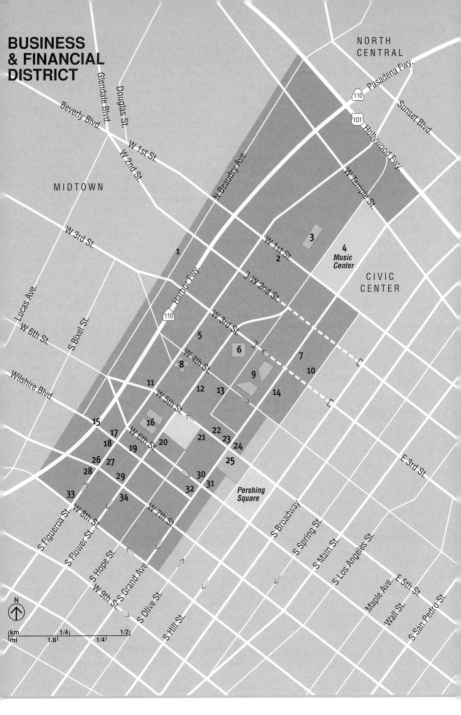

NORTH
CENTRAL

MIDTOWN

CIVIC
CENTER

4
Music
Center

Pershing
Square

N

km | 1/4 | 1/2
mi | 1/8 | 1/4

California. ♦ M-F, lunch; daily, dinner.
Reservations a must. 213/972.3331.
www.patinagroup.com

DOROTHY CHANDLER PAVILION

Designed by architect **Welton Becket,** the
Dorothy Chandler Pavilion can be an

exciting place to attend the opera or a
play. The former home of the the Academy
Awards (which moved to the new **Kodak
Theater** in Hollywood), it houses performances of the LA Opera under the
direction of Placido Domingo. ♦ Box office:
M-Sa, 213/972.7300; LA Opera,
213/972.7219

Restaurants/Clubs: Red | Hotels: Purple | Shops: Orange | Outdoors/Parks: Green | Sights/Culture: Blue

MARK TAPER FORUM

One of LA's most iconic buildings and the artistic core of the Center Theater Group, the 41-year-old venue recently emerged from a $30 million makeover designed by the architectural firm of **Rios Clementi Hale Studios** of Los Angeles and theatrical consultant Roger Morgan of **Sachs Morgan Studios.** The most notable exterior difference is the restoration of the 378-foot precast concrete mural relief. Inside you'll find a larger, spiffier lobby with terrazzo flooring and a radial grid-pattern ceiling. The theater itself boasts better seats, new appointments, and improved acoustics. Winner of virtually every theatrical award, The Taper was distinguished by having two plays that premiered there, *The Kentucky Cycle* and *Angels in America*, earn the Pulitzer Prize in Drama. ♦ M-Sa. 213/972.0700; www.taperahmanson.com

AHMANSON THEATER

This 2,140-seat theater has hosted a wide variety of dramas, musicals, comedies, and classic revivals since it opened with *Miss Saigon* in 1967. ♦ M-Sa. 213/972.0724; www.taperahmanson.com

PRECONCERT DINING

The Music Center offers a variety of casual dining choices such as is **Kendall's Brasserie** (213/972.7322), **Spotlight Café** on the plaza level (213/972.7565), and **Kendall's** (213/997.7322). Other choices for pre-theater dining include the **Taipan** (213/626.6688) and the **California Pizza Kitchen** (213/626.2616), in the Wells Fargo Center, and **Cicada** (213/655.5559), in the **Oviatt Building** (see page 33).

5 WORLD TRADE CENTER

Home to a number of import/export companies and law offices, the World Trade Center is linked by bridges to the Bonaventure Hotel, Bunker Hill Towers, and the Sheraton Grande Hotel. A passport office and currency exchange are located in its shopping arcade. ♦ 350 S Figueroa St (between W Fourth and W Third Sts). 213/489.3337

6 BANK OF AMERICA

The well-detailed 55-story tower was designed in 1974 by **AC Martin Partners**. It is set at an angle to the street and anchored by a red Alexander Calder stabile outside the main entrance. ♦ 345 S Hope St (between W Fourth and Flower Sts)

7 MUSEUM OF CONTEMPORARY ART (MOCA)

The 1986 building, recently renamed **MOCA Grand Avenue,** is a dazzling fusion of Western geometry and Eastern tradition. The first major US building by Japan's leading architect, **Arata Isozaki,** it is also one of the city's finest. A sequence of luminous galleries with exposed vaults open off a sunken courtyard. Isozaki has even indulged his fascination with Marilyn Monroe in the sensuous curve of the parapet overlooking the courtyard. Highlights in this widely acclaimed facility include works from Franz Kline, Claes Oldenburg, Louise Nevelson, and Mark Rothko. Throughout the year, artists, critics, and curators give informative tours of current exhibitions. In the courtyard is what may be the best museum gift shop in LA. Below the galleries is a steep 162-seat auditorium used for film, video, and performing arts. Every Thursday night the museum stays open late; there is a bar, free hors d'oeuvres, and in summer, live performances in the courtyard. Parking is available at First and Grand (Lot 167) and at the Music Center; rates in garages below the museum are very high. The museum's second facility, the **Geffen Contemporary,** is a few blocks away in Little Tokyo at 152 North Central Avenue (see page 22). Parking close to the Geffen is much more reasonable and the DASH shuttle will get you to MOCA. ♦ Admission; free Th, 5-8PM. Tu-Su; Th until 8PM. 250 S Grand Ave (between W Fourth and W First Sts). General information 213/621.2766; recording 213/626.6222. www.moca-la.org &

Within the Museum of Contemporary Art (MOCA):

PATINETTE

★★$ Probably the best restaurant to ever find its way into a museum, this one comes thanks to the creative efforts of Joachim Splichal, chef/owner of Patina, Cafe Pinot, Pinot Bistro, and Pinot Hollywood. Offering a Mediterranean menu with a rotating selection of appetizers, soups, sandwiches, salads, and yummy desserts in a casual setting, it provides an inexpensive way to sample this superchef's coveted cuisine. ♦ Continental ♦ Tu-Su, lunch and dinner. 213/626.1178

8 WESTIN BONAVENTURE HOTEL

$$$ "Buck Rogers beside the Freeway" best describes this 1976 **John Portman** design of five mirror-glass silos with glass-bubble elevators and a huge, fanciful atrium. FYI: There's a rumor going around that the hotel's 1,354 rooms may be converted into condos or apartments. For now, accommodations are traveler friendly and nicely appointed, but the hotel does quite a bustling convention business, so don't expect serenity. It's also a popular spot for lookie-loos who wander about trying to make sense

of the confusing eight levels of shops, fast-food places, and restaurants. Among these, the revolving **LA Prime,** a New York–style steak house, is notable for its prime cuts of beef served with a sweeping 360° view of the city and surrounding mountaintops. On a clear day you can even see the Pacific Ocean. Fitness/health amenities include a circular indoor running track with a multi-station weight training course and a 9,000-square-foot Asian-themed spa. There's also a half-acre garden deck and pool area for sun worshippers. For business travelers, there's a full-service center. Valet parking is available too. ♦ 404 S Figueroa St (at W Fourth St). 213/624.1000; fax 213/612.4800 ♿

9 WELLS FARGO CENTER

The twin knife-edge towers clad in polished brown granite and tinted glass were designed by **Skidmore, Owings & Merrill** in 1983 and developed by Maguire Thomas Partners. Between the towers is **The Court,** an exciting glass-walled garden designed by Lawrence Halprin, with sculpture by Jean Dubuffet, Joan Miró, Louise Nevelson, and Robert Graham. ♦ 350 S Hope St (between W Fourth and W Third Sts)

10 THE GRAND AVENUE PROJECT AND L.A. LIVE

Two major developments flanked by Walt Disney Concert Hall on the north and Staples Center on the south, slated to become the core of downtown Los Angeles, are currently under construction. The brainchild of billionaire Eli Broad and magnate Tim Leiweke, the ambitious $1.8 billion Grand Avenue venture will include high-end shopping outlets, condominiums, and a 16-acre public park. The $2.3 billion L.A. Live project is designed to entertain sports fans, conventioneers, and moviegoers with a 55-story convention center and two hotels: a JW Marriott and a Ritz-Carlton. Scheduled to open in 2010, that will add 1,001 guest rooms to the area, a 7,100-seat theater, a 14-screen Regal Cineplex, and a dozen restaurants (among them Fleming's Prime Steakhouse, Katsuya, a branch of Long Beach–based Yard House, and a Rosa Mexicano direct from New York). Also on the horizon are a Starbucks and a New Zealand Natural Ice Cream. Other plans call for a museum to showcase the history of the Grammys; a broadcast studio, Club Nokia; a 2,200-seat live music auditorium; and more venues. It's uncertain how far along the development will be by the time you read this, but we wanted to give you a heads-up

in case you happen to stroll by during construction and wonder what's up with that. ♦ In the meantime, should you like more information, go to www.aegworldwide.com or call 213/742.7850

Within The Grand Avenue Project and L.A. Live:

NOKIA THEATRE

The first venue to appear on the scene of this 5.6 million-square-foot entertainment emporium, the 7,100-seat NOKIA Theatre opened with a bang in October 2007 with a gala presentation of the Eagles and the Dixie Chicks. We're not sure what demographics they're after, but get this eclectic lineup of entertainers that finished out the year: Neil Young, John Fogerty, Anita Baker, and, well, Larry the Cable Guy. The theater will also host family, dance, and comedy acts, award shows (the 35th American Music Awards Show took place there in November 2007), conventions, and product launches. It is expected to become LA's most popular indoor venue for live performances. ♦ 777 Chick Hearn Ct, at L.A. Live. 213/763.6000. www.nokiatheatrelalive.com

10 OMNI LOS ANGELES HOTEL AT CALIFORNIA PLAZA

$$$ This 439-room luxury property, perched atop Bunker Hill, is perfect for business travelers who want to be close to downtown's business and financial district. It's a good-looking hotel with an interesting stylized lobby where Asia meets the West with a dramatic welded steel *Yellow Fin* by David Stomeyer sitting in a glass-walled atrium; a painted silk kimono done by California artist Marie-Laurie Ilie, housed in a Japanese frame; and black Chinese chairs by David Hockney. The rooms are equally arty, done in neoclassic style with an Asian flair yet plugged in for the techno-needy, with work desks, dataports, three phones, video games for the kids, plus the usual creature comforts (robes, minibars, televisions). For nourishment there's the pretty, magnolia tree–framed **Grand Café** (★★$$), serving breakfast, lunch, and dinner as well as Sunday brunch. The eclectic international cuisine, created by executive chef Peter Dean, leans on the healthy, low-cholesterol side. And to keep you in shape, the fitness center has all the right stuff, while a mini-spa helps you relax with facials, massages, and assorted body treatments. Additional services include a full business center, complimentary town car transportation within a three-mile area, and the Omni Kids program, which keeps the little tykes

---

Restaurants/Clubs: Red | Hotels: Purple | Shops: Orange | Outdoors/Parks: Green | Sights/Culture: Blue

amused. ♦ 251 S Olive St (between W Third and W Second Sts). 213/617.3300, 800-THE-OMNI; fax: 213/617.3399. www.omnilosangeles.com &

Within the Omni Los Angeles Hotel:

NOE

★★★$$$ Accentuated by warm colors, international artwork, wood and glass, and recessed pin ceiling lights, the handsome setting, created by famed Hollywood production designer Curtis Schnell, provides an apt showcase for artfully prepared dishes such as Dungeness crab–stuffed *loup de mer,* asparagus fettuccini, hazelnut-crusted ahi, sweet and sour spinach, wild Alaskan king salmon, butter-poached lobster, lemon curd ravioli with tapioca sauce, and miso-cured Colorado lamb. For a grand finale, opt for the banana tempura with boysenberries, banana walnut ice cream, and butterscotch sauce. Then, if puffing's your penchant, have a cigar and a cognac on the pleasant outdoor patio. ♦ American/Japanese fusion ♦ Daily, dinner. Reservations essential. 213/356.4100. www.noerestaurant.com/losangeles

11 CUIDAD

★★$$ This Latin American theme restaurant marches to its own salsa drum with a lively atmosphere, great waitstaff, and good food. Its mixed bag of Latin American cuisines was created by Mary Sue Milliken and Susan Feniger of Border Grill fame. You can enjoy Cuban sandwiches, Argentine empanadas, Brazilian moqueca, tapas, and assorted Hispanic drinks and wines. The atmosphere is colorful. The best time to go for dinner is after 8PM, when the theater crowd leaves for the show. The restaurant offers diners free shuttle service to the Music Center and Staples Center. ♦ M-F, lunch; daily, dinner. Reservations suggested for dinner. 445 S Figueroa St, Ste. 100 (at Fifth St). 213/486.5172. www.cuidad-la.com

12 444 FLOWER BUILDING

This undistinguished corporate tower replaced the 1935 Sunkist Building, with its hanging gardens and statuary. Known by many as the *LA Law* building, it was seen weekly in the opening credits for the TV series. Steps and escalators lead up from a palm-shaded plaza to an upper garden on Hope Street; along the way is a distinguished collection of modern artworks by Mark di Suvero, Michael Heizer, Frank Stella, Bruce Nauman, and Robert Rauschenberg. A pedestrian bridge over Flower Street connects the building with the Bonaventure Hotel. ♦ 444 Flower St (between W Fifth and W Fourth Sts)

13 STUART M. KETCHUM DOWNTOWN YMCA

This sleek coed facility features the latest equipment for sports enthusiasts: an indoor lap pool, a running track, and squash, racquetball, and tennis courts. ♦ Nonmembers pay a daily-use fee. 401 S Hope St (at W Fourth St). 213/624.2348

14 CALIFORNIA PLAZA

This 11.5-acre site developed by Bunker Hill Associates adheres to **Arthur Erikson Architects'** master plan with two slick-skinned office towers with curving glass walls anchored by granite. There's a residential tower, a spiral amphitheater, a museum, and a 1.5-acre outdoor perfor-mance space and garden. A restored version of the historic **Angel's Flight Railway** (the world's shortest railway) runs between Hill and Olive Streets. Outdoor con-certs—featuring popular music, classical tunes, and such one-of-a-kind entertain-ment as El Vez, a Latino Elvis imperson-ator—are some of the popular events. ♦ S Grand Ave (between W Fourth and W First Sts). 213/687.2000

15 HARBOR FREEWAY OVERPASS

Between Figueroa Street and Beaudry Avenue, Wilshire Boulevard passes over the Harbor Freeway. A few blocks north is the stack interchange where the Hollywood, Harbor, and Pasadena Freeways form the hub of the freeway system. Driving north gives you the closest view you will want of two unusually inept buildings: pseudoclassi-cal towers for Coast Savings and Home Savings.

16 CITY NATIONAL PLAZA

To replace the 1929 Atlantic Richfield Building, a flamboyant black-and-gold Art Deco tower, the Atlantic Richfield Co. (ARCO) commissioned **AC Martin Partners** in 1972 to design twin 52-story charcoal-gray shafts—the architectural equivalent of a sober business suit—to house its own expanded offices, and those of the Bank of America. Two 20-foot-high bronze doors from the old building are displayed in the lobby of the south tower. On the plaza is *Double Ascension,* a striking red helical sculpture by Herbert Bayer, who also designed the executive floors from the carpets on up. The escalators on Flower Street lead down to seven acres of subterranean shopping and eating, plus a church, fitness center, and post office. Yet another refurbishing in 2003, when Los Angeles developer James A. Thomas launched a $125 million face-lift, included lots of freestanding illuminated glass signs, several fountains, a European-style central public plaza, a restaurant in each plaza, and a major upgrade of the underground shopping complex. The design by architects **AC Martin Partners**, according to Thomas, intends to entice you inside. ◆ M-Sa. 515 S Flower St (between W Sixth and W Fifth Sts). 213/613.1900

17 FIG@WILSHIRE TOWER

Constructed in 1991 by **AC Martin Partners,** the granite, glass, and bronze tower has the dull and dated look of a chunky block—but don't let that stop you from seeing where all the design effort went. At its base, a 45-degree setback creates outdoor spaces that link the tower to the street. Interior screens stripe two dramatic 80-foot-high lobbies with light, accenting granite and marble floors and walls. ◆ 601 S Figueroa St (at W Sixth St)

18 WILSHIRE GRAND HOTEL

$$ At press time a $40 million renovation was making headway at this imposing 900-room hotel. Intended to increase the hotel's appeal to conventioneers as well as leisure travelers, the redo includes major enhancements and modernizations to public areas and rooms. The interior has been livened up with a more contemporary décor. Flat-screen TVs, high-speed Internet access, modern furnishings, and new bathrooms are going into every guest room. Each of the four restaurants is undergoing a face-lift. Amenities include a small fitness center and an outdoor pool. Guests who prefer more heavy-duty workouts than the in-house fitness center can get complimen-tary passes to nearby **Gold's Gym.** ◆ 930 Wilshire Blvd (between S-Figueroa and Francisco Sts). 213/688.7777, 800/773.2888. www.wilshiregrand.com

Within the Wilshire Grand:

KYOTO

★★$$ Designer sushi is served in a dramatic setting whose centerpiece is a 600-gallon aquarium filled with colorful coral and saltwater fish. Chef Horii Hitoshi's lovely offerings include sashimi, crab legs, red snapper, and a delightful tempura bar. ◆ Japanese/Seafood ◆ M-F, lunch and dinner. Valet parking available. 213/896.3812

SEOUL JUNG

★★★$$ Chef Seek Soo Kim creates an exotic Korean menu centering on pork, beef, fish, and chicken. All are skillfully prepared on your marble-tabletop barbecue, in the style of the chef's homeland. ◆ Korean ◆ M-F, lunch and dinner; Sa, Su, dinner. 213/629.4321

CITY GRILL

★$$$ City Grill's tasty Cobb salad helps business execs stick to their diets. ◆ California ◆ M-F, lunch and dinner. 213/623.5971

CARDINI

★★$$$$ New York architects **Voorzanger and Mills** designed the stunning postmodern interior of this restaurant in crisp tones of gray and blue. The space is beautifully lit and divided into enclosures by arches, columns, and open grilles. Standout dishes include thin slices of veal with an herb-laden sauce; black ravioli filled with shrimp, cream, and chives; and risotto with seafood and porcini mushrooms. ◆ Italian ◆ M-F, lunch. Reservations recommended. 213/896.3822

19 TAKAMI SUSHI & ROBATA RESTAURANT + ELEVATE LOUNGE

★★★$$$ Wow, what a place for some sushi and then some! Situated atop of an office building on the 21st floor, this upscale club/restaurant rocks with the well-heeled, designer-draped crowd who come for the food, scene, and high-energy action. The food's fab, though the service can be spotty. But the awesome view of downtown LA is worth the wait. Ask for an outdoor table and sip a signature beverage while poring through the extensive menu. That's how we bided our time until diving into amazing appetizers like edamame with garlic butter and soy sauce, vegetable tempura, poki martini (spicy tuna poki with three layers of caviar mashed potatoes), and beef robata. All that before entrées of New York steak and asparagus and Chilean sea bass. And we still had room for a crème brûlée trio of green tea, vanilla, and pistachio, and an apple spring roll topped with cinnamon and walnut caramel sauce. Stay for the late-night action in the 6,000-square-foot Elevate Lounge, where downtowners get down 'til the wee small hours. ◆ Japanese ◆ Reservations advised. 811 Wilshire Blvd (at S Flower St). 213/236.9600. www.takamisushi.com; www.elevatelounge.com

20 CALIFORNIA CLUB

For years LA was in effect run by members of this private club. The Renaissance-style

---

brick building, designed in 1930 by **Robert Farquhar,** is still a staid and elegant bastion of power and old money. Accept an invitation if you get so lucky; the food is surprisingly good. ◆ 538 S Flower St (between W Sixth and W Fifth Sts). 213/622.1391 ⅏

21 RICHARD J. RIORDAN CENTRAL LIBRARY

Designed in 1930 by **Bertram Goodhue and Carleton Winslow Sr.,** this LA landmark—named for the former mayor of Los Angeles—combines Beaux Arts monumentality with touches of Byzantine, Egyptian, and Roman styles in the surface ornament and incised lettering. There's even a hint of Art Deco. The building underwent a $214 million restoration in 1986, and a 1997 renovation by **Hardy Holzman Pfeiffer** added a lovely, bench-lined strolling garden and the Tom Bradley Wing, featuring an eight-story glass atrium and a children's reading room. Of special interest is Dean Cornwell's four-panel mural, which covers 48 square feet and is illustrated with 300 heroic-size figures that depict the history of California. As you enter at street level, notice the vaulted ceiling painted by Petropoulos. ◆ The hours change from time to time, so call ahead. 630 W Fifth St (between S Grand Ave and Flower St). 213/228.7000 ⅏

21 CAFE PINOT

★★★$$ Right outside the Central Library, this lively spot is superchef Joachim Splichal's gourmet version of a casual brasserie. Top items on the menu include a delightfully cheesy French onion soup; polenta with rock shrimp, pancetta, and asparagus; and escargot in wine sauce served on a brioche. Lighter spa cuisine is offered as well. Be sure to sample the homemade ice cream. There's also outdoor seating in a glorious patio filled with olive trees. ◆ California/French ◆ M-F, lunch and dinner; Sa, dinner. 700 W Fifth St (between S Grand Ave and Flower St). 213/239.6500. www.patinagroup.com ⅏

22 FIRST INTERSTATE WORLD CENTER

It's been called the tallest building in the West: a 1,017-foot, 75-story tower designed in 1990 by **Pei Cobb Freed & Partners Architects/Harold Fredenburg** and developed by Maguire Thomas Partners. The architects achieved an interplay between orthogonal and circular geometries, which are revealed in the setbacks that lead up to a circular crown. A number of attorneys and other professionals have their offices in this prestigious building. ◆ 633 W Fifth St (between S Grand Ave and Flower St)

At First Interstate World Center:

BUNKER HILL STEPS

Test your endurance by climbing this monumental stairway, designed in 1990 by Lawrence Halprin. The wide steps wrap up and around the base of the First Interstate tower, linking Bunker Hill to Hope Street (the two halves of the business district) and forming part of a sequence of landscaped pedestrian areas that Halprin calls "choreography for the urban dance." To come are his West Lawn for the library and Hope Street Promenade leading down to Grand Hope Park.

23 ONE BUNKER HILL

The former Southern California Edison building, built in 1931 by **Allison & Allison,** is a handsome Art Deco corner block with a lobby mural by Hugo Ballin. The building has been elegantly restored. ◆ S Grand Ave and W Fifth St

24 THE GAS COMPANY

Based on the plans of **Skidmore, Owings & Merrill/R. Keating** and developed by Maguire Thomas Partners, this elegant 62-story high-rise of polished granite and tinted glass steps and tapers around a core of boat-shaped elliptical blue glass. The shape of the 1991 building intentionally resembles the blue gas flame that is now the official symbol of The Gas Company. The lobby, reached by an escalator, faces a water garden and a 300-foot-high Frank Stella mural painted on the adjacent Pacific Bell/AT&T Building. The colorful, abstract *Dusk* is part of Stella's Moby-Dick series, which explores motion and travel themes. ◆ 555 W Fifth St (at S Grand Ave)

25 THE MILLENNIUM BILTMORE HOTEL

$$$ This Italianate Beaux Arts structure was originally constructed in 1923 by **Schultze & Weaver** and was long considered a social hub. In 1927, at a lavish banquet here, Douglas Fairbanks Sr. announced that the newly incorporated Academy of Motion Picture Arts and Sciences would begin giving out awards to recognize distinctive achievement in the movies. The palatial décor of the public rooms has been refurbished and regilded several times over the years. All of its 683 rooms are adorned with original artwork, and display nice touches such as chairs upholstered in imported peacock-design tapestry.

Bathrooms boast creamy beige fixtures and accents of marble and gold. The Premier Level rooms (floors 10 and 11) are ideal for business travelers, with fully stocked desks, voice mail, and data port capabilities. A private Premier Level Club Lounge offers concierge service, complimentary continental breakfast, and evening hors d'oeuvres. The Presidential Suite has a private elevator; the Music Suite a grand piano. The nondescript health club is crammed with out-of-date equipment, which hopefully will be updated soon. The indoor pool, however, is more appealing. There's also a full-service business center with all the latest techno gadgets, plus a sports bar, an outdoor pool, and child-care and banquet rooms. The **LA Conservancy** (213/623.2489) offers tours of the hotel. ♦ 506 S Grand Ave (at W Fifth St). 213/624.1011, 866/866.8086 in CA; fax 213/612.1545. www.millennium-hotels.com or www.thebiltmore.com &

Within the Millennium Biltmore Hotel:

GALLERY BAR

Cheers! Here's the perfect place to sip one of the best martinis in town while enjoying some fine live jazz performances on Saturday nights. ♦ Daily, 4PM–2AM. 213/624.1011

GRAND AVENUE SPORTS BAR

Grab a bar stool or booth at this mega-saloon and watch your favorite sporting events on any of a dozen TV monitors. Go on the weekend and enjoy a hearty breakfast with your sports. ♦ Sports Bar/American. ♦ M-Sa, dinner (until Sunday during football season). 213/612.1595

RENDEZVOUS COURT

Afternoon tea is served English fashion in this elegant Rococo-style lounge, where you can also brush up on your manners at etiquette classes held throughout the year. ♦ Reservations suggested. 213/612.1562

26 LA INC. THE CONVENTION & VISITORS BUREAU

Maps, flyers, and advice on Southern California's attractions are available from a helpful staff that can converse in English, Spanish, Japanese, French, German, and Italian. Tickets to TV tapings and discount coupons are sometimes offered. A multilingual events hotline is also available. ♦ M-Sa. 685 S Figueroa St (at W Seventh St).

213/689.8822, 800/228.2452. www.lacvb.com

27 ENGINE COMPANY NO. 28

★★$$$ This 1912 landmark firehouse has been reborn as a stylish bar and grill. It's just the place to unwind with a cocktail and comfort food: grilled fish, garlic chicken, and spicy french fries. The wine list is excellent. ♦ American ♦ M-F, lunch and dinner; Sa, Su, dinner 5-9PM. Reservations recommended. 644 S Figueroa St (between W Seventh St and Wilshire Blvd). 213/624.6996. www.engineco.com &

28 7 & FIG @ ERNST AND YOUNG PLAZA

This urbane complex is found at the foot of Citicorp Plaza, three 42-story towers designed by **Skidmore, Owings & Merrill**. The sunken, palm-shaded patio is covered by a 144-foot canopy and ringed with three levels of specialty stores, as well as a Robinsons-May department store. Other tenants include Ann Taylor, Doubleday Books, and Johnston and Murphy. Choose between the cafés and restaurants or brown-bag it on a bench in the leafy, street-level plaza. The **Jerde Partnership** created this people-friendly space in a restrained neo-Victorian style. There's validated parking with a minimum purchase. ♦ M-Sa. 735 S Figueroa St (between W Eighth and W Seventh Sts). 213/955.7150. www.7Fig.com

29 FINE ARTS BUILDING

Designed by **Walker & Eisen** in 1925, this splendidly eclectic landmark was first built as a complex of artists' studios enclosing an exhibition hall, and was later converted to office space. Brenda Levin & Associates restored the Romanesque façade and the high-ceiling tiled lobby with its gargoyles, fountain, and fanciful murals, and remodeled the interiors. ♦ 811 W Seventh St (between Flower and S Figueroa Sts)

30 HILTON CHECKERS HOTEL

$$$$ This small luxury hotel was created within the shell of the Mayflower, itself a posh establishment when it opened in 1927. The Mayflower has undergone several ownership changes, the Hilton group being its most recent. The 200 guest rooms and suites are furnished in a traditional style, with muted colors; niceties include writing desks and marble baths. Every room has three telephones, and the hotel offers a full range of electronic equipment, including personal fax machines, as well as 24-hour

---

Restaurants/Clubs: Red | Hotels: Purple | Shops: Orange | Outdoors/Parks: Green | Sights/Culture: Blue

room service. There are also meeting rooms, limousine service, a multilingual staff, and a rooftop spa with a tiny pool. ♦ 535 S Grand Ave (between W Sixth and W Fifth Sts). 213/624.0000, 800/757. HILTON; fax 213/626.9906. www.hilton.com &

31 WATER GRILL

★★$$ If seafood's your thing, this is the place. Begin your meal with mouthwatering oysters, then plow through a menu of exquisitely prepared seasonal fresh fish. Located on the ground floor of the Pacific Mutual Building, the softly lit dining room is done in leather and mohair. ♦ Seafood ♦ M-F, lunch and dinner; Sa, Su, dinner. Reservations recommended. 544 S Grand Ave (between W Sixth and W Fifth Sts). 213/891.0900 &

31 CARAVAN BOOK STORE

This fine antiquarian bookseller specializes in California history and memorabilia. ♦ M-Sa. 550 S Grand Ave (at W Sixth St). 213/626.9944

32 CASEY'S BAR

$$ This is a popular after-work meeting place for office workers. Simple fare is served in a setting of white-tile floors, dark paneling, and tin ceilings. ♦ American ♦ M-F, lunch and dinner. Reservations recommended. 613 S Grand Ave (between Wilshire Blvd and W Sixth St). 213/629.2353

33 777 TOWER

Part of the Citicorp Plaza and home to a number of law firms and other profession-als, this 53-story skyline standout, designed by **Cesar Pelli & Associates** in 1991, has a crisp profile of off-white metal that's luminous in sunlight. Indented corners with flared accents emphasize its vertical height, curving form, and solidity. The three-story lobby is glass-walled on the east and south, while a double-height colonnade faces the busy **Seventh Market Place** next door. ♦ 777 S Figueroa St (at W Eighth St)

34 MACY'S PLAZA

Unfortunately, this indoor mall isn't quite as appealing as it once was. It still attracts lots of locals who shop at Macy's, Victoria's Secret, and a few other stores and work out at a bare-bones branch of Bally's Fitness. Actually, it's worth a visit just to get a sense of the ethnicity and diversity of LA's downtown population. You'll feel like you're in another country. ♦ Daily. 750 W Seventh St (at Flower St). Mall information: 213/624.2891

COMMERCIAL & EXPOSITION PARK

A unique mix of interesting things to do and see . . .

This area conveys an intriguing complexity, with severa shops and hotels to the north; commercial, wholesale, manufacturing, and distribution sites to the east; and **Exposition Park** and the **University of Southern California (USC)** to the south. **Pershing Square,** the hub of the downtown business area, is active during regular business hours but almost deserted at night. Near the **Coliseum** and the **Shrine Auditorium** (the site of such events as the Grammy Awards and the American Music Awards), nighttime traffic jams occur when football and concert fans collide. The streets of the wholesale distribution centers are quiet until after midnight, when hundreds of trucks fill the roadways. And in the early dawn hours, movie crews may be filming on the deserted streets.

1 BLUE VELVET

★★$$ It's too hip and kind of quirky, with a knockout interior highlighted by silver metal and deep red and blue tones, and an outdoor swimming pool complete with chaises and an open fireplace where scenesters gather nightly for drinks. The real draw is the innovative drinks and bar food like sautéed shrimp with popcorn, Thai shrimp toast, tiny Monte Cristo sandwiches, and Spanish-style pizzas. Regular offerings range from black bean garlic-marinated tofu and fig salad starters to wild king salmon, meat and potatoes, Muscovy duck breast, and yummy desserts like brûléed peach, chocolate, and peanut butter bombe and coconut rum baba. ♦ Lounge/Restaurant ♦ Daily, lunch and dinner; dinner only on weekends. Reservations a must. 750 S Garland Ave (between W Seventh and W Eighth Sts). 213/239.0061

2 KAWADA HOTEL

$ Hidden on an undesirable stretch, this 116-room hotel built in the shell of a once-dilapidated 1920s brick building has retained its quaint exterior character with the original fire escapes and flower boxes. The interior is contemporary economy, with incredibly reasonable rates for downtown LA. ♦ 200 S Hill St (at W Second St). 213/621.4455, 800/752.9232; fax 213/687.4455. www.kawadahotel.com

3 BROADWAY

Considered the main shopping street for Los Angeles's Latino community, Broadway's crowded sidewalks and exotic sounds and smells give it an intensely urban quality— much like upper Broadway in New York, or even Mexico City. But changing tastes, neglect, and speculative greed threaten the architectural legacy of the prewar years, when Broadway was LA's "Great White Way."

The once beautiful façades have been covered in plastic signs, the terrazzo sidewalk ornament is cracked and filthy, and, worst of all, the upper stories of several buildings have been lopped off in order to reduce tax assessments. Local restoration groups are working to protect the remaining structures.

3 HISTORIC THEATER DISTRICT

The first district of its kind to be listed on the National Register of Historic Places, this strip of theaters stretches from Third Street to Olympic Boulevard. They are open to the public by LA Conservancy tour only. Noteworthy sights include the **Million Dollar Theater** (307 S Broadway, at W Third St), a stunning building with a Churrigueresque exterior and a lavish Baroque interior; the **United Artists** (933 S Broadway, between W Olympic Blvd and W Ninth St), a **Walker & Eisen**–designed Spanish Gothic tower housing a cathedral-like theater that was financed by Mary Pickford, Douglas Fairbanks, and Charlie Chaplin; and the **Los Angeles Theater** (615 S Broadway, at W Sixth St), a Baroque structure designed by **S. Charles Lee** that is thought by many to be the finest theater in the city (parts of the movie *Batman Forever* were shot here). The **Orpheum Theatre** (842 S Broadway) mimics the Paris Opera with its polished brass doors, silk wall panels, marble pilasters, chandeliers, and bare-breasted bronze females on the lighting fixtures. Live performances, entertainment, weddings, fashion shows, and special events are held here regularly. The **LA Conservancy** (213/623.2489) offers guided tours of the district. ♦ S Broadway (between W Olympic Blvd and W Third St). Events hotline, 213/430.4219. www.LAconservancy.org

3 GRAND CENTRAL PUBLIC MARKET

Don't miss this indoor bazaar, which extends from Broadway to Hill Street. Ira Yellin, a developer with the vision to see Broadway's potential, commissioned Brenda Levin to undertake a major restoration. The stalls sell a wide range of food, from fish tacos to soups. Plastic wrap is unknown here— butchers use waxed paper and fruit and vegetable vendors select your produce from beautiful piles (don't help yourself) and brown-bag it. If you're thirsty, stop at **Tropical Zone Juice Bar**. ♦ Daily. 317 S Broadway (between W Fourth and W Third Sts). 213/624.2378

4 BRADBURY BUILDING

LA's most extraordinary interior is a Victorian treasure that was, in its time, futuristic. This office building was designed in 1893 by architectural draftsman **George Wyman,** who was inspired by a message from his dead brother, received via a Ouija board. Behind the plain brick façade is a skylit interior court that is a marvel of dark foliate grillwork, tiled stairs, polished wood, marble, and open-cage elevators. It was used to memorable effect in the movie *Blade Runner,* itself a vision of the future. Only the lobby level is open to the public. ♦ M-Sa. 304 S Broadway (at W Third St). 213/626.1893

5 SPRING STREET

What was once called the "Wall Street of the West" is slowly recovering from a long period of neglect. This National Register Historical District showcases a treasury of buildings from the first three decades of the century. Many have been imaginatively recycled. The huge **Ronald Reagan State Office Building** between Third and Fourth Streets, along with lofts and apartments, were added.

6 TITLE GUARANTEE & TRUST BUILDING

John and Donald Parkinson's romanticized 1930 skyscraper has a Gothic crown and zigzag details on the façade. The building now houses luxury rental apartments. ♦ 401 W Fifth St (at S Hill St)

7 PERSHING SQUARE

SITE Projects, the New York architects best known for their surreal Best Co. stores, won a 1986 competition with a proposal to transform this site into an undulating landscape, but their plan was rejected by neighboring property owners who said it lacked accessibility. Working with developer Maguire Thomas Partners and the Community Redevelopment Agency, the property owners instead hired Mexico City architect **Ricardo Legorreta** to design a $14 million renovation plan with landscape architect **Hanna Olin.** The layout includes an amphitheater for public performances, an eye-catching 120-foot purple campanile (Legorreta's signature), and large shade trees. A crack in the ground was placed there to suggest earthquake damage. There's a large outdoor ice-skating rink open November through January. ♦ Bounded by S Hill and Olive Sts, and W Sixth and W Fifth Sts

8 OVIATT BUILDING

Designed in 1928 by **Walker & Eisen,** this was formerly an exclusive men's store, built for haberdasher James Oviatt, who had fallen in love with Art Deco during his many

---

buying trips to Paris. Oviatt commissioned the decorative glass from **René Lalique,** imported the furnishings from France, and lived in a marvelous zigzag penthouse above the shop. In 1976, the building was bought by developer Wayne Ratkovich, who hired architect Brenda Levin to restore its original glories and leased the upper floors as offices. You can rent the thirteenth-floor penthouse for catered parties of up to 50 and dance under the stars on the 1,500-square-foot rooftop. ♦ 617 Olive St

(between W Seventh and W Sixth Sts). 213/622.6096

9 JEWELRY DISTRICT

Though this papery building does nothing for Pershing Square, the 1982 interactive neon artwork that runs the length of its façade— *Generators of the Cylinder* by Canadian Michael Hayden—is worth a look. If you're more interested in flashing diamonds than in flashing lights, the old jewelry district, offering

highly competitive prices, extends a block south on Hill Street between Sixth and Seventh Streets. ♦ 550 S Hill St (at W Sixth St)

10 ALEXANDRIA HOTEL

$$ A fine hotel when it opened in 1906, the 400-room Alexandria once welcomed Theodore Roosevelt, Enrico Caruso, Sarah Bernhardt, and the first generation of moviemakers. Today it is a residence hotel only. ♦ 501 S Spring St (at W Fifth St). 213/626.7484

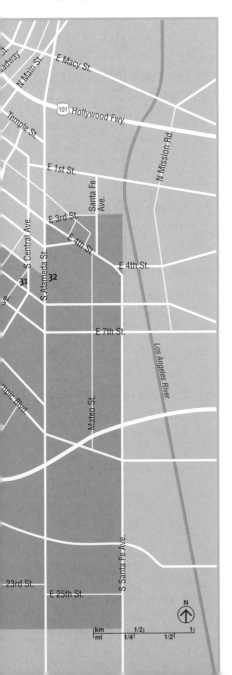

11 CONTINENTAL BUILDING

At 175 feet in height, this was LA's first skyscraper, an ornate pile designed in 1904 by **John Parkinson,** the architect of 17 other surviving buildings on the street. ♦ 408 S Spring St (at W Fourth St)

12 ZUCCA

★★★$$ Another Patina Group/Joachim Splichal winner, this popular indoor/outdoor downtown eatery is big with the theater crowd and Splichal groupies who will follow him anywhere. The clubby room is done in rich woods, Venetian crystal chandeliers, and treasures imported from Italy. The bar is always hopping and the tables are pretty much filled nightly. The menu takes an Italian twist and everything tastes great, from the antipasto to specialties such as *bistecca alla fiorentina*, roasted lamb sirloin with purple artichokes, and roasted striped sea bass. ♦ Italian. ♦ M-F, lunch and dinner; daily, dinner. Reservations necessary. 801 S Figueroa St (at W Eighth St). 213/614.7800; e-mail: zucca@patinagroup.com. www.patinagroup.com

13 THE ORIGINAL PANTRY

★★$ This 1924 restaurant is the best place in town for hearty breakfast food served in generous portions. Later in the day, steaks, chops, meat loaf, and more are featured, as well as great coleslaw, sourdough bread, and hash browns. Owned by LA mayor Richard Riordan (who also is a frequent patron), the place never closes. Next door is the **Pantry's Bake & Sandwich Shoppe,** which offers just what the name promises (open daily, 6AM-3PM). ♦ American ♦ Daily, 24 hours. 877 S Figueroa St (at W Ninth St). 213/972.9279 ⅃

13 RIORDAN'S TAVERN

★★★$$$$ Not content to own two restaurants (**The Original Pantry,** above, and **Gladstone's Malibu,** which he saved from extinction), former LA Mayor Richard J. Riordan opened this New York–style neighborhood tavern in 2007. The handsome mahogany bar acts as the centerpiece of the stylish restaurant/pub while exposed brick walls plastered with photos of the man himself, distressed wood floors, sports memorabilia, and hunter greens set the mood for lunch, dinner, or what the owner calls "stiff" drinks. Evening fare includes New York, bone-in beef chop, filet mignon, and Porterhouse steaks, beef burgers, lobster tails, chicken, salmon, or combos. Lunch offerings include hand-carved sandwiches made with freshly baked breads and beef, lamb, or pork; salads (the Caesar rules); crab cakes; and cool coleslaw. They also serve the best cheesecake in LA, and we do mean the best. ♦ American Chophouse

◆ Daily, lunch and dinner. Reservations advised. 875 S Figueroa St (at Ninth St, next door to Original Pantry). 213/627.6879. www.riordanstavern.com

14 O HOTEL

$$ Hip, trendy, and so New York, this tiny 68-room boutique hotel is the perfect place for budget seekers with champagne tastes. Set in a historic 1920s building in the heart of LA's financial district, the place rings with great vibes. Rooms are quite compact but well-appointed with queen or double beds, flat-screen TVs, high-speed Internet access, MP3 hookups on alarm clocks, minibars, small bathrooms with showers, and get this, old-fashioned phones. The attractive lobby houses a little restaurant for breakfast, lunch, and dinner and a lounge for cocktails. There's also a spa and fitness room. Room rates vary depending on demand and could be anywhere from $90 to $140 daily; can't beat that. ◆ 819 S Flower St (at W Ninth St). 213/623.9904; fax 213/614.8010. www.ohotelgroup.com

15 STORY BUILDING & GARAGE

Morgan, Walls & Clements designed the 1916 Beaux Arts tower, faced in white terra-cotta and with superb zigzag garage gates. The garage was designed by **Clement Stiles** in 1934. ◆ S Broadway and W Sixth St

16 BROADWAY SPRING ARCADE

An Australian company turned this enormous skylit space linking Broadway and Spring Street into a three-level shopping arcade. The 1923 Spanish Renaissance office block has been fully renovated into residential units and retail outlets. ◆ 542 S Broadway (between W Sixth and W Fifth Sts)

17 LOS ANGELES CENTER STUDIOS

Originally a bank designed in 1916 by **John Parkinson**, this building was dramatically remodeled and expanded by John Sergio Fisher and Associates into a complex of four small, steeply raked theaters leading out of the original banking hall. Failing to garner broader public support, the center has become a major player in film and television productions, to which it leases state-of-the-art, high-tech soundstages, 72 furnished dressing rooms, a commissary, and screening rooms. ◆ 1201 W Fifth St (at Spring St). 213/534.3000; fax 213/534.3001.www.lacenterstudios.com

18 FIGUEROA HOTEL

$$ This 280-room hotel has a superb location near the **Los Angeles Convention Center.** Amenities include an enormous swimming pool and **The Clay Pit** restaurant. ◆ 939 S Figueroa St (between W Olympic Blvd and W Ninth St). 213/627.8971, 800/421.9092; fax 213/689.0305

19 GRAND HOPE PARK

🅟 This two-acre park, designed by **Lawrence Halprin,** comprises a series of outdoor rooms created by trellises, a fountain, a clock tower, and trees, all enhanced by the work of leading local artists. It is the hub of the **South Park development,** a residential/commercial/office neighbor-hood bounded by Main and Eighth Streets and the Harbor and Santa Monica Freeways. A landscaped promenade along South Hope Street links the park with **Bunker Hill Steps** and the renovated library. ◆ W Ninth and S Hope Sts

20 CLIFTON'S BROOKDALE CAFETERIA

$ You'll find a redwood forest interior with a waterfall and stuffed moose at this cafeteria. On the sidewalk are early-1930s terrazzo roundels depicting city landmarks. ◆ American ◆ Daily, breakfast, lunch, and dinner. 648 S Broadway (between W Seventh and W Sixth Sts). 213/627.1673 ও

21 SPRING STREET TOWERS

Schultze & Weaver's handsome 1924 Beaux Arts bank has been recycled as an office building, though the exterior has changed little. ◆ 117 W Seventh St (between S Los Angeles and S Spring Sts)

22 HOLIDAY INN CITY CENTER

$$ This 195-room hotel is convenient to the commercial center of downtown, and popular with business travelers. ◆ 1020 S Figueroa St (between W 11th St and W Olympic Blvd). 213/748.1291, 800/628.5240. www.holidayinnLA.com

23 FASHION INSTITUTE OF DESIGN AND MERCHANDISING

The **Jerde Partnership**'s characteristically eclectic 1990 design comprises a four-story arcade and terrace overlooking **Grand Hope Park.** The complex houses a fashion museum and gallery, shops, video production facilities, classrooms, and offices. Make a note to visit the adjacent gallery during the month after the Academy Awards nomina-tions are announced. That's when they dress mannequins in the actual costumes worn by Oscar candidates. It's really worth it. ◆ 919 S Grand Ave (between W Olympic Blvd and W Ninth St). 213/624.1200. www.fidm.edu

24 RALPHS FRESH FARE

We're not usually in the habit of including grocery stores, but this mega food shop, part of the Ralphs supermarket chain, is definitely worth noting. Debatably the most popular of its kind, locals swamp to this Dean & Deluca–like yuppie grocery market day and night, many to take out food from the fantastic deli section, which carries everything from beef Wellington to tuna salads and beyond. There's also a major wine cellar and regular tastings, a pharmacy, dry cleaner's, and organic food section. ♦ Daily. W Ninth St, between S Broadway and S Grand Ave

25 EASTERN COLUMBIA BUILDING

Formerly the Eastern Columbia, constructed in 1929 by **Claude Beelman,** this is downtown's finest Art Deco building since the Richfield Tower was razed. The 13-story tower, faced in turquoise terra-cotta with dark-blue and gold trim and ornamented with oddly twisted zigzag moldings, now houses luxury condos. ♦ 849 S Broadway (between W Ninth and W Eighth Sts)

26 LOS ANGELES CONVENTION CENTER

This municipal facility has been tripled in size, to 810,000 square feet, to lure major conventions, trade shows, and public events such as the Auto Show in January and the Travel Show in the spring. Twin 155-foot-high glass-and-steel lobby pavilions mark the $287 million project, designed by **Gruen Associates/Pei Cobb Freed & Partners Architects** on a 63-acre site. One of the most striking features is a massive curve of light-refracting blue-green glass just north of the intersection of the Santa Monica and Harbor Freeways. A four-acre open plaza named for late city councilman Gilbert W. Lindsay fronts Figueroa Street. As part of the Art-in-Architecture program, more than 60,000 feet of artist Alexis Smith's terrazzo designs pave the floors, including a world map design featuring medallions derived from early Pacific Rim cultures. ♦ 1201 S Figueroa St (between Venice Blvd and W 11th St). 213/741.1151

Adjacent to the Convention Center:

STAPLES CENTER

Brace yourselves, sports fans, this $403 million, behemoth athletic arena/entertainment emporium took on a new glam appearance after the addition of $10 million of amenities aimed at the comfort-crazed upscale market. We're talking high-tech LED video screens, plush carpeting, and cushy seats. Now X Games followers, concertgoers, and sports buffs can wallow in the lap of luxury while taking in the action. In the meantime outside the arena, Staples owner AEG and its billionaire proprietor, Philip Anschutz, are in the middle of a billion-dollar development next door that includes a 1,200-room, 55-story hotel and condo complex north of the facility, the 7,000-seat **Nokia Theatre,** chic shops, restaurants, and a TV studio. Staples Center is home to the LA Lakers and LA Clippers basketball teams, LA Kings hockey team, X Games, and LA Avengers arena football team. The complex is also used for concerts, ice shows (such as the 2002 Figure Skating Championship), and events (this is where the 2000 Democratic Convention assembled). An ideal venue for any event, the center has 23 refreshments stands, 1,200 television monitors, 55 rest rooms, over a dozen meeting rooms, 2,500 premier seats (roughly 20,000 total seating occupancy), and 160 high-priced ($900 to $7,000 a night) luxury suites (where Jack Nicholson, Tom Hanks, and other well-heeled sorts view events in style while being catered to by waiters and cocktail waitpersons). The suites, which can accommodate 20 to 140 people, are sold by event or season. Those who can't afford this kind of luxury have their pick of thousands of less expensive options. ♦ 1111 S Figueroa St. 213/742.7100; fax: 213/742.7269. www.staplescenter.com &

27 HERALD EXAMINER BUILDING

Julia Morgan, the first woman trained at the Ecole des Beaux Arts in Paris and the designer of William Randolph Hearst's San Simeon castle, created this Spanish Mission Revival design in 1912, inspired by the California Building from the 1893 Chicago World's Fair. The newspaper is now defunct, but in 2005 the Hearst Corporation, which owns the property, hired developer Urban Partners to restore and convert the property into a residential and retail complex with two towers designed by award-winning architect **Thom Mayne.** The plans call for a 37-story complex with 330 units and a 23-story structure with 235 condos. ♦ 1111 S Broadway (at W 11th St)

28 MAYAN

An upscale nightclub now occupies what was once the **Mayan Theatre,** built in 1927 by **Morgan, Walls & Clements**. The auditorium, which opened with a Gershwin revue and then was long relegated to porn, now contains a two-level dance floor and bar, popular among movie stars and top models. Warrior priests glare from the façade; inside is looming statuary and a riot of ornament inspired by an excavated Mayan tomb (much as King Tut's launched a fad for ancient Egypt in the early 1920s). Next door is the **Belasco**, another theater by the same architects, and now available for rental. Across the street is **Tony's Burger**, a 1932 log cabin, while presiding over the parking lot is Kent Twitchell's 70-foot mural of Ed Ruscha—just one of LA's surreal juxtapositions. ♦ F, Sa. 1038 S Hill St (between W 11th St and W Olympic Blvd). 213/746.4287

29 LA FASHION DISTRICT

Los Angeles has been a major center for high-quality garments at bargain prices since the 1930s, well before the advent of the outlet mall. First gaining fame for women's sportswear were Cole of California, Catalina, and Rose Marie Reid, three companies that transformed the nation's beaches. Today, jobbers and discount stores offering low prices on everything from children's wear to leather coats to knockoff T-shirts line Los Angeles Street from Seventh Street down to Washington Boulevard. A concentration of retail womenswear bargains can be found in the **Cooper Building** (860 S Los Angeles St, at E Ninth St; 213/622.1139). Across the street is **Academy Award Clothes** (821 S Los Angeles St; 213/622.9125), with a huge selection of quality men's suits and formalwear, and courteous service. ♦ Bounded by S San Pedro St and S Broadway, and Washington Blvd and Seventh St. www.fashiondistrict.org

30 LOS ANGELES FLOWER MARKET

As at the **Wholesale Produce Market** (see below), the action here begins in the wee hours of the morning. The **American Floral Exchange** and the **Growers' Wholesale Terminal** are huge halls of flowers reflecting the seasons that Southern California doesn't have. Wholesalers are willing to sell a box to anyone, and Wall Street is lined with stalls where smaller merchants offer potted plants to the public at substantial discounts. The best bargains are to be had after 9AM, and on Saturday mornings when the traders clear out their stocks for the weekend. ♦ M, W, 8AM-12PM; Tu, Th-Sa, 6AM-11PM. 754 Wall St (between W Eighth and W Seventh Sts). 213/622.1966

31 THE FISHERMAN'S OUTLET

★$ You can either buy fish to take home at this retail and wholesale establishment or eat at outdoor tables. There are a dozen varieties to choose from—broiled, deep-fried, or Cajun-style—in large portions at rock-bottom prices. ♦ Seafood ♦ M-Sa, 10AM-2:30PM, lunch. 529 S Central Ave (between E Sixth St and Ceres Ave). 213/627.7231 ♿

32 CIRRUS GALLERY

Contemporary paintings and fine art prints by Southern California artists are showcased here. ♦ Tu-Sa. 542 S Alameda St (between E Sixth and E Fifth Sts). 213/680.3473

33 SBC BUILDING

This 32-story commercial structure has an observation deck with an outstanding view of downtown LA's high-rises. ♦ Free. M-F. 1150 Olive St (at W 12th St). 213/742.2111

34 WHOLESALE PRODUCE MARKET

A cornucopia of produce, sold by the lug or the bushel only, is available every weekday from 3AM to noon. The market is divided into two main sections: **Produce Court,** off Ninth Street just west of Central Avenue; and **Merchant Street,** off Eighth Street just west of Central Avenue. ♦ No phone

35 COCA-COLA BUILDING

In 1937, **Robert Derrah** took five plain industrial buildings and redesigned them so they would resemble an ocean liner. The streamlined forms, hatch covers, portholes, and flying bridge bring the semblance of a little salt air to the land of asphalt. Inset at the corners are two enormous replicas of Coke bottles, a reminder that the soft-drink giant used to be housed here. ♦ 1334 S Central Ave (between E 14th and E 12th Sts)

36 NORTH UNIVERSITY PARK

Feisty local preservation groups have protected a concentration of handsome late-Victorian houses that were laid out after the 1880s' population explosion linked this prosperous residential neighborhood to downtown by streetcar. The residents have restored several of the finest examples, including the **Bassett House** (2653 S Hoover St) and the **Miller and Herriott House** (1163 W 27th St), all of which are private residences. ♦ Bounded by S Hoover St and Orchard Ave, and W 27th St and W Adams Blvd

37 THE INN AT 657

$ Here is a small, charming hotel with a friendly personality and an ideal downtown location. The 11 suites, which used to be separate apartments, are individually decorated with a mixture of contemporary furnishings and antiques; all have private baths and face either the garden or the patio. The amiable innkeeper, Patsy Carter, cooks up a lavish breakfast each morning (included in the rate) that may feature an egg dish, potato pancakes or hash browns, steak, fresh fruit, and croissants. ♦ 657 W 23rd St (between Harbor Fwy and Estrella Ave). 213/741.2200, 800/347.7512. www.patsysinn657.com ♿

38 DOHENY MANSION AND CHESTER PLACE

Thirteen grand and expensive houses were built here at the turn of the century on one block of a 15-acre residential park. The mansion, considered to be the finest structure on the block, was designed in 1900 by **Theodore Eisen** and **Sumner P. Hunt** for Oliver Posey. Shortly after its construction, oilman Edward Doheny bought the home. Few alterations have been made to the French Gothic château exterior. The house and park are now owned by **Mount St. Mary's College.** ♦ 8 Chester Pl (between W Adams Blvd and W 23rd St). 213/746.0450

39 STIMSON HOUSE

Originally designed in 1891 for prominent lumberman Douglas Stimson, this Queen Anne–style house has a tower and details reminiscent of a medieval fortress. The building is now occupied by the **Convent of the Infant of Prague** and is closed to the public. ♦ 2421 S Figueroa St (between W Adams Blvd and Harbor Fwy)

40 ST. VINCENT DE PAUL ROMAN CATHOLIC CHURCH

Oilman Edward Doheny donated the funds for this church, designed by **Albert C. Martin** in 1925 in the ornate Spanish style known as Churrigueresque, patterned after Baroque scrolled silverwork. The interior is decorated in brightly colored tiles and contains ceiling decorations painted by Giovanni Smeraldi. ♦ 621 W Adams Blvd (at S Figueroa St)

41 AUTOMOBILE CLUB OF SOUTHERN CALIFORNIA

This handsome Mission Revival building was completed in 1923. Services offered to members include insurance, towing, travel planning, and maps. Wall maps can be purchased by nonmembers. Check out the early road signs displayed in the courtyard. ♦ M-F. 2601 S Figueroa St (at W Adams Blvd). 213/741.3111

42 HEBREW UNION COLLEGE/ JEWISH INSTITUTE OF RELIGION

This institute of Jewish higher learning opened in 1954. The **Frances-Henry Library of Judaica** contains a special collection of material on the American Jewish experience. Changing exhibitions are also offered. ♦ Free. Hebrew Union College, M-F. S Hoover St (between W 32nd and W 30th Sts). 213/749.3424

43 UNIVERSITY OF SOUTHERN CALIFORNIA (USC)

Founded in 1880, USC is the oldest major independent coeducational nonsectarian

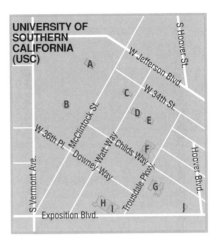

UNIVERSITY OF SOUTHERN CALIFORNIA (USC)

university on the West Coast, with a student body that's grown from 53 at its founding to 31,000. Among the professional schools are architecture, law, medicine, dentistry, social work, education, public administration, engineering, gerontology, cinema, performing arts, pharmacology, and international relations. The campus has 191 buildings on 152 acres, and is open daily year-round; free hour-long walking tours of the campus are available. ♦ M-F. Bounded by S Figueroa St and Vermont Ave, and Exposition and W-Jefferson Blvds. General information 213/740.2311

Within the University of Southern California (the letters preceding the entries refer to the map above):

A McDONALD'S OLYMPIC SWIM STADIUM

This is where USC hosts its swimming and diving events. Closed to the public. ♦ Off McClintock St and W 34th St. 213/740.5127

B DAVID X. MARKS TENNIS STADIUM

USC tennis matches are held here. Closed to the public. ♦ 213/740.5127

C ARNOLD SCHOENBERG INSTITUTE

This complex, angular structure, designed in 1978 by **Adrian Wilson & Associates,** houses the archive of the great 20th-century composer and a re-creation of the Brentwood studio in which he worked as an exile for the last 17 years of his life. Concerts of contemporary music are given in a small auditorium. ♦ Free. M-F. 3443 Watt Way. 213/740.4049

D BING THEATRE

In 1995, a version of the opera *The Ruffians* debuted at this little theater. ♦ Box office: M-F. 213/740.1249

E NORRIS CINEMA THEATRE

Film programs in this luxurious theater are open to the public most evenings. ♦ Free. 213/740.1946

F BOVARD ADMINISTRATION BUILDING

John and Donald Parkinson's 1921 Romanesque brick block contains the 1,600-seat **Norris Auditorium,** which is used for a variety of cultural events.

G HANCOCK MEMORIAL MUSEUM

Original furnishings from a now-demolished mansion are incorporated into historical rooms. ♦ Free. M-F, by appointment. 213/740.5140

H FISHER GALLERY

Offers three rotating painting and photography exhibits featuring different artists, eras, and styles. ♦ Free. Tu-Sa, Aug-May. 823 Exposition Blvd. 213/740.4561

I MUDD HALL

Since its opening in 1930, this has been an important philosophy library. The building was modeled on a medieval Tuscan monastery. ♦ M-F. 213/740.7434

J WIDNEY ALUMNI HOUSE

Built in 1880, this two-story clapboard house is furnished in period style.

44 SHRINE AUDITORIUM

This movie-set mosque, designed for and still used by the Shriners, was built in 1926. Neglected for years after the construction of the **Music Center,** the cavernous auditorium gained worldwide recognition as the site of the annual Grammy Awards and the Academy Award ceremonies, now staged in the **Kodak Theater** in Hollywood. Concerts are also held here. ♦ 665 W Jefferson Blvd (at Royal St). 213/749.5123, concert information 213/748.4141

45 SECOND BAPTIST CHURCH

Paul Williams's 1925 Lombardesque-Romanesque church serves as a center for African-American community activities. ♦ Daily. 2412 Griffith Ave (at E 24th St). 213/748.0318

46 RADISSON HOTEL AT USC

$$ This comfortable 240-room hotel is located across the street from USC's **Davidson Conference Center.** Facilities include a swimming pool, restaurant, and complimentary transportation to area attractions. ♦ 3540 S Figueroa St (between Exposition and W Jefferson Blvds). 213/748.4141, 800/333.3333; fax 213/746.3255. www.radisson.com

47 EXPOSITION PARK

This is the location of the **Memorial Coliseum, Sports Arena,** the **Museums of Science and Industry, Space,** and **Natural History,** a community clubhouse, and several landscaped areas, including a rose garden. The park began as a casual open-air market, and in 1872 was formally deeded as an agricultural park for farmers to exhibit their products. Fairs and carnivals on the grounds were organized by the Southern California Agricultural Society, including occasional horse races (and sometimes camel races) on the lot to the rear of the park. In the early twentieth century, it was home to bicycle and automobile competitions. During the park's decline in the early 1890s, it became a hangout for society's lower elements and home to three saloons. The transformation of the rowdy park into a major state, county, and city museum center was accomplished by Judge William Miller Bowen after the park's seductive attractions had made truants of the students in Sunday school classes he taught nearby. One Sunday he followed his class to discover their secret destination (a saloon), then spearheaded a drive to create a landmark of worthwhile cultural significance on the site of the infamous watering hole. By 1910, work on the **County Museum of Natural History** had begun. ♦ Bounded by S Figueroa St and Menlo Ave, and South Park Dr and Exposition Blvd

Within Exposition Park:

NATURAL HISTORY MUSEUM OF LOS ANGELES COUNTY

This handsome Spanish Renaissance building was restored in 1988 for the museum's seventy-fifth anniversary. Some of the finest traveling exhibitions in LA are presented here, on topics as varied as Hollywood, nomads, volcanoes, and Indonesian court art. But the image of the museum is indelibly set by its celebrated collections of reptile and mammal fossils (including several dinosaurs), its innovative **Schreiber Hall of Birds,** and its minerals and pre-Columbian artifacts. The **Hall of American History** shows machinery and memorabilia. Native American and folk art festivals are presented every year, and the annual **Dinosaur Ball** is a major social event. Children and adults will enjoy the **Discovery Center,** where they learn by handling and working with artifacts. The **Insect Zoo** features over 25 live insect exhibits, including giant beetles and hissing cockroaches. The museum also has a bookstore, a gift shop, and a cafeteria serving low-priced meals. ♦ Admission; free on the first Tu of every month. M-Su; daily in summer. 900 Exposition Blvd (at Menlo Ave). General information 213/763.3515. www.nhm.org

CALIFORNIA AFRO-AMERICAN MUSEUM

This museum is dedicated to African-American achievements in politics, education, athletics, and the arts. The front part of the museum is a 13,000-square-foot sculpture court with a sloping space-frame ceiling covered with tinted glass. Inside are a research library, theater, and gift shop. ♦ Free. Tu-Su. 600 State Dr (between S Figueroa St and N Coliseum Dr). 213/744.7432

CALIFORNIA MUSEUM OF SCIENCE AND INDUSTRY AEROSPACE HALL

A black-walled hangar, with echoes of radomes and space-assembly buildings, and an F-104 Starfighter pinned to the façade, seemingly frozen in flight, catch your eye when you first see this museum, designed by **Frank Gehry** in 1984. Inside, open walkways give you close-ups of suspended planes: a 1920 Wright glider, a 1927 Mono Coupe, a T-38 Air Force Trainer, and a Gemini 11 space capsule. ♦ Free. Daily. 700 State Dr (between S Figueroa St and N Coliseum Dr). 213/744.7400

Next to California Museum of Science and Industry Aerospace Hall:

IMAX THEATER

Frank Gehry's octagonal theater shows IMAX films on a five-story-high, 70-foot-wide screen. ♦ Admission. Call for schedule. 213/744.2014. www.californiasciencecenter.com

CALIFORNIA MUSEUM OF SCIENCE AND INDUSTRY

A great place for kids of all ages, this museum gets more visitors each year than any other LA museum. Its exciting displays include the **Mark Taper Hall of Economics**

and Finance, **Charles Eames**'s **Mathematica,** talking computers, and the **Kinsey Hall of Health.** Innovative exhibitions allow you to check your health, understand electricity and earthquakes, and explore DC-3 and DC-8 aircraft. There's a gift shop and a **McDonald's** cafeteria, too. ♦ Free. Daily. 213/744.7400

EXPOSITION PARK ROSE GARDEN

This sunken garden contains more than 19,000 rosebushes representing 190-plus varieties. At the center are latticework gazebos. When the roses are in bloom, this is the most fragrant spot in town. ♦ Reservations required for weddings. 701 State Dr (between S Figueroa St and N Coliseum Dr). 213/748.4772

LOS ANGELES MEMORIAL COLISEUM & SPORTS ARENA

Built in 1923, the Coliseum was the major venue for the **1984 Olympics,** as it was for the **1932 Games.** It has also been the site of two Super Bowls (in 1967 and 1974) and a papal visit (in 1987). The stadium was damaged during by the 1994 Northridge earthquake and was later remodeled, though since the Raiders returned to Oakland the space is often empty, aside from hosting **USC football games,** other sporting events, and the occasional concert. ♦ 3911 S Figueroa St (between S Park and State Drs). 213/748.6136

In front of Los Angeles Memorial Coliseum:

OLYMPIC ARCH

Robert Graham's massive sculpture in front of the Coliseum is a permanent memento of the **1984 Summer Olympics.** It is topped by two headless bronze nudes; water polo player Terry Schroeder was the model for the male figure.

SPORTS ARENA

Built in 1958, this sister facility to the Coliseum is used as a multipurpose indoor sports and entertainment facility. The main auditorium is home to the **LA Clippers,** the **USC basketball team,** and the **Ice Dogs** (LA's member of the International Hockey League). In addition, the stadium hosts ice shows, track meets, car shows, concerts, rodeos, wrestling, and conventions. ♦ 3939 S Figueroa St (at S Park Dr). 213/748.6131

Restaurants/Clubs: Red | Hotels: Purple | Shops: Orange | Outdoors/Parks: Green | Sights/Culture: Blue

MIDTOWN

We're talking an eclectic, ethnic infusion here . . .

Los Angeles's Midtown neighborhood begins where downtown stops and ends just before Beverly Hills and the Westside begin. The easternmost section, from the **Harbor Freeway** to **Lafayette Park**, is an eclectic melting pot of immigrants from Central America, Mexico, Southeast Asia, and Korea. **La Brea Avenue** to the west is a booming area, with landmark commercial buildings that date back to the 1920s combined with modern-day restaurants and retail outlets. In the 1930s, **Wilshire Boulevard** from La Brea to Fairfax Avenue was developed into a prestigious business and shopping district that was dubbed Miracle Mile; following a long decline, this strip has been extensively rebuilt. The final section, west to **La Cienega** and **Robertson Boulevards,** is a fashionable residential district, studded with design showrooms and art galleries.

Wilshire Boulevard, the backbone of this corpulent entity, was originally a trail followed by the Yang-Na Indians from their Elysian Hills settlement to the tar pits of Hancock Park, where they obtained pitch to waterproof their homes. The bustling boulevard, which runs 16 miles west to the ocean, was named after **H. Gaylord Wilshire** (1861-1927), a puckish entrepreneur from Ohio who made and lost fortunes in orange and walnut farming, gold mining, therapeutic electric belts, and real estate development. The thoroughfare didn't reach its current renown until oil fever captured the city and Edward Doheny struck a small pool after digging with a shovel 16 feet into a hillside near First Street and Glendale Boulevard. By 1905 the area was dotted with oil wells, and fortunes were made—among them the Hancock family's, whose farm included the tar pits near Wilshire Boulevard and Fairfax Avenue. This field was soon exhausted, leaving only the tar pits and a few camouflaged wells as reminders of the boom years. Today the famous **La Brea Tar Pits** showcase fossils from over one million years ago.

1 TRASHY LINGERIE

Diaphanous, lacy, and racy only begins to describe the ultrasexy array of intimate apparel sold here. The enticing window displays stop traffic. However, a membership fee is charged to discourage voyeurs from lingering in the store. ♦ M-Sa. 402 N La Cienega Blvd (at Oakwood Ave). 310/652.4543. www.trashy.com

2 CANTER'S FAIRFAX RESTAURANT DELICATESSEN AND BAKERY

★$ A legend in its own time, this is the largest, liveliest deli on Fairfax, and is a popular breakfast spot with the lox-and-bagel crowd and morning people who like to wake up with big, hearty plates of food. The interior never changes. In fact, it's remained virtually untouched since Doris Day was a girl. The corned beef hash and eggs are a must, any sandwich will satisfy, and the pastrami is top grade. The neon sign on the façade is a classic. ♦ Deli ♦ Daily, 24 hours. 419 N-Fairfax Ave (between Oakwood and Rosewood Aves). 323/651.2030

3 AL'S NEWS

A profusion of newspapers and magazines line the racks here. ♦ Daily. 370 N Fairfax Ave (at Oakwood Ave). 323/935.8525

4 RAPPORT CO.

This is the place to shop for top-quality home furnishings and accessories. You're bound to find some really cool pieces to decorate your home or apartment, and the sales staff is friendly and helpful. ♦ Tu-Sa. 435 N La Brea Ave (between Oakwood and Rosewood Aves). 323/930.1500

5 LA BREA AVENUE

La Brea bustles with art galleries, design-oriented stores, and restaurants, especially around the junction with Melrose Avenue and south to Wilshire Boulevard, where they're housed in Art Deco and Spanish 1930s buildings. Leading galleries include **Couturier Gallery** (166 N La Brea Ave; 323/933.5557); **Iturralde Gallery** (116 S La Brea Ave; 323/937.4267); **Silkroads** (145 N La Brea Ave; 323/857.5588); **P.F.A**, which stands for Perrell Fine Art (also at 1435 N La Brea Ave; 323/933.8629); and **Fahey/Klein Photography** (148 N La Brea Ave; 323/934.2250). Bargain hunters should stop at the **Buffalo Exchange** (131 N La Brea Ave; 323/938.8604, www.buffaloexchange.com) for cheap designer vintage clothing. They buy, sell, and trade trendy duds of all kinds. Wannabe

comics should check out the **Acme Comedy Theatre** (135 N La Brea Ave; 323/788.3851), which offers classes in improvisation. And if you love pizza but adhere only to kosher food, grab a slice or a pie at **Pizza Mayvan** (140 N La Brea Ave; 323/857.0353).

6 THE IVY–LA DESSERTS

★★★$$$ Perennially hip, it's so in to lunch at the Ivy but not that easy to get a reservation. Dinner's a tough ticket, too, and there's always a long wait unless you're somebody. But the setting is pretty, the food good, and, well, it's just the place to go. The décor reflects a Southwestern feeling, with adobe walls, open hearths, antiques, and an ivy-strewn terrace. Simple dishes are best: Try the corn chowder and mesquite-grilled shrimp. But save room for the desserts that made this restaurant's reputation, especially the lemon cake topped with white chocolate mousse. And carry some home from LA Desserts, which shares space with the restaurant. ♦ American ♦ M-Sa, lunch and dinner; Su, brunch, lunch, and dinner. Reservations required. 113 N Robertson Blvd (between Alden Dr and Beverly Blvd). 310/274.8303 ♿

7 PACIFIC THEATER BUILDING

This mall/office complex of white stucco across the street from The Ivy–LA Desserts houses shops, restaurants, retail outlets, and a movie theater. The layout features a charming, well-landscaped courtyard. ♦ 120 N Robertson Blvd (between Alden Dr and Beverly Blvd)

Within the Pacific Theater Building:

PAIGE

Ultrachic and trendy, this 1,200-square-foot designer denim boutique caught the eyes (and slim hips) of Tinseltown fashionistas the minute it opened. After all, the proprietor is none other than supermodel Paige Adams-Geller (ergo the name). Designed to please discerning shoppers of both sexes, the décor favors an androgynous look of dark browns and cream lighted by crystal chandeliers, with leather couches and a special coffee bar with flat-screen TVs. It's the place to be seen while browsing through Paige's designer jeans and denims collections or looking for necklaces and rings by Virgins Saints & Angels. ♦ Daily. 16 N Robertson Blvd. 310/274.6726. www.paigepremiumdenim.com

Los Angelenos are the largest consumers of seafood in the United States, eating some $1.5 billion worth annually.

NEWSROOM

★★$ Healthy food is the specialty at this eatery. The menu features generous portions of Caesar salad (in several low-fat variations using just egg whites), turkey burgers, and reduced- and low-fat chicken and vegetarian dishes. True vegans will delight in the "Moroccan mixed-up wild grains" (grilled chopped vegetables tossed with couscous, four kinds of rice, and Moroccan spices). Breakfast is served all day. The large dining room is sparsely decorated, with simple wooden furnishings; there's also a bar and a take-out counter. The service is friendly and efficient. ◆ Health food ◆ Daily, lunch and dinner. 310/652.4444 &

7 CHAYA BRASSERIE

★★★$$ The marvelous interior by Elyse Grinstein and Jeff Daniels combines a Japanese esthetic (skylit, pine-framed bamboo grove and upturned parasol lampshades) with the friendly informality of a Parisian brasserie. Chefs Goto Shingi and Shigefumi Tachibe pull off the same East-meets-West magic in such innovative dishes as tuna tartare and seaweed salad, plus Japanese-accented French and Italian fare. There's a hot bar scene, too. ◆ Japanese/French/Italian ◆ M-F, lunch and dinner; Sa, Su, dinner. Reservations recommended. 8741 Alden Dr (at N Robertson Blvd). 310/859.8833. Also at Venice Renaissance Building, 110 Navy St (at Main St), Venice. 310/396.1179. www.thechaya.com &

8 CEDARS SINAI MEDICAL CENTER

Though it's inspirational for the philanthropy that made it possible (and fashionable because of the celebrities and other bigwigs who come for the medical services), this hospital's unimaginative gigantism makes it a fit companion for the Beverly Center. A bright spark, architecturally, is the outwardly inconspicuous cancer clinic, designed by Morphosis in 1988. ◆ 8700 Beverly Blvd (between N San Vicente and N Robertson Blvds). 310/855.5000

9 HOTEL SOFITEL

$$$ An absolute knockout following $35 million makeover, this 297-room hotel boasts a vivid personality created by designers Cheryl Rowley and Yabu Pushelberg. The award-winning creative team transformed every nook and cranny into what they call a "fusion of European sophistication with the energetic pulse of Hollywood." The mood begins when you walk into the striking silver, black, and glass lobby, greeted by a startling stainless steel abstract sculpture by Damon Hidreth. One of a series of Gordian knots, the piece stands 16 feet high and definitely catches the eye. The hotel houses an extensive art collection, so if you're interested, pick up information at the front desk. Besides the gorgeous interior, one of the most noticeable traits of this hotel is the cordial, efficient staff. Another is **Simon** (★★★$$$), the three-meal-a-day restaurant named after chef Kerry Simon (of Simon's Kitchen and Bar in the Hard Rock Hotel, Las Vegas), which sports a large outdoor dining patio; and a cutting-edge after-hours club, **Stone Rose,** created by scenester Rande Gerber, who also decorated the rooms with lacquers in cream, cinnabar, and chartreuse, Macassar ebony, and limed white oak finishes paired with velvet and faux leather upholstery. All accommodations boast 32-inch plasma TVs, laptop connections, and oversized rain showers in the bathroom. If price is no object, opt for a Penthouse Suite—a two-room affair with balconies, big comfy beds, flat-screen TVs, huge bath-rooms, floor-to-ceiling windows with curtains that go up and down with the push of a button, and lots of space to romp around. The fitness center, purportedly the largest hotel facility of its kind in the area, is effectively put together with the latest equipment, nicely laid for comfort. There are lots of chilled bottles of water, newspapers, fruit, and two complimentary Internet-accessible computers, just in case you need an e-mail fix while working out. Personal trainers are available. Another asset is the LeSpa, an urban sanctuary offering head-to-toe treatments by well-trained therapists, with an entire menu of therapies just for men like the Executive manicure or pedicure, the Flip Flop pedicure, Java Jolt scrub, and Bare Necessity chest treatment. Of course there are plenty of options for women, too, like a fabulous customized aromatherapy facial (ask for Vanessa), scrubs, rubs, and soothing soaks. The hotel also sports an outdoor pool. ◆ 8555 Beverly Blvd (between N La Cienega Blvd and Beverly Pl).

310/278.5444, 800/521.7772 (direct to hotel), 800/763.4835 (Sofitel reservations); fax 310/657.2816. www.sofitel.com; sofitel.losangeles@accor.com

10 BEVERLY CENTER

This eight-story bastion of consumerism provides a stylish, upbeat, contemporary spot in which to shop till you drop. A 32-by-46-foot shoji screen showcases the Grand Court displaying a pixilated California landscape on 252 panels. The Café L.A. food court on level 8 features an outdoor rooftop patio and terrace restaurant providing great views of the areas below. Level 6 sports **Wave and Bar Restaurant** (★★$), an unusual dining venue for a mall that actually serves great food. And even deserves two stars. Open from 11AM until the last shop closes, Wave offers an inviting bar or several tables on which to sample the eclectic California/Asian cuisine. The service is unusually competent; the prices are moderate, and it's well worth a stop even if you just go for tapas (prawn rolls, salmon asparagus, melted brie with candied walnuts and garlic). There are also great soups, salads, and sandwiches. Anchored by Bloomingdale's and Macy's. Beverly Center proffers all the essentials for maxing out the credit card with more than 160 outlets such as Club Monaco, BOSS, Laundry by Shelli Segal, ISSI, Up Against the Wall, Williams-Sonoma Grande Cuisine, Traffic, Lucky Brand Dungarees, and DKNY. In addition to the food court, several full-service chain restaurants provide fuel for shoppers, including P.F. Chang's China Bistro, Starbucks, Quiznos, California Pizza Kitchen, and others. Late movies are offered on the 13 screens on level 8. Beverly Center attracts its share of tinseltown types. So, keep your eyes wide open. You just might spot Ben Affleck, Matthew Perry, Drew Barrymore, Jackie Chan, Jennifer Lopez, and even Tom Cruise—or so the P.R. folks for Beverly Center claim, anyway. You'll also find ample parking on four open decks. ♦ 8500 Beverly Blvd (bounded by La Cienega and San Vicente Blvds, and W Third St and Beverly Blvd). 310/854.0070. www.beverlycenter.com

11 ÉLAN

$$ If you like your hotels small, cozy, and uncluttered, this one's for you. Situated just a stroll from **Beverly Center,** boutiques, shops, and restaurants, the 50-room, ultra-techno-styled charmer offers royal deluxe, 200-thread-count bedding, down comforters and pillows, 25-inch TVs, high-speed Internet, two phones, voice mail, mini fridge, coffeemaker, and robes in every tidy room. There's no restaurant, but food can be ordered in from a restaurant (Jan's) across the street, and a free continental breakfast is served in the cyber-lounge daily. There is a small fitness center and accessibility to a nearby health club. ♦ 8435 Beverly Blvd. 323/658.6663, 888/611.0398. www.elanhotel.com

11 FUN FURNITURE

Treat the kids to whimsical architect-designed pieces such as a skyscraper dresser, a taxi toy box, or a fire-engine bed at this unique children's furnishings shop. ♦ Daily. 8451 Beverly Blvd (between N Croft Ave and N Alfred St). 323/655.2711

11 CORONET THEATER

Set back in an almost hidden courtyard, this intimate playhouse features children's theater productions by the Serendipity Theater Company. ♦ 366 N La Cienega Blvd (between Beverly Blvd and Oakwood Ave). 310/657.7377

11 CORONET PUB

This cute little neighborhood watering hole is popular with actors, writers, and musicians. ♦ M-Sa, until 2AM. 370 N La Cienega Blvd (between Beverly Blvd and Oakwood Ave). 310/659.4583

12 BEVERLY CONNECTION

This attractively designed, three-story mall sits just across La Cienega Boulevard from Beverly Center and acts as somewhat of an annex to the larger facility. Tenants include Old Navy, Marshalls, Starbucks, Sports Chalet, Long's Drugs (which actually resides in the landmark Rexall drug building), Soupplantation, and at press time a few empty spaces. There's plenty of validated parking. ♦ Daily. 100 N La Cienega Blvd (between W Third St and Beverly Blvd)

13 KINGS ROAD CAFE

★$ Folks congregate outside while waiting for tables at this happening café. The clientele is an eclectic mix of writers, artists, and industry execs who go there to sip rich espresso, cappuccino, or *caffè lattes* and munch on gourmet sandwiches prepared with fresh-baked sourdough bread and fillings such as herb-roasted chicken, Black Forest ham, fontina cheese, onions, and roasted eggplant. The croissants and pastries are good, too. ♦ Coffeehouse ♦ Daily, until midnight. 8361 Beverly Blvd (at N Kings Rd). 323/655.9044

14 I. MARTIN IMPORTS

This place is a haven for anyone in training for the Tour de France, or who wants to race up the side of Mount Wilson riding the best bike money can buy. ◆ Daily. 8330 Beverly Blvd (at N Flores St). 323/653.6900. www.imartin.com

14 MANDARETTE

★★$$ The food is good and portions are intentionally small so you can sample several choices. Ask your waiter to help you choose from the eclectic selection of regional Chinese dishes. The room is smart and simple, with white walls and accents of sky blue and a most calming shade of celadon. ◆ Chinese ◆ Daily, lunch and dinner. 8386 Beverly Blvd (at N Orlando Ave). 323/655.6115 ₺

15 PASTIS

★★★$$ This special little find dishes out great food, from a delightful tuna tartare and asparagus salad to spicy Chilean sea bass on a bed of wild mushrooms, lovely lamb as only the French can fix, and fabulous salads, with friendly service and moderate prices. The place is always packed, so call ahead. ◆ French ◆ Daily, dinner. Reservations recommended. 8114 Beverly Blvd (between N Crescent Heights Blvd and N Kilkea Dr). 323/655.8822 ₺

16 MIMOSA

★★★$$ This charming French bistro showcases the culinary flair of Jean-Pierre Bosc, one of LA's finest chefs. The bistro-style menu is a throwback to Bosc's French background with such dishes as French onion soup, leeks vinaigrette, macaroni and cheese gratin, roasted chicken, and filet of sole. Desserts are equally yummy, from the fresh fruit "minestrone" and sherbet to the sinfully rich crème brûlée. All are served in a soothing room with plank floors and pale yellow walls adorned with photographs of friends, family, and customers, or on a patio that's heated on cool days. ◆ French/Italian ◆ M-F, lunch and dinner; Sa, dinner. Reservations recommended. 8009 Beverly Blvd (at N Edinburgh Ave). 323/655.8895

17 FAIRFAX AVENUE

Since World War II, this has been Main Street for the Jewish community of Los Angeles. Although the majority of Los Angeles Jews currently reside on the Westside and in the San Fernando Valley, the Eastern European Jewish tradition continues as a strong influence in this area. Alas, an influx of young, affluent professionals and eagle-eyed investors has dramatically changed the focus of the neighborhood, now dubbed Fairfax Village by city officials. Mom-and-pop shops, in business for decades, have been pushed away by soaring rents. Designer jeans and upscale boutiques are quickly replacing bagels-and-lox shops and small grocery stores. Fairfax Village spans a seven-block area from kitschy Melrose Avenue on the north to the upscale Grove to the south. Hipper residents favor the ongoing yuppification of Fairfax, while the senior contingent obviously looks upon it with great sadness and disdain. It's the dawn of a new era, folks.

18 CBS TELEVISION CITY

This massive complex of television studios and offices was built in 1952 by **Pereira & Luckman** and renovated in 1976 by Gin Wong Associates. Free tickets to shows can be picked up at the information window; age restrictions vary. For groups of 20 or more, call 323/852.2455. ◆ Daily. 7800 Beverly Blvd (between N Genesee and N Fairfax Aves). 323/852.2624

19 AUTHENTIC CAFE

★★$ Be prepared to stand in line most of the time at this tiny, terminally trendy spot. Rest assured, the tasty, generous portions, always served with a smile, are worth the wait. Tortilla-crusted chicken breast, Jamaican jerk chicken, Asian noodle salad, marinated and wood-grilled Yucatecan chicken, and skirt steaks are among the best choices. ◆ International ◆ Daily, breakfast, lunch, and dinner. No reservations. 7605 Beverly Blvd (between N Curson and N Stanley Aves). 323/939.4626

19 SONRISA FURNITURE

Here's the place to pick up some unique pieces for home or office made from vintage American steel, much of it recycled from medical facilities. There are great industrial-looking bookshelves, desks, and cabinets. ◆ M-Sa. 7609 Beverly Blvd (between N Curson and N Stanley Aves). 323/935.8438

20 A. J. HEINSBERGEN COMPANY

This tiny medieval brick castle, with drawbridge and moat, is still occupied by the design company that built it in 1925. ◆ 7415 Beverly Blvd (between N Martel Ave and N Vista St). 323/934.1134

21 GRACE

★★$$$ Cutting-edge hip with waiters donned in safari chic, this is one of the top spots for LA's young and restless. The over-the-top

Restaurants/Clubs: Red | **Hotels: Purple** | **Shops: Orange** | **Outdoors/Parks: Green** | **Sights/Culture: Blue**

47

design features a frivolous but tasty menu that begins with a soup tasting and moves along to John Dory accompanied by potato gnocchi or salmon with Catalan-style peppers stuffed with brandade, braised short ribs with langoustines, or a bacon-wrapped saddle of rabbit. Vegans can enjoy tofu stuffed into peppers alongside basmati rice and butternut squash. Dress outrageously hip and you'll fit right in. ♦ French ♦ Dinner, Tu-Su. Reservations a must. 7630 Beverly Blvd (between N Fuller and N Martel Aves). 323/934.4400; fax: 323/934.0485. www.gracerestaurant.net

22 SKANK WORLD

It looks like a Goodwill store with punk overtones, but this is the place to find classic 1950s furniture at affordable prices, including Eames plywood chairs and the rare example of Alvar Aalto. ♦ Opens at 2:15PM Tu-Sa or by appointment (323/965.1757). 7221 Beverly Blvd (between N Formosa Ave and N Alta Vista Blvd). 323/939.7858 &

23 STEVE TURNER GALLERY

This gallery features American modernist paintings from the 1930s and 1940s, and international poster design from 1910 to 1950. ♦ W-Su. 7220 Beverly Blvd (between N Formosa Ave and N Alta Vista Blvd). 323/931.1185

23 INSOMNIA

★★$ This stylish literary coffeehouse, operated by UCLA graduates and frequented by aspiring screenwriters, is set in a converted Art Deco building. Fresh breads, pastries, and light fare sustain those who are reading, playing chess, or listening to the Wednesday- and Sunday-night readings of poetry and fiction. ♦ Coffeehouse ♦ Daily. 7286 Beverly Blvd (between N Alta Vista Blvd and N Poinsettia Pl). 323/931.4943

24 EAST INDIA GRILL

★$$ Enjoy original dishes such as basil-coconut curries, tandoori ribs, and savory soups at this friendly bistro. ♦ Indian ♦ Daily, lunch and dinner. 345 N La Brea Ave (between Beverly Blvd and Oakwood Ave). 323/936.8844. www.eastindiagrill.com

25 HANCOCK PARK

Captain G. Allan Hancock—son of Henry Hancock, who bought Rancho La Brea in 1860—began this exclusive residential section in the 1910s. The palatial mansions were once owned by such notable California families as the Dohenys, Huntingtons, Van Nuyses, Jansses, Bannings, Crockers, and others. ♦ Bounded by S Lucerne, Larchmont, and Wilshire Blvds and Highland and Melrose Aves

26 LARCHMONT VILLAGE

Don't miss this shopping street of small-town charm and urban sophistication. Nearby is the Wilton Historic District, a modest area of California bungalows dating from 1907 to 1925. ♦ N Larchmont Blvd (between W First St and Beverly Blvd)

At Larchmont Village:

PRADO

★$$ The setting—pale-blue walls, painted angels floating above the chandeliers—enhances the cuisine prepared by chef Javier Prado. The dishes, while exotic, are often overspiced, and the tiny room is sometimes overwhelmed with diners. ♦ Caribbean ♦ M-Sa, lunch and dinner; Su, dinner. Reservations recommended. 244 N Larchmont Blvd. 323/467.3871

27 CHAN DARAE

★$$ The slightly sleeker, fancier spin-off of the Thai favorite in Hollywood is a winner with the Hancock Park crowd. Specialties include sausage with ginger and lime, stuffed chicken wings, barbecued beef, and flamed banana fritters with coconut and sesame seed. ♦ Thai ♦ M-F, lunch and dinner; Sa, Su, dinner. Reservations recommended. 310 N Larchmont Blvd (at Beverly Blvd). 323/467.1052. www.chandarae.com

28 KENTUCKY FRIED CHICKEN

The architecture is the attraction here, not the food. **Grinstein/Daniels** created this superb piece of innovative 1990 design, with a curving façade and floating geometric masses. ♦ 340 N Western Ave (at Oakwood Ave)

29 CASA CARNITAS

★$ Kitsch décor, Latino crowds, and Mexican music create an appropriate context for searingly soulful food. Rich Yucatecan specialties include excellent fish and shellfish, pork-and-black-bean stew, and fried plantains. ♦ Mexican ♦ Daily, lunch and dinner. 4067 Beverly Blvd (between N Kenmore and N Alexandria Aves). 323/667.9953

30 FOUR SEASONS HOTEL

$$$$ This is about as good as a hotel gets, with outstanding service and style. Each of the 179 rooms and 106 suites is outrageously comfortable and luxurious. But then, this is what one comes to expect of this prestigious hotel chain. The public areas are exquisite, with fine furnishings, marble floors, fine art (including a Picasso in the lobby), and fresh floral arrangements everywhere. The hotel spa is one of the prettiest in town, with aromatic scented

treatment rooms, top-notch therapists, and a fitness-friendly, outdoor/tented workout area. There's also a charming garden, a terrace pool with a café, and complimentary limo service to Rodeo Drive in Beverly Hills. ♦ 300 S Doheny Dr (at W Third St). 310/273.2222, 800/332.3442; fax 310/859.3874. www.fourseasons.com ♿

Within the Four Seasons:

GARDEN'S

★★★$$$ This exquisite dining room is perfect for a special occasion with its consistently excellent service and sensational food: Try the banana lemongrass and coconut soup, ahi tuna tartare and avocado timbale (it's amazing), Maine lobster pot stickers, Moroccan spice–roasted Maine lobster, licorice-roasted John Dory fillet with wild mushroom couscous, truffle-scented wild mushroom risotto with shaved Parmesan (outrageously delicious), or from the grill, an 8-ounce Kobe rib-eye, 12-ounce veal chop, 12-ounce rack of lamb, or organic chicken breast. A divine finale is the chocolate truffle cake with banana rum ice cream. For a slice of LA life, go early and grab a seat at the bar, or settle down in one of the cushy chairs in **Windows Lounge** adjacent to the restaurant and enjoy cocktails with the affluent young "in" crowd who pack the place nightly. There's a tasty bar menu to nosh on. ♦ California ♦ Daily, breakfast, lunch, and dinner. 310/273.2222, ext 2171

31 MICHEL RICHARD

★$$ There are tables for *petit déjeuner*, salad-and-quiche lunches, and steak-and-shrimp dinners. Each dessert is a work of art. ♦ French ♦ Daily, breakfast, lunch, and dinner. 310 S Robertson Blvd (between Burton Way and W Third St). 310/275.5707

32 LOCANDA VENETA

★★★$$ Owner Jean Louis de Mori and chef Massimo Ormani head up this terrific trattoria that continues to lure foodies with such winners as handmade mozzarella, duck, chicken dumplings with onion confit, organic free-range chicken grilled with sage and lemon zest in a spicy garlic sauce, and any of the pastas or risottos—not to mention the vanilla ice cream with chocolate sauce. ♦ Italian ♦ M-F, lunch and dinner; Sa, dinner only. 8638 W Third St (between Willaman Dr and Hamel Rd). 310/274.1893 ♿

32 ORSO

★★$$ This great-looking trattoria boasts the most seductive patio in town. The bread is

fabulous, the hand-painted plates gorgeous, the service friendly (if casual and a bit hands-off), and the cosmopolitan clientele star-studded. The ambitious menu changes daily, but you can always get such delicacies as pan-fried calf's liver or a margarita pizza, and if you're there at the right time, veal kidney, tripe, dandelion greens, and Italian cheeses, along with pastas and grilled fish. However, some dishes are overpriced. ♦ Italian ♦ Daily, lunch and dinner. Reservations recommended. 8706 W Third St (at Hamel Rd). 310/274.7144 ♿

32 BAREFOOT

★★$$ Light and dark wood, aged copper, stone, and floral prints are blended to great effect in this restaurant, with its cozy bar and airy rooftop terrace. The creative menu features sautéed whitefish, stuffed chicken breast with goat cheese, and seafood risotto du jour. Don't miss the crème brûlée—it's gotten raves all over town. Because it stays open until midnight, this is a perfect place for late-night dining. ♦ California/Italian ♦ M-F, lunch and dinner; Sa, Su, brunch, lunch, and dinner. 8722 W Third St (between Hamel Rd and Arnaz Dr). 310/276.6223 ♿

33 THIRD STREET

This booming half-mile corridor hosts a collection of worthwhile little restaurants, antiques shops, and lots of hair salons. Hip without the hype, Third Street is more off the beaten path than offbeat. The street's denizens, mainly apartment dwellers who reside north and south of Sunset Strip, can stroll around the corner and grab a sandwich at **Who's on Third,** walk in for a restyled coif at **Object Hair Salon,** purchase new threads at **Atlas Clothing Co.,** and wash those threads at the **Washing Machine** self-serve laundry. ♦ Between S Sweetzer Ave and S La Cienega Blvd

34 THE TRAVELER'S BOOKCASE

Browse through an extensive collection of books for armchair globe-trotters and serious adventurers at this delightful shop. ♦ Daily. 8375 W Third St (between S Kings Rd and S Orlando Ave). 323/655.0575

34 THE COOK'S LIBRARY

Owner Ellen Rose turned her hobby into an occupation when she opened the only LA store that concentrates entirely on cookbooks—new, old, and out-of-print. ♦ M-Sa. 8373 W Third St (between S Kings Rd and S Orlando Ave). 323/655.3141

Restaurants/Clubs: Red | Hotels: Purple | Shops: Orange | Outdoors/Parks: Green | Sights/Culture: Blue

35 ARNIE MORTON'S THE STEAK HOUSE

★★★$$$ This carnivore's paradise serves the biggest, juiciest steaks you've ever eaten—and possibly the most expensive, too. Grilled to taste, beef just doesn't get any better than the melt-in-your-mouth filet mignon, New York, porterhouse, and rib-eye steaks accompanied by à la carte piles of mashed or fried potatoes, asparagus, or fresh spinach sautéed with mushrooms. The New York cheesecake, chocolate velvet cake, and Key Lime pie wage a conspiracy against your diet resolutions. ♦ American ♦ Daily, dinner. Reservations recommended. 435 S La Cienega Blvd (at Colgate Ave). 310/246.1501. www.mortons.com

36 BEVERLY PLAZA HOTEL

$$ This attractive 98-room hotel is recommended for those who want to shop 'til they drop at nearby **Beverly Center** (see page 46). The rooms are charming and come with terry robes, coffeemaker, natural soaps and shampoos, daily newspaper, fresh fruit, and yummy chocolates at turndown. There's a pool, fitness center, spa, and free transportation within a five-mile radius of the hotel. ♦ 8384 W Third St (at S Orlando Ave). 323/658.6600, 800/624.6835; fax 323/653.3464 &

37 THE LITTLE DOOR

★★★$$$ Organic, Mediterranean-style cuisine attracts health-minded gourmets to this trendy bistro. A favorite of models and celebrities, the handsome St. Barth's–style eatery features wide curtained windows, rich wood furnishings, and soft lighting. Chef Nicolas Peter's seasonally changing menu is downright spectacular, with spinach ricotta and potato gnocchi primavera, veal shank osso buco, foie gras with poached figs, goat cheese and pistachio tart, and celery root-crusted sea bass. The primo tables are out front or in the back room. ♦ French/Mediterranean ♦ Daily, dinner. 8164 W Third St (between S Crescent Heights Blvd and S La Jolla Ave). 323/951.1210

38 SOFI RESTAURANT

★$$ This lively, family-run restaurant serves excellent moussaka and other Greek specialties. ♦ Greek ♦ Daily, dinner. 8030 W Third St (between S Edinburgh Ave and S Crescent Heights Blvd). 323/651.0346

39 AOC

★★$$ This chic neighborhood-style restaurant run by partners Suzanne Groin and Caroline Styne, of Lucques fame, is one of the hottest tickets in town. The scene's a hoot, with a mix of the young and restless, Cosmopolitan-swirling set and foodies just there for the great eats. The name stands for Appellation d'Origine Controlée, an official French classification for wines and cheeses. Designed more like a tapas "tasting menu," portions are small. Waiters suggest sharing, and so do we. Choose from dishes of braised pork cheeks; skewers of lamb, skirt steak, and arroz Negro with squid, roasted date, Parmesan, and bacon; duck fat potatoes; and brioche with prosciutto, Gruyère, and egg. The wine list is sensational, with 50 choices by the glass. ♦ French with a California flair ♦ Daily, dinner. Reservations required. 8022 W Third St (between S Fairfax Ave and Crescent Heights Blvd). 323/653.6359

40 FARMERS' MARKET

A favorite with locals and tourists, this market was established in 1934 as a cooperative where local farmers could sell their produce. Today, more than 160 vendors set up shop every day, including dozens of stalls offering hot and cold dishes from around the world. Go to **Johnny Rockets** (Stall 706) for the best burgers and hot fudge sundaes; **Sushi A Go Go** (No. 618) for yummy sushi, or **Du-pars** (No. 210) for yummy pancake breakfasts. Browse around the retailers, munch on a nosh here, an entrée there, but save room for pastry at **Thee's Continental Bakery** (Stall 361) or **Thee's Pie Shop** (Stall 530), and find a seat beneath the umbrellas and awnings. **Mr. Marcel Gourmet Grocery** (Stall 150) sells all sorts of gourmet treats; try **Farm Fresh Produce** (Stall 816) for exotic fruits. Several of the fruit and nut stalls will create and ship gift boxes, as will some of the confectioneries, where you can watch candy being made. Complete your outing with a stop at **Light My Fire** (Stall 230), where you can pick up hot spices from around the world. ♦ Daily. 6333 W Third St (corner of S Fairfax Ave and Third St). Three hours free parking. 323/933.9211; www.farmersmarketla.com

Within the Farmers' Market:

KOKOMO

★$ The New Age counter here offers great granola, gumbo, and BLTs. ♦ American ♦ Daily, breakfast, lunch, and dinner. 323/933.0773

GUMBO POT

★$ Spicy gumbo, fresh oysters, blackened fish, and meat loaf are the specialties, and the weekend brunches are hearty. ♦ Cajun/Creole ♦ M-F, breakfast, lunch, and dinner; Sa, Su, breakfast, brunch, lunch, and dinner. 323/933.0358

MONSIEUR MARCEL

★★$$ This petite café offers a little taste of the French countryside. It's quite a find, kind of lost in the middle of stalls and shops, with it starched white cloths covering the pretty tables and remarkably good food at decent prices. The brief menu offers steaks and seafood as well as cheese and meat plates for lighter appetites. There's a nice wine list, which for some odd reason lists only imported selections. Across the way is Monsieur Marcel's grocery, where you can find expensive, hard-to-get cheeses and gourmet fare. ♦ French ♦ Daily, lunch and dinner. Reservations a must for dinner. Stall 150. 323/939.7792. www.breadwineandcheese.com

40 THE GROVE AT FARMERS' MARKET

A major departure from the over-the-top-consumerism of Beverly Center, this picture-postcard pretty, European-village-like mall, which attracts shoppers, moviegoers, and even busloads of tour groups by the droves, is one of the most successful commercial centers in the city. The stunning 640,000-square-foot annex to Farmers' Market provides a study in architectural styles ranging from Italian Renaissance to Art Deco. An assortment of retail outlets, anchored by Nordstrom, offers consumers opportunities to buy just about anything under one multimillion-dollar roof. You have Abercrombie & Fitch, All American Sausage Co., Amadeus Spa, Apple Computers, Banana Republic, Barnes and Noble, Lucky Brand Dungarees, Gap, Victoria's Secret, several restaurants, and an acoustically advanced multiplex movie theater. ♦ 189 The Grove Drive (between W Third St and Beverly Blvd). 888/315.8883, 323/900.8000. www.thegrovela.com

Within The Grove at Farmers' Market:

THE WHISPER LOUNGE

★★★$$ Whether you go to The Grove to shop or browse, it's worth a trip just to eat at this wildly popular indoor/outdoor spot. The food is deliciously prepared from organic, locally grown produce and it's yummy from soups to desserts. Our fave raves include the Kobe beef sliders (three juicy burgers on buns), Gorgonzola tart with Zinfandel-poached pear, Whisper fries (man, are they crisp and good), spinach and ricotta ravioli, or cedar-plank roasted salmon. Wine lovers should go on Tuesday nights when bottles of wine are half price and corkage fees are waived if you bring your own. There's also live jazz on Monday, Wednesday, and Friday to enhance your dining pleasure. ♦ California Fresh ♦ Daily, lunch and dinner. Suite F-90B. 323/931.0102. www.whisperloungela.com

41 FARFALLA

★★$$ This larger version of the North Central LA trattoria on Hillhurst Avenue serves delicious pizza, pasta, and desserts to a smartly dressed film industry crowd. Any dish with eggplant is worth a try. ♦ Italian ♦ M-F, lunch and dinner; Sa, dinner. Reservations recommended. 143 N La Brea Ave (between W First St and Beverly Blvd). 323/938.2504

41 PATINA

Choose from custom-made hats in felt and straw, trimmed with vintage lace, ribbons, and flowers, in period and contemporary styles. ♦ W-Sa; M, Tu, by appointment. 119 N La Brea Ave (between W First St and Beverly Blvd). 323/931.6931

42 AMERICAN RAG COMPANY

This is where to pick up hip and trendy recycled duds at designer prices. You'll find racks and racks of blue jeans, cool jackets, and American Rag Cie shoes. Next door is a home-furnishings store and the **Maison et Cafe** (No. 148) for a quick lunch or espresso. ♦ Daily. 150 S La Brea Ave (between W Second and W First Sts). 323/935.3154

42 SONORA CAFÉ

★★$$ This gourmet cousin of LA's beloved Mexican eatery **El Cholo** serves deliciously sophisticated Mexican-influenced Southwestern dishes such as Texas barbecue pork chop with sweet potato tamale and mango-papaya salsa, chicken enchiladas, Southwestern mixed grill with Texas antelope, Sonoma quail, venison sausage, and roasted poblano-tomatillo salsa. Desserts take on a continental twist, with offerings like flourless chocolate cake, lime tart, eggnog cheese-cake, and a to-die-for trio of crème brûlée (vanilla, coffee, and chocolate). The margaritas are really robust. The dining room has a warm Southwestern feel, with wood floors, large chandeliers, and antique rugs, and a lovely patio encourages outdoor dining. ♦ Southwestern/Mexican ♦ Tu-F, lunch and dinner; Tu-Su, dinner. Reservations advised.

---

180 S La Brea Ave (at W Second St). 323/857.1800 ♿

43 FORMER SELIG STORE

This streamlined gem designed in black-and-gold glazed terra-cotta and glass brick dates back to 1931. ♦ S Western Ave and W Third St

44 SHIBUCHO

★★$$ Sushi and sashimi of high quality are served in a traditional, woodsy interior with pebble floors. ♦ Japanese ♦ M-Sa, dinner until midnight. 3114 Beverly Blvd (between S Vendome and S Dillon Sts). 213/387.8498

45 TOMMY'S

$ More than a million people have enjoyed a burger or two at this legendary hamburger joint (circa 1946). Best known for its world-class chili burgers and chili cheese burgers, now available at more than two dozen locations throughout the Southland, Tommy's is the place to go when you want quality beef ground into the best burger you've ever eaten. It's just a funky, little stand and there is always a line. But believe us, it's worth the wait. Extra portions of tomato, chili, onions, or pickles are on the house. ♦ Burgers ♦ Daily. 2575 W Beverly Blvd (at Rampart Blvd). 213/389.9060. www.originaltommys.com

46 BROOKLYN BAGEL BAKERY

The bagels here will bring tears to the eyes of New York expatriates—the crisp, shiny crusts garnished with onion are great. ♦ Daily. 2217 Beverly Blvd (between N Lake St and Roselake Ave). 213/413.4114

47 PARK LA BREA HOUSING AND TOWERS

Built in the 1940s, the large Regency Moderne complex of low- and high-rise garden apartments is surrounded by a 176-acre park. ♦ Bounded by Cochran and S-Fairfax Aves, and W Sixth and W Third Sts

48 IL LITERATURE

An eclectic mix of books, frames, candles, cards, and unique gifts is stocked here. ♦ Daily. 456 S La Brea Ave (between W Sixth and W Fourth Sts). 323/937.3505

49 WILSHIRE CREST

$$ This 34-room hotel has great rates, with a daily continental breakfast thrown in. ♦ 6301 Orange St (at S Crescent Heights Blvd). 323/936.5131; fax 323/936.2013

50 MUSEUM OF CONTEMPORARY ART (MOCA)

At press time, this extension of the **Los Angeles County Museum of Art** (LACMA;

see next page), was undergoing a major $200 million transformation. ♦ 6067 Wilshire Blvd (at S Fairfax Ave). 323/857.6000 ♿

51 LOS ANGELES MUSEUM OF THE HOLOCAUST

This archival storehouse honors the survivors and six million Jewish victims of Nazi persecution and internment. The gallery displays photomurals, documents, artifacts, and memorabilia recounting this tragic period in history. Names of the victims are inscribed on the walls of the **Martyrs Memorial,** designed to resemble the cattle-car transports that carried millions to their deaths. In a wing dedicated to the children of the Holocaust is a scaled model of Terezin, a concentration camp that imprisoned 15,000 youths between 1942 and 1944. Also here is the **Jewish Community Library,** which contains literature on Jewish history and culture. ♦ Free. Gallery: M-F, Su. Library: M-F. 6006 Wilshire Blvd (at S Ogden Dr). 323/761.8176

51 PETERSEN AUTOMOTIVE MUSEUM

This 340,000-square-foot exhibition space showcases the largest automotive collection in the country. There's also a restaurant. ♦ Admission. Tu-Su. 6060 Wilshire Blvd (at S Fairfax Ave). 323/930.CARS. www.petersen.org

52 LA BREA TAR PITS

The tar (*brea* in Spanish) that seeps from these pits was used by Native Americans and early settlers to seal boats and roofs. In 1906, geologists discovered the pits had entrapped 200 varieties of mammals, plants, birds, reptiles, and insects from the Pleistocene Era and preserved them as fossils. Disneyesque sculptures of doomed mammals add a surreal touch. ♦ Hancock Park, Wilshire Blvd (between S Curson Ave and S Ogden Dr)

At the La Brea Tar Pits:

GEORGE C. PAGE MUSEUM OF LA BREA DISCOVERIES

Established in 1977 within grassy berms topped by a steel-frame canopy, the museum offers exhibitions, films, and demonstrations describing the evolution of the pits. Children will revel in the holographic displays (which give flesh to the bones of a tiger and a woman that were excavated here) and in a hands-on demonstration of how sticky tar is. Summer visitors can watch paleontologists at work in Pit 91. There's a gift shop, and free parking is available in back. ♦ Admission. Tu-Su. 5801 Wilshire Blvd. 323/936.2230

52 LOS ANGELES COUNTY MUSEUM OF ART (LACMA)

At press time, LACMA was undergoing a comprehensive $200 million transformation spearheaded by world-renowned architect **Renzo Piano.** When the new campus is completed, visitors will enter through a grand entrance—a sheltered area off Wilshire Boulevard that will house art installations and information. A covered concourse will link the 20-acre, 1/3-mile-long facility from LACMA West to the Japanese Pavilion. The historic Ahmanson Building will serve as the gateway to LACMA East. The museum experience will be enhanced with diffused natural light from the ceiling. Once completed, the permanent collection of Western artworks by Degas, Monet, and Gauguin and fine holdings of Asian and Near Eastern art, costumes, and textiles will be reinstalled, but in a more exciting, innovative environment. Serving as the centerpiece of LACMA will be the **Broad Contemporary Art Museum (BCAM),** a three-story, 60,000-square-foot gallery, named for trustee Eli Broad and his wife Edythe, where 200 works of postwar art will be on display. One of the largest column-free art spaces in the country, the Italian travertine BCAM building houses six loftlike 8,300-square-foot gallery spaces on each level. The glass-roofed third story is dedicated to works by Los Angeles conceptual artist John Baldessari, Jeff Koons, Andy Warhol, Ed Ruscha, and the late, great Roy Lichtenstein. Level 2 displays include works by British artist Damien Hirt, Jean-Michel Basquiat, Chris Burden, Robert Longo, and others. The first floor is devoted to the work of Richard Serra—whose Band sculptures were purchased by the museum with funds donated by the Broads along with 30 additional drawings. Other additions include the **Boone Children's Gallery** at LACMA West, which will contain a restaurant, gallery space, an education area, and book and design stores. LACMA is the largest encyclopedic museum in the US and the only one of its kind to make contemporary art a principal area of activity. ♦ Admission; free the second Tuesday of each month and after 5PM. Open every day but Wednesday, Thanksgiving, and Christmas. 5905 Wilshire Blvd (between S Curson and S Fairfax Aves). Recording 323/857.6000. www.lacma.org

53 EL REY

This streamlined movie house, designed by **W. Clifford Balch** in 1936, has led a checkered life, going from thriving Wall Street nightclub and restaurant to lively theater and, finally, to a flophouse for the homeless. Recently reborn, the Art Deco theater is now alive with the sounds of music, movie wrap parties, fund-raisers, and other special events. ♦ 5519 Wilshire Blvd (between Dunsmuir and Burnside Aves)

54 COMMERCIAL BUILDING

Frank M. Tyler's 1927 twin turrets look like towering Japanese origami. ♦ 5464 Wilshire Blvd (between Cochran and Dunsmuir Aves)

55 THE DARK ROOM

The façade of Marcus P. Miller's 1935 building is that of a period camera in black vitrolite. ♦ 5370 Wilshire Blvd (between S Detroit St and Cloverdale Ave)

55 DOMINGUEZ-WILSHIRE BUILDING

In 1997, Los Angeles's Art Deco Society joined forces with the owners of this 1930 **Morgan, Walls & Clements** structure to completely restore the finely detailed tower and two-story retail base to its former glory. ♦ 5410 Wilshire Blvd (at Cloverdale Ave)

55 OGAMDO

★★$$ Just press the doorbell-like buzzer at your table and a waiter quickly appears, decked out in a Laotian sailor suit. Set in a 112-year-old brick building, which once housed the offices of Ozzy Osbourne's production company, the quirky room features antique railroad and nautical decorations, designed by co-owner Junho Lee. There's a colossal chandelier in one of the dining rooms and a real 15,000-pound ship in the backyard. The mixed menu offers lip-smacking Chinese and Korean dishes served to a background of tunes from the '50s and '60s. ♦ Chinese-Korean ♦ Tu-Su, lunch and dinner. Reservations suggested. 842 S La Brea Ave 323/936.1500

56 CAMPANILE

★★★$$$ Architect **Josh Schweitzer** placed a glass roof over a street-front courtyard of a 1928 Spanish-style building (once owned by Charlie Chaplin) to create a two-story atrium. The pretty tile fountain and signature tower that serves as the entrance to one of the most romantic dining spots in LA were kept intact. The menu is a rustic blend of Italian and California, with signature dishes such as prosciutto and melon, squash blossom and ricotta ravioli, risotto cakes with Portobello mushrooms, cedar-smoked king salmon, and

---

Restaurants/Clubs: Red | Hotels: Purple | Shops: Orange | Outdoors/Parks: Green | Sights/Culture: Blue

a big, juicy porterhouse steak. Sweet treats include macadamia nut tart, panna cotta, and chocolate sorbet, along with a selection of dessert and port wines. Late breakfast lovers should go for the Saturday and Sunday brunch (which starts at 9:30). The big, thick slices of French toast and the buttery scrambled eggs with creamed spinach are worth waiting for. ♦ Italian/California ♦ M-F, lunch and dinner; Sa, breakfast and dinner; Su, breakfast. Reservations required. 624 S La Brea Ave (between Wilshire Blvd and W Sixth St). 323/938.1447

57 MIRACLE MILE

In 1920, visionary A.W. Ross bought 18 acres of empty land along Wilshire Boulevard, which he then developed as a prestigious business and shopping district. A friend dubbed it "Miracle Mile." Ross closely supervised the designs of individual buildings, and a few relics survive ongoing redevelopment.

57 LUNA PARK

★★$$ Hot, hot, hot. This San Francisco import has hosted an SRO crowd since opening its smart and casual bar/restaurant in 2003. Bar noshing is big here, but tables and the private booths along the wall with closeable curtains also fill up nightly. The eclectic menu is interesting, really tasty, and surprisingly inexpensive. Sample fare includes vine-ripened tomatoes with fresh Burrata mozzarella that's amazing, mussels in a tangy herb broth with andouille sausage, pastas, pizzas, and one of the best steaks we've ever had, especially for the price. Desserts have improved over the years and are definitely worth the caloric splurge. Plan time to sip a trendy mojito at the bar. There's a nice wine list but a limited selection by the glass. ♦ French/Italian/Asian ♦ M-F, lunch and dinner; daily, dinner. Reservations suggested. 672 S La Brea Ave (at Wilshire Blvd). 323/934.2110. www.lunaparkla.com

57 RON MILLER HOME FURNISHINGS

Jessica Alba was spied browsing through this unusual outlet that looks more like an upscale garage sale than a retail shop. A treasure trove of adorable mosaic and bamboo bistro tables and benches, handcrafted fountains, and other fun finds, this is the place to go when you want to make a statement in your yard or home. Among the many treasures are antiques and paintings from France, distinctive patio pieces, outdoor furniture made from watercress, and accessories from Asia. The clientele of this 30-something business come from all over to pick through the wonderful but cramped display. ♦ Daily, 10AM-6PM. 600 S La Brea Ave (between Wilshire Blvd and W Sixth St). 323/930.0466

58 WILSHIRE EBELL THEATER AND CLUB

Because of its Renaissance-style façade, this 1924 building is popular with movie and television companies. The theater is noted for its cultural and educational programs as well as for stage plays. ♦ 4401 W Eighth St (at S Lucerne Blvd). 323/939.1128

59 GETTY HOUSE

This half-timbered English-style house, built in 1921, was donated to the city by the Getty Oil Company and was once used as the mayor's official home. It is now a private residence. ♦ 605 S Irving Blvd (at W Sixth St)

60 WILTERN CENTER

Another Art Deco masterpiece, this tower was designed by **Morgan, Walls & Clements** in 1931. Wayne Ratkovich rescued the building from an insurance company that wanted to clear the site. The corner tower and side wings are clad in green terra-cotta; closely spaced, lively moldings make the tower seem far more imposing than its 12 stories. Architect Brenda Levin restored them for lease as offices, stores, and the **Upstage Cafe** (213/739.9913). ♦ Wilshire Blvd and S Western Ave

Within the Wiltern Center:

WILTERN THEATRE

This grand theater has an imposing marquee and a patterned terrazzo forecourt. Built in 1931 by **G. Albert Lansburgh,** the venue has been restored by Brenda Levin and Anthony Heinsbergen Jr., son of the original interior designer, for use as a performing arts center. It is a fairyland of Art Deco ornament embellished in pink and green hues with gold trim. A masterly sequence of spaces guides the audience into an auditorium whose proscenium is crowned with a sunburst of low-relief skyscrapers. ♦ Box office: noon-6PM on the first day tickets are released and three hours before the event on show day. 3790 Wilshire Blvd. 213/380.5005

OPUS RESTAURANT

★★★$$$ Models, actors, actresses, fashionistas, and the just plain gorgeous hang out at this highly stylized, upscale nightspot/restaurant painted in burnt orange and burgundy, with high-back leather chairs and cozy leather banquettes. The "it" place to eat, drink, and be seen, Opus presents honestly good food that the chef calls "freestyle American cooking." The menu changes daily, but you can pretty much expect to find the spiced flatiron steak, which is outrageously good, along with dozens of superb appetizers (terrine of foie gras, salmon rillettes, paprika-laced calamari, yellowtail tartare), assorted pastas, wild salmon, and great salads. Tipplers hit the bar before and after dinner and tables fill up quickly, so make a reservation and arrive on time. There's an airy outdoor patio where the younger set congregate. ♦ Freestyle American. ♦ M-Sa, dinner. Reservations a must. 3760 Wilshire Blvd. 213/738.1600. www.opusrestaurant.net

61 ST. BASIL'S CATHOLIC CHURCH

The massive, modernist reinforced-concrete church was designed by **AC Martin Partners** in 1974. ♦ 3611 Wilshire Blvd (between S Kingsley Dr and S Harvard Blvd). 213/381.6191

62 WILSHIRE PLAZA HOTEL

$$ This 385-room hotel has a pool and small fitness room, along with a restaurant. ♦ 3515 Wilshire Blvd (at S Normandie Ave). 213/381.7411, 800/382.7411; fax 213/386.7379. www.wilshireplazahotel.com

63 CASSELL'S PATIO HAMBURGERS

★$ Homemade hamburgers, out-of-sight turkey burgers, potato salad, and fresh-squeezed lemonade are served at this landmark, no-frills joint. ♦ American ♦ Daily, lunch until 4PM. 3266 W Sixth St (at S Berendo St). 213/480.8668

64 I. MAGNIN WILSHIRE

The grandest Art Deco monument in LA was completed in 1928. Designed by **John & Donald Parkinson,** it was the city's most handsome store, from its stepped profile to its soaring green-crowned tower. The store closed in 1993 because of poor sales, but the exterior is still a sight to see. ♦ 3050 Wilshire Blvd (at S Westmoreland Ave)

65 CNA BUILDING

The mirrored slab of this 1972 building reflects the sky and the 1932 English Gothic First Congregational Church across the street. ♦ W Sixth St and S Commonwealth Ave

66 LAFAYETTE PARK

This park includes a recreation and senior citizens' center, tennis courts, a picnic area, and a scent garden with numerous fragrant flowers. ♦ 625 S Lafayette Park Pl (between Wilshire Blvd and W Sixth St). 213/387.9426

67 GRANADA BUILDING

Spanish Colonial architecture is combined with Mission-style arches and arcades in this 1927 building. ♦ 672 S Lafayette Park Pl (between S Hoover St and Wilshire Blvd)

68 OTIS SCHOOL OF ART AND DESIGN

LA's oldest college of art and design, established in 1918, offers undergraduate and master's degrees in fine and applied arts, plus public evening classes and varied community outreach programs. Kent Twitchell painted one of his best murals, a Holy Trinity of soap opera stars, on a wall overlooking Carondelet Street. The **Otis/ Parsons Art Gallery** presents notable exhibitions. ♦ Free. Tu-Sa. 2401 Wilshire Blvd (at S Park View St). 213/251.0500

68 LA FONDA

★$$ **Los Camperos,** one of the finest mariachi groups anywhere, entertains in this popular spot. The margaritas are especially good and the atmosphere is one of the most festive in town. ♦ Mexican ♦ W-Su, dinner. Reservations recommended. 2501 Wilshire Blvd (at S Carondelet St). 213/380.5055

69 BOB BAKER MARIONETTE THEATER

Since 1963, this has been one of LA's most delightful experiences for children of all ages. Ticket prices include refreshments and a backstage tour. ♦ Performances: Tu-Su. Reservations required. 1345 W First St (at Glendale Blvd). 213/250.9995. www.bobbakermarionettes.com

70 CARTHAY CIRCLE

Don't miss this charming, leafy neighborhood of 1930s stucco cottages that mix Spanish and Art Deco themes. Consistent in style and scale, this historic district is now threatened by predatory developers. ♦ Bounded by S Fairfax Ave and Schumacher Dr, and W Olympic and Wilshire Blvds

71 KOREATOWN

Rambling, repainted old bungalows, storefronts provisioned with Korean foodstuffs, and distinctive angular calligraphy identify this dynamic ethnic neighborhood, bounded roughly by Vermont and Western Avenues, Pico Boulevard, and Eighth Street. It is the hub

LA's city population topped 3,976,071 in 2006 with 10,245,572 people making their home in the entire Los Angeles County—making it the most populous county in the US.

THE BEST

Rick Dees

LA radio personality, morning drive-time host of KMVN 93.9 FM, The Rick Dees Weekly Top 40 Countdown

Southern California . . . 15 million people, and they all seem to be using the same freeway at the same time. Is there an oasis in this concrete desert? Is there a safe haven? YES!

LA has it all. The **Getty Center,** with its unbelievable array of priceless works of art, where you can take art lessons while sitting directly in front of invaluable masterpieces. The **Hollywood Bowl**—not only a historic landmark where countless legends have performed, but where I set the record for the smallest audience ever at a Hollywood Bowl event. Amazing teams like the **Los Angeles Lakers.** Good friend Chick Hearn delivered play-by-play to the likes of Magic Johnson and James Worthy; it's where Pat Riley broke records, and Phil Jackson delivered on the unbelievable promise of a "Three-Peat." **Dodger Stadium,** where MOVIN' 93.9 allowed me to throw the first pitch of the 2007 season (a 35-mile-an-hour fastball . . .).

The people of Los Angeles are the most intriguing individuals in the world. LA is the new melting pot of the US and I love the different flavors! Plus: where else can you drive down the 405 and from the freeway see the Goodyear Blimp parked at its **Blimp Base Airport** in Carson!

My favorite place for dinner is at the **Bel-Air Hotel.** Easily the most romantic. I like to take friends or to celebrate a special occasion. Walking across its entrance bridge, watching the swans swimming, and bumping into the likes of Angelina Jolie easily makes this one of my favorite places to get away from it all in the city. If anything can be called enjoying a slice of heaven on earth, it's dining at the Bel-Air Hotel. Remember to order the soufflé, and make sure to bring home some of Chef Bruno's AMAZING homemade cookies—absolutely unbelievable!

For Mexican food I go to **Don Cuco's** on Riverside Drive in Toluca Lake. I love the *pollo pibil*—half chicken marinated in achiote sauce and then broiled to perfection. *Muy caliente!* As the designated driver, I let my guests enjoy their amazing margaritas (one is enough—it'll do ya!).

When I crave pancakes, I head for **Du-Par's** in Studio City. In fact, I offered to swap them my own homemade peach cobbler recipe in exchange for their pancake recipe. Du-par's refused . . . Get the blueberry pancakes—you'll be glad you did.

---

for Korean cultural, social, and business life, but only a third of LA's 160,000 Koreans (the largest Korean population in the US) actually live here. It is now home to twice as many Latino immigrants, many from Central America.

72 TAYLOR'S STEAKHOUSE

★$$ This place is everything a steak house should be: a clubby, wood-paneled space with the finest meat, generous portions, and very reasonable prices. The menu offers seafood and chops as well as steak.
♦ American ♦ M-F, lunch and dinner; Sa, Su, dinner. 3361 W Eighth St (between S Normandie Ave and Irolo St). 213/382.8449. www.taylorssteakhouse.com

73 MACARTHUR PARK

One of LA's first public gardens, this was originally worthless swampland. In the 1880s, Mayor William H. Workman arranged to have topsoil brought in and planted trees and shrubbery. A lake was created by filling a low ravine with water, which inspired the name Westlake Park because of its geographical location in town. Later the park was renamed as a tribute to General Douglas MacArthur. Today it provides badly needed recreation space for local immigrant communities. It contains more than 80 species of rare plants and trees, a lake with paddleboats for rent, a small bandshell for summer entertainment, snack bars, and children's play areas. More than 11 site-specific artworks have been installed in the park, including Judy Simonian's *Pyramids* (two tiled ziggurats linked by a speaking tube), Eric Orr's *Water Spout* (which rises up to 500 feet from the lake), and George Herm's *Clock Tower* (constructed from discarded materials in the spirit of Watts Towers). The neon signs around the park and along Wilshire Boulevard have been relit to evoke the 1930s; especially notable is the marquee of the **Westlake Theatre,** a handsome 1926 movie palace overlooking the park. The area is currently threatened by drug-related violence, so be careful. ♦ Wilshire Blvd (between S Alvarado and S Park View Sts)

74 MARY ANDREWS CLARK MEMORIAL RESIDENCE OF THE YWCA

Arthur Benton designed this enormous French château in 1913. ♦ 306 Loma Dr (at W Third St)

According to the US Census Bureau, Los Angeles has a population density of 8,208 per square mile.

75 La Plancha

★$$ If you're looking for a gastronomic adventure, you've come to the right place. Specialties include meats and fish marinated in orange and lime, ripe plantain stuffed with cotija cheese, and *nactamales* (giant tamales). Beer, wine, and refreshing *cacao* (a chocolate drink) are also available. ◆ Nicaraguan ◆ Tu-Su, breakfast, lunch, and dinner. Reservations recommended. 2818 W Ninth St (between S Westmoreland and S Vermont Aves). 213/383.1449

75 Yongsusan

★$$ You can be your own barbecue chef at this lively restaurant, but come prepared for spicy food and clouds of smoke. ◆ Korean ◆ M-F, lunch and dinner; Sa, Su, dinner. 950 S Vermont Ave (between W Olympic Blvd and San Marino St). 213/388.3042

76 Langer's Delicatessen

★$ One of the few pastrami places that a New Yorker would applaud; other delectables include braised lamb shank and grilled liver and onions. ◆ Deli ◆ M-Sa, breakfast and lunch until 4PM. 704 S Alvarado St (at W Seventh St). 213/483.8050

77 Versailles

★★$ Built to accommodate loyal patrons from the Midtown area, this larger version of the original restaurant serves the same gutsy garlic chicken, pork with black beans, oxtail, and strong coffee. ◆ Cuban ◆ Daily, lunch and dinner. 1415 S La Cienega Blvd (between Alcott St and W Pico Blvd). 310/289.0392. Also at 10319 Venice Blvd (at Vinton Ave). 310/558.3168

78 Maurice's Snack 'n' Chat

★$$ This popular soul food restaurant serves large platters of meat loaf, short ribs, and liver and onions, accompanied by yams, beets, or black-eyed peas. ◆ Soul Food ◆ M-F, breakfast, lunch, and dinner; Sa, Su, breakfast and dinner. 5549 W Pico Blvd (at S Sierra Bonita Ave). 323/931.3877

79 South Bonnie Brae Street

Westlake (now MacArthur Park) was one of LA's first suburbs. Most of it has been rebuilt, but this street survives as a treasury of houses built in the 1890s. Among the standouts are **No. 818,** a regal Queen Anne with an immense veranda, elaborate woodwork, and several types of columns and piers; **No. 824,** the Charles B. Boothe and Carriage House, with its Islamic domed tower; and many on the **1000 block.** ◆ Between W 11th and W Eighth Sts

80 Loyola Law School

An idiosyncratic version of Thomas Jefferson's "Academical Village" has given new spirit to what was formerly a drab commuter school. Completed in 1987, **Frank Gehry**'s stylized versions of a classical temple and a Romanesque chapel are deployed on a tight-knit campus. Outside stairs create a forced-perspective centerpiece on the administration building and encourage social intercourse. The school has established a fine art collection that includes Claes Oldenburg's *Toppling Ladder,* a whimsical construction. ◆ 1441 W Olympic Blvd (at Valencia St). 323/736.1000

81 Alvarado Terrace

Laid out in the first decade of the century, this gently curving street is a fashionable suburb at the western boundary of the original pueblo of Los Angeles. It's a smorgasbord of architectural styles, including Queen Anne, Mission Revival, Shingle, and English Tudor. It's named after Juan Bautista Alvarado, the Mexican governor of California from 1836 to 1842. ◆ Between W Pico Blvd and S Hoover St

82 L'Adelita

★$ This Mexican and Central American emporium offers baked goods, fresh tortillas, tamales, *pupusas* (Salvadoran cornmeal turnovers), sandwiches, and hot entrées. ◆ Mexican/Central American ◆ Daily, breakfast, lunch, and dinner. 1287 S Union Ave (at W Pico Blvd). 213/487.0176. Also at 5812 Santa Monica Blvd (at N Van Ness Ave). 323/465.6526

83 St. Elmo's Village

Artist Roderick Sykes organized friends and neighbors to transform this derelict courtyard into a painted quilt of faces, figures, and inspirational messages whose verve would have delighted Picasso. ◆ Su, noon-6PM. 4830 St. Elmo Dr (between Rimpau Blvd and Longwood Ave). 323/936.3595

84 Fred's Bakery

Only in LA would bagels aspire to elegance, but these are good enough for movie stars. Other tempting treats include cakes, cookies, and fresh-baked breads. ◆ Daily. 2831 S Robertson Blvd (between Olin and Hargis Sts). 310/838.1204. www.fredsdeli.com

Restaurants/Clubs: Red | Hotels: Purple | Shops: Orange | Outdoors/Parks: Green | Sights/Culture: Blue

Tinseltown meets urbanity in a tale of two cities...

Hollywood exudes a seamy, underbelly sensibility, a little like New York's old 42nd Street. First-time visitors expect to see movie stars on every corner; instead they find hand- and footprints on the sidewalks or stars embedded in a Walk of Fame where celebrities rarely tread (save to immortalize their extremities in cement or dedicate their stars). *Hooray for Hollywood!* The city is finally digging out of its doldrums

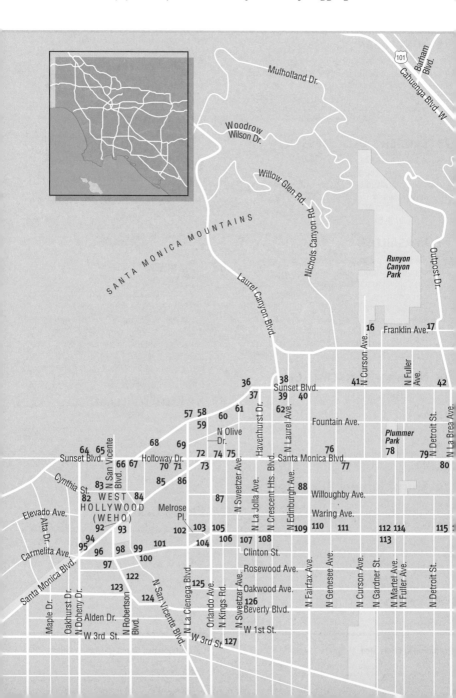

thanks to a colossal urban renewal designed to transform it into a modern-day million-dollar baby. More than 3,000 new luxury residences with million-dollar price tags and scores of additional businesses are currently under construction. A 300-room **W Hotel** is scheduled to open in the near future, along with a 350-room apartment house, 145 luxury condos, and 6,000 square feet of retail space, on 4½ acres of land at **Hollywood** Boulevard and Argyle, across the street from the **Pantages Theater**.

We hate to be the ones to break the news, but contrary to popular belief, the American film industry wasn't born in Hollywood. Actually, the fledgling business

of the "flickers" emerged from the borough of Queens in New York City, and didn't move west until the second decade of the 20th century, when the first movie moguls realized that their product could be made more conveniently year-round in sunny California. At first, they settled in an area of Los Angeles called Edendale (which today is **Silverlake, Echo Park,** and **Los Feliz**), but soon afterward they moved west to Hollywood, where the land was cheaper. Here, a legend was born: As a mecca for established and aspiring actors, directors, producers, and other film people, Hollywood came to symbolize glamour and excitement around the world. And it still does, even though most of the major studios have relocated (only **Paramount Pictures** remains).

Hollywood is divided economically and geographically into two communities: the flatlands and the hills. Older houses, elegant remnants of Hollywood's Golden Age, hide in the low hills to the north, secluded because of the confusing, narrow roads snaking into them. Small, often decrepit bungalows from the 1910s and 1920s, battered, faceless apartment buildings, and the characterless offices of small entertainment-industry service companies make up most of the rest of the "flats."

The hills, on the other hand, exhibit the rustic charms of **Nichols Canyon** and the raffish counterculture of **Laurel Canyon.** They feature a bizarre mixture of castles and cottages, Spanish haciendas and Moorish temples, and winding streets and wild areas of chaparral. Prosperous and settled, the hills appeal to literary and artistic types (some of the folks who live or have lived there include Reese Witherspoon, Jane Seymour, Jay Leno, Frank Zappa, Arsenio Hall, Kevin Costner, David Hockney, Marlon Brando, and Judy Collins). Recent immigrants, especially from Southeast Asia, Latin America, the Middle East, and the former Soviet Union, make up much of the lower flatlands population. Sadly, the part of Hollywood that the average tourist knows best is also one of the seediest sections of LA. World-famous stretches along Hollywood Boulevard, **Sunset Boulevard,** and **Vine Street** are often overcrowded, honky-tonk, or just run down. A major revitalization effort by the Community Redevelopment Agency has made the area more eye-pleasing, but if you're planning to stroll along the **Walk of Fame** to check out any of the 2,324 stars immortalized in concrete or their bronze and terrazzo foot- and handprints in front of **Mann's Chinese Theatre,** do so during daylight. Noncelebrity issues include the addition of an ambitious retail/residential/entertainment complex between Highland, Hollywood Boulevard, and Vine, which has greatly enhanced the area's appeal.

In contrast to Hollywood, recently titivated West Hollywood (WeHo)—a 1.9-square-mile pistol-shaped area in the flatlands west of Hollywood and east of Beverly Hills—exudes a tidy sophistication combined with a literally and figuratively gay attitude. An independent city since 1984, some 39,000 people make their home here, one-third of whom are gay or lesbian. Impeccably groomed like a tropical SoHo with bustling sidewalk cafés, beautifully landscaped plazas, and pretty foliage, WeHo provides a welcoming feeling for visitors. Designer showrooms, fashionable shops, restaurants, and hotels abound. The predominantly gay and lesbian community, with a small bohemian population, is generally more affluent than the rest of LA.

West Hollywood runs from Santa Monica Boulevard east to **La Brea Avenue** and west to **Doheny Drive.** But its boundaries—from **Beverly Boulevard** to the **Sunset Strip** in the west, narrowing to a few blocks in the east—are so ragged that it's more practical to describe the area's attractions along with those of Hollywood. WeHo's hub is a stretch of Santa Monica Boulevard from **La Cienega** to **Robertson Boulevard,** which sees most of the action. For help planning gay-friendly travel, sign on to gogaysocal.com—a special site designed to direct gays and lesbians to destinations in Palm Springs, San Diego, and of course WeHo.

Historically, Hollywood was a winter campground for the Cahuenga Indians and later, because of its proximity to the **Cahuenga Pass,** it became a way station on the Camino Real and a major stop on the Butterfield Stage route. When Harvey Wilcox registered the subdivision of Hollywood in 1887, it had few residents, and only 165 citizens participated in the 1903 vote to incorporate as a city. Wilcox's wife, Deaida, named the area after the Chicago summer home of a woman she met on the train, and she was its greatest supporter, giving land for churches and schools, keeping demon drink at bay, and welcoming French artist Paul de Longpre, whose garden became Hollywood's first tourist attraction. Hollywood surrendered its independence in 1910 to guarantee its access to city water, but it remained a staid farming community of citrus orchards and sheep, with unpaved streets lined with pepper trees and a scattering of houses.

Then moviemakers arrived from the East like the Goths invading Rome, taking over a saloon on Sunset as the first Hollywood film studio, hiring cowboys who rode over front lawns in the excitement of the chase, and greasing intersections to film motorists' skids. Today, although the big studios have moved on, their lots and stages have been taken over by small independents—many of which are producing the more interesting work to come out of Hollywood these days—and TV production facilities and recording studios still flourish here. However seedy, the reality and the myth still endure.

1 HOLLYWOOD SIGN

The 50-foot-high letters that sit near the summit of Mount Lee were first erected in 1923 to advertise **Hollywoodland,** a residential development. In 1949, the deteriorating sign and its acreage were deeded to the Hollywood Chamber of Commerce, which took down the "land" to create a civic advertisement. A new sign was erected in 1978. The sign has been a favorite target of stealthy typographers, from the one who blanked out the "H" to create "Ollywood" (for Iran-contra messenger Colonel Oliver North) to those who draped the sign in a gigantic yellow ribbon to honor the US troops in Desert Storm. Nowadays, there's a high-tech security system to keep visitors at a safe distance. ♦ Mount Lee Dr (north of Mulholland Hwy)

2 LAKE HOLLYWOOD

This reservoir up in the hills offers a splendid view of the Hollywood sign, a rustic jogging trail, and a sense of what this place must have looked like a hundred years ago.
♦ Daily. Lake Hollywood Dr (east of Barham Blvd)

3 VILLAGE COFFEE SHOP

★$ The good food and warm atmosphere make the tables worth waiting for in this homey rendezvous where actors, writers, and singers gather for leisurely meals and gab fests. ♦ American ♦ M-Sa, breakfast, lunch, and dinner; Su, 8AM-3PM. 2695 N Beachwood Dr (at Belden Dr). 323/467.5398

4 HOLLYWOOD BOWL

On 11 July 1922, conductor Alfred Hertz and the Los Angeles Philharmonic rang in the first season at the Hollywood Bowl with audiences seated on simple wooden benches situated on the natural hillside of Bolton Canyon. Today this amphitheater is one of the largest in the world, with a seating capacity just under 18,000. A truly magical way to enjoy music under the stars, the Bowl still hosts the summer season of the **Los Angeles Philharmonic,** visiting musicians, as well as jazz and pop concerts. Popular perennials include the Easter sunrise service, the Fourth of July, and closing-night concerts with fireworks. A $25 million face-lift reshaped, refined, and redesigned the Bowl in 2003, launching it into a new era with an innovative, larger, taller, more elliptical shell. The scalloped shape went untouched while a halo-like adjustable covering replaced the Frank Gehry–designed floating spheres, to improve the acoustics. New speaker columns were added to distribute sound more evenly. A 50-foot-wide turntable now allows the greatly enlarged stage to revolve so one act can perform while the other sets up. The seats are still hard, so bring a cushion for comfort. A blanket or shawl is also advisable, as the temperature drops at night. The **Rooftop Grill** serves supper alfresco (reservations required a week in advance); there's also **The Market Café** (serving gourmet sandwiches, salads, snacks, wine, and beer), as well as **Stuccato's,** a walk-up grab-and-go box meal takeout, and **Deli Market West,** where you can get Asian delicacies to munch on. For a really fun night of it, pack a picnic and arrive early—the Bowl fills up quickly. Many local restaurants and even some hotels (**Pinot Bistro** and **Hotel Bel-Air,** to name a couple) sell great picnic baskets designed for the Bowl. Parking at the Bowl on Highland Avenue is quite expensive and chaotic; a cheaper choice is the park-and-ride lots that provide free bus service from different parts of LA. For the Rooftop Grill and picnic baskets (order the previous day), call 323/850.1885. ◆ Grounds daily until dusk, July-Sept. 2301 N Highland Ave (at Cahuenga Blvd W). 323/850.2000. www.hollywoodbowl.org

At the Hollywood Bowl:

HOLLYWOOD BOWL MUSEUM

Exhibitions on the history of the Bowl include original drawings of concert shell prototypes by **Lloyd Wright** (son of Frank). Visitors may listen to tapes of Bowl performances in small booths. ◆ Tu-Sa. 323/850.2058. www.hollywoodbowl.org/museum

5 SAMUELS-NAVARRO HOUSE

Designed by architect **Lloyd Wright** in 1928, this house stretches horizontally along a natural ridge ending with a swimming pool (now enclosed) at one end and a garden at the other. Josh Schweitzer remodeled the private residence. ◆ 5609 Valley Oak Dr (off Verde Oak Dr)

6 LOFT TOWERS

With a nod to nearby **High Tower** (see below), Australian architects **Koning & Eizenberg** created a pair of suburban lofts, each of which comprises three 20-square-foot rooms for working and living. The 1987 residences are private. ◆ 6949 Camrose Dr (between Glencoe Way and N Sycamore Ave)

7 HIGH TOWER

This 1920 campanile is an elevator shaft that rises to the villas on either side. Stepped streets reinforce the impression of San Gimignano in the Hollywood Hills. ◆ High Tower Dr (south of Camrose Dr)

8 HOLLYWOOD HERITAGE MUSEUM

Cecil B. DeMille rented this horse barn in 1913 and used it as a set, offices, and changing rooms for *The Squaw Man,* the first feature-length movie shot in Hollywood. It originally stood at Selma Avenue and Vine Street, and was moved to its present site in 1985, where it was restored by **Hollywood Heritage** and furnished with exhibitions. ◆ Open to the public only when volunteers are on duty, so your best bet is to call before going. 2100 N Highland Ave (at Milner Ave). 323/874.2276

9 YAMASHIRO'S RESTAURANT

$$ Housed in a 600-year-old pagoda, imported by Adolphe and Eugene Bernheimer as an ornament for the Japanese palace and gardens they built in 1913, this is one of LA's most popular attractions. The food is okay, but the sunset view is dynamite and worth the price of a drink. ◆ Japanese ◆ Daily, cocktails and dinner. 1999 N Sycamore Ave (at Fitch Dr). 323/466.5125

10 FREEMAN HOUSE

The **Frank Lloyd Wright**-designed, Mayan-influenced 1924 residence was completely restored by USC. ◆ 1962 Glencoe Way (between Hillcrest Rd and Camrose Dr). No public phone number

11 WHITLEY HEIGHTS

Developed in the 1920s and 1930s by Hobart J. Whitley, these old Italian villa-style houses are built into the hillside. Marion Davies, Gloria Swanson, and Ethel Barrymore are among those who once lived here. ◆ North of Franklin Ave (between Cahuenga Blvd and N Highland Ave)

12 LA POUBELLE

★★$$ How to resist a brasserie that calls itself "The Garbage Pail"? French waiters

STEAMY NIGHTS IN HOLLYWOOD

thriving late-night scene takes over Hollywood after ours as a growing number of hot, trendy clubs compete or the young party crowd, which often includes Paris ilton and her brat pack. The action begins around 10PM rhen the belly-bearing, body-pierced, outrageously utfitted barely-out-of-puberty set arrives by car, cab, and mo, and continues until they close the bar. If you want to am with the trendy throngs, and get past the bouncers, 's essential to look cool and dress hip, and it helps if ou're considered "hot." Here's the coolest of the hottest:

ar Lubitsch, 7702 Santa Monica Blvd
323/654.1234)

asque, 1707 N Vine St (323/464.1654)

Cabana Club, 1430 N Cahuenga Blvd (323/463.0008)

Cinespace, 6356 Hollywood Blvd, 2nd floor (323/817.3456)

The Loft, Hollywood Blvd & Highland Ave (323/461.9820), 4th level

Mbar, 1253 N Vine St (323/856.0036)

Mood, 6623 Hollywood Blvd (323/464.6663)

Privilege, 8117 Sunset Blvd, WeHo (323/655.8000)

Vine Street Lounge, 1708 Vine St (323/468.0188)

Winston's, 7746 Santa Monica Blvd, WeHo (323/654.0105)

Please keep in mind that clubs come and go in this fickle town, so be sure to call before you head out.

shout orders to the kitchen, Edith Piaf recordings play, and owner Jacqueline Koster guides you through the menu. Crepes, omelettes, and coq au vin are staples. ♦ French/Italian ♦ Daily, dinner. 5907 Franklin Ave (at N Bronson Ave). 323/465.0807

13 AMERICAN FILM INSTITUTE (AFI)

Offices of the AFI and its **Center for Advanced Film Studies** now occupy what was once the campus of Immaculate Heart College. The **Louis B. Mayer Library,** open to serious film scholars, has the most extensive collection of movie scripts in the country. The AFI and its **Sony Video Center** presents regular screenings and classes, plus annual film and video festivals. ♦ 2021 N Western Ave (between Franklin Ave and Los Feliz Blvd). 323/856.7600

14 5390 FRANKLIN AVENUE

This flamboyant apartment building, formerly the **Château Elysée,** is now owned by the Church of Scientology. ♦ Between N Harvard Blvd and N Western Ave

15 SOWDEN HOUSE

This private residence was designed by Frank Lloyd Wright's son, **Lloyd Wright.** Built in 1926, its décor is a fusion of Mayan and Deco themes. The house is built around a courtyard with a unique entrance through a cave framed with decorative concrete blocks. ♦ 5121 Franklin Ave

(between N Normandie Ave and Laughlin Park Dr)

16 WATTLES MANSION & GARDENS

Hollywood Heritage restored this 1905 house and the formal gardens, which were a top tourist attraction in Hollywood's early years. Just beyond is a wilderness area that links up to **Runyon Canyon Park.** The staff is all volunteer workers, and because of this you never know when someone will be on duty to show you around. When someone is there, he or she will be happy to give you the five-minute tour. ♦ 1824 N Curson Ave (north of Hollywood Blvd). 323/874.4005 (or check at the Hollywood Studio Museum). 323/874.2276

17 CASE STUDY APARTMENTS

Adele Naude Santos's design for a villagelike cluster of low-income apartments was chosen by the Museum of Contemporary Art to be built as homage to the Case Study House Program that *Arts+Architecture* magazine ran from 1945 to 1966. ♦ Franklin and N La Brea Aves

Charlie Chaplin built an eclectic group of cottages for workers at his La Brea Avenue studio, including the Hampton Towers in West Hollywood.

Restaurants/Clubs: Red | Hotels: Purple | Shops: Orange | Outdoors/Parks: Green | Sights/Culture: Blue

18 MANN'S CHINESE THEATRE

Master showman Sid Grauman commissioned **Meyer & Holler** to create this fanciful Chinese temple in 1927 so that he would have a new stage for his prologues—extravagant spectacles keyed to the movies they accompanied. Legend has it that Norma Talmadge accidentally stepped into the wet cement of the forecourt, inspiring Sid to round up Mary Pickford and Douglas Fairbanks to repeat the trick with their hands and feet, thus inaugurating the world's largest autograph album. He also created the first gala premiere, lining Hollywood Boulevard with klieg lights as the limousines arrived for the opening night of DeMille's *King of Kings* on 18 May 1927. ♦ 6925 Hollywood Blvd (between Orchid Ave and N Orange Dr). 323/464.8111

19 HOLLYWOOD BOULEVARD

Originally laid out as Prospect Avenue and lined with ornate mansions, this stretch of road was rebuilt in the 1920s and 1930s as the movie colony's Main Street. For a decade or so, it boasted fashionable stores, hotels, and restaurants, though the movie stars came out only at night—for gala premieres at **Mann's Chinese Theatre** (see above) and other movie palaces. Hollywood Heritage, a lively preservation organization, secured official recognition for the heart of the boulevard as a National Historic District—though this doesn't seem to be protecting it from massive redevelopment. Look up to enjoy such treasures as the Gothic Moderne tower of the **Security Pacific Bank** at Highland Avenue, the lively zigzag façades, the streamlined drugstore on the corner of Cahuenga Boulevard, and the 1933 marquee of the **Hollywood Theatre** (which now houses the **Guinness World of Records Museum**). Look down for the thousands of terrazzo stars lining the **Walk of Fame,** commemorating celebrities from every branch of entertainment.

19 HOLLYWOOD ROOSEVELT HOTEL

$$ Zounds! You won't recognize this revved-up, highly charged Lalaland landmark. The interior is a mere memory of its former self. Once a staid old (it opened in 1937) spot, the place throbs with hip, attitudinal, drink-guzzling Generation X and Y'ers who hang at **Demme's Lobby Bar, Demme's Teddy's,** and **Demme's Tropicana** poolside bar—all named after proprietor Amada Scheer Demme. The 1927 landmark was the site of the first Academy Awards ceremony and the social hub of the movie colony. Errol Flynn invented his recipe for gin in a back room of the barber's shop; Scott Fitzgerald, Ernest Hemingway, and Salvador Dalí patronized the old **Cinegrill;** and Bill "Bojangles" Robinson taught Shirley Temple to tap dance up the lobby staircase—or so the legends go. The two-story Spanish Colonial lobby with its painted ceiling is worth stopping in to see All of the 335 rooms are soundproofed to drown out the street noises, and come with coffeemakers, minibars, hair dryers, and other amenities. David Hockney painted the Olympic-size pool. ♦ 7000 Hollywood Blvd (at N Orange Dr). 323/466.7000, 800/950.7667 in CA, 800/858.2244 in the US; fax 323/462.8056. www.hollywoodroosevelt.com; www.thompsonhotels.com ♿

Within the Hollywood Roosevelt:

DAKOTA RESTAURANT

★★★★$$$ Sizzling hot, this chic chophouse commingles glamour and great food for an impossibly delightful dining experience. Designed by the ubiquitous Dodd Mitchell, who seems to have the market cornered on LA restaurants, and created by the equally omnipresent Tim and Lisa Goodell (Meson G, Whist, and others), the coffered-ceilinged, leather-bound room (even tables are draped in leather) rocks nightly with young, rich, and restless scenesters and trendoids. The food is exceptional. The steak tartare couldn't be better, nor the Caesar salad more perfect. Steaks (the New York cut is heavenly) and chops (the veal chop is superb) rule the entrées, but you can find some tasty fish and poultry dishes as well as sashimi, crab cakes, and jumbo shrimp cocktails. Be sure to order sides of thickly sliced battered onion rings—they are the best. And while you're at it, get an order of truffle-sprinkled french fries. Desserts are enticing, a sweet finale to such a fine meal, especially the sticky toffee pudding with berry consommé covered in vanilla bean ice cream, Rocky Road brownie sundae with vanilla ice cream and toasted walnuts, or for chocoholics, the ganache tart. The handsome bar gets its buzz on around 9PM when the belly-bearing eye-candy cuties and Hollywood-good-looking guys make their grand entrances. ♦ Chophouse ♦ Daily, breakfast, lunch, and dinner. Reservations a must. 323/769.8888. www.dakota-restaurant.com

25 DEGREES

★$$ It's a diner, a coffee shop, a quirky hamburger joint where you can get a turkey or sirloin burger, a shake, fries, soups, and salads in a chimerical bordello-like setting designed by Dodd Mitchell with black and chrome mirrored tile, fuchsia wallpaper, oxblood leather booths wrapping around half moon–shaped wooden tables, and flat-screen televisions along the wall and behind the counter. FYI: The 25 refers to the temperature difference between medium-rare and well-done burgers. Hollywood Roosevelt's answer to a burger joint. ♦ Daily, lunch and dinner. 323/785.7244

19 LA FILM PERMIT OFFICE

Free daily listings of location filming are available here. ♦ M-F. 6922 Hollywood Blvd (between N Highland Ave and N Orange Dr), Suite 602. 323/485.5324

20 THE RENAISSANCE HOLLYWOOD HOTEL

$$$ This 640-room Marriott International hotel embodies the cornerstone of Hollywood's revitalization after a recent $29 million renovation. The 22-story, 637-room hotel boasts a midcentury-modern style with all the creature comforts a traveler would want: fitness center, swimming pool, restaurant, lounge, 50,000 square feet of multifunctional meeting space, a 30,000-square-foot Grand Ballroom with food catered by Wolfgang Puck, and a few over-the-top features, such as a pool deck that rises 50 feet in the air and a 3,500-square-foot Presidential suite with floor-to-ceiling glass windows. ♦ 1755 N Highland Ave (at Hollywood Blvd). 310/856.1200. www.renaissancehollywood.com

21 PACIFIC EL CAPITAN THEATER

Fields & Devereaux Architects artfully restored this 1926 single-screen movie palace, a magnificent blend of Baroque, Moorish, East Indian, and Churrigueresque ornamentation created by architects **Morgan, Walls & Clements** and theater designer G. Albert Lansburgh. A team of conservators re-created the stenciled ceiling coves, cornice moldings, and balcony boxes. Thanks to Disney's Buena Vista Pictures and Pacific Theaters, the preservation saved the elaborate interior from being partitioned into soulless multiscreen boxes. Today, perhaps in gratitude to its rescuer, the theater shows mostly Disney movies. Call for showings. ♦ 6838 Hollywood Blvd (between N Highland Ave and N Orange Dr). 323/467.7674

21 HOLLYWOOD & HIGHLAND

This $567 million, 1.3 million-square-foot retail and entertainment complex at Hollywood Boulevard and Highland Avenue spearheaded by TrizecHahn features a pair of elephants, replicated from the 1916 D. W. Griffith movie *Intolerance*, looming over the central courtyard. The massive production also includes the **Renaissance Hollywood Hotel** (see opposite), four movie theaters, nightclubs, a broadcast studio, and major shopping outlets such as Duty Free Stores, Aveda, Tommy Hilfiger, Louis Vuitton, Origins, Gap, Banana Republic, Benetton, Swatch, Café Med, Celine, a trendy bowling club, Lucky Jeans, Planet Funk, a second branch of Virgin Megastores, and more. But the main attraction is the spiffy 3,300-seat **Kodak Academy Awards Theatre,** the new home of the Oscars. Located on the northwest corner of Hollywood Boulevard and Highland Avenue, the facility was designed specifically for the annual event, with a dramatic entrance, cable tunnels, a red terrazzo floor, and a Governors Ballroom with views of Hollywood Boulevard and the Hollywood Hills. During the other 364 days of the year the theater hosts concerts and stage performances. Guided tours are offered daily, every half hour, and worth it just for a look at the 26 four-foot-wide by five-foot-high images of such Oscar winners as Grace Kelly, Jack Nicholson, Tom Hanks, and Marlon Brando. 323/308.6300, 323/308.6363. www.kodaktheatre.com. ♦ 6834 Hollywood Blvd (between N Highland and N La Brea Aves). Information 323/460.2626. www.hollywoodandhighland.com

Within the Hollywood & Highland Complex:

LUCKY STRIKE LANES

It's a bowling alley, it's a restaurant, it's hip, it's happening, and it's a lot of fun. Created by entrepreneurs Steven and Gillian Foster, this 12-lane upscale bowling alley/lounge attracts a high-visibility celebrity crowd and young trendoids who go as much to be seen as to throw strikes. Comforts include a custom lounge, billiards tables, outdoor smoking patio, private VIP room, and a bustling bar/restaurant (which is more like a food service than a sit-down facility). The food, which is served at the lanes or at the bar, is what you'd expect and a little more—burgers, hot dogs, and pizzas, skewered rock shrimp, baked clams, tomato cheese s'mores, Buffalo wings with a blue cheese dip—you get the picture. There are plenty of dessert options to fuel you for action. ♦ Daily, 11AM-2AM. 323/467.7776. www.bowlluckystrike.com

21 FREDERICK'S OF HOLLYWOOD

The venerable purveyor of sexy lingerie displays its wares in a lavish 4,500-square-foot undergarment emporium defined by vivid red awnings, huge wraparound windows, theatrical lighting fixtures, sensuous tones of scarlet, gold, and leopard, and luminous Swarovski crystal sconces. An oversized chandelier dangling from the 17-foot ceiling exemplifies the interior mood. For added eroticism, klieg lights strategically illuminate the bras, panties, teddies, corsets, thongs, and such, while "beauty spots" created by a solid crystal add a glamorous glow. Talk about giving new meaning to lingerie shopping! But there's more. Just to make shoppers feel relaxed and comfortable, they've added a lounge, a mezzanine level for customized consumption, and a Bra Bar, where women are personally fitted for the right size. ♦ 6751 Hollywood Blvd. 323/957.5953, 24-hour mail order 800/323.9525. www.fredericks.com

22 GUINNESS WORLD OF RECORDS MUSEUM

Oddities and world-record displays are featured in the refurbished **Hollywood Theatre,** Hollywood's first movie house. The most popular exhibit is the $30,000 tribute to singer Michael Jackson's *Thriller* album, which set a record when it sold 48 million copies. ♦ Admission. M-Th, Su, until midnight; F, Sa, until 2AM. 6764 Hollywood Blvd (between N McCadden Pl and N Highland Ave). 323/463.6433. www.guinessrecords.com

22 THE HOLLYWOOD WAX MUSEUM

Only in LA can you find more than 200 wax replicas of such famous figures as *Playboy*'s Hugh Hefner, who took his enshrined spot alongside a bevy of wax beauties. A bit spacey, you bet, but hey, this is Tinseltown. So go on over and take a look at the eerie likenesses of Marilyn Monroe, Pamela Anderson, Bob Hope, various sports figures, and even Hannibal the Cannibal Lecter, aptly ensconced in the Chamber of Horrors. ♦ Admission. Daily, 10AM to midnight, until 2AM on weekends. 6767 Hollywood Blvd (at N Highland Ave). 323/462.8860

22 HOLLYWOOD HISTORY MUSEUM

Housed in the recently restored Art Deco–style Max Factor Building, the museum's exhibits take you on a tour of Hollywood past and present. There's a restaurant, gift shop, and lounge. ♦ Admission. Daily. 1666 N Highland Ave (at Hollywood Blvd). 323/464.7776. www.hollywoodhistorymuseum.com

23 EGYPTIAN THEATER

Sid Grauman's first Off-Broadway movie palace, designed by **Meyer & Holler,** was inspired by the 1922 discovery of King Tut's tomb, complete with sphinxes, hieroglyphics, and winged cobras adorning the walls. Facing competition from multiplex movie houses, owner United Artists shut down the theater in 1992, but thanks to local preservationists, this national institution is making a comeback under **American Cinematheque.** They are currently restoring the theater to its original splendor, with period signs, a marquee, and an organ. Films on the history of Hollywood, independent and foreign flicks, documentaries, and classic film festivals will fill the schedule. ♦ 6712 Hollywood Blvd (between N Las Palmas Ave and N McCadden Pl)

23 PIG 'N WHISTLE

★★$$ This historic 1927 landmark still looks as it did when movie stars and moguls flooded the place after attending premieres at the **Egyptian Theater.** Redesigned and restored by noted architects **Morgan, Walls & Clements,** the restaurant relives the glamour that was Hollywood with a marquee sporting a dancing-pig-and-fife motif, hand-painted tiles, and hand-carved wood. The food is Hollywood bistro, with Scottish salmon, peppered filet, shepherd's pie, seafood salads, and an original selection of Pig 'n Whistle soda fountain drinks. After 10PM from Wednesday through Saturday, Pig 'n Whistle turns into a hip spot with live bands and performances. ♦ Hollywood Bistro ♦ Su-Th, 11AM-midnight; F, Sa, 11AM-2AM. 6714 Hollywood Blvd (between N Las Palmas and N Highland Aves, on the west side of the Egyptian Theater). 323/463.0000. www.pignwhistle.com

24 LES DEUX CAFÉ

★★★$$$$ Ooh la la! It doesn't get more French than this. We're talking waiters with an attitude and food that makes you want to sing praises to the chef. The entrance is in a dark parking lot, but don't let the location fool you: Eating here is an experience you won't want to miss if you really care about good food. The crowd is beautiful, with lots of models and showbiz types, all dressed in trendy black outfits, who arrive late and hang around the patio bar before dining. The menu, which changes frequently according to what's fresh and available, is French bistro with hearty soups, rigatoni with white bean ragout, and great desserts. ♦ French. ♦ Reservations *mai oui*! 1638 N Las Palmas Ave (between Sunset and Hollywood Blvds). 323/465.0509

25 MUSSO AND FRANK GRILL

★★★$$ Opened in 1919, Hollywood's oldest restaurant has hosted plenty of celebrities over the years. Gossip columnists Hedda Hopper and Louella Parsons held court here, and Dashiell Hammett, Papa Hemingway, F. Scott Fitzgerald, William Faulkner, and Aldous Huxley dined regularly at what was called the "Algonquin Round Table West." The place remains reassuring, with its paneled permanence, great martinis, and comfortable counter for solitary diners. The short ribs or macaroni and cheese (made with cheddar, Parmesan, and breadcrumbs) are sure winners. Waiters can be brusque unless they know you, however. ♦ American ♦ Tu-Sa, breakfast, lunch, and dinner. Reservations recommended for lunch and dinner. 6667 Hollywood Blvd (between Cherokee and N Las Palmas Aves). 323/467.7788 &

26 JANES HOUSE

Constructed in 1903, this last survivor of the Victorian mansions that lined the boulevard until the 1920s was the home of a family-run school whose famous students included the children of Douglas Fairbanks, Cecil B. DeMille, Thomas Ince, and Charlie Chaplin. It is currently an official **Visitors Information Center.** ♦ M-Sa. 6600 Hollywood Blvd (between N Hudson and Whitley Aves). 323/461.9520

27 FREDERICK'S OF HOLLYWOOD

Alas, Frederick's relocated to Hollywood and Highland (see page 65) in 2005. However, we thought you'd like to know about its original location, which is now a nightclub. The 1935 purple-and-pink Art Deco tower designed by **Frank Falgien** and **Bruce Marteney** is an appropriate symbol for the company's flamboyantly sexy apparel. During the 1992 riots, thieves made off with, among other items, Madonna's studded brassiere from the **Celebrity Lingerie Hall of Fame.** A few days later, a guilt-plagued young man handed a priest a bag containing Ava Gardner's pantaloons and a bra belonging to actress Katey Sagal, saying he was too afraid to return them himself. It took a few years longer for the Madonna bustier to find its way back. ♦ 6608 Hollywood Blvd (between N Hudson and Cherokee Aves)

28 LOS ANGELES CONTEMPORARY EXHIBITIONS (LACE)

This nonprofit interdisciplinary arts organization offers diverse gallery and community art programs. Since 1977, the group has presented significant audio/video performances, sculpture, drawings, paintings, and installation pieces by both emerging and well-known artists. There's also an art periodical bookstore. ♦ W-Su. 6522 Hollywood Blvd (between Wilcox and N Hudson Aves). 323/957.1777

29 IVAR AVENUE

This block above Yucca Street still has many 1920s and 1930s apartment buildings. The **Parva Sed** is where Nathanael West lived when he originally conceived the plan for *Day of the Locust.* Farther up the block is **El Nido,** the fictional home of the luckless screenwriter played by William Holden in the movie *Sunset Boulevard.* ♦ Between Yucca St and Hollywood Fwy

30 JOSEPH'S CAFE

★$ This long-established favorite serves fabulous gyros, lentil soup, and rice pudding. ♦ Greek/Mediterranean ♦ Daily, breakfast, lunch, and dinner. 1775 Ivar Ave (at Yucca St). 323/462.8697

31 HOLLYWOOD PALACE

This 1920s Art Deco landmark looks great after a million-dollar face-lift. The 1,200-seat, bi-level dance club boasts a state-of-the-art light-and-sound system and performances by groups like Green Day, Sterolab, and Nine Inch Nails (if you haven't heard of 'em, it's probably not your scene). There's a strict dress code: Be cool, but not in bad taste. ♦ Performances F and Sa nights, other events scheduled during week; call for program. Vine St (between Hollywood Blvd and Yucca St). 323/467.4571, recorded hotline 323/462.3000. www.hollywoodpalace.com

32 PANTAGES THEATER

Once a movie palace, the Pantages is now a showcase for Broadway musicals such as the Tony award–winning production of *The Lion King.* It's a dazzling example of adaptive reuse. Originally designed by **B. Marcus Priteca** in 1929, the theater rivals the **Wiltern** (see page 56) as an anthology of zigzag moderne, from the vaulted lobby to the fretted ceiling of the auditorium, designed by Anthony B. Heinsbergen. ♦ 6233 Hollywood Blvd (between Argyle Ave and Vine St). 323/468.1770. www.nederlander.com

32 COLLECTOR'S BOOK STORE

For film fans and collectors, this shop is a treasure trove of movie books, stills, and memorabilia. ♦ Tu-Sa. 6225 Hollywood Blvd (between Argyle Ave and Vine St). 323/467.3296

Restaurants/Clubs: Red | Hotels: Purple | Shops: Orange | Outdoors/Parks: Green | Sights/Culture: Blue

32 CAPITOL RECORDS TOWER

An example of programmatic architecture on an epic scale, this 1954 tower by **Welton Becket & Associates** looks like a stack of records topped by a stylus. A rooftop beacon flashes the word "Hollywood" in Morse code at night. In December, it's lit to create Hollywood's tallest Christmas tree. ◆ 1750 Vine St (at Yucca St). www.hollywoodandvine.com

33 FRANCES GOLDWYN REGIONAL BRANCH LIBRARY

To replace the Hollywood Library, which was destroyed by arson, **Frank Gehry** created this cluster of luminous boxes (the illumination comes from light bouncing off water in shallow reflecting pools) in 1986. So outdoorsy is the overall feel that you hardly notice how well the building is protected—"tighter security than the American Embassy designed for Damascus," says the architect. ◆ M-Sa; M, W until 8PM. 1623 N Ivar Ave (between Vine St and Hollywood Blvd). 323/467.1821

34 JAMES DOOLITTLE THEATER

This spot is one of the best places in LA to enjoy one-person shows and quality drama. ◆ 1615 Vine St (between Selma Ave and Hollywood Blvd). 323/462.6666

35 THE MUSIC BOX AT FONDA'S/ BLUE PALMS LOUNGE

Okay, there is no box office, so you must show up the night of the performance, concert, or event and hope for the best. Or you can buy two drinks in the Blue Palms Lounge at 6PM (two hours before doors open) and obtain limited VIP seating in the balcony. Call for schedule at the beginning of the week. ◆ 6126 Hollywood Blvd (between Gower St and El Centro Ave). 323/468.1700, 323/464.0808

36 CHATEAU MARMONT HOTEL

$$$ This 1927 Norman castle, where Greta Garbo stayed and John Belushi died, once guarded the approach to the Sunset Strip. The interior of the hotel is handsome and intimate enough to continue attracting movie and music celebrities. The 63 accommodations include 30 luxury suites with balconies and views, and cottages around the pool. The dining room is open 24 hours, as is room service. If you're into vintage wheels and power cars, take a peek into the parking garage: It will blow you away. ◆ 8221 Sunset Blvd (at Marmont La), West Hollywood. 323/656.1010, 800/242.8328; fax 323/655.5311

BAR MARMONT

★★★$$ A popular hideaway for young Hollywood stars seeking seclusion from fans, this casual spot is perfect for a romantic dinner. The food's good, especially the gnocchi, pork chop, and corn fritters. It's definitely a place to see stars, but be discreet; the ones who go here really don't want to be recognized. ◆ California Cuisine Daily, dinner. Reservations suggested. 323/650.0575. www.chateaumarmont.com

37 HOLLYWOOD HOUNDS

This one's for dog lovers. If you're traveling with Fido or just want to treat him to a "pawdicure," this canine day spa is the place to go. You can board your pups, throw them a birthday party or bark mitzvah, or even walk them down the aisle in holy muttramony at this wild and wonderful one-of-a-kind facility. There's even pick-up and delivery from your home or hotel. ◆ 8218 Sunset Blvd (just west of Crescent Hts and across the street from the Chateau Marmont). 332/650.5551

38 GREENBLATT'S DELICATESSEN

★$ This haven for expatriate New Yorkers serves typical deli fare (pastrami, cheese-cake, cold cuts, sides, etc.) to eat in, take home, or bring to the Hollywood Bowl in the summer. There's a full bar, a nifty wine cellar, and a friendly staff. ◆ Deli ◆ Daily until 2AM. 8017 Sunset Blvd (between N Laurel Ave and Laurel Canyon Blvd). 323/656.0606

39 GAUCHO GRILL

★$ Good, solid Argentinean-style steaks and chicken are smothered in garlic and served with French fries (or rice and salad). The décor encourages quick meals. Wear earplugs; it's loud. ◆ Argentinean ◆ Daily, lunch and dinner. 7980 Sunset Blvd (at N Laurel Ave), 323/656.4152. Also at 11754 San Vicente Blvd (at Gorham Ave). 310/447.7898; 11838 Ventura Blvd (between Blue Canyon Dr and Carpenter Ave), San Fernando Valley. 323/508.1030

39 8000 SUNSET STRIP

This contemporary Art Deco commercial complex housed the first US branch of the Virgin Megastore until it shut its doors in early 2008. At press time, the massive rental space was empty, but it was business as usual for the rest of the establishments. Like the lively coffee shop on the first floor aptly named **Buzz** (323/650.7742), serving dynamite espressos and pastries in an outdoor setting; a jam-packed **California Pizza Kitchen** (★★★$$ 323/654.0162) that is so popular you'd think they were giving away free food, open daily; a **Pinkberry,** the hottest yogurt franchise in town; and a **Burke Williams Day Spa** (323/822.9007). Up one story you'll find a six-screen Laemmle movie theater (323/848.3600); a Rockstar Energy Drink café (no phone number available); a branch of the hopping **Sushi Dan** (★★$$ 323/848.8583), open daily; and **Crunch** (323/654.4550), a hip and happening health club. ♦ Daily. 8000 Sunset Blvd (between N Laurel Ave and Crescent Heights Blvd)

40 DIRECTORS GUILD OF AMERICA

This overpowering curvilinear bronze-glass tower is a textbook example of how not to build on Sunset. Constructed in 1989, it is out of scale and character with everything around it. It does have three excellent auditoriums, though, which are currently being used by the **American Cinematheque** (323/461.9622) for public programs. ♦ 7920 Sunset Blvd (between N Fairfax and N Hayworth Aves). 310/289.2000

41 DAR MAGHREB

★$$$ The Arabian Nights décor and good renditions of the standard dishes (couscous, lamb, and quail) are popular with tour groups. ♦ Moroccan ♦ Daily, dinner. 7651 Sunset Blvd (at N Stanley Ave). 323/876.7651

42 FALCON

★★★$$$ This lofty lair, named for Falcon Lair, the luxurious sanctuary of silent-film star Rudolph Valentino, throbs with young sophisticates decked out in designer black. The minimalist décor, outdoor patio, and perceptive waitstaff add to the charm. The food doesn't hurt either. Get in the mood with an exotic martini—chocolate espresso, keylime, or Topaz. Then savor starters such as pan-seared diver scallops, beef carpaccio, or ahi tuna and keep the juices flowing with wild mushroom, grilled chicken, and goat cheese pizza; lobster chopped salad; herb-crusted pork tenderloin, or red-wine-braised beef short ribs, then finish with a succulent savory. ♦ California ♦ Tu-Sa, dinner. Reservations required. Valet parking. 7113 Sunset Blvd (at Poinsettia). 323/850.5350. www.falconslair.com

43 HOLLYWOOD HIGH SCHOOL

Decorative reliefs and uplifting inscriptions embellish the surface of these 1935 Streamline Moderne buildings. Farmers called the $67,000 three-story Roman temple–style school a "ridiculous piece of extravagance" when it was being built over a century ago.

The "piece of extravagance" schooled famous folk such as Judy Garland, Mickey Rooney, Sally Kellerman, James Garner, and Nobelist William Shockley—to name a few. ♦ Sunset Blvd and N Highland Ave

44 CAFE DES ARTISTES

★★$$ Picture yourself on a back street in Cannes while dining at Silvio de Mori's idyllic neighborhood French bistro with its leafy patio, cool dining room, and friendly service. Some of the most delicious *plats du jour* include macaroni and cheese, mussels, or steak with *pommes frites*. The trendy spot attracts a young, hip, late crowd. The Sunday brunch is very good, too. ♦ French ♦ Tu-F, lunch and dinner; Sa, dinner; Su, brunch, lunch, and dinner. Reservations recommended. 1534 N McCadden Pl (between Sunset Blvd and Selma Ave). 323/469.7300

44 STAGES TRILINGUAL THEATER

Paul Verdier produces some of LA's most innovative theater here, including plays by Ionesco, Marguerite Duras, and René-Daniel DuBois, in English, French, and Spanish. Seating is limited, so book well in advance ♦ 1540 N McCadden Pl (between Sunset Blvd and Selma Ave). General information 323/463.5356, box office 323/465.1010

45 CROSSROADS OF THE WORLD

Designed in 1936 by **Robert Derrah,** this is a paradigm of fantasy architecture in pristine condition: a liner (center building) sailing into a foreign port (surrounding English, French, Spanish, and Moorish shops). ♦ 6671 Sunset Blvd (at N Las Palmas Ave)

46 BEAUTY BAR

Only in LA or Hollywood (or New York, where it originated) could you find a bar where you can get a manicure with your martini. Well, actually, just order a froufrou drink like a Shampoo, Prell, or Platinum and the preening's on the house. No joke! It's a no-brainer that the '60s-styled place, with its hair dryers, retro bar stools, and vintage fixtures, attracts a young crowd, mostly single women (so if you're looking . . .). ♦ Doors open at 6PM and close 2AM most nights. 1638 Cahuenga Blvd (between Selma Ave and Hollywood Blvd). 323/464.7676. www.beautybar.com

---

Restaurants/Clubs: Red | Hotels: Purple | Shops: Orange | Outdoors/Parks: Green | Sights/Culture: Blue

47 CITIZEN SMITH

★★★$$$ Don your hippest Goth garb and join the young tattooed, pierced, belly-bearing trendoids who fill this sexy, quirky Thomas Schoos–designed room with its high ceilings, smoked mirrors, candlelit walls, booths covered in real Brazilian bull hides, and mahogany bar that spans the length of the dining area. The surreal setting is like a movie scene and oddly enough the chow, which the chef calls "hip, upscale comfort food," is quite tasty. We loved the jalapeño tuna tartare, the fried green tomatoes with smoked mozzarella, and the cedar-planked salmon. You can eat light fare (nachos, quesadillas, French onion soup, or salads), but do have dessert—they rock. Comfort Food. ◆ Reservations a must. M-F, lunch and dinner; Sa, Su, dinner. 1600 N Cahuenga Blvd (east corner of Selma and Cahuenga), Hollywood. 323/461.5001. www.citizensmith.com

48 GREEN DOOR

$$$$ This restaurant/lounge/salon is so new we haven't had a chance to rate it, but guessing by the recent owner (Johnny Zander, fresh from the Tropicana and Teddy's at the Hollywood Roosevelt, who also acts as nightly host), it should prove a winner. Please forgive us as hot clubs do come and go, just like its predecessor, Sterling Steakhouse. Designed to attract the Hollywood brat-pack Paris Hilton crowd and other young scenesters, the sexy club was designed like an old-world French salon with antique mirrors, dimly lit sconces, dark wood fixtures, and velvet drapes highlighted by a massive chandelier. There are three reveling spaces: an outdoor patio, a middle room with dance floor, and a lounge. A small, bistro-like supper club menu is available. ◆ Tu-F, 8:30PM-2AM. Reservations advised. 1439 Ivar Ave (a half block south of Sunset Blvd). 323/463.0008

49 ARCLIGHT HOLLYWOOD & CINERAMA DOME

Nothing beats this paradigm of movie theaters, dramatically housed on three levels with floor-to-ceiling glass windows, for watching the latest motion pictures projected on super state-of-the-art screens while ensconced in comfortable seats. The Cinerama Dome is the showcase of the 14-theater complex, with its deeply curved screen and technologically advanced sound and production values. A nifty feature at ArcLight is the reserved seating, for which you purchase a ticket in advance either online (www.arclightcinemas.com) or by phone (323/464.4226) and avoid waiting in line. In addition to late-run movies, the facility houses limited-engagement exhibits that focus on the film industry; a gift shop stocked with memorabilia, and a café bar open for snacks and meals from 11AM until 1AM daily. Night owls can extend their evening out at **Charcoal** ($$$★★), a swinging American grill/nightclub designed by Dodd Mitchell, with live DJs on Wednesday, Saturday, and Sunday nights. There's four-hour validated covered parking (you pay $1). ◆ 630 Sunset Blvd (at Ivar Ave). 323/464.4226. www.arclightcinemas.com

49 AMOEBA MUSIC

A whopping 200,000 people a month pass through this mega–music store to browse, buy, or sell collections of vintage or used records, tapes, CDs, rock 'n' roll posters, and other music memorabilia. The staff is friendly and helpful and they pay pretty well for your recyclables. You can take cash or credit to use within the store. There are great pickings from every genre and era. ◆ Daily. 6400 Sunset Blvd (next door to ArcLight Cinerama Dome). 323/245.6400; fax 323/465.6410. www.amoebamusic.com

50 SUNSET & VINE

Urban renewal hits Hollywood big-time with this ambitious 3½-acre development project by The Sagan Group and Bond Capital, which has transformed a large chunk of Sunset Boulevard and Vine Street into a major retail/residential/entertainment center that includes 300 residential units and 900,000 square feet of retail space with such shops as Borders Books and Bed, Bath & Beyond. 310/395.4250

51 OFF VINE

★$$ A shark juts through the roof of this frame house, heralding such dishes as tender filet mignon, super lamb chops, pork chops, and turkey burgers with three sauces. The chocolate soufflé is a must, as is the chocolate pecan caramel pie. ◆ California ◆ M-F, lunch and dinner; Sa, dinner; Su, brunch and dinner. Reservations recommended. 6263 Leland Way (between El Centro Ave and Vine St). 323/962.1900. www.offvine.com

52 HOLLYWOOD PALLADIUM

Since it opened in 1940, this Streamline Moderne structure has swung to the sounds of the Dorsey Brothers, Glenn Miller, Stan Kenton, and Lawrence Welk, and rocked to the beat of more contemporary acts like the Rolling Stones, Madonna, Black Flag, and Arctic Monkeys. Current attractions vary from dancing—on an 11,200-square-foot dance floor—to conventions, but big names still make frequent appearances. A full bar and à la carte dinners are offered. At press time, Live Nation concert promoters signed a 20-year lease agreement to run the Palladium and undertake a major renovation. The place will be shuttered during the restorative face-lift. ♦ Cover. Call for show times. 6215 Sunset Blvd (at El Centro Ave). 323/962.7600

53 EAT.ON SUNSET

★★★$$ Another member of uber chef Joachim Splichal's Patina Group, this boisterous bistro does a boffo business every day of the week. The inviting spot features a buzzing bar, cozy outdoor patio, and a fireside lounge where you can enjoy drinks and tapas. Menu items range from house-made pasta dishes to pork chops with caramelized apples and mac and cheese, or a super steak for two with fat fries and lettuce wedge salad with blue cheese dressing. If you like wine with your meal, buy it by the bottle—it's much cheaper that way. Or, since there's no corkage fee, bring your own. ♦ American Bistro ♦ M-F, lunch; Tu-Sa, dinner. Reservations suggested. Valet parking. 1448 N Gower St (at Sunset Blvd). 323/461.8800. www.patinagroup.com/eatSunset

54 STARSTEPS

A 40,000-pound steel sculpture by artist John David Mooney has been perched atop the **Metromedia TV** studio since 1981. Brightly illuminated at night, it seems to float above the freeway. ♦ Sunset Blvd (between N Wilton Pl and Hollywood Fwy)

55 PARU'S

★$ Standouts on Paru's vegetarian menu include the *masala dosa* (a foot-long lentil flour crepe filled with potato curry), *samosas* (turnovers), and *idli* (rice pancakes with lentil gravy). ♦ Indian Vegetarian ♦ Daily, lunch and dinner. 5140 Sunset Blvd (between N Normandie Ave and N Kingsley Dr). 323/661.7600

56 BARNSDALL PARK

Located at the top of a hill and ringed by olive trees, this oasis and cultural center is in the flatlands of eastern Hollywood. ♦ 4800 Hollywood Blvd (between N Vermont Ave and Edgemont St)

Within Barnsdall Park:

HOLLYHOCK HOUSE

Oil heiress Aline Barnsdall commissioned this house—architect **Frank Lloyd Wright**'s first in LA, completed in 1920—as part of a complex of cultural and residential structures. It has been restored and includes many of the original Wright furnishings. The guided tour is interesting. ♦ Admission. Tours, Tu-Su. 323/913.4157

MUNICIPAL ART GALLERY

This exhibition space is a visual forum for cutting-edge Southern California art. The theater presents a lively and varied bill of films and concerts. ♦ Admission. Tu-Su. 323/485.4581

JUNIOR ARTS CENTER

The center offers an extensive program of sophisticated and innovative studio art classes for children and young people ages 3 to 18. Designed for a young audience, the gallery's changing shows emphasize participation and activity. ♦ M-F. Gallery, Tu-Su. 323/485.4474

57 MILLENNIUM ON SUNSET

This expansive 110,000-square-foot contemporary commercial complex stretches east from La Cienega Boulevard to Sunset Plaza. An assortment of upscale shops and boutiques are housed in three separate buildings—including Madison for fine Italian shoes, O Boutique featuring French fashions, L'Occitane for cosmetics and beauty products, and Vertigo for women's clothes. Fitness buffs should head over to the amazing **Equinox West Hollywood,** a contemporary exercise emporium with all the appropriate amenities (310/289.1900, www.equinoxfitness.com). ♦ 8560-8590 Sunset Blvd, West Hollywood

Within Millennium on Sunset:

KETCHUP

★★$$$ What can we say about a place named after a condiment? Okay, it's kitschy, all done up in—you guessed it—red. Even the waitstaff has faux ketchup splashed on their shirts. It's actually quite sleek and inviting if you don't mind seeing red everywhere. The upstairs/downstairs dining offers vinyl booths or banquettes in which to enjoy "comfort" food like fries with five kinds of ketchup, buffalo chicken wings, tomato soup, sloppy Joes, mac 'n' cheese, Kobe beef hot dogs, and more. ♦ Upscale Diner Fare. ♦ Reservations suggested. M-Sa, dinner. 310/289.8590. www.dolcegroup.com/ketchup

58 THE COMEDY STORE

This place is perennially packed by folks who just want to laugh and comedians who go to practice their craft before a critical audience. It is probably the most important

Restaurants/Clubs: Red | **Hotels: Purple** | **Shops: Orange** | **Outdoors/Parks: Green** | **Sights/Culture: Blue**

71

showcase for comedians trying to break into show business. The **Main Room** presents established comics; the **Original Room** offers continuous shows of rising new comedians; and the **Belly Room** presents female talent. ◆ Two-drink minimum. Call for hours. 8433 Sunset Blvd (between N Kings and Queens Rds), West Hollywood. 323/656.6225

59 HOUSE OF BLUES

$$ The brainchild of Isaac Tigrett and "Blues Brother" Dan Aykroyd, this is one of a chain of eatery/nightclubs that pays homage to blues music and Southern cooking. There are nightly performances of blues and blues-inspired music. Food is served in **The Porch** (★★$$), which is separated from the showroom by soundproof glass to afford peaceful enjoyment of the Southwestern comfort cuisine. Wending your way through the menu can be fun, with everything from crispy Caesar salads and blackened chicken sandwiches to cedar plank–roasted salmon with Dijon glaze, voodoo shrimp with Dixie beer, rosemary cornbread, and pan-seared crab cakes. Yummy desserts include warm chocolate-chip pie with cookie-dough ice cream and peppermint sauce, white chocolate banana bread pudding with crème Anglaise and whipped cream, and a to-die-for chocolate pecan terrine. ◆ Southern ◆ Cover varies. Restaurant: M-Sa, lunch; daily, dinner (until midnight Su-Th, 1AM on F, Sa); Su, gospel brunch and dinner. Club: daily until 2AM. 8430 Sunset Blvd (at Olive Dr), West Hollywood. 323/848.5100. www.houseofblues.com or simply www.hob.com

59 MONDRIAN

$$$ Hip hotelier Ian Schrager (owner of boutique properties such as the Paramount, Royalton, and Morgans in New York and the Delano in Miami) keeps this 188-suite hotel on its trendy toes. French designer Philippe Starck restored the landmark building to its original splendor, in an all-white, contemporary California look. The place rules as the too-hip spot for movie and recording industry stars, moguls, and wannabes who jam the popular **Sky Bar** or bring their drinks down to the starlit pool (drinks are served in plastic for that purpose). Reservations are not easily gotten at this outrageously

expensive restaurant, although hotel guests have a better shot than nonguests. If sake's your preference, you'll find the largest selection in LA at the **Seabar**. ◆ 8440 Sunset Blvd (at Olive Dr), West Hollywood. 323/650.8999, 800/525.8029; fax 323/650.5215. www.mondrianhotel.com

Within the Mondrian:

ASIA DE CUBA

★★★$$$$ Ian Schrager picked a winner when he opened this quirky Asian/Cuban fusion restaurant. The trendoids who frequent the Sky Bar love the long, narrow dining room with its stark white walls and black-and-white lithographs. The creative menu includes duck tacos, mahi-mahi, oxtail spring rolls, black bean soup, satays, and some of the best pan-seared salmon ever made. Dieters beware: Desserts are served in huge portions, like a skyscraper of coconut and butter cream cake topped with chocolate sauce, or a banana split that serves two. ◆ Daily, lunch and dinner. Reservations vital, and earlier is better as the regulars dine fashionably late. 323/848.6000

59 THE GRAFTON

★★★$$$ According to the desk clerk, the price varies depending on occupancy of the hotel. No kidding. It could range from $119 to $399-plus a day, so call ahead. The place is about as cool as its next-door neighbor, with trendy minimalist designs and a young clientele. There are 108 rooms (including five lavish suites), all simply but nicely appointed according to feng shui. Facilities include a bistro, a stunning Venetian-influenced pool and garden with a graceful waterfall, a bar, and a fitness center. Assorted amenities include free morning tea and coffee served at the pool, wireless Internet, laptop in-room safes, iPod docking stations, and complimentary transportation around town. ◆ 8462 Sunset Blvd, West Hollywood (next door to Mondrian, near Olive Dr). 323/654.4600, 800/821.3660; fax 323/654.5918. www.graftonsunset.com

Within the Grafton:

BOA STEAKHOUSE

★★$$ Over-the-top trendy with an innovative design, this is where the steaks are prime and the clientele ripe, especially at night. At least twice there have been sightings of former president Bill Clinton eating here. We've been assured it wasn't a Hollywood double. Best menu choices are the New York steak or sirloin burger. All drinks are big and potent. The lounge rocks in the evening; so if

F. Scott Fitzgerald wrote *The Last Tycoon*, his great unfinished novel about Irving Thalberg and the Golden Age of Hollywood, in his Laurel Avenue apartment in West Hollywood.

you don't go for dinner, hop over for a drink and a great scene. Be sure to dress in your coolest duds. ♦ Daily, lunch and dinner. Reservations suggested. 323/650.8383

60 SUNSET TOWER

$$$$ Originally called the Sunset Tower Hotel, the name was changed to the Argyle several years ago. However, Jeff Klein (who created the Manhattan boutique hotel City Club) stepped into the picture in 2005 and elaborately restored it from top to bottom. Today it's a dazzling reminder of years gone by with an upbeat, contemporary ambience. Listed on the National Register of Historic Places, the hotel is rich in Hollywood lore (John Wayne was one former tenant of the twelfth-floor penthouse—where he reportedly kept a cow on the balcony). The hotel was restored to its original splendor in 1995 under the direction of designer David Becker, who added steel window frames and a multi-spandreled glass exterior. The 64 guest rooms include two townhouse suites, two penthouse suites, 41 one-bedroom suites, and 19 deluxe rooms, each tastefully appointed in Art Deco style, with striking pieces imported from Italy. In-room amenities include fax/copy machines, computer modem hookups, two-line phones, robes, TV, VCR, and large marble bathrooms stocked with Aveda products. The small rooftop pool is a popular gathering place for Hollywood celebs, and there's also a 6,000-square-foot spa, meeting facilities, a concierge, a bar/lounge, and a restaurant. ♦ 8358 Sunset Blvd (between N Sweetzer Ave and Olive Dr), West Hollywood. 323/654.7100, 800/225.2637; fax 323/654.9287. www.sunsettower.com

Within the Sunset Tower Hotel:

TOWER BAR

★★$$$$ The action begins after 8PM when the young and lovely arrive in droves to sit at the handsome bar before settling down to dinner. The dark, dramatic minimalist-designed room provides an elegant yet casual setting. Sweeping views from floor-to-ceiling windows enhance the mood. The crowd is a mix of LA's fashionistas, record company bigwigs, and celebrities who come dressed for the occasion in either designer jeans or evening togs and sip martinis, Manhattans, and cosmopolitans seemingly endlessly. Located off to the south side of the lobby, the new facility heralds the rebirth of the original Tower, which thrived as a Tinseltown watering hole during the late 1920s. The softly lit room echoes more of the past with wood-paneled walls and plush sofas nestled by windows that provide lingering views of the city. Adding to the glamour is a soundtrack of recordings of Nat King Cole, Billie Holiday, and others of their era. On balmy nights ask for a table on the outdoor terrace, with its unbeatable poolside setting and views. We almost forgot: They do serve food, too, and it is exceptional—especially the seafood tower, roasted lamb T-bone, grilled king salmon, and desserts. ♦ Daily, breakfast, lunch, and dinner. Reservations suggested for dinner. 323/848.6677

ARGYLE SALON & SPA

We're talking a 6,600-square-foot pamper palace dedicated to celestial indulgence. What's really cool is you get your own private spa suite, which has all the amenities of a hotel room: shower, tub, vanity, commode, etc. Estheticians and therapists, trained by noted Fifth Avenue day-spa doyenne Cornelia Zicu, come to you to perform their magical maneuvers, which in addition to the usual facial-to-foot care includes a four-handed stone massage and special scrub wraps. The bi-level emporium features a tranquil outdoor patio area with cabanas in which to relax even more after salubrious sessions.

61 THE STANDARD HOTEL

$ This place is so hip and trendy the name is actually written upside down on the marquee. Carved out of a '60s motel, this youth-driven, 138-room hotel caters to its clientele in a big way. Twenty-somethings love it for the wild and free ambience and the cool rooms, all with CD players and VCRs, cordless phones, and platform beds with condoms on the pillows. Although the price is right, the "kids" who stay here are hardly needy. The lobby rules with its pair of bubble-like glass swings, constant R&R or rap music, and a cozy corner with oversized, cushy seats and arcing lamps. There's a wacky 24-hour coffee shop and bar serving everything from sandwiches and pizza to sushi and ahi tuna. It attracts a wild-and-crazy crowd all through the night. There's also a smoking room, barbershop, gift shop, pink pool on a wide-open deck, and day passes to nearby **Crunch,** the hottest health club in town. And get this: the housekeepers don't rev up their vacuums until noon. ♦ 8300 Sunset Blvd, West Hollywood (between N Sweetzer Ave and Olive Dr). 323/650.9090; fax 323/650.2820. www.standardhotel.com

62 VILLA D'ESTE APARTMENTS

This 1928 structure is one of several lushly planted courtyard apartments in Los Angeles that evoke romantic Mediterranean villas. Other cherished examples are located within walking distance at **1400** and **1475 Havenhurst Drive, 8225 Fountain Avenue,** and **1338 North Harper Avenue.** All are private residences. ♦ 1355 Laurel Ave (between Fountain Ave and Sunset Blvd), West Hollywood

63 AMMO

★★★$$ One of the city's most popular catering concerns runs this neighborhood restaurant with élan. The décor is funky, with hanging paper lanterns, exposed pipes, and metal chairs. And the food's downright delicious. Go for breakfast and feast on 10-grain flapjacks, have a turkey burger for lunch, and enjoy anything from tuna tartare and beef carpaccio to grilled chicken, a double-cut pork chop, or pan-seared halibut for dinner. Or just drop by for a piece of chocolate mousse layer cake with mocha icing when you get a craving for sweets that just won't quit. ♦ American ♦ M-F, lunch; daily, dinner; Sa, Su, brunch. Reservations suggested for dinner. 1155 N Highland Ave (between Fountain Ave and Sunset Blvd). 323/871.2666. www.ammocafe.com

64 ROXY

This Art Deco dance club is jammed every night with a mix of hip young trendies, older fans of rock 'n' roll, and recording industry bigwigs. Rock and jazz performers, already famous or on the right path, are the headliners here. The club is frequently booked by the local music industry to showcase hot new talent. The Roxy is open nightly from 7:30PM to 2AM. For after-hours jamming, and celebrity spottings, head upstairs to **On the Rox,** one of the sizzlingest scenester spots in town. Once a private club for Roxy proprietor Lou Adler and his buddy Jack Nicholson, the one-room lounge experienced some rocky times until a recent rebirth by Adler's son Nic. Glamour was restored with fresh paint, artwork of vintage rock-and-rollers and contemporary music groups (Deftones, Incubus, Papa Roach), and a state-of-the-art sound system. On the Rox reigns as the "it" spot for the "in" crowd. ♦ F, Sa, 10PM-2AM. Cover. Show times vary, so call ahead for the schedule. 9009 Sunset Blvd (between Hilldale Ave and N Wetherly Dr), West Hollywood. 310/278.9457. www.theroxyonsunset.com

64 KEY CLUB

This cool, three-story nightspot with its red and blue metal trim is the place to go to see big-name performers (Pink, John Mayer, Macy Gray, and the Sharks are a few past headliners). There's dancing on weekends, when the name changes to **Elysium** (on Fridays) and **God's Kitchen** (on Saturdays). There's also a pleasant horseshoe-shaped restaurant on the second floor serving decent California cuisine, along with great views of the action and a plush VIP lounge. Hours vary depending on who's on stage, but it's always open 'til at least 2AM. ♦ 9039 Sunset Blvd (between N-Wetherly and N Doheny Drs), West-Hollywood. 310/274.5800. www.thekeyclub.com

64 TALESAI

★★$$ Some of LA's most distinctive food is served in this chic, upscale Thai restaurant. Specialties include *hor mok* (shrimp and squid with lemongrass, basil, and coconut), squid with chili, and *masman* lamb (with chili-coconut sauce, curry style). ♦ Thai ♦ M-F, lunch and dinner; Sa, dinner. Reservations recommended. 9043 Sunset Blvd (between N Wetherly and N Doheny Drs), West Hollywood. 310/275.9724

65 WHISKY À GO GO

Live rock music is the attraction at this thriving nightspot. There's dancing on the floor up front by the stage. ♦ Cover. Call for hours. 8901 Sunset Blvd (at Clark St), West Hollywood. 310/652.4202

65 DUKES

★$ This popular West Hollywood coffee shop has a fast pace, good food, and a friendly feel. They seat you wherever they can, which is usually with strangers—but they won't be strangers for long. Expect a long wait for brunch on Sunday. ♦ Coffee shop ♦ M-F, breakfast, lunch, and dinner; Sa, Su, breakfast and lunch until 4PM. 8909 Sunset Blvd (between Clark St and Hilldale Ave), West Hollywood. 310/652.9411

66 THE VIPER ROOM

Hot groups like Pearl Jam and REM drop by regularly for a few impromptu sets at this cool music club. On a somewhat creepier note, this is also the place where actor River Phoenix died in 1994 after a particularly wild night. The clientele's dress code runs from miniskirts with work boots to tight jeans and tank tops. ♦ Cover. M-Sa, until 2AM. 8852 Sunset Blvd (at Larrabee St), West Hollywood. 310/358.1880

66 LONDON WEST HOLLYWOOD

$$$$ The Blackstone Real Estate Group, which purchased the property formerly known as Le Bel Age, closed the hotel in 2007 during a major head-to-toe overhaul by David Collins, who also designed London NYC in midtown Manhattan as well as The Blue Bar at Berkeley, among other restaurants. When it reopens, there will be lots of wow factors like an exclusive Golden

Door Spa, a restaurant from British chef and Fox TV celebrity Gordon Ramsay, concierge service by Quintessentially, bathrooms by Waterworks, and more. ♦ 1020 N San Vicente Blvd (between Cynthia St and Sunset Blvd), West Hollywood. 310/854.1111, reservations only; fax 310/854.0926. www.luxuryresorts.com &

67 BOOK SOUP

This marvelous store specializes in current and classic literature, books on the arts, and a remarkable choice of American and foreign magazines. ♦ Daily, until midnight. 8818 Sunset Blvd (between Holloway Dr and Larrabee St), West Hollywood. 310/659.3110

68 MEL'S DRIVE-IN

★★$ This fun spot serves the usual diner fare—hamburgers, shakes, fries—as well as vegetarian dishes. All the action takes place indoors (sorry, no car service), with booths, counter service, and a jukebox. ♦ Daily, 24 hours. 8585 Sunset Blvd (between Londonderry Pl and Sunset Plaza Dr), West Hollywood. 310/854.7200

68 SUNSET PLAZA

Fashionistas looking for haute couture need go no farther than this genteel strip of high-end shops spread out along Sunset Strip just east of Larrabee. Leading the list of top spots to shop is On Sunset (No. 8711; 310/289.8711, www.onsunset.net), a super-upscale designer haven, with helpful sales personnel and no attitude. You'll find everything here from casual to ultrachic with labels like Dolce and Gabbana, Jean-Paul Gaultier, Transit, DKNY, and Nigel. While the price tags may produce sticker shock, co-owners Shauna Stein and Lauralee Bell (star of TV's *The Young and the Restless*) run two major sales in June and January worth checking out. We scooped up an adorable designer number marked down from $670 to $135. If you don't find what you're looking for there, continue your search at these shops: **Nicole Miller** (No. 8633; 310/652.1629) for the designer's colorful clothing and accessories; **Oliver Peoples** (No. 8642; 310/657.2553) for optical-wear; **Origins** (No. 8645; 310/659.2797) for aromatherapy items and cosmetics; **Plaza Kids** (No. 8646; 310/652.1675) for the young jet set; **A/X Armani Exchange** (No. 8700; 310/659.0171); **Hugo Boss Shop** (No. 8625; 310/360.6931); **Dolce & Gabbana** (No. 8641; 310/360.7272); and **Club Monaco** (cool clothes for men and women) (No. 8569; 310/659.3821). ♦ 8589-8720

Sunset Blvd (at Sunset Plaza Dr), West Hollywood. 310/652.7137

At Sunset Plaza:

CAFE MED

★★$ This fun indoor-outdoor café is perfect for the budget conscious. Daily specials might include rack of lamb, risotto with seafood, and Dover sole. ♦ Mediterranean ♦ Daily, lunch and dinner. Reservations recommended for large parties. No. 8615. 310/652.0445 &

OLEHENRIKSEN

Bliss out at this special Zen-like oasis with a leisurely soak in a scented hydrotherapy tub surrounded by calming votive candles (there are actually two tubs, so bring a close friend). Then have a superb hot rock massage, or a 1½-hour sports massage from Michael that will leave you limp all over, or any of a number of top-notch treatments personally created by Danish dynamo Ole Henriksen, skin care guru to the stars. We do mean big-name celebs (Lisa Kudrow, Carmen Electra, Nelly Furtado, Ellen DeGeneres, Ellen Barkin, Mario Lopez, Jessica Alba, and Keifer Sutherland) so keep your eyes open if you're into stargazing. We recently spotted Kirk Douglas, a faithful customer for over 30 years, leaving the premises. There were other familiar faces relaxing and sipping herbal tea in the meditation room—a Zen-like den, where water drips gently down copper chains that hang in front of a rock-formation wall and comfy chairs rest below Japanese-inspired canvas floats that hang from the ceiling. If you really want to indulge yourself, opt for the Deluxe African Red Tea, two hours of pure pleasure designed to leave you relaxed and shimmering. The salubrious session begins with an organic sugar mixed with essential oils body scrub followed by an application of a body mask made from pure African red tea and yogurt, a heavenly scalp massage followed with an organic condi-tioner, and a half-hour deep tissue massage. Pure nirvana. ♦ 8622A W Sunset Blvd (in Sunset Plaza on the south side of Sunset Blvd, West Hollywood). 310/854.7700. ww.olehenriksen.com. OleHenriksen treatments are also available at Shutters at the Beach in Santa Monica in a sparkling facility designed by Michael Smith. 1 Pico Blvd (at Appian Way). 310/458.0030. A word of advice: If you go to one of his day spas, be sure to pick up supplies of OleHenriksen's botanically based product line Face/Body—perhaps some of the best beauty products available. And when you need more, just call 800/327.0331.

OleHenriksen treatments and products can also be found in 300 locations worldwide (including Nordstrom's, Sephora, and Victoria's Secret), just in case you run out.

69 SUNSET MARQUIS

$$$$ This oasis hidden in the midst of Hollywood caters to show and music biz types. Billy Joel, U2, Bruce Springsteen, and the like appreciate perks like 24-hour security and room service, multiline phones, and a workout room with two trainers. There are 102 sensational suites, but the really big spenders opt for one of the 52 palatial one- and two-bedroom villas that come with a personal butler (you haven't lived until you've experienced butler service, trust us) or the Presidential Villa, which has three fireplaces, a screening room, three baths, two bedrooms, and an office. There's a chic poolside restaurant (serving limited menus for breakfast, lunch, and dinner) and walk-up bar. An especially attractive perk for visiting recording stars and producers is the acoustically engineered 1,200-square-foot recording studio, set in an underground garage. There's also a small spa and compact fitness room (for those requiring a more heavy-duty workout, free passes are provided to the nearby Equinox health club). ◆ 1200 Alta Loma Rd (between Holloway Dr and Sunset Blvd), West Hollywood. 310/657.1333, 800/858.9758; fax 310/652.5300. www.sunsetmarquis.com

Within the Sunset Marquis:

BAR 1200

This late-night bar pulsates with a hip Hollywood crowd after 11PM, making it a prime stargazing spot. The dimly lit room with comfortable upholstered sofas is also perfect for a romantic rendezvous. ◆ Cover. Daily, until 2AM. 310/657.1333

70 THE CHAMBERLAIN

$$ The trendy Kor Hotel Group runs this 112-all-suite boutique hotel with its signature charismatic, or should we say "Korismatic," flair. Designed by David McCauley, a protégé of Kelly Wearstler of kwid, the pied-a-terre-style property sits squirreled away in a tree-lined residential area in West Hollywood just a few steps from Sunset Boulevard. The décor reflects diverse accents of neoclassi-cal, Moorish, and English Modern sophistica-tion with a twinge of hominess. Touches include queen-size beds covered by 250-thread-count cotton sheets and down

Hollywood High School alumni include Linda Evans, Carol Burnett, Ricky Nelson, and Warren Christopher.

comforters, gas log–burning fireplaces, balconies, LCD flat-panel TVs, refrigerators, and Carrera marble bathrooms stocked with Italian robes and luxurious hair and body care products. There's also a pay-as-you-use Beauty Bar (beware of sticker shock) stocked with organic skin care products from Sundari, Aesop, and Sante Verde. Striped carpeting and signature Kor grays add to the appeal. A handy business traveler bonus is the large, in-room workstation equipped with high-speed Internet access, two-line speakerphone, private voice mail, and a safe for laptops. World Wide Web access is available from just about anywhere in the hotel. An American bistro tucked just off the lobby provides an engaging garden greenhouse setting for breakfast, lunch, and dinner. Adjacent to the café is an inviting lounge with an extensive list of wines by the glass, along with a selection of creative martinis. Another pleasant touch is the rooftop pool deck, where you can enjoy an awesome view of the area while relaxing in a cushy chaise or in a private cabana. For a special treat, contact room service to request breakfast, lunch, or even dinner served by the pool. There's a fitness center on the lower level. Additional conveniences include a concierge, valet parking, and a meeting room for small groups. ◆ 1000 Westmont Dr (at W Knoll Dr), West Hollywood. 310/657.7400, 800/201.9652. www.chamberlainwesthollywood.com

71 ROSAMUND FELSEN GALLERY

New and established LA artists, including Mike Kelley, Chris Burden, and Roy Dowell, are showcased here. ◆ Tu-Sa. 8525 Santa Monica Blvd (at West Knoll Dr), West Hollywood. 310/652.9172

72 PALIHOUSE HOLLOWAY

$$ A unique concept unveils at this Bohemian-style boutique urban lodge, where the minimum stay is 14 days. These home-away-from-home accommodations are perfect for families or business travelers who want all the usual hotel services but with an apartment-like atmosphere. The inviting condos and suites purvey an understated elegance reminiscent of classic New Orleans French Quarter with a European flair. Amenities include a courtyard brasserie, an espresso bar, and a lobby living-room lounge. Guest quarters range from 800 to 1,900 square feet and come with dish-washer, washer/dryer, DVD player, hardwood floors, Calcutta marble bathrooms, fully equipped kitchens, LCD TVs, spacious closets and wardrobes, luxurious European pillows and bed linens, and expansive terraces with city or hillside views. ◆ 8465 Holloway Dr (near La Cienega Blvd), West

Hollywood. 323/656.4100.
www.palihouse.com

72 ORIGINAL BARNEY'S BEANERY

★★★$$ Man, this quirky roadhouse has attracted a steady flow of characters to its barroom doors since it opened in 1920, when Santa Monica Boulevard was called Route 66! Celebrities made the place famous, first Greta Garbo, and later Clark Gable, Jim Morrison, Jimi Hendrix, and Janis Joplin (who is said to have consumed her last beer there). Today's regulars include Drew Carey, Adam Sandler, and Quentin Tarantino, who hang out, eat, drink, and shoot pool, and normal folks who hang out, eat, drink, and shoot pool—it's all fun. There's lots of noise, several televisions turned on at one time, a satellite dish, more than 132 kinds of imported and domestic beer, and really tasty food. What more could you want? We go for the ambience, but also to eat amazing onion rings, 37 kinds of chili, juicy burgers, pizzas, burritos, breakfast items all day long, and huge salads that would fill an elephant, along with a few hundred other yummy items. ♦ American Roadhouse Comfort Food ♦ M-F, lunch and dinner, 11AM-2AM; Sa, Su, breakfast, lunch, and dinner, 9AM-2AM. 8447 Santa Monica Blvd (near La Cienega Blvd), West Hollywood. 310/654.2287. Also at 1351 Third St (Third St Promenade), Santa Monica. 310/656.5777; 99 E Colorado Blvd, Old Town Pasadena. 310/405.9777. www.barneysbeanery.com

73 CAFÉ LA BOHÈME

★★★$$ What a pleasant place to dine! Recently transformed by award-winning designer Margaret O'Brien with new touches that include private booths, lots of wicker, a lounge/bar, and vibrant artwork. Chef Christine Banta still mans the kitchen, dishing out choices such as octopus or warm sliced sirloin salads, catfish with black rice, miso-glazed salmon, and a 55-day dry-aged steak. The place has great vibes and food and a friendly attitude. ♦ American Bistro with French and Japanese influences ♦ Daily, dinner. Reservations required. 8400 Santa Monica Blvd (at N Orlando Ave), West Hollywood. 323/848.2360 ὑ

74 HUGO'S

★★★$$ Such head-turning stars as Julia Roberts, Bette Midler, and Geena Davis, as well as funnyman Jerry Seinfeld, have been spotted breakfasting at this hip spot. Many a million-dollar deal has been made over pumpkin pancakes, pasta alla Mamma (linguine, eggs, garlic, and Hugo's secret seasoning), and the healthy protein scramble—egg whites with chicken, mushrooms, and broccoli. Go early; primo window tables fill up fast. ♦ Italian ♦ Daily, breakfast, lunch, and dinner. 8401 Santa Monica Blvd (between N Kings Rd and Olive Dr), West Hollywood. 323/654.3993 ὑ

74 GLOBE PLAYHOUSE

The charming replica of Shakespeare's wooden O-shaped theater is host to the Bard's plays and dramatic readings of his sonnets. ♦ 1107 N Kings Rd (between Santa Monica Blvd and Fountain Ave), West Hollywood. 323/654.5623

75 O-BAR

★★★$$ You feel good the minute you walk into this dynamite-looking restaurant thanks to the cheerfully welcoming hosts and waitstaff. The décor is a knockout, with large chunks of raw, recycled glass, bamboo floors, pebble-crusted columns, and replica busts of classical sculpture set under a high ceiling. Extraordinary-looking white powder-coated iron reeds hang in synthesis over the two-sided bar. Adding to the look, created by SCHOOS Incorporated (a design firm that also owns the restaurant), is a glassed-in meditation garden. Located in the center of activity in WeHo, the restaurant attracts a large gay crowd, but thanks to amiable and above-average-looking waiters and waitresses, everybody feels at home here. The food is innovative and good if you stick to less complicated offerings. Signature dishes include lobster macaroni and cheese, pot roast, short ribs, and butternut squash ravioli. Desserts here are sinfully rich, especially the best banana split you'll ever eat, made with tons of chocolate, ice cream, cookies, and plenty of calories. ♦ Asian Fusion/California ♦ Daily, dinner. Reservations suggested. 8279 Santa Monica Blvd (at N Sweetzer Ave). 323/822.3300. www.obarrestaurant.com

76 THE PLEASURE CHEST

The catalog of naughtiness here is as prosaically displayed as produce in a supermarket. ♦ Daily, until 1AM. 7733 Santa Monica Blvd (at N Genesee Ave), West Hollywood. 323/650.1022

77 VODA SPA

Not your typical day spa—which is why we've included it—this place esthetically engulfs you the minute you walk through the designer door. In LA speak, it's just too fab for words. The name, *voda*, which means

Restaurants/Clubs: Red | Hotels: Purple | Shops: Orange | Outdoors/Parks: Green | Sights/Culture: Blue

water in Russian, personifies this eccentric sanctuary where amazing European, Asian, and Russian-style therapies are proffered in a stylish setting that includes traditional Russian *banyas* (saunas), a large indoor pool, cold plunge, Jacuzzi, and water everywhere. You can eat breakfast, lunch, or dinner at the voda café (featuring light gourmet fare) or relax in the soothing v room bar and lounge. The two-story, 14,000-square-foot facility is a designer's dream with 10 gorgeous pampering rooms, walls of Venetian plaster, black granite, special imported glass-covered lockers, an outdoor terrace where smokers can light up, and lots of ambience. You can spend an entire day here hopping from one therapy to the next, eating, drinking, or just blissing out. If you're game, you can try a *platza*—a rigorous rub done with a bundle of oak or birch branches called a *venik*. Hmmm, maybe just a rub, Siberian wildberry scrub, or a caviar body wrap. Tempted? ◆ Treatments are offered 10AM to 10PM daily, but the place is open M-F, 9AM-midnight; Sa, Su, 10AM-10PM. 7700 Santa Monica Blvd (between N Curson and N Genesee Aves), West Hollywood. 323/654.4411. www.vodaspa.com

78 PLUMMER PARK

Part of a ranch that operated as a farm and dairy from 1877 to 1943, this three-acre park now contains recreational facilities and the original **Plummer home** (323/848.6530). A **farmers' market** is held here every Monday from 10AM to 2PM. ◆ 7377 Santa Monica Blvd (between N Fuller Ave and N Vista St), West Hollywood

79 JONES HOLLYWOOD CAFE

★★★$$ This hip, clublike restaurant attracts young trendies in designer jeans who go for the good food and fun ambience. The menu offers a blend of California and continental fare, including calamari, grilled ahi tuna, grilled Portobello mushrooms with polenta, and a large selection of salads. The setting is casual, with tables draped in red-and-white checkered oilcloths, a large banquette adorned with a bandana-like print, and Jack Daniel's bottles standing behind chicken wire on a shelf. An eclectic mix of recorded music plays in the background. ◆ California/Continental ◆ M-F, lunch and dinner; Sa, Su, dinner. Reservations required for dinner. 7205 Santa Monica Blvd (at N Formosa Ave), West Hollywood. 323/850.1726

80 WEST HOLLYWOOD GATEWAY

Locals rejoiced when this urban commercial center opened in 2004 because they no longer needed to drive long distances to get their shopping fix at **Target,** one of the most popular department stores in the Southland

and the cornerstone of this 252,000-square-foot indoor shopping complex. An attractive addition to WeHo, the building also houses electronics outlet **Best Buy,** a gigantic liquor store called **Beverages & More,** a **Starbucks,** and assorted eateries (including **Baja Fresh**) sprinkled here and there—all under one roof. Be sure to check out **ULTA,** a cosmetics emporium stocked with every imaginable brand of beauty product. Specialists are on hand to help you select the right preparations for your skin. While you're there, why not have your eyebrows shaped, makeup done, or hair colored and/or cut at the affordable Style Bar? Hey, it's also a great place for celebrity spotting. Rachel Bilson, Adam Brody, Tori Amos, Paula Abdul, Kelly Osbourne, and Jason Lee are customers. There's one-hour free underground parking. ◆ Corner of Santa Monica Blvd and La Brea Ave

81 MAROUCH

★★★$ This little sleeper gained recognition in Zagat as one of the best of its kind in the city. It's plain and simple, with a storefront façade, but the food's delicious. Middle Eastern appetizers such as tabouleh, falafel, and dishes like *kibbeh* (veal mixed with crushed wheat stuffed with ground beef and pine nuts), *shawarma* (beef topped with sesame sauce), *shawarma* chicken, *lekkos ramly* (fresh sea bass), and assorted baklavas for dessert make for a perfect meal. There's a tiny patio for smokers who can't resist, and a belly dancer who entertains on weekends. What more can you ask for? ◆ Lebanese ◆ Tu-Su lunch and dinner. Reservations recommended for four or more. 4905 Santa Monica Blvd (at N Edgemont St). 323/662.9325

82 858 NORTH DOHENY DRIVE

Frank Lloyd Wright designed this concrete-block house with a dramatic two-story living room in 1928. A private residence, it's located on a tiny corner lot. ◆ At Vista Grande St, West Hollywood

83 LE MONTROSE

$$$ Located one block from Beverly Hills and just south of the Sunset Strip in a quiet residential area, this little charmer boasts a lobby with Art Nouveau furniture and 133 tastefully decorated suites (including 45 executive suites). Many feature kitchenettes, sunken living rooms, balconies, and VCRs, and such luxuries as fax machines, fireplaces, irons and ironing boards, and terry-cloth robes. A fruit basket and mineral water are in each executive suite upon guests' arrival, and homemade cookies and milk are served upon their departure. There's a fitness center with a sauna, a

rooftop heated pool with private cabanas, a Jacuzzi, and a lighted tennis court. The **Library** restaurant is open to hotel guests and their friends only. Visiting rock bands and performers make this their Los Angeles home. ♦ 900 Hammond St (at Cynthia St), West Hollywood. 310/855.1115, 800/776.0666; fax 310/657.9192. www.lemontrose.com &

84 ELEVEN

★★★★$$$$ Wow, what a spot for dining, drinking, and eyeing the beautiful people who do just that at this super-sexy nightclub/restaurant, which was carved out of a historic building constructed in 1922 as First National Bank of Sherman and later became a sound studio where artists such as Donna Summer, Prince, and Patti LaBelle recorded albums. Created by legendary Hollywood mogul Sid Krofft, the restaurant is divided into two areas: a bar for small bites and drinks downstairs and a sophisticated loft section up a flight defined by wood floors, exposed beam ceiling, and geometric sconces made of raw silk. The waitstaff is impossibly good-looking and the food sensational, especially the crispy duck salad, truffle risotto, sashimi, porcini salad, asparagus soup, crispy-skin black bass, pan-roasted prime rib eye, and macadamia nut-crusted maple-leaf duck breast. Outrageously delicious desserts include a chocolate crème brûlée, New York cheese-cake, or chocolate mousse tart with caramel pecans and vanilla whipped cream. FYI: Wines are very pricey. ♦ California Gourmet. ♦ Reservations a must. Tu-Su, dinner; Sa, Su, brunch; special events Monday nights. 8811 Santa Monica Blvd (at Larrabee St), West Hollywood. 310/855.0800. www.eleven.la.com

84 VALADON

$$ This intimate 80-room hotel features split-level suites, some with kitchenettes, and a rooftop heated pool, gym, and spa. Room service is available. ♦ 8822 Cynthia St (at Larrabee St), West Hollywood. 310/854.1114; fax 310/657.2623. www.valadonhotel.com

85 RAMADA PLAZA WEST HOLLYWOOD

$$ The Art Deco/Miami–South Beach façade, featuring bright pastels and colorful accents, seems a little out of place on this stretch of Santa Monica Boulevard, but you get used to it. The colorful metal flower sculptures by Peter Shire were left intact. Accommodations include 175 rooms, of which 20 are two-bedroom corporate apartments and eight are studio units. Panini Café serves breakfast, lunch, and dinner. There's a fully equipped fitness center and a branch of Wells Fargo Bank. Several sidewalk cafés (Starbucks, Jamba Juice) are just a stroll from the entrance along the boulevard. ♦ 8585 Santa Monica Blvd (between West Knoll and Westmount Drs), West Hollywood. 310/652.6400, 800/845.8585; fax 310/652.4207. www.ramada-wh.com

86 BENVENUTO

★★★$$ Oozing with ambience, this tiny trattoria dishes out great Italian food in an inviting café that once served as a recording studio for Jim Morrison and The Doors. It's now a popular late-night rendezvous for celebrities, who linger over espresso and cappuccino after meals of focaccia and olive oil, pizza, fresh fish, and divine desserts. ♦ Italian ♦ Tu-F, lunch and dinner; Sa, Su, dinner. 8512 Santa Monica Blvd (at N La Cienega Blvd), West Hollywood. 310/659.8635 &

87 MAC CENTER FOR ART AND ARCHITECTURE/ L.A. SCHINDLER HOUSE

LA's most innovative house has been lovingly restored. **Rudolph Schindler** came from Vienna to work with Frank Lloyd Wright, and built this studio/residence in 1921. He lived and worked here until his death in 1953. Inspired by a desert camp, the architect combined tilt-up concrete slab walls, canvas canopies, and open-air sleeping lofts—techniques and spatial treatments that were novel at the time. Richard Neutra lived here in the late 1920s, and the house was a meeting place for the avant-garde.

Restaurants/Clubs: Red | Hotels: Purple | Shops: Orange | Outdoors/Parks: Green | Sights/Culture: Blue

♦ Admission. Free on F, 4-6PM. W-Su, 11AM-6PM and by appointment. 835 N Kings Rd (between Waring and Willoughby Aves), West Hollywood. 323/651.1510. www.maccenter.com

88 LOLA'S

★★$$ Don't let the cottage fool you—this place rocks with the crowd of barflies who gather nightly. It can get loud and rowdy, but the food's worth it, and so are the martinis, of which there are over 50 listed, from the famous apple martini to cantaloupe, banana, and beyond. The vaulted ceiling shelters a décor of wrought-iron chairs upholstered in cheetah-patterned velveteen, a cozy alcove with leopard-skin sofas, and an antique billiards table. Some of the fish dishes are heavenly, and the garlic mashed potatoes, seared ahi, chicken satay, and meat loaf are real winners. And yes, there is a Lola Dunswsorth, owner and ubiquitous hostess. ♦ Eclectic ♦ Daily, dinner. Reservations recommended. Valet parking available. 945 N Fairfax Ave (between Willoughby Ave and Romaine St), West Hollywood. 213/736.5652 ♿

89 BURNETT MILLER

Minimalist and conceptual American and European artworks and installations by Charles Ray and Wolfgang Laib are featured. ♦ Tu-Sa. 964 N La Brea Ave (between Willoughby Ave and Romaine St). No phone

90 PROPAGANDA FILMS

Franklin Israel's brilliant 1988 adaptation of an old warehouse features sculptural enclosures in a cavernous space. ♦ 940 N Mansfield Ave (between Willoughby Ave and Romaine St)

91 HOLLYWOOD MEMORIAL CEMETERY

Ⓟ A galaxy of top stars found refuge from their fans in this 65-acre oasis. Douglas Fairbanks has the most elaborate memorial, and Valentino is in wall crypt No. 1205, though the lady in black who used to bring flowers on the anniversary of his death comes no more. Here, too, are Cecil B. DeMille, Tyrone Power, and Peter Lorre. Close by is the **Beth Olam Cemetery,** where rests mobster Bugsy Siegel. ♦ Daily. 6000 Santa Monica Blvd (between N Van Ness Ave and Gower St). 323/469.1181

92 MARGO LEAVIN GALLERY

Claes Oldenburg, John Baldessari, and Alexis Smith strike again, with a blade slicing through the stucco façade like a knife through pastry. It's just the thing to enliven a side street and win attention for serious contemporary art. ♦ Tu-Sa. 817

Hilldale Ave (between Santa Monica Blvd and Keith Ave), West Hollywood. 310/273.0603. Also at 812 N Robertson Blvd (between Santa Monica Blvd and Keith Ave), West Hollywood

92 BIN 8945 WINE BAR AND BISTRO

★★★$$ This wildly popular place pours great wines to accompany bistro offerings such as charcuterie plates, jerk chicken, steak frites, and Munster melts oozing with cheese from Alsace on thick *pain rustique* topped with sautéed wild mushrooms. An eclectic crowd of wine know-it-alls and want-to-learns squeeze into the tiny place, where the noise overpowers any conversation, but who's listening? ♦ Bistro/Wine Bar ♦ Tu-Su, dinner. Reservations necessary. 8945 Santa Monica Blvd (near N Robertson Blvd), West Hollywood. 310/550.8945. www.bin8945.com

93 THE ABBEY FOOD & BAR

★★★$$ A coffee shop, restaurant, and swinging late-night bar rolled into 16,000 square feet of stylized space, this Abbey ranks among WeHo's top places to be and be seen. The **Finlandia Ice Bar** is packed with gay and heterosexual couples sipping assorted varieties of the potent cocktail. The moody, upscale décor provides a perfect setting to trysting and drinking, with intimate outdoor cabanas and lots of private nooks and crannies. Don't underestimate the food—it's quite good, whether you go for breakfast, lunch, or dinner. ♦ M-Th, 7AM-2AM; F, 7AM-3AM; Sa, 8AM-3AM; Su, 8AM-2AM. 692 N Robertson Blvd (between Melrose Ave and Santa Monica Blvd), West Hollywood. 310/289.8410. www.abbeyfoodandbar.com

94 PALM RESTAURANT

★★★$$$ Big juicy steaks and large lobsters are the big sellers here along with super side orders of onion rings, mashed potatoes, creamed spinach, and fries. Portions are big, but if you have room left, go for the New York cheesecake or crème brûlée. The dining room is always jammed, but the waiters are speedy. ♦ American ♦ M-F, lunch and dinner; Sa, Su, dinner. Reservations recommended. 9001 Santa Monica Blvd (between N Robertson Blvd and N Doheny Dr), West Hollywood. 310/550.8811. Also in downtown LA at 1100 S Flower St. 213/763.4600. www.thepalm.com ♿

95 DOUG WESTON'S TROUBADOR

This long-established rock 'n' roll shrine now specializes in heavy-metal bands. ♦ Cover. Call for schedule. 9081 Santa Monica Blvd (at N Doheny Dr), West Hollywood. 310/276.6168

95 LA MASIA

★★★$$ Celebrate a special occasion at this versatile restaurant, which has a tapas bar upstairs and Latin jazz and salsa music downstairs from 9PM. Paella and other standard Spanish fare is served. ◆ Spanish ◆ M-F, dinner; Sa, brunch and dinner. Reservations recommended. 9077 Santa Monica Blvd (between Nemo St and N Doheny Dr), West Hollywood. 310/273.7066

96 JAN TURNER GALLERY

Tony Delap, John Alexander, Guy Dill, and the late Carlos Almarez are among the artists shown here, where innovative landscapes are a specialty. The gallery shares its space with **Turner/Krull** (310/271.1536), which shows 19th- and 20th-century photography. ◆ M-Sa. 9006 Melrose Ave (at N Almont Dr), West Hollywood. 310/271.4453

96 MAXFIELD

Shop here for avant-garde couture at drop-dead prices in a spare concrete shell designed by Larry Totah. The window display is often worth a detour. ◆ M-Sa. 8825 Melrose Ave (between N Robertson Blvd and N La Peer Dr), West Hollywood. 310/274.8800

97 JAY WOLF

Designer Waldo Fernandez adds his signature decorative touches to this sophisticated imported menswear store. ◆ M-Sa. 517 N Robertson Blvd (between Rangely and Melrose Aves), West Hollywood. 310/273.9893

98 FAT FISH

★★$$ Locals love this little spot at night (probably because there is no valet parking at lunchtime and it's difficult finding a place to park your car). The dining area is roomy and minimally decorated. The service is sometimes slow. There's a pleasant patio for alfresco dining or drinks and a little bar hidden off in the back. The menu centers around fresh fish with an Asian twist, such as grilled salmon with long beans, and seared bass carefully marinated in sake and miso with candied ginger, baby choy sum, lemongrass, and basil mousse. There's also duck breast, sushi, and other choices. ◆ Asian Bistro ◆ M-F, lunch and dinner. Reservations suggested. 616 N Robertson Blvd (between Melrose Ave and Santa Monica Blvd), West Hollywood. 310/659.3882. www.fatfishla.com

98 HEDLEY'S

★★$ Forget fancy-schmansy spots; this simple little joint dishes out great food at low prices in a fun, family-style atmosphere. Go for lunch or dinner and enjoy home-style cooking such as pork loin with grilled yams, roasted turkey with stuffing, tofu steak seasoned with ginger, veggie burgers, or even a New York steak for half the price you'd pay anywhere else. The ambience combined with the price attracts a big crowd day and night that jams into the tiny dining room or outside patio. There's a small selection of wines and beers and luscious desserts such as peach and blueberry cobbler with oat strudel, Key lime pie, or warm chocolate bread pudding. There are napkins on the tables and smiles on the waitstaff's faces. ◆ American ◆ Tu-F, lunch and dinner; Sa, Su, brunch and dinner. Reservations required for large parties. 640 N Robertson Blvd (between Melrose Ave and Santa Monica Blvd). 310/659.2009

98 KINARA

This charming, transcendental day spa owned, operated, and conceived by Olga Lorencin and Christine Splichal, wife of LA super chef Joachim Splichal, is designed to calm and relax through exotic treatments created by Lorencin. You feel the bliss the minute you walk through its glassed front portals. The mood is friendly and honest, and the treatments are divine. Products are natural, herbal concoctions that are beneficial to your skin. A pleasant plus is a yummy restaurant where you can dine inside or out, all day until 7PM on a charming patio. The menu relies on organic, healthy fare created by Joachim Splichal. ◆ Tu-Su. 656 N Robertson Blvd (a block south of Santa Monica Blvd). 310/657.9188. www.kinaraspa.com

99 PACIFIC DESIGN CENTER (THE BLUE WHALE)

These mammoth, glass-clad geometric structures by **Cesar Pelli** and **Gruen Associates** house around 130 interior furnishings and accessories showrooms. The public may visit **Center Blue** or **Center Green;** most showrooms allow you to browse on your own, but purchasing requires the services of an interior-design professional. Visitors can learn more about the designers and their work by taking a free one-hour tour. On the plaza that separates the center from San Vicente Boulevard is the **MOCA Gallery,** which presents high-quality art and design exhibitions (213/626.6222). Throughout the

Restaurants/Clubs: **Red** | Hotels: **Purple** | Shops: **Orange** | Outdoors/Parks: **Green** | Sights/Culture: **Blue**

81

year, public exhibitions are held. ♦ M-F. Tours: M-F, 10AM. Reservations required for large groups. 8687 Melrose Ave (at N San Vicente Blvd), West Hollywood. 310/657.0800. www.pdclacworldnet.att.net

Within the Pacific Design Center:

CHRIS MICHAELS

★★$$ A pleasant place to get a quick bite while browsing around the Center, offering morning coffee and pastries and lunchtime salads, sandwiches, soup, and turkey chili. ♦ American ♦ M-F, breakfast and lunch. Reservations not required. 310/289.8877

DESIGN CAFÉ

$ Housed in steel, this very simple eatery offers alfresco dining on a charming patio facing Melrose Avenue. ♦ M-F, breakfast and lunch. 310/657 0800

RED SEVEN BY WOLFGANG PUCK

★★$$ Named in celebration of the celebrity chef's seventh restaurant, this striking crimson gem is highlighted by vivid red glass and Puck's inspirational cuisine. This is also "Wolfie's" second Design Center location. ♦ Asian Fusion ♦ Daily, lunch and dinner. 310/360.6409. www.wolfgangpuck.com

WP/WOLFGANG PUCK

★★$$ The menu's nearly identical to his Red Seven, but this spot, located on the third floor, is also available for catered events. ♦ M-F, lunch. 310/652.3933. www.wolfgangpuck.com

100 ROBERT KUO LTD & KUO DESIGN

Right across from the **Pacific Design Center** (see page 81), this marvelous shop offers very impressive limited-edition and one-of-a-kind repoussé and cloisonné pieces created by Chinese artist Robert Kuo. You'll also find the most unusual pieces of jewelry created by Alice Kuo, Robert's wife. ♦ M-F; Sa, noon-4PM. 8686 Melrose Ave (at N San Vicente Blvd), West Hollywood. 310/855.1555

100 NISHIMURA

★★★$$$ Keep your eyes open, as it's easy to miss the tiny building that houses this upscale sushi joint. The gracious entrance sits off to the side next to a pretty garden. An inviting portal, adorned with a bright blue basin filled with water and a bamboo ladle, opens to a modern, white-walled, high-ceilinged room decorated with brilliant ceramic pieces by Mineo Mizuno. Once inside, you'll find some of the best sushi this side of the Orient presented on hand-painted ceramic plates. Owned and operated by master sushi chef Hiro Nishimura, who made his mark at Katsu in Los Feliz, the place is perfect for digging into Nishimura's tantalizing concoctions. The lightly grilled *unagi* (eel) threaded on a bamboo skewer, dabbed with miso and green peppers, is fantastic. So are the steamed razor clams, oysters, or scallops and octopus sushi and sashimi. For tipplers, there's a large selection of Japanese beers and sakes. ♦ Sushi Bar ♦ M-F, lunch; M-Sa, dinner. Reservations advised. 8684 Melrose Ave (across the street from the Pacific Design Center). 310/659.4770

101 BODHI TREE

Books on philosophy, health, women's issues, astrology, and religion stock the shelves, along with herbs, soaps, and tarot cards. ♦ Daily, until 11PM. 8585 Melrose Ave (between Westmount and Westbourne Drs), West Hollywood. 310/659.1733. www.bodhitree.com

101 LE PAIN QUOTIDIEN

★★$$ This charming white-shingled café would deserve three stars if only they used cloth napkins; paper doesn't hack it for us. Still, the food and service are great and the prices are affordable. There's outdoor seating on a long, inviting porch, where most folks sit. Belgian-born chef/owner Alain Coumont's cuisine is a healthy mix of organic and fresh produce, simply prepared but quite tasty. We loved the Portobello mushrooms stuffed with curried chicken and the braised boneless short ribs. A great choice for vegetarians is the lasagna stuffed with tofu and cheese. There are also gourmet sandwiches like brie with pecans and seafood choices. *Le pain quotidien* means "daily bread," which is the LPQ's specialty and truly about as good as it gets (loaves are available for purchase at the little retail outlet by the entrance). You'll want to take a few loaves home and while you're at it, a muffin or dessert or two. Speaking of sweets, desserts are luscious, especially the fruit tarts. ♦ California with some French twists ♦ Daily, 7AM-10:30PM. Reservations suggested for dinner. 8607 Melrose Ave (corner of Westbourne, 2 blocks west of La Cienega Blvd). 310/854.3700. Also at 9730 Little Santa Monica Blvd (between Bedford and Camden). 310/859.1100; and 11702 Barrington Ct (corner of Barrington and Sunset Blvd). 310/476.0969. Both open 7AM-7:30PM. www.painquotidien.com

102 LE PARC

$$$ This 150-room all-suite hotel has an inviting marble lobby and pretty accommoda-

tions stocked with CD players and terry robes. There are also tennis courts, a rooftop swimming pool, a fitness facility, and a garden. ♦ 733 West Knoll Dr (between Melrose Ave and Sherwood Dr), West Hollywood. 310/855.8888, 800/578.4837; fax 310/659.7812. www.leparcsuites.com

Within Le Parc:

KNOLL AT LE PARC

$$$ This intimate café secreted on the third floor of the hotel has had its share of chefs, so we decided not to rate the food. However, the room itself deserves three stars. When we sampled the menu during the reign of our favorite chef, David Slay, who opened the restaurant, it was remarkable, especially the crispy fried spinach with Parmesan cheese, gourmet pastas, and flatiron steak—which is still on the menu along with grilled lamb chops, New York steak, and assorted poultry. If you're not too hungry, you can grab a sandwich or salad. The intimate room provides a romantic setting with its hardwood floor, gracious bar with high-back chairs, fireplace, attractive artwork, and fresh floral arrangements. The waitstaff is efficient and cordial. ♦ Mediterranean ♦ Daily, breakfast, lunch, and dinner. Reservations required for dinner. 310/855.8888, ext. 4421

103 KOI

★★★$$$ This stylish, feng shui–correct, impossibly delicious Japanese restaurant is such a magnet for celebrities that the management has had to call in the Los Angeles Police Department to call off the tenacious paparazzi hounding their guests. Geez, can't Lindsay Lohan, Paris Hilton, Madonna, Bruce Willis, and Venus Williams eat in peace? Of course, calling the cops gets you in the newspapers, but you wouldn't think that Koi needed any more publicity. The place is packed nightly, and not just because of the eye-candy celebs— the food is outstanding. If you have a yen for creative Japanese and don't mind the flashbulbs popping off around you, this is the place to go. Anyway, the paparazzi have been ordered to step away from the entrance and keep to restricted areas. The indoor and outdoor dining areas are equally inviting with Buddhas and bamboo, ornately carved wooden doors, and a popular bar and lounge. Koi's Zen-like interior actually sparkles, and so does the food. The crispy salmon skin salad, with just the right amount of zest, and tangy tuna tartare with avocado in a crisp wonton are superb; the spicy seared albacore with crispy onion is another winner, as is the

Kobe–style filet mignon Toban-Yaki, black cod bronzed with miso, and any tempura on the menu. The bar bustles with the young and hip, who sip drinks before and after dinner. It's a scene, and worth showing up for. ♦ Japanese-inspired with California accents ♦ M-F, lunch and dinner; daily, dinner. Reservations recommended, especially for dinner. Valet parking available. 730 N La Cienega Blvd (near Melrose Pl). 310/659.9449

104 LUCQUES

★★★$$$ French for "olive," Lucques (pronounced Luke, no "s") is a foodie's paradise where the in crowd goes to savor chef Suzanne Goin's fabulous French fare. Dress casual chic, preferably in something black. Sip some wine, then feast on some jumbo asparagus, Tuscan bean soup, saddle of rabbit, grilled club steak for two, or the fish du jour. Finish with vanilla pot de crème or some other delightful dessert. ♦ French ♦ Tu-Sa, lunch; daily, dinner. Reservations a must (request a table in the garden, among the cool crowd). 8474 Melrose Ave (one-half block east of N La Cienega Blvd), West Hollywood. 323/655.6277. www.lucques.com &

104 TASTE

★★★$ So chic yet relatively cheap, this stylish, hip, and juicy gem is one of the hottest spots around. An eclectic crowd, some dressed in jeans, others in suit and tie and dressier togs, pack the place nightly. The patio is outrageously popular, especially during warm nights—heat lamps go on when the temperature drops. The handsome interior features dark wood floors and buttercup-yellow and chocolate-brown walls adorned with big round mirrors. Unusual lanternlike chandeliers hang from the ceiling. A miniature Japanese-style garden behind a glass wall adds to the ambience. The best inside table is perched by open floor-to-ceiling windows overlooking the patio. The diverse menu features lots of yummy appetizers, such as pizzetta drowned in roasted pears and caramelized onion and topped with Gorgonzola and walnuts, ahi tuna tartare, sweet corn chowder, and wild salmon (in season), which is absolutely superb. Blackened salmon salad, orange ginger shrimp, and the grilled New York steak are also winners, and the berry cobbler hit the spot. Tipplers should note that only beer and wine are served. The waitstaff is exceptional—no attitude, friendly, and efficient. ♦ California ♦ Tu-Su, lunch; daily, dinner. Reservations advised. 8454 Melrose Ave (a few steps from Ago and east of La

Cienega Blvd), West Hollywood.
323/852.6888; fax 323/852.4888.
www.ilovetaste.com

104 AGO

★★★$$$ Named for noted chef Agostino
Sciandri, this uptown trattoria, with its wood-
burning pizza oven, tempts with such artfully
prepared dishes as *costata di manzo* (18-
ounce rib eye), *fritto misto di mare* (batter-
fried seafood), Tuscan-style chicken cooked
in wine and herbs, grilled polenta with salt
cod in a spicy tomato sauce, and Agostino's
signature steak Florentine. The charming
room, set under corrugated roofing and
halogen spotlights, is a throwback to the
Tuscan countryside, with a villa courtyard
shaded by six 30-foot-high Italian cypress
trees and four olive trees on a terra-cotta
floor. The waitstaff is delightful, and the crowd
comes in late. ♦ Italian ♦ M-F, lunch; daily,
dinner. Reservations recommended. 8478
Melrose Ave (at Clinton St), West Hollywood.
323/655.6333

105 GEMINI G.E.L.

Fine art prints by David Hockney, Jasper
Johns, Robert Rauschenberg, and Ellsworth
Kelly are spotlighted in this workshop/gallery
designed by **Frank Gehry.** ♦ M-F. 8365
Melrose Ave (between N Kings Rd and
N Orlando Ave). 323/651.0513

106 KIYO HIGASHI

The work of Larry Bell, Penelope Krebs, Guy
Williams, and Lies Kraal is shown in this
austerely handsome space. ♦ Tu-Sa. 8332
Melrose Ave (at N Flores St).
323/655.2482

107 DAILEY RARE BOOKS & FINE PRINTS

This shop carries art and illustrated books
and literary first editions. ♦ Tu-Sa. 8216
Melrose Ave (between N La Jolla and
N Harper Aves). 323/658.8515

107 DOLCE

★★★$$ Little Italy meets LA at this modish
hot spot filled with lovely, lean women baring
pierced bodies and taut bare bellies who
mostly hang at the bar and make lots of
noise. Designed by Douglas Dodd (who
created interiors for Falcon, Avenue, and
Katana), the clubby room is swathed in
black leather and so is much of the young
clientele. The food's good, from the
antipasto to the assorted pasta, meat, and
fish dishes (go for the halibut or sea bass).
The Caesar salad is one of the best in town.
The crepes stuffed with ricotta, the prime rib,
and the risottos are not to be missed.
♦ Italian ♦ Daily, dinner. Reservations

essential. 8284 Melrose Ave (at N Sweetzer
Ave). 323/852.7174

108 FRED SEGAL

It's *so* overpriced. But the "I want to be hip"
set that shops here doesn't care. Racks and
display tables are filled with everything
trendy, from T-shirts to shoes. Sales clerks
have attitude. The parking lot's filled with
Mercedes, Porsches, Z-3s, and other cool
wheels. And, for the less privileged style-
seekers, there is a sale every September
that's so popular, parking spots are filled for
six blocks around—which only goes to show
you there's no shame in bargain hunting.
♦ Daily. 8100 Melrose Ave (at N Crescent
Heights Blvd). 323/651.4129

108 FRED SEGAL MAURO CAFÉ

★★★$$ Adjacent to **Fred Segal,** this hip,
happening café is often filled with young
celebs (Naomi Watts, Nicole Ritchie, Patrick
Dempsey), writers, agents, and Hilton-like
celebutantes who go for their morning
caffeine fix, late lunches, and afternoon wine
or cocktails. The food's surprisingly
scrumptious, especially the spaghetti or
pasta dishes, panini, salads, yummy Italian
pastries, and rich chocolate goodies. There's
a tiny sidewalk dining section and a take-out
food deli at either end of the restaurant. FYI:
The coffee's kick-butt. ♦ Bistro/Café
♦ Reservations advised. Daily, 7AM-7PM.
8112 Melrose Ave (next door to Fred Segal).
323/653.2874

108 IMPROVISATION

The bar here is two or three deep on
weekends, but you can catch the best (and
worst) of stand-up comedy every night. Top
names sometimes stop in to watch a show or
try out new material. ♦ Cover. Daily; call for
performance times. 6182 Melrose Ave
(between N Kilkea Dr and N La Jolla Ave).
323/651.2583

109 AGENT PROVOCATEUR

This London-based lingerie boutique was
put together by Joseph Corre (son of the
fashion world's Vivienne Westwood and
former Sex Pistols manager Malcolm
McLaren) and his wife, Serina Reese. The
sensuous shop was a big hit with
Tinseltown's A-list crowd: Naomi Campbell,
Kate Moss, Madonna, Courtney Love, and
Oscar winners Gwyneth Paltrow and Julia
Roberts. If you're looking for a sexy gift, or
something naughty for yourself, you're
bound to find it among the fabulous
international collection of mink collars,
slave chains, bustiers, corsets, panties,
and nighties. There's a private little
dressing room for the timid. ♦ M-Sa,
11AM-7PM. 7961 Melrose Ave (between

N Fairfax Ave and N Edinburgh Ave).
323/653.0229

109 CARLITOS GARDEL

★★$$$ Terrific Argentinean food is served in
this contemporary, bustling restaurant. For a
real treat ask for the nightly special, which is
always amazing. The menu changes often,
but you'll usually find a 24-ounce bone-in rib
eye, rack of lamb, or a tasty paella, and
superb gnocchi (Argentina was heavily
settled by Italians). There's a good selection
of Argentinean wines, too. ♦ Argentinean ♦
M-F, lunch and dinner; Sa, Su, dinner.
Reservations recommended. 7963 Melrose
Ave (between N Hayworth and N Edinburgh
Aves). 323/655.0891

110 GENGHIS COHEN

★$$ Catering to a neighborhood crowd and
a smattering of show-biz types, this
upscale Szechuan restaurant serves black-
bean crab, crackerjack shrimp, and *kung
pau* chicken (in a sauce of red chilies,
peanuts, soy, and scallions). We love this
place but were a little disappointed with the
fare last visit, though not enough not to
return. The décor has a stylish New York
feel. ♦ Chinese ♦ Daily, lunch and dinner.
740 N Fairfax Ave (between Melrose and
Waring Aves). 323/653.0640 &

111 MATRIX THEATRE COMPANY

As good as any Off-Broadway theater, this
adventurous, Equity-waiver playhouse
received the LA Drama Critics' Circle Award
for its productions of *The Tavern* and *The
Seagull* in 1994. Other shows have included
Samuel Beckett's *Endgame,* Harold Pinter's
Betrayal and *The Homecoming,* Lyle Kessler's
Orphans, and Simon Gray's *The Common
Pursuit.* ♦ 7657 Melrose Ave (between N
Stanley and N Spaulding Aves).
323/852.1445. www.tix.com

111 TABLE 8

★★$$ Smack in the middle of quirky
Melrose and perched aptly enough under a
body-piercing salon, this replacement for
Bouchon fast became an in spot when it
opened in 2003. The restaurant features a
minimalist 1960s New York–style décor with
lots of banquettes and comfy chairs. Co-
owner chef Govind Armstrong offers an
inventive seasonal menu that plays on fresh
vegetables. The Kobe-style beef or Kurobuta
pork are worth ordering. Desserts are
spectacular here, especially the peach
crisp. There's a lounge menu for light fare
like grilled cheese sandwiches or asparagus

and morel omelettes and a jiggy bar.
♦ French Bistro ♦ Daily, dinner. Reserva-
tions suggested. 7661 Melrose Ave
(between N Stanley and N Spaulding Aves).
323/782.8558

112 LA EYEWORKS

Eyeglasses are treated as art in this shop,
which has a stark setting and inventive
displays to rival the best galleries. Both
classic and outrageous frames of high
quality are sold at high prices. ♦ Daily. 7407
Melrose Ave (between N Martel Ave and N
Vista St). 323/653.8255

the foundry
ON MELROSE

112 THE FOUNDRY ON MELROSE

★★★$$$ What a winner, with a casual
outdoor dining patio highlighted by a lovely
18-foot-tall olive tree, a fireplace, sofas
and booths, and an equally inviting indoor
area with a mahogany piano bar, fire-
orange walls covered with huge mirrors,
polished concrete floors, antique light
fixtures, and sconces made from vintage
heat registers. The inspiring cuisine,
created by Eric Greenspan, formerly
executive chef of **Patina,** skillfully befits the
setting. Greenspan alters the menu weekly,
or on a whim, doing creative takes on sea
bass (maybe in a curry sauce, or possibly
grilled or sautéed), tuna tartare (in a lovely
melon soup), Maui onion soup in poached
bone marrow, poached Jidori chicken, beef
short ribs, and his amazing caramel–tonka
bean crème brûlée with tonka bean ice
cream. There's a reasonably priced wine list
and a talented sommelier to help you with
selections. Request a table under the olive
tree. ♦ California ♦ Reservations a must.
Tu-Su, dinner. 7465 Melrose Ave (between
N Martel Ave and Gardner St), West
Hollywood. 323/651.0915.
www.thefoundryonmelrose.com

The first issue of the *Los Angeles Times,* published in
1881, was delivered by horse-drawn wagons and
carriages.

Restaurants/Clubs: **Red** | Hotels: **Purple** | Shops: **Orange** | Outdoors/Parks: **Green** | Sights/Culture: **Blue**

113 LONDON BOOTS

Shoes, boots, and accessories imported from Europe fill the shelves of this jolly good shop. The styles are quirky, funky, and SoHo-ish. ♦ Daily. 7400 Melrose Ave (at N Martel Ave). 323/866.1801

114 VIA BRAZIL

Or should we say viva Brazil? This boutique brings us cool bikinis, tees, tanks, skin-tight jeans, dresses, and accessories direct from the South American country. ♦ Daily. 7374 Melrose Ave (between N Fuller and N Martel Aves). 323/788.1703

115 PINK'S FAMOUS CHILI DOGS

★$ Serving what are arguably the city's best hot dogs, hamburgers, and tamales since 1939, this funky little place is an LA institution. The chili dogs are what make this place world famous. ♦ American/ Takeout ♦ M-Th, until midnight; F, Sa, until 3AM; Su, until 2AM. 709 N La Brea Ave (between Melrose and Waring Aves). 323/931.4223

115 M CAFÉ DE CHAYA

★★$ Macrobiotics rejoice: We found the perfect place to indulge your dietary discipline. Everything on the menu at this cute little joint, created by Shigefumi Tachibe (of Chaya Brasserie and Chaya Venice) and chef Lee Gross (who used to cook for Gwyneth Paltrow), is authentic. You can eat in or take out from this deli-like shop/restaurant, where you order at the counter and they bring your food to an indoor or patio table, if you're eating there. Selections include assorted bento boxes (we loved the tofu assortment) and various panini, which they call "paninos" (the "Tuscano," with white bean spread, spicy seitan faux salami, caramelized onions, and arugula on house-baked focaccia, was fabulous). There are even macrobiotic-friendly desserts, including a fantastic tofu cheesecake, chocolate tart, and Linzer tort. Other delicious creations include rice bowls, hearty soups (split pea and barley is a winner), sushi, and sandwiches that strictly adhere to macrobiotic principles. ♦ Macrobiotic ♦ Daily, 9AM-9PM. No reservations. 7119 Melrose Ave (just west of La Brea Ave). 323/525.0588; fax 323/525.0310. www.mcafechaya.com. Home delivery: 310/278.3955 or www.whycookla.com

116 DANZIGER STUDIO

It was this minimalist house/studio built for designer Lou Danziger in 1965 that launched **Frank Gehry**'s career. Three blank stucco boxes, adroitly positioned, transform LA's industrial vernacular into high art. It's a private residence. ♦ 7001 Melrose Ave (at N Sycamore Ave)

117 MELROSE AVENUE

Innovative restaurants, galleries, design stores, and shops selling radical, kitschy vintage, and used clothing line this funky street where sidewalks are always thronged and parking is difficult. Wear comfortable shoes for the three-mile stroll from Highland west to Doheny. For racy adult gifts and videos, browse around **Drake's** (No. 7566; 323/651.5600). Stop for a jolt of joe and dessert at **Caffe Luna** (No. 7463; 323/655.8647) or some of the best Mexican food north of the border at **Antonio's** (No. 7470; 323/655.0480), where mariachis serenade while you dine. Pick up some really outrageous vintage outfits at **Aardvark's** (No. 7579; 323/655.6769) or begin a great gallery hop at **Tasende** (No. 8808; 310/276.8686), then continue on to **Chac-Mool** (No. 8920; 310/550.6872) and **William A. Karges Fine Art** (No. 9001; 310/276.8551). If you're looking for unusual bling, stop by **B. Boheme** (9013½; 310/902.3334), where you'll find one-of-a-kind pieces. For your reading pleasure, **A Different Light** (No. 8853; 310/854.6601) provides a mix of lesbian and gay and conventional literature. The once less trodden stretch of Melrose west of Fairfax between Hayworth Avenue and Melrose Place now pulsates with fashionistas in search of designer duds, vintage togs, and footwear. The eclectic selection includes shops such as **Spirituali** (No. 7928, 323/653.3471), which specializes in Indian styles; **Miu Miu** (No. 8025; 323/651.0072), where you can find Prada for less; **Betsey Johnson** (No. 8050; 323/852.1534), for trendy labels; **Xin** (No. 8064; 323/653.2188), for custom-made Italian footwear; the old standby **Miss Sixty** (No. 8070; 323/655.1460); and **Non** (No. 8250; 323/653.8850), for mother-to-be clothes that last. There's also a cutting-edge branch of **Frederic Fekkai Salon**, with 1,400 square feet of ultrachic preening space for LA's elite tucked away on the second floor of a picturesque Spanish Mission–style building (8457 Melrose Pl at N Alfred; 310/655.7800), and a wild coffeehouse called **Kaffee Wien** (8629½; 310/855.1136), complete with silver tray service, authentic Viennese pastries, and even free Wi-Fi, not to mention about a

During a trip to Los Angeles, Noël Coward once observed, "There is something so delightfully real about what is phony about what is real here."

dozen or so more opportunities to max out that credit card.

118 PIZZERIA MOZZO

★★★$$$ If you can get into this hot spot, you're in for a real treat. It's the toughest ticket in town and has been since super LA chef Nancy Silverton and New York culinary impresario Mario Batali opened the designer pizza palace in 2007. Silverton's painstakingly prepared wood-oven-baked pizzas (fennel sausage, egg, and *guanciale* pie, or the Margherita) are amazing, but so are the antipastos, salads, and desserts (the Meyer lemon gelato pie will make your taste buds explode). The place is packed from opening to closing. There is some-times room at the pizza bar or wine bar if a table isn't important to you. ♦ Pizzeria ♦ Daily, noon to midnight. Reservations should be made weeks in advance and with good luck. 641 N Highland (between Clinton St and Melrose Ave). 323/297.0101. www.mozza-la.com

119 PROVIDENCE

★★★★$$$$ Seafood captures top billing on the menu at this fashionable restaurant, and it's truly superb. Chef/co-owner Michael Cimarusti displays his skills in a handsome, candlelit room with brown fabric walls surrounding a minimalist interior. Best bets range from Copper River salmon (in season) to lobster and striped bass. Other palate pleasers include a Kobe-style beef rib eye and a Muscovy duck breast, and of course delectable desserts. The two-page menu includes a prix-fixe option as well as à la carte choices; either side is astronomical and the wine prices are shocking, so plan this for a big splurge. ♦ California/Continental ♦ Reservations a must. W-F, lunch; M-Sa, dinner. 5955 Melrose Ave (between Cole and Wilcox Aves). 323/460.4170. www.providenceLA.com

120 PARAMOUNT STUDIOS

The last of the major studios in Hollywood. The original entrance gate, through which Gloria Swanson was driven by Erich von Stroheim in *Sunset Boulevard*, is tucked away at the end of Bronson Avenue, its purpose supplanted by a new double gate on Melrose. The stages along Gower Street were formerly part of **RKO Studios,** and the trademark globe can be seen at the corner. The studio is closed to the public, but the site is full of atmosphere. ♦ 5555 Melrose Ave (between Bronson Ave and Gower St)

121 CHA CHA CHA

★★$ The crowds just keep on coming to this little out-of-the-way hot spot, which has an infectiously friendly spirit, spicy food, and wonderful daily specials. The corn tamale with golden caviar, the corn chowder, the giant shrimp in black pepper sauce, and the chicken *poblano* (in a sauce with chocolate and almonds) are real winners. ♦ Latin/Caribbean ♦ Daily, lunch and dinner; Sunday brunch is not to be missed. Reservations recommended. 656 N Virgil Ave (at Melrose Ave). 323/664.7723. & Also at 762 Pacific Ave (at W Eighth St), Long Beach. 310/436.3900

122 IL PICCOLINO

★★★$$$ Silvio de Mori, the charming, debonair host with the most, and partner Eddie Kerkhofs take turns running this popular neighborhood eatery. The inviting room is actually an enclosed patio with retractable sides that has been spruced up with tropical foliage, candles, ceiling fans, interesting artwork on the walls, nicely set tables, and an outdoor dining area separated by an etched glass wall. There's a serving room highlighted by a floor-to-ceiling wine rack. The crowd is a mix of old Hollywood/Friars Club types and neighbor-hood walk-ins, the food exceptional. We savored the tuna carpaccio sprinkled with truffle oil and capers on a bed of arugula, the Burrata cheese with heirloom tomatoes,

---

Some of Southern California's shakiest quakes:

17 January 1994 in Northridge: 6.6 magnitude, 55 deaths, 1,000 injuries, $30 billion in damages

28 June 1992 in Landers and Big Bear Lake: 7.4 and 6.5 magnitude (respectively), one death, 350 injuries, $92 million in damages

28 February 1990 in Upland: 5.5 magnitude, no deaths, 38 injuries, $10.4 million in damages

1 October 1987 in Whittier Narrows: 5.9 magnitude, eight deaths, more than 200 injuries, $358 million in damages

8 July 1986 in North Palm Springs: 5.9 magnitude, no deaths or injuries, $5.3 million in damages

9 February 1971 in Sylmar/San Fernando Valley: 6.4 magnitude, 58 deaths, 2,000 injuries, $511 million in damages

21 July 1952 in Tehachapi: 7.7 magnitude, 12 deaths, 18 injuries, $50 million in damages

---

Restaurants/Clubs: Red | Hotels: Purple | Shops: Orange | Outdoors/Parks: Green | Sights/Culture: Blue

THE BEST

Diana Rosen

Writer/author of books on tea and coffee, and 30-year resident of LA

Great Stuff About LA:

Anything and everything you can imagine is available in Los Angeles. It's hip, it's hep, it's what's happening. And, yes, it's cooler than New Yawk City! More theater and art galleries than in NYC, too!

The Netsuke Room at the Japanese Pavilion in the **Los Angeles County Museum of Art (LACMA)** is a treasure of hundreds of intricately carved sculptures that tell reams of stories despite its small size. Exquisite! Also at LACMA, the Betty Asher Collection of whimsical teacups from the best contemporary artists in America.

The sunny California look and feel of the main lobby of the **Peninsula Beverly Hills,** and its perfect afternoon tea.

Before or after any venture downtown, I stop at the **Brooklyn Bagel Bakery** on Beverly; it's not the same since they put up barriers so you can't peer into the vats of boiling water, but they still make the best poppy-seed bagels anywhere, and the price is right!

Driving along **Sunset Boulevard,** beginning at the Beverly Hills Hotel and going west, and fantasizing about which home I'll buy when I win the lottery.

The pure Americana of **Dodger Stadium,** with instant replay on giant screens, always off-key organ for the music, and a pig-out on hot dogs, popcorn, drippy nachos, and watery Coke (forget the yuppie stuff like sushi). Oh, do you go to see the game?

Walking the many enclaves throughout the city practicing "Safe Shopping"—a.k.a. looky-looing. I don't drive (believe it or not), so I walk, bus, or cab it. Best deal in town: the 25-cent **DASH** with various routes to Beachwood Canyon, Korea Town, Hollywood, Van Nuys/Studio City, and throughout Downtown LA. Short trips in air-conditioned comfort . . . for a quarter!

The strolling shopping choices are legion, but **Silverlake** is a flashback to the '60s with a yuppie edge; **Melrose** is a trend-lover's passion; the theater districts of **NoHo** and **Santa Monica Boulevard** between El Centro and west of Fairfax offer exciting entertainment; **Chado Tea Rooms** in LA and Pasadena and **Le Palais des The** in Beverly Hills are gourmet tea lovers' passions; and in between shopping splurges, the $3 **Regency** and $4.50 **Los Feliz** theaters satisfy the yen for company while watching all the movies you want to without breaking the bank or waiting for the DVD.

fresh tortellini stuffed with asparagus, cheese fondue and hazelnuts, and the Italian sea bass, which was prepared to perfection. The building is somewhat hidden from the street and easy to miss, so keep your eyes wide open. The charming patio is ideal for a meal or before-and-after drinks. ♦ Mediterranean ♦ M-Sa, lunch and dinner. Reservations suggested. 350 N Robertson Blvd (at Beverly Blvd). 310/659.2220

123 MADEO

★★$$$ The chic dining experience here is worth the price. Superb veal chops, sea bass, extraordinary risotto, and delicious desserts are just some of the specialties. It helps if you know Italian, as the staff doesn't speak much English. ♦ Italian ♦ M-F, lunch; daily, dinner. Reservations recommended. 8897 Beverly Blvd (between N Robertson Blvd and N Almont Dr), West Hollywood. 310/859.0242 &

124 DOMINICK'S

★★★$$ "New York, New York" . . . Frank Sinatra and his Rat Pack, Marilyn Monroe, and Billy Wilder were among the select friends allowed to sip martinis and eat pasta in swanky booths at this exclusive Hollywood hideout back in its heyday of the late 1940s. The current owners, Warner Ebbink and Brandon Boudet, practice a more liberal policy at their New York–style Italian eatery. You almost expect to see Old Blue Eyes at the marble bar. The retro décor sports a Manhattan rooftop feel with a family-style table and brick fireplace on the patio, and dark woods and red booths inside. Incurable romantics or couples looking for a cool spot to tryst will appreciate the sexy, intimate atmosphere. Oh yeah, the food's good, too, especially the osso buco, veal Parmesan, whitefish piccata, and ricotta fritters with chocolate hazelnut sauce. ♦ Italian ♦ Daily, dinner. Reservations suggested. 8715 Beverly Blvd (between San Vicente and Robertson Blvds), West Hollywood. 310/652.2335

124 TAIL-O'-THE-PUP

$ This hot dog stand, built in 1946, is the most celebrated of LA's few remaining programmatic structures. Hot dogs are sold from a 17-foot-long wiener in a bun. Don't miss it. ♦ Daily. 329 N San Vicente Blvd (between Beverly Blvd and Ashcroft Ave), West Hollywood. 310/652.4517

125 SONA

★★★$$$ Hot, hot, hot, this throwback to fine dining is the brainchild of co-chef/owners David and Michelle Meyers, who have a self-professed passion for food, which is a good thing for chefs and diners alike. With the help of Parisian architect Anthony Eckelberry, they created a minimalist room done in white, gray, and black, highlighted by a wine-decanting table carved from a six-ton granite boulder by Japanese sculptor Yoshikawa. The cuisine is an outrageously creative combination of Asian, French, and California. Go for the tasting menu and enjoy small bites of foie gras with blood plum blaze, tuna tartare with pickled watermelon rind, red and yellow tomato soup with vodka crème fraiche, miso-marinated prime beef, and fried lotus chips. You can order off the menu or just take a seat and ask the chef to surprise you—which he will with multiple mouthwatering courses paired with appropriate wines and served on Izabel Lam china along with Reidel stemware. ◆ Modern French ◆ Tu-Sa, dinner. Reservations essential. 401 N La Cienega Blvd (between Beverly Blvd and Melrose Ave). 310/659.7708. www.sonarestaurant.com

126 JAR

★★★$$ Super chef/owner Suzanne Tracht showcases her culinary talents at this over-the-top hip WeHo eatery. Whimsically prepared fare (braised pork belly, pot roast, garlic French fries) mixes with steaks (prime porterhouse, 16-ounce New York, rib eye), pork chops, fish, and veggies, and desserts like heaping portions of chocolate pudding and banana cream pie. Tracht recently opened a signature restaurant at the Renaissance Long Beach Hotel serving pretty much the same menu—all good. ◆ American Chophouse ◆ Dinner nightly, and a boffo Sunday brunch 10AM-2PM. Reservations required. 8225 Beverly Blvd (between N La Jolla and N Sweetzer Aves). 323/655.6566. www.thejar.com

127 ORTOLAN

★★★$$$$ Chef Christophe Eme and his partner, actress Jeri Ryan (*Boston Public*), took over the former Linq in 2005 and transformed it into an extravagant French restaurant named after a peacock. No price was spared on the décor, which impresses with crystal chandeliers, long cream-colored winged leather banquettes, and stunning glasses. They even embossed the name of the restaurant on the bottom of the menu. It didn't take long for word of mouth to attract LA foodies and young entertainment-industry types who savor a glam atmosphere. The beautifully prepared dishes taste as good as they look. The bistro-like menu features Eme's signature langoustines served on chickpea purée, rabbit meatballs with rosemary gnocchi, lamb wrapped in filo, salmon with chorizo and Parmesan, and squab. The float-in-your-mouth pear clafoutis is a must-have. An attractive bar is so hidden in a back room you don't notice it until you go to the rest room. You'll fit in better with the décor if you dress up for the occasion. ◆ French ◆ M-F, dinner. Reservations required. 8338 W Third St (between N Sweetzer Ave and N Kings Rd). 323/653.3300. www.ortolanrestaurant.com

---

BEVERLY HILLS/ CENTURY CITY

Money, moguls, and movie stars, and mo' money . . .

Somehow you just find it difficult to differentiate fantasy from reality while strolling around the gilded sidewalks of this haughty hamlet. The home of rich, famous, and buff-bodied beauties, where plastic surgery and liposuction are household words and limousines, Mercedes, Rolls-Royces, and vintage wheels are the rides of choice. Beverly Hills is all about looks and appearances. Neat and clean, chockablock with expensive adult toy stores and lined with Old World buildings, this is a gilded paradise of tree-shaded streets, low crime, and narcissistic opulence. Multimillion-dollar homes, defined by backyard swimming pools, impeccably manicured lawns, and tennis courts, epitomize the residential areas north and south of **Sunset Boulevard**, but less extravagant residences and modest apartments can be found high up in the hills and south of **Wilshire Boulevard**. Hollywood moguls, mavens, and movie stars began moving to Beverly Hills in the 1920s, on the heels of one of its most famous couples, Mary Pickford and Douglas Fairbanks, who first set up house at what is now known as Pickfair. Beverly Hills flaunts its wealth in a manner that has gone out of style elsewhere, but hey, that's because it can.

Until the 1880s, what is now Beverly Hills was just a bunch of lima bean farms. According to local legend, founder **Burton Green** picked the original name, Beverly Farms, from a place in Massachusetts where President William Howard Taft vacationed. In 1907, Wilbur Cook designed the present city for the Rodeo Land and Water Company, laying out the triangular grid of business streets at a 45-degree angle to Wilshire and the

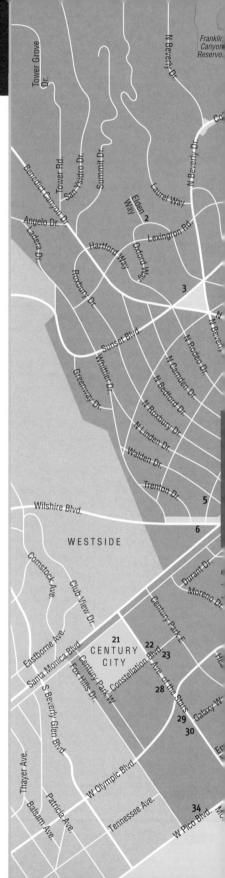

curving residential streets north to Sunset. The Olmsted brothers created the picturesque streets that wind through the hills above Sunset Boulevard as though in a landscaped park. One of the first buildings was the **Beverly Hills Hotel**, which was completed around 1912, but much of the surrounding area remained undeveloped until long after. As late as 1946, agent Leland Hayward was offered a snake-infested tract of hilly land in a prime location at a bargain price; that miserable property is today's affluent **Trousdale Estates**. The residential streets are lushly planted with stately and well-trimmed shrubbery and flowers. In spring, gorgeous jacarandas bloom along **Palm** and **Whittier Drives**. The houses, when not obscured by perfectly preened hedges or high walls, exhibit every known architectural style and many hybrids.

Tourists flock here to shop (unless you have a big budget, prepare for a major price shock), stargaze (especially along **Rodeo Drive**, where celebrity-toting limousines line up in front of the chic shops and boutiques), and generally to ogle the good life. The main retail area—bounded by **North Cañon Drive**, Wilshire Boulevard, and **Santa Monica Boulevard South**—is known as the **Golden Triangle**. Rodeo Drive, which slices north and south through this gilded gateway, is LA's answer to London's Bond Street, Rome's Via Condotti, and Paris's Rue du Faubourg-St-Honoré. From Armani to Versace, Cartier to Tiffany, Chanel to Hermès, every top fashion name is represented in this high-rent retail district and along the blocks of Wilshire Boulevard. The pedestrian-friendly area features wide sidewalks shaded by stately palms and flowering trees. **Century City** sits strategically between Beverly Hills and the booming Westside. Once Twentieth Century-Fox's backlot, it was sold in the late 1950s and developed by the Alcoa Corporation. Lacking the glitz of its neighbors, the sterile commercial center offers no street life and little redeeming architecture. It does, however, boast the deluxe **Hyatt Century Plaza Hotel**, the **Intercontinental Los Angeles Century City**, and **Westfield Century City**, a consumer haven of boutiques and outlets sprawled over 18 acres.

---

1 GREYSTONE PARK

Oil millionaire Edward L. Doheny built this 55-room English Tudor mansion for his son in 1928. Long abandoned, it was used as a set for The Loved One and later leased by the American Film Institute. City authorities seem unable to decide what to do with the house, which is closed to the public. But the 16-acre garden, with its balustraded terraces and grassy slopes, is one of LA's loveliest public parks. ♦ Daily. 905 Loma Vista Dr (at Doheny Rd). Concert and event information 310/550.4654

2 VIRGINIA ROBINSON GARDENS

Forget touring the homes of the stars; by calling a week in advance, you can enjoy the oldest residence in Beverly Hills, plus six acres of lush gardens, groves of palms, azaleas, and camellias in spring. It's a treasury of rarities and specimen trees,

including the largest monkey hand tree in California. ♦ Admission. Tu-F, 10-11:30AM, 1-2:30PM. 1008 Elden Way (just north of N Crescent Dr). 310/276.5367

3 BEVERLY HILLS HOTEL

$$$$ This doyenne of LA is nicknamed "the Pink Palace." A sprawling Mission Revival hotel that is seen as the unofficial symbol of the city and its hedonistic lifestyle, the graceful building was constructed in 1912, enhanced in the 1940s, and restored, remodeled, and renovated several times since. The 12 acres of lush tropical gardens are cleverly landscaped to prevent intrusion from traffic noise and prying eyes. The 194 rooms are large, modern, and lavishly decorated. A fitness center, two tennis courts, five meeting spaces, an inviting pool with cabanas, a LaPrairie full-service spa, and a glamorous swinging saloon called Bar Nineteen12 are added amenities. The

property also hosts the legendary **Polo Lounge** (see below) and the **Fountain Coffee Shop** (★★★$$), which also hosts the rich and famous, many who go regularly for awesome breakfasts at the counter. ◆ 9641 Sunset Blvd (between N Crescent Dr and Hartford Way). 310/276.2251, 800/283.8885; fax 310/887.2887. www.thebeverlyhillshotel.com

Within the Beverly Hills Hotel:

THE POLO LOUNGE

★★★★$$$$ Industry bigwigs congregate for lunch, drinks, and fashionably late dinners at this eternally chic celebrity-centric landmark. The scene starts at the brooding bar before and after lunch and well past dinner. The food's great whether you go for a salad or an extravagant entrée. ◆ California Cuisine ◆ Daily, lunch and dinner. Reservations required. 310/276.2251

4 IL CIELO

★★★$$ White tablecloths set with candles, flowers, and fine china, a good bottle of wine, and a stellar menu makes a perfect setting for *amore* at this oh-so-romantic Italian eatery. You can dine indoors in the white-walled room with its trompe l'oeil sky or alfresco in either of two charming courtyards. Wherever you choose to sit, you'll love everything on the menu, from assorted risotto to a whole *brazino* (striped bass). ◆ Northern Italian ◆ M-F, lunch and dinner; Sa, dinner. 9018 Burton Way (between N Almont and N Wetherly Drs). 310/276.9990 &

4 PRATESI

Hand-embroidered silk sheets, cashmere blankets, and huge fluffy towels for millionaires can be found here. ◆ M-Sa. 9024 Burton Way (between N Almont and N Wetherly Drs). 310/274.7661

5 SPADENA HOUSE

Hansel and Gretel would have lived here if they'd made it big with their screenplay. The thatch-roof house was designed by **Henry Oliver** in 1921 as a combined movie set and office. It's a private residence. ◆ Walden Dr and Carmelita Ave

6 BEVERLY HILTON HOTEL

$$$ *Oh what $80 million can do!* Well, for starters, reinvent a hotel that for the last half century served as a political and celebrity stomping ground that hosted dignitaries such as Presidents Clinton and Nixon, moguls like Steve Forbes and Bill Gates, and more than 175 red-carpet events annually. An original Conrad Hilton property circa 1955, it was owned by the late Merv Griffin from 1987 until 2003, when he sold it to businessman Beny Alagem, one of the founders of Packard Bell, and Oasis West Realty, who infused new life into the slumping facility with an ambitious face-lift. Executive architect Gensler, along with project manager Anthony Mason and a design team from HBA/Hirsch-Bedner Associates, orchestrated the facility's new look. We are truly impressed with the transformation of the guest rooms from drab to dynamic. Each of the 559 rooms sports youthful vibes, with floor-to-ceiling windows and obligatory upscale accessories such as custom pillowtop mattresses, silk blankets, 220-thread-count linens, spa-style bathrooms stocked with L'Occitane bath products, 42-inch HDTV plasma screens, and techno toys like wireless Internet and Bose Wave radios. You can escape to serenity in a cushy chaise by the Aqua Star Pool, which the company claims is the largest in Beverly Hills. Trader Vic's, an institution since the hotel's inception, is now a popular lounge relocated adjacent to the pool. Frou-frou umbrella drinks are still proffered (order a rum-laced Suffering Bastard if you're not driving), along with Asian appetizers, but in a more vibrant atmosphere. There's also the charming Aqua Star Spa, offering the whole nine yards of pamper options, and a pleasant salon (The Bellezza Salon), where celebs can often be spotted under hair dryers or in stylist chairs. ◆ 9876 Wilshire Blvd (just west of Santa Monica Blvd). 310/274.7777, 800/HILTONS; fax 310/285.1313. www.beverlyhilton.com &

Within the Beverly Hilton Hotel:

CIRCA 55

★★★$$$ Reflecting a retro-chic mid-'50s mood, this indoor/outdoor restaurant is the perfect place to dine when you don't feel like leaving the hotel. The service echoes the hotel's ambience: warm, friendly, and efficient. There's a good wine list, albeit pricey, but on Wednesday "Wine" nights they offer a selection of bottles at half price. Go for the 18-ounce prime bone-in rib eye with truffle butter, the steamed halibut, or butter-poached Maine lobster with wild mushrooms. Do dessert—the selection is yummy, especially the fruit tarts. ◆ Daily, breakfast, lunch, and dinner. 310/887.6055

7 KATE MANTILINI

★★$$ When owner Marilyn Lewis requested a roadside café, the architects at Morphosis gave her one of the most exciting interiors in LA, spread out in layered space, indirectly lit, with a jagged steel sundial extending from the floor through the ceiling. Enclosed

---

Restaurants/Clubs: Red | Hotels: Purple | Shops: Orange | Outdoors/Parks: Green | Sights/Culture: Blue

booths line the 100-foot-long outer wall. The restaurant is named for a boxing promoter of the 1940s, and the menu pays homage to Hollywood's famous Musso and Frank Grill, offering hearty meat loaf with crisp kale, roast chicken with mashed potatoes, and a delectable calf's brain omelette. ♦ American ♦ M-F, breakfast, lunch, and dinner; Sa, Su, brunch and dinner. 9101 Wilshire Blvd (at N Doheny Dr). 310/278.3699 ♿

8 ACADEMY OF MOTION PICTURE ARTS & SCIENCES

LA's finest thousand-seat theater houses Oscars and lobby exhibitions, plus occasional public screenings. ♦ 8949 Wilshire Blvd (between N La Peer and N Almont Drs). 310/247.3000

9 WILSHIRE-ROBERTSON PLAZA

Designed by the provocative firm **Arquitectonica** in 1990, this commercial block stands out from the tedious succession of savings and loan offices. ♦ 8750 Wilshire Blvd (at S Robertson Blvd)

10 SLS AT BEVERLY HILLS

$$$ At press time Le Meridien had been taken over by Starwood Hotels Luxury Collection and was closed for extensive renovations. When it reopens it will sport a chic, new look conceptualized by Philippe Starck, and be renamed SLS at Beverly Hills. Each of the 295 rooms will reflect Starck's signature style with clean lines and earth tones. All rooms will have sitting areas, work desks, robes, slippers, and the usual modern-day techno toys and flat-screen TVs. A health club and fitness center will be available free of charge. Additional planned amenities include the Humbel Abode Spa, an enhanced pool area, and a restaurant and lounge. ♦ 465 N La Cienega Blvd (at Clifton Way). 310/247.0400; fax 310/247.0315, 800/343.9236, 800/325.3538, or 800/323.3589. www.starwoodhotels.com ♿

11 FOGO DE CHÃO

★★$$$ It feels like a scene from the last days of Pompeii: You're seated under half-moon chandeliers in a noisy, cavernous room scented by *churrasco* roasting over an open wood-burning fire, awaiting an eating orgy served and prepared by costumed *churrasqueiros*, or gaucho chefs, who stop by your table with 15 different cuts of meat on individual skewers. Choices include *picanha* (part of the sirloin), filet mignon, *alcatra* (from top sirloin), *costela* (beef ribs), *fraldinha* (from the butt of the sirloin), chicken, and sausages. And it keeps on coming until you ask them to stop. Red and green chips, placed on the table, are used to beckon waiters to bring more food (green) or stop (red). The price-fixed repast also includes several side dishes, such as polenta, bananas, and garlic mashed potatoes, also replenished regularly. If that doesn't satisfy, there's a massive salad bar included in the tab (which you can order in lieu of the meat courses). Desserts cost extra and are probably pointless, but the caramelized cheesecake is a real winner just in case. ♦ Brazilian Steak House ♦ M-Th, lunch and dinner; F-Su, dinner. Reservations suggested for dinner. 133 N La Cienega Blvd (between Wilshire Blvd and Clifton Way). 310/289.7755. www.fogodechao.com

12 GONPACHI

★★$$$ Not your typical Japanese restaurant, this 11,000-square-foot eating emporium sports everything from an amazing Zen garden to entertainment offerings like Japanese drums, martial arts and ninja exhibitions, and of course your typical Japanese menu. You can watch the soba master work his noodle magic in a glassed-in room, then enjoy the freshly made buckwheat treats served chilled on bamboo mats with a daikon and wasabi sauce. Other good choices include Zaru tofu, tuna tartare, shrimp fritters, and sushi rolls. Desserts are so-so. The bodacious lower-level dining room provides a good view of the kitchen, while the mezzanine allows a sweeping sight of the lively action below. ♦ Japanese Fusion ♦ Reservations a must. Daily, dinner. 134 N La Cienega Blvd (between Wilshire Blvd and Clifton Way). 310/659.8887. www.globaldiningca.com

13 LAWRY'S PRIME RIB

★★$$ Prime rib is always the *plat du jour* at this carnivore's emporium set in retro 1940s décor. It seems silly to go here unless you're into beef, but for those who aren't, there are other choices on the menu. There's always a fairly long wait for a table. ♦ American ♦ Daily, dinner. 100 N La Cienega Blvd (between Wilshire Blvd and Clifton Way). 310/652.2827 ♿

14 THE STINKING ROSE

★★★$$ Garlic lovers rejoice, this eccentric eatery is for you. Everything about it reeks of the zesty clove from pictures on the walls to tangy menu choices such as garlic-roasted prime rib, Dungeness killer crab roasted in secret garlic sauce, and Yukon Gold garlic-mashed potatoes. There's even a 40-clove garlic chicken and an appetizer of garlic cloves roasted in olive oil, and a special dining area called "Garlywood" as an homage to Tinsel Town. It's all good. ♦ Garlic-infused American ♦ Daily, lunch and dinner. Reservations suggested. 55 N La Cienega Blvd (between Wilshire Blvd and Clifton Way). 310/652.7673. www.thestinkingrose.com

15 TANZORE

★★$$$ Once again the owners of the former Gaylord changed the name and altered the concept. It's still Indian, but metro-trendier. For starters, there's a cushy lounge with projection TVs displaying catwalking models and music videos. The décor is lavish, with high-back booths, banquettes, a pool that slices the dining area in half, and vibrant colors. The food's as good as ever, with familiar entrées such as tandoori lamb chops, lamb curry, chicken dishes, fried crab cakes, and killer prawns. ♦ Indian ♦ M-F, lunch; daily, dinner. Reservations suggested. 50 N La Cienega Blvd (between Wilshire Blvd and Clifton Way). 310/652.3894

16 THE LODGE

★★$$$ Just what this town needs is another steak house. But that hasn't stopped meat lovers from flocking to this rather eccentric establishment. We do mean eccentric, with double fieldstone fireplaces, tree-trunk pillars, floor-to-ceiling faux fur drapes, a twig chandelier, and other quirky touches. One of more than a dozen carnivore-centric restaurants to open in a year, this one is more décor than food. Still, you can get a decent New York steak or veal chop, really tasty onion rings, and a deliciously sweet vanilla-bean cheesecake or banana split. ♦ Steak House ♦ Reservations required. Daily, dinner. 14 N La Cienega Blvd (near Wilshire Blvd). 310/854.0024

17 WILSHIRE THEATRE

The stylish zigzag movie house, designed by **S. Charles Lee** for Fox in 1929, has been restored as a stage for musicals and dramas. ♦ 8440 Wilshire Blvd (near S La Cienega Blvd). 323/655.0111. www.wtbh.org

18 RUTH'S CHRIS STEAK HOUSE

★★$$$ Some say this acclaimed restaurant serves the best steaks in town. Order your favorite cut from their traditional menu. ♦ American ♦ Daily, dinner. 224 S Beverly Dr (between Gregory Way and Charleville Blvd). 310/859.8744. www.ruthschris.com

19 ROSEBUD CAKES

Head here for a selection of delicious cakes and other delectable confections. ♦ Tu-Sa; Su, 10AM-noon (pickups only). 311 S Robertson Blvd (between Olympic Blvd and Gregory Way). 310/657.6207. www.rosebudcakes.com

20 CENTER FOR MOTION PICTURE STUDY

Fran Offenhauser and Michael J. Mekeel did the imaginative conversion of this 1928 landmark building. The project represented a triumph for local preservationists, offsetting the loss of the zigzag Beverly Theater on North Beverly Drive. The **Margaret Herrick Library,** with one of the country's finest collections of film books, magazines, and archival treasures, is open without charge to serious students of cinema. ♦ Free. M-F. Tours on first day of the month at 10AM by reservation only. 333 S La Cienega Blvd (between W Olympic Blvd and Gregory Way). 310/247.3000

21 WESTFIELD CENTURY CITY

One of LA's earliest malls remains a mere shadow of its former self after a mega-makeover enhanced, enlarged, and transformed every square foot into a more contemporary complex of consumerism. The ongoing face-lift began with the expansion of **Gelson's Super Markets** (one of LA's finest food stores), followed by the addition of a two-level 15-screen, ultramodern AMC Theatre. Other additions include new dining venues and more upscale boutiques in which to max out that credit card. **Bloomingdale's** and **Macy's** are currently the stalwart anchors of more than 100 outlets proffering virtually anything you might want, from shaving essentials at the **Art of Shaving** to vitamins at **Great Earth.** Other retailers of note include **Café Coton** (a men's shirt shop), **United Colors of Benetton, Movado, Coach, Apple, Bose, Crabtree & Evelyn, Abercrombie and Fitch, Gap, Tiffany's, Crate & Barrel,** a branch of the New York **Metropolitan Museum of Art Gift Shop,** and many more. Of course, there are plenty of places to fuel so you won't drop after you shop, such as Coral Tree Café, Red Rock Chili, Hana Grill, Seik-Shi-Susi, French 75, and Ummba Grill. So you don't get exhausted and end your shopping spree, Westfield has created a **Shopping Concierge Center** (310/277.3898), whose staff can assist you with theater tickets, directions, and advice on where to find goods and services. ♦ Daily. Free parking with

---

Restaurants/Clubs: Red | Hotels: Purple | Shops: Orange | Outdoors/Parks: Green | Sights/Culture: Blue

validation. Complimentary valet parking when you spend $250 or more. 10250 Santa Monica Blvd S (between Avenue of the Stars and Century Park W). 310/277.3898. www.westfieldshoppingtowncenturycity.com Within Westfield Century City:

PINK TACO

★★$$ What a scene! This high-energy eatery from the famous Morton family of restaurateurs definitely pleases the senses with 10,000 square feet of kitschy cantina-like space adorned with low-rider bikes, rusted tin roofs, funky murals, and hot pink walls. Lest we forget bright orange umbrellas, floorboards made from recycled wood, and delicious south-of-the-border fare like nachos, tacos, enchiladas, *sabana de pollo*, *carne asada*, and the signature Mexico City hot dogs made with pork chorizo stuffed with cheese and jalapeños wrapped in crispy bacon. Wash it all down with refreshing mojitos, beer, or wine. ♦ Mexican Cantina ♦ Daily, lunch and dinner. Top level of the mall facing Santa Monica Blvd. 310/789.1000. www.pinktaco.com

22 CENTURY CLUB

★★$$$ This gargantuan space (25,000 square feet) is a combination café/nightclub, with three dance floors and patio and indoor dining areas. There is a mix of entertainment styles: For example, on Mondays they play the blues; on Fridays, the score heats up with Latin salsa; on Sundays, rap and hip-hop are highlighted. The "it" spot among LA scenesters, this place is ultrachic, over-the-top elegant, and always happening. There's a strictly enforced dress code: "upscale attire" and a real attitude. You'll love the food at **Wolcano** (★★★$$$)—a mix of Asian (including sushi) and California cuisines. ♦ M-F, lunch and dinner; Sa, Su, dinner. 10131 Constellation Blvd (at Avenue of the Stars). 310/553.6000. www.centuryclub.com ♿

23 CRAFT

★★★★$$$$ Imported from New York's Gramercy Park by star chef Tom Colicchio, this wildly popular place is as attractive as the clientele—mostly CAA and ICM agents and their clients who can afford the tab. From artfully crafted appetizers like Nova Scotia lobster with lemon comfit and big-eye tuna with horseradish, to wild mushrooms sides, Wagyu beef and sea bass wrapped in prosciutto, and an outrageous black mission

fig tart with vanilla crème fraiche, every meal is choreographed to perfection. We're not kidding about the four dollar signs, either; this place is beyond pricey. ♦ Seasonal California Cuisine ♦ W-F, lunch; M-Sa, dinner. Reservations a must. 10100 Constellation Blvd. 310/279.4180

24 WOSK APARTMENT

Frank Gehry and **Miriam Wosk**'s surreal 1983 penthouse—with its gold ziggurat, blue dome, black marble arch, and turquoise-tile walls clustered atop a pink apartment building—juices up an otherwise bland street. It's a private residence. ♦ 440 S Roxbury Dr (between S Bedford Dr and Olympic Blvd)

25 BEVERLY DRIVE

A less costly alternative to "rich man's" Rodeo Drive, the burgeoning 200 block of Beverly Drive south of Wilshire Blvd appeals to the budget-conscious crowd with less pricey salons, shops, and restaurants. Just head over at lunch time when hordes of local workers make a beeline for places like **California Pizza Kitchen** (207 S; 310/275.1101), **Chin Chin** (206 S; 310/248.5252), **Pinkberry** (240A), and **Burger 90210** (242 S), where gourmet patties are flipped into buns. The street also sports enterprising businesses such as **Lola et Moi** (238^1/2 S; 310/276.5652), a cute boutique with spirographic designs in hot pink, orange, lime green, and turquoise lining the walls and whimsical "couture" fashions for tiny tots and kids 6 months to 12 years old; **Close Shave** (230 S; 310/888.2898), where guys can get an old-fashioned barbershop-like shave, shoeshine, fingernail clipping, and even a drink; and **Girlfriends Beverly Hills** (202^1/2 S; 310/285.0741), specializing in original silk tops and dresses, shoes, and trendy accessories. There are many more places to shop and eat, so you just have to go there.

26 AVALON HOTEL

$$ This is one of LA's best-kept secrets, and the TV, film, recording, and other entertainment types who stay here like it that way. If you prefer small, out-of-the way hotels, this legendary triplex hideaway on the southern tip of Beverly Hills is for you. Carved from a 1950s relic that once hosted Marilyn Monroe and served as a location for the *I Love Lucy* show, the hotel's interior was reinvented by Kelly Wearstler of KWID

Designs, with a hip and cozy décor defined by sharp curves and clean lines. Each of the 88 recently renovated homey rooms features Charles Eames–inspired chairs, George Nelson bubble lamps, and Isamu Noguchi tables highlighted by bright colors and equipped with the usual TV, CD, iPods loaded with iTRAIN fitness programs, Internet access, fax, and room service (which is the dining option of choice for its Tinseltown clientele). In-room manicures, pedicures, facials, massages, and even acupuncture are available. There's also an outdoor pool. **Blue on Blue Restaurant** (★★$$) is a fun, cheery three-meals-a-day eatery with good food and signature drinks like "A Walk in Space," with Pearl vodka, watermelon liqueur, and Tang, or the "Librarian's Martini"—Southern Comfort, amaretto, and fresh limes and cranberries. ♦ California ♦ Daily from 7AM. ♦ 9400 W Olympic Blvd (corner of Beverly Dr). 310/277.5221, 800/535.4715. www.avalon-hotel.com

27 CHRISTOPHER HANSEN

In 1990, **Kirkpatrick Associates** designed this museum-like setting for custom audio installations and home-entertainment centers. ♦ M-Sa. 8822 Olympic Blvd (between S Robertson Blvd and S Clark Dr). 310/858.8112

28 HYATT REGENCY

$$$$ You don't have to be rich *and* famous to stay at this opulent landmark—just rich. The original hotel, an elliptical block designed by **Minoru Yamasaki,** opened in 1966. In October 2005, Sunstone Investors, Inc., a real estate investment trust based in San Clemente, purchased the former Century Plaza Hotel, embarked on a $22.5 million renovation, and turned it into Hyatt Regency. The hotel boasts a primo Regency Level Club floor, which provides privileges for a price such as continental breakfasts and evening snacks and cocktails served in a private lounge, a showcase lobby, and a world-class, 30,000-square-foot, Asian-themed day spa. There are 727 rooms (all with balconies) attractively designed with cherry wood paneling, unique glass vanities, porcelain flooring, polished chrome, and lavish bathrooms. In-room extras include Internet access, 27-inch televisions, robes, deluxe bath products, safes, three phones, and private bars. As always, the Plaza's focus is banquet and convention groups, and there's plenty of space dedicated to both. There's also a 10-acre garden with an oversized pool. ♦ Valet and self-parking. 2025 Avenue of the Stars (between W Olympic and Constellation Blvds). 310/277.2000; fax 310/551.3355. www.hyatt.com

29 FOX PLAZA

Johnson, Fain & Pereira Associates' 1987 design represents the most dramatic addition to Century City since the original twin towers. This handsome 34-story office tower is faceted like a crystal, banded in salmon granite and gray-tinted glass, and positioned to dominate the sweep of Olympic Boulevard and the Midtown skyline. ♦ 2121 Avenue of the Stars (between W Pico and W Olympic Blvds). 310/282.0047

30 INTERCONTINENTAL LOS ANGELES CENTURY CITY

$$$$ The Intercontinental Hotels personified luxury when they took over the former Park Hyatt in 2007 and converted nearly half of the hotel's 367 rooms into suites. The company also transformed the lobby into an inviting Japanese-style area with comfortable chairs and a lively bar/lounge. Definitely designed for business travelers, all rooms are fitted with essentials such as flat-screen TVs, iPods, balconies, fine toiletries, multiple phones, and more. The 181-suite property features an exterior peach pyramid design with a softly tinted interior décor. Guests are pampered with such special services as packing and unpacking of luggage on request, limousine service, and a 24-hour mending and pressing service. Each comfortable, recently refurbished room comes with a terry-cloth robe, fine toiletries, multiple phones, and a balcony. There is a restaurant, a serene spa with three Zen-inspired villas in which to succumb to salubrious treatments, a small but well-equipped fitness center, and a swimming pool and sundeck with an inviting Jacuzzi. The hotel also offers extensive business services along with family and corporate business specials. ♦ 2151 Avenue of the Stars (between W Pico and W Olympic Blvds). 310/284.6500; fax 310/284.6501, 800/633.8464. www.intercontinental.com/losangeles &

Within the Intercontinental Los Angeles Century City:

PARK GRILL RESTAURANT

★★★$$$ You're in for a surprising treat at this lobbyside restaurant, where chef Vincent Cachot pleases your palate with innovative dishes such as crab cake with smoked trout or pan-seared diver scallops with black truffle butter, seared black mission fig salad, organic salmon steak, single seared wild sea bass, and a Wagyu Kobe beef rib eye that melts in your mouth. Desserts are equally tasty, especially the plate of Chef Vincent's cookies or the duet of panna cotta (berries, fruit, toasted brioche, and almond cream). ◆ Daily, breakfast, lunch, and dinner. Reservations suggested for dinner. 310/284.6500

31 THE TOWER BEVERLY HILLS HOTEL

$$$ A hotel of many incarnations, the former Loews Beverly Hills was purchased by Cipriani USA in October 2007 and closed during a $50 million head-to-toe renovation and name change. At press time, the hotel was expected to reopen by fall of 2008. Situated on a quiet hillside a bit off the beaten track, just outside of Beverly Hills proper, the hotel was a perfect choice of the prestigious Italian hotel company that plans to replace all existing accommodations with 115 suites and to add a lavish spa, fitness center, and, direct from Italy, a Harry's Bar. ◆ 1224 S Beverwil Dr (at W Pico Blvd), Beverly Hills. 310/277.2800

32 SPARK WOODFIRE GRILL

★★$$ Housed in a picturesque three-story building with pumpkin-colored walls, this place provides a homey setting for its Cal-Mediterranean cuisine. There are dining areas on all three floors, with the lowest level catering to live music. The menu begins with pizza and continues to salads, freshly prepared pasta, and spit-roasted chicken. And there's comfort food like baby back ribs, so tender they fall off the bone, and meat loaf like Mama used to make. You can also order a Kansas City steak with blue cheese. ◆ California/Mediterranean ◆ M-F, lunch; daily, dinner. Reservations suggested for dinner. 9575 W Pico Blvd (between Smithwood and Edris Drs). 310/277.0133. www.sparkwoodfiregrill.com

33 MUSEUM OF TOLERANCE

This high-tech multimedia center was created to raise everyone's consciousness of bigotry and racism, with a focus on the Nazi Holocaust and prejudice in American history. The new **Point of View Diner** (which serves no food) encourages visitors, through video monitors, to consider the moral responsibility of such social issues as First Amendment rights and drunk driving. ◆ Admission. M-F, Su. 9786 W Pico Blvd (at S Roxbury Dr). 310/553.8403. www.weisenthal.com

34 TWENTIETH CENTURY-FOX FILM CORP

This film company has survived more predators than a maiden in a melodrama.

There are no tours offered here, but you can drive up to the gate and get a glimpse of the *Hello, Dolly!* street, a re-creation of turn-of-the-century New York. This was Hollywood's first studio planned for sound, created by pioneer William Fox, who then lost control of the company he had established. Darryl Zanuck ruled here over such eminent subjects as Shirley Temple, Carmen Miranda, and director John Ford. It was also home to Marilyn Monroe, *Cleopatra*, and *M.A.S.H.* ◆ 10201 W Pico Blvd (between Avenue of the Stars and Fox Hills Dr). 310/369.1000

35 BEVERLY HILLS CITY HALL

The unique scroll ornament and colorful aquatile dome of **William Gage**'s splendid 1932 Baroque pile were scrubbed clean in a recent restoration. ◆ 455 N Rexford Dr (at Santa Monica Blvd)

35 BEVERLY HILLS CIVIC CENTER

Architect **Charles Moore** won a competition with his romantic/historical design for a diagonal sequence of three landscaped courtyards that link the library, fire and police stations, offices, and parking to the remodeled City Hall. The grand vista toward the hills works well, but the buildings have the insubstantial quality of a movie set—you wonder if they will still be there next week. Repetitive rusticated arches and tile inserts along the courtyard compete with the frilly decoration of old City Hall. ◆ N Rexford Dr (between Santa Monica Blvd S and Santa Monica Blvd)

36 US POST OFFICE

Ralph Flewelling created this noble 1933 structure in the Italian Renaissance style, with terra-cotta, brick, and classically framed windows and doors. This may be the only post office in the country (or even the world) that offers valet parking. It could also end up being the only mail center with a museum-quality retail store, café, theater, and visitors information center, if the Beverly Hills Cultural Center Foundation raises enough funds for the project. ◆ 9300 Santa Monica Blvd S (at N Crescent Dr)

37 UNION 76 GAS STATION

The swooping cantilevered 1950s concrete canopy is extraordinarily daring for this area. ◆ N Rexford Dr and Santa Monica Blvd S

38 RAFFLES L'ERMITAGE HOTEL

$$$$ Hidden in a residential section on the fringes of Beverly Hills, this stylish hotel attracts a big record company/entertainment industry crowd who appreciate its off-the-beaten-track location and luxurious digs. The décor is minimalist/Asian modern accented by maple, marble, and interesting works of art. The 124 suites are spacious and

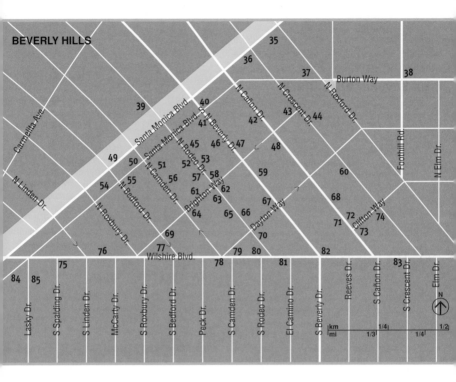

BEVERLY HILLS

sumptuous, with plush carpeting, silk-covered queen-sized beds, and English sycamore furnishings. Lovely latticework separates the bedroom from a well-stocked bar (with free soft drinks) and walk-in closet, and the lavish marble-and-tile bath offers an array of Aveda amenities. Other enticing touches include 40-inch televisions, CD/DVD players, free local calls, fax machines, and cell phones. There's a cozy library bar with a fireplace; the Writer's Bar, where scribes ponder over scripts on their laptops; the bustling Jaan Patio, famous for its Billionaire margarita made with 1942 Don Julio tequila; an attractive rooftop deck and pool populated by young celebs; a nicely equipped fitness center; and a spa, along with a very accommodating staff. While room service is the preferred mode of dining among the celebrity in-house guests (many rarely leave their suite), the restaurant (see below) is definitely worth trying. ♦ 9291 Burton Way (at Foothill Rd). 310/278.3344; fax 310/278.8247. www.beverlyhills.raffles.com

Within Raffles L'Ermitage Hotel:

JAAN RESTAURANT AT RAFFLES

★★★$$$ The seasonally changing, light, and lively menu excites the palate whether you order à la carte or opt for the six-course tasting menu (we recommend the latter), but be sure to ask for the fresh halibut served on potato gnocchi or foie gras pâté. The gorgeous dining area sits under a dome ceiling. Dancing fountains, lit up at night, visible through a floor-to-ceiling window add to the romance of the room. A striking Oriental flower arrangement provides a regal centerpiece for the dining area. The adjacent lounge overflows with before- and after-dinner drinkers, while an outdoor patio attracts those who still smoke. ♦ Daily, lunch and dinner. Reservations advised. 310/278.3344

RAFFLES AMRITA SPA

This pretty little pamper spot, named after a mystic nectar of the gods, offers an array of salubrious services from facials to pedicures. Conveniently located on the eighth floor, just below the rooftop pool and adjacent to the fitness center, the spa features Zen-like treatment rooms, changing rooms for men and women with steam baths, showers, and lockers, and a superb staff. A recent massage ranked as one of the top 10 ever experienced by a self-admitted spa snob. ♦ Daily, 6AM–10PM.

39 O'NEILL HOUSE

Antonio Gaudí is alive and well in Beverly Hills! The architect would be proud of the writhing stucco on **Don Ramos**'s 1989 Art

---

Nouveau house, and of the more whimsical guest house behind. It's a private residence. ♦ 507 N Rodeo Dr (between Santa Monica Blvd and Carmelita Ave)

40 BEVERLY HILLS DINER

★$ A real retro, fast-food (they make a burger in 4 minutes) diner with horseshoe-shaped counter and booths along the side wall and even jukeboxes playing oldies. The menu features New York–style sandwiches (the egg salad is yummy and generous), burgers (beef, turkey, and vegan), hot dogs, salads, shakes, malts, floats, banana splits, hot fudge sundaes, and apple or cherry pie. Take-out orders are accepted. ♦ Diner ♦ M-Su, 11AM-10PM. 474 N Beverly Dr (at Santa Monica Blvd S). 310/271.2227. www.bhdiner.com

41 THE PALEY CENTER FOR MEDIA

Architect **Richard Meier** redesigned this former bank building to house the 23,000-square-foot museum. Visitors can choose from more than 60,000 television and radio programs and commercials to watch at private consoles. Special exhibits are shown in a 150-seat theater as well. ♦ Admission. W-Su. 465 N Beverly Dr (at Santa Monica Blvd S). 310/786.1000

42 CARROLL & CO.

Proffering menswear for the old guard—including such odd bedfellows as Ronald Reagan, George McGovern, and Gregory Peck—this popular, upscale shop moved here in 1997. ♦ M-Sa. 425 N Cañon Dr (between Brighton Way and Santa Monica Blvd S). 310/273.9060

43 THE CRESCENT HOTEL

$$ Get a load of this: Every room comes with Apple iPod Minis offering a custom play list of funk, disco, hip-hop, jazz, and down-tempo sounds, programmed by Gray V (www.grayv.com). It's just one of the clever perks proffered by loungeSleep Hotels, proprietors of this 35-room boutique property designed by the ubiquitous Dodd Mitchell. Accommodations are furnished with obligatory yuppie accoutrements such as Italian linens, down comforters, custom bathrooms, lush robes, high-end hair and skin products, flat-screen TVs, free wireless Internet service, and entertainment centers with DVD/CD players. A useful amenity is the Federal Express overnight mail envelope placed in each closet. ♦ 403 N Crescent Dr (at Brighton Way). 310/247.0505. www.crescentbh.com

Within The Crescent Hotel:

BOE

★★$$ This intimate restaurant (*boe* is an acronym for "Bacchus, Orpheus, Epicurus")

offers indoor/outdoor dining with a fireplace visible from both areas. Request a table on the inviting patio, which is nicely sheltered from the street and shaded by umbrellas. The eclectic American menu features dishes such as Southwest scrambled eggs with chorizo chilies, avocados, and tortillas in the morning, a blackened po' boy sandwich for lunch, and a grilled flatiron steak with purple Peruvians, sunburst squash, and mushrooms for dinner. The adjacent bar/lounge attracts a nightly crowd of tipplers willing to shell out $12 for a martini, or trendy quaffs like Berry Jitos (dark rum with fruit) or Mount My Mango (more rum with Fruja mango and orange juice). ♦ American ♦ Daily, breakfast, lunch, and dinner. In-room massages are available, as are discounted day passes for use at the **Sports Club LA** (9560 Wilshire Blvd).

44 WESTERN ATLAS

Paul Williams's 1940 American Federal Revival office building has a grand portico. ♦ 360 N Crescent Dr (between Dayton Way and Santa Monica Blvd S)

45 POLO/RALPH LAUREN

No, you haven't wandered into an English country house; it's just the latest of Lauren's emporia for visiting squires and Anglophiles. ♦ M-Sa. 444 N Rodeo Dr (between Brighton Way and Santa Monica Blvd S). 310/281.7200

46 THE FARM OF BEVERLY HILLS

★★$$ This friendly eatery offers generous portions of comforting home-style fare. At times inconsistent, the food is generally very good, and the place is packed night and day. Favorites include halibut with warm red and yellow tomatoes, grilled marinated steak with shoestring potatoes and three-grain mustard sauce, and rotisserie chicken. The deli offers food to go—perfect for a picnic at the beach or the Hollywood Bowl. ♦ American ♦ M-F, breakfast, lunch, and dinner; Sa, Su, brunch and dinner. 439 N Beverly Dr (between Brighton Way and Santa Monica Blvd S). 310/273.5578 ♿

47 NATE 'N' AL

★$$ Big-name stars often frequent this celebrated deli on weekends to read their Sunday newspapers and visit with friends. ♦ Deli ♦ Daily, breakfast, lunch, and dinner. 414 N Beverly Dr (between Brighton Way and Santa Monica Blvd S). 310/274.0101

48 E. BALDI

★★★$$$ Foodies flock to this little charmer for some of the best Italian cuisine this side of the old country. We're talking carpaccio and polentas to die for, lasagna, gnocchi, and veal dishes done to perfection. And divine desserts. ♦ Italian ♦ M-F, lunch and dinner; Sa, dinner. Reservations a must. 375 N Cañon Dr (at Brighton Way). 310/248.2633

49 CACTUS GARDEN

Cacti and succulents from around the world occupy one section of the most handsome landscaping to be found on any city boulevard. ♦ Santa Monica Blvd (between N Camden and N Bedford Drs)

50 SPRINKLES CUPCAKES

Move over, Krispy Kreme! The stream of people waiting to satisfy their sweet tooth stretches down the block. You'd think they'd never seen a cupcake before. Well, maybe not the designer varieties that change here daily. If it's Monday there's vanilla, dark chocolate, red velvet, carrot, lemon, mocha, chocolate coconut, and more. On Tuesday there's all of the above plus strawberry, Wednesday's treat is ginger lemon, on Thursday they add dark chocolate to the list, Friday it's chai latte, and if it's Saturday you can also have peanut butter chocolate or black & white. ♦ M-Sa. 9635 Santa Monica Blvd S (between N Roxbury and N Camden Drs). 310/273.9765; fax 310/274.7890. www.sprinklescupcakes.com

51 LA SCALA

★★★$$$ An institution once known for its celebrity clientele, snooty service, and steep prices, this spot has a new attitude. It is now a kinder, gentler neighborhood restaurant, serving good food with a smile, including ever-changing pasta dishes, osso buco, and fresh fish. The wine list is excellent. ♦ Italian ♦ M-Sa, lunch and dinner. Reservations recommended. 434 N Camden Dr (between Brighton Way and Santa Monica Blvd S). 310/275.0579 &. Also at 3821 Riverside Dr (between Hollywood Way and Kenwood St), Burbank. 818/846.6800 &; 11740 San Vicente Blvd (at Gorham Ave), Brentwood. 310/826.6100

52 FRETTE

Exquisite Italian lingerie and table, bath, and bed linens are sold here. ♦ Daily. 449 N Rodeo Dr (between Brighton Way and Santa Monica Blvd S). 310/273.8540

53 GIORGIO ARMANI

The largest and glitziest of Italian designer Giorgio Armani's ultrastylish clothing stores attracts Steven Spielberg, Sir Elton John, and other big-name regular customers. ♦ Daily. 436 N Rodeo Dr (between Brighton Way and Santa Monica Blvd S). 310/271.5555

53 HERMÈS

Designed by Rena Dumas, this behemoth haute couture emporium, with towering archways, lush greenery, and slender furnishings, is designed to provide an appropriately elegant backdrop for Hermès signature scarves, high fashion, and leather goods. ♦ M-Sa. 434 N Rodeo Dr (between Brighton Way and Santa Monica Blvd S). 310/278.6440

54 ALLURE PILATES SPA

Part Pilates studio, part pamper spa, this unique 2,800-square-foot, three-level city spa attracts the buff-body crowd who stay that way working out with high-energy, good-looking instructors hand-picked by proprietor Anita Neumann. Trust us, these workouts are guaranteed to whip you into shape. There's a pleasant reception area, a lower-level workout area complete with Pilates Reformers, and an upstairs mini-spa in which to succumb to the talents of massage and facial therapists and get waxed, oxygen boosted, hydrated, scrubbed, peeled or de-cellulited—all at reasonable prices. Do sign up for the hour-long Kung Yo session—a fusion of yoga and spiritual martial arts. It's fun and effective. Although attractive, the facility is rather bare bones, with a noticeable lack of saunas, steam baths, or lockers. ♦ M-Sa. 9701 Santa Monica Blvd S (at N Roxbury Dr). 310/777.0201. www.Allurepilatesspa.com

54 CAFÉ MARLY

$ Cheap eats in Beverly Hills, impossible but true at this adorable French café offering salads (Niçoise, paysanne), panini, beignets, crepes, and assorted egg dishes and breakfast plates. What's more, you can enjoy all the above on Thursday nights accompanied by live music. ♦ French Country ♦ M-Sa, breakfast, lunch, and dinner. Reservations suggested for dinner. There's also takeout and free delivery anywhere in town. 9669-2 Santa Monica Blvd (between N Roxbury and N Bedford Drs). 310/271.7274; fax 310/271.7258

55 CRUSTACEAN

★★★$$$ Like its San Francisco namesake, this dynamite Eurasian eatery features food as attractive as the place itself. An awesome aquarium, built into the floor, winds from the entrance to the dining room. Chef/owner Helene An's busy open kitchen creates such scrumptious tapas as prawn-filled rice-paper rolls and lemongrass-sesame beef satay. Artfully prepared entrées include Chilean sea bass pan-seared with ginger-citrus reduction and rack of lamb flambéed in Chardonnay. ♦ Eurasian ♦ M-Sa, lunch and dinner. Reservations required. Valet parking available. 9646 Santa Monica Blvd S (at N Bedford Dr). 310/205.8990

56 MANDARIN

★★$$$ Peking duck, braised lamb, and Beggar's Chicken highlight the Mandarin menu at this fun eatery. ♦ Chinese ♦ M-F, lunch and dinner; Sa, Su, dinner. Reservations recommended. 430 N Camden Dr (between Brighton Way and Santa Monica Blvd S). 310/859.0638, 323/272.0267

57 RODEO COLLECTION

Within this pink marble shopping mall are upscale designer boutiques such as La Perla, Sumer Collection, Sonia Rykiel, Stuart Weitzman shoes, and Fila. ♦ Daily. 433 N Rodeo Dr (between Brighton Way and Santa Monica Blvd S)

58 CHANEL

This fabulous flagship of high designer couture reeks of Chanel. Extravagantly laid out over 14,700 square feet of prime space, the extravagantly appointed shop was designed to evoke Coco Chanel's Paris residence. Even if you can't afford the pricey baubles, bangles, and fashion, it's worth a visit to marvel over the beauty excess can buy. Buy lipstick or something affordable, then stroll around this virtual art gallery filled with stunning commissioned works of art and amazing pieces like a strand of pearls magnified in Murano glass. ♦ Daily. 400 N Rodeo Dr (at Brighton Way). 310/278.5500

59 TASCHEN BOOKSTORE

This highbrow bookstore, operated by the German-based Taschen Company, specializes in scholarly and pop coffee-table books of various genres from photography to sex. Designed by Philippe Starck, the stunning 3,000-square-foot literary emporium looks more like an art gallery than a bookstore. Careful cerebral touches include a private glassed-in reading room on the mezzanine and a relaxing terrace area. To keep you on your intellectual toes, there are regularly scheduled events and lectures as well as special weeks highlighting celebrity curators. ♦ Daily. 354 N Beverly Dr (between Dayton and Brighton Ways). 310/274.4300. www.taschen.com

60 WHOLE FOODS MARKET

This bustling yuppie haven is the place to stock up on fresh organic produce, meat raised humanely and without hormones, healthy breads, yummy natural desserts, and other politically correct goodies. ♦ Daily. 239 N Crescent Dr (between Clifton and Dayton Ways). 310/274.3360. Also at 3476 Centinela Ave (at Palms Blvd), Westside. 310/391.5209

61 EMPORIO ARMANI

You can really bust your budget at this posh Italian designer-wear emporium, but hey, his stuff's worth it. ♦ 9533 Brighton Way (between N Rodeo and N Camden Drs). 310/271.7790

62 LUXE HOTEL RODEO DRIVE

$$$ A special little find in the heart of Beverly Hills, this minimalist 86-room hotel, designed by Vicente Wolf, blends classic and contemporary styles through the use of copper, marble, and glass. Each adorable room comes with upscale features such as Frette linens, signature robes, Rene Furterer toiletries, and CD players. Other in-room amenities include speedy Internet access, 32-inch flat-screen televisions, and 24-hour room service. There are two Valentino boutiques (one for him, the other for her) at the entrance of the hotel, where big-budget shoppers can find exquisite designer duds. Even if you can't afford the price tags, just browsing through these chic shops is a trip. And, who knows, you just might spot a favorite celebrity or two. Since there is no pool or tennis courts, guests are free to use the facilities at the sister property, the **Summit Belair.** ♦ 360 N Rodeo Dr (between Dayton and Brighton Ways). 310/273.0300, 800.HOTEL.411; fax 310/859.8730. www.luxehotels.com ♿

63 BANG & OLUFSEN

The selection of high-concept electronic systems at this massive, museum-like shop will delight the senses of any audiophile. The Danish company's showroom houses wide-screen and interactive digital televisions, sound systems, computers, and other high-end play toys and gadgets. If you're into high design and equipment that looks like an artistic piece of furniture, this is the place. ♦ Daily except Christmas, Columbus Day, and Easter. 369 N Rodeo Dr (between Dayton and Brighton Ways). 310/247.7785. www.bangandolufsen.com

64 PREGO

★★$$ Tantalizing pizzas are prepared in wood-burning ovens, but the pies hardly upstage the carpaccio, gnocchi, pasta, and grilled entrées. This is an attractive, bustling restaurant with a lively (separate) bar scene and service that is tremendously congenial, if a bit harried. ♦ Italian ♦ M-Sa, lunch and dinner; Su, dinner. 362 N Camden Dr (between Wilshire Blvd and Brighton Way). 310/277.7346 ৬

65 GIORGIO BEVERLY HILLS

This tiny boutique offers a great selection of signature scents, body products, and pricey designer casual wear and jewelry, and shares space with BCBG Max Azria, which carries cutting-edge women's clothing. ♦ Daily. 327 N Rodeo Dr (between Dayton and Brighton Ways). 310/275.2550

66 DAVID ORGELL

The sparkle of superb jewelry and antique English silver will catch your eye at this smart boutique. ♦ M-Sa. 320 N Rodeo Dr (between Dayton and Brighton Ways). 310/273.6660

67 IL FORNAIO

★★$ One of the few bargains in an otherwise pricey town, this bright and cheerful café serves great food—from hearty soups and salads to pizzas, pastas, and fish. The bakery turns out designer breads (whole wheat and olive, walnut, rosemary, potato) and yummy desserts. ♦ Italian Bakery/Café ♦ Bakery: daily. Café: daily, breakfast, lunch, and dinner. 301 N Beverly Dr (at Dayton Way). 310/550.8330 ৬. Also at 1800 Rosecrans Ave (at Manhattan Village Mall, corner of Sepulveda Blvd), Manhattan Beach. 310/725.9555

68 MASTRO'S STEAKHOUSE

★★★$$$ This stylish steak house appeals to meat eaters with big, juicy prime rib beef and great service. The 18-ounce Kansas City strip of 40-ounce porterhouse is recommended. Be sure to order the baked potato or fried onion rings on the side. There's a great bar and drinks are large, like everything else served here. ♦ Steak House ♦ M-F, lunch; daily, dinner. Reservations necessary. 246 N Cañon Dr (between Clifton and Dayton Ways). 310/888.8782

69 NELSON J SALON

Only dream about lustrous, shiny hair? You can make it a reality at this spiffy salon where the owner, celebrity stylist Nelson Chan, performs his magical signature deep-conditioning treatment that takes the dull, dryness, frizz, and damage out. We tried it; it works. Why else would some of Hollywood's top stars (Sarah Michele Gellar, Heather Graham, Alicia Silverstone, Devon Aoki) fly him on location or send limos to fetch him home? This guy's good, and his spacious salon has a no-attitude appeal and great style with metallic mirrored ceiling tiles, blue texture-stained concrete floors, and the most comfortable shampoo chairs we've ever sat in. Even better are the prices, which are several cuts below par in this pricey town. Products are all-natural and nontoxic; services include cut, color, blow dry, conditioning, nail care, and Saturday massages. ♦ Tu-Sa, 9AM-5PM. 350 N Bedford Dr (between Brighton Way and Wilshire Blvd). 310/274.1553. www.nelsonstudio.com

70 2 RODEO

Across the street from 1 Rodeo resides the crowning jewel of the boulevard. Perched atop Spanish-style steps is an ersatz European village with a cobblestone street designed by Kaplan/McLaughlin/Diaz in 1990. The corner of Rodeo and Wilshire houses the largest **Tiffany & Co.** store outside of New York. Other tony tenants include José Eber, Cartier, Pierre Deux, Sulka, Jimmy Choo, and Judith Ripka. Perhaps the most striking occupant, though, is **Gianni Versace**—in a Greco-Roman acropolis featuring fluted Corinthian columns, mosaic tile floors, and a dramatic glass oculus, and offering high-fashion men's and women's clothing (310/205.3921). ♦ N Rodeo Dr (between Wilshire Blvd and Dayton Way)

71 MONTAGE HOTEL & GARDENS

$$$$ An offspring of the Laguna Beach Montage, the property was under construction at press time and scheduled to open in the fall of 2008. If its beachfront sister is any indication, this 201-room, 7-story deluxe hotel is bound to be a knockout. The design features a Spanish Colonial Revival exterior and a classic Mediterranean Revival interior created by Hill Glazier Architects of Palo Alto and Darrell Schmitt Design Associates of LA. Each ritzy room is 500 square feet (the Presidential Suite takes up 2,000 square feet) and features all the amenities you'd expect (lots of marble, tile, oversize tubs, LCD TVs, plush robes and linens, feather-top beds, high-speed Internet, I-dock, and more). There are also 25 penthouse condominiums, a rooftop pool, a 20,000-square-foot spa, and three restaurants. In keeping with its "old-style Hollywood meets modern-day luxury" theme, a massive art collection celebrates the golden era of Beverly Hills in the 1920s and 1930s. ♦ 225 N Cañon Dr (between Wilshire Blvd and Dayton Way). For information only, call 310/274.0011. www.montagebeverlyhills.com

---

Restaurants/Clubs: Red | Hotels: Purple | Shops: Orange | Outdoors/Parks: Green | Sights/Culture: Blue

72 THE WINE MERCHANT

Dennis Overstreet relocated his wine and spirit shop into this three-story building, providing customers with more space in which to taste wine, sample cheese and caviar, take classes, or store their personal wine collections. There's an impressive wine cellar on the lower level and an inviting tasting lounge on the top floor. The company also offers private wine tastings at the shop or in your home. ♦ M-Sa. 228 N Cañon Dr (between Clifton and Dayton Ways). 310/278.7322. www.winemerchantbh.com

73 SPAGO BEVERLY HILLS

★★★★$$$$ Call right now to book a reservation at this shining star of super chef Wolfgang Puck's culinary empire. Puck's former wife, Barbara Lazaroff, and architect Stephen Jones are responsible for the inviting design, which wraps the dining area around a garden patio where tall, willowy pepper trees and two-century-old olive trees shade a fountain. Menu favorites include sweet corn soup spiced with lobster nuggets; rare beef on the bone, thickly sliced with potato and garlic purée whipped with Cantal cheese; and simply prepared fresh fish such as whole dorado or turbot. The desserts are to die for: crepes with berries and cheese dumplings stuffed with apricots or plums. The place hops nightly with major industry players and celebrities who get top priority for primo tables. ♦ California ♦ M-Sa, lunch and dinner; Su, dinner. Reservations essential; be sure to call weeks in advance to assure a table at the usual dinner time (7:30PM and on). Valet parking available. 176 N Cañon Dr (at Clifton Way). 310/385.0880 &

74 THE CRESCENT BEVERLY HILLS

While we don't often list apartment houses, we made an exception since you are most likely to wonder about this Class A structure with its limestone, radius glass, and metal trim exterior on the corner of Crescent and Wilshire whose name and design seem to belong to a boutique hotel. The intricate building actually houses 88 high-priced ($5,000 to $7,000 a month) luxury apartments in an exquisite structure designed by **VTBS** (Van Tilburg, Banvard and Soderbergh of Santa Monica). If you're interested and can afford the rent, amenities include a fitness and business center, concierge, doorman, and underground parking. ♦ 155 N Crescent Dr (just behind Spago). 310/385.1924

75 MOSAIC HOTEL

$$ Devotees of boutique hotels will enjoy this 57-room charmer with its stylish interior and warm ambience. Amenities include a fitness room outfitted with a treadmill, Elliptical machine, weights, and exercise videos, and free laptops set up in the lobby to check your e-mail or surf the net. Each attractive room comes with upscale toiletries as well as Frette sheets, towels, and robes. Planning on a long stay? Opt for a Fab Four lifestyle suite furnished with gourmet kitchens, whirlpool spas, plasma-screen TVs, and lots of techno gadgets. There is a full-service restaurant with an active bar where you can nosh on tapas, and 24-hour room service. ♦ 125 S Spalding Dr (just south of Wilshire Blvd). 310/278.0303, 800/463.4466. www.mosaic.com

76 BRITESMILE SPA

While we try to avoid chains of any kind, this one's well worth mentioning. First of all, it's in Beverly Hills, and that means celebrities, especially given the emphasis on teeth whitening. No place does it mean more than in a town full of folks who are paid to flash their pearly whites in front of the cameras. The spa sparkles with white walls offset by displays of BriteSmile products wrapped in bright blue packaging. The hour-long whitening process takes place in a private cubicle where you can relax on a comfortable reclining chair and watch TV or nap. It's pricey (about $600) but painless and effective, and the results are worth it, especially when you take a look at the before-and-after photos the dentist takes of your teeth. You might even spot a star on your way out who no doubt will flash you a smile. ♦ M-Sa. 9725 Wilshire Blvd (between N Roxbury and N Linden Drs). 310/385.8016

76 DR. LANCER THERAPEUTICS INC

Want to see stars? Go to this posh penthouse dermatology office during the month before the Academy Awards presentations and you're bound to run into some of Hollywood's most famous faces, who go for facial tune-ups to prepare them for those harsh close-ups and bright, unforgiving lights. The really big names sneak in by private elevator, from which they are whisked into one of Dr. Harold Lancer's treatment rooms where the amiable, talented dermatologist performs face-saving manipulations with Botox injections or special noninvasive therapies such as microepidermabrasion and what he calls the "Lancer Glow." Of course, you don't have to be famous to make an appointment. But be prepared for his outright honesty. Once he examines your skin and prescribes the proper remedies you will love the results. It's not cheap, but you couldn't be in better hands. After all, we did catch glimpses of Madonna, Cher, and even a few more youthful starlets stepping out of the elevator. And let's face it: If they trust their faces to Dr. Lancer, you can be sure he's good. ♦ 9735 Wilshire Blvd (at N Roxbury Dr), The Penthouse. 310/278.8444

77 BARRY REITMAN AT JUAN JUAN CENTER

Get a fabulous new coif or simply treat your tresses to some tender loving care from Barry Reitman. The supertalented cosmetician has spent two decades coloring, styling, and trimming the luxuriant manes of famous folk and ordinary people. But unlike some Beverly Hills celebrity hair care–givers, Reitman works without the attitude or inflated prices. He's a hoot to watch as he sculpts, creates, colors, cuts, and maneuvers your mane into what he likes to call "award-winning" coifs. ♦ Appointments only. W-Sa, and Sundays on request. 9675 Wilshire Blvd (between N Bedford and N Roxbury Drs). 310/278.4247; cell 818/427.8770

78 WILSHIRE BOULEVARD

Upscale department and specialty stores line this stylish stretch of LA's Main Street, where handsome old buildings and contemporary slick glass high-rises reflect a mix of architectural styles. The boulevard, shaded by lofty palm trees, boasts a lively pedestrian scene. Shopping highlights include **Niketown; Burberry** (No. 9560; 310/246.0896); **Neiman Marcus** (No. 9700; 310/550.5900); and **Saks Fifth Avenue** (No. 9600; 310/275.4211).

78 BARNEYS

The LA branch of the New York department store is a five-level, 108,000-square-foot shopping emporium of cutting-edge fashions (at inflated prices), along with a Chelsea Passage Gift Department offering collectibles from all over the world. ♦ 9570 Wilshire Blvd (between S Camden and Peck Drs). 310/276.4400

Within Barneys:

BARNEY GREENGRASS

★★$$ The hoopla over this department-store dining room amazes us. Folks literally eat this place up. Perched in a compact space on the top floor, the shop-till-you-drop crowd flock here for breakfast before beginning their spending sprees on Rodeo, and lunch *après* the upscale shopping bags are filled to the brim. Theatrical agents go to fuel up for a day

of power dealing. The biggest draws are deli-like offerings such as salmon, sturgeon, and cod, but there are also soups and salads. ♦ American/Deli ♦ Daily, lunch and dinner. 310/777.5877

78 THE SPORTS CLUB LA-BEVERLY HILLS

This swank $25 million offspring of the fast-growing chain of elite health clubs takes fitness to new heights. Pass through the Zen-like lobby, adorned with bamboo gardens and waterfalls, and you enter a 10,000-square-foot gym, a Cardiovascular Center with 100 pieces of select equipment, each with a personal TV. There's also a Flexibility Center, Functional Training Performance Center, and four exercise studios. Members stay in shape through REV group cycling, Pilates, yoga, aerobics, and specially designed classes. *Après*-workout amenities include Splash, a destination day spa, a boutique, and Oliver Café, operated by famed restaurateur Mario Oliver and open for breakfast, lunch, and dinner. The Sports Club LA has branches in Washington DC, Boston, San Francisco, Miami, and Orange County. ♦ 9601 Wilshire Blvd (at Camden Dr). 310/888.8100. www.thesportsclubla.com

79 THE GRILL ON THE ALLEY

★★★$$$ Chef John Sola has won applause for his assurance with corned beef hash, braised short ribs, and Cobb salad, along with oak-charcoal-grilled fish and meats. One of the most popular restaurants in the city, this is a place with a warm, woodsy setting, professional waiters, and huge helpings at fair prices. ♦ American ♦ M-Sa, lunch and dinner. Reservations required. 9560 Dayton Way (at Wilshire Blvd). 310/276.0615 &

80 1 RODEO

This building, fronted by a whimsical pastiche of Palladio-style façades by Johannes Van Tilburg, houses such swank boutiques as Bulgari and Denmark Jeweler. ♦ 201 N Rodeo Dr (at Wilshire Blvd)

81 BEVERLY WILSHIRE, A FOUR SEASONS HOTEL

$$$$ The doyenne of luxury hotels, thanks in part to the fine management by Four Seasons Hotel and Resort, this stellar property was originally designed by **Walker & Eisen** in 1928. Today the completely renovated 402-room (of which 123 are suites) hotel boasts a brighter yet still luxurious look that unites

marble with mahogany, plush carpeting, and outstanding works of art. Each room is sumptuously appointed with every creature comfort imaginable. A dramatic 5,000-square-foot, three-bedroom penthouse suite is worth all of the $8,000 a day it commands from the rich and famous who stay there regularly. Besides spectacular views from a wraparound balcony, the suite has a Jacuzzi tub in an over-the-top marble bathroom, an entertainment center, a formal dining room, a butler's pantry, and special privileges. The service throughout the hotel is *par excellence*, from the 24-hour concierges to the fastidious room stewards on every floor. On the ground floor is a handsome, clubby bar where well-heeled guests might enjoy an after-dinner cognac or cigar. Other amenities include a full-service spa, a well-equipped fitness center (with amenities like TV monitors, towels, ice water, coffee, fruit and nuts, and attendants on hand), and an outdoor swimming pool. And to keep you well coiffed, the **Lea Journo Salon** offers the gamut of hair care services along with manicures, pedicures, and makeup applications. For an appointment, call 310/385.7007. ♦ 9500 Wilshire Blvd (at El Camino Dr). 310/275.5200, 800/545.4000; fax 310/274.2851. www.regenthotels.com ♦

Within the Beverly Wilshire, A Four Seasons Hotel:

THE BLVD

★★★$$$$ Set beneath a high ceiling and flanked by bird's-eye maple paneling, the handsome room pulsates with a lively crowd perched at the beautiful onyx bar sipping trendy drinks like "baccaratinis," served in cobalt blue Baccarat crystal martini glasses that cost a mere $185—but hey, you can keep the glass. Tables, impeccably set with fine china and crystal on leather place mats, buzz with contented, obviously well-heeled diners savoring the outrageously delicious, pricey fare. A recent dinner of mouthwatering tuna tartare, as-good-as-it-gets Caesar salad, a cooked-to-order prime filet, and Hawaiian snapper made us swoon, and a delicately delicious cheesecake and outstanding tarte Tatin proved heavenly. If you don't mind the traffic noise, request a table on the Wilshire Boulevard patio, where the really cool crowd dines. ♦ California ♦ Daily, breakfast, lunch, afternoon tea, and dinner. Reservations required for dinner. 310/275.5200.

At press time a **Wolfgang Puck Steakhouse,** designed by noted architect Richard Meier, was scheduled to replace The Regent Beverly Wilshire Dining Room. According to the designer, the new room will blend contemporary and classic elements with vibrant, "mystical" colors.

CUT A WOLFGANG PUCK STEAKHOUSE

★★★$$$ Whatever celebrity chef Wolfgang Puck touches turns to gold and this chic, contemporary steak house is no exception. Designed by noted architect Richard Meier, the lively room is a masterpiece of minimalism with wood floors, see-through glassed-in kitchen, and special swivel chairs designed for the high-visibility clientele who want to be able to turn easily in order to see and be seen. The menu opens with an *amuse-bouche* (starter) gone wild theme that includes tiny Kobe burger sliders, Kobe steak sashimi, an amazing foie gras, and other tempting treats. The true headliners are the tender, delicious prime cuts of beef that rule the menu, like the 100% Wagyu beef from Kagoshima Prefecture, porterhouse, New York, or rib eye, and the amazing deserts. The restaurant is booked weeks in advance, so call ahead. Get there early and enjoy an adult beverage in the swinging Sidebar lounge. ♦ Steak House ♦ M-Sa, dinner. Reservations a must. 310/276.8500. www.wolfgangpuck.com

82 STERLING PLAZA

The stunning Art Deco office tower built by Louis B. Mayer in 1929 as the MGM Building has been beautifully refurbished. Ironically, the movie company has moved a block away behind a bland white-marble-and-black-glass façade. Mayer would not have approved. ♦ Wilshire Blvd and Beverly Dr

83 THOMPSON BEVERLY HILLS

$$$ The former Beverly Pavilion Hotel was reinvented by Thompson Hotels in 2007 and turned into a chic, contemporary-style, 107-room boutique property with the help of top designer Dodd Mitchell. The bad news is the rates more than doubled. But the place pulsates with young vibes and the rooms are nifty with sleek, modern furnishings, white oak floors, glass accents, platform beds, marbled baths with oversize showers, linens by Sferra, and private balconies. There's a Japanese restaurant called Bond Street Beverly Hills, a bustling bar, a rooftop pool, a member's-only rooftop bar, and a fancy, glass-enclosed fitness center with views of the Hollywood Hills and downtown LA. FYI: Parking's $22 a night. ♦ 9360 Wilshire Blvd (at S Crescent Dr). 310/273.1400, 800/441.5050; fax 310/859.8730. www.thompsonhotels.com ♦

84 PENINSULA BEVERLY HILLS

$$$$ This bustling French Renaissance–style hotel offers 196 well-appointed rooms (including 32 suites and 5 two-story villas) and outstanding service, making it a favorite

of well-heeled celebrities and business travelers. Along with spectacular landscaped grounds, the low-rise hotel boasts fine antiques, European marbles, polished woods, and tapestries. It offers courtesy chauffeured Rolls-Royce service in Beverly Hills and Century City. Other amenities include a rooftop pool designed for privacy and indulgence with lavish cabanas, food and beverage service, and amazing views. The Spa provides a cocoon-like sanctuary in which to enjoy world-class facials, massages, and body treatments, while the well-equipped fitness center features everything to keep you fit. There's also a full-service business center. During the Oscars, Tinseltown rules the property with presenters and award hopefuls holed up in swank suites. Although the rich and famous are regulars here, this is one hotel that truly does treat all guests equally—maybe you won't be upgraded to a suite, but you will get the same service as everybody else. ♦ 9882 Santa Monica Blvd S (between Lasky Dr and Charleville Blvd). 310/551.2888, 800/462.7899; fax 310/788.2319. www.peninsula.com &

Within the Peninsula Beverly Hills:

THE BELVEDERE

★★★★$$$$ Classic and exquisitely designed, with big windows and a comfortable ambience, it's worth a trip even if you're not staying at the hotel. The award-winning restaurant provides a fitting showcase for outstanding dishes like Nantucket bay scallops with baby leeks, chorizo, cannellini beans, and roasted pepper broth; charred corn and sweet potato bisque with lightly smoked duck; Alaskan salmon; roasted lamb loin with artichoke chickpea fritters and twice-cooked eggplant; line-caught sea bream with organic brown rice, shiitake mushrooms, and ruby grapefruit; and potato-crusted Chilean sea bass that melts in your mouth. Desserts are also divine, particularly the Valrhona Manjari chocolate obsessions with caramel ice cream, chocolate soufflé tart with melted bananas, and warm apple tart with cinnamon ice cream and caramel sauce. If you have trouble deciding, you can order the bite-size sampler plate. Sunday brunch at the Belvedere is a special-occasion event with fabulous food and endless glasses of Champagne. ♦ Continental ♦ M-Sa, breakfast, lunch, and dinner; Su, brunch and dinner. Reservations recommended; jacket required. 310/788.2306

85 MAISON 140

$$ Located in a residential area on the periphery of the shopping district, this adorable 45-room boutique hotel oozes charm. A bit 18th-century France, a tad modern, the Kelly Wearstler–designed hotel has interesting touches such as dormers with potted topiaries, a white-lacquered floor-to-ceiling screen of suspended classical ceiling medallions resting on the foyer's black hardwood floor, crystal French chandeliers, Lucite bar stools, and gobs of hand-selected antiques. Each colorfully charming (and little) room contains vintage pieces and custom-designed appointments like overstuffed French Bergère chairs and Rothko-inspired oil paintings, along with contemporary must-haves: cordless phone, high-speed Internet access, data ports, minibars, and safes. There's no restaurant, but you can order light snacks at the lively Bar Noir, a fun tippling spot that stages a monthly cheese and wine tasting event called Vin et Fromage. A generous complimentary continental breakfast makes the moderate price even more attractive. ♦ 140 Lasky Dr (between Charleville Blvd and Santa Monica Blvd S). 310/281.4000, 800/432.5444; fax 310/281.4001. www.maison140.com

Restaurants/Clubs: **Red** | Hotels: **Purple** | Shops: **Orange** | Outdoors/Parks: **Green** | Sights/Culture: **Blue**

107

WESTSIDE

Yuppie heaven...
Too trendy, so chic, the Westside is where privileged power players live in self-indulgent excess. Pricey cars, household staffs, and designer everything defines this side of Los Angeles. Space, greenery, picturesque hills, clean air, and proximity to the ocean—and a good deal of snob appeal—are the palpable attractions

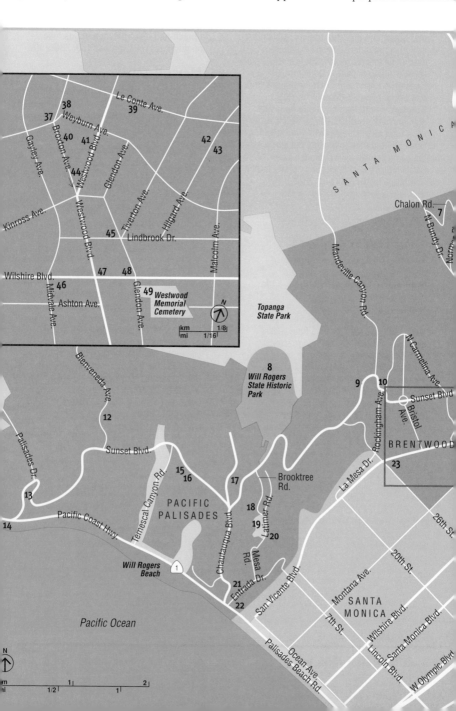

of this region, located just west of Interstate 405. With cool ocean breezes, air conditioning is rarely needed, even during the height of summer. The area is primarily residential, with a sharp contrast between the modest houses and apartments that predominate south of Wilshire Boulevard and the lushly planted estates of Bel Air, Brentwood, and Pacific Palisades to the north of that axis.

Private tennis courts, swimming pools, Porsches, Mercedes, BMW Z4s, Range Rovers, and high-end SUVs are commonplace in this affluent area, which also hap-

pens to sport five major country clubs. But unlike Beverly Hills, which flaunts its wealth, the golden ghettoes of the Westside are somewhat restrained.

Just east of I-405 but often included as part of the Westside is **Westwood Village,** an upscale residential area that also houses the **University of California at Los Angeles** (UCLA). Originally part of the 1843 land grant of Rancho San Jose de Buenos Ayres, Westwood became the John Wolfskill Ranch after 1884. In 1919, Arthur Letts, founder of the Broadway and Bullock's department stores, bought the farmland and then sold it to the Janss Company. In 1926, Westwood was annexed to Los Angeles in a civic enlargement that included a large portion of the Santa Monica Mountains, the Pacific Palisades, and Brentwood. In 1929, when UCLA opened its Westwood campus, the Janss Company had already built 2,000 houses and a shopping district called Westwood Village.

Westwood Village is your typical college town with a croissant shop or cookie store on virtually every block, scores of pizza places and ice cream and frozen yogurt parlors, and hamburger and falafel joints interspersed among restaurants, shops, and movie theaters. The main intersection at Wilshire and Westwood Boulevards is one of the city's busiest. The **Village Center Westwood** at Weyburn and Tiverton Avenues has 13 movie screens, 26,000 square feet of restaurant space, and a five-story retail/residential building. And although high rents drove out several quality stores in previous years, a major gentrification and civic push is now drawing many back, luring fine dining establishments and slowly filling up some of the empty retail spaces. Because parking is difficult, many merchants offer one hour free with a minimum purchase at their shops.

Although founded in 1917 by entrepreneur/developer Harry Culver, **Culver City** has emerged as the new kid on the Westside block and is quickly becoming a little culinary center. Restaurants keep popping up along the stretch of Culver Boulevard and Main Street, while local shops, boutiques, and art galleries are gaining interest with out-of-towners. If you haven't explored this charming area, you really should.

BEL AIR

This posh hillside community, developed by Alphonzo E. Bell in the early 1920s, rapidly became a preferred location for stars and other celebrities who valued the privacy and the views. There's not much for the outsider to see along the winding roads with their Mediterranean names, since the best houses are hidden from sight.

1 MULHOLLAND GRILL

★★$$ Barbara Lazaroff originally helped transform this tiny storefront into the colorful, cavelike southwestern restaurant Shane. It was so adorable that when the new Italian owners took it over, they retained the décor and simply added tablecloths. The ambience is lively, the food superbly prepared, especially the seafood risotto with shrimp, scallops, and Manila clams sautéed with garlic, white wine, parsley, and tomato sauce; the *salada bella* (baby arugula with goat cheese and sun-dried tomatoes); *tonno di sicilia* (seared center-cut crusted ahi tuna with Italian peppers and sesame seeds over julienned mixed vegetables and crispy carrots in an orange ponzu sauce); and *osso buco agnello* (lamb shank with vegetables in Tuscan-style red wine sauce served with polenta). For dessert there's a flourless chocolate cake à la mode, chocolate truffle oozing with dark chocolate, and caramelized banana tart. ♦ Italian ♦ M-F, lunch and dinner; Sa, Su, dinner. Reservations recommended. 2932 Beverly Glen Cir (north of N Beverly Glen Blvd). 310/470.6223 &

2 BEL AIR BAR & GRILL

★★★$$ After touring **The Getty Center** (see page 112), drive a mile down the road for a bite to eat at this handsome neighborhood restaurant/bar carved out of a 60-year-old ranch house. The retro '50s supper-club décor is replete with French mahogany-framed countryside doors, cushy booths, banquettes, and a real brick-wall fireplace set under a high vaulted ceiling. The night scene is filled with well-heeled locals and foodies who drive from other parts of town to sample the simple but tasty selection of items like grilled swordfish with garlic shrimp, New York steak with Gorgonzola mashed potatoes, and braised veal Bolognese that melts in your mouth (no kidding). There are also creative sandwiches such as a house-cured salmon with dill mayo, tomatoes, and capers, and the Bel-Air Club, which is stacked with grilled chicken, Canadian bacon, and avocado served on panini bread, as well as pastas and more. For your sweet tooth, the caramelized banana split, chocolate soufflé, and apple tart à la mode do the trick. ♦ American Bar and Grill ♦ M-F, lunch and dinner; daily, bar open 'til 2AM. Reservations required. 662 N Sepulveda Blvd (just north of Sunset Blvd at Moraga Drive, about a mile from the Getty). 310/440.5544; fax 310/475.5492. www.belairbarandgrill.com &

3 HOTEL BEL-AIR

$$$$ This ultra-exclusive 94-room hideaway, nestled in a wooded canyon among 11 pastoral acres, is the place to stay for a special occasion. Not only is it like no other LA hotel, when you're there it feels as if you're in a different country. Yet it is just minutes from Beverly Hills and other metropolitan areas. Even the entry waxes poetic as you stroll across the bucolic bridge past towering sycamores, over the tranquil lake inhabited by four graceful white swans, into the gracious European-style lobby, where you are greeted like an old friend. Thanks to the able guidance of managing director Carlos Lopes, this elite hideaway continues to redefine luxury with special touches such as elegant tea service delivered to your room a few minutes after you check in, bottled water and fruit provided poolside throughout the day, and attentive guest service personnel. For an extraordinary, albeit budget-busting, treat, book the Grace Kelly, Swan Lake, or Spa suite. Each provides the ultimate in luxurious living. At press time a lavish 12,000-square-foot, two-story spa was under construction at the hotel that will include 10 private treatment room suites, a yoga and Pilates studio, an organic juice bar, plunge pools, oversized Jacuzzis, and a 1,000-square-foot fitness facility. Also in the works are three residential spa suite guest rooms fitted with saunas, steam baths, Swiss showers, and spa wardrobes. Until the spa opens, you can enjoy a variety of treatments in the privacy of your own room. If you feel like having a facial, makeup, hairstyling, manicure, pedicure, body wrap, scrub, or massage, simply dial the concierge staff and a therapist will arrive within a couple of hours. If you have unruly tots in tote who need some etiquette training, you might want to consider enrolling them in the hotel's unique Petite Protocol workshop. The half-day session, headed by an internationally recognized instructor, teaches basic manners and decorum from writing thank-you notes to serving food and beverages. Sessions with Ms. Manners cost $250 a tiny head and include a child's-size multi-course lunch with the chef. Classes are held three or four times a year. For information or reservations, call 310/207.5175.

You can't help but love any of the 92 uniquely designed Tuscan-influenced rooms and suites, neatly tucked within rambling Mission-style buildings. Each exudes a distinctive charm provided by needlepoint rugs, canopy beds, wood-burning fireplaces, natural stone or marble, and always-lovely floral arrangements. One of the most exceptional is the Chanock Suite, a freestanding bungalow (named after a former guest who resided in the hotel for more than 40 years) that boasts terra-cotta-paved floors, a limestone fireplace from France, and French doors that open to a walled back garden lush with azaleas, camellias, philodendrons, and a large silk-floss tree. The very pricey hotel caters to a very high-end clientele comprised mostly of movie stars and music industry mavens. Attention to privacy and discretion make you feel like the only guest in residence. During the day, the rich, famous, handsome, and beautiful-bodied congregate at the pool for sunning, reading, lunching, and drinking. A nice touch is the pitchers of ice water, tons of towels, and bowls of fresh fruit set out on the deck for all to enjoy. There's also a nicely equipped fitness center with a legend: It was carved out of Marilyn Monroe's favorite bungalow. The inviting center features high-quality state-of-the-art equipment and apparatus. It's free and open 24 hours. ♦ 701 Stone Canyon Rd (at Chalon Rd). 310/472.1211, 800/648.4097; fax 310/476.5890. www.hotelbelair.com

Within the Hotel Bel-Air:

THE RESTAURANT

★★★★$$$$ Designer Leo A. Daly redesigned and redefined the courtly dining room with a palette of "Tuscan-inspired colors" such as butter cream, terra-cotta, and gold illuminated by a Venetian chandelier. They softly glazed the walls with a hand-applied parchment finish and added Spanish Baroque mirrors against a wall of mid-century modern–inspired leather banquettes to allow total visibility of the room and its occupants. A blazing fireplace enhances the mood and warms the room on chilly nights. When you've finished dining, take a tour of the herb garden and wine terrace. The food is simply divine but no surprise with chef Douglas Dodd and chef de cuisine Bruno Lopez—two talent culinarians—creating the menus. Along with favorites such as the tortilla soup and white bisque with truffle flan, the chefs prepare delicately cooked daurade with just the right touch of flavors, a mouth-watering rack of lamb, wildflower honey-lacquered duck, and mustard-crusted salmon. Scrumptious desserts include fresh doughnut Parisienne with fondue and a knockout Grand Marnier soufflé. Take a few foodie friends out for a night at "Table One"—specially prepared chef's dinners for eight people served in a charming room adjacent to the kitchen, where diners can watch the action through a glass window; make reservations at least two weeks in advance. The more casual terrace overlooking the swan-filled lake offers a tranquil spot to enjoy a hearty breakfast. ♦ California/French ♦ Daily, breakfast, lunch, and dinner. 310/472.1211. www.hotelbelair.com

THE CHAMPAGNE BAR

Before or after dinner it's simply de rigueur to stop in here for an adult beverage served at the friendly bar or in the cozy lounge beside the roaring fireplace. Enjoy a killer martini, glass of fine wine, or vintage Champagne while you sit back and listen to piano music performed by the talented Antonio Castillo de la Gala. If you enjoy sampling wines, be sure to stop by for the weekly tastings featuring hand-selected picks from California and the world.

4 UCLA HANNAH CARTER JAPANESE GARDEN

Ⓟ The enchanted garden, designed by Nagao Sakurai in 1961, is a tranquil retreat amid private estates, with rocks, wooden structures, trees, and plants imported from Japan. Behind the teahouse is a Hawaiian garden. ♦ Free. Tu-W. Reservations required. 10619 Bellagio Rd (between Stone Canyon Rd and Siena Way). UCLA Visitor's Center: 310/825.4574

5 THE GETTY CENTER

Richard Meier designed this billion-dollar paean to fine art that opened in December 1997 with much worldwide brouhaha and press. Perched dramatically on 110 hilltop acres in the Santa Monica Mountains, seven stunning, low-scale geometric-shaped pavilions—each devoted to a period in art history—are linked by bridges and lush formal gardens. Half the project sits underground, where all the buildings are connected. The amazing, crisply detailed complex, with rough travertine marble cladding alternated with metallic-finished porcelain steel panels, offers changing exhibits along with the extensive Getty art collection. The center unites several programs of the J. Paul Getty Trust: a study center for comparative archeology and culture, the **Getty Conservation Institute,** and the **Getty Center for History of Art and Humanities.** Orientation talks and gallery lectures are given daily, concerts are held Friday afternoons and evenings, and educational programs are offered regularly. A pleasant restaurant/café has outdoor seating on balconies and terraces with awesome views of the Pacific. ♦ Fee for parking only. Tu-Su. Note: Parking reservations are no longer required, but spaces are limited. Visitors may take the MTA bus no. 561 or the Santa Monica Big Blue bus no. 4; request a museum pass from the driver. 1200 Getty Center Dr (west of San Diego Fwy). 310/440.7300, 310/440.7722. www.getty.edu ♿

6 HOTEL ANGELENO

$$ Carved out of a dazzling landmark circular building that once housed a Holiday Inn, the highly stylized, yuppie-driven hotel was designed and reinvented by Jofusion Inc. Each attractive accommodation provides all the essentials of an upscale boutique property, such as 300-thread-count Italian cotton linens, feather duvets, down-around pillows, private balconies, the usual rapid web connections, CD player, workstations with ergonomic chairs (lest you rest), plasma flat-screen TVs, free HBO, aromatherapy bath products, and coffeemakers. There's an outdoor pool, an indoor fitness center, and a business center with Macs and PCs. If you want to visit the nearby **Getty,** all you have to do is call for the complimentary shuttle, which also takes guests to Westwood, Brentwood, or UCLA. ♦ 170 N Church Lane (just off the 405 Fwy). 310/476.6411, 866 /964.2788. www.hotelangeleno.com

Within Hotel Angeleno:

WEST

★★ $$$ What a setting for a restaurant—the penthouse floor of this impressive circular structure, where awesome panoramic views complement an extensive Italian-inspired menu. Created by Kitchen Table Partners and design director/co-owner Joanna Perlman, the highly stylized WEST reflects a postwar-era Italy with dramatic chandeliers, rich cherry wood ceilings, Carrera marble tables, and cushy banquettes. Specialties include 24–48-ounce grilled Florentine T-bone steaks, Dijon-crusted rack of lamb, and a 16-ounce veal chop, with à la carte sides. ♦ Cal-Italian ♦ Daily, breakfast, lunch, and dinner. Reservations suggested for dinner. 310/481.7878. www.westatangeleno.com

6 THE LUXE

$$$ Few people know about this little gem hidden away on seven acres just below **The Getty Center.** It's a little off the beaten track but perfect for a peaceful hideaway. There are 162 rooms equipped with the usual business tech tools as well as the usual hair dryers, robes, and amenities. Recreational facilities include a pool, spa, fitness center, and tennis courts. **On Sunset** (★★$$) is a perfect place to enjoy breakfast, lunch, or dinner indoors or out on the patio. ♦ Daily. 11461 Sunset Blvd (between Church La and N Gunston Dr). 310/476.6571, 800/HOTEL411; fax 310/471.6310. www.luxehotels.com

PACIFIC PALISADES

Now one of the most affluent communities in and around Los Angeles, with real estate values that have skyrocketed to supersonic levels, Pacific Palisades was founded in 1922 as a new Chautauqua by the Southern Conference of the Methodist Episcopal Church. Highlighted by a western border of oceanfront bluffs that frequently crumble down onto the Pacific Coast Highway, particularly after bad rainfalls, the Palisades boasts the highest median income of any area in the city of Los Angeles—we're talking big bucks here, folks. Film and television stars, moguls, mavens, and even some wannabes make up the majority of the residents, who pay a premium for the prestigious address and lifestyle. You would think that streets would be named after some of the famous Hollywood folk who live or lived here, but instead, many bear the names of Methodist Church bishops.

7 MOUNT SAINT MARY'S COLLEGE

The small, private liberal arts college sits atop a hill with one of the most beautiful views in the city. ♦ 12001 Chalon Rd (between Norman Pl and N Bundy Dr). 310/476.2237

Within Mount St. Mary's College:

CHAMBER MUSIC IN HISTORIC SITES

Among the annual attractions that make Los Angeles a mecca for music lovers is this series of concerts organized by Dr. Mary Ann Bonino for the Da Camera Society of Mount St. Mary's College. Many of the performances, by top groups and soloists, are held under the Tiffany glass dome of the **Doheny Mansion,** the society's home. But that's just for starters. The Bartok String Quartet has performed in Frank Lloyd Wright's Ennis-Brown House; Prague's Music da Camera in the Grand Salon of the *Queen Mary;* the New World Basset Horn Trio in a former Masonic lodge. ♦ 310/440.1351

8 WILL ROGERS STATE HISTORIC PARK

This 187-acre park was the home of cowboy/humorist/writer/performer Will Rogers between 1924 and 1935. Inside the house is memorabilia from his busy career. A nearby visitor's center sells "Rogersiana" and shows a 10-minute film on his life, narrated by friends and family. Rogers was an avid polo player, and his 900-by-300-foot polo field is the site of matches on the weekend year-round, weather permitting. The extensive grounds and the chaparral-covered hills invite hiking and picnicking. No barbecues are allowed. ♦ Free. Daily. 14253 Sunset Blvd (between Amalfi Dr and Rivas Canyon Rd). 310/454.8212

9 CLIFF MAY OFFICE

Cliff May, renowned master of the California ranch-style house, designed this wood-paneled studio in 1952. It is tucked into a corner lot on Sunset Boulevard near his residences on Riviera Ranch and Old Oak Roads. Immediately recognizable with their broad shingle roofs and stucco walls, most of the homes are partially visible through the foliage, with the exception of May's former residence, Mandalay, which is gated and hidden by plantings. ♦ 13151 Sunset Blvd (at Riviera Ranch Rd)

10 TEMPLE HOUSE

As a child, actress Shirley Temple lived with her parents in this delightful small-scale European farmhouse designed by **John Byers** and **Edla Muir** in 1936. It's a private residence. ♦ 231 N Rockingham Ave (between Sunset Blvd and Oakmont Dr)

11 MARIA'S CUCINA

★$ Standout pizza with a variety of toppings is the highlight of this mostly take-out place. ♦ Pizza/Takeout ♦ Daily. 11723 Barrington Ct (just south of S Barrington Ave). 310/476.6112

12 ST. MATTHEW'S EPISCOPAL CHURCH

Charles Moore of Moore Ruble Yudell worked closely with the parishioners when designing this replacement for a church destroyed by fire. The result is indisputably modern, but the subtle use of historic design elements, from Renaissance to California Craftsman, grounds the building in tradition. ♦ 1030 Bienveneda Ave (between Las Pulgas Rd and El Hito Cir). 310/454.1358

13 SELF-REALIZATION FELLOWSHIP LAKE SHRINE

Once a movie set, the open-air temple was founded in 1950 by followers of Paramah-ansa Yogananda. Ponds, lakes, waterfalls, windmills, and gazebos make this a pleasant place for walking or meditation. ♦ Tu-Su. 17190 Sunset Blvd (between Pacific Coast Hwy and Marquez Pl). 310/454.4114

14 GLADSTONE'S MALIBU

★★$ One of the best beachfront restaurants for a casual meal, this funky fish house offers alfresco picnic-style dining. Fish is the dish here—mahimahi, Fanny Bay oysters, Maine lobster, halibut—served with a huge salad. FYI: Cocktails here are legendary and desserts big and decadent. ♦ Seafood ♦ Daily, breakfast, lunch, and dinner. Reservations recommended. 17300 Pacific Coast Hwy (at Sunset Blvd). 310/454.3474. www.gladstones.com

15 GELSON'S MARKET

A cornucopia of fresh produce, specialty meat cuts, and exotica fills the shelves. ♦ Daily, until 10PM. 15424 Sunset Blvd (at Via de la Paz). 310/459.4483

15 TIVOLI CAFE

★$$ An upscale spot, this place offers designer pizzas, sandwiches, and tiramisù, along with daily specials. ♦ Italian ♦ Daily, lunch and dinner. 15306 Sunset Blvd (at Swarthmore Ave). 310/459.7685

16 MODO MIO CUCINA RUSTICA

★★$$ A little taste of Italy, tucked away on a side street, oozing with charm, reeking of garlic, and serving some of the best risotto, gnocchi, and cioppino this side of owner Rino Brigliadori's native country. ♦ Italian

♦ M-F, lunch and dinner; Sa, Su, dinner. Reservations recommended. 15200 Sunset Blvd (at La Cruz Dr). 310/459.0979

17 BRIDGES HOUSE

In 1989, **Robert Bridges** designed and engineered this woodsy three-level house/office atop concrete piers. It rises from a precipitous site 70 feet above the traffic on Sunset Boulevard. It's a private residence. ♦ 820 Chautauqua Blvd (between Sunset Blvd and Gallaudet Pl)

18 KAPPE HOUSE

The founder of the Southern California Institute of Architecture, **Raymond Kappe**, built this expansively scaled concrete-and-wood home for himself. It's a private residence. ♦ 715 Brooktree Rd (between Hightree Rd and Ranch La)

19 RUSTIC CANYON RECREATION CENTER

The quiet sylvan glade is perfect for picnics and barbecues. ♦ 601 Latimer Rd (between Hilltree and Brooktree Rds). Groups of more than 20 should call ahead: 310/454.5734

20 UPLIFTERS CLUB CABINS

In the early 1920s, an offshoot group of the Los Angeles Athletic Club (L. Frank Baum, author of the *Wizard of Oz* books, was one member of this splinter group) built cottages in the hills of the Pacific Palisades. Many of the residences were log cabins, but some were intended as stage sets. They are now private residences. ♦ Nos. 1, 3, 18 Latimer Rd (just north of Upper Mesa Rd); nos. 31, 32, 34, 38 Haldeman Rd (between Latimer and Brooktree Rds)

21 CHANNEL ROAD INN

$ A bit off the beaten track (but not too far, and worth the trip), this small, luxurious inn oozes charm, and the price is right. Designed in 1910 by **Frank Kegley** as the home of oil magnate Thomas McCall and his family, the Colonial Revival–style structure still features many of its original characteristics, including stately fireplaces, birch wood floors, and cream-colored walls. The public areas are plush and comfortable, with furniture upholstered in pastel silks and lavender-accented Oriental carpeting, and each of the 14 rooms (two with Jacuzzis) and suites is attractively decorated with an antique four-poster bed and lace bedspread or Amish quilt. All rooms have private baths; two suites feature fireplaces. The rate includes a continental breakfast and afternoon refreshments such as wine and cheese.

♦ 219 W Channel Rd (between E Rustic Rd and Chautauqua Blvd). 310/459.1920. www.channelroadinn.com &

22 MARIX TEX MEX PLAYA

★$$ This branch of the rambunctious West Hollywood restaurant offers the usual Southwestern/Mexican-style fare, from nachos and tostadas to chili rellenos and *mas*, all easily washed down with some of the best margaritas mixed north of the border. ♦ Tex-Mex ♦ Daily, lunch and dinner. 118 Entrada Dr (between Ocean Way and Pacific Coast Hwy). 310/459.8596

BRENTWOOD

hic, casual, and countrified, this section of town is opulated with stucco and clapboard cottages and uge, sprawling mansions.

an Vicente Boulevard is Brentwood's main drag. he attractive, coral tree–shaded street is popular with joggers, walkers, and cyclists. The roads that ind up into the hills have an even more rustic feel. Most of the activity centers around the sleek, nultistory **Brentwood Gardens complex** with its igh-end fashion boutiques and patio dining at the California Pizza Kitchen (310/826.3573). Across he street is an outdoor mall, **Brentwood Town & Country,** home to **Flowers with Love** 310/207.3075), a petite but colorful floral stand.

23 BRENTWOOD COUNTRY MART

This red barn houses a post office and more than 26 shops, including an espresso bar and a fresh juice bar. Standouts include the **Brentwood Camera Shop** (310/394.0256), **Hansel 'n Gretel,** for really adorable clothing and stuff for kids (310/394.2619), **Loupilou** for adult clothing (310/394.4118), and **Shokos,** where you can pick up gorgeous floral arrangements or flowers (310/394.1856). This is a favorite shopping spot for local celebrity residents. ♦ 26th St and San Vicente Blvd. 310/395.6714

24 DUTTON'S BOOKSTORE

Saved by the bell, this landmark bookstore almost saw extinction, but influential locals made enough of a stink to keep it running. Music and the humanities are the strong suits here, but there's a good choice of new and used books in every major field, plus CDs and tapes, readings, and book signings. The service is expert and friendly. ♦ Daily; M-F until 9PM. 11975 San Vicente Blvd (near S Bundy Dr). 310/476.6263. Also at 5146 Laurel Canyon Blvd (between Hartsook St and Magnolia Blvd) San Fernando Valley. 818/769.3866; 3806 W

Magnolia Blvd (at Screenland Dr), Burbank. 818/840.8003

25 DAILY GRILL

★★$$ Sibling of **The Grill** in Beverly Hills (see page 106), this place is located upstairs in an upmarket mall. The mood is fun and the food dependable. Chicken potpie, Cobb salad, great onion rings, french fries, and rice-pudding pie are favorite choices. ♦ American ♦ Daily, lunch and dinner. 11677 San Vicente Blvd (near S Barrington Ave). 310/442.0044

25 CORAL TREE CAFÉ

★★★$$ What a great getaway, smack in the heart of town. Impeccably prepared and tasty organic food is dished out in an adorable cottage-like environment packed with locals and celebrity regulars (we sat right across from Dustin Hoffman). Only hitch is you have to stand in line to order your soups (the French onion is topped with gobs of delicious cheese), sandwiches (stuffed with egg or chicken salad), salads (a Greek salmon salad was wonderful), and amazing coffees and desserts. ♦ Café ♦ Daily, breakfast, lunch, and dinner. 11645 San Vicente Blvd (near S Barrington Ave). 310/979.8733. www.coraltreecafe.net

26 TOSCANA

★★★$$ Splendid rustic food is served in a bright, modern restaurant that hums with a crowd of satisfied diners at lunch and dinner. Standouts from chef Pietro Topputo's menu include pizzas and perfect risottos, a variety of grilled meats including an authentic *battuta al rosmarino* (pounded tenderloin with rosemary and garlic), and *salmone alla rugola* (poached salmon with arugula, lemon, and extra-virgin olive oil). In season, fresh porcini mushrooms are served with the grilled items. There's a marvelous list of wines by the glass or bottle to enhance the meal. For dessert, the tiramisù is unbeatable. ♦ Italian ♦ M-Sa, lunch and dinner; Su, dinner. Reservations recommended. 11633 San Vicente Blvd (near S Barrington Ave). 310/820.2448

T O S C A N A

27 SAWTELLE VETERANS' CHAPEL

This picturesque white gingerbread chapel was designed by **J. Lee Burton** at the turn of the century. It's part of the Sawtelle Veterans' Hospital complex, one of the first veterans' facilities opened in the US after the Civil War. ♦ Wilshire Blvd and Bonsall Ave

---

Restaurants/Clubs: Red | Hotels: Purple | Shops: Orange | Outdoors/Parks: Green | Sights/Culture: Blue

27 WADSWORTH THEATER

Located near the Veterans' Chapel, the auditorium is used by UCLA for chamber music, plays, and special film screenings. Free jazz concerts are offered on the first Sunday of the month; call for details. ◆ Eisenhower Ave (near Bonsall Ave). 310/825.2101

28 VINCENTI RISTORANTE

★★★$$ Chef Gino Angelini creates show-stopping dishes such as *strozzaprette* (handmade pasta spirals) in a spicy lobster sauce, blackened red snapper, and tripe simmered in tomato with Parmesan flan. The ambience is contemporary yet old world, with a sleek marble bar, burnished aubergine walls, and rounded booths. ◆ Italian ◆ Tu-Th, Sa, Su, dinner; F, lunch and dinner. Reservations recommended. 11930 San Vicente Blvd (between Montana Ave and S Bundy Dr). 310/207.0127 &

28 PECORINO

★★★$$$ Next door to Vincenti and equally good, this neighborhood eatery, named after an Italian sheep's milk cheese, oozes with old-world ambience. Exposed brick walls, chandeliers, ironwork, and an open kitchen combined with nice touches like top-of-the-line olive oil and thick crusty bread, add to its charm. The food is wonderful, from luscious, thin-sliced carpaccio to pasta with clams and stuffed veal chops. In between you can savor salads prepared with crispy greens and ripe tomatoes (we hate it when they aren't ripe), bruschettas, and a braised beef served with mashed potatoes. Yummy dessert choices include crème brûlée, tiramisù, a warm pear gratin, and more. ◆ Italian ◆ M-Sa, lunch and dinner. Reservations required. 11604 San Vicente Blvd. 310/571.3800, www.pecorinorestaurant.com

29 GAUCHO GRILL

★$ This meat-eaters' haven in waistline-conscious Brentwood is similar to its Hollywood sister. The great take-out menu features Argentinean-style ribs designed for 2 or 10. ◆ Argentinean ◆ Daily, lunch and dinner. 11754 San Vicente Blvd (at Gorham Ave). 310/447.7898

30 BERTY'S

★$$ Try the blue-crab ravioli and a grilled veal chop before moving on to a tempting dessert. This restaurant is casual, with a cool, tranquil environment. ◆ California ◆ M-F, lunch and dinner; Sa, dinner. Reservations recommended on weekends. 11712 San Vicente Blvd (at S Barrington Ave). 310/207.6169

30 CHIN CHIN

★★$ Brent Saville designed this offshoot of the popular café on Sunset Strip. Dim sum and other light Chinese dishes are served in a bright tiled room and on a handsome roof terrace with large white umbrellas. ◆ Chinese ◆ Daily, lunch and dinner. 11740 San Vicente Blvd (at Gorham Ave). 310/826.2525. Also at several southland locations, including 8618 Sunset Blvd (between Alta Loma Rd and Palm Ave), West Hollywood. 310/652.1818; 12215 Ventura Blvd (between Laurel Canyon Blvd and Laurelgrove Ave), San Fernando Valley. 818/985.9090; 13455 Maxella Ave (at De Rey Ave), Marina del Rey. 310/823.9999

31 NEW YORK BAGEL COMPANY

★$ To the delight of his friends and bagel aficionados, ex–New Yorker Dave Rosen brought his bagel business to the sunnier pastures of Los Angeles. Slap everything from cream cheese and lox to fruit jams on 11 varieties of the ringed rolls, including cinnamon raisin, pumpernickel, garlic, and sesame. Rosen's old friend, master architect **Frank Gehry,** created a design for this deli/diner (located in the Brentwood Town & Country outdoor mall) that reminds patrons the best bagels come from the Big Apple: A 33-foot-long replica of the Chrysler Building floats over the high-ceilinged structure like an armored zeppelin. ◆ Deli ◆ Daily, breakfast and lunch. 11640 San Vicente Blvd (near S Barrington Ave). 310/820.1050

32 INDIA'S OVEN

★★$$ Great tandoori chicken and curries are served in a posh second-floor restaurant. ◆ Indian ◆ Daily, lunch and dinner. 11645 Wilshire Blvd (between S Barrington and Federal Aves). 310/207.5522

WESTWOOD AREA

33 TISCHLER HOUSE

This geometrically sculptured house was designed by **Rudolph Schindler** in 1949; the private residence was one of the architect's last and most successful works. ◆ 175 Greenfield Ave (between Cashmere St and Sunset Blvd)

34 UNIVERSITY OF CALIFORNIA AT LOS ANGELES (UCLA)

This world-renowned university has grown to be a city within the city. It was established in 1919 as the University of California's "Southern Branch," a small two-year college

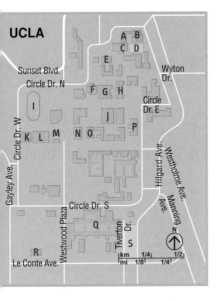

UCLA

Sunset Blvd.
Circle Dr. N
Wyton Dr.
Circle Dr. E
Gayley Ave.
Circle Dr. W
Hilgard Ave.
Westholme Ave.
Manning Ave.
Circle Dr. S
Westwood Plaza
Tiverton Dr.
Le Conte Ave.

km 1/4 1/2
mi 1/8 1/4

The fledgling institution grew rapidly, and in 1929 moved to Westwood. Today, UCLA has the largest enrollment (37,600 students) of the nine University of California campuses. The first four buildings—Italian Romanesque brick palazzos laid out around a grassy quadrangle known as the **Royal Quad**—remain the best. The 419-acre campus is beautifully landscaped, with plenty of paths for walking, jogging, or quiet reverie. Many of the departments and professional schools have exceptional reputations, including chemistry, earth and space sciences, philosophy, linguistics, history, medicine, law, the John E. Anderson Graduate School of Management, and theater, film, and television. Library holdings total more than 6.1 million volumes—among the world's largest.

The best way to get to the campus is by bicycle or shuttle bus; cars are restricted to a few ring roads. Local authorities have covered the area with meters and created ordinances that restrict parking, often by permit only. RTD, Santa Monica, and Culver City bus lines have direct routes to UCLA.

Free **Campus Express buses** circulate from Westwood Village through the campus every five minutes on weekdays. Limited parking is available in campus structures; access tokens are sold at the information kiosks on Westwood and Sunset Boulevards and Hilgard Avenue. ◆ 405 Hilgard Ave (between Le Conte Ave and

Sunset Blvd). 310/825.4321. www.UCLA.edu/resources.html

Within the University of California at Los Angeles (the letters preceding the following entries refer to the map above):

34 UCLA–WESTWOOD CENTER

Restored and refurbished in the 1960s by A. Quincy Jones, this pleasant compound houses a theater and a second-floor photographic exhibit chronicling the history of Westwood Village. ◆ Exhibit hours: Daily. 10886 Le Conte Ave (between Tiverton Ave and Westwood Blvd). 310/208.4108

A UCLA WIGHT ART GALLERY

A vital, innovative force within the Southern California art community, the gallery is located within the **Dickson Art Center.** It encompasses exhibition galleries as well as the **Grunwald Center for the Graphic Arts** and the **Franklin Murphy Sculpture Garden.** Exhibitions are complemented by a wide range of programs, including lectures, tours, educational workshops, and publications. The museum shop sells books, posters, jewelry, and crafts. ◆ Free. Grunwald Center: Open by appointment. Wight Art Gallery: Tu-Su. Docent tours: Sa, Su, 1:30PM or by appointment. 310/825.3281

B UCLA FILM AND TELEVISION ARCHIVE

Screenings of more than 500 films a year are a major activity in the former Melnitz Hall, dedicated to the preservation, study, and exhibition of the moving image. In addition, the archive presents major retrospectives, festivals, tributes, and documentaries. The **Archive Research and Study Center** (310/206.5388), located in Powell Library, makes available to the UCLA community and general public on-site viewing of archival material for research purposes. ◆ Information about public screenings: 310/206.8013

C UNIVERSITY RESEARCH LIBRARY

Designed by **A. Quincy Jones** in 1964, this library houses a superb reference collection. It's open to the public for reading; loans are available to the university community and library card purchasers. Exhibitions of literary material from the Department of Special Collections are displayed on the first floor. ◆ For hours, call 310/825.8301. Reference desk 310/825.1323

Restaurants/Clubs: **Red** | Hotels: **Purple** | Shops: **Orange** | Outdoors/Parks: **Green** | Sights/Culture: **Blue**

D Franklin Murphy Sculpture Garden

This idyllic five-acre greensward looks its best when the jacaranda trees bloom in April. Major works by Jean Arp, Henri Matisse, Joan Miró, Henry Moore, Auguste Rodin, David Smith, Francisco Zuniga, and others are here.

E North Campus Student Center

This popular campus dining spot offers the same low prices as all UCLA restaurant facilities. ♦ M-Sa. 310/206.0720

F Fowler Museum of Cultural History

The three-story museum houses one of the nation's leading collections of African, Oceanic, and American Indian art and cultural artifacts, with more than 750,000 pieces in all. There are also four exhibition galleries, an amphitheater, a museum store, and a library. ♦ Free. W-Su. 310/825.4361

G Royce Hall

Designed by **Allison & Allison** in 1919, this is part of the original quadrangle, with classrooms, offices, and an auditorium that is a year-round venue for big-name artists and professional music, dance, and theatrical presentations. ♦ UCLA Central Ticket Office 310/825.2101

H Haines Hall

This 1928 building, also one of the original buildings on the quadrangle, houses classrooms.

I Drake Stadium

The track-and-field stadium seats 11,000. ♦ Event information 310/825.4546

J Powell Library

Located here is the college library, which houses the undergraduate collection. The rotunda and grand staircase of the 1928 building are notable. ♦ Reference desk 310/825.1938

K LA Tennis Center

Built for the 1984 Summer Olympics, the center is the current home of the annual Volvo Tennis/Los Angeles Men's Tournament. ♦ Event information 310/825.5995

L Pauley Pavilion

Welton Becket & Associates designed this 1965 home of the UCLA Bruins women's and men's basketball teams. Concerts, cultural events, gymnastic meets, and volleyball games are also held. ♦ UCLA Central Ticket Office 310/825.2101, 310/825.4546

M UCLA Athletics Hall of Fame

A two-story display of trophies, photos, and memorabilia relating to the UCLA athletic tradition is located in the J.D. Morgan Intercollegiate Athletics Center. ♦ M-F. 310/825.8699

N Ackerman Student Union

A bustling center of campus activity, the union houses the **Student's Store** and the **Treehouse Restaurant.** Actually several restaurants in one, the eatery has fresh fruit and salads and a full meal section, all at very low prices. The store on the first floor carries a fine selection of academic books, with a full range of UCLA insignia merchandise in the "Bearwear" department. ♦ For hours, call 310/825.7711

O Kerckhoff Hall

Student activity offices and a moderately priced coffeehouse are located here. ♦ Coffeehouse, daily. 310/206.0729

P Schoenberg Hall

The hall is named for the Austrian composer **Arnold Schoenberg,** who was a professor of music at UCLA from 1936 to 1951. The departments of music, musicology, ethnomusicology, and systematic musicology are located here, as well as the **Schoenberg Auditorium** and the **Jan Popper Theater**. ♦ UCLA Central Ticket Office 310/825.2101

Q Center for Health Sciences

The entire southern end of the campus is occupied by one of the largest medical complexes in the nation. The UCLA Hospital and Clinics, also in the center, operates a 24-hour emergency room, which is reached via an entrance at Tiverton Dr and Le Conte Ave. ♦ Emergency 310/825.2111, physicians referral: 800/825.2631

R Visitors' Center

Walking tours depart from Room 1417 of the Ueberroth Building on weekdays at 10:30AM and 1:30PM. Free maps in English, Japanese, Spanish, and French are available there. ♦ M-F. 10945 Le Conte Ave (between Westwood Plaza and Gayley Ave). 310/825.4321, group tour information 310/825.8764

S Mathias Botanical Gardens

This eight-acre shaded canyon was planted to create a peaceful, woodsy retreat with mature specimens of unusual size. There are no restroom facilities. ◆ Free. Daily. Tiverton Dr (north of Le Conte Ave). 310/825.3620

35 STRATHMORE APARTMENTS

When **Richard Neutra**'s modern bungalow court rose from a then-empty hillside in 1937, its stark lines attracted such tenants as Orson Welles, Charles and Ray Eames, Clifford Odets, and Luise Rainer. A private residence, it remains one of the best preserved of several Neutra apartment buildings in and around the village. ◆ 11005 Strathmore Dr (at Glenrock Ave)

36 BEVERLY HILLS PLAZA HOTEL

$$$ This low-key, reliable hotel in a converted apartment building has a homey feeling that makes it popular with guests on extended visits. Each of the 116 suites has a living room, dining area, kitchen, and one or more bedrooms. After sightseeing, take a dip in the pool. The restaurant features steak, pastas, seafood, and salads. ◆ 10300 Wilshire Blvd (at Comstock Ave). 310/275.5575, 800/800.1234; fax 310/278.3325. www.placestostay.com &

37 MANN'S VILLAGE THEATRE

This marvelous 1931 Spanish Moderne tower still dominates the village. Architect **P.O. Lewis** designed the gleaming white-stucco moldings, porte cochere with freestanding box office, and golden flourishes within. Fox Studios built a chain of Spanish theaters before the Depression put them out of business; the Deco "FOX" sign that crowns the tower has been refurbished and relit, and today the theater shows first-run films. ◆ 961 Broxton Ave (at Weyburn Ave). 310/208.5576

38 MANN'S BRUIN THEATRE

Denoted by a sensuously curved and neon-lit marquee, this streamlined 1937 movie house carries the design signature of architect **S. Charles Lee**. ◆ 948 Broxton Ave (at Weyburn Ave). 310/208.8998

39 GEFFEN PLAYHOUSE

A $17 million face-lift transformed this little theater into a major player with dramatic improvements that include wider, more comfortable, roomier seats, improved sight lines that provide great views of the stage no matter where you sit, and even upgraded rest rooms. The facility sports two stages: the 522-seat **Geffen Main Theater** and the 117-seat **Audrey Skirball Kenis Theater,** where intimate readings and eclectic programming are offered. The main auditorium is designed for easy accessibility to the physically challenged, allowing patrons to enter directly from the lobby without the need to climb stairs. Great theater happens here with productions such as *Cat on a Hot Tin Roof* starring John Goodman, *Third* starring Christine Lahti, *The Female of the Species* featuring Annette Bening, and special Geffen-commissioned plays. ◆ 10886 Le Conte Ave (between Westwood Blvd and Tiverton Ave), Westwood. 310/208.5454. www.geffenplayhouse.com

40 MYSTERY BOOK STORE

This intriguing bookshop attracts fans of spies, sleuths, gumshoes, and all sorts of unsavory sorts. ◆ Daily. 1036 C Broxton Ave (between Kinross and Weyburn Aves). 310/659.2959, 800/821.9017. www.mystery-bookstore.com. For orders: orders@mystery-bookstore.com &

41 BEL AIR CAMERA

This 45-year-old shop offers a wide range of photo, audio, and video equipment at competitive prices, with expert service. ◆ Daily. 10925 Kinross Ave (at Gayley Ave). 310/208.5150

42 HILGARD HOUSE HOTEL

$$ The elegant, 47-room hotel is located a few minutes from the village and UCLA. Complimentary continental breakfast is served. ◆ 927 Hilgard Ave (between Weyburn and Le Conte Aves). 310/208.3945, 800/826.3934; fax 310/208.1972

43 W LOS ANGELES– WESTWOOD HOTEL

$$$$ Wow! Re-styled in 2007, this youth market–driven 258-suite hotel is sleeker and sexier than ever. Designed by New York–based Thom Filicia and the W Design team, rooms resemble bodacious bungalows done in faux bois wallpaper and dark graphic carpet, with charcoal-colored doors and honeycomb peek-a-boo windows connecting the bedroom to the bathroom. All are appointed with Eames chairs, techno tools, sharp-lined white and tan custom-made furniture, bliss spa products, and of course the perfunctory plasma-screen TVs and DVD/CD players. Extra comforts include pillow-top mattresses, feather beds, 350-count linens, minibars, oversized desks, and Whatever/Whenever service that claims no request goes unfulfilled. Lots of "wow" factors prevail, like **The Backyard** (★★$$), a casual poolside restaurant, serving Mediterranean fare for lunch and dinner, and a

---

Restaurants/Clubs: Red | Hotels: Purple | Shops: Orange | Outdoors/Parks: Green | Sights/Culture: Blue

whimsical bonfire—a cluster of mini fire-pits with s'more-making stations and signature drinks—where picnics, movie screenings, game nights, and fashion shows are staged on various nights. The attractive indoor eatery **NineThirty** (★★$$$) serves "farm to table" seasonal American cuisine daily for breakfast, lunch, and dinner. **The Whiskey Blue Bar,** designed like an exotic or possibly "erotic" Polynesian hideaway, features a special VIP room filled with four-poster beds and seductive murals on the wall. They literally pamper your pants off at the 7,000-square-foot spa imported from New York called **bliss,** with head-to-toe treatments and quirky touches like movies-while-you-manicure nail stations and a brownie buffet. There's also the **Sweat,** an energized fitness center equipped with every essential. Heightening the seductive vibes is a sensuous pool area with intelliChaises, where you can order food and drinks or get your wireless fix without getting up; cabanas equipped with flat-screen TVs, DVD players, and daybeds; and glass lanterns to enhance the mood at night. Additional amenities include meeting rooms, valet parking, and concierge service. ♦ 930 Hilgard Ave (between Weyburn and Le Conte Aves). 310/208.8765, 800/421.2317, 888/627.7135; fax 310/824.0355; 877-WHOTELS. www.whotels.com &

44 TANINO RISTORANTE BAR

★★★$$ From the Italianate Renaissance arches above the sidewalk café to the original 1920s interior design (modeled after the Pitti Palace in Florence), it doesn't get more Italian than this. A bustling bar sets the mood for a festive feast of chef/owner Tanino Drago's culinary delights. Begin with a fantastic antipasto and/or soup such as *pappa al pomodoro* (thick bread and tomato soup) and continue on with *pasta incaciata* (penne with beef ragu, peas, boiled eggs, and provolone cheese, baked in an eggplant dome), risotto with squid ink and calamari, roasted leg of veal with polenta, or lamb shank osso buco. Then, for a grand finale, a tiramisù, *torta al cioccolato* (flourless chocolate cake with raspberry sauce), or panna cotta—all equally delicious. ♦ Italian ♦ Daily, dinner; M-F, lunch. Reservations suggested. 1043 Westwood Blvd (between Kinross and Weyburn Aves). 310/208.0444; fax 310/208.2344. www.tanino.com &

44 YAMATO WESTWOOD

Much to our dismay, Eurochow closed its doors in 2007. It will reopen as Yamato Westwood. The creation of Ken Oyadomari, president of Yamato Enterprises, LLC, the menu will offer classical Japanese cuisine in a room designed by New York–based YT Design that among other touches—like 30-foot ceilings, natural wood chairs and benches, ebony tabletops, and ground-floor and mezzanine dining rooms—will house a Sake Wall. Daily, dinner. Reservations recommended. 1099 Westwood Blvd (at Kinross Ave). 310/209.0066

45 GARDENS ON GLENDON

★★$$ This popular, savvy restaurant is set in a Spanish-style brick rotunda. The hamburgers, salmon tartare, pizzas, salads, and grills justify the high prices. ♦ California ♦ Tu-Su, lunch; daily, dinner. Reservations recommended. 1139 Glendon Ave (at Lindbrook Dr). 310/824.1818 www.opentable.com

45 NAPA VALLEY GRILLE

★★$$ Wine and food is what this place is all about. Seasonal products are paired with one of the 700 wines carefully chosen from the vast wine cellar. Signature dishes include ahi tuna tartare, grilled Maine scallops, short ribs, and cioppino. Dessert offerings include brown butter Margo blueberry tart and chocolate torte. Designed by Bay Area architect Mark Stevens, the sprawling restaurant is inviting in warm earth tones and rough-hewn materials, accented by a life-size hand-painted mural of the Napa Valley in springtime. Two fireplaces keep the room warm on cool winter nights and an attractive garden is welcoming for warm-weather alfresco dining. ♦ California ♦ Reservations recommended. M-F, lunch; daily, dinner. 1100 Glendon Ave (one block north of Wilshire Blvd at the corner of Tiverton). 310/824.3322; fax 310/824.3232. www.napavalleygrille.com

46 THE TOWER

This striped marble concoction was designed in 1988 by the meister of slick, **Helmut Jahn.** Its pretentiousness is all the more obvious amid the mediocrity of Westwood's high-rises. ♦ 10940 Wilshire Blvd (at Midvale Ave)

47 UCLA HAMMER MUSEUM AND CULTURAL CENTER

The late chairman of Occidental Petroleum broke a pledge to donate his art to the Los Angeles County Museum of Art (LACMA) in order to build this monument, which squats beneath his corporate tower. Designed by **Edward Larrabee Barnes,** the museum opened in 1990, shortly after Hammer's death. The basic concept of this museum is to promote and interpret the works of underrepresented, up-and-coming artists. It is also a showcase for the **Armand Hammer Collection** of Old Master, Impressionist, and

Post-Impressionist paintings, such as the works of Mary Cassatt, Claude Monet, Pissarro, Rembrandt, and Vincent van Gogh. The **Contemporaries Collection** highlights the painting, sculpture, and lithography of 19th-century French satirist Honoré Daumier and his peers. There's also the must-see **Franklin D. Murphy Sculpture Gardens,** an outdoor collection spread out on five acres of land at the northern end of UCLA's campus, showcasing such greats as Jean Arp, Isamu Noguchi, and Auguste Rodin. A recent $25 million enhancement added features such as an auditorium with TV and movie archives, a courtyard bookstore, a Great Hall lecture area for educational programs, a café/restaurant/coffee bar, and a new entrance on Lindbrook that provides better accessibility for the physically challenged. Thanks to a $5 million donation by Audrey L. Wilder, widow of famed director/writer Billy Wilder, the museum now sports a 288-seat theater named after her husband, who died in 2002 at the age of 95. ♦ Tu-Su. 10899 Wilshire Blvd (at Westwood Blvd). 310/443.7020; fax 310/443.7099. www.hammer.ucla.educ ♿

48 PALOMINO

★★$$$ This eclectic urban eatery was a hit the minute it opened. The mood is friendly and the décor a blend of rare African quartered Sapele veneers, sliced mahogany, and broken-stripe Makore veneer accented by Spanish Roo Alicante marble floors and countertops and Italian Vagli Calicatta Roas bar tabletops. Gorgeous hand-blown chandeliers and pendant lamps by artist Martin Blan and reproductions of Expressionist wall art by Northwest artists Kevin Koch and Shawn Hair complete the leitmotif. The food may seem almost a secondary consideration, but it isn't. Everything's quite tasty, especially signature dishes like rotisserie chicken, applewood-grilled wild Alaskan halibut, and oven-roasted garlic prawns. The seafood sampler (salmon, scallops, and prawns with sun-dried tomato risotto and raspberry vinaigrette), paella, and rotisserie pork loin are also winners. ♦ American/Southern European Bistro ♦ Reservations suggested. M-F, lunch; daily, dinner. Valet parking. 10877 Wilshire Blvd (corner of Glendon Ave). 310/208.1960; fax 310/208.3366. www.palomino-euro-bistro.com ♿

49 WESTWOOD MEMORIAL CEMETERY

ⓟ The graves of Marilyn Monroe, Natalie Wood, and Buddy Rich are tucked away behind the Avco Center movie houses. ♦ Daily. 1218

Glendon Ave (between Wellworth Ave and Wilshire Blvd). 310/474.1579

50 CENTURY WILSHIRE HOTEL & SUITES

$$ This 99-room hotel is the perfect budget-saver with its pretty garden patio, outdoor pool, and free parking. Most units have fully equipped kitchens. ♦ 10776 Wilshire Blvd (between Selby and Malcolm Aves). 310/474.4506, 800/421.7223; fax 310/474.2535. www.centurywilshirehotel.com

51 BEL AIR CAVIAR MERCHANT

This roe shop sells 15 varieties of caviar packaged to go or to ship anywhere in the country. ♦ W, Th, F. 10423 Santa Monica Blvd (between S Beverly Glen Blvd and Pandora Ave). 310/474.9518

52 LA BRUSCHETTA

★★★$$ The elegant service and décor here are as savory as the excellent Northern Italian cuisine. The portions are hearty, and there's a very enticing wine list. Recommended are the osso buco (veal shank), roasted squab, and any pasta dish. ♦ Italian ♦ M-F, lunch and dinner; Sa, dinner. 1621 Westwood Blvd (between Massachusetts and Ohio Aves). 310/477.1052 ♿

53 SHAMSHIRY

★$ The setting may be bare-bones, but this popular family restaurant serves huge portions of shish kebab, chicken faisanjan (braised in pomegranate sauce), and pilaf. ♦ Persian ♦ Daily, lunch and dinner. 1712 Westwood Blvd (between Santa Monica Blvd and Massachusetts Ave). 310/474.1410

54 MORMON TEMPLE

Designed by **Edward Anderson** in 1955, this is the largest temple of the Church of Jesus Christ of Latter Day Saints outside of Salt Lake City. The 257-foot tower crowned with a 15-foot gold-leaf statue of the angel Moroni is a familiar landmark on the LA skyline. It's open only to church members, but visitors may tour the grounds and the Visitor Information Center. ♦ Daily until 9PM. 10777 Santa Monica Blvd (between Manning and Selby Aves). 310/474.1549

55 LA CACHETTE

★★★$$$$ An uptown clientele frequents this charming Provençal bistro, where chef/owner Jean François Meteigner's amazing cuisine is showcased in a romantic setting of yellow walls adorned with Impressionist paintings and pale yellow fabrics, banquettes

---

Restaurants/Clubs: Red | Hotels: Purple | Shops: Orange | Outdoors/Parks: Green | Sights/Culture: Blue

upholstered in Pierre Deux cloths, taffeta window coverings, cedar paneling, and wood beams. A stunning handcrafted blue glass bar with matching cocktail tables provides the centerpiece of the room. Do be sure to take a look at the maître d' station. Designed by Meteigner and created by woodcarvers Enkeboll Design of Culver City, six panels depict the life of wine. All and all it's the food that counts, and the chef outdoes himself with delicious renditions of just about anything on the menu. Some fave raves include his napoleon of sautéed foie gras; foie gras terrine with rhubarb and strawberry chutney and orange sauce; spicy ahi tuna tartare flavored with Korean chili paste, served with a crispy potato waffle; Maine lobster salad served warm; white Peking duck done two ways; bouillabaisse, and any fresh fish du jour. For a delightfully different lunch, try the scrambled eggs wrapped in smoked salmon or the smoked whitefish salad. Meteigner adds specials daily and seasonally. Desserts are also divine, especially the tarts, soufflés, and baked chocolate mousse. ♦ French ♦ M-F, lunch and dinner; Sa, Su, dinner. Reservations a must. Valet parking mandatory. 10506 Santa Monica Blvd S (between Thayer and Fairburn Aves). 310/470.4992; fax 310/470.7451. www.lacachetterestaurant.com

56 LA BOTTEGA

★★$ Stop for a bite at this deli/restaurant before or after an art film at the neighboring Nuart or Royal Theaters. The extensive menu features everything from great antipasti to homemade pasta and pizzas, sandwiches, and heartier fare. The risotto *pescatore* with calamari, shrimp, clams, and mussels in a red sauce is a winner. ♦ Italian ♦ Daily, lunch and dinner. 11363 Santa Monica Blvd (at Purdue Ave). 310/477.7777

56 THE ISLE OF CALIFORNIA

The much-faded classic mural, created in the late 1960s by the LA Fine Arts Squad, shows the rugged Arizona coastline after the "Big One" has sent California off into the Pacific. ♦ Santa Monica Blvd and Butler Ave

57 NOOK

★★★$$ Hidden away in a tiny nondescript minimall, this little gem is difficult to find but well worth the effort. The tiny room seats only 30 people in an attractive space under an exposed beam and ductwork ceiling, with polished concrete flooring and cylindrical light fixtures hanging from above. There's a communal table in the center for large groups, one intimate booth, a row of banquettes, and an attractive bar where you can eat and drink. It really belongs in a more accessible location. Nevertheless, the bistro-like cuisine will make your palate sing. The Caesar salad rivals any prepared in fancier establishments, the soups (such as house-made lentil vegetable with feta and lemon mint) are rich and hearty, and the entrées, including maple mustard–glazed rib eye, grilled flatiron steak, and Oregon tilapia, are delicious. You don't have to eat large, either: You can have a burger with Gruyère cheese, a bowl of brown rice with sautéed tofu or chicken, or even a catfish burrito. The waitstaff is exceptional. Desserts are chocolate-centric and yummy, and the coffee is wonderfully rich. ♦ American Bistro ♦ M-F, lunch and dinner; Sa, dinner. 11628 Santa Monica Blvd (between Federal and Barry Aves). 310/207.5160; fax 310/207.5220. www.nookbistro.com

58 JAVAN

★$ This Persian restaurant has a crisp black-and-white interior and delicious offbeat dishes. Specials have included *zereshk polo* (chicken with rice pilaf flavored with dried barberries), *gheymeh* (lamb shank with split yellow peas), and steamed spinach with tart yogurt. Baklava is the dessert of choice. ♦ Persian ♦ Daily lunch and dinner. 11500 Santa Monica Blvd (between Federal and Butler Aves). 310/207.5555

59 NUART THEATER

One of LA's last surviving movie repertory houses, this theater shows adventurous new work, theme series, classics, and camp favorites. Notice the fine streamline neon marquee. ♦ 11272 Santa Monica Blvd (at Sawtelle Blvd). 310/478.6379

60 THE SPORTS CLUB LA

This acropolis of fitness is typically filled with an all-star cast of body-conscious celebrities such as Dyan Cannon, Linda Fiorentino, Marisa Tomei, Dennis Rodman, Diana Ross, Justin Timberlake, Katie Holmes, Sarah Michelle Geller, Adam Sandler, Jennifer Garner, plus many directors, screenwriters, and more. Famous and trendy, the lavish body-buffing emporium offers yoga and exercise classes, carpeted aerobics rooms, and locker rooms with steam baths, saunas, whirlpools, towels, toiletries, and lots of telephones. Personal trainers are available for a fee. Scripts are pored over, big movie deals are made, and singles meet at the bar or one of the two power restaurants. There's not only valet parking, but you can have your car washed, waxed, and/or detailed while you

THE BEST

Steve Wallace

Founder/Owner Wally's Wine & Spirits, philanthropist/general partner in the Food Company's Broadway Deli, Capo and Cora's Coffee Shoppe, Brentwood Restaurant & Lounge, and BrassCap American Brasserie

Being a native of Los Angeles, I love the **Hollywood Bowl.** It is a magical experience attending a concert under the stars with a nice picnic and bottle of good wine.

I like to take a day off and fish the backside of **Catalina Island** for Calico bass and sand dabs.

Playing Texas hold 'em no limit poker at the **Commerce Club.**

On a sunny California day, I like to ride my motorcycle to the rock store on Mulholland Highway.

Eating at **Phillips BBQ.** Walking along old Malibu Road and stopping in **Wylies Bait Shop** on Pacific Coast Highway.

Strolling around the gorgeous grounds of the **Hotel Bel-Air** and having breakfast on the patio.

---

work out. Now a thriving chain, Sports Club LA is expanding faster than Rambo's biceps, with reciprocal memberships available in New York, Washington DC, San Francisco, Orange County, Miami, and Boston. ◆ Daily. 1835 S Sepulveda Blvd (between Missouri and Nebraska Aves). 310/473.1447. Also in Beverly Hills at 9601 Wilshire Blvd (at Camden Dr). 310/888.8100. www.thesportsclub.LA.com

61 WALLY'S LIQUOR AND GOURMET FOODS

Within this high-tech California redwood store is the best in food and wine, including boutique vineyard labels unavailable elsewhere, and a cheese department that includes buffalo mozzarella, California goat cheese, pizzas, and chili dogs. The ever-present owner, Steve Wallace, is an expert on California wines. ◆ Daily. 2107 Westwood Blvd (between W Olympic Blvd and Mississippi Ave). 310/475.0606, 888/9.WALLYS. www.wallywine.com

62 KOUTOUBIA

★★$$$ Named for a famous mosque in Marrakesh, this tent, with its hassocks and low brass tables, is a showcase of the cuisine of the Magreb. Chef/owner Michael Ohayon is a master of couscous and *tajines* (well-done lamb cooked with onion, parsley, cilantro, honey, and raisins), but will prepare special treats if you call ahead—fresh brains with coriander sauce, *b'stilla* (flaky pastry stuffed with chicken, cinnamon, and spices) with squab, and sea bass with red chilies. Delicious anise bread accompanies every entrée. For dessert there's a luscious mango tartin. ◆ Moroccan ◆ Tu-Su, dinner. 2116 Westwood Blvd (between W Olympic Blvd and Mississippi Ave). 310/475.0729 &

63 ODYSSEY THEATRE

Founded by artistic director Ron Sossi in 1969, this three-stage avant-garde theater offers innovative and experimental productions. ◆ 2055 S Sepulveda Blvd (between Mississippi and La Grange Aves). 310/477.2055. www.odysseytheatre.com

63 SERVICE STATION

No it's not for cars. This unique concept, created by Fred Sutherland, entrepreneur/nightclub designer, provides salubrious services for men who want to feel macho while having a haircut, massage, facial, hand and foot care, or a simple shave. Sutherland describes his bi-level day spa as a mix between a Le Mans pit stop and a James Bond hideout. ◆ 2000 Cotner Ave (between Mississippi and Missouri Aves). 310/268.0333

64 SAWTELLE BOULEVARD

Named for a subdivision that didn't take, this area is now a Japanese/Mexican community of restaurants and small businesses, most related to the gardening trade. ◆ Between W Olympic and Santa Monica Blvds

64 HIDE SUSHI

★★$$ The counter chefs never get a moment's rest in this perpetually crowded café, but they seem to relish the attention and praise for the excellent sushi delicacies and finger appetizers. ◆ Japanese ◆ Tu-Su, lunch and dinner. 2040 Sawtelle Blvd (between Mississippi and La Grange Aves). 310/477.7242

65 MATTEO'S

★★★$$$$ This celebrity hangout caters to the older generation, especially on Sunday nights. A long bar near the entrance

---

Restaurants/Clubs: Red | Hotels: Purple | Shops: Orange | Outdoors/Parks: Green | Sights/Culture: Blue

provides the perfect place to see and be seen; in the main dining room, try for a booth against the wall for better people-watching. In addition to antipasti and great pasta, the menu offers such signature dishes as chicken Beckerman (roasted with parsley, garlic, and roasted potatoes), veal Matteo with eggplant parmigiana, and baked ziti with ricotta and marinara sauce. The service is exceptional—it's attentive without being fawning, friendly without being overly familiar. ◆ Italian ◆ Tu-Su, dinner. Reservations required. 2321 Westwood Blvd (between W Pico Blvd and Tennessee Ave). 310/475.4521

66 WESTSIDE PAVILION

Architect **Jon Jerde** (of San Diego's Horton Plaza fame) makes retail whimsical in this 1985 indoor shopping mall, centered around an elongated glass-vaulted atrium and accented with trendy paste-on Postmodern design. **Nordstrom** anchors three levels of retail establishments. A skybridge above Westwood Boulevard connects the mall to another complex that has similar details. A 1950s-style merry-go-round (310/446.8811) and **Disney Store** (310/474.7022) are appropriate tenants, given the mall's theatricality. ◆ Daily. 10800 W Pico Blvd (between Westwood Blvd and Overland Ave). 310/474.6255. www.westsidepavilion.com

Within Westside Pavilion:

NORDSTROM

The stock and service are exemplary at this branch of the Seattle-based chain. Shoes and stylish American clothes are specialties. ◆ Daily. 310/470.6155

THE LANDMARK

This mega-movie theater complex redefines film-going with special, 50-seat screening rooms furnished with sofas, side tables, and love seats designed to make you feel at home. For those who prefer conventional seating, the $20 million complex offers 12 other venues, all fitted with extra-wide cushy chairs. To further enhance your night out there is a lobby wine bar and concessions offering gourmet snacks such as La Brea Bakery pretzels served with a choice of mustards like raspberry wasabi, popcorn done in sunflower oil and served with real butter, vegan cookies, low-carb pizzas, all-natural yogurts, and if that's not enough, chocolate Tim Tam biscuits direct from Australia. Movie-going doesn't get much better than this. 310/470.0492. www.landmarktheatres.com

67 LAX LUGGAGE

One of a row of discount stores, this shop has good prices on name-brand bags.

◆ Daily. 2233 S Sepulveda Blvd (between Tennessee Ave and W Olympic Blvd). 310/478.2661

68 WINE HOUSE

Their huge and eclectic stock of wines, beers, and spirits is competitively priced. ◆ Daily. 2311 Cotner Ave (between W Pico Blvd and Tennessee Ave). 310/479.3731

69 RENT-A-WRECK

Owner Dave Schwartz has successfully franchised his idea worldwide, but he still manages this original facility. Once just a place to "rent a wreck," it now has hundreds of cars of every make, model, and year. Vintage Mustang convertibles are a specialty here. The scruffy surfaces are deceptive; the old cars rarely let you down and will dramatize your disdain of conventional status symbols. In the land of Mercedes, a battered Chevy is king. However, you might feel even better in a late-model Rolls, Corvette, or Porsche. And while you're deciding, there are free bagels to nosh on and dozens of magazines to read. ◆ Daily. 12333 W Pico Blvd (at Centinela Ave). 310/826.7555, 800/995.0994. wrentwreck@aol.com

70 BOMBAY CAFÉ

★★$ The combination of excellent tandoori-style food and low prices keeps this place hopping day and night. An open kitchen provides a firsthand view of the chef's specials along with fragrant, appetite-teasing aromas. Everything on the menu is worthy of praise, from the tandoori chicken to the samosas and beyond. There are fun, tasty samplers and great curries. ◆ Indian ◆ M-F, lunch and dinner; Sa, Su, dinner. 12021 W Pico Blvd (at S Bundy Dr). 310/473.3388. www.bombaycafe-la.com

71 CHAN DARAE

★★$$ Don Carsten's neon-accented interior glows with rich lacquers, and the kitchen also sparkles with vegetable soup (crammed with goodies), huge and flavorful shrimp, pan-fried noodles with chicken, and beef *panang* (in a thick curry gravy). This is the third in a family that began in Hollywood and Larchmont Village. ◆ Thai ◆ Daily, lunch and dinner. 11940 W Pico Blvd (between Granville Ave and S Bundy Dr). 310/479.4461. www.chandarae.com

72 PETAL HOUSE

Architect **Eric Moss** has taken a modest suburban house and, using the simplest materials, opened it up like a flower. This is a private residence. ◆ 2828 Midvale Ave (between Coventry Pl and Brookhaven Ave)

73 TRADER JOE'S

Known as the "poor man's gourmet shop," this is the place to find really great deals on wine, champagne, liquor, cheese, coffee, chocolate, and nuts, plus exotica that are wittily described in the monthly catalog. There are branches all over town. ◆ Daily. 10850 National Blvd (at Westwood Blvd). 310/470.1917. Also at 8611 Santa Monica Blvd, West Hollywood. 310/657.0152; 7304 Santa Monica Blvd, West Hollywood. 323/851.9772; 2730 Hyperion Ave. 323/665.6774; 263 S La Brea Ave. 323/965.1989

74 CUCINA PARADISO

★★$$$ It looks, smells, and sounds like Little Italy with wooden chairs, tables covered in white linen, and Old Country tunes providing a musical background. And *mamma mia*, the food is fantastic and the waitstaff exceptional! Plan to feast—everything is wonderful. Begin with lovely garlic-laced, sautéed scampi and move along to pumpkin and ricotta cheese ravioli, grilled wild salmon in puttanesca sauce, lamb cooked to perfection, or tender, pan-roasted filet mignon. End with a delightful panna cotta al caramello. Of course, these aren't the only choices—there are plenty of other pastas, fish, chicken, and an out-of-sight Caesar salad. ◆ Italian ◆ M-F, lunch; daily, dinner. Reservations suggested. 3387 Motor Ave (near Woodbine St), Culver City. 310/830.2500. www.cucinaparadiso.net

75 VERSAILLES

★★$ The roast pork with black beans, chicken with garlic, and paella are all delicious in this modest restaurant. For dessert, stick with the flan. ◆ Cuban ◆ Daily, lunch and dinner. 10319 Venice Blvd (between Vinton and Motor Aves). 310/558.3168

76 WONDERFUL WORLD ART GALLERY/WONDERFUL WORLD OF ANIMATION

If you love comic books and animation art, this is the place. Owner Debbie Weiss's amazing gallery makes you feel like a kid as you browse through cels, comic strips, and commemorative artworks such as original *Peanuts* comic strips by Charles Schulz; cels from *Snow White* and *SpongeBob*, *Pirates of the Caribbean*, *Didactic Duck*, and *Emily the Strange;* and the celebrated cast of *The Simpsons.* ◆ M-Sa. 9517 Culver Blvd (between Watseka Ave and Washington Blvd). 310/836.4992. www.wwagallery.com

SANTA MONICA/VENICE

Oh to ride a scooter or roller blade down by the seashore in a thong bikini . . .
Youth-oriented, high energy, and *mojo-motivated* are active terms that best describe this dynamic duo of adjacent seaside communities. Beach seekers were attracted to this area more than a century ago—so much so that they spent a half-day riding in a stagecoach just to get from downtown Los Angeles for overnight camping trips in **Santa Monica Canyon**. Today a similar trip could take nearly as long due to the heavy traffic that often throttles the city. But, all kidding aside, it really should take only about 20 to 40 minutes by freeway, and if you're lucky it sometimes does. On a typical hot summer Sunday, commuting sybarites sit in bumper-to-bumper for nearly 40 miles driving up and down the **Pacific Coast Highway** especially around Santa Monica and Venice with their long, unbroken line of beaches—the most accessible to the city. Sun, surf, sand, cool ocean breezes, and smog-free air lure millions of visitors to the Los Angeles County coast, but don't expect the Pacific to be balmy: It's very rare for the water temperature to reach 70 degrees, even in midsummer.

SANTA MONICA

Santa Monica, and the original amusement area of **Ocean Park** to the south, started out as a seaside resort in the 1870s. Hotels and stores sprouted up soon after, attracting year-round residents. In 1887, Santa Monica was incorporated as an independent city, and in the 1930s led a dual existence as both a quiet residential suburb and bustling haven for offshore gambling ships. But the opening of the **Santa Monica Freeway** in 1966 permanently altered the sleepier tempo. Affluent, family-oriented residents mostly populate the northern sector of Santa Monica. The central and southern parts attract the upwardly mobile and young singles drawn to an upscale, casual lifestyle. This well-heeled populace once began their relocation by moving to rent-controlled apartments or leased condos until they'd saved enough for a down payment on a house, but the dot-com riches of the '90s afforded many the opportunity to buy right away, and they did. And once the deed was signed, a devoted remodeling began that would put Martha Stewart to shame. A $15 million face-lift of the six-block area between **Ocean Avenue** and **Seventh Street** further enhanced the city's oceanfront charm. Sidewalks were widened and embellished with mosaic tiles patterned after Japanese kimonos. Visitors can find their way around with the aid of 35 sandblasted granite map tiles. Streetlights, made in Barcelona, brighten the boulevards, while a dozen stainless-steel bronze and art-glass bus shelters make waiting for a bus more pleasurable. There are even electronic touch-screen kiosks offering visitor information at the touch of a finger. For a virtual tour of the town, go to www.Santamonica.com. To live in Santa Monica it's simply *de rigueur* to be, or at least look, hip.

1 LA MESA DRIVE

Huge Moreton Bay fig trees canopy this lovely street, which is lined with fine Spanish-Colonial 1920s houses by **John Byers**. Examples are at **nos. 1923, 2102, and 2153.** They are all private residences. ♦ From about 19th St to 25th St

2 WILSHIRE BOOKS

A diverse collection of new and used books is found here. ♦ Daily. 3018 Wilshire Blvd (between Berkeley and Stanford Sts). 310/828.3115

3 GEHRY HOUSE

Renovated by master architect **Frank Gehry** himself, this is a mecca for students of architecture but an outrage to the neighbors. Gehry described the original Dutch-gabled cottage as "a dumb little house with charm." In 1978, he built a carapace of corrugated metal, plywood, chain link, and glass around the house, creating a design statement that might have been concocted by a Russian Constructivist of the early 1920s. It's a private residence. ♦ 22nd St and Washington-Ave

4 SONNY MCLEANS BOSTON IRISH PUB AND RESTAURANT

This cozy place is a fun spot for a light meal and bit of ale, music, pool, and darts. ♦ Irish ♦ Daily; bar until 2AM. 2615 Wilshire Blvd (between Princeton and 26th Sts). 310/828.9839

5 DRAGO

★★$$ Another bellissimo production of Celestino Drago and his brothers, this one features an old-world charm imparted by the late designer Brent Saville, who went for the understated with Italian tiled floors and a kitchen framed by artwork from local talent. The food is consistently Celestino *buono*, especially the *branzino* (striped bass) and grilled veal chop. The signature panna cotta with fresh berries completes a fine dining experience. ♦ Italian ♦ Daily, dinner; M-F, lunch. Reservations suggested. 2628 Wilshire Blvd (at 26th St). 310/828.1585

6 PACIFIC DINING CAR

★★$$ This Westside branch serves up the same high-quality steaks, prime ribs, and lobster as its flagship on West Sixth Street in downtown LA (which has been around since 1921). It's a great spot for a power breakfast or lunch or a lively dinner. ♦ American ♦ Daily, breakfast, lunch, and dinner. 2700 Wilshire Blvd. 310/453.4000. www.pacificdiningcar.com

7 WILSHIRE RESTAURANT

★★★$$$ This Thomas Schoos–designed culinary showcase is nothing like anything we've ever experienced in Los Angeles. While we'd like to say "over the top," it's more "outside the box," with several electrifying dining nooks, rooms, cozy spots, and areas in which to eat, drink, or listen to live music on the weekend. What's more, the place is a scenester's delight, jammed with the truly "beautiful" people, mostly young and trendily dressed—especially the female contingent, who either went to the same plastic surgeon or were naturally overendowed with ample cleavage, which they proudly displayed. To set the scene, Schoos combined dark woods with canvas-covered ceilings, billowing curtains, amber candles blazing from assorted perches on the walls, sideboards, tables, and antique mirrors that exaggerate the décor. A flaming torchlit flower box separates the outdoor dining patio from the cigar lounge. Each room reveals a unique warm atmosphere. Plush leather banquettes hide behind intricate latticework to provide an intimate seating arrangement. An attractive amber-lit bar sits under coffered ceilings in the main dining area. The seasonally changing menu offers farm-fresh organic foods, with excellent presentations of fish, meats, and desserts, especially the peach tart with lemon amaretto sabayon, an assortment of yummy cookies, and a caramel cream pie with sautéed bananas and candied coconut. Best choices include white corn and fingerling potato soup, tartare of yellowfin tuna, and wild mushroom ravioli, risotto du jour, black bass with wild mushroom dumplings, wood-grilled Maine lobster, oak-grilled sirloin steak, and veal short ribs. The waitstaff is exceptional and helpful. There's actually a bouncer at the door for the late-night crowd, so don your chicest, trendiest togs and you'll fit right in. ♦ American ♦ M-F, lunch; daily, dinner. Reservations required. 2454 Wilshire Blvd (between Chelsea Ave and 25th St). 310/586.1707. www.wilshirerestaurant.com

8 CABANA

This South Beach–style shop, with its pink-and-white striped store awning and cabana dressing rooms, features the casual-chic couture and home accessories of Lilly Pulitzer, noted East Coast fashion designer of society mavens from Boston to Palm Beach. LA fashionistas love the place, which also carries stylish shoes by Miss Trish of Capri, Eliza Gray handbags, and belts and bling by Sophia & Chloe. Owner Laura Lieblich designed a very hospitable shop with a flat-panel television for watching sports events or children's shows and a portable icemaker for making drinks. ♦ Tu-Su. 1511a Montana Ave (between 16th and 15th Sts). 310/394.5123

9 LE MARMITON

For the most elegant of picnics, or when you would love to eat in a very fine French restaurant but can't afford it, this takeout is the answer. ♦ Daily. 1327 Montana Ave (between 14th and 13th Sts). 310/393.7716

10 CAFE MONTANA

★$ This local favorite is flooded with natural light and has a contemporary interior design by Eddie Silkaitis. The pleasing menu emphasizes soups, salads, and grilled fresh fish, plus excellent breakfasts and desserts. ♦ California ♦ Daily, breakfast, lunch, and dinner. Reservations recommended. 1534 Montana Ave (at 16th St). 310/829.3990

11 PALMETTO

The skin, hair, and bath products are natural and therapeutic at this upscale store. The handsomely packaged soaps and scents have attracted such celebrity customers as Demi Moore, Annette Bening, Lauren Bacall,

---

Restaurants/Clubs: Red | Hotels: Purple | Shops: Orange | Outdoors/Parks: Green | Sights/Culture: Blue

and Angela Lansbury. ♦ Daily. 1034 Montana Ave (at 11th St). 310/395.6687

12 THE AMBROSE

$ Set in a residential part of town, next door to St. John's Hospital, this 76-room hideaway is the perfect place for chilling out, especially *après* surgery. The Gustav Stickley–inspired early California artisan design includes a fireplace library, inviting entry foyer/living room, and study. Rooms come with two-tone cherry wood–paneled vestibules, beds covered with pretty chenille spreads, terraces, and bathrooms touched with chrome, limestone countertops, and Gasgon blue floors. A complimentary breakfast buffet is served in the living room. Room service, provided by local restaurants, is available (but not always 24 hours, as the management claims). Amenities include a recreation room stocked with fitness videos, chilled towels, and lockers where frequent guests can store their workout gear. To sweeten your stay the hotel also offers free underground parking, free wireless high-speed Internet access in guest rooms and public areas, and complimentary transportation to downtown Santa Monica via the hotel's own London taxi. You can also stroll a block up to Wilshire Boulevard and browse at the Gap, Borders Books, or a number of shops and boutiques that line the street. If you're up to it, walk the 17 blocks to the Third Street Promenade. For a good workout, trek the mile and a half more to the beach. ♦ 1255 20th St (at Arizona Ave). 877/AMBROSE, 310/315.1555; fax 310/315.1556. www.ambrosehotel.com

13 LA FARM

★★★$$ A wooden gate with a steer's head leads to this noisy, hip, and citified version of the rural and rustic, with a lovely patio surprisingly situated in an office building. Jean-Pierre Peiny, former chef of the genteel **La Serre,** offers corned beef and cabbage, but the menu is primarily cosmopolitan and worldly. Try fresh salmon marinated in aquavit or zucchini tempura. ♦ International ♦ M-F, breakfast, lunch, and dinner; Sa, dinner. 3000 W Olympic Blvd (between Centinela Ave and Stewart St). 310/449.4000

14 FRENCH RAGS

Savvy designer Brenda French turned her cottage industry into a thriving fashion emporium with her unique knitwear for women. Her styles appeal to the likes of Hillary Rodham Clinton, Ann Richards, and Barbara Boxer (to drop a few fan names). You can have an entire wardrobe created by Brenda or one of her consultants while you sip some coffee, tea, or wine. Price tags are moderately high, but the quality and style is exceptional and long-lasting. There's also a sales rack to browse through for prêt-à-porter items. Call for an appointment or just drop by to browse through the showroom; you'll love it. ♦ 11599 Tennessee Ave (near Colby and Olympic Blvd), 310/479.5648, 800/347.5270. www.frenchrags.com

15 BRASS CAP

★★★$$$ Noted restaurateur Bruce Marder carved this brooding brasserie out of the old Beach House. The food is as good as you'd expect from this superchef, mostly French with the usual escargots, steak au poivre, and great fish, and a prime New York steak that melts in your mouth. Marder also utilizes wonderful white truffles to embellish certain dishes, such as a great beef carpaccio drizzled with the luscious oil and tiny slivers. His desserts are scrumptious, too. Service is exceptional and the clientele a mix of locals, celebrities, and out-of-towners. The attractive interior is separated into two sections: a dark front room and a back area with a lengthy bar, flat-screen TVs, and an adjacent patio. ♦ French/American Brasserie. ♦ Reservations necessary. Daily, dinner. 100 W Channel Rd (between Channel and Entrada Dr). 310/454.4544

16 BACK ON THE BEACH

★★$$ Hardly the Ritz of restaurants, but barrels of fun and good food, this bougainvillea-shaded shack, smack on the sand at Santa Monica Beach, provides bird's-eye views of roller-bladers, joggers, and buff bodies exercising along the strand. It's the perfect place to begin a day at the beach with yummy breakfast quesadillas, pancakes, French toast, or a feta-tomato-spinach omelette. Then work off your morning meal and return for lunch and order Fred's Salad (named after owner Fred Deni), a combo of romaine lettuce, chicken salad, grilled potatoes, lemon herb dressing, and blue cheese, sprinkled with Parmesan cheese. There's also a full dinner menu with salmon, steak, and other options, but the café is most popular during daytime hours. ♦ California ♦ Daily, breakfast and lunch; Tu-Su, dinner until 9PM in summer, 5PM in winter. Reservations accepted for indoor dining; eating on the sand is first come, first served. 445 Pacific Coast Hwy (1½ miles north of the Pier, between California Incline and Entrada Dr). 310/393.8282. www.backonthebeachcafe.com

17 THE MASSAGE PLACE & PETIT SPA

This will rub you the right way. In an era of triple-digit massage rates, it's refreshing to find a place that offers great rubs for less. Granted, there are no frills. You won't find a

Jacuzzi, steam room, or sauna. But there are showers and 20 top therapists who do Swedish, deep tissue, sports, acupressure, pregnancy, and reflexology massages for $64 for an hour and a half of pure bliss. ♦ Daily. Appointments suggested, but they take walk-ins when there's availability. 625-C Montana Ave (between Sixth and Seventh Sts). Also at 2901 Ocean Park, Santa Monica (at 29th St). 310/399.9484; 2805 Abbot Kinney Blvd (at Washington Blvd), Marina del Rey. 310/306.5166; and 245 Main St (corner of Rose Ave). 310/399.5566

18 MONTANA AVENUE

Slicing through the ritzy residential areas of Santa Monica and Brentwood, this perky street offers 11 blocks of shopping options, from funky furnishings and vintage clothing to cutting-edge fashions and string bikinis. At last count there were more than two dozen women's clothing stores, 21 hair and beauty shops, 9 laundries and dry cleaners, 20-plus restaurants and gourmet takeouts, 19 gift boutiques, and a half dozen specialty stores, plus offices of 12 doctors and 10 dentists. This is a fun place to window-shop and celebrity-watch—stars are best spotted in the more upscale stores, although they also can be seen browsing in the funkier establishments. ♦ Between 17th and Seventh Sts

18 VINCENZO

★★$$ Yes, there is a Vincenzo and he's very proud of his homemade pastas, pastries, and breads. The rest of the menu's pretty typical, with seafood, veal chops, and rack of lamb. Vincenzo recommends the tiramisù, cannoli, or fresh fruit pie for dessert, and you should listen to him. ♦ Italian. ♦ Tu-Su, dinner. Reservations recommended. 714 Montana Ave (between Lincoln Blvd and Seventh St). 310/395.6619

19 BEST WESTERN GATEWAY HOTEL

$$ This 125-room, four-story hotel, centrally located at a busy intersection, is a modern version of the familiar Best Westerns. Suites are available. There's no restaurant on-site, but there is an **International House of Pancakes** next door. ♦ 1920 Santa Monica Blvd (at 20th St). 310/829.9100, 800/937.8376; fax 310/829.9211

20 BERGAMOT STATION

Art lovers will feel like kids in a candy store at this five-acre art center, where 33 galleries are housed in a former trolley car station designed by architect **Frederick Fisher.** Some of the city's most prestigious galleries are housed here, including the **Robert Berman Gallery** (310/315.9506), **Patricia Correla Gallery** (310/264.1760), **Frumkin/Duval Gallery** (310/453.1850), **Rosamund Felsen Gallery** (310/453.6463), **Frank Lloyd Gallery** (310/264.3866), **Gallery of Functional Art** (310/829.6990), and **Shoshana Wayne Gallery** (310/451.3773). ♦ 2525 Michigan Ave (northeast of Cloverfield Blvd). General information 310/829.5854

21 VALENTINO

★★★★$$$$ Sicilian-born owner Piero Selvaggio and his talented chefs make culinary magic at this popular Italian restaurant. Among the mouthwatering signature dishes are the smoked mozzarella-stuffed black cod with roasted tomato sauce; bucatini with ricotta and zucchini; beef carpaccio with capers and radicchio; mushroom timbale with saffron; marinated shiitake mushrooms, French beans, and sliced mozzarella; Maine lobster salad with couscous, olives, and orange-infused oil or potato-and-spinach gnocchi in a Gorgonzola sauce; perfect pastas; and risotto. There's also a great grilled squab in honey-fig and red wine sauce, osso buco braised in veal stock with mushrooms and Marsala, super shrimp and scallop dishes, Dover sole, and leg of lamb. Desserts are to die for. To truly sample the chef's culinary talents, go for the tasting menu, which might include warm Australian crab with Tuscan beans and spelt, prime Angus beef tenderloin with Raschera fondue, Tuscan kale, and mushroom tart, along with Italian savories such as *lamponi con zabaglione al moscato gratinato e gelato. Buon appetito!* All the desserts are *magnifico,* but the marscapone teardrop with chocolate sorbet and zabaglione, Italian rice pudding with strawberry, and balsamic sorbet are sure winners. The captain will happily help you create a special menu for the evening and suggest the proper wine pairings from the 115-page list—one of the best in the country. Expect an enjoyable evening with friendly service in a gorgeous room that combines elegance, comfort, and striking contemporary style. FYI: Should you book a cruise on Crystal Cruises' *Crystal Symphony* or *Harmony* you'll find Piero's food served in the alternative Prego restaurant on board. ♦ Italian ♦ M-Sa, dinner; F, lunch and dinner. Reservations recommended. 3115 Pico Blvd (between Centinela Ave and Stewart St). 310/829.4313. www.valentinorestaurant.com &

Restaurants/Clubs: Red | Hotels: Purple | Shops: Orange | Outdoors/Parks: Green | Sights/Culture: Blue

22 CALIFORNIA MAP & TRAVEL CENTER

Owner Sheldon Mars has LA's best stock of maps, both local and of other areas of the country and the world. ♦ Daily. 3312 Pico Blvd (between 34th and 33rd Sts). 310/396.6277

23 OCEANA SANTA MONICA

$$$ This little charmer sits across the street from the ocean and worlds apart from the hustle and bustle of the big city. Its 63 rooms were painstakingly designed by Cheryl Rowley with vibrant colors and quirky touches. Rooms feature large flat-screen TVs, wireless Internet, full kitchens with dining areas, private balconies, ocean views, Aveda bath products, terry robes, and Egyptian cotton linens. There's a charming courtyard with an inviting swimming pool and fitness center. Other touches include free high-speed Internet service, a business center, concierge service, and a lounge restaurant created by Jonathan Morr from New York's Bond Street, offering versions of comfort food. ♦ 849 Ocean Ave (between Idaho and Montana Aves). 310/393.0486, 310/458.1182, 800/777.0758. www.oceanahotelgroup.com

24 EL CHOLO

★★$ Formerly **Tampico Tilly's,** this clone of Ron Salisbury's popular Mexican eatery recreates the ambience of his original Midtown location. The romantic entry leads to a gracious patio with a flower-filled Guadalajara-style fountain and hand-painted walls by local artist Sally Lamb. Everything is authentic Mexican, from the tasty margaritas and nachos to the enchiladas, tostadas, green corn tamales, and fajitas. ♦ Mexican ♦ Daily, lunch and dinner. Valet parking available. 1025 Wilshire Blvd (between 11th and 10th Sts). 310/899.1106. Also at 1121 S Western Ave (between Country Club Dr and W 11th St), Midtown. 321/734.2773; 958 S Fair Oaks Ave (between California and E Del Mar), Pasadena. 626/441.4353

25 MELISSE

★★★$$$$ This popular spot is a must-do if you happen to enjoy spectacular food served in a room oozing with ambience. Talented chef/owner Josiah Citrin's California/Mediterranean cuisine—which Citrin say is "based on classical French techniques and all natural ingredients"—is simply sensational. For a true sampling of the chef's skills, order the tasting menu. Selections change regularly and may include dishes such as sweet pea soup made with Greek yogurt mint mousse, asparagus risotto, morel mushrooms in a red wine reduction, Wagu Kobe beef, and desserts like sticky toffee pudding with mocha ice cream or our favorite, raspberry-apricot tart with pistachio bavarois and raspberry sorbet. Burn calories and save a few bucks by parking on one of the side streets. ♦ French/ California. ♦ Daily, dinner; W-F, lunch. Reservations a must. 1104 Wilshire Blvd (at 11th St), Santa Monica. 310/395.0881. www.melisse.com

26 SANTA MONICA SEAFOOD

Shop here for the largest, freshest selection of fish outside of downtown. ♦ M-Sa. 1205 Colorado Ave (at 12th St). 310/393.5244

27 BUFFALO CLUB

★★★$$$$ This star-filled club, owned by TV producer Anthony Yerkovitch (best known for *Miami Vice*), does not enjoy the best location: It's off the beaten track, in a somewhat seedy neighborhood. But the ambience of the elegant, mahogany-accented dining room and the hearty American fare offer a memorable dining experience—that is, *if* you can get in: The place is about as snobby as it gets. If you can name-drop your way through the door, you'll soon be rubbing elbows with such LA luminaries as Robert De Niro, Quentin Tarantino, Arnold Schwarzenegger, and Maria Shriver. Signature dishes include hush puppies with lamb chops, onion rings made with chili, pork roast, oyster shooters, Buffalo wings, shrimp and lobster dumplings, and great pork chops. For a dessert sensation, try the pecan pie crumble sundae with bittersweet chocolate sauce. ♦ American ♦ M-Sa, dinner; M-F, lunch. Reservations required (and very hard to get). 1520 Olympic Blvd (between 16th and 15th Sts). 310/450.8600. www.buffaloclub.com ♿

28 JOSIE

★★★$$$ Chef Josie LeBlach (formerly with Remi and Saddle Peak Lodge) and spouse Frank Delzio took over the former 2424 Pico Restaurant and transformed it into an elegant eatery with banquettes upholstered in light green, pretty framed prints, and soft lighting. The extensive menu has something for every taste, from sautéed sardines fried with celery leaves and ravioli stuffed with oxtail to Texas wild boar, vegetarian barley prepared like risotto, and campfire trout. If you want a special dish, call 48 hours in advance and Josie will prepare it. ♦ American, with French and Italian Influences ♦ Dinner, nightly. Reservations recommended. 2424 Pico Blvd (between 25th and 24th Sts). 310/581.9888. www.josierestaurant.com ♿

29 SUN TECH TOWN HOUSES

Urban Forms designed this striking high-tech terrace of condominiums in 1981. A similarly scaled group, with a false classical façade, is located at **2332 28th Street.** These are private residences. ♦ 2433 Pearl St (at 25th St)

30 IL FORNO

★$$ Exceptional pizza and pasta are served in a noisy, crowded room. ♦ Italian ♦ M-F, lunch and dinner; Sa, dinner. 2901 Ocean Park Blvd (at 29th St). 310/450.1241. www.ilfornocafe.com

31 THE HUMP

★★★$$$ Just one floor up in the building that houses Typhoon, this outstanding Japanese restaurant offers a creative menu in a unique setting. Your entry into this Asian delight, designed by architect Stephen Jones, begins when you walk through intricate steel doors onto pebble stone floors. Propeller-shaped fans hang from a ceiling made of mahogany, bamboo, and seagrass. Seating is in teak/leather chairs from Indonesia, and food is served in Asiatic ceramic or pieces of bamboo. There's also an observation deck with a telescope where you can watch the planes taking off or landing. Chef Hiro Nishimura's cuisine matches the view. Begin with a cup of sake and feast on miso soup, assorted tempuras, grilled salmon skin and crabmeat salad, tuna sashimi (with cilantro, ginger, and garlic), broiled or steamed black cod, soft-shelled crabs, *y-ma-dai* (steamed whitefish with shiitake mushrooms), and other delights. There's also a sushi bar to die for. ♦ Japanese ♦ Tu-F, lunch; daily, dinner. Reservations a must. At Santa Monica Airport, 3221 Donald Douglas Loop S (off 28th St and upstairs from Typhoon). 310/313.0977. www.typhoon.biz

32 BAY CITIES IMPORTING

Mediterranean foods, a deli counter, sandwiches, pastas, cheeses, wines, and extra-virgin olive oils make this a one-stop shop for creating your favorite meal. ♦ Daily. 1517 Lincoln Blvd (between Colorado Ave and Broadway). 310/395.8279

33 HUNTLEY HOTEL

$$$ South Beach meets Santa Monica at this spiffy 209-room luxury hotel. All gussied up and glamorized after a $15 million renovation, the interior is absolutely stunning. The lobby embodies the essence of the design with a clever union of minimalism and retro set on high-glossed hardwood floors. Artistic touches include leather bed-like lounges and designer chairs adorned with fur pillows, stingray-skin lamps, a piranha wall, and a wall filled with 300 white-lacquered ceramic fish. The white, bronze, and black color scheme emboldens the area. Each room boasts a unique décor created by ace designers Meri Meis and Thomas Schoos. All come equipped with yuppie-centric amenities like 42-inch plasma-screen televisions with mirrored backs that swivel to face either the bed or the sofa or are hung on the wall. Martini lovers will appreciate the shaker and glasses set on the minibar. Fix a drink, then sit in one of the cushy chairs and catch the awesome view from the wall-to-wall windows. Other touches include fur rugs and sharkskin-covered chairs, Matteo linens and robes, tufted caramel suede headboards, vintage mirrors, high-design work areas with wireless high-speed Internet hookup, gorgeous marble and granite bathrooms with rain showers, and in some rooms, separate tubs. There's a small fitness room with ample equipment. In addition to the interior appeal, the Huntley offers an ideal location close to the beach, shops, and Third Street Promenade. Book a room on a high floor for the best views. We're partial to #1613, but they are all spiffy. ♦ 111 Second St (between Wilshire Blvd and California Ave). 310/394.5454; fax 310/458.9776. www.thehuntleyhotel.com

Within the Huntley Hotel:

THE PENTHOUSE

★★★$$$ Wear sunglasses if you go up to this top-floor restaurant during daylight—it's bright, and we're not kidding. The stark white room filled with white lacquered cabanas covered by white gauze curtains, coupled with sun blaring in from the wide windows, is blinding. The eye-appealing Thomas Schoos beach design juxtaposes sea-foam greens, pale blues, and rich chocolate with hints of bronze and daring orange accents showcased by Murano chandeliers. A mother-of-pearl fireplace and 19-foot backlit circular vintage chrome bar complete the décor. The noise level can be excruciating thanks to the crowds of high-energy trendies tippling at the bar on mojitos and martinis, and the foodies who pack the tables. The ocean view—which, on clear day, stretches west to Palos Verdes Peninsula and east to Hollywood—is spectacular, and the food, if you order right, scrumptious. An 18-ounce bone-in rib eye steak melted in the mouth,

---

Restaurants/Clubs: Red | Hotels: Purple | Shops: Orange | Outdoors/Parks: Green | Sights/Culture: Blue

tuna tartare was heavenly, asparagus and a plate of field mushrooms were cooked just right, and fresh halibut was wonderful. Desserts are good, too. ◆ California ◆ Daily, breakfast, lunch, and dinner. Reservations days in advance a must. Valet parking is a bit stiff, so try to find space on the street. 310/393.8080

34 THE FAIRMONT MIRAMAR HOTEL

$$ Situated on the bluffs above Santa Monica, this legendary 302-room luxury hotel has the ambience of a private seaside residence. LA-based designer Virginia Ball of VB Designs Inc. is responsible for the modern design of this century-old property. In addition to hotel rooms there are 32 superspecial bungalows with private patios hidden among tropical flowers and palm trees. We suggest staying in one of the completely renovated bi-level units, which feature an upstairs living room and balcony, a sauna, and a whirlpool bath (where Greta Garbo, Humphrey Bogart, Betty Grable, Marilyn Monroe, and other box-office biggies bedded down in decades past). Other accommodations include 176 ocean-view rooms and suites and a "historic" wing with oversized rooms. Special amenities include in-room coffeemakers, robes, two-line phones, data ports, Nintendo games, minibars, and daily newspaper. Facilities include a bi-level fitness complex where you can look out at the ocean while you pump, flex, and sweat it out on the latest machines. There's also **Club Sante Spa,** with a steam room, sauna, and whirlpool, a gamut of salubrious treatments, and an outdoor pool. There are two places to eat: **The Grille** for California cuisine served indoors or alfresco on the patio, and **Koi Pond,** where local luminaries like to go for casual fare. The enormous Moreton Bay fig tree in the center courtyard was planted in the 19th century. ◆ 101 Wilshire Blvd (at Ocean Ave). 310/576.7777, 800/866.5577; fax 310/458.7912. www.fairmont.com/santamonica.htm

35 MICHAEL'S

★★★★$$$ Any meal at this Michael McCarty white-on-white restaurant is a magical experience. The cutting-edge restaurateur pioneered the new California cuisine, and also has a talent for breaking imported chefs in to the LA scene. His most recent prize is chef de cuisine Olivier Rousselle, a Parisian who earned his toque abroad in a busy bistro, Boodle's gentlemen's club in London, where under chef Keith Podmore he cooked for London luminaries and members of the royal family.

After a stint in South Africa's wine country at La Couronne Hotel, he returned to the London, where he cooked at several trendy eateries. Then, *voilà,* Michael discovered him. Like those of his predecessors, Rousselle's menu is both sensational and seasonal. If it's summer, you might find items such as oysters on the half shell, chilled avocado soup, hazelnut-crusted goat cheese, ahi tuna tartare, roasted sardines, seared California squab and foie gras, or grilled Mediterranean *loup de mer.* The best dessert is the lemon crème brûlée. And from zee pastry cart, your very own apple crumble pie with caramel ice cream, hot Valrhona chocolate fudge cake, or the cookie and confection plate are sure to please the sweet tooth. Adding to the culinary enjoyment is the flower-filled patio with its big white umbrellas and the works of David Hockney and Jasper Johns that adorn the dining room walls, not to mention the beautiful people who frequent this popular spot. Do dress up for the occasion in fashionably casual attire. ◆ California ◆ M-Sa, dinner; M-F, lunch and dinner. Reservations required. 1147 Third St (between Wilshire Blvd and California Ave). 310/451.0843. www.michaelssantamonica.com

36 THIRD STREET PROMENADE

This three-block pedestrian street with its faded stucco façade has been landscaped (with topiary dinosaur fountains) and given a major face-lift, revealing such architectural gems as the **Keller Building** (at Broadway), restored by Frank Dimsterr, and the **W.T. Grant Building** (1300 block). Architect **Johannes Van Tilburg** designed the block at Arizona Avenue in the style of the Viennese Werkstatte. The area is home to the best specialty bookstores west of New York's SoHo, including **Arcana Books on the Arts** (no. 1229; 310/458.1499), as well as a rare book dealer, **Kenneth Karmiole** (two blocks away at 509 Wilshire Blvd; 310/451.4342). A bustling nightlife thrives throughout the outdoor mall, thanks to several movie theaters and a good selection of restaurants and bars, many with sidewalk patios. The shops are a mixed bag of everything from optical boutiques and New Age crystal shops to clothing outlets such as **Clothes Minded** (no. 1452), where everything costs $15 or less; **French Connection** (no. 1418); **Miss Sixty** (no. 1334); **Old Navy** (no. 1234); **Lucky Brand Jeans and Casual Wear** (no. 1215); **Johnny Rockets** (no. 1322); and **Pink Ice** (no. 1340), the place to find outrageously hip, tattoo/pierced-friendly fashions. ◆ Daily. Most of the shops stay open late. On Wednesday, California farmers market their produce on Arizona Avenue between Fourth and Second Streets. ◆ Between Broadway and Wilshire Blvd

36 LOCANDA DEL LAGO

★★★$$ A spunky Italian trattoria, it has oversize windows that face the bustling promenade. Bring a big appetite and dig into chef Enrico Gladuo's wonderful Northern Italian menu: *mossarella ala Sorrentina* (fresh mozzarella and tomato with oregano and basil), *carpaccio di bue all'Albese* (thin slices of raw beef tenderloin brushed with lemon-truffle dressing and shaved Parmesan and celery), fillet of trout coated in a porcini mushroom breading, *fritto misto* (calamari, white shrimp, and lightly fried freshwater smelts), and the best risottos you've ever tasted. ♦ Italian ♦ Daily, lunch and dinner. Reservations recommended. 231 Arizona Ave (at Third St Promenade). 310/451.3525

37 SHANGRI-LA HOTEL

$$$ Like the monastery in the classic 1937 movie *Lost Horizon*, this is a 55-room Streamline Moderne gem, and—with its view over **Palisades Park** and the ocean—it's almost as idyllic. Please note: At press time the hotel was closed for a major $25 million renovation that will dramatically transform its appearance from head to toe with new guest rooms, a lobby restaurant, lounge, elevated pool with private cabanas, and more. The hotel is conveniently located within walking distance of shops and the beach. ♦ 1301 Ocean Ave (at Arizona Ave). 310/394.2791, 800/345.STAY. www.shangrila-hotel.com, www.meridianla.com

38 BRAVO CUCINA

★$$ This is a charming sidewalk café to stop for a bite while strolling the Promenade. Pasta's the specialty here and it's *molto bene*. ♦ Italian ♦ Daily, lunch and dinner. 1319 Third St Promenade (between Santa Monica Blvd and Arizona Ave). 310/394.0374

39 HOOTERS

$$ It all depends on how you feel about scantily clad waitresses in tight T-shirts serving you chicken wings, hot dogs, hamburgers, and other greasy food in a noisy, high-octane environment. If the idea appeals, this two-hundred-and-thirtieth member of the quirky chain serves food as spicy as its women. ♦ Daily. 321 Santa Monica Blvd (between Fourth and Third Sts). 310/458.7555

40 BURKE WILLIAMS DAY SPA AND MASSAGE CENTER

When this fortress of salubrious indulgence opened in Santa Monica more than a decade ago, it was the only act in town of its kind. Pamper seekers flocked here for the ultimate massage. It was truly one of the best. In 2005, the spa relocated to a larger, more luxurious facility just down the street. The elegant, Mediterranean-style interior provides 22,000 square feet of space in which to enjoy whirlpool baths, scrubs, rubs, facials, sunbathing (in a coed solarium), and relaxation in an indoor or outdoor lounge, both with fireplaces and cushy chaises. To really bliss you out there are two major hot tubs: the Zen Jacuzzi (for tranquillity) and the Social Jacuzzi, which is just like is sounds. The company, which now operates 11 day spas statewide, recently added a signature cosmetics collection called H2V. You can still enjoy a top-notch rub if you get the right therapist. Unfortunately, some regulars have experienced more misses than hits. But it still packs them in, somewhat to the consternation of regulars who feel it's become too factory-like. Still, it's convenient for locals, and the facility itself is quite pleasant and attractively put together. ♦ Daily. 1358 Fourth St (between Santa Monica Blvd and Arizona Ave). 310/587.3366. Also at 8000 Sunset Blvd (at Laurel Ave), Hollywood. 310/833.9007; 39 Mills Place, Pasadena. 626/440.1222; 27741 Crown Valley Pkwy, Mission Viejo. 949/367.9717; 20 City Blvd, West Bldg, Orange. 714/769.1360; and 15301 Ventura Blvd, Sherman Oaks. 818/789.3339. www.burkewilliamsspa.com

41 OCEAN AVENUE SEAFOOD

★★$$ Superlative fresh fish, raw oysters, and genuine New England clam chowder are served in a yuppified Las Vegas setting. Patio dining overlooks **Palisades Park**. ♦ Seafood ♦ Daily, lunch and dinner. Reservations recommended. 1401 Ocean Ave (at Santa Monica Blvd). 310/394.5669

41 BOA

★★$$$ Floor-to-ceiling windows illuminate this boisterous beachfront steak house. The glamorous setting, highlighted by a driftwood tree lodged in the middle of the room, provides an ideal spot for sipping drinks and sinking your teeth into big, juicy signature steaks like the Wagyu Kobe beef filet. All meats arrive with a choice of sauces and rubs such as Worcestershire/peppercorn or creamed horseradish and blue cheese. If the patio's open (usually on warm days), you might want to consider sitting out there in the fresh ocean air. To feel like a kid again, or as a treat for the kids, order the carnival-style cotton candy, to go or eat in.

Restaurants/Clubs: Red | Hotels: Purple | Shops: Orange | Outdoors/Parks: Green | Sights/Culture: Blue

There's also an amazing Meyer lemon crème brûlée. Much of the action happens at the swing bar before and after dinner. ◆ Steak House ◆ Daily, lunch and dinner. Reservations suggested. 101 Santa Monica Blvd (at Ocean Ave). 310/899.4466

41 POMP SALON

When your hair is stressed out or your nails need some TLC, this highly stylized salon is the place to go. The team of estheticians really know their stuff, whether you're in the mood for a whole new look or just crave a cut, style, or blow dry, a manicure or pedicure, or a relaxing scalp treatment (which is great but not long enough). The room, designed by salon owner Lisa Dixon, exudes warmth and relaxation through a color scheme of beige, sand, and blue embraced by mirrors, artwork (which is for sale), sleek wooden flooring, and lots of glass. There's a tranquil waiting room where you can sip complimentary teas, juices, Borba Skin Balance Water, coffee, or tea. There are also comfy massage chairs to sit in during treatments. It's a great place to bring a wedding party to preen for the big event. ◆ Tu-Sa; Th until 9PM. 1421 Ocean Ave, Suite B (between Broadway and Santa Monica Blvd). 310/393.1543. www.pompsalon.com

42 YE OLDE KING'S HEAD

$ Members of the local British colony tend to congregate for dart games and a sustenance of fish-and-chips and warm beer at this traditional English pub. ◆ English ◆ Daily, lunch and dinner; bar until 2AM. 116 Santa Monica Blvd (between Second St and Ocean Ave). 310/451.1402

43 JIRAFFE

★★★$$$ Chef Raphael Lunetta (formerly of **Jackson's**) continue to please diners with great food and a comfortable setting. The two-story dining room features big, arched windows, dark-wood library chairs, and attractive ironwork sconces. Tables are set with retro-French silverware, white tablecloths, and baskets filled with thick, buttery brioches. The creative menu includes such heavenly choices as truffled artichoke hearts, wild mushroom salad, fresh fig and arugula salad, ahi tuna tartare, seafood, lamb, and rabbit. ◆ American ◆ Daily, dinner. Reservations required. 502 Santa Monica Blvd (at Fifth St). 310/917.6671

44 VODA BAR & RESTAURANT

★★★$$$ The name translates to "water" in several languages, but vodka drinks are really the big draw here, with lots of different brands and types served with caviar. Stone walls accentuated by brown carpets and candles set the scene for the hip young crowd that frequents this lively spot. The eclectic menu ranges from designer pizzas to hearty steaks. ◆ Italian ◆ M-Sa, dinner. Reservations a must. 1449 Second St (near Santa Monica Blvd). 310/394.9774

45 URBAN OUTFITTERS

Steel girders frame 10 huge panels of floor-to-ceiling windows on the façade of this converted meatpacking plant, which now houses a funky sportswear shop for hip young metropolitanites. The raw, cavernous interior, with its open beamed ceiling and cement floor, showcases trendy labels such as Bull Dog, Wheat, Free People, and Anthropology. ◆ Daily. 1440 Third St Promenade (between Broadway and Santa Monica Blvd). 310/394.1404

46 GOTHAM HALL/SESSIONS

Bon vivants and just plain night owls will enjoy this two-story European-style club, spread out in a mammoth six-room facility. The scene is young and hip, and often outlandish (there's a TV screen running replays of Jerry Springer's "Transsexual Tales," and performers in diamond-studded black-leather bikinis), with DJs from local radio stations spinning the latest hits. ◆ Cover. Must be 21 or older. F, Sa, 10PM-2AM. 1431 Third St Promenade (between Broadway and Santa Monica Blvd). 310/394.8865

47 BORDER GRILL

★★$$ Half Mexican cantina, half punk nightclub (designed by Josh Schweitzer), this place literally vibrates with sound and color. Chefs Mary Sue Miliken and Susan Fenniger are known for their inventive cuisine, everything from green corn tamales and shrimp ceviche to bread soup, braised duck, and lamb tacos. Communal tables are provided for single diners and those without reservations. ◆ Mexican ◆ Tu-Su, lunch; daily, dinner. Reservations recommended. 1445 Fourth St (between Broadway and Santa Monica Blvd). 310/451.1655. www.bordergrill.com

48 PALISADES PARK

This park is one of the oldest and best maintained in the city, and the steep, crumbly cliffs along the edge of the ocean are a traditional spot for Angelenos to watch the sunset fade over the ocean. Towering palms and semitropical trees form beautiful bowers for strolling or jogging, as well as a haven for the elderly, who gather here to gossip and play chess, and for the homeless. Steps lead down to the beach. ◆ Ocean Ave (between Colorado Ave and Adelaide Dr)

49 CARMEL BY THE SEA

$ This well-kept economy hotel with 102 rooms and eight suites is close to **Santa Monica Place.** There's a convenient coffee shop just outside the building. ♦ 201 Broadway (at Second St). 310/451.2469

50 LONE WOLF

Celebrities James Belushi and Chuck Norris opened this bustling cigar shop, where smokers can relax in oversize leather chairs and puff to their heart's content on private-label brands and selections from around the world. Humidors keep the stogies fresh. ♦ M-F, 10AM-10PM; Sa, 10AM-11PM; Su, 10AM-8PM. 223B Broadway (between Third St Promenade and Second St). 310/458.5441

51 BROADWAY DELI

$ Steven Erlich designed this stripped Deco interior with stylish simplicity. They serve sandwiches, salads, grills, and deli basics, plus a good choice of beers and wines by the glass. ♦ Deli ♦ Daily. 1457 Third St Promenade (at Broadway). 310/451.0616

52 I CUGINI

★$ Owned by the same successful restaurateurs who opened **Water Grill** downtown and **Ocean Avenue Seafood** down the street, this restaurant has a split personality: noisy at night inside; quiet and candlelit on the outdoor patio, where diners enjoy views of **Palisades Park** and the Pacific Ocean. The veal chops, sea bass, and spaghetti with seafood are popular entrées. The décor is turn-of-the-century Northern Italian, with mahogany wainscoting, marble accents, and cove ceilings. A lobby bakery sells fresh rosemary bread sticks, spinach bread, and an olive purée that's great for spreading on bread. ♦ Italian ♦ Daily, lunch and dinner. 1501 Ocean Ave (at Broadway). 310/451.4595

53 FRED SEGAL FOR A BETTER ECOLOGY

The burgers are turkey; the bed sheets, clothing, face products, and paints are bleach- and chemical-free; and ecology and energy information is displayed alongside products. But don't confuse this complex with earthier, more bohemian stores: It has upscale fare for environmentalists who drive Range Rovers. ♦ Daily. 420 Broadway (between Fifth and Fourth Sts). 310/394.6448

54 FRED SEGAL

A spin-off of its Melrose sister, this cluster of specialty stores is like a tiny village under one roof, with gourmet takeout and an espresso bar; youthful, hip, and classy upscale goods; and a DJ spinning oldies and Top 40 hits. Hats, jewelry, clothing, and scents for women, a pricey kids' shop with handmade quilts, men's clothing and gifts, and the latest eyewear are all available. The latest addition is a sleek, contemporary day spa proffering the gamut of head-to-toe services from professional hair-color consultations to a grooming parlor for men. The quirky décor includes doohickeys such as a graffiti pole, an oversized black-and-white cowhide-covered bench in the waiting room, Takara Belmont wall-mounted shampoo bowls, and stylists and manicure stations on wheels for faster service. And for those really in the fast lane, a concierge who makes dinner reservations, arranges alterations and dry cleaning, walks and/or grooms your dog, has your car washed or detailed, gets theater tickets, and more. What more can you ask for? 310/451.5155 ♦ Daily. 500 Broadway (at Fifth St). 310/393.2322

55 IVY AT THE SHORE

★★$$$ This informal oceanfront version of the more stylish Ivy in Midtown is spacious and airy, with big rattan chairs and an outdoor terrace. Although the food has fallen from foodie grace, it's still worth a visit. The menu includes crab cakes, grilled fresh fish, steaks, pasta, and salads. It's a good place to bring out-of-town visitors looking for the elusive "LA lifestyle." ♦ California ♦ Daily, lunch and dinner. Reservations recommended. 1535 Ocean Ave (between Colorado Ave and Broadway). 310/393.3113

55 TENGU JAPANESE/SUSHI

★★$$ This fun little spot dishes out yummy sushi and ocean views. It's a great place to start a dine-around or enjoy a full meal like the Omakase—an assortment of the chef's signature dishes like Mizore roll (crab, avocado, seared albacore) and red snapper carpaccio; wash it down with the house-infused chilled pineapple sake. ♦ Japanese ♦ Su, Sa, lunch and dinner. Reservations suggested. 1541 Ocean Ave, Suite 120 (between Colorado Ave and Broadway). 310/587.2222

55 ABODE

★★$$$ Hidden away on a terra-cotta-tiled courtyard, this adorable restaurant was designed by Franklin Studios to reflect the seaside location with alfresco dining set among banana trees and succulents. The interior is defined by tangerine high-backed leather chairs and black walnut tables. Floor-to-ceiling cream-colored geometric wood screens highlight the room. The chefs obviously have fun with the menu, creating innovative dishes such as pear-parsnip cappuccino soup with truffles and coffee, pork osso bucco cooked in cider for five hours, and yummy desserts like piña colada floats with rum soda and apple, *Manchego*, and rosemary sorbets. ♦ Contemporary American ♦ M-Sa, dinner; Su, brunch. Reservations suggested. 1541 Ocean Ave (between Colorado Ave and Broadway, in a courtyard behind Tengu Sushi). 310/394.3463. www.aboderestaurant.com

56 SANTA MONICA PLACE

Architect **Frank Gehry**'s 1979-81 design of this huge white skylit galleria features three levels of shops. The cutaway façade with its balcony views of the ocean, the mesh screen on the parking garage, and the asymmetrical plan show that an architectural intelligence rather than a cookie-cutter mind was involved. The complex includes **Eddie Bauer, Compagnie BX** (Michael Glasser's boutique), **Natural Wonders, Cotton Kids,** more than a dozen specialty carts selling everything from candles to jewelry, and 150 other stores as well as the **Santa Monica Visitor's Center** (at no. 203). If you need help navigating the area, drop into this state-of-the-art help center where a multilingual staff can assist with hotel reservations or tickets to attractions and give advice on restaurants. There are also interactive computer displays. 310/393.7593. The **USC School of Fine Arts** shows innovative Southern California artists in its **Atelier.** ♦ Daily. Bounded by Fourth and Second Sts, and Colorado Ave and Broadway. 310/394.1049. www.santamonicaplace.com

57 SANTA MONICA PIER

The aroma of popcorn, cotton candy, and corn dogs, the soft resonance of the boardwalk underfoot, the calliope of the merry-go-round, and the metallic din of the penny arcade characterize this pier, which really began as two piers. Built side by side between 1909 and 1921, the piers were threatened with demolition in 1973 and badly damaged by storms 10 years later. Citizens rallied to save them, and the city backed a Pier Restoration Corporation development plan that resulted in such additions as the **UCLA Ocean Discovery Center** (310/393.6149), a hands-on aquarium/learning center focusing on the study of underwater sea life. Open to the public daily 11AM to 5PM, the facility offers computer links to scientific sources around the world, tanks filled with many kinds of sea creatures, and a small auditorium for lectures. **Pacific Park** (310/260.8744), a two-acre "fun zone" at the southwest corner of the pier, features 12 rides, including a roller coaster and a giant Ferris wheel that soars 100 feet above the ocean. There's also a food court, arcade games, strolling performers, shops, and boutiques. www.pacpark.com.

The **Looff Hippodrome**'s **Philadelphia Toboggan carousel** is the most popular activity on the pier. Brought to the pier in 1947 and restored in 1981, the carousel played a supporting role in the movie *The Sting*. Free concerts with dancing under the stars are presented regularly in the summer. At night, the long strand of white lights along the pier's edge creates a poetic landmark for those coming down the coast highway from the north. **Perry's Beach Club** (320 Santa Monica Pier, 310/393.9778) offers 1½-hour guided bike tours through historic Santa Monica that include a goody bag of freebies and coupons, three-hour bike rental, lock, and protective gear. Nearby, the architectural firm **Moore, Ruble, and Yudell** created **Carousel Park** (Colorado and Ocean Avenues) as a stepped gateway to the pier, an open theater for beach sports, and a children's park with a dragon made of river-washed granite boulders. To the south, the same architects have landscaped a section of **Ocean Park Beach,** and the entire three-mile stretch of beach has been turned into the **Natural Elements Sculpture Park.** Already installed in this park is Douglas Hollis's *Wind Harp* (singing beach chairs). Carl Cheng's *Santa Monica Art Tool* is a concrete roller towed by a tractor to imprint a miniature metropolis on the sand. ♦ Fee for Pacific Park rides and carousel. Pacific Park and Looff Hippodrome: daily. Carousel Park: Tu-Su in summer; Sa, Su in winter. Shuttle buses run from the parking structure at 2030 Barnard Way. Colorado Ave (just southwest of Ocean Ave). General information 310/260.8747

58 SANTA MONICA FREEWAY

Known as the "Christopher Columbus Transcontinental Highway," it sweeps through a curved tunnel to Route 1, setting you on a new course filled with dramatic scenery.

59 ANGELS ATTIC MUSEUM

Miniatures, toys, and dolls are displayed in this restored Victorian-style house, while tea and cookies are served on the porch from 12:30 to 3:30PM. ♦ Admission. Th-Su. 516 Colorado Ave (between Sixth and Fifth Sts). 310/394.8331

60 DOUBLETREE SUITES

$$$ Sweeping views, a terrace restaurant, business center, outdoor pool, and fitness facilities are only some of the amenities provided at this all-suite hotel (formerly **Guest Quarters**). It's a great buy for families, as the 253 suites here each sleep four. ♦ 1707 Fourth St (at Santa Monica Fwy). 310/395.3332, 800/222.8733 (weekends only); fax 310/458.6493. www.doubletreeSantaMonica.com

61 SANTA MONICA CIVIC CENTER

The complex includes the **Santa Monica Civic Auditorium** (310/393.9961), which presents big-name rock and jazz concerts, exhibitions, and trade shows. ♦ Bounded by Fourth and Main Sts, and Pico Blvd and Santa Monica Fwy

62 SHERATON DELFINA

$$$ The Kor Hotel Group's design dream team revamped this 308-room hotel from top to bottom to create a real stunner. The hospitable lobby bears an urban motif emphasized by espresso browns and Tibetan blues. There are cozy areas set up with cushy chairs and sofas in which to relax or have a drink. An interesting array of artwork and photographs fill the length of the back wall from top to bottom. Accommodations are inviting, with special Sweet Sleeper beds with textured leather headboards, Lucite lamps, fine linens, and bath and body products, and now-necessities such as flat-screen TVs, large workspaces with desks, high-speed Internet, and digital safes. There are two restaurants: The lively **Lobby Bistro & Lounge** (★★★ $$) enjoys an inviting poolside setting under an attractive atrium and is a pleasant place to enjoy some fun "small plates" of exceptional food. Go for the fish and chips at lunch, some of the best we've tasted this side of England. Breakfast, lunch, and dinner are served daily. **Perla** ($$), located on the mezzanine level, was under renovation during our visit, so we didn't sample the fare. It is open for dinner daily. While almost unheard of, parking is complimentary—a real bonus considering most hotels charge upwards of $18 a night to house your car. Another perk is free shuttle service to local attractions—which is recommended, since it's not easy finding parking spaces in town. If you book a "club floor" or oceanfront room, they throw in a complimentary continental breakfast and evening hors d'oeuvres and snacks served in a private cabana near the pool. Leisure-time offerings include a swimming pool and fitness room. The location is perfect: The beach is an easy four-block walk or jog away: shops and restaurants are only a little farther, and quite manageable by foot. There's also a guest laundry for folks who like to wash their own clothes. ♦ 530 Pico Blvd (between Fourth St and Lincoln Blvd). 888/627.8532, 310/399.9344; fax 310/399.2504. www.sheratondelfina.com

63 LOEWS SANTA MONICA BEACH HOTEL

$$$$ This attractive luxury hotel just above the beach provides sweeping views of the sea. Just a short walk from the **Santa Monica Pier,** it offers 350 recently renovated rooms and suites flanking a lofty glass-roofed atrium, out of which flow the restaurants and a half-covered pool. The spa and fitness center, operated by trainer-to-the-stars Jackson Sousa, is one of the best of the hotel variety. **Ocean Vine** (★★★ $$$) features creative California cuisine in a casual setting. There's also a fireside lounge for drinks and tapas. An array of business facilities and meeting spaces is available. ♦ California ♦ Reservations suggested. Daily, breakfast and lunch; Tu-Sa, dinner. 310.576.3180. 1700 Ocean Ave (between Seaview and Seaside Terrs). 310/458.6700, 800/223.0888; fax 310/458.0020. www.loewshotels.com ♿

63 SEGWAY LOS ANGELES

For a fun tour of Santa Monica, book the guided California Dreamin' tour offered here. The latest rage throughout Southern California, Segways are self-balancing, electric-powered devices (they hate it when we call them "scooters," but that's what they look like to us) that employ gyroscopes and tilt sensors to emulate human equilibrium—a pretty nifty way to tool around town, especially on this two-hour trek that runs along the shoreline, on the Boardwalk, past the Pier, Muscle Beach, and other interesting sights. If you haven't hopped on a Segway before, don't worry—a 15-minute tutorial is provided. When last we looked, the tour tab was $75 a person. ♦ M-Sa. 1660 Ocean Ave (between Pico Blvd and Colorado Ave). 310/395.1395. www.segway.la

63 LE MERIGOT

$$$ Although there are 175 rooms, Le Merigot (a JW Marriott beach hotel and spa) has the feel of a smaller, more intimate hotel thanks to a friendly staff and relaxed atmosphere. Even the lobby is serene with its large, open spaces and comfy chairs and sofas. All the rooms are spacious and nicely

---

Restaurants/Clubs: Red | Hotels: Purple | Shops: Orange | Outdoors/Parks: Green | Sights/Culture: Blue

appointed, with an understated elegance. The linens are Frette and the toiletries are from Bare Escentuals. There are feather beds, robes, slippers, 24-hour mending and pressing of clothing, free shoe shine, newspaper, fax, cellular phone, and even the option of having someone pack and unpack your bags. (For a real treat, book room no. 449, which comes with a big balcony and great views of the sea.) There's an inviting lobby bar **Le Troquet,** where drinks, hors d'oeuvres, and cigars are proffered. A well-equipped fitness room and nice-sized pool help keep guests in shape, while a full-service spa provides the ultimate in pampering treatments—massages here are not to be missed. Le Merigot opened on New Year's Day Y2K. Be sure to ask about the family and other assorted packages. The hotel is literally steps from the sea and Santa Monica's shopping areas. ♦ 1740 Ocean Ave (between Pico Blvd and Colorado Ave). 310/395.9700, 888/539.7899; fax 310/395.9200. www.lemerigothotel.com or www.marriott.com

Within Le Merigot:

CEZANNE RESTAURANT

★★★$$$ Hardly your average hotel restaurant, this one's a real winner, with great food and homey service. Hidden down a short flight of stairs, the attractive room seems designed for couples, complete with a piano player who keeps it soft and light. The menu begins with tasty starters such as lobster bisque, wild mushroom spring rolls, and spicy ahi tuna tartare (really good), and moves along to fresh salads (the Caesar is super) and perfectly prepared wild California king salmon, Alaskan cod, Dover sole meunière, black truffle mac and cheese, lamb, steaks, and yummy desserts such as opera cake and lemon shortcake with strawberries. ♦ French with a Pacific Rim Twist ♦ Daily, breakfast, lunch, and dinner. Reservations required for dinner. 310/395.9700

64 VIDIOTS

This is the place to rent or buy unique independent, foreign, and cult movies. ♦ Daily. 302 Pico Blvd (at Third St). 310/392.8508

65 MARLOW'S BOOKS

And here's where to pick up new and used books of all kinds, along with sheet music and magazines. ♦ Daily. 2314 Lincoln Blvd (between Kensington Rd and Strand St). 310/392.9161

66 VICEROY

$$$ Interior designer Kelly Wearstler performed miracles on the aging landmark Pacific Shore Hotel when hired by the Kor

Hotel Group, who took over the place in 2002, to do the remodel. The result is an over-the-top stunning design with lots of white, splashes of yellow, charcoal, and minimalism mixed with Colonial—cane and wicker furnishings combine with chandeliers, oversized chairs, and chaises done in white faux leather. It's hip and happening, with 170 sleek rooms done in blinding white with yellowish trim. Nice touches include 300-thread-count Frette sheets, surround-sound CD/DVD players, and attractive tile baths with lavish amenities. For those who prefer the very best, the pay-as-you-use Beauty Bar features high-end ayurvedic and botanical-based organic skin care products from Sundari, Aesop, and Santa Verde. The two pools double as a guest facility, providing a meeting place for after-work locals who flop on oversized chaises and sip martinis and other libations. There's also a fitness center outfitted with Technogym equipment, LCD screens, and hardwood floors, and a popular restaurant called **Whist** (see below). ♦ 1819 Ocean Ave (at Pico Blvd). 800/622.8711, 310/260.7500; fax 310/260.7517. www.viceroysantamonica.com

Within the Viceroy:

WHIST

★★★$$$ A crowd scene on almost any night of the week, this quirky-looking restaurant combines metallic wallpaper with pentagonal, Escher-esque glass chandeliers, a limed wood floor, wingback chaises, smoky mirrors, and a green-mirrored wall filled with 250 pieces of English china. The noise level (mostly from high-testosterone tipplers) makes conversation difficult. The food is so good you'll want to concentrate on what you're eating anyway. Frequent visits never disappoint and in fact prove better than the last, if that's possible. We're talking a Caesar salad prepared to perfection, or an amazing Belgian endive salad vinaigrette with St. Agur blue cheese, apples, and toasted pecans that goes beyond the bar. Then a sautéed foie gras with cranberry compote and a toasted brioche that surpasses, or a seared ahi tuna with heirloom tomatoes, white beans, and sautéed spinach that will make your taste buds sing. Then a wild king salmon on lentils or an unsurpassed grilled Angus prime rib. Even vegans get a culinary treat with the roasted pumpkin served on mascarpone polenta with seasonal vegetables. Bring a big appetite and save room for desserts, which are equally divine. ♦ California ♦ Daily, breakfast, lunch, and dinner. Reservations a must for dinner. 310/451.8711

67 SHUTTERS ON THE BEACH

$$$$ Antebellum unites with modern-day luxury at this 198-room plantation-style beachfront budget-buster. It seems like a

whole lot of reinventing is going on in the hotel industry, and Shutters is right in step with the trend. Los Angeles–based designer Michael S. Smith put his talents to work enhancing guest rooms with oak hardwood floors, hand-knotted Tibetan wool rugs, oversized desks with all the high-tech Internet gadgets, four-poster beds, built-in 32-inch LCD TV screens, built-in bookcases with a relaxation library, coffeemakers, and even an in-room wine cellar. He also put 10-inch flat-screen LCDs in the bathroom. The hotel has gone outside the box to make your traveling experience hassle-free with departure services and amenities such as prearranged airport transportation, preprinted boarding passes, take-out meals to bring on your flight, neck pillows, and luggage straps. They'll even gas up your car on request (for the cost of fuel, of course). All you have to do is hit the "dreams" button on your phone to have your requests filled. Creature comforts include pretty terry robes, in-room and outdoor Jacuzzis, a health club, a pool, two restaurants, and a plucky waterfront saloon called **Pedals.** One of the best amenities is the **OleHenriksen** day spa. One branch of the West Hollywood facility, the transcendental pamper spot offers hand-picked, trained therapists who provide head-to-toe treatments. Facials are about as good as it gets. Call the concierge for appointments at 310/458.0030. (OleHenriksen is also located at 8622A W Sunset Blvd, in Sunset Plaza on the south side of Sunset Blvd, West Hollywood. 310/854.7700.) www.olehenriksen.com ♦ 1 Pico Blvd (at Appian Way). 310/458.0030, 800/336.3000; fax 310/458.4859 ♿

67 CASA DEL MAR

$$$$ This 129-room sister of **Shutters** hotel sits just across the street from its sibling yet is worlds apart. Originally built as a beach club/hotel nearly 75 years ago, the historic landmark underwent a $60 million face-lift before reopening in 1999. The lobby lounge caught on quickly with locals (who jam the place nightly), and the charming hotel rooms have lured lots of business. There's a phenomenal restaurant, a nice-size pool, and all the usual upscale amenities. Pamper seekers can enjoy top-notch therapies at the modest **Murad Spa** (created by noted dermatologist Dr. Howard Murad). Located on the lower level, the facility includes a nicely equipped fitness room, just to the left of the entrance, stocked with modern exercise machines and equipment. Just past the reception desk is a cozy sitting room in which to relax before and after treatments. Spa services, designed by Dr. Murad, run the

scale from facials to foot care and are actually quite good, as well as pricey. Lockers and showers are available, but there are no steam baths or saunas. Should you want to sweat it out, you can go next door to Shutters and luxuriate at the One Spa for no extra fee. ♦ 1910 Ocean Front Walk (across the street from Shutters at Pico Blvd). 310/581.5533. www.hotelcasadelmar.com

Within Casa del Mar:

CATCH

★★★$$$ Sweeping views of the sea from oversized windows and a casual-chic atmosphere provide the perfect setting for sampling exceptional cuisine. In fact, on a recent visit the food at the recently redecorated beachfront restaurant was better than ever, especially the plate of delicately seasoned white asparagus, perfectly spiced tuna tartare, a sushi sampler, and a faultless Caesar salad, and a superbly prepared pan-roasted John Dory, a crispy-skin king salmon, and a melt-in-your-mouth beef rib eye, along with yummy desserts like the walnut baklava with cinnamon ice cream and Pinot Noir syrup, warm chocolate truffle cake, and a mascarpone cheesecake with roasted cherry sauce and hazelnut tuile that made our taste buds sing. ♦ California Cuisine ♦ Daily, breakfast, lunch and dinner. Reservations a must for lunch and dinner. 310/581.7714

67 CORA'S COFFEE SHOPPE

★★$$ This funky little indoor/outdoor joint dishes out hearty, delicious breakfasts. The rich illy coffee will jump-start your day; the cappuccinos are potent and delicious. In addition to the usual egg dishes, there are wonderful frittatas, omelettes, and pancakes. You can actually have breakfast all day, or opt for luncheon/dinner–like fare: prime rib sandwich, rotisserie organic half chicken, or a Caesar salad with white truffle oil. This is quite a popular spot, so you may have to wait for a table, especially one on the patio. ♦ Daily until 9PM. No reservations. 1802 Ocean Ave (at Pico Blvd). 310/451.9562

68 SANTA MONICA VISITORS CENTER

The friendly folk who man this new center can help you with hotels, restaurants, attractions, and even directions. There's high-speed wireless Internet access, souvenir shops, and a display about the area. ♦ 1920 Main St, Suite B (1 block south of Pico Blvd). 310/393.7593, 800/544.5319. www.santamonica.com

Restaurants/Clubs: Red | Hotels: Purple | Shops: Orange | Outdoors/Parks: Green | Sights/Culture: Blue

69 MAIN STREET

Slightly south of Santa Monica proper is Ocean Park, once a seaside resort with thousands of tiny beach cottages and a large Coney Island–style amusement park. The neighborhood now includes an active shopping and trendy dining area covering several blocks of this street. It's a pleasant place for walking and window-shopping. There is a high concentration of restaurants, many with rear patios or sidewalk seating.

70 HORATIO WEST COURT

These impressively modern two-story apartments, designed by **Irving Gill** in 1919, were far ahead of their time. They are private residences. ♦ 140 Hollister Ave (between Neilson Way and Ocean Ave)

71 HIGHLIGHTS

Owners Ron Rezek and Lori Thomsen have displayed their choice of the "50 best lights in the world," and can order up many more if you still can't find just the right lamp. Call ahead if you plan to drop by at lunchtime. ♦ M-Sa. 2427 Main St (between Ocean Park Blvd and Hollister Ave). 310/450.5886

71 EDGEMAR

Developer Abby Sher commissioned **Frank Gehry** to design this urban village in 1989. The mixed-use development points to the numbing mediocrity of the minimalls elsewhere in the city. Instead of the typical façade with a car park in front, Gehry has created a cluster of unique sculptural forms (high-tech, streamlined, and minimalist) that relate well to neighboring buildings and define a series of pedestrian spaces. An eclectic mix of businesses occupies the development, including an art museum, an upscale restaurant, and retail stores offering functional art, pricey retro children's clothing, business services, records, and **Ben & Jerry's** ice cream. ♦ 2435 Main St (between Ocean Park Blvd and Hollister Ave)

72 CALIFORNIA HERITAGE MUSEUM

Period rooms, local archives, and photographs are preserved in this restored 19th-century house designed by **Sumner P. Hunt** for Roy Jones, a son of one of the city's founders. ♦ Admission. W-Su. 2612 Main St (at Ocean Park Blvd). 310/392.8537

73 MAX STUDIO

Trendy Generation Y'ers shop here for Leon Max's casuals, suits, and special dresses. ♦ Daily. 2712 Main St (between Ashland Ave and Hill St). 310/396.3963. www.maxstudio.com

74 JADIS

Even if you're not a set designer, you might get a kick out of Parke Meek's place of movie props. Meek makes scientific and industrial props that have appeared in such films as *Batman, Casper, Mystery Men*, and *Waterworld*, as well as TV's *The X Files*. His kitschy window displays are reason enough to visit the shop—and Meek always welcomes visitors. ♦ 2701 Main St (right next door to Paris 1900 at Hill St). Call ahead to be sure someone's there, if you want to go inside. 323/396.3477

74 PARIS 1900

Martha Stewart meets Laura Ashley at this adorable boutique, which carries a wonderful assortment of white vintage lace gowns, bridal accessories, antique table linens, bedding, and museum-quality antique clothing and accessories. ♦ M-Sa by appointment, or take a chance and stop by; if someone's there they'll let you in. 2703 Main St (at Hill St). 310/396.0405. www.paris1900.com

74 CHINOIS ON MAIN

★★★★$$$$ **Wolfgang Puck**'s noisy, crowded, and expensive restaurant is not to be missed by anyone who loves indulging in inventive cuisine in the most stylish of settings. Puck's creations fuse East and West. Try the warm curried oysters, Cantonese duck, barbecued salmon, or ginger-stuffed whole sizzling catfish with sweet pepper sauce. Desserts are special here, the standout being an assortment of three petites crèmes brûlées. Barbara Lazaroff (Puck's former wife) did the wonderful décor, which incorporates a fine screen by Miriam Wosk. Ask for a table away from the open kitchen. ♦ French/Chinese ♦ Daily, dinner; W-F, lunch and dinner. Reservations required. 2709 Main St (between Ashland Ave and Hill St). 310/392.9025

75 HOMEWORKS

You will certainly find unusual items at this novelty gift shop, which prides itself on its oddball eclectic inventory. ♦ Daily. 2923 Main St (between Pier and Ashland Aves). 310/396.0101

76 ENTERPRISE FISH COMPANY

★★$$ This fish-eater's haven captures the seafaring ambience of the Chesapeake Bay and the Pacific Northwest. Steamed mussels, chunky clam chowder, and fried calamari are great openers for swordfish, mahimahi, orange roughy, and fresh Pacific salmon broiled on an open mesquite grill. Japanese tourists come here by the busload. ♦ Seafood ♦ Daily, lunch and dinner. Reservations recommended. 174 Kinney St (at Main St). 310/392.8366

VENICE

t the turn of the century, tobacco magnate Abbot Kinney tried to create a model community fashioned fter Venice, Italy, that would spur Americans to chieve their own cultural renaissance. A network of anals drained the marshy land and fed into the **Grand agoon,** and a three-day opening celebration, eginning on 4 July 1905, featured gondola and camel des. The community was briefly self-governing, but in 925, residents voted for annexation by the city of LA, vhich soon paved over all but three of the original 16 niles of canals and closed the speakeasies and ambling houses that thrived during Prohibition. The rcades along **Windward Avenue** and a few surviving vaterways to the south (which are slowly being efurbished) are all that survive of Kinney's grand esign.

ut Venice and neighboring **Ocean Park** continued to ourish as "Coney Island West," defying the bluenoses nd devastation by storm and fire. Flanking the oardwalks and several piers were Arabian bath-ouses and Egyptian bazaars, roller coasters, and reak shows. As the area became more raffish and run-own, it lured those who couldn't afford to live—or idn't feel at home—elsewhere. Beats gave way to ippies and Hell's Angels to drug gangs, with the lderly, the artistic, and the adventurous finally settling ere in a crazy quilt of humanity. The diversity is on isplay in the weekend circus on **Ocean Front Walk,** vhere jocks, executives, panhandlers, hipsters, amilies, bikini-clad women, and cops in shorts romenade or roll along the famed **Venice Beach oardwalk** on every imaginable wheeled device. It has ecome a compulsory stop for tourists from Tokyo to opeka. You can rent skates or bikes and join the cene. For a map of **Venice Beach,** contact the **Venice hamber of Commerce** (310/396.7016, ww.venice.net/chamber) and ask for the *Venice isitors Map,* a valuable guide to the area's rich election of public art, historic sites, and more.

ferment of cultural activity away from this colorful raziness are the studios and galleries of leading rtists, many of which can be explored on the annual rt Walk (for more information, call 310/392.8630). ome of LA's most adventurous new architecture and estaurants are slotted in amid the peeling stucco and lapboard cottages. The greatest threats today are om crime and gentrification, not physical deteriora-on. When there's no room at the beach parking lots, ou can leave your car in the city lot at Abbot Kinney

and Venice Boulevards and ride to the beach on the DASH shuttle, which runs every 15 minutes on Saturday and Sunday.

77 VENICE RENAISSANCE BUILDING

Johannes Van Tilburg's design for this 1990 building was lauded for its mixed-use concept. The 34-foot-high ballerina clown sculpture mounted at its southeast prow has become a landmark; the bizarre kinetic work unites the contrasting images of a classical performer and a lowbrow comedian. Artist Jonathan Borofsky designed the vulgar, kitschy image to echo Venice and to contrast the upscale site. ♦ Rose Ave and Main St

Within the Venice Renaissance Building:

CHAYA VENICE

★★$$ This stunning restaurant was designed by Grinstein/Daniels, who created the interior for **Chaya Brasserie** in West Hollywood and **El Chaya** in Hollywood. Bronze and copper, natu-ral woods and stone, and a Japanese ceiling mural achieve a pleasing harmony. And the food is equally enjoyable, especially the miso or spicy white bean soup, shrimp and pork pot stickers, and paella. For dessert, the brownie sundae and the "Banana, Banana, Banana" tart coated in chocolate are musts. ♦ International ♦ M-F, lunch and dinner; Sa, dinner; Su, brunch, lunch, and dinner. Reservations recommended. 110 Navy St (at Main St). 310/396.1179. www.thechaya.com

78 340 MAIN BUILDING

Designed by **Frank Gehry,** this unique building has two sections flanking the entry—a boat-shaped white office wing on the north and an innovative abstract tree form made of copper-clad steel on the south—which were already designed when former tenant Jay Chiat pushed for an entry solution. Gehry grabbed a nearby Claes Oldenburg maquette of a pair of binoculars and placed it on the model as an example. Chiat liked it. The result is an unusual building (completed in 1991) designed to create a three-part streetscape in scale with the neighborhood. The structure still appears massive because it reaches the edge of the site (to compensate for coastal height limits). The treelike form creates a sunscreen for the west-facing building, and the binoculars contain two small meeting rooms. ♦ 340 Main St (at Rose Ave)

79 VENICE BISTRO

★$$ Mexican-American dishes, including pasta and a variety of salads, are served at

---

Restaurants/Clubs: Red **|** Hotels: Purple **|** Shops: Orange **|** Outdoors/Parks: Green **|** Sights/Culture: Blue this popular patio restaurant. There's live music Wednesday through Sunday evenings. ◆ Mexican/American ◆ Daily, lunch and dinner. 323 Ocean Front Walk (between Dudley and Rose Aves). 310/392.3997

80 FIG TREE

$$ Grilled fish and flavorful vegetarian dishes are served both indoors and on a peaceful patio just off the boardwalk. ◆ California ◆ Daily, breakfast, lunch, and dinner. 429 Ocean Front Walk (between Paloma and Dudley Aves). 310/392.4937

81 ABBOT KINNEY BOULEVARD

Move over, Melrose and Montana Avenues: This Venice Beach thoroughfare, buzzing with trendy shops, restaurants, and gathering spots, is about to eat your shorts. The hip, cool, and the oh-so-happening eternally-on-the-cell-phone crowd can't get enough of this quirky commercial mecca where funk meets high-end architecture and cutesy cottages and spiffy new buildings perch side by side. Just a few highlights include **Primitivo Wine Bistro,** a fun spot for a glass of wine, tapas, salads, and desserts that buzzes to a Brazilian beat (at 1025 Abbot Kinney Blvd, 310/396.5353, www.primitvowinebistro.com); **Jin Patisserie,** where baked goods are works of art (1202 Abbot Kinney Blvd, 310/399.8801, www.jinpatisserie.com); and **Equator Books,** when you need a cultural fix of rare and vintage reading materials. You'll find a large collection of out-of-print surfing titles, Japanese lit, and Black studies, along with the works of various artists (1102 Abbot Kinney Blvd, 310/399.5544). And that's not all: There's a **Scentiments,** specializing in floral designs from natural materials (1331 Abbot Kinney Blvd, 310/399.4110, www.scentimentsflowers.com), and lots of other shops, clothing boutiques, sushi joints, and bars. For a creative, definitely different eating experience, check out **3 Square + Baker** (★★$$), Hans and Patti Rockenwagner's quirky café where folks flock for unique creations such as Bavarian breakfast meat loaf with eggs and a pretzel roll with caramelized onions, corn crepes stuffed with Black Forest ham, avocado fries with fire-roasted salsa, pretzel burgers, apple pancakes, or more traditional goulash, sandwiches, and mini sandwich samplers and salads. The popular spot is open for breakfast and lunch weekdays, 8AM-3PM, and weekends, 9AM-4PM with dinner 5PM-10PM, Tu-Sa. The bakery operates daily, 7AM-6PM (1121 Abbot Kinney Blvd at San Juan Ave, 310/399.6504, www.rockenwagner.com).

81 JOE'S RESTAURANT

★★★$$ Yes, there really is a Joe: chef Joe Miller, who staffs the kitchen and creates good, honest California food at modest prices. We love the relaxed atmosphere, especially for a leisurely lunch, but dinner's great, too. Everything the chef makes rocks. A few recommendations include the tuna tartare and smoked salmon starter, house-made English pea tortellini with devil's gulch pork rillette, truffle-parsnip puree, and grapefruit gremolata. If you really want a taste of Miller's efforts, go for the prix-fixe menu. Rewards for finishing your plate include decadent desserts. The room has a New York/San Francisco flair, a laid-back elegance that makes you want to dress up. There's a welcoming outdoor patio (heated in winter). The service is consistently efficient. ◆ California ◆ Tu-Su, lunch and dinner. Reservations suggested. 1023 Abbot Kinney Blvd (near Broadway). 310/399.5811. www.JoesRestaurant.com

81 LILLY'S FRENCH CAFÉ & BAR

$$ Chef Francis Bey treats diners to delicious French fare in a California-casual bi-level patio setting. The roasted chicken breast; goat cheese, wild mushroom, and leek tart; and juicy sirloin steak are ooh la la and there are yummy desserts. ◆ French ◆ Daily, lunch and dinner. Reservations suggested for dinner. 1301 Abbot Kinney Blvd (between Westminster Ave and Broadway). 310/314.0004. www.lillysfrenchcafe.com

81 AXE

★★$$$ This eclectic little café dishes out some dandy eats, from the grilled flatbread smothered with hummus, eggplant, and caramelized onions to the poached halibut or duck leg laced with plum, orange, and cilantro. And for dessert, a chocolate brownie pudding will satisfy your sweet tooth. ◆ Eclectic ◆ Reservations suggested. Tu-F, lunch; Tu-Su, dinner. 1009 Abbot Kinney Blvd (between Brooks Ave and Broadway). 310/664.9787

82 CAPLIN HOUSE

This quirky house by **Frederick Fisher** was built in 1979 for the editor of *Wet* magazine; the design was a stylistic statement for both the architect and the client. It's a private residence. ◆ 229 San Juan Ave (between Riviera Ave and Main St)

83 SPILLER HOUSE

In 1980, **Frank Gehry** designed this pair of houses, each with two parking spaces and a garden, shoehorned onto a very tiny plot. They combine a corrugated-steel exterior

The city of Santa Monica collects more than $5 million in parking fees yearly.

with a woodsy interior, thus creating an archetypal low-cost Venice landmark. This is a private residence. ♦ 39 Horizon Ave (between Pacific Ave and Speedway)

84 HAL'S BAR & GRILL

★$$ A favorite with local artists, this place has a casual interior and offers salads, pasta, and other basic fare. ♦ California ♦ Daily, lunch and dinner; Sa, Su, brunch and dinner. Reservations recommended. 1349 Abbot Kinney Blvd (between California and Santa Clara Aves). 310/396.3105. www.halsbarandgrill.com

85 BEYOND BAROQUE LITERARY/ ARTS CENTER

Don't miss the adventurous readings, lectures, and performances that sustain the bohemian tradition of Venice. Abbot Kinney would have approved. Call ahead for program information. ♦ 681 Venice Blvd (between Oakwood and Shell Aves). 310/822.3006

86 SIDEWALK CAFE

$ Skateboarders and young "dig me" types go here to enjoy salads, pizzas, and burgers. ♦ American ♦ Daily, breakfast, lunch, and dinner. 1401 Ocean Front Walk (at Horizon Ave). 310/399.5547

87 WINDWARD CIRCLE

From 1905 to 1929 it was known as the "Grand Lagoon." Architect **Steven Erlich** has tried to awaken its ghosts with three complementary buildings that use concrete-filled culvert pipes to suggest Venetian porticoes. The giant **Race Through the Clouds roller coaster** finds an echo in the neon loop of a retail block; metal frames flank a food market, recalling the steam-driven dredgers that excavated the canals. A residential block occupies the site of the **Antlers Hotel,** which was demolished in 1960. To the south is a post office containing Edward Biberman's mural of the history of Venice. ♦ Main St and Windward Ave

At Windward Circle:

HAMA SUSHI

★$$$ This well-lit eatery decorated with blond wood furnishings is a favorite neighborhood sushi bar. If perchance you're not in the mood for sushi, try the lobster dynamite (lobster sautéed in soy sauce with mushrooms). ♦ Japanese ♦ Daily, dinner. 213 Windward Ave. 310/396.8783. www.restaurant-hama.com

88 CAPRI

★★$$ Owner Alana Hamilton Cooke offers superb food in a minimalist setting. Menu highlights include tuna tartare, halibut ceviche, spinach ravioli, Angus filet, and some impressive pastas and risottos. Cooke boasts a hand-picked, reasonably priced wine list with selections from Italy, France, and California. Save room for wonderful desserts, like panna cotta and molten flourless chocolate cake. ♦ Italian ♦ Daily, dinner. Reservations recommended on weekends. 1616 Abbot Kinney Blvd (between S Venice Blvd and Rialto Ave). 310/392.8777

89 VENICE MURAL

Terry Schoonhoven's large, much-faded mural shows a mirror image of the city on a very clear day, with the distant mountains in view. Venice is full of murals—one of the best, Jon Werhle's *The Fall of Icarus*, is a block north—and in fact French filmmaker Agnes Varda, a local resident, did a poetic documentary about them called *Murs Murs*. A local agency, SPARC, is commissioning more murals to be created with city funds. ♦ Windward Ave and Speedway

90 L.A. LOUVER GALLERY

Works by important LA artists, including David Hockney, Ed Moses, Tony Berlant, and Michael McMillen, are showcased here. ♦ Tu-Sa. 55 S Venice Blvd (at Pacific Ave). 310/822.4955. Also at 77 Market St (at Pacific Ave). 310/822.4955

91 JAMES BEACH

★★★$$ James Evans's popular neighbor-hood eatery sports spare white walls, classic "potato chip" chairs created by Charles Eames, and cozy booths by the back wall. The food continues to garner rave reviews from critics and patrons, especially the "Towering Shrimp Louis" (a mound of plump pink shrimp on crisp iceberg lettuce), tuna tartare, grilled Portobello mushrooms with spinach and mashed potatoes, hearty chicken potpie, turkey burgers, and sandwiches. ♦ American ♦ Daily, dinner; W-F, lunch; Sa, Su, brunch. Reservations recommended. Valet parking available. 60 S Venice Blvd (at Pacific Ave). 310/823.5396

92 VENICE CANALS

A frail remnant of Abbot Kinney's vision can be found along this succession of side canals and Venetian bridges. The city would like to fill the canals in, so catch them while you can. ♦ Southeast of S Venice Blvd and Strongs Dr

Restaurants/Clubs: Red | Hotels: Purple | Shops: Orange | Outdoors/Parks: Green | Sights/Culture: Blue

93 NORTON HOUSE

Frank Gehry created this 1984 house for a
Japanese-American artist (notice the log *torii*
over the gate, two upright beams supporting
a concave crosspiece that are typical of a
Shinto temple gateway) and her screenwriter
husband, who works at a lifeguard shelter
overlooking the beach. Gehry's design
provides privacy and complexity on a
minuscule site. This is a private residence.
♦ 2509 Ocean Front Walk (between 26th
and 25th Aves)

94 THE VENICE BEACH HOUSE

$$ Just off the oceanfront, this charming
bed-and-breakfast is located in a quiet part
of Venice. Each of the nine rooms is
individually decorated. ♦ 15 30th Ave
(between Pacific Ave and Speedway).
310/823.1966. www.venicebeachhouse.com

95 SIAMESE GARDEN

★★$$ The specialties served in this
delightful little place include barbecued
chicken, grilled shrimp, glass noodle crab
claws, and the best pad Thai noodles in LA.
The courtyard is delightful, too. ♦ Thai
♦ Daily, dinner. Reservations recommended.
301 Washington St (at Strongs Dr).
310/821.0098. www.siamesegarden.com

MARINA DEL REY

Pulsating with the young, the tan, the blond, and the
restless, this waterfront community was laid out in the
1960s on marshy land between Venice Beach and LAX
(see map on page 126). It's the world's largest
artificial yacht harbor, with moorings for 5,300 private
pleasure craft. Visit www.visitthemarina.com

96 MARINA INTERNATIONAL HOTEL AND BUNGALOWS

$ The main attractions at this waterfront
property are the 24 European-style
bungalows and the commanding views of
the marina from any of 134 rooms. A free
airport shuttle is available to hotel guests.
The **Crystal Fountain** restaurant serves
breakfast, lunch, and dinner daily. ♦ 4200
Admiralty Way (at Palawan Way).
310/301.2000, 800/862.7462 in CA,
800/882.4000 in US; fax 310/301.8867.
www.marinaintlhotel.com

97 RITZ-CARLTON MARINA DEL REY

$$$$ A recent $12 million face-lift breathed
some air into this formerly stuffy hotel. It's
still a Ritz, albeit younger and more
contemporary-looking. The 306 opulent
guest rooms boast Italian marble bathrooms,
stocked with Bulgari toiletries, terry robes,
and hair dryers. Other comforts include a
minibar, multiple phones, Frette linens, flat-
screen TVs, DVD players, and the usual
techno gadgets. Guests on the exceptional
46-room **Club Floor** are treated to
complimentary breakfast, light meals and
drinks, and other special services. As one
would expect from a Ritz, amenities include
just about anything your heart de-
sires . . . just ask. The hotel's dinner
restaurant, **Jer-ne,** features creative
California cuisine (see below). The **Wave
Restaurant and Bar** offers light fare and
drinks by the pool, in season. The centerpiece of the makeover is **The Boutique Spa,**
where they pamper you (for a price—nearly
$200 for a 60-minute rub) with upscale
products such as Prada Beauty, Murad,
Payot, and Mama Mio in eight gorgeous
treatment rooms or a couples suite. There's
also a waterfront fitness center where you
can spin, YAS (a combo of spinning and
yoga), or just work out on the latest
equipment. The oversized, eco-conscious
pool is filled with seawater. There are also
bicycle rentals on the property. ♦ 4375
Admiralty Way (at Via Regatta).
800/241.3333, 310/823.1700; fax
310/823.8421. www.ritzcarlton.com

Within the Ritz-Carlton Marina del Rey:

JER-NE

★★★$$$ Quite good for a hotel facility, this
inviting room overlooking the marina excels
with great food and service. Signatures
dishes include almond-dusted calamari,
roasted Kurobuta pork, scallops, soufflés,
warm hazelnut cake, and our favorite—
blueberry crepes with honey lavender ice
cream. ♦ California Regional Cuisine ♦ Daily
dinner. Reservations advised. 310/823.1700

98 CAFE DEL REY

★★★$$$ Just too trendy for words, with all
the typical Westside accoutrements (sleek
interiors and beautiful people), coupled with
a magnificent view of the marina and great
food, this restaurant is the area's best. The
menu offers choices such as curry-blackened
ahi tuna, boar bacon–wrapped filet mignon,
and "globally inspired cuisine" with choices
such as Thai shellfish sausage, black
spaghetti, assorted fish, beef, salads, and
pastas. The sinfully rich signature dessert is a
white chocolate croissant pudding. ♦ Pan-
Pacific Infusion ♦ M-F, lunch; M-Sa, dinner;
Su, brunch. Reservations recommended.
4451 Admiralty Way (between Bali Way and
Via Regatta). 310/823.6395

99 VILLA MARINA MARKETPLACE

A 1989 complex and a more-than-20-year-
old center are oddly combined in this

shopping area, which spans both sides of the street. Merchants include **Gelson's** gourmet supermarket, **Petals & Wax** (which carries cute candles and gifts), **Electronics Boutique, Gap,** and **Tower Records,** plus 12 movie screens and a Southern restaurant. ◆ 13450 Maxella Ave (between Glencoe Ave and Lincoln Blvd). 310/827.0253

Within Villa Marina Marketplace:

SOUPLANTATION

★★$ A healthful version of the all-you-can-eat smorgasbord, this salad-and-soup bar offers a wide array of fresh vegetables, fruits, and breads. Unlike most shopping-center restaurants, it's airy and light. ◆ American ◆ Daily, lunch and dinner. 310/305.7669

99 AUNT KIZZY'S BACK PORCH

★★$ Catfish, fried chicken, short ribs, and smothered pork chops, just like in the Old South, are served in a cabin-style restaurant. ◆ Southern ◆ Daily, lunch and dinner. 4325 Glencoe Ave (between Mindanao Way and Maxella Ave). 310/578.1005

00 THE CHEESECAKE FACTORY

$$ Specialty drinks are the name of the game at this branch of the popular restaurant chain. Sip a Flying Gorilla or Strawberry Creamsicle while looking out over the boat slips. Then enjoy a meal of really big portions of whatever you order—so big you'll need a doggie bag. And, if you really want to kiss your diet good-bye, order a slice of one of the 35 varieties of cheesecake. ◆ American ◆ Daily, lunch and dinner. 4142 Via Marina (between Panay and Admiralty Ways). 310/306.3344. There are a half dozen or so Cheesecake Factory restaurants throughout the Southland; two

other very popular ones are at 364 N Beverly Dr (one block south of Santa Monica Blvd S), Beverly Hills. 310/278.7270; and 11647 San Vicente Blvd (between Barrington and Darlington Aves), Brentwood. 310/826.7111 (popular with a young "uptown crowd")

101 MARINA DEL REY HOTEL

$$ An ideal base for sailors, this nautical-style, 157-room hotel is surrounded by water on three sides. The **Waterfront Grill** restaurant overlooks the marina's main channel. Additional facilities include a pool, lounge, bike and skate rentals, and complimentary use of LA Fitness Center. ◆ 13534 Bali Way (southwest of Admiralty Way). 310/301.1000, 800/862.7462 in CA, 800/882.4000 in the US; fax 310/301.8167

102 BURTON CHACE PARK

🅟 This park is perfect for yacht watching, fishing, kite flying, or moon gazing. Picnic facilities (with rest rooms) attract families. ◆ Mindanao Way (southwest of Admiralty Way)

103 FISHERMAN'S VILLAGE

Grab a bike, put on a pair of skates, or simply stroll along a 26-mile-long coastal path that stretches from Malibu south to Palos Verdes. Or just stop by for a picnic or to rent a boat, windsurf, whale watch (in season), or enjoy other aquatic sports. Be sure to check out the Sunday-afternoon jazz concerts that enliven this tourist attraction of quaint restaurants (with marginal food) and shops. It's also the perfect venue for yacht watching along the marina channel, or to hop on one of the many harbor cruises. ◆ 13755 Fiji Way (southeast of Admiralty Way). 310/823.5411

MALIBU/THE CANYONS

Where the rich and famous play in the sun and surf . . .

Sun, surf, movie stars, and multimillion-dollar beachfront homes hidden behind gilded gates epitomize the mystique of celebrity-packed Malibu, a high-rent district where the mountains meet the sea and reality and illusion sometimes clash

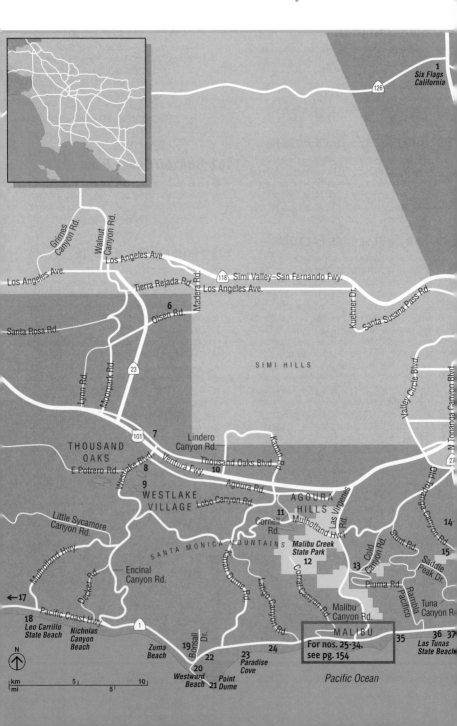

For nos. 25-34, see pg. 154

discordantly. Just about everything you've heard about its laid-back hedonism is true. Bikini-clad sunbathers, die-hard surfers, and star-struck tourists eager for a glimpse of a famous resident all succumb to the allure. Rural, hilly, and isolated from the city, Malibu is about the same size as the rancho it replaced, and tends to hide its riches: Exclusive estates along the **Pacific Coast Highway** reveal only their usually scruffy backsides or hide behind anonymous gates, and Malibu's scatter-shot commercial strip is as ordinary and undistinguished as those of most beach towns, making one wonder just where Malibu actually is.

The Chumash Indians were the area's earliest settlers; in 1887, wealthy easterner Frederick Rindge bought the Topanga-Malibu-Sequit rancho, an expanse that included more than 22 miles of pristine Pacific oceanfront. Rindge built a private railroad and pier, planted alfalfa, and spent the rest of his life trying to shut out newcomers, even taking his argument to the Supreme Court. The government eventually prevailed, however, and in 1929 the Pacific Coast Highway (then the **Roosevelt Highway**) officially opened, paving the way for more development. The first film star to settle in **Malibu Beach** was Anna Q. Nilsson, who built a house on a deserted beach just west of **Malibu Creek** in 1928. Clara Bow, Gloria Swanson, Ronald Colman, and Frank Capra soon followed, and by 1930 the area had been dubbed the "Malibu Motion Picture Colony." Now simply "The Colony," Malibu Beach is still home to a host of celebrities who own houses and estates along the beaches or in the canyons.

The chaparral-covered **Santa Monica Mountains**, which separate the Los Angeles basin from the **San Fernando Valley**, provides a haven for hikers. Affluent homeowners, who have carved a place of their own in the hills and canyons, enjoy breathtaking views along with their privacy. For an up-close and personal 360-degree panorama of ocean, mountains, and the San Fernando Valley, drive up into the hills to the end of Corral Canyon Road, beyond **Malibu Canyon**, and climb to the boulders on the crest of the hill. While the canyon-marked hills trap the smog in the flatlands of the city they define, they also give urban dwellers a rim of rural wilderness.

Alas, there are often problems in Paradise. Devastating mudslides, caused by infrequent but heavy rains in an otherwise arid area, have reduced palatial homes to tumbles of plywood, and the ever-present threat of brushfires keeps residents' hoses at the ready. But for every blow Mother Nature deals them, Malibu dwellers just shrug philosophically—and rebuild. Once you see this magical place, you'll understand why.

SANTA CLARITA VALLEY

One of the fastest-growing areas in Southern California, this picturesque valley surrounded by majestic mountains is blessed with clean air, a low crime rate, and some of the friendliest people in Los Angeles County. Credit **Six Flags Magic Mountain** for putting the area on the map and a major development company for attracting businesses and residents.

1 SIX FLAGS CALIFORNIA

For more than 30 years, **Six Flags Magic Mountain** has offered thrill rides and grand spectacles to delight both kids and adults. Known as the "Xtreme" park for its daredevil rides, it also made the *Guinness Book of Records* for having the most roller coasters of any attraction. ♦ Magic Mountain Pkwy (west of Golden State Fwy). 818/367.5965

At Six Flags California:

SIX FLAGS MAGIC MOUNTAIN: THE XTREME PARK!

This gigantic theme park gets its name from the fast and scary thrill rides offered. Spread out on 260 beautifully landscaped acres atop the rolling hills west of Santa Clarita, this is the kick-ass amusement park of all times, with 15 roller coasters to test your mettle. For true white-knuckle thrills, there's **Déjà Vu,** a super-boomerang roller coaster that plummets 196 feet and flies at a speed of 65 mph over the outside of a vertical loop and a giant 110-foot-tall boomerang turn. If that's not scary enough, climb onboard **X,** where you race in prototype vehicles that spin 360 degrees forward or backward and let you fall (albeit safely) 299 feet to the ground, headfirst, facedown, and race at 76 mph spinning head-over-heels through a huge 3,600-foot twisting steel maze—we're feeling dizzy just writing about it. The two make **Colossus** seem tame even though it's billed as the largest, fastest, highest, and steepest wooden roller coaster ever built. After you've ridden 9,200 feet at speeds of up to 65 mph, you won't want to argue the point. **Zonga,** a loopy, 112-foot-tall roller-coaster ride featuring wild blue, purple, red, yellow, and green towering metal twists-four full-circle, full-tilt loops and two big back-to-back circuits—marks the sixth and wildest roller coaster added to the park's 35 rides in the last six years. Then there's **Scream!** And you surely will after riding this Guinness Book world record winner, with its flying chairs hurtling at mega-speeds through the air and no track above your head or coach around the seats. Now that's Xtreme. The **Revolution** offers a 360-degree vertical loop at 60 mph; the **Shock Wave** gives thrill-seekers the opportunity to loop the loop while standing up; the **Gold Rusher** is a theme roller coaster on which you become a passenger aboard a runaway mine train; and **Flashback** is the world's only hairpin-drop roller coaster, with six spiral dives. If you enjoy getting drenched try the **Tidal Wave,** which takes you by boat over a 50-foot waterfall; the **Jet Stream,** which whisks you across the water in speedboats; and the **Roaring Rapids,** a whitewater rafting trip straight out of *The River Wild.* For extreme adventure of the bungee-jumping kind, **Dive Devil** dares participants, who are strapped in a harness and suspended from steel cables, to dive from towers more than 150 feet tall. "Fliers" plunge in a 50-foot freefall, reaching 60 mph and swing only six feet from the ground before arching back up.

For those who would prefer to watch someone else perform fantastic feats, check out the **Batman Begins Stunt Show,** where stuntmen dangle from wires, fall from buildings, crash motorcycles, and ride the Batmobile onto the stage. Assorted pyrotechnics, an exploding aqueduct, and crumbling buildings enhance the excitement. The **Lazer Dome** presents a live show featuring enough acrobatics, in-line skating, and stunts to satisfy any kid's craving for spectacle. For views of the surrounding territory, take the **Eagle's Flight Tramway,** a 40-degree inclined funicular, to the top of the mountain, or the **Sky Tower,** a ride to the observation deck of a 384-foot space-needle structure.

Nor is the past forgotten here. The **Grand Carousel** is an exquisitely restored 1912 merry-go-round. At **Spillikin Handcrafters Junction,** traditional American crafts such as glassblowing and blacksmithing are demonstrated, and the goods are sold in quaint shops.

Nighttime attractions for teenagers include **Back Street,** a high-energy city block, and **After Hours,** a high-tech dance club. The **Magic Moments Theater** presents *California Dreamin';* and there's plenty of rocking at the **Contempo Pavilion.** Divers and dolphins star at the **Aqua Theater.** A fireworks extrava-ganza explodes over **Mystic Lake** nightly through summer.

Bugs Bunny, Daffy Duck, Wile E. Coyote, and other Warner Brothers cartoon characters welcome youngsters to the six-acre **Bugs Bunny World** with its 15 pint-size rides, and kids can enjoy a magic show through the summer in the **Valencia Falls Pavilion.** And be sure to check out the petting zoo.

Food is plentiful in the park, although it's recommended that you wait a half-hour after meals before hitting the larger rides. The **Four Winds** offers a delicious salad buffet at lunchtime and hot meals in the evening. The **Timbermill** serves hearty American-style food. **Food Etc.** is a fast-food restaurant with a surprisingly sophisticated décor by Shari Canepa. ♦ Admission (one fee covers all rides and attractions, except Dive Devil). Daily, Memorial Day through Labor Day; Sa, Su, and school holidays the rest of the year. There are height and weight restrictions on some rides. 661/255.4111, 661/255.4100. www.sixflags.com

Six Flags Hurricane Harbor Water Park

Adjacent to Six Flags Magic Mountain, this water park has a tropical jungle setting with lagoons, rafting adventures, replicas of ancient ruins, and playful sea creatures, and provides fun for the whole family. Children love **Castaway Cove,** a pirate-themed water play area; **Shipwreck Shores,** a play area with swings and slides; and **Lizard Lagoon,** a 3.2-acre tropical paradise with a 7,000-square-foot, $3\frac{1}{2}$-foot-deep pool with basketball hoops, a lizard slide, volleyball, and more. There are also fun rides for all ages, like open-flume body slides, high-speed flume rides, and a wave pool. ♦ Admission (a combination ticket can be bought for both Six Flags Magic Mountain and Six Flags Hurricane Harbor).

Daily, Memorial Day through Labor Day. 661/255.4111, 661/255.4100. www.sixflags.com

2 Hyatt Valencia

$$$ Situated in a self-contained community that resembles a movie set of a turn-of-the-century New York or European city—with its varied architecture that combines stark stone, wrought-iron balconies, and tile roofs—this 244-room hotel oozes with charm. The staff is friendly. Rooms are pleasantly appointed, many with terraces that look out onto the nearby golf course or mountains. An inviting courtyard hosts a heated pool nestled by a two-sided fireplace. The **Vines Restaurant and Bar** (★★$$) is a pleasant spot for breakfast, lunch, and dinner, with indoor and outdoor seating. A scrumptious buffet brunch is served on Sunday. Dinner menus have seasonal twists with French, Asian, Caribbean, and California influences. Winemakers' weekends are sponsored throughout the year. Just a short stroll from the hotel entrance awaits the centerpiece of the community, **Valencia Town Center** (661/287.9050), a major mall housing dozens of shops, cafés, restaurants, movie theaters, an IMAX 3-D theater, and a major sports club. Hyatt guests have the benefit of privileges at the TPC at Valencia, a 27-hole golf course designed by PGA Tour Design Services and Mike O'Meara. Six Flags Magic Mountain, the area's main attraction, is just a short drive down the road (see above). ♦ 24500 Town Center Dr (between Magic Mountain Pkwy and McBean Pkwy), Valencia. 661/799.1234; 800/233.1234. www.hyatt.valencia.com

3 California Institute of the Arts

Founded with an endowment from Walt Disney in 1970, Cal-Arts is an elite, cutting-edge college with schools of film, dance, theater, art, and music. Graduates here (including David Salle and Eric Fischl) have invigorated the fine arts world on both coasts. ♦ 24700 McBean Pkwy (just east of Golden State Fwy), Santa Clarita. 805/255.1050

4 William S. Hart Park

"While I was making pictures, the people gave me their nickels, dimes, and quarters. When I am gone, I want them to have my home." With this testament, silent-film cowboy star William S. Hart bequeathed his 253-acre ranch for use as a public park. Some 110 acres have been preserved as a wilderness area. The developed portion of the property includes an animal compound, picnic sites, and Hart's ranch-style home, **La Loma de los Vientos,** which contains paintings and sculpture by Charles M. Russell. ♦ Free. Park: daily. Museum: W-Su. 24151 San Fernando Rd (at Newhall Ave), Santa Clarita. 805/254.4584

5 PLACERITA CANYON PARK

This 314-acre native chaparral park is located in a canyon amid stands of California live oak. The **Nature Center** and self-guided tour are designed to illustrate the relationships of the plants and animals in the area. ♦ Free. Daily. 19152 Placerita Canyon Rd (east of Antelope Valley Fwy). 805/259.7721

SANTA MONICA MOUNTAINS

A national recreation area administered by the National Park Service, the Santa Monicas are part of a mountain chain that rises from the floor of the Pacific, forming the **Channel Islands,** the beach plateau, and a series of peaks that extend into the city center at heights averaging 1,000 to 2,000 feet. These mountains offer breathtaking views of the Los Angeles basin and the San Fernando Valley from their summits, while retaining a wild environment within their ridges and valleys. The slopes are covered with a collection of evergreen shrubs and scrubby trees known as chaparral. Other plant life includes chamise and sage on the lower, drier hills and a denser cover of scrub oak, sumac, wild lilac, and manzanita along the streambeds. The wild plants you see on these mountains were introduced only 200 years ago by the Franciscan padres. Fire is a major hazard in this region, as the plant life is bone-dry in the summer, and the smallest spark or flame can ignite a raging brushfire—you may remember watching the Santa Monicas burn on television in October 1993 in a firestorm that ultimately destroyed more than 175,000 acres, leveled 750 houses, and caused approximately $500 million in damage.

For a quick look at the wilderness and the housing that imperils it, cruise the length of **Mulholland Drive** and **Mulholland Highway,** which snake 50 miles along the crest of the Santa Monicas from the **Hollywood Freeway** to **Leo Carrillo State Beach.** The narrow country roads were named for the self-taught Irish engineer who developed the first major aqueduct in the city, thus spurring its rapid growth.

6 RONALD REAGAN MEMORIAL LIBRARY

Want to climb aboard *Air Force One* or learn more about the life and times of our former president? Then take the trip over the mountains to the Simi Valley for a visit to the memorial of all memorials. There you can take a peek into the young life of Ronald Reagan as you walk through a model of the Dixon Arch in Illinois, where his Eureka College letter sweater is on exhibit. Then enter a re-created studio where he began his broadcast career and move on to costumes, movie posters, and other artifacts that trace his big-screen days. You will even get a look at his love affair with his wife Nancy, contrasted by a piece of the Berlin Wall. The showstopper, however, is *Air Force One,* which sits under a pavilion and is open to visitors. ♦ Daily except Christmas, Thanksgiving, and New Year's Day. Admission. 40 Presidential Dr (between Madera and Olsen Rds), Simi Valley. 800/410.8354. www.reaganlibrary.org

7 ARIS INSTITUTE

Although Beverly Hills and LA's Westside boast the largest concentration of day spas per capita, there are a growing number of options for folks who live outside those areas, such as this unique facility. To make it in today's competitive day-spa world, it helps to be different, and Aris definitely distinguishes itself from the rest with what they call "energy balancing treatments." To accomplish their balancing act, therapists begin treatments by gently massaging your face and/or body with jeweled wands (emeralds and diamonds) or feather brushes. Life Resonance cosmetics, imported from Switzerland, designed to balance energy and revitalize, are used in each facial or massage. While it may sound gimmicky, the results are actually phenomenal. The therapists are well trained and some of the best available. Additional treatments include waxing, body glows and scrubs, and other specialty therapies. The place itself is comforting, with an enchanting meditation room and outdoor patio on which to relax before and after services. There's an attractive dressing room with lockers and an attentive staff. Aris is definitely a little charmer worth checking out. ♦ 3723 E Thousand Oaks Blvd (between S Westlake and E Thousand Oaks Blvds), Westlake Village. 805/449.1799; fax 805/449.2018. www.arisinstitute.com

8 TUSCANY

★★$$ Come here for serious eating in a remote location. Try the herb-flavored veal chops, cheese-stuffed chicken breast, and inventive antipasti. Tommaso Barletta runs a tight ship. ♦ Italian ♦ M-F, lunch and dinner; Sa, Su, dinner. 968 Westlake Blvd (at Townsgate Rd), No. 4. Thousand Oaks. 818/880.5642. www.tuscany-restaurant.com

9 BOCCACCIO'S

★★$$$ Despite its location in the midst of a housing development, this dependable standby offers a degree of sophisticated service, a formal, elegant atmosphere, and a truly marvelous oak-tree and lakeside view. Caesar salad, Xeal Oscar, escargots, crab cakes, and tiramisù are standouts. ♦ Italian/French ♦ M-F, lunch and dinner; Sa, Su, dinner. Reservations recommended. 32123 Lindero Canyon Rd (at Lakeview Canyon Rd), Westlake Village. 818/889.8300

10 FOUR SEASONS HOTEL WESTLAKE VILLAGE

$$$$ Luxury arrived at this burgeoning, somewhat drab area in 2007 with the opening of this spa-centric 270-room emporium of health and wellness. The 40,000-square-foot spa takes top billing with 28 treatment rooms, a head-spinning menu of therapies, and assorted feng shui–correct touches. The roomy, 12,000-square-foot fitness center is perfectly equipped. There's a meditation lawn for yoga and tai chi, an exercise path, and an impressive indoor Mediterranean-inspired lap pool where large sliding doors open to gardens embellished with white marble and blue agate. An inviting serenity pool sits just outside the spa and offers comfy chaises and cabanas in which to relax. There are two main restaurants: **Onyx** ($$$), featuring Japanese cuisine and sushi for lunch M-F and dinner daily; **Hamptons** (see below); and a casual spa café for light, healthy snacks. A bit of a stretch for Four Seasons, the hotel has a rather industrial-looking exterior. However, once inside it warms up. Public rooms are typical Four Seasons chic. Guest rooms are nicely appointed with desks, flat-screen TVs, marble baths, and subtle colors (pale yellow walls and blue and gold carpeting accented our room). There's 24-hour room service, a business center, and all the usual Four Seasons attention to details. Assorted packages are available, but don't expect bargain prices. The hotel attracts conventions, large groups, and people going through the medical program at the California Health & Longevity Institute (see below), which is housed in the hotel next door to the spa. ♦ 2 Dole Dr (off Via Colinas. Exit Hwy 101 on Lindero Canyon Rd, continue to Via Colinas). 818/575.3000; fax 818/575.3100. www.fourseasons.com/westlakevillage

Within the Four Seasons Westlake Village:

HAMPTONS

★★$$$ The chefs try hard but occasionally miss their mark in this large, lavish dining room, which attracts locals hungry for fine dining in an area lacking in such options. The emphasis is on choices: light fare or heavy, it's up to you. We went with the former with a

tasty ahi tuna tartare with mango sauce; an Alaskan wild salmon didn't pass muster, but the prime rib was close to perfect. The desserts were so-so, save for a delicious chocolate trio. ♦ California Cal-conscious/or not. M-Sa, dinner; Sa, Su, breakfast. Reservations suggested. 818/575.3000

CALIFORNIA HEALTH & LONGEVITY INSTITUTE

A unique concept where preventative health practices are taught and diagnostic measures are administered by a team of top professionals. A tour of the facility left us breathless as we viewed all the technologically advanced modern-day medical bells and whistles like echocardiogram with Doppler, bone density machine, digital mammography, DNA testing, Thallium Stress Test equipment, MRI, the "Bod Pod" (which they claim is the best test of body composition), and more. They also offer fitness, nutrition, weight loss, and other lifestyle-changing options. It's not cheap, but for those who can afford the tab, it sounds a lot better than the offerings most HMOs and PPOs offer. Many of the clients stay overnight at the hotel. ♦ On the Garden Level of the Four Seasons Westlake Village, adjacent to the spa. 888/575.1114. www.chi.com

11 PARAMOUNT RANCH

Since the early 1920s, westerns have been shot on the standing set of what was formerly a 4,000-acre expanse of hills. Ranger-guided hikes over the ranch and movie set are offered once a month, and 436 acres of wooded countryside are open daily for riding, walking, and picnicking. Silent films are shown under the stars in July and August. ♦ Free. Daily, dawn to dusk. 2813 Cornell Rd (north of Mulholland Hwy). 818/735.0876

12 MALIBU CREEK STATE PARK

Four thousand acres of park, including Malibu Creek, two-acre Century Lake, and ageless oaks, chapparal, and volcanic rock, are found here. There is excellent day hiking on almost 15 miles of trails, and camping is allowed. ♦ Parking fee. 28754 Mulholland Hwy (between Las Virgenes Rd and Lake Vista Dr). 818/880.0367

13 SADDLE PEAK LODGE

★★★$$$$ The hearty game food menu—exotic antelope, kangaroo, venison, and quail—is so befitting of the lodge-like atmosphere here, where a roaring fire, dimly lit hurricane lamps, cushy armchairs, and a high-beam ceiling hung with assorted stag's heads enhance the rustically elegant setting.

Restaurants/Clubs: Red | Hotels: Purple | Shops: Orange | Outdoors/Parks: Green | Sights/Culture: Blue

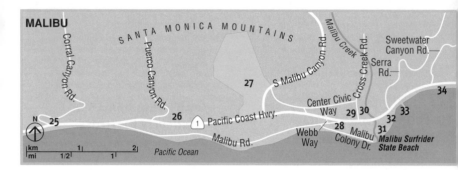

If game isn't your thing, there are other superb choices such as vodka-cured salmon, lobster and black truffle ravioli, and a carpetbagger steak. It's well worth the long drive. Lots of folks have discovered this hideaway, so be sure to make a reservation. ♦ American ♦ W-F, dinner; Sa, brunch and dinner; Su, brunch. Reservations required. 419 Cold Canyon Rd (between Piuma Rd and Mulholland Hwy). 310/456.7325. 818/222.3888. www.saddlepeaklodge.com

14 WILL GEER'S THEATRICUM BOTANICUM

This outdoor theater, established by the late Will Geer (grandpa on the TV show *The Waltons*), stages Shakespeare and new and classic modern plays from June through September. ♦ 1419 N Topanga Canyon Blvd (between Oakwood and Cheney Drs). 310/455.3723

15 TOPANGA CANYON

A quaint, artistic community shaded by bamboo and sycamore trees and covered with heavy brush and flowers, Topanga Canyon (whose name means "Mountains That Run into the Sea," as the long, curving canyon road really does) once boasted Jim Morrison, Charlie Chaplin, Peter Lorre, and Humphrey Bogart as residents. The quiet, bucolic setting still attracts celebrities, as well as screenwriters, producers, architects, teachers, and assorted hippies (though even before hand-painted VW buses, when only Mexicans wore huaraches, this was an alternative community). An eclectic group of homes (some looking pretty shabby, but surprisingly expensive) sit sheltered under groves of sycamores or scattered along the creek that flows through the base of the canyon. It's believed that Native American settlements date back at least 5,000 years. You can learn more about this interesting area at: www.topangaonline.com

15 INN OF THE SEVENTH RAY

★★$$ This charming, ephemeral eatery sits snugly perched off a funky canyon road about

four miles from the Coast Highway. Although it has always catered to vegetarians, there's now something for everybody on the New Age menu. And you can't beat the bucolic setting, where tables nestle outside beside a gently flowing stream, accompanied by Baroque and New Age melodies. Somehow dining here always calls for a bottle of crisp Chardonnay to accompany a meal of, say, agave-glazed vegan duck, lobster, halibut, or swordfish; outstanding freshly baked breads; and luscious desserts like macadamia nut pie or Vermont maple cheesecake. For those who care, all the fish is fresh and wild, the meat organically fed, and the poultry free range. ♦ California ♦ Daily, dinner; M-Sa, lunch; Su, brunch. Reservations recommended for brunch and dinner. 128 Old Topanga Canyon Rd (just west of N Topanga Canyon Blvd). 310/455.1311. www.innoftheseventhray.com

16 TOPANGA STATE PARK

With 9,000 untouched acres to explore and enjoy, this park offers a soothing respite from civilization. The high peaks beckon, with superb views of the ocean and the San Fernando Valley, while the grassy meadows and woodlands are perfect for picnics and long walks. A self-guided trail explains the ecology. Water and sanitary facilities are available in the park. You can camp in the backcountry for $1 a person. Note: There are no park signs, so keep a sharp lookout for the turnoff from Topanga Canyon Boulevard. ♦ Daily. Parking is only $2. 20825 Entrada Rd (off Topanga Canyon Blvd). 310/455.2465

17 POINT MUGU STATE PARK

The secluded and idyllic park, with 70 miles of trails, a tall-grass prairie preserve, beautiful sycamores, and lovely canyons, is excellent for day hikes and picnics. Advance camping reservations are required. ♦ Admission. 9000 Pacific Coast Hwy (between Pacific View and Las Posas Rds). 818/880.0350

18 LEO CARRILLO STATE BEACH

This beach was named for the Los Angeles–born actor, who died in 1961. A descendant of one of California's oldest families and son of the first mayor of Santa Monica, Carrillo became famous as Pancho, the sidekick on TV's *The Cisco Kid*. Surfers should head for the western end of the beach. ♦ Pacific Coast and Mulholland Hwys

19 ZUMA CANYON ORCHIDS

Prizewinning plants bred here are sent all over the world. ♦ M-Sa. 5949 Bonsall Dr (north of Pacific Coast Hwy). 310/457.9771. www.zumacanyonorchids.com

20 THE SUNSET RESTAURANT

★★$$$ Isn't it romantic to sit in a cozy room just across from sensational Zuma Beach, with 180-degree views of the ocean and Catalina Island, dining on fine food and maybe even spotting a whale or two in season? You bet it is at this precious spot that formerly housed the Gray Whale and several other restaurants during the past 150-plus years. Even with new owners, the food is still as amazing as the view, especially any fish dish. ♦ Continental ♦ Tu-Su, dinner. 6800 Westward Beach Rd (south of Pacific Coast Hwy). 310/589.1007. www.thesunsetrestaurant.com

21 POINT DUME

♦ This residential area with a hard-to-get-to beach was named in 1782 by George Vancouver, the English explorer, for Father Dumetz, a Jesuit at the **Ventura Mission.** Until the 20th century, Point Dume was high and peaked, but the top was shaved off to build a housing development. ♦ Westward Beach Rd (south of Pacific Coast Hwy)

22 ZOOMA SUSHI

★★★$ College students and casually dressed celebrities such as Emilio Estevez and Nick Nolte frequent this 25-seat sushi bar and restaurant located in architect **Ed Niles**'s woodsy office building. The most popular dish is the Vegas Roll—five kinds of fish rolled in seaweed, deep fried, and wrapped in spicy crab—but more traditional fare is also available. ♦ Japanese ♦ Daily, dinner. 29350 Pacific Coast Hwy (between Heathercliff and Westward Beach Rds). 310/457.4131. www.zomasushi.net

23 PARADISE COVE

♦ This private beach is full of nooks and crannies for walking and exploring. **The Sandcastle** (310/457.2503), a staid, inexplicably popular restaurant, overlooks the ocean. ♦ Admission. Paradise Cove Rd (south of Pacific Coast Hwy)

24 GEOFFREY'S

★★★★$$$$ One of the most magical spots in Los Angeles, where you get breathtaking 180-degree views of the ocean and awesome sunsets from the cliff-edge terrace. The eclectic menu includes grilled Portobello mushroom with Parmesan polenta, seafood paella, ahi tuna au poivre, pan-seared Chilean sea bass, and a Kobe "Platinum" sirloin. There's live piano music nightly. ♦ Cal-Asian/New American ♦ Daily, lunch and dinner; Su, brunch. 27400 Pacific Coast Hwy (at Escondido Beach Rd). 310/457.1519. www.geoffreysmalibu.com

25 BEAU RIVAGE

★★★$$$ This warm and cozy yet elegant roadhouse with a piano indoors and a patio out back has a rich, steeply priced menu that includes gnocchi, risottos, fish like bran-zino and Norwegian salmon steak, Long Island duckling, and filet mignon of Limousin beef—all done with a touch of France, Italy, Morocco, and Spain. ♦ Mediterranean ♦ W-F, dinner; Sa, Su, brunch and dinner. 26025 Pacific Coast Hwy (between Puerco Canyon and Corral Canyon Rds). 310/456.5733. www.beaurivagerestaurant.com

26 24955 PACIFIC COAST HIGHWAY

This crisp low-rise development designed by **Goldman Firth Architects** in 1989 lifts the spirits of motorists speeding by. ♦ Between John Tyler Dr and Puerco Canyon Rd

27 PEPPERDINE UNIVERSITY

Popularly known as "Surfers U" for its oceanfront site, Pepperdine is actually a respected institution that offers bachelor's and master's degrees in 50 major subject areas. It has a law school, four satellite centers in Southern California, and a year-in-Europe program at Heidelberg University. Also on campus is the **Frederick R. Weisman Museum of Art,** which displays pieces from the industrialist's personal collection of modern art, as well as changing exhibits on such themes as British photography, turn-of-the-century arts and crafts in America, and modern glass sculpture. ♦ Free. Tu-Su. 24255 Pacific Coast Hwy (at S Malibu Canyon Rd). General information 310/456.4000, museum 310/456.4851

28 MALIBU BEACH COLONY

"The Colony," as insiders call it, has been an exclusive and very private beach community for the famous and wealthy since 1926. Many of the multimillion-dollar beach cottages have bedrooms sufficient to sleep the cast of

---

Restaurants/Clubs: Red | Hotels: Purple | Shops: Orange | Outdoors/Parks: Green | Sights/Culture: Blue

Melrose Place and hot tubs big enough to soak the Olympic swim team. The drives and beach here are private, but the dramatic **Stevens House** by **John Lautner** can be seen from the Pacific Coast Highway as a double-height, concrete quarter-circle rising into the sky. ◆ Malibu Colony Dr (south of Malibu Rd)

29 NOBU MALIBU

★★★$$$ The Malibu cousin of **Matsuhisa** in LA and the sister of Nobu New York, this one is a little more affordable, but still has much the same great Japanese fusion menu. Order the *tiradito* plate, a pretty-as-a-picture flower-shaped dish of thinly sliced whitefish. Any sushi is superb, as are the whole grilled sizzling fish, chicken, lobster, and steak dishes. A fun dessert is the bento box filled with green-tea ice cream and chocolate soufflé. The broiled plums with a meringue puff and ginger ice cream with a cookie taste pretty good, too. ◆ Japanese ◆ Daily, dinner. Reservations suggested. Country Mart, 3835 Cross Creek Rd (between Pacific Coast Hwy and Civic Center Way). 310/317.9140. www.malibu.org

30 GUIDO'S

★$$ The flower-filled patio at this restaurant overlooking Malibu Creek is a lovely place for lunch; for dinner guests, there's a cozy interior. Smoked salmon, pasta with eggplant, risotto, and herbed roast chicken all come recommended. ◆ Italian ◆ Daily, lunch and dinner. Reservations recommended. 3874 Cross Creek Rd (north of Pacific Coast Hwy). 310/456.1979. www.guidosmalibu.com

31 SURFRIDER STATE BEACH

Affectionately known as "The Bu" by surfers, this beach has a world-famous right reef point break. The surfing here is best in August and September, when south swells are at their peak. ◆ Pacific Coast Hwy (between Sweetwater Canyon Rd and Malibu Colony Dr)

32 ADAMSON HOUSE

This romantic Spanish Colonial house, designed by **Stiles Clements** in 1929, is preserved just as its owner, Rhoda Rindge Adamson, left it at her death in 1962. It is a showcase of colorful Malibu tiles and a reminder of the imperious family that once owned 17,000 acres in and around Malibu. The house and adjoining **Malibu Lagoon Museum** are accessible only on guided tours, which take about 45 minutes. ◆ Admission. Tours: W-Sa, 11AM-3PM. 23200 Pacific Coast Hwy (at Serra Rd). 310/456.8432

33 MALIBU PIER

This landmark structure, built in 1906, is finally ready for the public after years of on-

again, off-again restorations. It's a pleasant place to stroll, gaze out to sea, and fish. It's also a favorite location site for television and movie productions. ◆ 23000 Pacific Coast Hwy (between Sweetwater Canyon and Serra Rds)

34 CASA MALIBU INN ON THE BEACH

$$ This charming historic hideaway, draped in bougainvillea and copa de oro, dates back to 1949, when it was a popular place for celebs to flee to for weekends. The 21 rooms and suites boast a contemporary style; each has a king-size or double bed, coffeemaker, and refrigerator; some also have private decks, fireplaces, and fully equipped kitchens. The **Catalina Suite,** once a favorite of Lana Turner's, features a cozy sitting room with a fireplace, bookshelves that reach the ceiling, a TV set, and a sofa bed. There's another fireplace in the bedroom, which also boasts a king-size four-poster bed and grand ocean views. Though the hotel does not have a restaurant, there are several in the neighborhood. ◆ 22752 Pacific Coast Hwy (just east of Sweetwater Canyon Rd). 310/456.2219, 800/831.0858; e-mail: casamalibu@earthlink.net ＆

34 LA SALSA

★$ A huge rooftop figure of a man in a sombrero marks this popular take-out place overlooking the ocean. The fresh vegetables, grilled chicken, fish, and meat tacos have won acclaim. ◆ Mexican/Takeout ◆ Daily, lunch and dinner. 22800 Pacific Coast Hwy (just east of Sweetwater Canyon Rd). 310/317.9476. www.lasalsa.com

34 MALIBU BEACH INN

$$$ This charming Spanish-style beachfront hotel sits smack on the silky sands of Malibu. Angelenos love it as a weekend getaway, and a growing number of jet-setting Europeans have also discovered its charm. While the best time to visit is during the balmy days of summer, it's equally appealing during winter months when you can hole up in your room next to the fireplace and gaze out to sea, or peer off your balcony during the day in search of a whale sighting. The beach is just steps away, the staff exude inviting warmth, and each of the hotel's 47 rooms is warm and cozy and comes with a fireplace, plasma TV, balcony, extravagant linens and towels, minibar, and, in ground-floor rooms, private Jacuzzi. A complimentary breakfast buffet is laid out each morning in the lobby. You can take your food outside to enjoy on the oceanfront verandah or eat indoors by a

roaring fireplace (turned on during chilly days). In the afternoon you can mingle and meet fellow guests in the lobby when complimentary tea, coffee, cheeses, crackers, and cookies are served, or enjoy the no-host wine bar and beach barbecue, which is available daily 11AM to 4PM. Room service is available from a limited in-house menu, or by delivery from local establishments. What's really nifty is they will serve your meal anywhere you'd like, on the glass-and-teak outdoor terrace, on the beach, or on your balcony. There are also plenty of places to eat within walking distance of the hotel. ♦ 22878 Pacific Coast Hwy (at Sweetwater Canyon Rd). 310/456.6444, 800/462.5428; fax 310/456.1499. www.malibubeachinn.com

35 ACKERBURG RESIDENCE

Designed by **Richard Meier & Partners,** this 1991 beachfront house translates Meier's white rational design into Southern California courtyard living. On the same strip of beach are the contrasting styles of two other renowned architects. **John Lautner**'s 1979 **Segal Residence,** a heavily landscaped curving wood and concrete house, is located at no. 22426, and a **Gwathmey, Siegel & Associates** wood-and-glass house is located at no. 22350. All three are private residences. ♦ 22466 Pacific Coast Hwy (between Carbon Canyon and Sweetwater Canyon Rds)

36 MOONSHADOWS

★★$$ California jamming down by the seaside. Ritz rides fill the parking lot of this funky-chic waterfront eatery. Definitely the spot to go get a handle on California beach culture, the place is filled to capacity day and night with tall, tan, and blond guys and girls socializing, dining, and catching the awesome ocean view. Waves slap against the patio as waiters race around carrying orders of seafood with mango spring rolls, flash-fried calamari, hanger steak, tiger shrimp with luscious seasonings, and other tasty treats. Go for the sunset—you won't be disappointed. ♦ Daily, lunch and dinner. Reservations recommended. 20356 Pacific Coast Hwy (between Big Rock Dr and Las Flores Canyon Rd). 310/456.3010. www.moonshadowsmalibu.com

37 LAS TUNAS STATE BEACH

🅟 The name does not refer to canned fish; it's Spanish for the fruit of the prickly pear cactus. ♦ Pacific Coast Hwy (between Tuna Canyon Rd and Big Rock Dr)

38 REEL INN RESTAURANT AND FRESH FISH MARKET

★$ Fresh fish is prepared in the kitchen daily, grilled or pan-blackened Cajun style, and served alongside hearty home-fried potatoes, Cajun rice, and coleslaw. The setting is rustic boathouse, with long wooden picnic tables and a patio. Celebrities like to slip in here unnoticed. However, should the American Land Conservancy have its way and turn the area on which it sits into a state park, the restaurant will become one of its victims. ♦ Seafood ♦ Daily, lunch and dinner. 18661 Pacific Coast Hwy (between S Topanga Canyon Blvd and Topanga Canyon La). 310/456.8221. Also at 1220 Third St Promenade (between Arizona Ave and Wilshire Blvd), Santa Monica. 310/395.5538; 2533 Pacific Coast Hwy (at Crenshaw Blvd), Torrance. 310/530.40470

39 THE GETTY VILLA

The **Getty Villa,** once the **J. Paul Getty Museum** (which has long since been relocated to West LA), represents a stunning piece of architecture that replicates the Villa dei Papiri. Perched above the Pacific Ocean on 64 acres of lavishly landscaped land with gorgeous gardens and views, the villa was designed by the Boston-based firm of **Machado and Silvetti Associates** to fuse contemporary designs with antiquity. The 28 galleries sport steel support systems hidden in the walls and floors. Features include a 250-seat auditorium and the 450-seat, open-air **Barbara and Lawrence Fleischman Theater.** Art lovers will feel like kids in a candy store as they wander by 44,000 Roman, Etruscan, and Greek antiquities and some 1,200 pieces of art. There are two dedicated educational areas, a Family Forum hands-on discovery room for families, and the TimeScape Room, which focuses on time, place, and artistic style in the ancient Mediterranean. The Villa also hosts the UCLA/Getty Master's Program on the Conservation of Ethnographic and Archaeological Materials—the first of its kind in the country. This place is a definite must-see for anyone interested in the arts. ♦ M-Th. Although admission is free, tickets are mandatory and must be requested in advance on the web site or by phone. 17985 Pacific Coast Hwy (at Coastline Dr). 310/440.7300, 310/440.7305 for the hearing impaired. www.getty.edu. For a free monthly newsletter, sign up at www.getty.edu/subscribe

---

Restaurants/Clubs: Red | Hotels: Purple | Shops: Orange | Outdoors/Parks: Green | Sights/Culture: Blue

SAN FERNANDO VALLEY

L ike, we're talking the other side of the mountain . . .

Made famous by the teens who shop till they drop at the local malls and speak a "Valley girl" language few adults can decipher, the sprawling San Fernando just keeps on growing. To really get a handle on its scope, take an evening drive along **Mulholland Drive** to the top of the LA basin and gaze straight down from the crest of the hills. On a clear night, it looks like Christmas, with countless twinkling lights illuminating the basin. Go during the day to catch a bird's-eye view of the

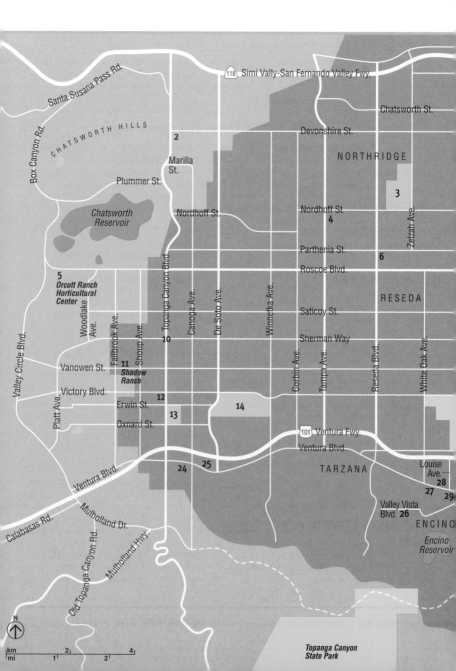

awesome **Santa Monica Mountains,** which separate the valley from the rest of the city. Although somewhat connected to Los Angeles, the Valley does have a distinctive personality: lots of space (most of it flat), high temperatures (the Valley is usually 10 to 20 degrees warmer than the LA basin), trauma (it was the epicenter of the 1994 Northridge earthquake), and traffic (an extended grid of seemingly endless boulevards and streets crossing its length and breadth, reinforcing its dominant car culture). For visitors from eastern American or European cities, the sprawl of the Valley could prove difficult to grasp: When the City of Los Angeles originally annexed the San Fernando Valley on 22 May 1915, it effected a land grab that added 177 square miles to its existing 108 square miles.

Until the early 1900s, land use in the Valley was limited to ranching and nonirrigated agriculture. Then speculators, anticipating the arrival of the **Owens River Aqueduct** in 1913, began to buy up thousands of acres of Valley property. To share in the water brought by the aqueduct, ranchers voted to join the municipality of Los Angeles. Property values soared, and people savvy enough to invest in real estate profited handsomely. Boom succeeded boom, and hundreds of thousands moved into the Valley, encouraged by jobs in the nearby aviation, electronics, and entertainment industries. Several decades of accelerated development made the area famous for rapid-start tract-house neighborhoods and instant shopping centers. The west and south sides of the Valley (Calabasas, Encino, Westlake Village, Toluca Lake) are the most affluent areas with large, almost mansion-like homes and big yards. Industry is heavily concentrated in the northern area around San Fernando, Sylmar, and Pacoima.

---

1 MISSION SAN FERNANDO REY DE ESPAÑA

Until the dissolution of the missions in the mid-1830s, San Fernando was an essential part of the economic life of Los Angeles, supplying a great portion of the foodstuffs for the fledgling community. Founded in 1797 by Friar Fermin Lasuen, the mission was completed in 1806 but was subsequently destroyed by an earthquake and replaced in 1818. History repeated itself in the 1971 Sylmar/San Fernando earthquake, when the church again sustained damage so grave that it had to be reconstructed. The adobe construction of the early period had a simple yet monumental quality that achieved richness through the repetition of structural elements. This quality is best observed in the 243-foot-long *convento,* where 19 semicircular arches supported by massive square pillars form a loggia over time-hollowed tiles. Tours of the mission include working, sleeping, and reception areas, giving visitors a sense of day-to-day life during the early days. ♦ Admission. Daily. 15151 San Fernando Mission Blvd (between Sharp Ave and Sepulveda Blvd). 818/361.0186

2 LES SISTERS SOUTHERN KITCHEN

★★$ More than 20 years old and still going strong, this authentic soul food restaurant specializes in Cajun/Creole cuisine. Best bites: barbecue chicken, ribs, hush puppies, Southern fried chicken, and gumbo; for dessert, buttermilk pie. There is no bar, and no alcohol is served. ♦ Cajun/Creole ♦ Tu-F, lunch; Tu-Su, dinner. Reservations recommended for five or more. 21818 Devonshire St (between Jordan and Vassar Aves), Chatsworth. 818/998.0755

3 CALIFORNIA STATE UNIVERSITY AT NORTHRIDGE (CSUN)

One of the most popular branches of the **California State University** system, CSUN offers undergraduate and graduate courses in liberal arts and science disciplines. Recent government cutbacks have forced the university to curtail programs and classes, making the traditional four-year baccalaureate pursuit more difficult. **Richard Neutra** designed the 1961 **Fine Arts Building.** ♦ 18111 Nordhoff St (between Zelzah and Darby Aves). 818/885.1200

4 ALEXIS GREEK RESTAURANT

★★$ This fun spot combines Greek and Portuguese food and ambience. The unusual menu has it all: roast leg of lamb, filet mignon strip steak, white bass baked in wine with mushrooms and feta cheese, spicy chicken pirii, six different Greek salads, and all sorts of wonderful sausages. It also boasts a lavish dessert menu that includes an outstanding tiramisù; light and delicious almond cookies made with egg whites, almonds, and sugar, and a different chocolate cake every night. Beer and wine are the only alcoholic beverages served. ♦ Greek/Portuguese ♦ MSa lunch; daily, dinner. 9034 Tampa Ave (at Nordhoff St). 818/349.9689

5 ORCUTT RANCH HORTICULTURAL CENTER

Ⓟ Originally part of a 200-acre estate belonging to William and Mary Orcutt, the extensive gardens, lush landscaping, and venerable trees accented by statuary are relaxing and lovely. Picnic spots, hiking trails, and horticultural demonstrations count among the attractions. Tours of the 1920 house designed by **C. G. Knipe** are given the last Sunday of each month from 2 to 5PM from September through June. ◆ Free. Ranch: daily. 23600 Roscoe Blvd (between Jason and March Aves). 818/346.7449

6 THAI BARBEQUE

★$ The great northern Thai/Laotian food at this restaurant is absolutely the spiciest in town, so unless you want smoke pouring out of your ears, don't ask them to make it hot. Not for everyone, but certainly interesting, is a jackfruit ice cream made with garbanzo beans. ◆ Thai ◆ M-F, lunch and dinner; Sa, Su, dinner. 8650 Reseda Blvd (at Parthenia St). 818/701.5712

7 94TH AERO SQUADRON HEADQUARTERS RESTAURANT

★$$ Located near the Van Nuys Airport, this 1973 version of a French farmhouse comes complete with bales of hay in the front yard. American standards—burgers, prime rib, fried chicken—make up the menu. It's a fun place to take the kids. ◆ American ◆ Daily, lunch and dinner. Reservations recommended. 16320 Raymer St (west of Woodley Ave). 818/994.7437

8 DR. HOGLY-WOGLY'S TYLER TEXAS BBQ

★★$ This is the real thing, tangy enough to bring tears to the eyes of a Lone Star exile. People line up to eat down-home ribs, links, chicken, and beans, despite the lack of amenities. ◆ Barbecue ◆ Daily, lunch and dinner. 8136 Sepulveda Blvd (between Sepulveda Pl and Roscoe Blvd). 818/780.6701

9 WESTERN BAGEL

Jalapeño and blueberry are among the two dozen varieties of freshly baked bagels sold here. ◆ Daily, 24 hours. 7814 Sepulveda Blvd (between Stagg and Raymer Sts). 818/786.5847. Also at 11628 Santa Monica Blvd (between Federal and Barry Aves). 310/826.0570

10 ANTIQUE ROW

More than 28 shops specialize in Americana, ranging from memorabilia to publications. ◆ Daily. Sherman Way and Topanga Canyon Blvd

11 SHADOW RANCH

This restored 1870 ranch house built by LA pioneer Albert Workman is located on nine acres that were once part of a 60,000-acre wheat ranch. The eucalyptus trees on the property were planted in the late 19th century by Workman, who brought them from Australia; they are purported to be the parent stand of the trees that are now one of the most prominent features of Southern California botany. The ranch is presently used as a community center. ◆ Free. Daily; Tu-Th until 9PM. 22633 Vanowen St (between Sale and Ponce Aves). 818/883.3637

12 ROY'S

★★★$$ Be prepared to feast. Owner/Chef Roy Yamaguchi does everything big, and this 7,200-square-foot, purple and terra-cotta yellow Valley branch of his restaurant empire is no exception. Wooden walls, adorned with Hawaiian paintings and torchlike sconces, surround the cheerful interior. Faux bamboo groves and ceiling fixtures that look like ocean swells continue the Island theme. Roy's signature display kitchen and sushi counter add to the ambience. There's a busy bar at the entrance occupied by the usual 20- and 30-something suspects. Absent from Los Angeles for several years, Roy hit the jackpot when he opened this location, which has been jam-packed from day one. It is well worth the trip over the hill, if you happen to be on the other side, to sink your teeth into such signature dishes as Roy's original Hawaiian blackened island ahi, Big Island–style ahi poke, or Hawaii Kai–style crispy crab cakes. Every item has an Island flavor and each dances the hula in your mouth. There's a decently priced three-course prix-fixe dinner, along with plenty of à la carte selections. Bring a big appetite and begin your food foray with a platter of Roy's Canoe Appetizers: Szechuan baby ribs, petite crab cakes, Chinatown chicken spring rolls, crispy seafood wontons, and steamed edamame. All the fish dishes (Roy's specialty) are divine. Trust us—the food is great. There's an extensive wine list to accompany the meal and luscious desserts to end it. Dress is casual here, with many patrons donning colorful Aloha shirts or Island-like togs. It keeps the theme flowing. ◆ Hawaiian Fusion ◆ Daily, dinner. Reservations suggested. 6363 Topanga Canyon Blvd (at Victory Blvd), Woodland Hills. 818/888.4801. www.royrestaurant.com

---

Restaurants/Clubs: Red | Hotels: Purple | Shops: Orange | Outdoors/Parks: Green | Sights/Culture: Blue

MAGICAL MULHOLLAND DRIVE

Mulholland Drive, LA's mountain roadway, twists along a ridge high above the **Los Angeles Basin** to the south and sprawling **San Fernando Valley** to the north. Here celebrities seclude themselves in hilltop mansions or gated estates far from the street; lovers drive up at night for the romantic setting enhanced by the twinkling lights of the city below; and Sunday drivers cruise to escape the week's pressures.

Named for William Mulholland, who engineered the aqueduct connecting LA and the San Fernando Valley, the two-lane road with numerous switchbacks opened in 1924. Apart from attracting celebrity residents such as Marlon Brando, Kevin Costner, and Arsenio Hall, it hasn't changed much since. Riding the ridge of the **Santa Monica Mountains** (an east-west spur of the Coastal Range referred to as the Hollywood Hills), Mulholland Drive rises 1,400 feet

above sea level—just high enough to afford spectacular views.

The 22-mile-long portion of the road between Hollywood and the San Diego Freeway at Bel-Air is the neighborhood known as **The Hills,** where well-heeled businesspeople, writers, entertainers, rock stars, and artsy-crafty sorts live the cantilevered life. Mule deer, bobcats, coyotes, great horned owls, red-tailed hawks, and even the odd mountain lion roam and roost along the canyon-riven roadway. There are few curbs here, lots of rural mailboxes, and plenty of native chaparral. The only commerce is a country store and the popular **Four Oaks Restaurant** in Beverly Glen Canyon. Yet just short drives away are all the important business addresses, restaurants, and nightspots of LA. The locals relish the relative isolation and have fought—somewhat successfully—to keep it.

13 WESTFIELD WOODLAND HILLS

This is one of the poshest of the indoor malls, with 80 upscale shops and boutiques, such as **818 Freight Dakota Blues** for jeans and sportswear. Also lining the tiled corridors are a state-of-the-art movie theater with stadium-like seating and a food court. Lighting, fountains, and indoor landscaping add to the cool elegance of the place. ♦ Daily; M-F until 9PM. 6100 Topanga Canyon Blvd (between Oxnard and Erwin Sts). 818/884.7090. www.westfield.com

14 LOS ANGELES PIERCE COLLEGE

This branch of the **Los Angeles Community College** system specializes in agriculture, horticulture, landscape architecture, and animal husbandry. ♦ 6201 Winnetka Ave (between Oxnard St and Victory Blvd). 818/347.0551

15 SEPULVEDA BASIN RECREATION AREA

The 2,000-acre basin is leased by the City of Los Angeles from the US Army Corps of Engineers. Within the park are three 18-hole golf courses, a 20-acre picnic area, a cricket field, a model airplane field, an archery range, and plenty of bicycle and roller-skating paths. ♦ Daily, sunrise to sunset. 17017 Burbank Blvd (between Balboa Blvd and Aldea Ave). General information 818/756.8189, golf reservations 213/485.5515

16 LOUISE BIANCO SKIN CARE

In a town sated with day spas, it's always a bonus when you find a talent like Louise Bianco. She's been called a "miracle worker," "facialist to the stars," and the "tops in town"—and rightly so. Relocated from her Beverly Hills salon, Bianco performs her magic in the comforts of her own home. If you need wrinkles ironed out or a facial pep-up, make an appointment with this wonder woman. Just one treatment lifts, rejuvenates, and even firms the skin. Follow the stars and book the microdermabrasion/oxygen, contour, glycolic acid, and oxygen or ultrasonic facial—your skin will thank us for it. After all, these are the treatments that keep her celebrity clientele looking great. While you're there, be sure to stock up on her signature cosmetics, such as Bianco's hand-tailored Microsomes, guaranteed to help you look more youthful. ♦ 13655 Chandler Blvd (between Woodman and Buffalo Aves), Sherman Oaks. For appointments: 818/786.2700; to order products: 800/782.3067. www.louisebianco.com

17 GREAT WALL OF LOS ANGELES

The world's longest mural (a half-mile and still unfinished) occupies the west wall of a concrete flood control channel and tells the history of California from the age of the dinosaurs to the present. Anger brings history to life, as in the revolutionary murals of Mexico City, and though this collaborative effort by more than 215 of the city's young people is no artistic masterpiece, it's a provocative learning experience for participants and visitors. Judy Baca has directed the project over the past dozen or so years for SPARC, a nonprofit Venice arts group. ♦ Coldwater Canyon Ave (between Burbank Blvd and Oxnard St)

18 NORAH'S PLACE

★$ Quinoa, the sacred grain of the Inca, is a key ingredient in the distinctive cuisine of Bolivia. So are a few of that country's 100-plus kinds of potatoes. Other dishes served here are more familiar—such as empanadas and *lomo saltado* (sirloin tips). Enjoy live folk music and dancing on weekends. ♦ Bolivian ♦ W-Su, dinner. 5667 Lankershim Blvd (between Burbank Blvd and Collins St). 818/980.6900

19 VALLEY DISCOUNT JEWELERS

What a delightful discovery—a jeweler whom we'd trust with the family gems, and have. Charming Armenian immigrant Greg Kalajian is the beloved shopkeeper, a gem master who can turn any piece of jewelry into a work of art, restore it, or fix it. Beloved and trusted by locals for more than 25 years, Kalajian has made rings for Hugh Hefner's three girlfriends, William Shatner, and CBS's popular show *According to Jim*. They also have the cheapest prices on watch batteries. ♦ Daily except holidays. 12119 Magnolia Blvd (at Laurel Canyon Blvd), Studio City. 818/761.8832

20 DUTTON'S BOOKSTORE

A well-stocked branch of the Brentwood store. ♦ Daily. 5146 Laurel Canyon Blvd (between Hartsook St and Magnolia Blvd). 818/769.3866. Also at 11975 San Vicente Blvd (at S Saltair Ave), 310/476.6263; 3806 W Magnolia Blvd (at Screenland Dr), Burbank. 818/840.8003

21 CHAING SHAN

★$$ Tasty Thai cooking is served in a nondescript setting. The beef curry and the special seafood dish, which includes shrimp, squid, and clams in a delicious spicy sauce, are highly recommended. ♦ Thai ♦ Daily, lunch and dinner. 5145 Colfax Ave (between Hartsook St and Magnolia Blvd). 818/760.1283

22 SALOMI

★$$ The curries here are exceedingly hot. For the faint of heart, there are also tamer tandoori and kabob dishes. ♦ Indian ♦ Daily, lunch and dinner. 5225 Lankershim

Blvd (between Magnolia Blvd and Weddington St). 818/506.0130

23 ARTE DE MEXICO

Create your own hacienda from the items in seven warehouses crammed with crafts from Mexico and the Southwest. ♦ Daily. 5356 Riverton Ave (north of Magnolia Blvd). 818/769.5090

24 THREE 6 NINE

Tammy Kranzo named her boutique salon "Three 6 Nine" for her favorite lucky numbers. Men and women flock from near and far (all the way from Palm Springs) to have their tresses stylishly trimmed, permed, and colored at this adorable, no-attitude salon with its Old European/Mediterranean décor. Big, colorful starfish hang from the exposed pipe ceiling, muted yellow tones cover the walls and floors, and plates of cookies, fruit, and assorted beverages are proffered freely. Many go for a makeover by superstylist Tammy Kranzo, the owner/operator and former head colorist for Sebastian International. If Tammy's not available, you'll be in good hands with any of her skilled staff. Besides being just about the best in the business, their prices are more affordable than those puff-puff shops over the mountain in Beverly Hills. And when you have your hair washed you get a dreamy, tension-reducing scalp massage. Tammy's organic shampoos, coloring, and conditioners leave your hair feeling soft and silky. ♦ M-Sa. 21132 Costanso (one block off Ventura Blvd, between Canoga Ave and Topanga Canyon Blvd). 818/347.1900

24 BROTHER'S SUSHI

★★$$ The sushi is wonderful, but don't miss the ultrafresh oysters or the crackly salmon skin. ♦ Japanese ♦ Tu-Sa, lunch and dinner. 21418 Ventura Blvd (at Canoga Ave). 818/992.1284

25 NICOLA'S KITCHEN

★★$$ Now that's Italian! We're talking house-made pastas, meatballs, and risotto recipes straight from the old country. Not surprising, since the family who runs the place is Italian. ♦ Italian ♦ Daily, lunch and dinner. Reservations suggested. 20969 Ventura Blvd (between Fallbrook and Royer Aves). 818/883.9477. www.nicolaskitchen.com

26 JUEL PARK

Edwina Skaff creates lingerie for perfectionists, continuing the tradition of her mother, Sue Drake, who joined the firm a year after its founding in 1929 and created

---

Restaurants/Clubs: Red | Hotels: Purple | Shops: Orange | Outdoors/Parks: Green | Sights/Culture: Blue

form-fitting, bias-cut silk gowns for Jean Harlow, Carole Lombard, and Norma Shearer. Custom-made negligees and teddies come in satin, lace, and organdy. ◆ By appointment only. 17940 Rancho St (between Zelzah and Lindley Aves). 818/609.7342

27 DOMINGO'S

Pick up imported cheeses, salami, olive oil, pastas, and great sandwiches and other food to go at this family-run Italian grocery/deli. ◆ Tu-Su. 17548 Ventura Blvd (between Encino and Texhoma Aves). 818/981.4466

28 SKIN SPA

The south of France meets Encino at this delightful spa spread out atop the charming **Courtyard Center.** Owner Jonathan Baker provides a salubrious setting and high-quality service unmatched in the Valley. The tranquil facility has a terraced spa deck, a "Niagara" waterfall that massages your entire body with 20 jets, couples' suites for a massage *à deux*, a private therapy bath soak, and special full-body regimens that include massage with exotic oils, antioxidant skin treatments, and mud baths. If you're the "no pain, no gain" type, head for a **CHI sports massage,** 55 minutes focusing on every sore or overused muscle in the body. There's also a **SuperStretch**—85 blissful minutes of Pilates-style body movements combined with a super massage. You can also arrange an entire day of pampering, which includes spa treatments, catered lunch on the patio, leisurely soaks in the hot tubs, and even (for an extra charge) limousine service to and from your hotel. ◆ Tu-Su. 17401 Ventura Blvd (between Louise and Encino Aves). 818/995.3888, 877-SKIN SPA. www.skinspa.com

29 ENCINO TOWN CENTER

This little minimall has a couple of shops, one specializing in home furnishings, the other in bargain books. Its most distinguishing characteristic is an old oak tree estimated to be more than a thousand years old. The branches spread out 150 feet and the trunk measures more than eight feet in diameter. ◆ Daily; M-F until 9PM. 17200 Ventura Blvd (between Oak Park and Louise Aves). 818/788.6100

A contest to rename the San Fernando Valley was staged by the *Los Angeles Times* after surrounding neighborhoods began adopting fancy nicknames to improve their image.

The winning name in the tongue-in-cheek competition: Twenty-Nine Malls. Some runners-up: Beige-Air, Minimalia, McValley, Valle de Nada, and West Emphysema.

30 RANCHO DE LOS ENCINOS STATE HISTORICAL PARK

Leave the traffic behind and recall the stagecoach era, when dusty travelers stopped off here to refresh themselves. Among the five acres of expansive lawns, duck ponds, and tall eucalyptus are a nine-room adobe built in 1849 by Don Vicente de la Osa and a two-story limestone French-style home designed in 1870 by Eugene Garnier. ◆ Admission. Grounds: W-Su. Home tours: W-Su, 1-4PM. 16756 Moorpark St (at La Maida St). 818/784.4849

31 TEMPO

$ The taste of the Middle East served here will be welcome for those unfamiliar with its charm. Try the falafel, hummus, or shish kebab. ◆ Middle Eastern ◆ Daily, lunch and dinner. 16610 Ventura Blvd (at Rubio Ave). 818/905.5855. e-mail: tempo@venturablvd.com

32 BENIHANA OF TOKYO

★$$$ The *teppan*-grill tradition of Japan is raised to the level of theater by a chef trained to handle a knife like a samurai. ◆ Japanese ◆ Daily, lunch and dinner. Reservations required. 16226 Ventura Blvd (between Woodley and Libbit Aves). 818/788.7121

33 SHIHOYA

★★$$ This is another traditional sushi bar, where you are rewarded with outstandingly fresh and beautiful sashimi and sushi. ◆ Japanese ◆ M-F, lunch and dinner; Sa, dinner. 15489 Ventura Blvd (between Orion and Firmament Aves). 818/986.4461

34 LA FRITE

$$ A perfect place to stop for light crepes, omelettes, quiche, sandwiches, soups, and salads. ◆ French ◆ Daily, lunch and dinner. Reservations recommended. 15013 Ventura Blvd (between Lemona and Noble Aves). 818/990.1791. Also at 22616 Ventura Blvd (between Sale and Ponce Aves). 818/225.1331

35 PANZANELLA

★★$$ Three Drago brothers, Tanino, Calogero, and Giacomino, operate this Tuscan-style eatery featuring assorted pastas, risottos, and such. ◆ Italian ◆ Tu-F, lunch; M-Sa, dinner. Reservations suggested. 14928 Ventura Blvd (between Kester and Noble Aves). 818/784.4400

36 MILLENNIUM DENTAL SPA

Next time you need dental work, consider this unusual facility operated by Dr. Eddie

Siman, which actually pampers patients with manicures, pedicures, foot reflexology, and leg and ankle massages while in the chair during any procedure that lasts an hour or more. While the dentist does his stuff, your face is covered in hot towels, a scented seed pillow is placed over your eyes, and you can put on headphones to listen to DVDs. There's even an attractive aromatherapy, candlelit "relaxation room." Talk about taking the angst out of dentistry. Get this: You can even have your car washed and detailed while you're there. The best part is it's all included in Dr. Siman's fee. ♦ 14629 Ventura Blvd (between Kester Ave and Van Nuys Blvd), Sherman Oaks. 818/784.6666. 800/92.SMILE. www.youngersmiles.com

37 FORBIDDEN PLANET

This is the place for contemporary pop culture—American and European adult comics, fantasy, and science fiction—and artworks and collectibles. ♦ Daily. 14513 Ventura Blvd (at Van Nuys Blvd). 818/995.0151

38 ROBBIE MAC'S

★$ For cheap eats, it's hard to beat this family-style fun designer pizza joint. Brick walls, a hardwood floor, and a friendly staff add to the comfortable neighborhood ambience. The freshly made pies and pastas are tasty. The draft beer runs good and cold. (Wine is served, but no booze.) Sports fans have three TVs (one flat-screen) for their viewing pleasure. The New York–style cheesecake and chocolate mousse are killer desserts. ♦ Pizzas and Pastas ♦ Daily, 11AM to midnight. 14502 Ventura Blvd, Sherman Oaks (at Van Nuys Blvd). 818/906.3000

39 FAB'S ITALIAN KITCHEN

★$ This friendly restaurant and storehouse of imported specialties from the old country offers hearty pizzas and traditional pasta favorites. You can bring your own wine for a mere $5 corkage fee. ♦ Italian ♦ Daily, lunch and dinner. Reservations recommended for five or more. 4336 Van Nuys Blvd (at Dickens St). 818/995.2933

40 SUNKIST HEADQUARTERS BUILDING

This striking concrete crate was designed in 1969 by **AC Martin Partners.** ♦ 14130 Riverside Dr (at Hazeltine Ave)

41 WESTFIELD FASHION SQUARE

One of the first large indoor shopping malls built in the area. You can find just about anything you want at this two-story structure, from lingerie (Victoria's Secret) to sporting goods, household gadgets, jewelry (real and costume), shoes, and even vitamins (GNC). There's a fun food court where you can fuel up on pastries, pizza, frozen yogurt, ice cream, and assorted ethnic fare. ♦ Daily; M-F until 9PM, Sa until 7, Su until 6. 14006 Riverside Dr (at Hazeltine Ave). 818/783.0550

42 CAFE BIZOU

★★★$$ Gourmets discovered this wonderful French bistro the minute it opened, and it's now so popular that you need to make your reservation at least a week in advance. Decorated in beige and white, the pleasant, casual dining room is the perfect showcase for chef/owner Neil Rogers's creative menu, which includes such scrumptious specialties as shrimp and scallops served on a bed of black tagliarini mixed with tomato and basil, and salmon coated with sesame seeds presented on a bed of potato pancakes. Among the list of simple desserts, the tarte Tatin takes the cake. The very reasonable prices are another great attraction—you can even bring your own bottle of wine for an unheard-of low $2 corkage fee. ♦ Continental/French ♦ Daily, lunch and dinner; Sa, Su, brunch and dinner. Reservations required. 14016 Ventura Blvd (between Costello and Murietta Aves). 818/788.3536 &. Also at 91 N Raymond Ave (between Holly and Colorado Blvds), Pasadena. 626/792.9923; 2450 Colorado Ave (at Cloverfield Blvd), Santa Monica. 310/582.8203

43 SEÑOR FRED

★★★$ Andre Guerrero and Michael Lamb operate this sprightly eatery, named after Guerrero's son, on the heels of their successful MAX Restaurant about a mile down the boulevard. The design by interior architect Kristopher Keith echoes Mexico circa the turn of the 20th century, with two complementing areas. One offers oversized tooled-leather booths that seat 10, with dim lighting from hanging lamps covered by giant fabric-covered charcoal lampshades. The spacious dining room features freestanding tables and a stucco and tile-covered fireplace. A long, attractive walnut-stained bar, which takes up much of the place, is a popular gathering spot for local singles and couples. For non-barflies, there's a cozy lounge with an inviting couch. Tinted French doors lead to an outdoor patio, equipped with heat lamps for cool nights, where tables book up fast. It's a happy-go-lucky setting. Exceptional dishes include *Róbalo* (pan-roasted

---

Restaurants/Clubs: Red | **Hotels: Purple** | **Shops: Orange** | **Outdoors/Parks: Green** | **Sights/Culture: Blue**

sea bass accented with mango and black bean salsa tostada and topped off with a tangy sauce) and *Quesadilla de Huitlacoche* (prepared with the mushroom-like corn truffle filled with asadero cheese, epazote, and pieces of poblano chile and served with guacamole and other south-of-the-border-style dishes). The best desserts are the chocolate *con leche y galletas* flavored with cinnamon, almonds, and vanilla, served with freshly baked cookies; and the flan *con lima*. ♦ Mexican ♦ Daily, lunch and dinner. Reservations recommended for dinner. 13730 Ventura Blvd (at Mammoth Ave, just west of Woodman Ave), Sherman Oaks. 818/789.3200; fax 818/789.3232. www.SenorFred.com

44 PREZZO

★$$ The food is quite tasty at this favorite meeting place of the Valley's *jeunesse dorée*. Scallops in red pepper sauce, pasta with smoked chicken, and grilled swordfish come highly recommended. ♦ Italian ♦ Daily, dinner. Reservations recommended. 13625 Ventura Blvd (between Ventura Canyon and Woodman Aves). 818/905.8400

45 MAX

★★$$ Chef Andre Guerrero tipped his toque to Linq, where he worked culinary magic for two years, and opened his own little neighborhood charmer. Named after his son, the storefront eatery is adorned with white damask walls, cozy banquettes, and soft lighting. There's a special niche, off to the side of the main dining room, set aside for celebrities who like to go unnoticed. The food is a fusion of California and Asian with offerings such as shrimp and pork spring rolls; Thai lemongrass coconut soup; crab ravioli; tea-smoked salmon cured in soy sauce mirin and fresh ginger; roasted chicken; Applewood-smoked baby back ribs; New York pepper steak; and much more. The lemon mascarpone icebox cake, chocolate brownie, and brioche bread pudding should satisfy your sweet tooth. The service is good and the ambience inviting. ♦ California-Asian Fusion ♦ Daily, dinner; M-F, lunch. Reservations suggested for dinner. Valet parking available. 13355 Ventura Blvd (between Dixie Canyon and Fulton Aves), Sherman Oaks. 818/784.2915. www.maxrestaurant.com

46 THE GREAT GREEK

★$$ Greek food is served in an exuberant atmosphere here, but the appetizers are a better bet than the entrées. The 14-course banquet, intended to serve one, is enough for three people. There's music and dancing nightly. ♦ Greek ♦ Daily, lunch and dinner. Reservations recommended. 13362 Ventura Blvd (at Dixie Canyon Ave). 818/905.5250. www.greatgreek.com

46 MISTRAL

★$$$ This French bistro offers a warm atmosphere and a touch of Provence in the generous use of herbs to flavor the baked mussels and grilled steak. ♦ French ♦ M-F, lunch and dinner; Sa, dinner. Reservations recommended. 13422 Ventura Blvd (between Dixie Canyon and Greenbush Aves). 818/981.6650

47 IROHA SUSHI

★★$$ Excellent sushi is prepared at this quiet, caring bar that's well hidden from the street. ♦ Japanese ♦ M-Sa, lunch and dinner; Su, dinner. 12953 Ventura Blvd (between Coldwater Canyon and Ethel Aves). 818/990.9559

47 PINOT BISTRO

★★★$$$ High energy rocks this chic neighborhood eatery with young trendoids enjoying bistro fare created by one of LA's top chefs, Joachim Splichal. Not only is this a cool place to hang or hook up, the food rocks. Start with a plate of oysters, sautéed scallops with artichokes, asparagus, and tomato salad and move on to a nifty onion soup with gobs of melted cheese, a perfect lamb shank, or roasted Scottish salmon with tomato risotto. Leave room for yummy pastries, pies, and ice creams. This is the type of spot where local celebs like to linger over a leisurely meal, so star spotters should keep their eyes wide open. You never know who may be at the table next to yours. We saw some really high-profile types recently. Save a few bucks by going on Locals Night, which is held every Sunday, and sample an amazing three-course meal prepared by chef Charlie Schaffer. Sign up at the web site for special promotional events and discounts. ♦ French ♦ M-F, lunch and dinner; Sa, Su, dinner. 12969 Ventura Blvd (between Coldwater Canyon and Ethel Aves). 818/990.0500

47 MARRAKESH

★★$$ Couscous with lamb, chicken with olives, and *b'stilla* (chicken with spices, nuts, and fruit beneath a flaky pastry crust) are enjoyed amid authentic décor. ♦ Moroccan ♦ Daily, dinner. Reservations recommended. 13003 Ventura Blvd (between Coldwater Canyon and Ethel Aves). 818/788.6354

47 PINZ

The late, great James Dean bowled here years ago when it was called the Sports Center Bowl. Even under new management and a different name, it continues to attract young, attractive celebrities such as Jennifer Anniston, Brad Pitt, Cameron Diaz, Drew Barrymore, and that crowd. The appeal is the 32 state-of-the-art lanes, full game arcade, billiards, dancing, laser shows, and food and bar service from Jerry's Deli. Not to mention a private screening theater, comedy club, sushi bar, and a full schedule of theme nights held throughout the year. ◆ Daily. 12655 Ventura Blvd (across the street from La Knitterie Parisienne and next door to Jerry's Deli). 818/769.7600. www.pinzbowlingcenter.com

48 LA KNITTERIE PARISIENNE

If you want to learn how to knit, or already do but need some yarn, go see Edith Eig at her charming knitting emporium in Studio City. An amazing assortment of yarns (13,000 to be exact) include imported fibers such as silk, cotton, angora, linen, wool, mohair, corde, soutache, and hand-dyed and blended yarns. She also offers free knitting and crochet lessons. While you're there, browse through the collection of extraordinary sweaters and accessories. ◆ Daily. 12642 Ventura Blvd (between Whitsett and Coldwater Canyon Aves), Studio City. 818/766.1515; e-mail: laknitpar@earthlink.net. www.laknitterieparisienne.com

48 BISTRO GARDEN

★★★$$$ A popular meeting spot for the "ladies who lunch bunch" and well-heeled, mostly surgically enhanced Westsiders who trek over the mountain to gather and dish. The room is light and airy, with a traditional décor. The extensive menu includes signature dishes such as French onion or sweet potato, corn, and jalapeño soup; tuna tartare with ginger soy vinaigrette, goat cheese, and walnut cake; penne pasta with peppers, eggplant, zucchini, fresh mozzarella, and red bell pepper coulis; lemon pepper linguini with shiitake mushrooms, asparagus, sun-dried tomatoes, and extra-virgin olive oil; Parmesan risotto with beef tenderloin; broiled whitefish in lemon butter; braised Chilean sea bass in a Dijon mustard dill sauce; chicken curry; osso buco; grilled veal porterhouse; and on and on. Desserts worth the caloric splurge include a heavenly chocolate or pumpkin soufflé, crème brûlée, pineapple cheesecake, and chocolate mousse cake with vanilla sauce. ◆ French

Continental ◆ M-F, lunch and dinner; Sa, Su, dinner. Reservations recommended. 12950 Ventura Blvd (between Coldwater Canyon and Van Noord Aves). Valet parking. 818/501.0202; fax 818/501.2244. www.bistrogarden.com

49 TOMMY RAYS

★★$$ This is one of those fun neighborhood spots where locals gather for lunch and dinner during the week and breakfast on weekends. There's an inviting outdoor patio with bright red umbrellas shading aluminum tables. The indoor area sports a friendly bar (happy hour held daily from 3 to 6PM), along with booths and tables. The aura is warm and the food is nicely prepared by outgoing chef Tony Ramano, a first-generation Italian. Favorites include the classic Caesar salad, wild salmon, wild mushroom quesadilla, rack of lamb, and six different pastas dishes. The molten lava bundt cake's a killer. ◆ American with a European Twist ◆ Daily, lunch and dinner; 9:30AM-1AM on weekends. Reservations suggested. 12345 Ventura Blvd (between Laurel Canyon Blvd and Whitsett Ave), Studio City. 818/506.2412. www.tommyrayscafe.com

50 STORYOPOLIS

The best in children's book illustrations are displayed in this 6,000-square-foot showroom that is part shop, part gallery. Both the illustrations and the books themselves can be bought here. Operated by the eponymous production company that also makes films based on children's books, it presents craft and story hours the first Saturday of every month. Days of operation vary, so call ahead. ◆ 12348 Ventura Blvd (between Laurel Canyon Blvd and Whitsett Ave). 818/509.5600. www.Storyopolis.com

51 MEXICALI

★★$ This feisty little Mexican restaurant gets all dressed up in scarecrows and pumpkins in October and Christmas trees and lights in December, and offers a tasty menu with everything from enchiladas to ahi tuna. The garlic-and-chipotle-roasted chicken and the tortilla soup are superb. Cozy booths and a friendly staff make this a very special place. Go between 4PM and 7PM and get $1 off margaritas (they do make a mean margie here); and if it's Monday after 4PM, they give 30 percent off all food. ◆ Mexican ◆ Daily, lunch and dinner. 12161 Ventura Blvd (between Laurel Canyon Blvd and Laurelgrove Ave). 818/985.1744 ♿

Restaurants/Clubs: Red | Hotels: Purple | Shops: Orange | Outdoors/Parks: Green | Sights/Culture: Blue

51 ROMANOV

★★★$$$$ Dine like a czar or czarina at this over-the-top palatial restaurant/lounge/ steak house with a Russian twist. It's pricey, but worth splurging, if only to experience the fit-for-royalty room where trimmings go wild, beginning with an outrageously eccentric chandelier imported piece by piece from Russia, Fabergé egg lamps, gold-plated walls, and a 24-carat gold-leaf ceiling. To set the mood, there's a bodacious selection of vodkas, one served in a Fabergé egg that sells for $2,800 (if you can't afford to buy it, they'll be happy to show it to you). Nestle in a cozy booth and sink your teeth into assorted Russian appetizers (potato blini with smoked salmon and crème fraiche and caviar, pozharsky stuffed with ground beef and pork). Continue with borscht; the Czar salad, a good twist on Caesar; Colorado lamb chop, or czar and czarina cuts of prime rib. Desserts here are an acquired taste. The action starts around 8PM, when guests belly up to the bar to watch gypsy dancers strut their stuff. FYI: The chandelier is so unusual, Las Vegas's Steve Wynn has begged to buy it. ♦ Russian Steak House ♦ Daily, dinner. Reservations a must. 12229 Ventura Blvd, Studio City (on north side of the road between Laurel Canyon Blvd and Whitsett Ave). 818/760.3177. www.romanovia.com

52 DARI

Melanie Shatner, daughter of William Shatner, *Star Trek*'s Captain Kirk, and the irascible character Denny Crane on TV's *Boston Legal,* runs this earthly shop of trendy duds and accessories from designers such as Diane von Furstenberg, Laura Urbinati, and Isabella Fiore. ♦ Daily; Su until 5PM. 12184 Ventura Blvd (between Laurel Canyon Blvd and Whitsett Ave). 818/762.3274

52 ART'S DELI

★$ This full-service deli is a favorite among Valley denizens who hold court there, sometimes throughout the day. Pastrami is a house specialty. ♦ Deli ♦ Daily. 12224 Ventura Blvd (between Vantage and Laurelgrove Aves). 818.762.1221

53 OUT TAKE BISTRO

★★★$$ This chic little eatery proffers some of the best home-style cooking around. Few tables mean there's often a wait, but the food's well worth some patience. The eclectic menu includes wonton soup, Ukrainian borscht, Southwest turkey chili, spinach salad, Asian chicken satay, sandwiches, and pasta dishes. ♦ Café ♦ Daily, lunch and dinner. 11929 Ventura Blvd (between Colfax and Radford Aves). 818/769.0822

54 WINE BISTRO

★$$ Enjoy a variety of wines with a wonderful bistro menu served in a cozy woodsy setting. Start with escargots or pâté de foie gras with crusty French bread and continue with bouillabaisse, roasted duckling, or whitefish with sweet caramelized red onion. Luscious endings include crème brûlée, chocolate mousse cake, and a traditional cheese plate. ♦ French ♦ M-F, lunch and dinner; Sa, dinner. 11915 Ventura Blvd (between Colfax and Radford Aves). 818/766.6233

54 LA LOGGIA

★★$$ Movie moguls and power brokers keep this modern trattoria jumping. Its popularity hasn't waned since the day it opened—locals describe it as the Valley's answer to Spago. Pasta (linguini with seafood; angel hair with fresh tomatoes, garlic, and basil), risotto with saffron and asparagus, farm-raised roasted chicken au jus, and pork chop with caramelized Bartlett pears and Gorgonzola sauce are standouts. Forget calorie counting and finish with a scrumptious banana Napoleon, upside-down chocolate soufflé, or tiramisù. ♦ Northern Italian ♦ M-F, lunch and dinner; Sa, Su, dinner. 11814 Ventura Blvd (between Blue Canyon Dr and Carpenter Ave). 818/985.9222; e-mail: laloggia@earthlink. net. www.calendarlive.com/LaLoggia

54 TERU SUSHI

★$$ This hugely popular sushi bar launched what is now LA's favorite grazing fare. The theatrical presentation by the chefs adds flair to the other specialties as well. ♦ Japanese ♦ M-F, lunch and dinner; Sa, Su, dinner. 11940 Ventura Blvd (between Carpenter Ave and Laurel Canyon Blvd). 818/763.6201

54 FIREFLY

★★★$$$ Hidden in a vine-shrouded building—and we do mean concealed, with no signage—this is without doubt the hippest spot in the Valley. Fashion-plate, bare-bellied, tattooed, pierced, and trendy foodies flock from all over town to be part of this over-the-top scene. An open-air dining room, big bar lined with bookcases, velvet sofas, an outdoor fireplace, and dim lighting set the mood for the eclectic, seasonally

changing menu. Order the pan-roasted scallops served on a bed of succotash with vanilla-bean vinaigrette or the calamari sprinkled with almond flour if you see them on the list. Any salad will please your palate, and so will the Tahitian vanilla-bean crème brûlée or banana walnut cake. Dress as hip as your wardrobe allows. Bring a few friends; people tend to travel in groups here.
♦ American Eclectic ♦ M-Sa, dinner. Reservations necessary. 11720 Ventura Blvd (between Blue Canyon Dr and Carpenter Ave), Studio City. 818/762.1833. (Look for the vine-covered building, as there's no name posted.)

55 GELATO

★★$ This fun gathering spot dishes out 24 flavors of handmade gelato (pistachio, spicy chocolate, pink grapefruit, and more) along with bagels, croissants, cookies, and candies. A European-style coffee bar, set in a back room, churns out fresh, locally roasted brews. Drop by and relax in the indoor courtyard, where you can read newspapers like the *International Tribune*, play board games, or even take free Italian lessons on Thursdays. ♦ Coffee Bar ♦ M-Th, 7:30AM-10PM; F, Sa, until 11PM; Su, 9AM-10PM. 4342½ Tujunga Ave (between Moorpark St and Ventura Fwy). 818/487.1717

56 BARSAC BRASSERIE

★★$$ This charming little bistro caters to the nearby studio set, who dine here between scenes. The menu changes every three months, but you can usually count on items such as the quail salad, veal tortellini, ravioli stuffed with goat cheese, steamed wild salmon, or orange roughy to satisfy your taste buds. ♦ French ♦ M-F, lunch and dinner; Sa, dinner. 4212 Lankershim Blvd (between Cahuenga Blvd and Valley Spring La). 818/760.7081. www.barsac.com

57 AQ NAIL SPA

An oasis of tranquillity with refreshing mint green walls offset by bamboo and glass fixtures, this is one of the Valley's most inviting nail salons. The state-of-the-art massaging pedicure chairs provide heavenly comfort while the technician works on your toes. More than just a pretty place to have your nails done, the salon also offers facials, massages, and body treatments in a specially designed bamboo room. Prices are much more reasonable than you might expect from its uptown look. The service is good, but the staff can be somewhat standoffish. In addition to the usual nail care, you can have your hands and tootsies sea scrubbed, get them wrapped in a marine mask, or have calluses removed. ♦ Daily. 11239 Ventura Blvd, Suite 107 (between Vineland and Tujunga Aves), Studio City. 818/985.5159. www.aqnailspa.com

58 HORTOBAGY

★$$ Named after the plains region of Hungary, home of the fabled Hungarian horsemen, it's no surprise that the food here is solid, spicy, and unpretentious. There are stews, rich soups, grilled and breaded meats, and amazing homemade sausages, as well as a selection of Hungarian wines. Great dessert choices are the chocolate torte or plum dumpling. ♦ Hungarian ♦ M, dinner only; Tu-Su, lunch and dinner. Reservations recommended for four or more. 11138 Ventura Blvd (between Fruitland and Eureka Drs). 818/980.2273

58 SUSHI NOZAWA

★★$$ Victorian table manners are observed at this splendidly old-fashioned restaurant, but the stern warnings on what not to do or eat are worth it: Chef Nozawa offers some of the best sushi in town. ♦ Japanese ♦ M-F, lunch and dinner. 11288 Ventura Blvd (at Eureka Dr), Unit C. 818/508.7017

59 THE BAKED POTATO

Guitar gods Lee Ritenour and Larry Carlton got their starts here at one of LA's best-established clubs for contemporary jazz. It's loud and yet intimate. Twenty-one varieties of stuffed potatoes are served (shrimp-and-cheese are one of the favored choices). ♦ Cover. Daily, 7PM-2AM. 3787 Cahuenga Blvd (at Lankershim Blvd). 818/980.1615

L A's hidden treasures . . .
The 4,000-acre **Griffith Park** and the **Los Angeles** Zoo are the main attractions of this area just northeast of Hollywood. One of the largest urban green spaces
in America, it was named for Colonel Griffith J. Griffith, who bought the land in
1882 and then donated it to the city in 1896.

Two adjacent very distinctive communities, **Los Feliz** and **Silverlake,** sit south of the park. Built in the 1920s before the advent of pad construction, many of the houses here conform to the picturesque undulations of the land. The winding roads and tiled roofs massed on the slopes around the **Silver Lake Reservoir** resemble a Mediterranean hill town. The pretty lake provides the perfect setting for jogging, bicycling, or strolling. The region also boasts LA's highest concentration of modern architectural masterpieces, notably by **Richard Neutra, Rudolph Schindler,**

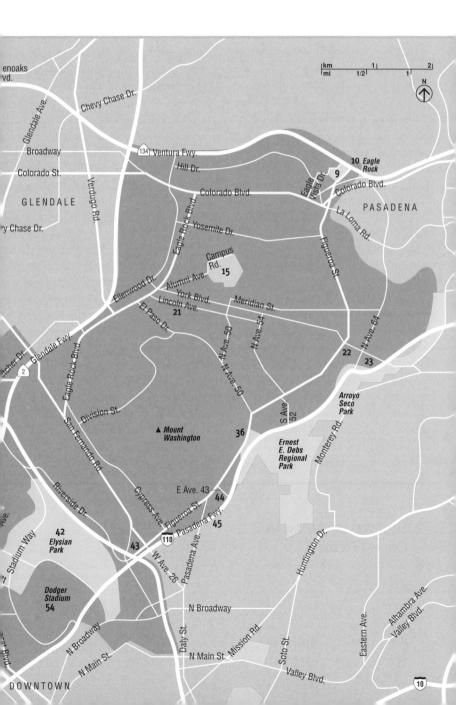

Gregory Ain, and **John Lautner.** Today Los Feliz and Silverlake are booming with young affluent adults and gays who are buying up and remodeling houses in droves. Both spots boast a thriving restaurant and late nightclub scene frequented by locals and scenesters from out of the area. Boutiques and quaint shops are also popping up everywhere. In the past couple of years, the two communities have quickly become the places to live and play in LA. Contrary to popular belief, Los Feliz's 90027 zip code beats Beverly Hills's 90210 as America's wealthiest address, with denizens past and present including Kirstie Alley, Geena Davis, Cecil B. DeMille, Colin Farrell, Al Jolson, Heidi Fleiss, Beck, and Red Hot Chili Peppers' Michael Balzary.

The first residents of North Central were the Yang-Na Indians, who camped in the **Elysian Park Hills** and hunted for small game with bows and arrows. Around 1910 moviemakers came to the neighborhood, among them Mack Sennett, who built his first studio near **Glendale Boulevard.** Today, North Central is predominantly a blue-collar Hispanic-American district, tucked into two pockets of steep hills and bordered by freeways at the northern end of downtown LA. The small frame houses perched high on the tightly woven streets give the appearance of a rural setting, and huge stands of eucalyptus trees run across the hillsides and into the canyons. Trails form a network through the overgrown wilderness across slopes and ravines leading up to **Mount Washington.** A mix of romance and economy makes this residential area attractive to creative young people.

The park is divided into two main parts: the flatlands, with their lush golf courses, picnic areas, pony and train rides, tennis courts, merry-go-round, zoo, museum of transportation, observatory, and **Greek Theatre;** and the mountainous central and western areas, undeveloped save for numerous hiking and horse trails. Four main entrances lead to the park: **Ferndell Drive,** off Los Feliz Boulevard, leading to the **Ferndell; Vermont Avenue,** off Los Feliz, leading to the Greek Theatre and the **Bird Sanctuary; Crystal Springs Drive,** off Los Feliz, leading to the **Ranger Station,** merry-go-round, and golf courses; and the junction of the **Golden State** and **Ventura Freeways,** leading to the zoo and museum. Rangers lead a hike on the first Saturday of the month at 9AM from the merry-go-round parking lot. **Sierra Club tours** include evening outings during full moons. There are no specific bike paths, but regular paved roads are open to cyclists; bikes aren't permitted on the fire roads or horse trails. Some of the 18 picnic areas in the park have benches and tables; those in the Ferndell and Vermont Canyon have barbecues and water. **Park Center** and **Mineral Wells** have some areas with cooking facilities. Visitors may also picnic on the grass. The park is open daily until 10PM.

---

1 EQUESTRIAN CENTER AND CRICKET FIELDS

🅟 Two fields are located in the center of the equestrian track near Riverside Drive. The track functions as a practice area and leads to all trails. There are 43 miles of horse trails within the park. Several commercial stables on the outskirts of the park rent horses by the hour. All accept cash only and require a security deposit. ◆ Daily. Riverside Dr and Main St, Burbank. 818/840.8401

2 TRAVEL TOWN

The romance of the rails lives on at this open-air museum of transportation, which displays many antique railroad and trolley cars, locomotives, planes, and automobiles. An enclosed structure houses fire trucks and a circus animal wagon. Many exhibits allow children to climb on board, a treat they'll not forget. Members of a model train club work-on an enormous train layout on Saturdays. ◆ Free. Daily. 5200 Zoo Dr (just north-of Griffith Park Dr). 323/662.5874. www.ci.la.ca.us/rap/grifmet/tt/information.htm

3 LIVE STEAMERS

The Los Angeles Live Steamers Club brings its tiny steam locomotives to an area just east of **Travel Town** each Sunday. The trains run on tracks only seven inches wide, but they're authentic in every detail and powerful enough to pull several fully loaded cars. Children get free rides and a chance to examine the miniatures. ♦ Su, 11AM-2:30PM. Zoo Dr (between Crystal Springs and Griffith Park Drs). 323/662.8030

4 AUTRY MUSEUM OF WESTERN HERITAGE

Gene Autry, the singing cowboy of movies, radio, and television, opened this wonderful tribute to the spirit of the West in 1988. Walt Disney Imagineering has brought the memorabilia, artwork, and movie clips to life so you can get a visceral sense of what it was like to be a settler, a cowboy, or a sheriff. Scholarship and showbiz are fruitfully combined, and the museum presents regular exhibitions along with the permanent collection. The architecture firm of **Widom Wein Cohen** designed the museum. ♦ Admission. Tu-Su. 4700 Western Heritage Way (at Zoo Dr). 323/667.2000. www.autry-museum.org

5 LOS ANGELES ZOO

Ⓟ The 75-acre zoo, which opened in 1966, has more than 2,000 animals grouped according to continent of origin. Many of the animals are in environments that simulate their natural habitats, with surrounding moats that allow you to see them without bars. The zoo preserves 78 endangered species. Explore the **Koala House** and the **Aviary,** ride a camel or an elephant, and take in a bird show. The **Animal Nursery** proudly displays the newest arrivals. And for those of you who enjoy seeing creepy, crawly creatures, there's **Spider City,** featuring 26 species such as jumping spiders, a bird-eating tarantula with a leg span of 12 inches, and some faux creations. The 4.5-acre **Pachyderm Forest** houses elephants, hippos, and other creatures in a setting of tropical hardwoods, lagoons, and an Asian topiary. **Sea Lions Cliffs** is a saltwater exhibit affording underwater viewing. Baby stroller and wheelchair rentals are available along with picnic tables, a snack bar, and a tram tour. ♦ Admission. Daily. 5333 Zoo Dr (just west of Golden State Fwy). General information

323/644.6400. A map of the zoo is available at www.lazoo.org

6 GOLF

Ⓟ Two 18-hole courses (**Harding** and **Wilson**) and two nine-hole courses (**Roosevelt** and **Los Feliz Pitch & Putt**) in the park are open to the public. City-registered golfers may make reservations. Others will be allowed on the green as space becomes available. ♦ Harding and Wilson: 4730 Crystal Springs Dr (between Los Feliz Blvd and Zoo Dr), 323/663.2555. Roosevelt: 2650 N Vermont Ave (at Commonwealth Canyon Dr), 323/665.2011. Los Feliz Pitch & Putt: 3207 Los Feliz Blvd (between Garden Ave and Golden State Fwy), 323/663.7758

7 MERRY-GO-ROUND

The well-preserved merry-go-round on the green was constructed in 1926 and moved to the park in 1936. ♦ Admission. Daily, mid-June to mid-Sept; Sa, Su, and LA public school holidays, mid-Sept to mid-June. Park Center Picnic Area (west of Griffith Park Blvd). 323/665.3051

8 RANGER STATION

Ⓟ The **Griffith Park Visitors' Center** operates here. Stop in to pick up information and free road and hiking trail maps. ♦ Daily until 10PM. 4730 Crystal Springs Dr (between Los Feliz Blvd and Zoo Dr). 323/913.7390; fax 323/485.8775

9 EAGLE ROCK PLAYGROUND CLUBHOUSE

Richard Neutra designed this building in 1953. It boasts a magnificent view. ♦ Figueroa St (between Colorado Blvd and Ventura Fwy)

10 EAGLE ROCK

Ⓟ The massive sandstone rock, 150 feet high, res embles an eagle in flight on its southwest side. Described by Dr. Carl Dentzel, late director of the Southwest Museum, as the most distinctive natural landmark in the city, it is visible from the Ventura Freeway traveling east from Glendale to Pasadena. ♦ N Figueroa St and Scholl Canyon Rd

11 SUNSET RANCH

Ⓟ The Old West flourishes in the heart of the city at this ranch, with photogenic stables and moonlit rides to the top of the mountains, where you'll have stupendous views of LA. Night rides every Friday at 5PM

Restaurants/Clubs: Red | Hotels: Purple | Shops: Orange | Outdoors/Parks: Green | Sights/Culture: Blue

are on a first-come, first-served basis; groups must make appointments on other nights. ◆ Daily. 3400 N Beachwood Dr (north of Franklin Ave). 323/469.5450

12 BIRD SANCTUARY

Rangers planted protective foliage to encourage birds to nest in this wooded canyon with ponds and a stream. Picnic while you keep an eye out for sparrows, hawks, and scrub jays, among others. ◆ Daily, dawn to dusk. Vermont Canyon Rd (between Commonwealth Canyon and Mount Hollywood Drs)

13 GRIFFITH-VERMONT CANYON TENNIS COURTS

Free play is available at the 12 day-use-only courts before 4PM. No reservations are taken. ◆ Fee after 4PM. Daily. Commonwealth Canyon Dr (between Vista del Valle Dr and N Vermont Ave)

14 TAM O'SHANTER INN

★★$$ **Lawry's** runs this haven for expatriate Scots. The prime rib is tops. But many folks go for the toad-in-the-hole and Scotch rarebit, mustard-encrusted pork, and the super salmon and swordfish. For true believers, haggis is served on Robert Burns's birthday. ◆ Scottish ◆ M-F, lunch and dinner; Sa, dinner; Su, brunch and dinner. Reservations recommended. 2980 Los Feliz Blvd (at Boyce Ave). 323/664.0228

15 OCCIDENTAL COLLEGE

This small liberal arts college, founded in 1887, was formerly affiliated with the Presbyterian Church. The campus core was designed by **Myron Hunt** after the college's move to the Eagle Rock area in 1914. Occidental figures as Tarzana College in Aldous Huxley's *After Many a Summer Dies the Swan.* The inventively designed **Keck Theatre** (323/259.2737) presents a wide range of plays and dance performances throughout the year. ◆ 1600 Campus Rd (at Alumni Ave). 323/259.2500

16 THE SAMUEL OSCHIN PLANETARIUM

The completion of a $63 million renovation and expansion enhanced the appeal of this popular attraction where you can see real stars up close through cutting-edge equipment and learn just about anything you ever wanted to know about the universe. Highlights of the 300-seat facility include a three-digital-laser projection system; a perforated aluminum projection dome, which is one of the world's largest at 75 feet; and a Zeiss Universarium Mark IX star projector, the most advanced in the universe. ◆ Tu-F, noon-10PM; Sa, Su, 10AM-10PM. 2800 Observatory Rd (between Vermont Canyon and Western Canyon Rds). 212/473.0800

17 GREEK THEATRE

This imposing amphitheater, with its distinctive 1930s façade, boasts attractive plaza areas with upscale concession stands, state-of-the-art sound and lighting systems, and an inviting picnic lawn area. The amphitheater presents mostly popular music from June through the first week of October. Box suppers may be purchased from concessionaires inside. Beer and wine are available. Bring a sweater—nights get chilly in LA. ◆ Admission. 2700 N Vermont Ave (north of Los Feliz Blvd). Tickets and schedules 323/665.5857, subscription information 323/468.1767. www.nederlander.com/greek.html

18 PONY RIDES

This safe, small track offers pony rides for children. ◆ Tu-Su. Crystal Springs Dr (north of Los Feliz Blvd). 323/664.3266

18 TRAIN RIDE

Another tiny train, but this one is for adults as well as children. ◆ Fee. Daily. 4400 Crystal Springs Dr (north of Los Feliz Blvd). 323/664.6788

19 SWIMMING POOL

An Olympic-size pool is open during the summer at the **Griffith Recreation Center.** ◆ Free. Daily, mid-June to mid-Sept. Riverside Dr and Los Feliz Blvd. 323/665.4372

20 CANELE

★★$$ This place goes to show good things do come in small packages. The tiny room packs a culinary wallop from the dandelion salad to coop's use omelettes starters. There's also roast chicken, a mean branzino, and authentic, crispy french fries. The orange butter cake provides a perfect finale. ◆ French with a Twist ◆ Tu-Su, dinner. No reservations. 3219 Glendale Blvd (between Edenhurst and Brunswick Aves). 323/666.7133. www.canele-la.com

21 SPARKLETT DRINKING WATER

Corporate LA is full of Islamic pastiches, and this 1929 mosque is one of the finest. The minarets came down in the 1971 earthquake and were rebuilt. ◆ 4500 Lincoln Ave (at N Ave 45)

22 SAN ENCINO ABBEY

The hybrid of California Mission and European Gothic styles was created by **Clyde Brown** between 1909 and 1925. Brown imported parts of old European castles and monasteries to create his own medieval environment. It's a private residence. ♦ 6211 Arroyo Glen St (at Figueroa St)

23 JUDSON STUDIOS

This studio has been well known for its stained-glass work since 1897. The Moorish and Craftsman-style building is owned by a fourth-generation Judson descendant. ♦ Lobby, M-F. 200 S Ave 66 (between Marmion Way and York Blvd). 323/255.0131

24 THE FERNDELL

Ⓟ This natural glade along a spring-fed stream is planted with native and exotic ferns. Paths and picnic tables make this an outstanding place to retreat from the world for an alfresco meal. ♦ Daily. Ferndell Dr (between Black Oak and Red Oak Drs)

25 ENNIS-BROWN HOUSE

Frank Lloyd Wright built this "Maya temple," the most impressive and best-sited of his concrete-block houses, on a hill overlooking the city in 1924. It is a private residence; however, tours are offered of the interior, which has been restored to its original appearance. ♦ Admission. Tours: Second Sa of each odd-numbered month from noon on. 2655 Glendower Ave (between Bryn Mawr Rd and N Catalina St). Tour reservations 323/660.0607

26 LOVELL HOUSE

Richard Neutra created LA's finest example of International-style architecture: a steel-framed, stucco-clad composition of stacked planes flowing out from a hillside. Completed in 1929, the design launched Neutra's 40-year career as the most productive and prestigious of LA's modern architects. This is a private residence. ♦ 4616 Dundee Dr (west of N Commonwealth Ave)

27 SANSUI

★$ "Healthy food in a peaceful room" is the goal of owner/chef Shinichi Kishi, and he delivers on both promises. The Shojin dinner includes 10 small vegetarian courses, and the music that wafts through sounds like wind on a mountaintop. ♦ Japanese ♦ M-F, lunch and dinner; Sa, Su, dinner. Reservations recommended for parties of five or more. 2040 Hillhurst Ave (at Price St). 323/660.3868

28 SAY CHEESE

This shop is a great neighborhood resource for fresh cheeses, teas, coffees, and

imported delicacies. ♦ Daily. 2800 Hyperion Ave (between Griffith Park Blvd and near Rowena Ave). 323/665.0545

29 FRED 62

★★$ This eccentric little coffee shop espouses the motto "Eat now, dine later." Perfect for families, the quirky menu offers kids such choices as MacDaddy and Cheese (macaroni and cheese) and Bearded Mr. Frenchy (French toast breaded with cornflakes). Adults might prefer the Thai Cobb salad, Seoul Caesar, or eggs and omelettes. ♦ Coffee Shop ♦ Daily, 24 hours. 1850 N Vermont Ave (at Russell Ave). 323/667.0062 &

30 ELECTRIC LOTUS

★★$$ The long, narrow restaurant, named after a nightclub in Goa, is definitely wired with the hip and happening (and young celebs) who go to enjoy Northern Indian cuisine and stay up late listening to live Indian music. The food's tasty and interesting, with offerings like chicken tikka masala, *palek paneer* (steamed spinach with tofu), tofu curry, and a choice of two desserts: rice pudding and yummy *gulab jamon* (pastry balls spiced with ginger and sweetened with honey). ♦ Indian ♦ Daily, lunch and dinner (open until midnight weeknights, 1AM weekends). Reservations. 4656 Franklin Ave (between Hillhurst and N Vermont Aves). 323/953.0040. www.electriclotus.com

31 EL CHAVO

$ The menu features *riñones fritos* (sautéed kidneys with chopped vegetables); tongue in Spanish sauce and mole; a wonderful, tender poached chicken; and excellent grilled steaks. The soft lighting is pleasant and the music is, thankfully, unobtrusive. ♦ Mexican ♦ Daily, dinner. 4441 Sunset Blvd (between N Hoover St and Sunset Dr). 323/664.0871. www.elchavo.com

32 CASITA DEL CAMPO

$ Go here for enjoyable eating on an outdoor patio. ♦ Mexican ♦ Daily, lunch and dinner. Reservations recommended. 1920 Hyperion Ave (between Landa St and Lyric Ave). 323/662.4255. www.casitadelcampo.com

33 OLIVE HOUSE

This wonderfully complex house was designed by **Rudolph Schindler,** Richard Neutra's compatriot and rival, who was more innovative but less successful in his LA career. This street has a uniquely rich concentration of classic modern houses, all of which are private residences. ♦ 2236 Micheltorena St (between Rock and Angus Sts)

Restaurants/Clubs: Red | Hotels: Purple | Shops: Orange | Outdoors/Parks: Green | Sights/Culture: Blue

34 RED LION TAVERN

★$ Not a nook for nibbling, this unpretentious, inexpensive neighborhood restaurant is the real home-cooked German article, with delicious food and lots of it: schnitzel, bratwurst, smoked pork loin, veal loaf, sauerkraut, potato salad, etc. There's also weiss beer on tap, and a fine selection of after-dinner liqueurs, such as kirschwasser, slivovitz, and apple schnapps. ◆ German ◆ Daily, lunch and dinner. Reservations recommended for parties of eight or more. 2366 Glendale Blvd (at Brier Ave). 323/662.5337

35 NEUTRA HOUSE

Richard Neutra built this daringly experimental house for himself in his first decade of work in 1933. When it was destroyed by fire in 1963, he created a more romantic version, completed one year later. On Silverlake's **2200 block** there's a concentration of Neutra houses dating from 1948 to 1961: nos. **2250, 2242, 2240, 2238, 2226, 2218, 2210,** and **2200.** All are private residences. ◆ 2300 Silverlake Blvd (between Earl St and Edgewater Terr)

36 SOUTHWEST MUSEUM OF THE AMERICAN INDIAN

One of the city's sleepers, this museum houses a magnificent collection of Native American art in a Mission-style building on Mount Washington overlooking the Pasadena Freeway. The permanent displays of art and artifacts from the Southwest, Great Plains, Northwest coast, and California have been dramatically improved over time. Notable among the holdings are the **Poole Collections** of American Indian basketry, Navajo blankets, pottery, and a full-size Blackfoot tepee. Loan exhibitions, lectures, and workshops for the entire family are held throughout the year. The **Festival of Native American Arts,** with food, music, and dance, is held every October. There is also a well-stocked gift and bookstore and the important **Braun Research Library** for scholarly reference. ◆ Admission. Tu-Su. 234 Museum Dr (just north of Marmion Way). 323/221.2164.www.southwestmuseum.org

37 EL CID FLAMENCO SHOW RESTAURANT

$$ The food in this Spanish Colonial cabaret is only run-of-the-mill, but the flamenco guitar and flamenco dancing are remarkable. It's located on the site of D.W. Griffith's studio, where the 150-foot-high set of *The Grand Babylon Hotel* rose in 1916. ◆ Mexican/Spanish ◆ W-Su, dinner. Reservations recommended. 4212 Sunset Blvd (at Myra Ave). 323/668.0318

38 CAFÉ STELLA

★★★ $$ This hip and happening brasserie serves fabulous country French food in a cozy yet lively setting. The *pomme frites* are crispy and authentic, the *steak frite* just like you'd get in France, and ooh la, the duck is superb. There are only 60 tables, so you may have to wait, but there's a pleasant patio for sipping an aperitif. ◆ French Brasserie ◆ Tu-Sa, lunch and dinner. Reservations suggested for dinner 3932 Sunset Blvd (in the Sunset Junction building near Sanborn Ave). 323/666.0265

39 SOMPUN THAI

★$ Excellent noodles and other great dishes are served in this family-style restaurant. Dine on the charming patio. ◆ Thai ◆ M, W-Su, lunch and dinner. 4156 Santa Monica Blvd (between Manzanita St and Myra Ave). 323/669.9906

40 TANTRA

★★★$$ The scene is tantra-lizing with seductive Bhangra music and subtle, sexy colors, designs, and scents. You feel like you walked into an opium den or forbidden garden. Designed by Sat Garg, the whimsical, mystical décor of mottled deep yellow plaster walls, a giant statue of Lord Ganesha (God of Prosperity), and plasma-screen television showing old Hollywood movies teases the senses, while the food rouses gastric juices into a frenzied state of pure delight. Every menu morsel is fantastic from the tandoori salmon kebob to the lamb biryani. The Tantra Platter is a winner, with salmon, green chicken tikka, and spinach tofu samosas served with masala cheese naan; as is the Jhinga Khichdi, an Indian-style risotto with red onion and coriander topped with a crispy prawn. The after-hours set fills the bar until early morning. ◆ Indian ◆ Daily, dinner. Reservations required. 3705 Sunset Blvd (between Edgecliff Dr and Lucille Ave). 323/663.8268. e-mail: tantrasunset@hotmail.com. www.tantrasunset.com

41 NETTY'S

$$ Soups, pasta, grilled chicken, and dishes of the day, to go or to eat at a few teensy tables, are the mainstays of the menu at this funky spot. ◆ American ◆ M-Sa, lunch and dinner. 1700 Silverlake Blvd (at Effie St). 323/662.8655

42 ELYSIAN PARK

The second-largest park (more than 600 acres) in the Los Angeles area occupies several hills and valleys. The parkland was set aside for public use at the founding of the city in 1781. The main part of it has been left in its natural state, its slopes covered with the shrubs and low trees known as chaparral and crisscrossed with hiking trails. A scenic plaza with a small artificial lake is located a quarter-mile north of the Academy Road/Pasadena Freeway intersection. There's also a children's play area. A café at the Police Academy is open to the public weekdays from 6AM to 3PM, serving hearty, reasonably priced meals. ♦ Free. Daily, until 9PM. 1880 Academy Dr (north of Academy Rd). 323/222.9136

43 LAWRY'S CALIFORNIA CENTER

The restaurant and gift shop have closed, and the building is now home to Lawry's corporate offices. Note the distinctive Spanish-style architecture. ♦ 570 W Ave 26 (between N Figueroa St and San Fernando Rd)

44 LUMMIS HOUSE

This unique owner-built residence was conceived and executed between 1898 and 1910 by Charles Fletcher Lummis, founder of the **Southwest Museum of the American Indian** (see page 176) and the first city librarian. Constructed of granite boulders from the nearby arroyo, hand-hewn timbers, and telephone poles, the structure is a romantic combination of styles. Most of the original furniture is gone, but the home and gardens remain as a monument to a most extraordinary man. ♦ Free. F-Su, noon-4PM. 200 E Ave 43 (at Midland St). 323/222.0546

45 HERITAGE SQUARE MUSEUM

The president of the National Trust described this as an "architectural petting zoo," and certainly these vintage houses had a greater impact on the city when they occupied their original sites. But just as zoos preserve endangered species, so the LA Cultural Heritage Board has rescued these eight historic buildings, built between 1865 and 1920, from the insatiable greed of developers. They include the **Hale House,** the **Palms Railroad Depot,** and the **Lincoln Avenue Methodist Church.** Ask about tours and special events. There's also a gift shop. ♦ Admission. F-Su, noon-4PM. 3800 N Homer St (south of E Ave 43). 626/449.0193

46 LONGEST STAIRCASE

The earliest movie makers built studios in Silverlake and filmed on its streets. Laurel and Hardy tried to carry a grand piano up these steps in *The Music Box* (1932). ♦ 927 N Vendome St (between N Dillon St and Sunset Blvd)

47 DUSTY'S

★★$ If you want to get a handle on what Silverlake residents are like, drop by this caffeine-driven eatery any time of the day. You'll find an eclectic mix of early and late risers dining under multicolored umbrellas on the patio or inside in wraparound upholstered booths, leisurely sipping killer-strength joes and/or munching on creative omelettes or eggs mixed with cheese, spinach, chicken, or other interesting ingredients. The menu also offers salads, soups, sandwiches, and a variety of burgers (vegan, turkey, lamb, crab, and of course traditional beef). ♦ American ♦ Daily, breakfast, lunch, and dinner. Reservations not necessary, but you may have to wait awhile. 3200 W Sunset Blvd (at Descanso Dr), Silverlake. 323/906.1018; fax 323/906.9356

48 OLIVE SUBSTATION

Restored by the Jerde Partnership, this 1907 structure was one of several Mission-style stations in the city taken over by the Pacific Electric Railway Company in 1911. It now houses a private office. ♦ 2798 Sunset Blvd (at N Occidental Blvd)

49 TAIX

★★★$$ The largest and oldest of LA's French restaurants, this dining spot offers fixed-price, full-course *très très* French meals. Favorites include signature roast chicken *fermière* (covered in a light Bordelaise sauce), a superior filet mignon served on Monday nights, a divine lamb shank on Wednesdays, about the best short ribs you'll ever eat on Fridays, and a duck à l'orange to make you drool on Saturdays. Although you get sherbet *après* your meal, the chocolate mousse or crème brûlée are well worth the splurge. Wines are the most reasonably priced around. ♦ French ♦ Daily, lunch and dinner. 1911 Sunset Blvd (at Reservoir St). 213/484.1265. www.taixfrench.com

50 BARRAGAN CAFE

★$$ This neighborhood favorite for Mexican food serves honestly prepared platters of the usual dishes (tacos, tostadas, enchiladas, rellenos) all dished out in combo plates with lots of chips and salsa. There's nightly entertainment in the bar. ♦ Mexican ♦ Daily, breakfast, lunch, and dinner. Reservations recommended. 1538 Sunset Blvd (between Laveta Terr and Echo Park Ave). 213/250.4256

51 ANGELUS TEMPLE

In the 1920s and 1930s, Aimee Semple McPherson preached her "Foursquare Gospel" within this circular structure. The large domed classical building was based on the design of the Mormon Tabernacle in Salt Lake City.

Restaurants/Clubs: Red | Hotels: Purple | Shops: Orange | Outdoors/Parks: Green | Sights/Culture: Blue

TINSELTOWN—TAKE ONE

Early moviemakers shot their scenes primarily in the streets of LA, making everyday life a part of the action. The Keystone Kops comedies, Harold Lloyd's *Safety Last* (1923), and Laurel and Hardy's *Big Business* (1929) document the city as it was then. Some of the best films featuring the City of Angels include the following:

American Wedding (2003) **Griffith Park** served as a backdrop for this *American Pie* sequel. Directed by Jesse Dylan, with Adam Herz, it centers on the wedding of Jim and Michelle.

Annie Hall (1977) Arguably Woody Allen's finest film, this stinging social comedy won Academy Awards for Best Picture, Actress (Diane Keaton), Director (Allen), and Screenplay (Allen and Marshall Brickman). In one scene, Alvy Singer (Allen) sits with Annie (Keaton) in the restaurant **The Source** and delivers the line that LA's greatest cultural contribution was its law allowing a right turn at a red traffic light.

The Big Lebowski (1998) Joel and Ethan Coen's darkly hilarious tale about an LA slacker (potently brought to life by Jeff Bridges) caught in a web of kidnap and murder features some nifty skewering of LA stereo-types, all in the name of entertainment. The Busby Berkeley–esque musical sequence is a highlight.

Blade Runner (1982) Ridley Scott's fantasy of LA in the year 2019 as a megalopolis of 90 million people makes inspired use of the **Bradbury Building** and Frank Lloyd Wright's **Ennis-Brown House.**

Boogie Nights (1997) This loving ode to the late-'70s porn industry that grew out of California makes the best use of LA's sprawling suburbs to tell the story of the rise and fall of Dirk Diggler (Mark Wahlberg) and his eclectic family of porn stars. Funny and heart-breaking.

Colors (1988) A violence-choked **East LA** is the setting for this police drama starring Robert Duvall and Sean Penn, but much of it was filmed in **Venice,** where director Dennis Hopper lives.

Day of the Locust (1975) Directed by John Schlesinger, the film takes a devastating look at moviemaking in the 1930s—the ultimate Hollywood horror story. It is in front of **Mann's Chinese Theatre** that Donald Sutherland incites the riot.

The Doors (1991) The Oliver Stone film biography stars Val Kilmer as legendary rock star Jim Morrison, following the UCLA film student/poet/musician from **Venice Beach** to **Sunset Boulevard** and the **Château Marmont.**

E.T. The Extra Terrestrial (1982) TV-perfect suburbia, as exemplified by the **San Fernando Valley,** is the setting for this Steven Spielberg movie, as well as many of his other films.

Falling Down (1993) Joel Schumacher's best film to date features a searing performance from Michael Douglas as "D-Fens," a man caught in LA's traffic hell who decides that he's had enough and sets out on a one-man vigilante rampage against all that's wrong with American society. Robert Duvall is especially affecting as the retiring cop who's chasing him down.

Grand Canyon (1991) Chance encounters change lives from **Brentwood** to **Inglewood** in Lawrence Kasdan's redemption film starring Danny Glover and Kevin Kline.

Lethal Weapon (1987) In this action flick and its three sequels, Mel Gibson and Danny Glover pull pranks and catch bad guys all over LA.

Magnolia (1999) P.T. Anderson's ambitious story about fathers and their children features frogs raining

---

♦ M-F. Services: Su, 10:45AM, 6PM; W, 7:30PM. 1100 Glendale Blvd (between Park Ave and Sunset Blvd). 213/484.1100

52 ECHO PARK

During the 1870s, **Echo Park Lake** provided water for nearby farms. In 1891, the land was donated to the city for use as a public park. Joseph Henry Tomlinson designed the layout utilizing the plan of a garden in Derbyshire, England. This 26-acre park is attractively landscaped with semitropical plants and a handsome lotus pond. The lake has paddle boats available for hourly rental. Special events include an annual celebration by the local Samoan community. ♦ Daily, until 10:30PM. Bounded by Echo Park Ave and Glendale Blvd, and Bellevue and Park Aves

53 ANGELINO HEIGHTS

This was LA's first commuter suburb, begun in the land boom of 1886 to 1887, when it was linked by cable car along Temple Street to the stores and offices downtown, just over a mile away. The hilltop site offered views and a cool refuge from the noise and dust of Spring Street. Professionals moved into Queen Anne and Eastlake houses, but the boom soon fizzled. The 1300 block of Carroll Avenue is a time capsule of the period, lovingly restored by its residents, who organize an annual house tour in May to raise money for improvements, including the installation of period streetlamps. It's a favorite location for film and television crews, but has kept an authentic neighborhood atmosphere, especially on the adjoining streets, where Craftsman bungalows are interspersed with own all over the city of angels, and some very brilliant performances from Tom Cruise, Julianne Moore, Melora Walters, and the rest of a stellar cast.

Meet the Fockers (2004) Ben Stiller, Robert De Niro, Barbra Streisand, and Dustin Hoffman are outrageous in this uproarious comedic sequel to *Meet the Parents*. Greg Focker (Stiller) invites the Byrnes, his future in-laws, to meet his parents (Hoffman, a latter-day hippie, and Streisand, a frank sex therapist). The hospital scene was shot at **St. Luke's Hospital** in **Pasadena**. Directed by Jay Roach.

Million Dollar Baby (2004) Clint Eastwood's Academy Award winner about a determined pugilist (Hilary Swank) boxing her way into a male-dominated world. Eastwood plays Swank's trainer.

Mulholland Drive (2001) The latest mind-warp from David Lynch is an endlessly fascinating homage to himself. Mixing the naïve sleuths of *Blue Velvet*, the bizarre denizens of *Twin Peaks*, the reality/fantasy witcheroo of *Lost Highway*, and none of *Dune*, this is Lynch's most provocative film in a long time.

The Player (1992) Robert Altman's insider view of today's movie business stars Tim Robbins as a studio dealmaker who kills a screenwriter. More than a dozen stars make cameo appearances in this ironic, funny, and accurate portrait of the industry.

Pretty Woman (1990) Julia Roberts got her big break in this chic flick playing a woman for hire. Most of the interior scenes were staged at the **Wilshire Beverly Regent** hotel in Beverly Hills, where Roberts's character shacked up with Richard Gere.

Ruthless People (1986) Designer Lilly Kilvert exploits the surreal juxtapositions of LA architecture to comic

effect in this viciously clever satire, starring Bette Midler and Danny DeVito.

Short Cuts (1993) A stark portrayal of virtually every layer of LA society, from the well-to-do to the poor, this intricate three-hour film by Robert Altman is based on a collection of Raymond Carver short stories. The large, all-star cast includes Jennifer Jason-Leigh, Tim Robbins, Madeleine Stowe, Jack Lemmon, Tom Waits, and Lily Tomlin.

Speed (1994) The ultimate proof that LA does indeed have public transportation—though you may not want to take it after watching this action thriller about a bomb-laden bus. Keanu Reeves plays the cop who has to defuse the situation, and Sandra Bullock got rave reviews as a plucky passenger. (A piece of future LA trivia: This is the first Hollywood movie to use the city's new subway system as a setting.)

The Sting (1973) Robert Redford tracks down a scruffy Paul Newman at the carousel on **Santa Monica Pier** in this classic romp about a pair of con men. Directed by George Roy Hill, it won seven Academy Awards, including Best Picture.

Swordfish (2001) Director Dominic Sena's sequel to *Gone in 60 Seconds* stars John Travolta as charismatic spy Gabriel Shear, who plots to rob billions of dollars in illegal government funds abetted by computer hacker Stanley Jobson (Hugh Jackman). Many scenes were shot at the artists' lofts/warehouse area in downtown Los Angeles.

10 (1979) At the end of this slight but trend-setting Blake Edwards picture, Dudley Moore watches as Bo Derek, the woman he has been chasing throughout the film, gets married to another man in **All Saints Episcopal Church** in Beverly Hills.

Victorians. For tour information and other events, call the **Carroll Avenue Restoration Foundation** at 213/626.9968. The houses are private residences. ♦ Carroll Ave (between Edgeware Rd E and Edgeware Rd W)

54 DODGER STADIUM

The Dodgers baseball team fled Brooklyn for the sunny skies of LA in 1958, but it wasn't until 1962 that the stadium designed by **Emil Prager** was completed. A $20 million renovation in 2005 saw the addition of 1,600 seats and improved dining facilities at the ballpark. The home of the "blue-and-white" is located at the heart of Chavez Ravine, and is surrounded by one of the world's largest parking lots. All levels of the stadium are well

supplied with food stands selling the famous Dodger Dogs; you might ask for the unadvertised spicy dog—a Polish sausage on an onion roll. And this is one of the only fields in America that sells sushi. It may not be the only ballpark serving martinis, but it's new to us. Yep, there's even a **Martini Bar** near the Dugout Club where you can sip baseball-themed mixtures such as the Brooklyn Dodger (apple martini), a Squeeze Play (Skyy Vodka with DeKuyper blue curaçao), or a Fernandomania, a commemorative drink to the famous southpaw (tequila with Grand Marnier). The ticket office is in the parking lot. ♦ Ticket office: M-Sa. 1000 Elysian Park Ave (at Stadium Way). 323/224.1400, 877/LAD-EVENTS. www.dodgers.com

Restaurants/Clubs: Red | Hotels: Purple | Shops: Orange | Outdoors/Parks: Green | Sights/Culture: Blue

BURBANK/GLENDALE

Beautiful downtown Burbank and environs . . .

Although the small, stubbornly independent Los Angeles County cities of Burbank and Glendale began life at the turn of the century as quiet, middle-class bedroom communities for settlers from the Midwest, today they have little in common. Glendale retains the aura of an unobtrusive, rather ordinary hometown, while Burbank is a thriving center for the entertainment industry, making it difficult to remember that the cities share a common location and a similar history. Both

are located at the eastern end of the **San Fernando Valley,** where the **Verdugo Mountains** to the north and the terminus of the **Santa Monica Mountains** at Griffith Park funnel into the Los Angeles Basin and the **San Gabriel Valley.** Each was originally part of **Mission San Fernando,** deeded in 1794 to José Maria Verdugo, the captain of the guards at the San Gabriel Mission. The 433-square-mile **Rancho San Rafael** remained in the Verdugo family until a financial crisis forced foreclosure in 1869. By 1883, 13 Americans had arrived and were farming a site they named Glendale (after the title of a painting one of them had seen), and in 1887 five speculators filed plans for the town. Within the year, real estate promoters founded another small town on the nearby site of the **Rancho La Providencia,** its name borrowed from physician/sheep rancher **Dr. David Burbank,** the former owner.

The two cities grew slowly until 1904, when the extension of the Pacific Electric Railway brought hundreds of new citizens. In 1906, Glendale became incorporated, and Burbank followed in 1911. **Tropico,** a competing city (and the site of photographer Edward Weston's first studio), sprang up south of Glendale that same year, its main economic activity being strawberry farming. Glendale annexed Tropico in 1918.

Many of Glendale's houses date from the 1920s, when it flourished as a suburban haven; more expensive subdivisions were later constructed on the steep mountain hillsides. Glendale retains a Main Street USA image on some of its older downtown streets. Minutes from downtown Los Angeles, its southern portion is predominantly commercial, while the northern side has its original residential grid filled with modest stucco houses.

Burbank too has a good number of simple houses attesting to its residential past (although it also has pricey enclaves like **Toluca Lake,** where Bob Hope had an opulent estate). But even though it's smaller than Glendale, it has a higher profile nationally for two reasons: aircraft construction and the motion picture and television industry. In 1914, Carl Laemmle was the first of the movie moguls to head "over the hill" from Hollywood when he turned a 230-acre

181

chicken ranch adjacent to Burbank into his **Universal City** production facility. The Burbank studio that has been the home of **Warner Bros.** for decades opened in 1918, and **Walt Disney Studios** came in 1940. Meanwhile, Allan Loughead (he later changed the spelling to Lockheed) opened an aircraft manufacturing facility in 1928, an event that eventually spawned a huge aerospace and electronics industry employing tens of thousands. Lockheed's airport eventually became the **Burbank-Glendale-Pasadena Airport,** until it was renamed **Bob Hope Airport** in 2006.

Burbank remained relatively quiet until the mid-1980s, when a construction boom created the **Media District,** a cluster of studios and industry offices in the area surrounding Warner Bros. A three-story height building restriction eventually gave way to the erection of skyscrapers. One of the major reasons for all the flurry of business activity is that Burbank imposes no gross receipts tax, as Los Angeles does.

With the explosion of growth in Burbank's entertainment industry, it hardly seemed to matter when the Lockheed Corporation, formerly the town's largest single employer, left town in 1990. Burbank bounced back almost immediately, and now Lockheed's huge property next to the airport has been turned into more production space for the area's studios. Today, Burbank's fame and fortune rests almost totally in the hands of its major film and television studios—Walt Disney, Warner Bros., Universal, **NBC,** and **SKG Dreamworks'** animation facility. However Burbank received a big blow in October 2007 when NBC announced plans to relocate its massive studios to nearby Universal City, devastating news for a city whose economy depends largely on the industry. With the exception of the Disney lot which is closed to visitors, guided studio tours are available to show "civilians" how all that incredibly lucrative fantasy is created.

1 THEODORE PAYNE FOUNDATION

The preservation and propagation of native California flora are the goals of this organization, which is named for the pioneer California botanist. There's a well-kept nature trail up the hillside and a nursery where seeds and plants are sold at reasonable prices. The book room offers informative literature. ♦ Free. W-Sa. 10459 Tuxford St (between Ledge and Wheatland Aves). 818/768.1802

2 MCGROARTY CULTURAL ARTS CENTER

This historic house is the former home of John Steven McGroarty, a congressman, poet, and historian. It's now operated by the City of Los Angeles as a showcase for mementos and a community arts center. ♦ Free. M-Sa. 7570 McGroarty Terr (at south end of Plainview Ave). 818/352.5285

3 MONTROSE BOWL

If you like tenpins and want to play where the rich and famous bowl, check out this charming, old-fashioned alley, which opened in 1936. Celebrities often rent the establishment for private parties; some of those who have include Tony Danza, Roseanne, Janet Jackson, and David Cassidy—check out their photos on the wall. ♦ 2334 Honolulu Ave (between Ocean View Blvd and Wickham Way). 818/249.3895

4 DESCANSO GARDENS

These 165-acre gardens are famous for their collection of camellias, with more than 600 varieties. The landscaping also includes azaleas, roses, and bulb flowers, all located in a mature California live-oak grove. The variety of plants ensures that there is almost always something blooming. (The camellias bloom from late December through early March.) Tea and cookies are served daily from 11AM to 4PM in a teahouse nestled in a Japanese-style garden featuring a stream that forms waterfalls and pools. If you're in town during the Christmas season, check out the special holiday garden and displays. ♦ Nominal admission. Daily. Tram tours on the hour: Tu-F, 1-3PM; Sa, Su, 11AM-3PM. 1418 Descanso Dr (between Encinas Dr and Verdugo Blvd), La Cañada-Flintridge. 818/952.4400. www.descanso.com

5 MIN'S KITCHEN

★★★$$ This casual Thai restaurant offers a good selection of authentically spicy fare, including seafood talay. The service is friendly, too. ♦ Thai ♦ Tu-Su, lunch and dinner. 1040 Foothill Blvd (at Chevy Chase Dr), La Cañada-Flintridge. 818/790.6074

6 JET PROPULSION LABORATORY (JPL)

More than 50 years ago, a group of **Cal Tech** graduates performed what one described as rather odd experiments in rocketry. Today, the laboratory covers 175 acres of the San Gabriel foothills and has 200 buildings. From the 1958 *Explorer 1,* America's first satellite, to the *Voyager* missions that blazed a trail to the edge of the solar system, it has brought the sights and sounds of space to scientists and into living rooms all over the world. Two-hour guided tours, offered on weekdays, include a multimedia presentation about the facility and a visit to the **Space Craft Museum.** ♦ Fee for tours. Call ahead for tour schedule. 4800 Oak Grove Dr (north of Foothill Blvd), La Cañada-Flintridge. 818/354.2180

7 BOB HOPE AIRPORT

Burbank Airport commissioners renamed Burbank-Glendale-Pasadena Airport "Bob Hope Airport" in 2006, marking the fifth time the name has been changed during the airport's then 73-year history. Hope, a longtime resident of Toluca Lake, died 27 July 2003, at the age of 100. Apparently he was somewhat envious when Orange County Airport was renamed "John Wayne Airport," and once remarked that it would be nice to have a facility named after him. The powers that be felt it would be a fitting tribute to the entertainer. The airport code remains "BUR," but the signage features Hope's name and likeness.

Six airlines serve a variety of domestic destinations, making this a convenient alternative to LAX for those living on the north side of LA. The airport is located between the Hollywood, Ventura, and Golden State Freeways. Adjoining the terminal are expensive short- and long-term parking lots, which can be entered from Empire Avenue. A free shuttle runs to a 24-hour economy lot located north of the airport on Hollywood Way. Ground transportation to and from the airport is available through **SuperShuttle** (818/556.6600). ♦ 2627 Hollywood Way (between Empire Ave and N San Fernando Blvd). 818/840.8847

8 BURBANK TOWN CENTER

You can shop 'til you drop or max out your plastic at more than 100 shops such as **Sears, Old Navy, Ikea** (located just outside the mall) **Idea, Mervyns,** and **Macy's.** There are also movie theaters and restaurants. The promenades between the stores make for interesting strolling. ♦ 201 E Magnolia Blvd (between N First and N Third Sts). 818/566.8617. www.burbanktowncenter.com &

9 BURBANK CITY HALL

This 1941 WPA Moderne classic is distinguished by its tall fretted screen, fountain, and jazzy lobby. ♦ E Olive Ave and N Third St

9 CHADAKA THAI

★★★$$ A welcome addition to Burbank's culinary scene, this chic and happening Thai eatery dishes out freshly prepared, spicy fare in a smart yet casual setting. If you like Thai food, you'll love it here. Big vases of ginger and tropical flowers brighten the attractive dining area as Buddha hovers over the dimly lighted bar, where Asian-inspired drinks are poured. Preparations include salads made with green papaya or pear and shrimp with toasted cashews, curries, noodles, seafood, fabulous fish and chicken dishes, and outstanding satays and pad Thai ♦ Thai ♦ Daily, lunch and dinner. Reservations suggested for dinner. 310 N San Fernando Blvd (between E Olive Ave and Magnolia Blvd). 818/848.8520. www.chadaka.com

10 BOULDER BUNGALOWS

These 1929 private bungalows are a good example of the use of boulders, which were popular building materials in the foothills in the 1920s. ♦ E Olive Ave and Ninth St

11 BRAND LIBRARY

Housed in an exotic "El Miradero" (meaning "view from a high place"), built in 1904 for Leslie C. Brand and inspired by the East Indian Pavilion at the 1893 Chicago World's Fair, this is a delightful place to do research or some quiet reading. Brand donated the white-domed Saracenic-style house and grounds to the city of Glendale with the stipulation that it be used as a public library and park. It is currently the art and music branch of the **Glendale Public Library,** housing a gallery for contemporary Southern California art, a lecture and concert auditorium, and an arts-and-crafts studio. The extensive, beautifully landscaped grounds are lovely for picnicking. The Queen Anne-style **Doctor's House,** furnished with period antiques, has been moved onto the grounds and restored. Tours of

Restaurants/Clubs: Red | **Hotels: Purple** | **Shops: Orange** | **Outdoors/Parks: Green** | **Sights/Culture: Blue**

183

the Doctor's House can be arranged. ♦ Free. Tu-Th, 1-6PM; F, Sa, 1-5PM. 1601 W Mountain St (at Grandview Ave). 818/548.2051

12 CATALINA VERDUGO ADOBE

Part of the original **Rancho San Rafael,** this single-story adobe was built in 1875 for José Maria Verdugo's blind daughter, Doña Catalina. It is now a private residence. ♦ 2211 Bonita Dr (off Opechee Way)

13 AUTOBOOKS-AEROBOOKS

Plane and car aficionados will love this shop specializing in automobiles, airplanes, and relevant merchandise. More than five decades old, the retail outlet fosters a dedicated clientele of luminaries such as Jay Leno, who has his own reserved parking spot in front; Nicolas Cage; and Tim Allen, to name a few. Drop by on Saturday mornings for what owner Chet Knox calls a "Cruise-In" where writers, automobile clubs, and car lovers congregate over coffee and pastries and enjoy a miniature car show highlighting hot rods, convertibles, and vintage wheels. ♦ Tu-Sa. 3524 W Magnolia Blvd (between N Hollywood Way and Buena Vista St). 818/845.0707. www.autobooks-aerobooks.com

14 CASA ADOBE DE SAN RAFAEL

Thomas A. Sanchez, onetime sheriff of Los Angeles County, lived on Rancho San Rafael. Huge eucalyptus trees planted by Phineas Banning, founder of the Los Angeles Harbor, surround this one-story hacienda. The historic house was restored in 1932 by the city of Glendale. ♦ Free. W, Su, 1-4PM. 1330 Dorothy Dr (between W Stocker and Spencer Sts). No phone

15 FIRST CHURCH OF CHRIST, SCIENTIST

Moore, Ruble, and Yudell designed this beautifully lit church in the Arts and Crafts tradition in 1989. ♦ 1320 N Brand Blvd (between E Randolph and E Mountain Sts)

16 DERBY HOUSE

This 1926 house by **Lloyd Wright** (Frank's son) is a superb example of the architect's precast concrete-block houses, patterned after pre-Columbian designs. Also in the neighborhood are Lloyd Wright's **Calori House** (3021 E Chevy Chase Dr), a free interpretation of the Spanish Colonial Revival style, and his **Lewis House** (2948 Graceland Way, south of Golf Club Dr). All three are private residences. ♦ 2535 E Chevy Chase Dr (between St. Andrews and Kennington Drs)

17 SAFARI INN/ANABELLE

$ These surprisingly inexpensive side-by-side small hotels provide lots of comfort and extras in any of their combined 102 oversized rooms (47 at Anabelle, 55 at Safari), all with safes, voice mail, free local calls, iron and board, robes, and mini refrigerator. There's even free shuttle service to the local airport; a great bistro and lounge for breakfast, lunch, dinner, and/or drinks; a fitness room; a swimming pool; and a sun deck—and you can't beat the location: just a stone's throw from Burbank, Disney, NBC Studios, and Warner Bros. studios, seven miles from Universal Studios, and 10 miles from Hollywood. ♦ 1911 W Olive Ave (between N Parish Pl and N Lamer St). 818/845.8586, 800/782.4373, 800/426.0670; fax 818/845.0054. www.westcoasthotels.com/anabelle

18 FRENCH 75 BURBANK

★★$$ Ooh la la, this place brings us back to a bistro in the Left Bank with its deep leather booths, tin ceilings, and ornate period lighting and artwork and Bohemian décor. Grab a seat at the Rouge Bar, order a martini or Champagne cocktail, and seize the mood. Then sit down and enjoy signature offerings like French onion soup, braised short ribs, beef stroganoff, Burgundy escargots, prime flatiron steak, or a filet mignon served with a choice of sauces (Chimichurri, Cabernet, or Roquefort). Finish with a hot chocolate soufflé for *deux.* ♦ French Bistro ♦ M-F, lunch and dinner; Sa, Su, dinner. Reservations required. 3400 W Olive Ave (between Ventura Fwy and Buena Vista St). 818/955.5100. www.french75burbank.com

19 ARNIE MORTON'S THE STEAK HOUSE

★★★$$$$ This Valley version of the Chicago-based nationwide chain dishes otherworldly cuts of beef that almost melt in your mouth in a clubby-looking setting of mahogany paneling, leather banquettes, and walls festooned with celebrity photos and LeRoy Neiman serigraphs. The cooked-to-order double filet mignon or 24-to-48-ounce porterhouse will satisfy any carnivore and perhaps Fido, too (doggie bags are prevalent here). Should you be dining with non-beef lovers, they too can find contentment in the lemon oregano chicken, broiled Block Island swordfish, or Sicilian veal chop. Be sure to order a soufflé for two (chocolate, Grand Marnier, or lemon). The Key lime pie is also good, and the fresh raspberries or strawberries are a lighter choice if you ask them to omit the Sabayon sauce. ♦ Steak House ♦ M-F, lunch and dinner; Sa, Su, dinner. Reservations advised. 3400 W Olive Ave (between Riverside Dr and Alameda Ave), Burbank. 818/238.0424. Also at 435 S La Cienega Blvd (at Colgate

The Best

Steve Harvey

"Only in LA" columnist for the *Los Angeles Times*

Some of my favorite things in Southern California:

Plunking a quarter into the tabletop jukeboxes for two tunes at **Johnnie's Pastrami** in Culver City.

Seeing the grin on my then eight-year-old son Jamie's face when **Dodger Stadium** vendor Richard Aller unleashed his trademark cry, "Nuts!"

Dining upstairs at **Philippe's** near Chinatown and wondering if any of the patrons around me know that the many doorways indicate it was probably a brothel a century or so ago.

Playing the eighteenth hole on the **Rancho Park Golf Course** and knowing I'll probably fare better than Arnold Palmer did at the 1961 Los Angeles Open. Probably. (Palmer shot a 12 on that hole.)

Gazing at the statuary at **USC,** including the sculpture of a student in a football uniform gazing at a football atop Bridge Hall, the gargoyle who appears to be giving a one-fingered salute outside Mudd Hall, and the cement monkey thumbing his nose at former chancellor Rufus B. Von "KleinSmid" on the **Student Union Building**—reportedly an architect's sly revenge against the interfering Von KleinSmid.

Showing visitors the photo display of scary-looking characters inside the **Original Pantry Cafe** on Figueroa Street—ex-waiters whose grim visages reinforce the urban myth that the eatery used to hire ex-cons to wait tables.

Spelunking inside the dark caverns of **Acres of Books** in Long Beach, an ancient warehouse with 6.5 miles of shelves on which are balanced 750,000 second-hand tomes, give or take a few Micheners. I never forget my flashlight.

Checking out LA's oldest homicide victim—a reconstructed skeleton of a 9,000-year-old female called **La Brea Woman** at the Page Museum on Wilshire Boulevard. Scientists believe she died from a blow to the head. The crime is unsolved.

Ave), Midtown. 310/246.1501. www.mortons.com

20 NBC Television Studios

Famous as the home of *The Tonight Show*, where Jay Leno rules as king of the late-night talk shows, this is the largest color facility in the US. At least for right now. In October 2007, NBC announced it will be moving the entire complex two miles away to Universal City, leaving some 34 acres of prime real estate up for grabs. While the new studios aren't slated to open until 2011, plans are to relocate the *The Tonight Show* sooner, but no date was set at press time. Tickets to attend tapings of NBC shows are available, some on a standby basis. Out-of-state visitors should write to: Tickets, NBC Television, 3000 W Alameda Ave, Burbank, CA 91523. No tickets will be sent out of state, but a letter of priority will be returned, which gives you priority at the Burbank ticket line. Because of frequent changes in availability, it is recommended that anyone wishing to attend a taping call the studio for current information. Don't miss the 70-minute tour through a number of soundstages, *The Tonight Show* studio, the prop warehouse, and the wardrobe department. ◆ Admission; show tickets free. Taping times vary. Tour: M-F. 3000 W Alameda Ave (between Bob Hope Dr and W Olive Ave). General information 818/840.3538, recorded information 818/840.3537

21 Circle 'K' Stables

🏇 This equestrian center appeals to couples and families who go to spend the day horseback riding through the picturesque trails of **Griffith Park.** Group rides can be arranged in advance. ◆ Daily. 914 S Mariposa St (south of Riverside Dr). 818/843.9890

22 Bar 'S' Stables

🏇 Another equestrian's delight, this one offers more than 45 horses to mount. It's popular with adults, and children over the age of seven can ride any of the more than 45 horses. Group rides with guides are available. Riding lessons are offered by appointment only. ◆ Daily. 1850 Riverside Dr (between Western Ave and Main St). 818/242.8443

23 Gennaro's

★$$$ Discreet décor, honest food (including clam soup, Caesar salad, and osso buco), and a solid wine list are the elements at work here. ◆ Italian ◆ M-F, lunch and dinner; Sa, dinner. Reservations recommended. 1109 N Brand Blvd (between W Dryden and W Stocker Sts). 818/243.6231. www.gennarosristorante.com &

Restaurants/Clubs: Red | Hotels: Purple | Shops: Orange | Outdoors/Parks: Green | Sights/Culture: Blue

24 HILTON GLENDALE HOTEL

$$$ Situated at the eastern door to the San Fernando Valley, this 19-story, 351-room glass-sheathed luxury hotel perfectly matches Glendale's contemporary skyline and affords panoramic views of the San Gabriel Mountains and downtown Los Angeles. Within is **Porter's Steakhouse,** a gourmet restaurant offering a wide selection of continental cuisine, plus three bar/lounges, a three-meal-a-day restaurant, a pool and Jacuzzi, and a health club. There are convention facilities, too. ◆ 100 W Glenoaks Blvd (at N Brand Blvd). 818/956.5466, 800-HILTONS; fax 818/956.5490. www.hilton.com

25 BOB'S BIG BOY

$ This is the nation's oldest in the acclaimed coffee shop chain, built in 1949 by owner Bob Wian and architect **Wayne McAllister.** Through preservation efforts, it is the only one of the original six not yet demolished. ◆ Coffee Shop ◆ Daily, 24 hours. 4211 Riverside Dr (at W Alameda Ave). 818/843.9334

26 FALCON THEATRE

Noted producer/director Garry Marshall founded this 130-seat theater in order to "bridge the gap between Hollywood and legitimate theater." Workshops, children's summer acting classes, and assorted performances are offered throughout the year. There's plenty of parking, comfortable seats (bought from a synagogue), and cake by the slice at the concession stand. It's open whenever there's a show, so call ahead. ◆ 4252 Riverside Dr (at N Rose St). 818/955.8004. www.falcontheatre.com

27 SMOKE HOUSE

★$$ This long-established steak house (circa 1946) takes care of the thing that really matters: meat. They age their own and grill it over hickory. ◆ Steak House ◆ Daily, lunch and dinner. Reservations recommended. 4420 Lakeside Dr (at W Olive Ave). 818/845.3731

28 WARNER BROS. STUDIOS

Movie buffs will enjoy this unique museum, offering more than 75 years of cinema memorabilia, including a massive wardrobe section. Visitors can take guided tours through the studios, observing live productions and rehearsals. It's a good idea to wear comfortable walking shoes. In contrast to the **Universal Studios** tours (see page 187), these are an introduction to the actual behind-the-scenes technical workings of the motion picture crafts. A limited amount of photography is permitted, and keep a sharp eye out—you never know whom you're going to run into. ◆ Admission. Tours: M-F, 9AM-3PM. Reservations required. 4000 Warner Blvd (corner of Olive Ave and Hollywood Way). 818/954.1744. www.warnerbros.com

29 THE EXCHANGE

A unique collection of upscale shops and boutiques, plus fine restaurants and movie theaters. ◆ Bounded by N Louise St and N Brand Blvd, and E Broadway and E Wilson Ave

29 FAR NIENTE

★$$ The rich menu draws crowds, though the cooking is uneven. Penne Far Niente or the veal chops are winners, though; and the chocolate soufflé is a good bet and should take care of your calorie intake for the week. ◆ Italian ◆ M-F, lunch and dinner; Sa, Su, dinner. Reservations recommended. 204½ N Brand Blvd (between E Wilson and E California Aves). 818/242.3835. www.farniente.com &

29 THE ALEX THEATRE

The fluted pylon of this dramatic 1939 Streamline Moderne movie house once dominated the cityscape along Glendale's Brand Boulevard. After becoming a victim of the rise of multiplex movie theaters nearby, the theater closed down for a time. Now completely restored, it's the perfect setting for shows, performances, concerts, and movies. ◆ 216 N Brand Blvd (between E Wilson and E California Aves). 818/243.2539. www.alextheatre.com

30 GLENDALE GALLERIA

This complex of more than 150 shops, boutiques, and restaurants is anchored by **Macy's, Nordstrom,** and **JC Penney.** There's ample parking. ◆ Daily; M-F until 9PM. S Central Ave (between W Colorado St and W Broadway). 818/240.9481. www.glendalegalleria.com

31 SCARANTINOS

★$ Home-cooked minestrone, chicken rollatini, baked zucchini, and spaghetti Napoletana are the top orders here. Bring your best appetite—the portions are generous. ◆ Italian ◆ M-F, lunch; Sa, Su, dinner. 1524 E Colorado St (between Lincoln Ave and Lafayette St), 818/247.9777. www.scarantinos.com, www.scarantinospasadena.com.

32 FOREST LAWN

◉ Founder Hubert Eaton envisioned "the greenest, most enchanting park you ever saw in your life . . . vistas of sparkling lawns, with shaded arborways and garden retreats and beautiful, noble statuary." The cemetery contains reproductions of **The Church of the Recessional,** modeled after a 10th-century English church; **Wee Kirk o' the Heather,** a copy of a 14th-century church in Glencairn, Scotland; and the **English church** in Thomas Gray's poem "Elegy in a Country Church-yard." All three may be visited when they're not being used for services.

The **Memorial Court of Honor** in the **Great Mausoleum** contains a stained-glass interpretation of Leonardo da Vinci's *The Last Supper.* The world's largest religious painting (measuring 195 feet by 45 feet), *The Crucifixion* by Jan Stykam, is displayed every hour on the hour in the **Hall of Crucifixion-Resurrection.** A companion behemoth, *The Resurrection* by Robert Clark, is revealed every hour on the half hour in the same hall. The **Court of Freedom** displays objects from American history as well as a 20-by-30-foot mosaic copy of *The Signing of the Declaration of Independence.* Additional attractions include the collection of originals of every coin mentioned in the Bible; the **Court of David,** containing a reproduction of Michelangelo's famous sculpture; and the chance to pay your respects to the earthly remains of Hollywood luminaries such as Clark Gable, W.C. Fields, Nat King Cole, and Jean Harlow. The exact whereabouts of graves are never disclosed by the staff. ◆ Free. Daily. 1712 S Glendale Ave (between San Fernando and Mission Rds). 818/241.4151

33 CAMPO DE CAHUENGA

The treaty ending the war between Mexico and the United States was signed here on 13 January 1847 by Lt. Col. John C. Frémont and General Andreas Pico in a historic meeting that opened the way for California's entry into the Union. The declaration was known as the Treaty of Cahuenga, after the building constructed by Thomas Feliz in 1845. The existing structure is a 1923 replica of the original, which was demolished in 1900. Unfortunately, it's no longer open to the public. ◆ 3919 Lankershim Blvd (between Ventura Blvd and Bluffside Dr)

34 SHERATON UNIVERSAL HOTEL

$$ Casual California-style living and attractive weekend packages add to the appeal of this 436-room hotel. Located smack on the backlot of Universal Studios, the hotel caters to business travelers, groups (there are lots of meeting and banquet facilities), and folks who want to be close to the theme park. Facilities

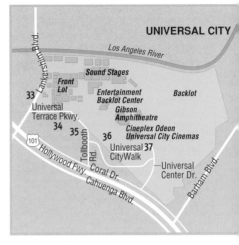

include a casual dining room (with rather mundane food), bar/lounge, outdoor pool, and health club. Rooms are typical Sheraton (save for some spiffier suites and special Club Floor accommodations), with the usual furnishings and amenities. ◆ 333 Universal Terrace Pkwy (east of Lankershim Blvd). 818/980.1212, 800/325.3535; fax 818/985.4980. www.sheraton.com

35 HILTON UNIVERSAL CITY AND TOWERS

$$ This attractive, 24-story steel-and-glass tower features 483 spacious, nicely appointed rooms that provide welcome amenities such as coffeemakers, daily newspaper delivery, three phones, iron and ironing board, fax machines, voice mail, writing desks, and safes. In addition to the lobby lounge, with a big-screen television and light menu, the pleasant restaurant serves California cuisine. Facilities include an outdoor pool with private cabanas, fitness center, and 17 meeting rooms. ◆ 555 Universal Terrace Pkwy (east of Lankershim Blvd). 818/506.2500, 800/727.7110; fax 818/509.2058. www.hilton.com &

36 UNIVERSAL STUDIOS HOLLYWOOD

Anticipating the need for a huge backlot, movie mogul Carl Laemmle moved his studio from Hollywood to the undeveloped hills of Universal City in 1915. This visionary augmented his revenues with the first studio tour: For a mere quarter, visitors could watch films being shot. The tour was discontinued when it proved distracting to moviemakers, but in 1964 a tram ride was inaugurated. It has since drawn more than 80 million visitors, making it the most popular manmade attraction in the US after Disney's two theme parks.

Compulsively humorous guides accompany the 45-minute studio tram tour around the lot, bringing you face-to-face with a 30-foot-high **King Kong** (smell the bananas on his breath!) and the giant mechanical shark from *Jaws.* You will barely survive an avalanche, a collapsing bridge, an earthquake registering 8.3 on the Richter scale (although some Angelenos feel this is in poor taste following the real 1994 quake), and the parting of the Red Sea. The tour takes you behind the scenes of the original movie sets from Steven Spielberg's *War of the Worlds* as you enter a small town devastated by the dramatic crash of a 747 jetliner. Reality meets fantasy during a stop at "**Fear Factor Live.**" Billed as "the most intense audience participatory attraction ever created for a theme park," the show allows audience members to compete with each other in assorted stunts such as blasting each other with water and air and spinning the Wheel of Fear. If you're still not afraid, you will be once you experience **Van Helsing: Fortress Dracula.** Set in 19th-century Transylvania, the spine-chilling experience mirrors the intensity and suspense of the movie as you stroll through a world possessed by souls "that plague man's deepest nightmares": Dracula, Frankenstein, and the Wolf Man. Prepare to be frightened. If you really want to be terrified, hop on the Revenge of the Mummy ride, a high-speed, death-defying indoor roller coaster ride of terror through Egyptian catacombs while filmmaker Stephen Sommer's "Mummy" movies flash on screens in a 60,000-square-foot soundstage. Visitors are invited to participate in demonstrations on the special-effects stages that reveal the astounding developments in movie magic, from the early years to today's creations by director Spielberg. Experience 10,000 degrees of excitement in **Backdraft,** based on Ron Howard's film about firefighters.

From the tram you can glimpse more than 500 outdoor sets, ranging from the **Bates Motel** from *Psycho* to *Kojak.* Artificially aged streets are redressed for every new movie and TV series: Here are the New England village; Six Points, Texas; and Old Mexico you've seen a hundred times in different guises on the screen. After the tour, wander at will into live shows, including the **Animal Planet Live!** For more thrills, there's **The Simpsons,** based on the long running TV show—a hoot-a-minute thrilling ride through Springfield with Bart, Lisa, and Maggie; **Shrek 4-D,** starring voice-overs by Mike Myers, Eddie Murphy, Cameron Diaz, and

John Lithgow; **Spiderman Rocks**—a musical performance portraying Marvel Comics' Peter Parker; **Revenge of the Mummy,** a high-speed, breathtaking rollercoaster ride; and **Terminator 2:3D. Jurassic Park** still thrills all ages with its realistically re-created prehistoric dinosaurs. Star look-alikes (from Charlie Chaplin and Marilyn Monroe to the Phantom of the Opera) will pose with you for photos, and special celebrations are held in the center throughout the year. A **Studio Center** facility features the futuristic **Universal Starway** people-mover plus **Lucy: A Tribute,** open-to-the-public video production stages, and the **Studio C Commissary.** Food stands and gift stores abound, and there are 50 acres of free parking.

For those who hate crowded buses, book the special **VIP Experience,** a personal tour in a comfortable private tram that whisks you hassle-free around the park. It's $199 well spent considering the perks: elegant continental breakfast, unlimited food options throughout the day, entry to normally off-limits areas, front-of-the-line privileges, reserved show seating, a commemorative photo, and lounge access. Several attractive, money-saving ticket options are also available, such as an **Annual Pass,** which gives you unlimited visits; **Hollywood CityPass,** which includes entry to Universal as well as other area attractions; **Front of Line Pass,** which affords front-of-the-line privileges, reserved show seating, and a souvenir photo; and more, so check them out before you head to the park. Memorabilia collectors should head for the new **Wardrobe Department** store where you can pick up clothing, cue cards, props, and assorted souvenirs from such popular television shows as *Will and Grace, Passions, Crossing Jordan,* and *American Dreams.* For easy access, print your ticket on the Internet by logging on to www.UniversalStudiosHollywood.com.
♦ Admission. Call ahead for hours and tours. 100 Universal City Plaza. 818/508.9600, 818/622.3036, or 800/UNIVERSAL. www.universalstudioshollywood.com

37 UNIVERSAL CITYWALK

It's Rodeo Drive, Melrose Avenue, Venice Beach, and Hollywood Boulevard all rolled into one jazzy, neon-lighted retail complex designed by **Jon Jerde** of Jerde Partnership. The bustling open-air promenade houses several dozen individual façades, each dedicated to a different architectural style of Southern California, surrounded by signature animated graphics, towering palm trees, plants, flowers, fountains, Postmodern ornaments, and brightly colored awnings, trellises, and canopies. While some urban critics initially dismissed the structure as an artificial and contrived mishmash, visitors—most of whom are locals or tourists who stroll over from **Universal Studios Hollywood**, the cinema complex, or the **Universal Amphitheatre**—not only love it, many stay until the lights go out. ♦ 100 Universal City Plaza (north of Hollywood Fwy). www.citywalkhollywood.com

Within Universal CityWalk (There are currently more than 60 venues represented; here are just a few prime examples. Please note, all restaurants are open from 11AM to 10 or 11PM daily):

Camacho's Cantina

★$ This Mexican restaurant is decorated in the charming style of LA's historic Olvera Street. The atmosphere is everything; the food is ordinary. ♦ Mexican ♦ Daily, lunch and dinner; Su, brunch and dinner. 818/622.3333 &

B. B. King's Blues Club

★★$$ This is the second link in this chain of music and supper clubs owned by the blues legend. King reportedly opened this branch because his guitar, Lucille, wanted to go to Hollywood. Patrons can enjoy tasty Southern food like fried catfish and Mississippi mud pie as they listen to the blues music played live by top artists (including, sometimes, King himself). The place keeps late hours—until 1AM during the week and 2AM on weekends. ♦ Southern ♦ M-Sa, lunch and dinner; Su, brunch and dinner. 717/622.5480 &

Tu Tu Tango

★★$$ The chimerical vibe at this bohemian-style café makes you feel like dancing. The room is adorned with wall-to-wall artwork and enlivened by paintings in progress, spontaneous song and dance performances, and visits from psychics, tarot card readers, and body painters. The delicious tapas, chicken potpie, and steak with mashed potatoes are best bets. ♦ Spanish/Eclectic ♦ Daily, lunch and dinner. 818/769.2222

Hard Rock Café Hollywood

★★$$ Okay, it's a chain, but you can still find exceptional burgers, shakes, salads, and fries at this zany spot, filled with such rock 'n' roll memorabilia as musical instruments and costumes once used by Jimi Hendrix, the Rolling Stones, the Beatles, Elvis, and Billy Idol, plus ZZ Top's pumpkin-

colored Cadillac convertible rotating from the ceiling. ♦ American. ♦ Daily, lunch and dinner. 818/622.7625

Versailles

★★$$ This is where to stop for a quick bite of delicious Cuban-style garlic-soaked chicken, fried plantains, and other ethnic specialties. The service is *muy rapido* and the food is *muy bueno*. ♦ Cuban ♦ Daily, lunch and dinner. 818/505.0093

Andrew's Panda Inn

★$ An eclectic take on traditional Chinese cuisine is dished out here. ♦ Chinese ♦ Daily, lunch and dinner. 818/487.6889

Jillian's High Life Lanes

★★$$ Play video games, do some over-the-top bowling, and enjoy electronic simulation attractions, dancing, music, sports, and media viewing along with some mighty fine food. ♦ American. ♦ Daily, lunch and dinner. 818/985.8234

Bubba Gump Shrimp

★★$$ Named for the 1994 hit movie *Forrest Gump,* this theme restaurant serves shrimp every which way and up. You can have them fajita style, with lobster, in linguini, New Orleans fashion, fried, or sautéed. If you're not into crustaceans, there are burgers and salads. Wash it all down with a killer margarita. ♦ Seafood ♦ Daily, lunch and dinner. 818/753.4867

Adjacent to Universal CityWalk:

Gibson Amphitheatre at Universal City Walk

The 6,000-seat amphitheater was renamed in 2005 under a 10-year deal with Nashville-based musical instrument maker Gibson Guitar Corp. The concert hall also received a major face-lift that included the addition of a luxury skybox suite, along with a new design that includes a guitar of illuminated instrument-shaped sculptures decorated by stars. The theater presents a full range of entertainment year-round. ♦ 818/980.9421, ticket charge line 818/622.4405

The New City Walk Cinemas

This newly remodeled movie complex houses one of Southern California's largest IMAX venues, along with a 1,400-car parking garage. ♦ 818/508.0711

Restaurants/Clubs: Red | Hotels: Purple | Shops: Orange | Outdoors/Parks: Green | Sights/Culture: Blue

PASADENA

Home of the Rose Bowl . . .
Pasadena's claim to fame rests on a single day's activities: the annual New Year's Day **Tournament of Roses Parade** and the post-parade **Rose Bowl** football game. Parade festivities have been held here yearly since 1890, when citizens first draped garlands of fresh blossoms over horse-and-buggy teams and carts in a celebration of the Southland's mild winter climate. 1 January 2008 marked the 119th Tournament of Roses Parade and the 94th Rose Bowl game. The "Battle of the Flowers" originally climaxed with a gala Roman chariot race. The races were thought to be too dangerous, however, so a substitute event—the national football college championship game known as the Rose Bowl—has been held since 1916.

Those who feel overwhelmed by the epic scale and relentlessly wholesome quality of the Roses Parade may enjoy a rival venture, the November **Doo Dah Parade**, which has fast become an institution. The Doo Dah has no floats, no queens (except, perhaps, in drag), and, best of all, no television celebrities. Its stars are the precision

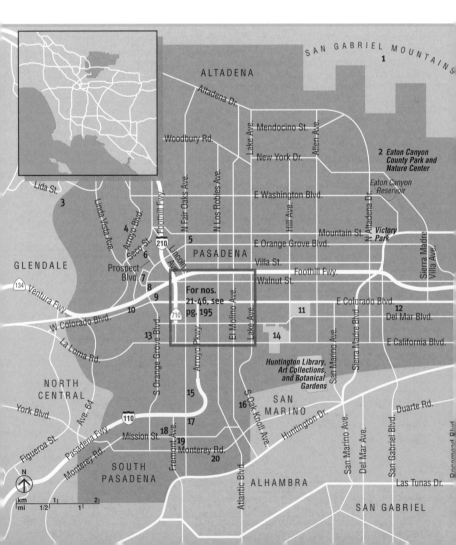

riefcase drill team and assorted zanies with lawnmowers, supermarket carts, and
odd musical instruments.

Pasadena had a false start in 1873, after Midwestern pioneers established a farming community here, giving it a name that means "Crown of the Valley" in the
Chippewa Indian language. The tiny settlement exploded during the land boom of
1886, when Pasadena had 53 active real estate agencies for a population of less than
4,500. Promoters arranged five daily trains to Los Angeles and a special Theater
Express to the downtown area three nights a week. Salespeople advertised the region's sunny, healthful climate, hotels were quickly erected, and get-rich-quick
schemes proliferated. The city incorporated in 1886, but the boom collapsed, the
population dwindled, and once-clamored-for town lots grew weeds. But soon the
clear air, citrus blooms, and mountain views (now but a memory) began to draw a
steady stream of affluent Easterners. The **Ritz-Carlton Huntington Hotel & Spa** and
the **Hotel Green** (now converted to apartments) are reminders of an era when this
was a fashionable winter resort. And the Craftsman bungalows, designed by architects Charles and Henry Greene, evidence that some travelers stayed on.

Pasadena's population increased through several small booms in the 1920s, until it
became the most important suburb of Los Angeles. LA's first freeway—the 1942 Arroyo Seco Parkway—stimulated commuter traffic. Today, Pasadena has 140,000 residents, a mixture of old money to the south and low income to the north, along with
opulent houses, lush gardens, and outstanding scientific and cultural resources.

1 SAN GABRIEL MOUNTAINS

P True wilderness is found in the San Gabriel
Mountains, which were inaccessible to
anyone but a seasoned adventurer until
1935 when the **Angeles Crest Highway**
(Route 2) opened. The highway begins in La
Cañada-Flintridge and leads to the
691,000-acre **Angeles National Forest.**
Some of the more remote sections of the
region have colorful histories. The discovery
of placer gold deposits triggered a small
gold rush as early as 1843 near the east
and west forks of the San Gabriel River.
Gold fever revived during the Depression,
when jobless Southern Californians
improvised camps and panned for
hardscrabble gold with kitchen utensils.
During the boom of the 1880s, Angelenos
made the horse trail up 5,710-foot Mount
Wilson a favorite vacation spot. Professor
T.S.C. Lowe opened the **Mount Lowe
Railroad** in 1893 to bring delighted tourists
3,000 feet up the steep incline to the mock-
Alpine hamlet near Echo Mountain's peak.
Fire destroyed the railway, but the famous
Mount Wilson Observatory (free;
626/793.3100) still stands near the peak
of the mountain. The observatory grounds
and an astronomical photo exhibition are
open Saturday and Sunday.

The San Gabriels are popular for hiking,
bicycling, fishing, bird watching, and, in
winter, a variety of snow sports. The quiet
trails are seldom crowded. There are great
contrasts in vegetation and terrain; water
makes all the difference (Crystal Lake is
one of the most spectacular sights). One
moment you may be walking in a fern dell,
the next taking in an arid chaparral
landscape. Wildflowers abound, including
poppies, Indian paintbrush, lupines, and
wild tiger lilies. Skunk cabbage grows near
springs, and pine trees flourish at altitudes
of more than 5,000 feet. Three levels of
ranges add variety to hiking pleasure. The
front slopes near **Altadena** are good for
day hikes, with well-maintained trails
leading through waterfalls and pools and
near cliffs and ravines. In places such as
Bear Canyon, the middle ranges take you
to the last reserves of mountain lions and
bighorn sheep in Southern California. At
the top of the range, many of the slopes
are stark—a rugged rock-climber's
paradise. One of the most challenging of
the higher areas is 10,064-foot Mount San

Restaurants/Clubs: Red | Hotels: Purple | Shops: Orange | Outdoors/Parks: Green | Sights/Culture: Blue

Antonio, or **Old Baldy,** the county's highest peak. Much is virgin territory, so the thrill of trailblazing is still available. Visitors are advised to stop at the **Red Box Ranger Station** for trail and road information. To phone ahead, dial 0 for the operator and ask for Red Box Ranger Station no. 2.

2 EATON CANYON COUNTY PARK AND NATURE CENTER

You can see native California plants at this 184-acre park just east of central Pasadena. The small museum contains displays of the area's ecology and gives leaflets for self-guided tours through the canyon. The **Naturalist's Room** houses live animals and natural history objects.◆ Free. Museum and park: daily. Naturalist's Room: Sa. Docent-led nature walks: Sa, 9AM. 1750 N Altadena Dr (between New York Dr and Canyon Close Rd). 626/821.3246

3 ART CENTER COLLEGE OF DESIGN

Established in 1930, the art center has an international reputation as a school of industrial design, photography, graphics, illustration, film, and fine arts. The Miesian steel-frame bridge that spans a ravine and now is an integral feature of the college was designed by Craig Ellwood and opened in 1976. The hilly 175-acre campus is an idyllic setting for artworks. Changing exhibitions of work by students and established artists and designers are held in the center's gallery. ◆ Campus and gallery: Tu, W, F-Su, noon-5PM; Th, noon-9PM. 1700 Lida St (between Pegfair La and Figueroa St). 626/396.2200. A second facility, the **Art Center College of Design South Campus,** is located in a renovated building that was the original home of America's first supersonic wind tunnel. Classes, lectures, and exhibits are ongoing there. 950 S Raymond Ave (same phone)

4 THE ROSE BOWL

Since 1902, the Midwest has met the West here in the most famous college football match of all, and **UCLA** plays its home games here. Recent highlights among the special events held here include the **1993 Super Bowl, 1994 World Cup** soccer finals, and the **1999 Women's Soccer Finals.**
◆ 1001 Rose Bowl Dr (just north of N Arroyo Blvd). 626/577.3100

Los Angeles' Wins in the Rose Bowl:

1923	USC over Penn State	14-2
1932	USC over Tulane	21-12
1933	USC over Pittsburgh	35-0

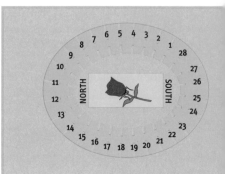

1939	USC over Duke	7-3
1940	USC over Tennessee	14-0
1944	USC over Washington	25-0
1945	USC over Tennessee	25-0
1953	USC over Wisconsin	7-0
1963	USC over Wisconsin	42-37
1966	UCLA over Michigan	14-12
1968	USC over Indiana	14-3
1970	USC over Michigan	10-3
1973	USC over Ohio State	42-17
1975	USC over Ohio State	18-17
1976	UCLA over Ohio State	23-10
1977	USC over Michigan	14-6
1979	USC over Michigan	17-10
1980	USC over Ohio State	17-16
1983	UCLA over Michigan	24-14
1984	UCLA over Illinois	45-9
1985	USC over Ohio State	20-17
1986	UCLA over Iowa	45-28
1990	USC over Michigan	17-10
1996	USC over Northwestern	41-32
2004	USC over Michigan	28-14
2007	USC over Michigan	32-18

4 KIDSPACE MUSEUM

Designed for children ages 2 to 12, the museum is housed in a spiffy $13.5 million complex designed by LA architect **Michael Maltzan.** The 18,000-square-foot facility features galleries and a theater in which the interactive exhibits are showcased. ◆ 480 N Arroyo Blvd (at Seco St, next door to the Rose Bowl). 626/449.9144. www.kidspacemuseum.org

5 JAMES IPEKJIAN

Cabinetmaker James Ipekjian designs furniture and carries handcrafted reproductions of **Greene and Greene** furniture. Call ahead for an appointment to visit the showroom. ♦768 N Fair Oaks Ave (between E Orange Grove Blvd and Painter St). 626/792.5025

6 PROSPECT BOULEVARD

The stone entrance gates at Orange Grove and Prospect Boulevards were designed by **Charles** and **Henry Greene** in the 1910s. Along this boulevard lined with camphor trees is the Greenes' 1906 **Bentz House** at No. 657. At No. 781 is **Alfred** and **Arthur Heineman**'s **Hindry House,** half hidden behind shrubbery. A narrow street entered from the southwest side of the boulevard is Prospect Crescent, which leads to **Frank Lloyd Wright**'s 1923 **Millard House** at No. 645. (The studio house near the pond was designed by Wright's son **Lloyd** in 1926.) The house is set in a ravine, and there's a better view from below on Rosemont Avenue. All are private residences. ♦ Between N Orange Grove Blvd and Seco St

7 GAMBLE HOUSE

This 1908 house designed by **Charles** and **Henry Greene** is a masterpiece of craftsmanship and planning, from the polished teak and original furnishings to the cross-ventilation that provides natural air conditioning. The architects and designers have appointed it beautifully with tables, chairs, and Tiffany glassworks. The best known of the Craftsman-style bungalows was commissioned by Cincinnati's Gamble family (of Proctor & Gamble), who, like other affluent sun-starved Easterners, wintered here at the turn of the century. The USC School of Architecture now maintains it for visiting scholars. Docents lead public tours, pointing out the Japanese-influenced deep overhanging roofs and crafted woodwork. Next door, at 2 Westmoreland Place, is the **Cole House,** also designed by the Greenes; this 1906 house is now part of the Neighborhood Church. ♦ Admission. Tours: Th-Su, noon-3PM. 4 Westmoreland Pl (just north of Arroyo Terr). 626/793.3334. www.gamblehouse.org

7 ARROYO TERRACE

West of Westmoreland Place is the loop of Arroyo Terrace, with its colony of bungalows designed by **Charles** and **Henry Greene.** All are worth noting, although some are in better condition than others. They are: **Charles Sumner Greene House** (1906) at no. 368; **White Sisters House** (1903) at no. 370, home of Charles Greene's sisters-in-law; **Van Rossen–Neill House** (1903, 1906) at no. 400, which has a wall of burnt clinker brick and Arroyo boulders; **Hawkes House** (1906)

at no. 408, which resembles a Swiss chalet; **Willet House** (1905) at no. 424, a remodeled bungalow; and, at no. 440, the **Ranney House** (1907). Also notable is the Greenes' **Duncan-Irwin House** (1900, 1906), which is close by at 240 North Grand Avenue. All are private residences. ♦ Between Westmoreland Pl and Live Oaks Ave

8 PASADENA MUSEUM OF HISTORY

Designed by **Robert Farquhar** in 1905, this neoclassical residence was formerly the home of the Finnish consul. The main floor retains its original furnishings, including antiques and paintings, while the basement houses a display of memorabilia, paintings, and photographs chronicling Pasadena's history. The adjacent library is open to researchers as well as the general public. The beautifully landscaped grounds (four acres total) encompass a wandering stream with several pools, as well as the **Sauna House,** a replica of a 16th-century Finnish farmhouse with a display of Finnish folk art. This museum is also known as the **Fenyes Mansion.** ♦ Admission. Th-Su, 1-4PM. 470 W Walnut St (at N Orange Grove Blvd). 626/577.1660

9 NORTON SIMON MUSEUM

One of America's greatest collections of European, East Indian, and Southeast Asian art is housed in this 1969 **Ladd and Kelsey** building. Norton Simon installed his holdings at these spacious galleries after the failure of the Pasadena Museum of Modern Art (a good idea later reborn as **MOCA**). Notable pieces include Old Master paintings and drawings by Rubens, Rembrandt, Raphael, Botticelli, and Zurbarán; Goya etchings; Impressionist paintings and sculpture, including works by Cézanne, Toulouse-Lautrec, Renoir, and van Gogh; a large Degas selection, including an exquisite series of small bronze dancers; and works by Picasso, Matisse, and the German Expressionists. So rich is the permanent collection that outstanding exhibitions can be generated in-house without recourse to outside loans. The museum shop has one of the finest selections of art books in the city. The museum was renovated in 2000 under the direction of noted architect **Frank Gehry,** who reconfigured the galleries and added a seven-acre sculpture garden. ♦ Admission. W, Th, noon-6PM, F, Sa-M, noon-9PM. 411 W Colorado Blvd (between N Pasadena Ave and N Orange Grove Blvd). 626/449.6840. www.nortonsimon.org

10 COLORADO STREET BRIDGE

Pasadena's 1913 *Pont du Gard* has graceful concrete arches that span the Arroyo Seco. A local and national landmark, the bridge was closed in 1987 for a $27.4 million restoration and reopened in 1994. Dubbed "Suicide Bridge" because of the number of people (approximately 100) who have jumped to their deaths 160 feet below, it features a new spiked suicide-prevention fence and replicas of the original ornamental balustrade and lampposts. ♦ W Colorado Blvd (between Arroyo Blvd and N San Rafael Ave)

11 PASADENA CITY COLLEGE

The two-year accredited college is part of the **Pasadena Area Community District.** ♦ 1570 E Colorado Blvd (between S Bonnie and S Hill Aves). 626/585.7123

12 ACAPULCO

★$ The crab enchilada is famous at this casual spot, which offers imaginative interpretations of Mexican favorites. ♦ Mexican ♦ Daily, lunch and dinner. 2936 E Colorado Blvd (at El Nido Ave). 626/795.4248

13 TOURNAMENT HOUSE AND WRIGLEY GARDENS

This Italian Renaissance–style house, once owned by chewing-gum magnate William Wrigley Jr., is surrounded by a rolling lawn and well-kept gardens. An example of the grand mansions found on the boulevard in the first decades of the century, it is now the headquarters of the Tournament of Roses Association. ♦ Garden: daily. Tours: Tu, 2PM Feb-Aug. 391 S Orange Grove Blvd (between Lockehaven and Arbor Sts). 626/449.4100

14 CALIFORNIA INSTITUTE OF TECHNOLOGY

Albert Einstein once taught at this institute, which is world-famous for physics, engineering, and astronomy. The faculty and alumni have won 26 Nobel Prizes, and the school has spawned a plethora of high-tech firms in the area. It is a far cry from Throop University, its forerunner, founded in 1891 to "foster higher appreciation of the value and dignity of intelligent manual labor." Architect **Bertram Goodhue** laid out the plan of the institute in 1930, which was inspired by a medieval scholastic cloister. Other buildings of that era were designed by **Gordon Kaufman,** notably the Spanish Renaissance **Atheneum Faculty Club** at 551 South Hill Avenue. ♦ Campus tours: M-F, 2PM Jan-June, Sept-Nov. Architectural

tours: 11AM the fourth Th of every month (reservations required). 1201 E California Blvd (between S Hill and S Wilson Aves). 626/395.6327

Within the California Institute of Technology:

BECKMAN & RAMO AUDITORIUM

This auditorium hosts lectures, concerts, films, plays, and dance performances. ♦ 332 S Michigan Ave (just south of E Del Mar Blvd). Schedule and tickets 626/395.4562

15 THE RAYMOND

★★★$$$ Carefully prepared and refreshingly homespun food is served in this charming turn-of-the-century California bungalow, once home to the Raymond Hotel caretakers. The menu changes weekly but usually includes veal, chicken, and beef entrées; steamed vegetables; and delicious, old-fashioned desserts. Colorfully landscaped patios offer quiet, bucolic dining. ♦ American ♦ Tu-Su, lunch and dinner. Reservations recommended. 1250 S Fair Oaks Ave (at Columbia St), South Pasadena. 626/441.3136

16 LANGHAM, HUNTINGTON HOTEL & SPA

$$$$ The prestigious Langham Hotel Group took over this 392-room former **Ritz Carlton Huntington Hotel & Spa** in January 2008 with plans for a $25 million renovation and a hike in already pretty pricey room rates. Details were sketchy at press time, but expect major changes in restaurants, rooms, and the spa. ♦ 1401 S Oak Knoll Ave (at Wentworth Ave). 626/568.3900; fax 626/792.6613, 800/588.9141. www.langhamhotels.com

17 BRISTOL FARMS

You'll find the freshest produce and fish, a dazzling array of wines and groceries, and exemplary service at this four-star market. ♦ Daily, until 9PM. 606 S Fair Oaks Ave (at Grevelia St), South Pasadena. 626/441.5450. Also at 837 Silver Spur Rd (between Crenshaw and Hawthorne Blvds), Rolling Hills Estates. 310/541.9157

18 BUSTER'S ICE CREAM & COFFEE STOP

★$ From blended yogurts to frosted mocha drinks, this place whips up a variety of delicious beverages to enjoy with the mellow live music that's featured five nights a week. Just off the railroad tracks, it's worth a visit, even with the occasional rattling as a locomotive rumbles by. ♦ Coffeehouse

♦ Daily; Tu-Su until 11PM. 1006 Mission St (between Fairview and Meridian Aves), South Pasadena. 626/441.0744

19 RESTAURANT SHIRO

★★★$$ Chef Hideo Yamashiro left **Cafe Jacoulet** to open this storefront restaurant, a great boon to the neighborhood. The freshness of the fish and the delicacy of the sauces have won acclaim. Standouts include seafood salad, ravioli stuffed with shrimp and salmon mousse, and sizzling catfish.
♦ French/Japanese ♦ W-F, lunch and dinner; Sa, Su, dinner. Reservations required. 1505 Mission St (at Mound Ave), South Pasadena. 626/799.4774. www.shirorestaurant.com

20 MILTIMORE HOUSE

Irving Gill designed this purified Mission Revival house in 1911. It is a private residence. ♦ 1301 Chelten Way (between Edgewood Dr and Monterey Rd), South Pasadena

21 PASADENA PUBLIC LIBRARY

The Renaissance-style building at the north end of the **Civic Center** axis was designed by **Hunt and Chambers** in 1927. ♦ Daily. 285 E Walnut St (between N Euclid and Garfield Aves). 626/744.4052

22 ARMORY CENTER FOR THE ARTS

Contemporary art shows are held at the center, which also has workshops offering kids hands-on experience of the arts.
♦ Free. Daily. 145 N Raymond Ave (between E Holly and E Walnut Sts). 626/792.5101

23 PLAZA LAS FUENTES

The $200 million, six-acre development by Maguire Thomas Partners, comprising a hotel, offices, retail, and restaurants to the east of **City Hall**, was designed by **Moore, Ruble, and Yudell** in 1989. In a break with the concrete boxes that have proliferated in recent years, the architects integrated buildings and gardens, drawing on the Beaux Arts spirit of the **Civic Center** as well as the Hispanic tradition. Pedestrian spaces are enlivened by fountains, with low buildings and plantings to soften the impact. Lawrence Halprin was the landscape architect. ♦ Bounded by N Los Robles and N Euclid Aves, and E Colorado Blvd and E Walnut St

Within Plaza Las Fuentes:

THE WESTIN PASADENA

$$$ This Four Diamond, 350-room property shines from its attractive lobby, fitted with

rich cherry-wood latticework and a limestone floor, to the contemporary public rooms and restful guest rooms. Amenities include a high-tech business center, a Westin WORKOUT·Reebok gym, and a restaurant. Accommodations feature Westin's signature Heavenly Bed, flat-screen TVs (albeit small by today's standard at 27 inches), upgraded bathrooms with Heavenly Showers (you get an invigorating spray), and a vanity area.
♦ 626/792.2727; fax 626/795.7669. www.westin.com

24 PASADENA CITY HALL

John Bakewell Jr. and **Arthur Brown Jr.** designed this bold, three-dimensional domed Italian Renaissance–style building in 1925. (The same firm designed San Francisco's City Hall.) Its distinguishing tile dome rises more than 200 feet. Listed on the National Register of Historic Places, the structure underwent a major $117 million restoration between 2004 and 2007. Equally impressive are the formal courtyard garden and fountain. ♦ 100 N Garfield Ave (between E Union and Ramona Sts). 626/744.4755. www.cityofpasadena.net

25 PASADENA MUSEUM OF CALIFORNIA ART

The newest addition to Pasadena's cultural scene was made possible by a $3 million gift from art collectors Bob and Arlene Oltman and local residents. The 30,000-square-foot, three-story museum features a dramatic entrance enhanced by fluctuating natural lighting from an overhead oculus. The second floor provides 8,000 square feet of gallery space and a bookstore. The Oltmans actually live in a 5,000-square-foot residence on the third level, while a rooftop terrace offers accessibility to the public. All exhibits are dedicated to in-state artists, architects, and designers from 1850 to the present. ♦ W-Su. Admission. 490 East Union St (at N Los Robles Ave, just east of Pacific Asia Museum). 626/568.3665

26 YUJEAN KANG'S

★$$ Dine on a variety of gourmet Chinese dishes such as tea-smoked duck in black bean sauce and catfish with kumquats and passionfruit sauce—served sparingly but elegantly, much like the setting. ♦ Chinese ♦ Daily, lunch and dinner. Reservations recommended. 67 N Raymond Ave (between E Union and E Holly Sts). 626/585.0855. Also in West Hollywood at 8826 Melrose Ave (between La Cienega and Robertson Blvds). 310/288.0806

26 XIOMARA

★★$$ Chef/owner Xiomara Ardolina bestows her culinary talents on this establishment, creating original dishes with a Cuban flair. Popular choices include ahi tuna, lamb malanga, Chilean sea bass on corn *guizo* (stew), and seared pork hash. ♦ Cuban ♦ M-F, lunch and dinner; Sa, dinner. Reservations recommended. 69 N Raymond Ave (between E Union and E Holly Sts). 626/796.2520

27 MI PIACE

★★$ This restaurant is always busy, and with good reason. The excellent and well-priced Italian fare is served in a cheerful, bright, high-ceilinged interior. ♦ Italian ♦ Daily, lunch and dinner. Reservations recommended for four or more. 25 E Colorado Blvd (between N Raymond and N Fair Oaks Aves). 626/795.3131

27 AKBAR

★★$ This funky little spot dishes out great tandoori fare to eat in or take out. Best bets

are coco lamb done in coconut sauce flavored with fennel, *bhartha* (roasted eggplant sautéed with tomatoes and peas), and tandoori-grilled Chilean sea bass marinated in herbs. And for dessert, *kesari kheer* (rice pudding infused with saffron, nuts, and raisins) and mango cheesecake are sure winners. There's a surprisingly good wine list with personal selections from chef Avinash Kapoor. ♦ Indian ♦ Daily, lunch and dinner. 44 N Fair Oaks Ave (at Union St). 626/577.9916; fax 626/577.9919. Also in Marina del Rey at 3115 Washington Blvd (one block west of Lincoln). 310/574.0666; fax 310/821.6686 &

28 PACIFIC ASIA MUSEUM

Grace Nicholson commissioned the firm of **Mayberry, Marston, and Van Pelt** in 1924 to design a traditional Northern Chinese building to house her extensive collection of Far Eastern art. The building, an imaginative amalgam of rare beauty and serenity, features changing exhibitions on the arts of the Far East and Pacific Basin. There's also a Korean Gallery with sculptures, paintings, and decorative works of art. ♦ Admission. W-Su. 46 N Los Robles Ave (between E Colorado Blvd and E Union St). 626/449.2742. www.pacificasiamuseum.org

28 WARNER BUILDING

Don't miss the sensational Art Deco frieze of seashells on this 1927 building. ♦ 481 E Colorado Blvd (between N Oakland and N Los Robles Aves)

29 THE ICE HOUSE

You just might catch tomorrow's top talent at this friendly night spot, as this is the place where Lily Tomlin, Robin Williams, and Steve Martin got their starts. Blues musicians perform live at a small club. ♦ Cover. Shows Tu-Su. Club: Th-Sa, until 2AM. 24 N Mentor Ave (between E Colorado Blvd and E Union St). 626/577.1894

30 OLD PASADENA

Who would expect to see the kind of action usually reserved for Melrose Avenue or Westwood Village in this bastion of old money? Though more tempered than their Westside counterparts, the streets of Old Pasadena bustle around small-scale vintage buildings, with several cinema complexes and interesting gift and antiques stores sharing the spotlight. Both sides of **Colorado**

Pasadena issues more than 400 film permits a year and has hosted shoots for such recent movies as *Hocus Pocus*, *Love Affair*, and *Significant Others*. Gamble House in Pasadena posed as Christopher Lloyd's *Back to the Future* digs, and *Beverly Hills Cop I* and *II*, *War of the Roses*, and *Witches of Eastwick* were all filmed in houses on the campus of the California Institute of Technology. Even the popular 1960s TV sitcom *The Beverly Hillbillies* was shot in a house on Pasadena's Oakland Avenue because 20th Century-Fox couldn't find a house in Beverly Hills that it thought looked enough like Beverly Hills.

LA boasts the longest bus in the U.S. The Metro Orange Line bus stretches 65 feet and holds 100 passengers.

Boulevard between Arroyo Parkway and Pasadena Avenue are lined with small boutiques and eateries. Along **Holly Street,** shops sell antiques and memorabilia.

30 Z GALLERIE

An affordable designer collection of gifts and home accessories is sold here, along with a wide selection of poster art. ◆ Daily, until 10PM. 42 W Colorado Blvd (between S Fair Oaks and S De Lacey Aves). 626/578.1538. Also at 230 Pine Ave (between E Maple Way and E Third St), Long Beach. 562/491.0766

31 DISTANT LANDS

Run by Adrian Kalvinskas, this traveler's bookstore offers maps, videos, and more than 8,000 book titles. ◆ Daily; F, Sa, until 9PM. 54 S Raymond Ave (between E Green St and E Colorado Blvd). 626/449.3220

32 PASEO COLORADO

This three-block-long indoor/outdoor shopping/condominium complex has everything under one urban roof, such as a **Macy's** department store, a multiscreen movie theater, a gourmet market, a health club, sidewalk cafés, and restaurants. ◆ East Colorado Blvd (between S Los Robles and S Marengo Aves). 626/795.8891. www.paseocolorado.com

33 PASADENA PLAYHOUSE

Founded in 1917, this theater flourished for more than 50 years, nurturing the careers of Gene Hackman, Kim Stanley, William Holden, and other leading actors. After closing in 1969 and staying dark for nearly 20 years, the 1925 building was elaborately restored and reopened in 1986 with Shaw's *Arms and the Man* in the proscenium-arch auditorium. There is also an Equity-waiver performance space. Both are flourishing under artistic director Sheldon Epps. Behind-the-scenes tours are led by theater alumni. ◆ 39 S El Molino Ave (at E Green St). Tickets 626/359.PLAY. www.pasadenaplayhouse.org

34 BISTRO 45

★★$$ Ensconced in a 1939 Art Deco building, this unpretentious and elegant California-style French bistro is light and airy by day and romantic by night. Food served with artistry fits the bistro mold: pan-roasted sweetbreads, roasted lamb, and a hearty cassoulet with fresh sausage, duck, rabbit, and white beans. ◆ California/French ◆ Tu-F, lunch and dinner; Sa, Su, dinner. Reservations recommended. 45 S Mentor Ave (between E Green St and E Colorado Blvd). 626/795.2478. www.bistro45.com

35 PASADENA POST OFFICE

Oscar Wenderoth designed this Italian Renaissance building in 1913. ◆ 1022 E Colorado Blvd (at S Catalina Ave)

36 AUX DELICES

Old Town residents get an early start with a variety of croissants and pastries at this French-style bakery and café. ◆ Daily, until 10PM. 16 W Colorado Blvd (between S Fair Oaks and S De Lacey Aves). 626/796.1630

36 PENNY LANE

Shop here for new, used, and cutout CDs, tapes, and LPs. ◆ Daily, until 11PM. 12 W Colorado Blvd (between S Fair Oaks and S De Lacey Aves). 626/564.0161

37 HOTEL GREEN APARTMENTS

This is one of the two remaining examples of Pasadena's grand hotel era (the other is the former **Ritz-Carlton Huntington Hotel**). Architect **Frederick Roehrig's** Moorish and Spanish Colonial design is an immense extension to the older Hotel Green structure, originally known as the Webster Hotel, built in 1890 for promoter E.C. Webster and patent medicine manufacturer Colonel G.G. Green. In the 1920s, Roehrig more than tripled the hotel's size with elaborate bridged and arched additions, including the domed and turreted **Castle Green Apartments** (built across the street in 1897), and these apartments, which have been renovated and modernized as a senior citizens' home. ◆ 50 E Green St (between S Raymond and S Fair Oaks Aves)

If LA County were a state, it would be the eighth largest in population.

LA County is home to 88 incorporated cities.

38 PASADENA CIVIC AUDITORIUM

Built in 1932, this hall is the attractive home of the **Pasadena Symphony Orchestra,** music and dance events, and Broadway musicals. Don't miss a concert that showcases the mighty 1920s Moeller, the largest theater organ west of the Mississippi. The Italian Renaissance building is the centerpiece of a convention center. It is currently undergoing a whopping $121 million renovation and expansion. ♦ 300 E Green St (between S Euclid and S Marengo Aves). 626/449.7360

39 HILTON PASADENA

$$$ This attractive 13-story, 296-room hotel features an inviting lobby with striped couches, steel blue high-back chairs, and fabric artwork hanging from the ceiling. There's a wide-open bar area with two plasma TVs, a piano, and a nouveau seating area. Amenities include a large, well-equipped gym and a restaurant. Guest rooms are attractively appointed. There's also a club lounge with a concierge. The Hilton is nicely located within walking distance of Old Pasadena, the convention center, and the business district. ♦ 168 S Los Robles Ave (between Cordova and El Dorado Sts). 626/577.1000, 800/445.8667; fax 626/584.3148. www.pasadena.hilton.com

40 CELESTINO OF PASADENA

★★★$$$ This neighborhood trattoria (formerly **Il Pastaio**), created by Celestino Drago and his three brothers, Giacomino, Calogero, and Tanino, specializes in antipasto, carpaccio, fresh and dried pasta, and risotto. Signature dishes include pumpkin lasagna, chestnut soup with sautéed duck liver, and roasted rabbit in sweet-and-sour sauce. All pastas and desserts, like the amazing hot chocolate ravioli with chocolate sorbet, are made in-house. The dining room is warmly decorated with antique pine furnishings, forest green walls, and touches of green-and-black marble. A charming patio provides alfresco dining. ♦ Italian ♦ M-F, lunch and dinner; Sa, dinner. 141 S Lake Ave (between Cordova and E Green Sts). 626/795.4006 &

41 LAKE AVENUE

One of Pasadena's main shopping streets, it has numerous specialty shops clustered around **Macy's.** Three arcades are notable: **The Commons** (quality food stores); **The Colonnade** and **Burlington Arcade** (elegant imports); and **Haskett Court** (flowers, toys, and curios from "merrie England"). The Shops on Lake Avenue, a 333,766-square-foot high-end shopping center, opened in the spring of 2003, bringing 27 more shops and restaurants to the area. ♦ Corner of Lake Ave and Del Mar Blvd. ♦ Eclectic ♦ 110 S Lake Ave (between Cordova and E Green Sts). 626/795.8950 &

41 CROCODILE CAFE

★★$ A junior version of the **Parkway Grill,** this café serves eclectic, trendy cuisine—including barbecued chicken, pizza, and spicy chicken salad—in a noisy, popular room. ♦ California ♦ Daily, lunch and dinner 140 S Lake Ave (between Cordova and E Green Sts). 626/449.9900

42 FOLK TREE

Folk art, fine art, and books, mostly from Latin America, are sold here. Don't miss the seasonal theme exhibitions. Down the street is the **Folk Tree Collection** (217 S Fair Oaks Ave; 626/795.8733), specializing in ethnic-inspired beads, clothing, and textiles and rustic crafts and furniture. ♦ Daily. 199 S Fair Oaks Ave (at Valley St). 626/793.4828

43 PARKWAY GRILL

★★$$$ This is the place to chow down on some outstanding contemporary California cuisine in the aggressively creative tradition of Spago: pizzas, oysters with corncakes, pasta, and, of course, grilled beef short ribs. The obligatory bustling open kitchen is the centerpiece of the warm and attractive high-beamed brick room. ♦ California ♦ M-F, Su, lunch and dinner; Sa, dinner. Reservations recommended. 510 S Arroyo Pkwy (between E California Blvd and E Bellevue Dr). 626/795.1001

43 ARROYO CHOP HOUSE

★★★$$$ Bob and Gregg Smith opened this swank steak house next door to their popular **Parkway Grill,** much to the delight of Pasadena carnivores. In addition to some of the finest prime steaks and marbled cuts around, they also serve a great veal chop and rotisserie chicken; choice nonmeat options include fresh fish, corn on the cob, and divine sautéed wild mushrooms. Cigar smokers can puff away on the special smoking patio. ♦ Steak House ♦ Daily, dinner. Reservations required. Valet parking available. 536 S Arroyo Pkwy (between E California Blvd and E Bellevue Dr). 626/577.7463

44 BURGER CONTINENTAL

★$ Gourmet hamburgers in native or exotic dress are offered at the self-serve counter or in the sit-down restaurant. Middle Eastern specialties are one of the surprises on this menu, and belly dancers perform on weekends. The rear patio is shaded by trees during the day and lit with Christmas bulbs in the evening. ♦ American/Middle Eastern

♦ Daily, breakfast, lunch, and dinner. 535 S Lake Ave (between E California and E Del Mar Blvds). 626/792.6634

45 PIE 'N' BURGER

★★$ Stop here for possibly the juiciest burgers in town—as good as the ones grilled in your own backyard. Remember to ask the waitress for a generous supply of napkins for the juices and dressing that drip with every bite. Top your meal off with a slice of old-fashioned peach-apple pie. ♦ American ♦ Daily, breakfast, lunch, and dinner. 913 E California Blvd (between S Catalina and S Lake Aves). 626/795.1123. Also at 9537 Las Tunas Dr (at Primrose Ave), Temple City. 626/287.5797

46 ROSE TREE COTTAGE

★$ Take tea in true English fashion—fine china, finger sandwiches, and all the trimmings—at this charming cottage/British gift shop. Offered daily at 1:00, 2:30, and 4PM, the service is so popular you have to reserve a table a week in advance. At press time the owners were debating a move to 801 S Pasadena Avenue, so do call ahead. ♦ English ♦ Daily, until 5:30PM. 824 E California Blvd (between S Lake and S Hudson Aves). 626/793.3337. www.rosetreecottage.com

---

Restaurants/Clubs: Red | Hotels: Purple | Shops: Orange | Outdoors/Parks: Green | Sights/Culture: Blue

SAN GABRIEL VALLEY

The other Valley . . .

The San Gabriel Valley was the site of the first settlement in the Los Angeles region around 1771, when 14 soldiers, four mule drivers, and two priests chose a spot near the banks of the San Gabriel River and Rio Hondo to found the **Mission San Gabriel Archangel.** By the time California became part of the Union, the valley was a well-known stomping ground along the route to Los Angeles. Several towns popped up in the San Gabriel region, as "ranchos" were broken up into small farm tracts. One of the first was **El Monte,** which started as a trading post and became the region's hog-ranching center. The site of **Alhambra** is part of the former **Rancho San Pascual,** which was ac-

quired by J. D. Shorb and Benjamin D. Wilson. Shorb and Wilson laid out a subdivision n 1874 and named it after Washington Irving's novel *The Alhambra.* Irving's "stern, melancholy country" reminded them of the landscape around the tract.

The next big development boom came in 1903, when **Arcadia** and **San Marino** were founded by two of the wealthiest men of the times. E.J. "Lucky" Baldwin named his subdivision Arcadia after the district in Greece whose poetic name meant "a place of rural simplicity," while Henry E. Huntington named his palatial estate after the Republic of San Marino and created a small, independent city of luxurious houses.

In the 1920s and 1930s, the San Gabriel Valley was a near paradise, dense with orange, lemon, and walnut groves interspersed with such exotic attractions as lion, ostrich, and reptile farms. Over the past two decades, the Anglo population has sharply declined as Latinos and Asians have flocked to the area. And the small communities of the valley, nearly all independent cities, have sprawled one into another, creating a large suburban region of small stucco houses extending some 30 miles.

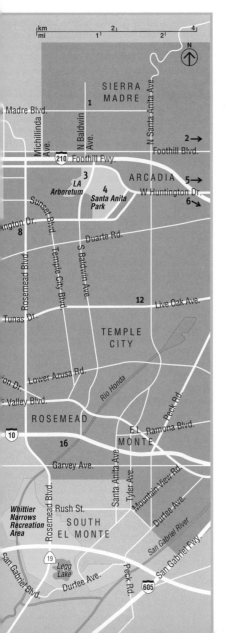

1 RESTAURANT LOZANO

★$$ The lively folksy setting provides a backdrop for black bean soup, stuffed peppers, AHA-approved burgers, and other flavorful, healthy dishes. ♦ Southwestern ♦ M-F, lunch; M-Su, dinner. Reservations recommended. 44 N Baldwin Ave (between E Sierra Madre Blvd and E Montecito Ave), Sierra Madre. 626/355.5945

2 AZTEC HOTEL

$$ This hotel, with its wonderfully eccentric, freshly restored stucco façade, was built in 1925 on a design by **Robert Stacy-Judd,** an enthusiastic advocate of the pre-Columbian Revival style. ♦ 311 W Foothill Blvd (between N Magnolia and Melrose Aves), Monrovia. 626/358.3231

3 LA ARBORETUM

There's no need to go to Africa or Brazil to visit a jungle—a trip to the arboretum and the lake where Humphrey Bogart heroically pulled the *African Queen* through the slimy muck, leeches and all, is certainly more economical. Located on a 127-acre portion of the former **Rancho Santa Anita,** the arboretum houses plant specimens from all over the world, arranged by continent of origin. The lake in the middle of the property is spring fed, a result of natural waters seeping up along the Raymond Fault, which runs across the property. The Gabrieleno Indians used this as a water source for hundreds of years before E.J. "Lucky" Baldwin, a high-living and often outrageous silver-mining magnate, bought the ranch in 1875. The Baldwin property was not only a working ranch but one of the earliest

FIT FOR STARDOM

In a city where your figure can be your fortune, Angelenos are quite possibly the most physically active people in the world. Spawned in the late 1970s and early 1980s by exercise gurus Richard Simmons and Jane Fonda, the fitness frenzy has touched an entire population of stars, wannabes, and just plain folk. Legions of joggers, power walkers, bicyclers, hikers, skaters, roller-bladers, bodybuilders, and surfers fill city streets, beaches, and gyms large and small. To most, exercise is considered tantamount to a religious experience.

Actually, fitness folk were doing their thing long before the advent of home exercise videotapes and posh health clubs. Back in the early 1930s, bodybuilders (remember Charles Atlas and the 97-pound weakling?) were pumping iron and doing calisthenics on what came to be known as **Muscle Beach,** just south of the Santa Monica Pier. Many Muscle Beach regulars went on to fitness fame and fortune, among them gymnasts Steve Hug and Cathy Rigby, Vic and Armand Tanny, Jack LaLanne, and Harold Zinkin (who developed the Universal weight machine).

Though a few diehards still lift barbells on the beach, modern-day muscle-seekers have turned to other venues where they can tone up in air-conditioned comfort—and maybe spot a celebrity or two. Herewith, some of our favorite fitness haunts.

Crunch

This super-hip "no attitude" workout emporium attracts a low-key celebrity crowd and ordinary folks who go to use the state-of-the-art equipment and/or participate in the quirky workouts. We're talking classes called "Live Wire 2K"—hip-hop meets funk energetic workout; "Pole Dancing"—sexy, challenging slithering; "Hula Hoop Pilates," to swivel away tummy bulge; "Cardio Striptease"—yep, and, well, you get the picture. It's

zany, it's fun, and it's effective. Tamer offerings include traditional Pilates, yoga, and super stretch classes. Men's and women's locker rooms have steam baths, saunas, and showers; bring your own lock. Monthly and yearly memberships are available. Free day and weekly passes are usually offered on the web site. ♦ M-F, 5AM-midnight; Sa, Su, 7AM-10PM. 8000 Sunset Blvd (second level) (between Crescent Hgts and Laurel). 323/654.4550; fax 323/654.3935. www.crunch.com

The Golden Door

For the ultimate fitness fix, the rich and famous hole up at the salubrious Golden Door Spa in Escondido, California, an elitist boot camp combining serious body toning and cardiovascular workouts with plenty of pampering. While they won't reveal the list of celebs who frequent the Japanese-style resort, we can tell you they rank among the biggest names in show business. And with a tab close to $8,000 for the all-inclusive week, you can see why. Only 40 guests a week are allowed through its shiny brass gates—mostly women, except during a few men's and coed weeks yearly. Although guests jet in (many in private planes) from all over the world, Angelenos often comprise the majority. There's no place else that whittles you down to size while pulverizing you to a pulp with massages, herbal wraps, foot, face, and assorted other treatments. A typical day begins with a heavy-duty hike up mountain trails. Then comes breakfast in bed followed by nonstop fitness options that range from the hot new Chi walking/running to Pilates, water works, posture, stretch, cardio, dance, circuit training, yoga, meditation, and more. In between you are squirreled away for your daily dose of heavenly treatments (massages are in your room). The hand-picked staff pampers every guest, famous or not. The spa cuisine combines fresh vegetables from the Door's garden with healthy entrées and even divine

botanical collections in the Southland. Witness several exceedingly tall *Washingtonia robusta* palm trees—at 121 feet they might set a world record. Peacocks and guinea fowl roam among the lush plantings, delightful with their vivid promenades and startling with their raucous cries. Demonstration gardens show California domestic horticulture at its best. A snack bar offers refreshments; a shop sells books and gifts. ♦ Admission. Daily. 301 N Baldwin Ave (across from the Santa Anita racetrack), Arcadia. 626/821.3222. www.arboretum.org

4 SANTA ANITA PARK

🅟 Thoroughbred horses race against the backdrop of the San Gabriel Mountains on one of the most beautiful racetracks in the country. The park features a lushly land-

scaped infield, a children's playground, and numerous eating places that run the gamut from hot dogs to haute cuisine. Weekdays, the public is invited to watch morning workouts (a continental breakfast is served at **Clocker's Corner**); on Saturday and Sunday, a free tram tour of the grounds is offered. The action in the saddling enclosure and walking ring may be viewed just before post time. In addition to the regular season, the Oak Tree Racing Association sponsors thoroughbred racing from October through mid-November. ♦ Admission. Season: 26 Dec to late Apr. Post time: 1PM. Morning workouts: 7:30-9:30AM. Tram tours: Sa, Su, 8AM. 285 W Huntington Dr (between N Santa Anita and S Baldwin Aves), Arcadia. 626/574.7223. www.santaanita.com

Within Santa Anita Park:

ow-calorie desserts. There is nothing quite like a week at he Golden Door to rejuvenate, refresh, and reduce. Go ust before Academy Awards week and you'll find many ontenders working hard to fit into their slinky designer gowns. 800/424.0777. www.goldendoor.com

Gold's Gym

This bodacious bodybuilding facility attracts celebrities and starlets from nearby Paramount Studios, aspiring actors, and ordinary folk. Even superstars feel at home here. Rows and rows of weight machines, nearly all occupied, line this serious muscle factory. There are lockers and showers, as well as a helpful staff. Cost is $15 a day, $567 a year (subject to change). Although there are dozens of Gold's branches throughout the Southland, this is the coolest spot to pump and flex. ♦ M-F, 5AM-11PM; Sa, Su, 7AM-9PM. 1016 Cole Ave (between Romaine St and Santa Monica Blvd). 323/462.7012

Joe's Gym

Mariel Hemingway, Sharon Stone, Jamie Lee Curtis, and Jane March are alumni of this workout haven specializing in savvy toning tactics combined with state-of-the-art matrix exercise equipment. The gym also features plasma TVs on all cardio equipment and four big-screen plasmas. There are no formal classes, but a knowledgeable staff teaches you proper techniques on the machines. Also available is computerized nutritional analysis and a staff chiropractor to work out the kinks. The cost is $20 for a day pass or $700 a year for unlimited use of the facility, and an additional $40 to $100 an hour for a personal trainer. ♦ M-F, 5AM-10PM; Sa, 6AM-6PM; Su, 8AM-4PM. 11601 Wilshire Blvd (in the World Savings Bldg at the corner of Wilshire Blvd and Federal Hwy). 310/966.1999. www.joesgym.net

LA Private Trainers Lifestyle Centers

A host of hard-bodied celebrities stay in shape at this hip, holistic health center. Robin Del Pesco, owner/president/CEO and a personal trainer, caters his centers to the aesthetic self-improvement (nutrition, behavior modification, and lifestyle) and overall physical conditioning of baby boomers. Of course, all ages can join, but these clubs focus on *restoring* health. Call for rates and information to book a one-on-one with a personal trainer (which you must do in order to gain access to the facility). ♦ M-F, 6AM-9PM; Sa, Su, 6AM-noon. 16542 Ventura Blvd (at Havehurst). 818/501.5142. www.laprivatetrainers.com

If you don't have time to go to the gym, get fit while you sightsee with Cheryl Anker Agata, a running tour guide who takes tourists and locals on jogging tours of the city designed to keep visitors fit while they explore the area. The running enthusiast launched her company, **Off 'N Running Tours,** in July 1994 and runs with each group, happily tailoring trips to fit any request. One of her most popular routes is up to **Holmby Hills,** past the **Playboy Mansion,** past the former estate of Aaron and Candy Spelling and Humphrey Bogart's old home, down around the **Beverly Hills Hotel** and bungalows, and over to **Beverly Drive** past more celebrity homes. Refreshments are provided during the tour and you get a "Running Keeps Me off the Street" T-shirt when you arrive at the finish line. Although the physically fit Cheryl can easily run 12 miles or more at a time, she leaves the distance up to her clients, most of whom, she says, prefer a 5- or 6-mile jaunt. The cost of the Saturday morning run is $55. For more information or to book a running tour, contact Cheryl at 310/246.1418 or at www.offnrunningtours.com

FRONTRUNNER RESTAURANT

★★$$$ One of the most elegant eateries of any sports site, this stylish luncheon spot is located in the Club House, where 400 feet of floor-to-ceiling sliding glass walls provide a 180-degree view of the finish line and the San Gabriel Mountains. Designed by Ray Gal, the décor is straight out of colonial Asia, with bamboo, rattan, ceiling fans, and mahogany and hand-carved wooden fixtures. For your betting convenience there's a nine-inch Sony TV and a pari-mutuel machine on every tabletop—which detract from the elegance, but gamblers like it. The menu is an eclectic assortment of everything from macadamia-crusted sea bass and grilled Sonoma lamb

chops to pizzas, sandwiches, and hamburgers. And for dessert, the flourless chocolate cake and espresso anglaise, caramelized banana Napoleon with rum sauce, and raspberry cheesecake are well worth the caloric splurge. Access to the Club House is by an admission fee that's also applicable for seats at the track. ♦ Open during racing season only (Dec-Apr), 11AM-4PM. 626/574.1035

5 MONROVIA HISTORICAL MUSEUM

Built in the early 1920s and once the offices and changing rooms for the municipal pool, this Spanish Colonial Revival structure was saved from demolition to safeguard Monrovia memorabilia. Though the

---

Restaurants/Clubs: Red | Hotels: Purple | Shops: Orange | Outdoors/Parks: Green | Sights/Culture: Blue

collections may not have mass appeal, the museum will interest those who enjoy discovering long-lost treasures in an attic. Among the highlights are items chronicling the life of city founder William Monroe, and relics from the San Marino estate of General George Patton. ◆ Free. W, Th, Su, 1-4PM. 742 E Lemon Ave (between S Mountain and S Shamrock Aves), Monrovia. 626/357.9537

6 RAGING WATERS

Families flock to this 44-acre water park extravaganza, where waves, water slides, and a sandy beach offer welcome relief from scorching days. Revive yourself with **Thunder Rapids,** a five-person rafting adventure that culminates in a six-story drop; **High Extreme II,** a thrilling two-person raft ride; and **El Niño, the Ride,** which is guaranteed to get you soaked. ◆ Admission. Hours vary, so call ahead. 111 Raging Waters Dr (north of Via Verde), San Dimas. 909/802.2200. www.ragingwaters.com

7 HUNTINGTON LIBRARY, ART COLLECTIONS, AND BOTANICAL GARDENS

This 207-acre estate, formerly the home of pioneer railroad tycoon and philanthropist Henry E. Huntington (1850-1927), is one of the greatest attractions in Southern California. Designed by **Myron Hunt** and **Elmer Grey** in 1910, it now houses an art collection that emphasizes English and French painting of the 18th century. Among the works displayed are Gainsborough's *Blue Boy,* Lawrence's *Pinkie,* Reynolds's *Sarah Siddons as the Tragic Muse,* and Romney's *Lady Hamilton.* The gallery also exhibits an impressive collection of English and French porcelains, tapestries, graphics, drawings, and furniture. Acquisitions include a full-length Van Dyck portrait, *Mrs. Kirke,* and a late Turner canvas, *The Grand Canal, Venice.* The library, designed by Myron Hunt and H.C. Chambers in 1920, houses extensive holdings of English and American first editions, manuscripts, maps, letters, and incunabula. Displayed are a number of the most famous objects in the collection, including a Gutenberg Bible, the Ellesmere manuscript of Chaucer's *Canterbury Tales,* the double-elephant folio edition of Audubon's *Birds of America,* and an unsurpassed collection of the early editions of Shakespeare's works. In the west wing of the library is the **Arabella Huntington Memorial Collection** of French porcelain, furniture, sculpture, and Renaissance paintings.

With the 1984 opening of the **Virginia Steele Scott Gallery of American Art,** designed by Warner and Gray, the estate added another dimension to its collections. Works range in date from the 1730s to the 1930s, and include paintings by Mary Cassatt (*Breakfast in Bed*), Gilbert Stuart, Winslow Homer, John Singleton Copley, Edward Hopper, and Robert Henri. American artifacts and furniture, including pieces by Gustav Stickley, are matched with paintings from the appropriate period. A permanent exhibition features furniture and decorative arts designed by Charles and Henry Greene. The beautiful and lush gardens were designed and developed by William Hertrich beginning in 1904. In addition to expansive lawns and formal planting arrangements that incorporate 17th-century Italian sculpture, they contain extensive rose and camellia gardens, a **Shakespearean Garden** of plants mentioned by the Bard, and a number of annual beds. The **Japanese Garden** is entered through a gate overlooking a half-moon-shaped bridge spanning a koi pond. It features an authentically furnished 18th-century-style house, specimens of bonsai, and a **Zen Rock Garden.** The astonishing 12-acre **Desert Garden** has one of the largest plantings of unique cactus and succulent varieties in the world. ◆ Admission. Galleries and gardens: Tu-Su. English tea (served in the Tea Room, behind the mansion): Tu-F, 1-3:30PM; Sa, Su, noon-3:30PM. 1151 Oxford Rd (between Euston and Orlando Rds), San Marino. Second entrance on Orlando Rd (between Oxford and Avondale Rds). General information 626/405.2100, tearoom reservations 626/584.9337, directions 626/405.2274. www.huntington.org

8 CLEARMAN'S NORTHWOODS INN

★$$ Kitschy log cabin architecture says it all—the Yukon in the heart of San Gabriel. The floors are covered with sawdust and peanut shells, which waitresses in frilly cocktail dresses encourage customers to toss freely. Good-size entrées are accompanied by delicious cheese breads and two salads. If you can't decide, try the hearty sampler—a steak, scallop, and chicken combination. ◆ American ◆Daily, lunch and dinner. 7247 Rosemead Blvd (between E Fairview Ave and Huntington Dr), San Gabriel. 626/286.8284, 626/286.3579. Also at 14305 Firestone Blvd (between Phoebe and Valley View Aves), La Mirada. 714/994.4590. www.clearmansrestaurant.com

9 JULIENNE

★★$ Homemade bread, delicious salads, roast chicken, and daily specials are served at this charming café. ◆ French ◆ M-Sa, breakfast and lunch; dinner served only in summer, Th-F. 2649 Mission St (between El Molino and Los Robles Aves), San Marino. 626/441.2299. www.juliennetogo.com

10 EL MOLINO VIEJO

Erected in 1816, the first water-powered gristmill in Southern California is maintained by the California Historical Society.
♦ Admission. Tu-Su, 1-4PM. 1120 Old Mill Rd (between Mill La and S Oak Knoll Ave), San Marino. 626/449.5450

11 TOKYO LOBBY

★★$$ Decorated with folk art, this Japanese restaurant features generous entrées that appeal to Americans. ♦ Japanese ♦ M-F, lunch and dinner; Sa, Su, dinner. Reservations recommended for large parties. 927 E Las Tunas Dr (between Earle St and N Charlotte Ave), San Gabriel. 626/287.9972

12 ALEX DI PEPPE'S

★$$ Good pizza, good lasagna, and good value keep the regulars *molto contenti.*
♦ Italian ♦ M-Su, dinner. Reservations recommended on Friday and Saturday. 140 Las Tunas Dr (between S Santa Anita and El Monte Aves), Arcadia. 626/445.0544

13 WAHIB'S MIDDLE EAST RESTAURANT AND BAKERY

★$ Bargain is the key word in this tiny shack of a restaurant, whether you're indulging in an aromatic stew, kabobs (which you must call ahead to order), or stuffed lamb with yogurt. All the traditional starters and desserts are available, as well as beer and wine. ♦ Lebanese ♦ Daily, breakfast, lunch, and dinner. 910 E Main St (between S Valencia St and S Granada Ave), Alhambra. 626/576.1048. www.wahibmiddleeast.com

14 SAN GABRIEL CIVIC AUDITORIUM

Designed especially for John Steven Groarty's *Mission Play,* Arthur Benton's authentic Mission-style playhouse was modeled after the **Mission San Antonio de Padua** in Monterey County. Heraldic shields of the Spanish provinces, donated by Spanish king Alfonso XIII on the auditorium's opening in 1927, adorn the immense interior. The fine theater organ is used for concerts and to accompany silent movies. ♦ Box office: M-F, 10AM-5PM. 320 S Mission Dr (between S Santa Anita St and W Broadway), San Gabriel. 626/308.2865. www.sgcivic.org

14 MUSEUM OF THE SAN GABRIEL HISTORICAL ASSOCIATION

Visitors can obtain a walking-tour brochure from the headquarters of this society dedicated to the preservation of local history. At press time, a major historical site next door, the Victorian **Hayes House** (circa 1887), was undergoing restoration supervised by the museum. ♦ Free. W, Sa, Su, 1-4PM. 546 W Broadway (between S Santa Anita St and S Mission Dr), San Gabriel. 626/308.3223

14 MISSION SAN GABRIEL ARCHANGEL

Founded in 1771 by Fathers Pedro Cambon and Angel Somera, the present mission church consists of the renovated remains of the one built by Indian workers from 1791 to 1805. Constructed of stone, mortar, and brick, its capped buttresses and narrow windows were influenced by the style of the Cathedral of Cordova in Spain. The church originally had a vaulted roof, but it was damaged in the earthquake of 1803. In 1812, the church tower on the façade was toppled by another earthquake. When the church was completely restored in 1828, a bell tower was constructed on the north wall of the altar end. The bell-tower wall, with its three rows of arched openings, creates the characteristic image of the mission. ♦ 537 W Mission Dr (between Junípero Serra Dr and S Santa Anita St), San Gabriel. 626/282.5191

15 BABITA MEXICUISINE

★★$ The specialties of this local treasure include Yucatecan seafood dishes such as *pescado picado* (seared fresh catch of the day with bell pepper, tomato, jalapeño, and white wine), chicken tostadas topped with black bean paste, *cochinita pibil* (pork baked in banana leaves), and *carne asada* (skirt steak with salsa Mexicana). Try the bread pudding; you'll love it. ♦ Mexican ♦ Tu-F, lunch; Tu-Su, dinner. 1823 S San Gabriel Blvd (at E Norwood Pl), San Gabriel. 626/288.7265

16 EDWARD'S STEAK HOUSE

★$$ You can count on nicely grilled steaks and chops, a surprise or two (perhaps lamb shanks), and at least one fresh fish entrée. The sawdust-on-the-floor informality makes this place a good choice when you're with the kids. ♦ American ♦ M-F, lunch and dinner; Sa, Su, dinner. 9600 Flair Dr (at Fletcher Ave), El Monte. 626/442.2400. www.edward.steakhouse.com

---

Restaurants/Clubs: Red | Hotels: Purple | Shops: Orange | Outdoors/Parks: Green | Sights/Culture: Blue

SOUTH AND EAST CENTRAL

Watt's up with this . . .

Edged by mountains and water and scored by railroad tracks, freeways, and rivers, South and East Central embody the true Los Angeles basin. The flat geography is a main attraction to industry, which provides the economic base of the area. Development relles on the Southern Pacific Railroad and the Pacific Electric Inter-Urban Railroad, transportation giants that bought up huge tracts of land as they built their lines, and later subdivided their holdings into a series of communities for workers and their families.

The wide-open expanses, right-angled streets, and unimpeded vistas seemed familiar to newcomers from the Midwest and the South, who headed this way in response to the boosterism and land fever of the 1880s and 1920s. Many of these communities have remained unincorporated; like the jigsaw patterns of the other parts of Los Angeles County, the boundaries between city and county hop, skip, and jump around each other.

Culver City was formerly home to three major motion picture studios: **Metro-Goldwyn-Mayer, Selznick International Studios,** and **Hal Roach Studios.** At one time, this small town produced half the films made in the United States.

From **Boyle Heights** to **Whittier Hills**, East LA has the largest concentration of Latinos in the United States, while **Monterey Park** is the preferred destination for Chinese immigrants and rivals Chinatown for authentic cuisine. South Central—from **Baldwin Hills** to the plains area that includes **Watts, Willowbrook, and Compton**—is home to the country's largest concentration of African-American residents, as well as a burgeoning Latino population. This area ranges from affluent hillside homes on the west to inner-city neighborhoods that have neatly trimmed older houses as well as run-down, dilapidated streets where the area's gangs congregate. Although the ethnic mix makes the area more vital and interesting, it also can be a source of tension and crime; some of the historic sites are worth seeing, but we highly recommend visiting only during daylight hours.

1 LOS ANGELES COUNTY USC MEDICAL CENTER

The highly visible 20-story Moderne structure, completed in 1934, covers 89 acres and is one of the largest general acute-care hospitals in the country. The **University of Southern California Health Sciences Campus,** located seven miles northeast of the main campus, serves USC's Schools of Medicine and Pharmacy, the University Hospital, the Doheny Eye Institute, and the Kenneth Norris Jr. Comprehensive Cancer Center. The hospital is a training ground for students from the USC School of Medicine. ◆ Medical Center: 1975 Zonal Ave (between San Pablo and Biggy Sts). 323/342.2000; hospital: 1200 N State St (between Marengo St and Zonal Ave). 323/226.2622

2 LINCOLN PARK

More than 300 varieties of trees—a number of them rare and enormous—grace this 46-acre park. Some date back to the 1870s, when the park was created. ◆ Daily; M-F, until 9PM. 3501 Valley Blvd (between N Soto and N Main Sts). 213/847.1726

Within Lincoln Park:

PLAZA DE LA RAZA

This charming lakeside park houses an educational/cultural center devoted to LA's Spanish-speaking population, with activities including musical performances, dance, drama, and seasonal festivals based on themes related to Mexican holidays and family life. ◆ Nominal admission. 323/223.2475

3 CALIFORNIA STATE UNIVERSITY AT LOS ANGELES

A branch of the large **California State University** system. ◆ 5151 State University Dr (between San Bernardino Fwy and N Eastern Ave). 323/343.3000

4 OCEAN STAR SEAFOOD

★★$$ The chefs create no-frills authentic Cantonese seafood, including steamed live shrimp and scallops, baked lobster, and fish prepared in several distinctive ways. Duck soup with citrus peel and beef hot pot are likewise recommended. On Atlantic Boulevard, a much larger branch of this restaurant serves a variety of seafood delicacies in a palatial dining room with private banquet rooms. ◆ Chinese ◆ Daily, lunch and dinner. Reservations recommended for 10 or more. 145 N Atlantic Blvd (between W Garvey and W Emerson Aves), Monterey Park. 626/308.2128

5 COCARY

★$ This frantic and fun Mongolian restaurant lets you select (from refrigerated cases down one wall) such delicacies as tiger prawns, baby clams, and fish dumplings to grill or simmer in a pot at your table. Bring a crowd of friends and a big appetite. ◆ Mongolian ◆ Daily, lunch and dinner. 112 N Garfield Ave (at W Garvey Ave), Monterey Park. 626/573.0691

6 DIAMOND BAKERY

A wide selection of pastries and cakes offered at this place is complemented by a variety of *bao*—puffy steamed or fried rice-flour rolls filled with beef or chicken. ◆ Daily 744 W Garvey Ave (at S Atlantic Blvd), Monterey Park. 626/289.5171

6 LITTLE SHEEP

★★$$ The extraordinary preparations of shrimp, crab, and sole put most Western seafood restaurants to shame. This place is crowded at lunchtime. ♦ Mongolian ♦ Daily, lunch and dinner. 120 S Atlantic Blvd (between W Newmark and W Garvey Aves), Monterey Park. 626/282.1089

7 YI-MEI DELI

This small, crowded deli and bakery features a wide selection of Chinese fast foods and sweets, including a popular soybean soup served with *yu jow gwui*, a tasty deep-fried bread. ♦ Daily. 736 S Atlantic Blvd (between El Mercado Ave and El Portal Pl), Monterey Park. 626/284.9306. Also at 18414 Colima Rd (at Batson Ave), Rowland Heights. 626/854.9246

8 HOLLENBECK PARK

 This 21-acre park was donated to the city in 1892. A lovely stand of jacaranda sits amid stately old trees and provides a pleasant setting for recreational programs sponsored by the clubhouse. ♦ M-F, until 10PM; Sa, Su, noon-4PM. 415 S St. Louis St (at E Fourth St). 323/261.0113

9 EL MERCADO

Experience the flavor of Mexico without leaving LA County at this south-of-the-border-style complex of bustling food markets, shops, and restaurants. The main floor houses stalls filled with all the ingredients necessary for Mexican cooking. The walls on this level are lined with a *tortillaria*, a bakery, snack bars with food to go, and delicatessens. The mezzanine has a series of cafeteria-style restaurants. Mariachis perform here from noon until midnight and happily accept special requests for a small donation. Shops in the basement sell everything from furniture to Mexican crafts and utilitarian domestic goods. ♦ Shops: Daily. Restaurants: Daily until midnight. 3425 E First St (between N Indiana and N Lorena Sts). 323/268.3451

10 EAST LOS ANGELES COLLEGE

This two-year community college offers a variety of undergraduate courses and occupational programs. It was one of the first colleges to offer free, noncredit courses to anyone in the community. ♦ 1301 Avenida Cesar Chavez (between Collegian and Bleakwood Aves), Monterey Park. 323/265.8650

11 WHITTIER NARROWS NATURE CENTER

 An enormous variety of birds, plants, and animals find sanctuary in this 419-acre nature center, located along the **San Gabriel River.** The small museum has exhibitions that describe the aquatic environment. Take a great hike along the nature trails. ♦ Free. Daily. 1000 N Durfee Ave (off Pomona and San Gabriel River Fwys). 626/575.5523

12 DO-NUT HOLE

This 1958 structure is one of the city's great pop monuments. Drive through the two giant doughnuts and pick up one (or a bag) for the road, any hour of the day or night. ♦ Daily, until midnight. 15300 Amar Rd (at Elliott Ave), La Puente. 626/968.2912

13 WORKMAN & TEMPLE FAMILY HOMESTEAD MUSEUM

Relive the colorful history of Los Angeles, from the first American settlers of the 1840s (when California was still under Mexican rule) through the boom years of the 1870s and 1920s. Each of these formative decades is dramatically evoked by historic buildings on a six-acre site restored by the City of Industry as an educational showpiece. The major attraction is a 26-room **Spanish Revival house,** built in the 1920s with the profits from an oil strike and furnished in period style, complete with a windup Victrola and a bearskin rug in the hall. The original mid-19th-century adobe, an English-style manor house, a lacy gazebo, and a private cemetery are also featured. ♦ Free. Tours available on the hour between 1 and 4PM. 15415 E Don Julian Rd (between Hacienda Blvd and Turnbull Canyon Rd), City of Industry. 626/968.8492

14 EZ NEW WEB LAUNDROMAT & CAFÉ

This place takes the drudge out of washday with an inviting facility in which to surf the web, eat, drink, or just plain lounge while waiting for your wash at any of 50 self-service washers and dryers. The café offers a menu of fresh fruit smoothies, coffee, and Frappuccinos (prepared by an in-house barrista), assorted beverages, panini sandwiches, pasta, vegetables, and fresh-baked pastries. And get this, there's even a boutique filled with clothing, handbags, jewelry, bath products, cups, mugs, and handmade dog collars. ♦ Daily, 6AM-10PM. 6144 Washington Blvd (between Culver and

La Cienega Blvds), Culver City. 310/559.6182. www.ezdays.com

15 WILLIAM GRANT STILL ARTS CENTER

Named for the famous late African-American composer and longtime resident of LA, the center offers exhibitions, festivals, and workshops. ◆ Free. Daily, noon-5PM. 2520 West View St (just north of W Adams Blvd). 323/734.1164

16 CLARK MEMORIAL LIBRARY

English literature and music of the 17th and 18th centuries are well represented in this research library, bequeathed to UCLA in 1934 by William Andrews Clark Jr. in memory of his father, Senator William A. Clark. The Italian Renaissance building is decorated with murals and ceiling paintings by Allyn Cox, and furnished with period antiques. Formal gardens cover the underground vaults. Tours can be arranged by appointment only. ◆ Open to researchers M-F. 2520 Cimarron St (at W Adams Blvd). 323/731.8529. www.humnet.ucla.edu/humnet/clarklib

17 HAROLD & BELLE'S

★★$$ An LA institution that began as a pool hall, this fun spot dishes out generous helpings of catfish strips, spicy gumbo, jambalaya, hot sausage, shrimp creole, and barbecued ribs. ◆ Cajun/Creole ◆ Daily, lunch and dinner. Reservations recommended. 2920 W Jefferson Blvd (between 9th and 10th Aves). 323/735.9023

18 SONY PICTURES STUDIOS

How the mighty have fallen! Once an empire with five lots, theaters and studios around the world, and "more stars than there are in heaven," Metro-Goldwyn-Mayer (MGM) has surrendered its last piece of turf to the producer of TV's *Dallas* and *Falcon Crest* and now occupies a bland Beverly Hills office building. Meanwhile, Columbia Pictures, born on Gower Street's "Poverty Row" the same year as MGM, relocated here from Burbank—a poor-wretch-makes-good story worthy of the movies. You can see the exteriors of the two major buildings on the lot: the 1916 **Triangle Company office**, with its classical colonnades, that MGM took over in 1924; and the monumental Moderne **Thalberg**

Building of 1939, named for MGM's legendary head of production. It is also the lot where later productions such as *Jeopardy!* and *Men in Black* were filmed. ◆ Although closed to the public, two-hour walking tours are offered by appointment for a fee (323/529.8687). 10202 Washington Blvd (between Madison and Overland Aves), Culver City. 310/244.4000

19 CULVER STUDIOS

King Kong roared, Atlanta burned, and "Boy Wonder" Orson Welles directed *Citizen Kane* on this historic piece of land. Its Southern plantation-style offices were built by pioneer producer Thomas Ince, later housed RKO, and were the trademark of David O. Selznick's company long before he built Tara on the land cleared by torching the surviving sets of Cecil B. De Mille's *King of Kings*. All of this history has gone with the wind, leaving only the façade and a cluster of vintage rental stages. ◆ Closed to the public. 9336 Washington Blvd (between Ince Blvd and Van Buren Pl), Culver City. No general public phone number

20 BALDWIN HILLS VILLAGE

Here is a rare model of planned housing that became a tight-knit community. Completed on the eve of America's entry into World War II, this 80-acre complex of one- and two-story studio to three-bedroom dwellings was considered a progressive urban experiment. Though many units had private walled gardens, the complex was well integrated, with its generous landscape of spacious lawns and giant sycamores and oaks. It was renamed **Village Green** in the mid-1970s when the units were converted into condominiums, all of which are private residences. ◆ 5300 Rodeo Rd (between S Sycamore Ave and Hauser Blvd)

21 KENNETH HAHN STATE RECREATIONAL AREA

Once an oil reservoir, this grassy 315-acre park (named for the longtime LA County supervisor) represents a sound, public-oriented, adaptive reuse solution for an otherwise bleak landscape of unimproved oil wells nodding away like mechanical storks. A forest was planted with 140 trees and shrubs from around the world, representing every nation that competed in the 1984 Summer Olympics. The park has hiking trails and two lakes for fishing. ◆ 4100 S La Cienega Blvd (between Stocker and Aladdin Sts). 323/291.0199

22 MUSEUM IN BLACK

This collection includes more than 1,000 pieces of traditional African art and African-

American memorabilia. There is a shop with items for sale. ♦ Free. Tu-Sa. 4331 Degnan Blvd (between W 43rd Pl and W 43rd St). 310/904.8117

23 DWAH BOOKSHOP

One of the few stores of its kind specializing in African-American, Islamic, and children's literature. ♦ M-Sa. 4801 Crenshaw Blvd (between W 48th St and Brynhurst Ave). 323/299.0335

24 FARMER JOHN'S PIG MURALS

Little pigs romp and play in a life-size trompe l'oeil farm landscape that blends in with the building it's painted on. Live trees are indistinguishable from painted ones, and pigs peer into windows both real and painted. The murals were painted in 1957 by film studio artist Leslie A. Grimes. When Grimes fell to his death from a scaffold in 1968, the Arco Sign Company assumed responsibility for maintaining and extending the murals. ♦ 3049 E Vernon Ave (between Downey Rd and S Soto St), Vernon

25 THE CITADEL

This Assyrian fortress, only nine miles from downtown LA, offers 38 pseudo-discount outlets such as **Geoffrey Beene, Benetton, Old Navy, Joan & David, Perry Ellis, Eddie Bauer, Corning Revere, DKNY,** and **Nike.** Don't expect big bargains, though: 10-20% is more realistic. There's a stylish food court to fuel you for your shopping spree. Designed by **Morgan, Walls & Clements** in 1929 as an impressive façade for the Samson Tire and Rubber Factory and later remodeled and redeveloped by the Trammell Crow Company into its current incarnation, the 130,000-square-foot cut-rate emporium is the closest of its kind to the city. ♦ Daily. 100-150 Citadel Dr (between Tubeway Ave and Atlantic Blvd), City of Commerce. 323/888.1724

26 WINNIE AND SUTCH COMPANY BUILDING

These structures, designed by **William E. Myer** in 1939, represent the best examples of Streamline Moderne architecture in LA since the Pan Pacific Auditorium was torched by vandals in 1989. The grounds, landscaped with flowers and shrubs, were designed to draw attention away from the building's

industrial purpose. ♦ 5610 S Soto St (between E Slauson Ave and E 54th St), Huntington Park

27 PIO PICO STATE HISTORIC PARK/CASA DE PIO PICO

Don Pio Pico, former governor of California, built this hacienda on his 9,000-acre **El Ranchito** in 1850. The U-shaped house, which has recently been renovated, is a 13-room, two-story adobe mansion with two- to three-foot-thick walls. Covered porches link the side wings to the central portion of the house; a well is located in the courtyard. Guided tours of the house are offered. ♦ Free. W-Su. 6003 Pioneer Blvd (at Whittier Blvd), Whittier. 562/695.1217

28 WESTFIELD FOX HILLS

Macy's and **JC Penney** anchor this shopping mall, with 137 other stores on three floors selling everything from fresh-roasted nuts to bolts of fabric and clothing for all ages. The electronic game center is a popular spot with youngsters. ♦ Daily; M-F until 9PM. Sepulveda Blvd and Slauson Ave, Culver City. 310/390.5073. www.foxhills@westfield.com

29 HARRIET'S CHEESECAKES UNLIMITED

Choose from 50 flavors of cheesecake. If the exquisite French vanilla is too tame for you, try the chocolate amaretto, apple 'n' spice, or coffee flavors. ♦ Tu-Sa. 1515 Centinela Ave (between N Cedar and Beach Sts), Inglewood. 310/419.2259

30 MAIN POST OFFICE

LA's main mail distribution center is the nation's largest single-level post office, the size of 10 football fields. It processes five and a half million pieces of mail per day. ♦ Window service: M-Sa. 7001 S Central Ave (between E Florence and E Gage Aves). General information 323/585.1723, 323/585.1705, or 800/275.8777

31 CENTINELA ADOBE

Built in 1834 for Ignacio Machado, this well-preserved house is made of adobe with a wood-shingle roof, and furnished with 19th-century antiques. Some of the original planting is maintained. Within the site are a research library and the office once used by Daniel Freeman, whose 22,000 acres became the city of Inglewood. ♦ Free. W, Su, 2-4PM. 7634 Midfield Ave (between W 82nd and W 76th Sts), Inglewood. General information 310/649.6272. Tours 310/677.1154

There are more than 30,000 swimming pools in Palm Springs alone, both in hotels and private homes.

Restaurants/Clubs: Red | Hotels: Purple | Shops: Orange | Outdoors/Parks: Green | Sights/Culture: Blue

32 ACADEMY THEATRE

This 1939 Streamline Moderne landmark, designed by **S. Charles Lee,** is notable for its spiral-finned tower. The building is now used as a church. ♦ 3100 Manchester Blvd (at Crenshaw Blvd), Inglewood

33 HOLLYWOOD PARK

Thoroughbred racing occurs April through July and mid-November through December on a track landscaped with lagoons and tropical trees. A computer-operated screen offers patrons a view of the back stretch, as well as stop-action replays of photo finishes and racing statistics. Refreshments are available at the elegant **Turf Club Terrace, International Food Fair, Paddock Club,** and **Hollywood Bar.** The children's play area, designated **North Park,** now features a carousel. ♦ Admission. Call for post times. 1050 S Prairie Ave (between Century Blvd and W 90th St), Inglewood. 310/419.1500; race results: 888/338.7223. www.hollywoodpark.com

34 WATTS TRAIN STATION

Restored as a railroad museum and office for the Department of Water and Power, the 1904 depot is meant as a symbol of the Community Redevelopment Agency's efforts to revitalize Watts. The **Metro Rail** Red Line from Long Beach to downtown LA stops close by—much as the Big Red Cable Cars used to. ♦ E 103rd St and Grandee Ave

35 WATTS TOWERS

Paris has the Eiffel Tower, Barcelona has the Sagrada Familia cathedral, and LA has the Watts Towers. One of the world's greatest works of folk art, they were designed by Sam Rodia, an unlettered plasterer who created these masterpieces between 1921 and 1954 from salvaged steel rods, dismantled pipe structures, bed frames, and cement. He worked alone, building without a conscious plan (though he may have been inspired by childhood memories of similar structures used in an annual fiesta held near Naples) and scaling the heights of his work using a window-washer's belt and bucket. "How could I have been helped?" asked Rodia. "I couldn't tell anyone what to do. . . . Most of the time I didn't know myself." Rodia's glistening fretwork grew slowly over the years until the central tower topped out at 99.5 feet tall. Glass bottle fragments, ceramic tiles, china plates, and more than 25,000 seashells embellish his creation, encrusting the surface so thickly that they seem to be the primary building material, forming skin that has the calcified delicacy of coral.

When the towers were completed, Rodia deeded his property to a neighbor and left LA forever. He died in 1965 in Martinez, California, unwilling to the end to talk about his life's work. The spires were disfigured by vandals and threatened with demolition, but citizens rallied and saved them. The three towers have been completely renovated thanks to the Cultural Affairs Department of Los Angeles, and officially declared a National Historic Landmark. Public access to the interior is limited to weekends from noon to 4PM. Cultural events and exhibits are held here, such as the Day of the Drum, an ethnic foods and music festival celebrated in late September. Be aware of the high crime rate in the area, especially now that the parking lot was recently bulldozed to make room for a $4.7 million youth arts center. ♦ 1765 E 107th St (east of Graham Ave). 213/847.4646 or 213/485.1795. www.trywatts.com

Within the Watts Towers:

WATTS TOWERS ART CENTER

This community art center hosts exhibitions, art classes, and music, dance, and poetry readings. ♦ Tu-Sa. 213/847.4646

36 ALL AMERICAN HOME CENTER

This family-owned home-improvement store comprises 21 departments on four acres, with another six acres for parking. It claims to be the best-stocked store in the US and, more important, it motivates its staff through profit sharing. So, if you want to build your dream house . . . ♦ Daily. 7201 E Firestone Blvd (between Old River School Rd and Garfield Ave), Downey. 562/927.8666. www.aahc.com

37 HERITAGE PARK

The restored 1880s ranch and history museum are located in six acres of gardens. Close by is the 1919 **Clarke Estate,** one of the best-preserved works by landmark architect **Irving Gill.** ♦ Free. Heritage Park Dr (south of Telegraph Rd), Santa Fe Springs. 562/946.6476

The Lakers basketball team moved to Los Angeles from Minneapolis in 1960.

38 EL POLLO INKA

★$ Marinated spit-roasted chicken is the signature dish, but just as delicious is the lamb stew served with rice and beans. ♦ Peruvian ♦ Daily, lunch and dinner. 15400-D Hawthorne Blvd (at W 154th St), Lawndale. 310/676.6665

39 KAMPACHI

$$ While many sushi bars offer tempura and other batter-dipped dishes, this Japanese eatery concentrates solely on raw, fresh seafood. ♦ Japanese ♦ M-F, lunch and dinner; Sa, Su, dinner. Reservations recommended. 1425 W Artesia Blvd (between Normandie and Western Aves), Gardena. 310/515.1391

40 GOODYEAR BLIMP

One of the best-known, best-loved corporate symbols in the US is 192 feet long, 59 feet high, 50 feet in diameter, and 202,700 cubic feet in volume. Deflated, the dirigible weighs 12,000 pounds; filled with helium, its weight drops to 150 pounds. Its cruising speed is 35mph; its top speed, 53mph. The normal cruising altitude of 1,000 to 1,500 feet gives the blimp and its logo maximum recognition from the ground. In addition to advertising, the blimp acts as a camera platform for TV coverage of sports and public events, and assists the American Cetacean Society with the annual count of the California gray whales during their winter migration. Officially named the *Columbia*, the blimp travels six months out of the year, but you're most likely to see it on the ground in the early morning or at twilight from the intersection of the Harbor and San Diego Freeways. ♦ 19200 S Main St (between San Diego Fwy and E 192nd St), Carson. 323/770.0456. www.goodyearblimp.com

41 DOMINGUEZ RANCH ADOBE

A relic of the Spanish settlement of California, the adobe sits on property owned by Juan José Dominguez, a soldier who accompanied Father Serra on the original expedition from Mexico to found the California missions. In 1782, Dominguez was rewarded for his service with a land grant covering the harbor area south of the **Pueblo de Los Angeles,** more than 75,000 acres. His nephew built an adobe in 1826, and its interior has been restored as a historical museum, displaying many of the original furnishings. The adobe is now part of the **Dominguez Memorial Seminary,** operated by the Claretian Order. ♦ Free. Tu, W, 1-4PM; second and third Sunday of every month, 1-4PM. Groups of more than 15 must make advance reservations. 18127 S Alameda St (between Laurel Park Rd and Gardena Fwy, Compton). 310/631.5981

42 LA MIRADA THEATRE FOR THE PERFORMING ARTS

This big, breezy theater features Tony award–winning performers, Off-Broadway productions, musicals, symphonies, and fabulous children's shows. ♦ 14900 La Mirada Blvd (between Ocaso and Rosecrans Aves), La Mirada. Box office 562/944.9801, 714/944.6310. www.lamiradatheatre.com

---

Restaurants/Clubs: Red | Hotels: Purple | Shops: Orange | Outdoors/Parks: Green | Sights/Culture: Blue

SOUTH BAY/LONG BEACH

By the bay, by the beautiful bay, but it's really an ocean . . .

A cluster of colorful beachside communities burrows beside California's jagged coastline between Venice and Naples. Distinctively different, each provides an idyllic setting for swimming, sailing, surfing, and fishing. The rocky outcrop of the

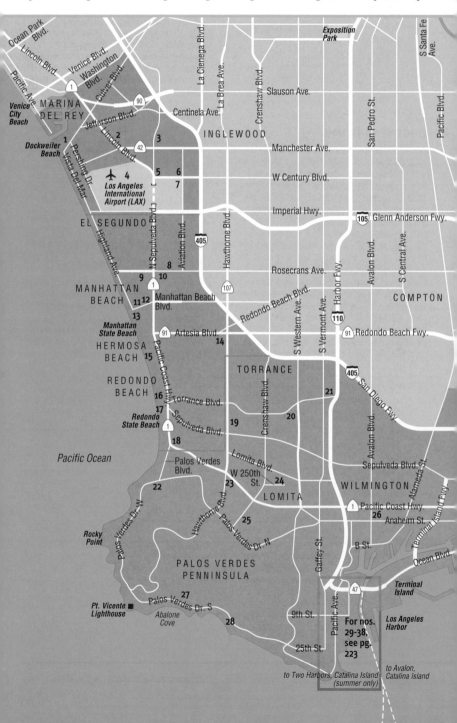

For nos. 29-38, see pg. 223

Palos Verdes peninsula, and the industrial enclave around **Los Angeles Harbor**, **San Pedro**, and **Long Beach**, breaks up the South Bay area's sandy expanses. Farther inland is **Los Angeles International Airport (LAX)**, the third-busiest airport in the world. Note: The area code of most phone numbers in Long Beach, Lakewood, Whittier, Downey, Pico Rivera, and Norwalk is 562.

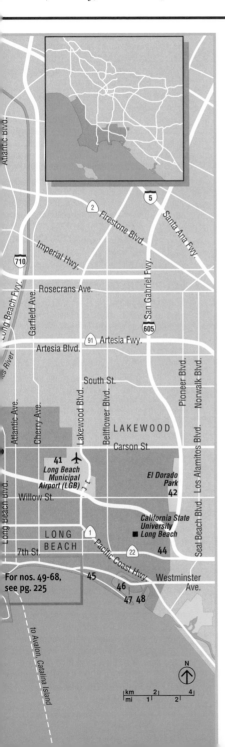

1 INN AT PLAYA DEL REY

$$ Just a few blocks from the beach and a five-minute drive from LAX, this luxurious bed-and-breakfast is a real find. Each of the 22 guest rooms is decorated in charming Cape Cod style; all feature private baths, phones (with voice mail), cable TV, computer hookups, and views of the Channel; some also boast canopied beds, sunken Jacuzzi tubs, fireplaces, and decks or porches. Rates include full breakfast, afternoon tea, and wine and hors d'oeuvres in the evening. Guests may use the inn's bicycles to ride on a nearby path that overlooks the ocean, and there's also a bird sanctuary just outside the breakfast room. ◆ 435 Culver Blvd (at Pershing Dr). 310/574.1920. www.innatplayadelrey.com &

2 LOYOLA MARYMOUNT UNIVERSITY

Founded in 1865, this successor to St. Vincent's (the first college in Los Angeles) is now a coed private Catholic university. ◆ Loyola Blvd and W 80th St. 310/338.2700

3 LOYOLA THEATER

A luxurious former preview theater for Twentieth Century-Fox has been gutted and turned into offices. The 1946 swan's-neck façade survives. ◆ N Sepulveda Blvd and W Manchester Ave

4 LOS ANGELES INTERNATIONAL AIRPORT (LAX)

A general flying field in the early 1920s, LAX was first known as the Municipal Airport of Los Angeles. The postwar building boom and westward migration prompted city planners to greatly expand the airport between 1959 and 1962, with William Pereira Associates supervising the master plan. The airport was again expanded for the 1984 Olympic Games, and the five-level **Tom Bradley International Terminal** was added. In 1996, the terminal's mezzanine was redesigned to include a central waterfall, grand staircase, and gourmet food concessions. Close to a million flights and upwards of 65 million passengers pass through any of the four east-west runways of the 3,500-acre site annually. The LA regional airport system includes Ontario International Airport to the east, Bob Hope Airport to the north, and Long Beach Municipal Airport and John Wayne Airport (Orange County) to the south. For detailed information on airlines, airport transportation, and parking, see "Airports" in the Orientation chapter on page TK.

5 SHERATON GATEWAY LOS ANGELES AIRPORT HOTEL

$$ Operated by the trendy Kor Hotel Group, this 802-room "boutique on the block" welcomes you in through a dramatic, stylized lobby decked out with modern fixtures set in a palette of charcoal, black, navy, and crimson. Each lavishly quirky room and suite is appointed with black-wash ebony furnishings, occasional tables with red faux ostrich finishes, Lucite lamps, and textured leather headboards on the beds. Amenities and gadgets include high-speed Internet hookup and Wi-Fi conveniently placed in public areas. The yuppified pool area is picture perfect with black-and-white cabanas (a big trend among LA hotels these days), palm trees, and assorted plants and flowers. A fully equipped, 1,240-square-foot fitness center and a Starbucks café (to help jump-start your workout) enhance the enjoyment. An added convenience is the free shuttle service to the beach and shops. Room service is available around the clock. Although primarily targeted to business travelers, Kor's touches make it more inviting for families and couples. But it's still an airport facility, albeit a rather unusual one. ♦ 6101 W Century Blvd (between Airport Blvd and Vicksburg Ave). 310/642.1111, 800/325.3535; fax 310/410.1267. www.sheratonlosangeles.com

Within the Sheraton Gateway Hotel:

SHULA'S 347

★★★$$$$ Kor's craftsmen created this handsome hip-o-centric room as the perfect showcase for the various cuts of prime steak offered at this restaurant named after ex–Miami Dolphin coach Don Shula, who owns the spot. Given its uptown chic, with a retro décor of dark woods, lanterns, a wild chandelier with three deer heads intertwining, and a bunch of flat-screen TVs tuned into sports channels, you easily forget you're a stone's throw from LAX. Each "custom aged" certified Angus beefsteak is truly exceptional, especially a perfectly grilled "Shula cut" filet mignon and porterhouse. Tasty side dishes to consider include garlic mashed potatoes, sautéed mushrooms, and string beans. If you're not too hungry, order a hamburger; it's the best we've ever tasted. We also loved the freshly baked cookies, but every

dessert was yummy. Non–meat eaters have several options, such as fresh fish, lobster tails, shrimp, or hearty salads. ♦ Daily, dinner. Reservations suggested. 310/642.4820. www.donshula.com

6 RENAISSANCE MONTURA HOTEL, LOS ANGELES

$$$ There are 499 guest rooms and 16 function rooms, which tells you this hotel caters primarily to the business traveler, though it does offer somewhat of an intimate style and personal attention. The décor is upscale and more contemporary after a $10 million face-lift, with polished brass and mahogany appointments, marble floors, and a $10 million art collection. The rooms and suites feature marble baths, large sound-proofed windows, fax machines, phones with voice mail, and coffeemakers. There are two restaurants (a steak house and a brasserie), an espresso bar, a lobby lounge, a fitness center, pool, and Jacuzzi; secretarial services are available. ♦ 9620 Airport Blvd (between W 98th and W 96th Sts). 310/337.2800, 800/647.6437 in CA, 800/228.9898 in the US; fax 310/216.6681. www.renaissancehotels.com ♿

7 FOUR POINTS SHERATON

$$$ Both business travelers and vacationers will find this 573-room hotel accommodating, especially with its 24-hour check-in/check-out feature that allows you a full day's stay no matter what time you arrive. Guest rooms are pleasantly furnished and chock full of extras such as Four Comfort beds with Sealy Posturepedic Plush Top mattresses, feather and down pillows, coffeemakers, irons and boards, and sleep-friendly blackout drapes. Wi-Fi hookups can be found throughout the property. Special executive-floor rooms come with all that plus Wi-Fi, complimentary water on arrival, and full American breakfasts. There are a couple of decent restaurants: **Palm Grill** ($$), where you can have breakfast, lunch, or dinner, a cup of Starbucks, a glass of Naked Juice, a slice of fantastic cheesecake, or a special anti–jet lag Body Clock meal (open 6AM-11PM); and **T.H. Brewsters,** a brew pub featuring an actual beer sommelier (no joke), light bar food, televised sporting events, and pop music (open 1PM-2AM). There's also 24-hour room service. The business and fitness centers are also open around the clock. For your recreational needs, there's an Olympic-size pool, a huge sundeck, and a billiards/game room. Free shuttle service to and from LAX is also part of the deal. ♦ 9750 Airport Blvd (at 98th St). 310/645.4600, 800-LAXHOTEL (direct), 800/325-3535; fax 310/649.7047. www.fourpointslax.com

EL SEGUNDO AND MANHATTAN, HERMOSA, AND REDONDO BEACHES

A jumble of pastel cottages, posh condos, and huge beachfront homes that were once summer getaways are now year-round residences in a series of permanent communities. **El Segundo** has the least-developed waterfront and is hemmed in by the airport and a huge oil refinery. With its extravagant houses, pricey apartment complexes, and upscale restaurants, **Manhattan Beach** is a magnet for an affluent society of both married couples and swinging singles. South of Manhattan Beach is **Hermosa Beach,** the prototypical beach town with its concentration of surfers, volleyballers, and sun worshippers. And farther south is **Redondo Beach,** a mixture of the well-heeled new and the slightly seedy old, with a wonderful pier and marina complex offering boutiques, shops, and eateries galore.

8 HOUSTON'S

★★$ One of the most popular places in the beach area, this casual, friendly restaurant serves old-fashioned American food with some newfangled twists. The menu ranges from simple (but juicy) hamburgers and ribs to creative dishes like tortilla soup, grilled chicken salad, eggless Caesar salad, and spinach-and-artichoke dip. The dining room is handsomely decked out, with dark maple and cherry wood accents, a stone floor, and a long, marble-topped bar. ◆ American ◆ Daily, lunch and dinner. 1550-A Rosecrans Ave (between Apollo and S Nash Sts), El Segundo. 310/643.7211. Also at 10250 Santa Monica Blvd (at Century Park W), Century City. 310/557.1285; 5921 Owensmouth Ave (at Oxnard), Woodland Hills. 818/348.1095; 320 S Arroyo Pkwy (at Del Mar Ave), Pasadena. 626/577.6001 &

9 THE BELAMAR

$$$ This hip, happening, and over-the-top hotel provides a pleasant place to stay if you want to be near the beach or airport. The attractive 127-room boutique property features modern styling, a friendly staff, and stunning rooms with lots of marble and tile, old-fashioned phones, work desks, luxurious bed coverings, high-count cotton sheets, flat-screen TVs, free high-speed Internet access, and plush robes. Bottled water is served with nightly turndown service, and a free *LA Times* is delivered each morning to your door. Amenities include a sparsely equipped fitness room, in-room spa treatments, and an attractive outdoor pool and Jacuzzi next to a pleasant courtyard. Complimentary shuttle service is provided to and from LAX and anywhere within a two-mile radius of the hotel. There's a well-landscaped hiking trail across Valley Drive that runs about four miles to Torrance. Belamar offers a variety of packages and specials but seems to cater mostly to meetings and convention groups. ◆ 3501 Sepulveda Blvd (at N Valley Dr), Manhattan Beach. 310/545.8466. www.thebelamar.com

10 MANHATTAN BEACH MARRIOTT

$$$ This 385-room hotel offers comfortable but not exceptional accommodations designed for the in-and-out business traveler, for whom there's a special "Room that Works" equipped with a big work desk, ergonomic chairs, data ports, and other aids of the trade. Amenities include a nine-hole golf course, shuttle service to the airport and to the beach (complimentary), concierge service, a full-service health club, and a pool. There's also Bleachers Sports Bar, the Terrace Restaurant (which is open for breakfast, lunch, and dinner), a lobby bar, and a Pizza Hut. ◆ 1400 Parkview Ave (east of Village Dr), Manhattan Beach. 310/546.7511, 800/228.9290; fax 310/546.7520. www.marriotthotels.com &

11 CAFE PIERRE

★★$$ More than 30 years old and still going strong, this popular eatery draws locals and out-of-towners who go for the fabulous French fare. Begin with the charcuterie and work your way through *steak au poivre* and other signature dishes. ◆ California/French Bistro ◆ M-F, lunch and dinner; Sa, Su, dinner. 317 Manhattan Beach Blvd (between N Morningside Dr and Valley Dr and N Highland Ave), Manhattan Beach. 310/545.5252. www.cafepierre.com

12 METLOX PLAZA

This 64,000-square-foot shopping village, named after the pottery factory that once stood there, houses boutiques and restaurants set around a charming courtyard highlighted by a large fireplace. Some interesting places to check out include the rather quirky **Buster & Sullivan,** which is about as over-the-top as it gets. We're talking a shop entirely for dogs. For starters, there's a deli counter filled with pastries that resemble people food, such as pretzels, cannolis, tarts, and cookies, but are made from canine-friendly ingredients. If that's not cutesy enough, there are dresses, sweaters, coats, toys (like a Jimmy Chew shoe to gnaw on), pillows, and other canine accessories. It's worth checking out even if you don't own a dog (310/802.1410, www.busterandsullivan.com).

Restaurants/Clubs: Red | Hotels: Purple | Shops: Orange | Outdoors/Parks: Green | Sights/Culture: Blue

There's also a trendy denim outlet called **True Religion** (310/406.3882, www.truereligionbrandjeans.com); a branch of the bakery **Le Pain Quotidien** (310/545.6422, www.lepainquotidien.com); **pomodoro**, an Italian restaurant chain (310/545.5401); **Deliboys,** a massive deli where you can eat in or go for take-out food (310/441.2483, www.labite.com or www.DeliBoys.com); a branch of the stationery shop **Papyrus** (310/802.1209); **Petros,** a really great Greek restaurant (see below; a special relaxation oasis called **Trilogy Spa,** a day spa (www.trilogyspa.com) (see below); **Cold Stone Creamery** (www.coldstonecreamery.com); and an extraordinarily eccentric hotel called **Shade** (see below). 451 Manhattan Beach Blvd (at North Valley Dr)

Also within Metlox Plaza:

SHADE

$$$ This unconventional breezy little 38-room boutique hotel attracts the privileged, entitled demographic of the Paris Hilton degree, along with the new young, restless, and beautiful Hollywood "rat pack," or what we like to call "the just barely out of puberty crowd." Fashioned by the Emmy Award–winning "lifestylist" designer from the Discovery Home Channel, Christopher Lowell, the hotel oozes with outside-the-box amenities. Which is exactly what Michael Zislis, the entrepreneurial proprietor, intended. "We're over the top," he boasts. "We want to be different. It's all about having an unforgettable experience with great service." The raffish décor commingles seaside casualness with exaggerated lavishness. The gorgeous lobby provides a fun setting for revelers with its bustling bar that sees nonstop action nightly after 5PM, and an adjacent outdoor patio where drinks, small bites, and breakfast are served. There is a "virtual" restaurant, which basically translates into a menu (you won't see a kitchen) of small bites that's available from noon to late evening, and a full breakfast menu available in your room, the lobby, or out on the patio (which is preferable, since there are no real dining tables in the lobby area, just sofas and side tables). Each finely tuned room is designed for utmost comfort with king-size Tempur-Pedic beds covered by 400-thread-count Mascioni linens, feather duvets, a "pillow library" with a choice of options on which to lay your head, and a table that can be rolled up from the foot of the bed. Of course, there are flat-screen Panasonic TVs and CD and DVD players (and free movies at the front desk). Rooms are equipped with chromatherapy illumination systems that provide customized lighting at the touch of a dial (amber, blue, lavender, and green), and a Sanijet spa tub built for two (hidden behind frosted-glass shoji-like screens) complete with color therapy and rain showers complement the bathrooms. There are also Lavazza espresso machines (a real treat for java junkies, which we find particularly pleasing). Some rooms have cyclone gas fireplaces with gas jets that propel flames in spiral tubing. When you're not trotting off to the beach, you can head up to the inviting rooftop Skydeck for a swim in the stainless steel pool, sunbathing, a yoga class, or a session on the spinning bike. One of our pet perks is the availability of complimentary strand cruiser bicycles that provide a healthy, hassle-free means of transportation to the beach or around town. It's not easy finding a parking space for cars in this bustling beach community. ♦ 1221 Valley Dr (at Manhattan Beach Blvd), Manhattan Beach. 310/546.4995, 866/98SHADE. www.shadehotel.com

TRILOGY SPA

This sweet oasis, powered by heady Polynesian ingredients and therapies, provides the perfect spot to zone out, relax, and succumb to amazing head-to-toe treatments by exceptional therapists. It also boasts one of the nicest spa staffs, who truly go out of their way to please. A men's facial proved outstanding—he looked years younger. An 80-minute hand, hot stone, and acupressure massage applied by a skillful therapist made us swoon. There are two peaceful relaxation areas: one indoors, the other on a rooftop deck where couples can snuggle in oversize lounges. Even the locker room exceeds the bar with complimentary offerings like body scrubs du jour to use freely, soaking tubs, gads of toiletries, and a steam for men and sauna for women. Products are naturally scented with ingredients like plumeria, and effective. ♦ 310/760.0044. Also at 1301 Manhattan Ave, Hermosa Beach. 310/318.3511. www.trilogyspa.com

PETROS

★★★$$$ Great Greek, we never expected to find a Greek restaurant this good so far from Greece! We're talking attractively presented gourmet dishes such as feta-crusted Colorado rack of lamb, or Horiatiki flatbread pizza like none we've ever tasted done with a thin, crispy dough topped with vine-ripe tomatoes, olives, avocado, onions, capers, and Epirus feta; also amazing are the Greek sea bass filet, grilled swordfish, and assorted delicacies prepared by chef/owner Petros, an entrepreneur who decided he'd rather cook, and he does it well. Everything on the menu is great—trust us, we tried it all. The baklava and *bougasta*—vanilla bean seminola custard with house-made ice cream—are to die for. ♦ Greek ♦ Daily, lunch and dinner. ♦ Reservations suggested. 310/545.4100. www.petrosrestaurant.com

13 ROCK 'N FISH

★★★$$ This San Francisco/New York–style restaurant serves—forks-down—the best fresh fish in town. Melt-in-your-mouth halibut, salmon, tuna, and swordfish are simply grilled and delicious. Of course, there are many other choices, from soups, salads, and sandwiches to assorted shrimp or Kapalua ribs, steaks, and more—all fantastic, thanks to fussy hands-on owner Michael Zislis, who also owns **Shade** hotel. Signature dishes include teriyaki chicken, sticky rice, and Navy Grog. There is seating on an outdoor patio (with a retractable roof) or indoors beside a large, bustling bar. ◆ Fish House ◆ Daily, lunch and dinner. Reservations essentials. 120 Manhattan Beach Blvd, Manhattan Beach. 310/379.9900. www.rocknfishmb.com

13 AVENUE

★★★$$$ This urban, uptown–style restaurant serves great food in a sophisti-cated setting. Menu choices include heirloom tomato gazpacho, seared foie gras, roasted pepper–mascarpone terrine, wild salmon, swordfish, braised short ribs, leg of lamb, and more perfectly prepared options. ◆ Continental/American ◆ W-Su, dinner; Su, brunch. Reservations advised. 1141 Manhattan Ave (at 11th Pl), Manhattan Beach. 310/802.1973. www.avenuemb.com

14 SOUTH BAY GALLERIA

Vaulted skylights, fountains, and tropical shrubbery provide the perfect setting for this yuppie-centric shopping sanctuary. There are even "roving ambassadors" who help consumers with their packages, wheelchairs, or children; a Kid's Club that provides diversions for youngsters while the parents shop 'til they drop; and The Galleria Gaitors, a walking club that teaches you how to get more exercise out of your shopping sprees. You can max out your credit card at **Nordstrom, Abercrombie & Fitch, Ann Taylor, Nine West,** and several cool boutiques. ◆ Daily. 1815 Hawthorne Blvd (at Artesia Blvd), Redondo Beach, 1/4 mile west of the 405 Fwy. 310/371.7546. www.southbaygalleria.com

15 HERMOSA BEACH PIER STRAND

This area near the fishing pier provides a charming, palm tree–lined walkway for strolling along with benches, cafés, and restaurants. Merchants include **Lapperts** (29 Pier Ave; 310/318.3953), the Hawaiian ice-cream vendor that scoops out the best sundaes this side of the islands; **Shirt Tales** (34 Pier Ave;

310/379.1073), a tiny but well-stocked T-shirt shop; and **Treasure Chest** (50 Pier Ave; 310/372.5644), a cool vintage outlet with far-out LA styles. Farther out on the pier is a tackle shop (310/372.2124) that rents equip-ment and sells bait. ◆ Pier: daily, 24 hours. Pier Ave (between Hermosa Ave and Hermosa Beach Pier), Hermosa Beach

Along the Hermosa Beach Pier Strand:

IL BOCCACCIO

★★$$ Pungent scents of garlic and aged Italian cheeses permeate this old-world trattoria, where good food is complemented by rich wood, white linens, and attentive service. The menu offers pastas, pizzas, great polenta, seafood, and more. ◆ Italian ◆ Daily, dinner. 39 Pier Ave. 310/376.0211

CAFÉ BONAPARTE FRENCH BAKERY CAFÉ

Hearty sandwiches, soups, and salads and yummy desserts, pastries, muffins, coffees, teas, and juices can be taken to go or enjoyed on the adjacent patio (where a big basket filled with books keeps the kids entertained). ◆ Daily, 6AM-midnight. 37 Pier Ave. 310/374.0026

THE LIGHTHOUSE CAFE

This is one of the best and oldest jazz clubs in Los Angeles. The fine music and top-flight performers have kept its doors open since the 1950s. Enjoy a weekend brunch enhanced by live jazz. ◆ Cover. Daily. 30 Pier Ave. 310/372.6911

HENNESSEY'S TAVERN

★★$ Big with the beach crowd, who throng here from dawn through midnight, this place is known for its unpretentious yet eclectic offerings: Irish nachos, quesadillas, Southern fried chicken, Caesar salad, burgers, sandwiches, and drinks. Rooftop dining overlooks the ocean. The lower-level bar is a happening watering spot, with its TV and friendly barkeeps. ◆ American/Irish/Mexican ◆ Daily, breakfast, lunch, and dinner. 8 Pier Ave. 310/372.5759

THE BEACH HOUSE

$$ A nifty spot, smack on a sandy beach along the picturesque 26-mile Strand, this 96-room hotel is centrally located within walking distance of boutiques, lively bars, and restaurants. Great oceanfront rooms called "lofts" boast balconies from which to ogle buff-bodied volleyball players competing on the beach below. Each room sports a

---

Restaurants/Clubs: **Red** | Hotels: **Purple** | Shops: **Orange** | Outdoors/Parks: **Green** | Sights/Culture: **Blue**

wood-burning fireplace, Frette linens and bathrooms, a microwave, stove, refrigerator, and coffeemaker, and a living area separated by a king-size bed. Free extras include wireless Internet anywhere in the hotel plus a satisfying continental breakfast that includes great New York–style bagels, freshly squeezed orange juice, and other nifty morning fare. Guests can also order food to go from local eateries. Top-quality spa treatments are available through WholeLife Consultants (310/614.7455) in your room or in a special little spa suite on the second floor. During our visit, a sports massage was outstanding. There is also a tiny fitness room with an adjacent outdoor Jacuzzi. You can even learn how to play volleyball from a professional player/trainer for a fee. ♦ 1300 The Strand, Hermosa Beach. 310/374.3001, 888/895.4559. www.beach-house.com

15 COMEDY & MAGIC CLUB

Some of comedy's finest—Jay Leno, Rodney Dangerfield, Robin Williams, Garry Shandling—occasionally hit the stage here to try out new material. But even the lesser-known comedians and magicians at this Art Deco spot will keep you giggling. ♦ Cover. Hours vary; call ahead for show times. Reservations required. 1018 Hermosa Ave (between 10th St and Pier Ave), Hermosa Beach. 310/372.1193

16 SPLASH

★★$$ At this chic dining spot overlooking the Marina, Moroccan-born chef Malik Mekibes creates miracles with his sophisticated fusion cuisine. Start with an exotic appetizer like dim sum filled with truffles and foie gras and move along to the Chilean sea bass steamed in a banana leaf with date purée, saffron-scented apple, and quince compote, or the horseradish-encrusted salmon served on Thai rice with a heady vodka orange sauce. The glass-walled dining room is a dramatic leitmotif of purple, gold, and teal under a metal grid ceiling with a floor-to-ceiling aquarium, whimsical food art, and great ocean views. ♦ Eclectic California/Mediterranean ♦ Daily, breakfast, lunch, and dinner. Reservations recommended. Valet parking available. 350 N Harbor Dr (at Beryl St), Redondo Beach. 310/798.5348 &

17 PORTOFINO HOTEL AND YACHT CLUB

$$$ This spiffy 46-year-old Redondo Beach landmark looks great after an $11 million head-to-toe face-lift. Each of the 161 guest rooms reflects the hotel's waterfront location with soft cream-colored walls and furnishings. Best accommodations face the water. Amenities include a stunning lobby where complimentary coffee is served each morning, a tiny workout room, an inviting outdoor pool and Jacuzzi, and a freestanding restaurant located across the driveway, overlooking a marina, called **Baleen** (★★$$$), open daily for breakfast, lunch, and dinner. ♦ 160 Portofino Way (west of N Harbor Dr), Redondo Beach. 310/379.8481; fax 310/372.7329, 800/468.4192. www.hotelportofino.com

17 REDONDO BEACH PIER & FISHERMAN'S WHARF

This sprawling waterfront commercial center attracts tourists and locals who come to stroll the boardwalk, shop, or dine in an assortment of casual and high-end restaurants. There are dozens of places to buy fresh fish to cook at home, T-shirts, bathing suits, souvenirs, and clothing or to grab quick bites of take-out food.

Places of note within the complex include **El Torito,** 100 G Fisherman's Wharf (310/376.0547), part of a chain that serves *muy bueno* Mexican fare; **Hats & Things,** 208 Fisherman's Wharf (310/376.3203), the place to buy really cool caps and hats; **New Starboard Attitude,** 202 Fisherman's Wharf (310/379.5144), a super hip jazz/blues club; **Old Tony's,** 210 Fisherman's Wharf (310/374.1442), a landmark Italian eatery; and **Zeppy's Pizza,** 203 Fisherman's Wharf (310/372.8364), for a great slice of the pie. ♦ Coral Way (west of S Catalina Ave), Redondo Beach. www.redondopier.com

17 RIVIERA VILLAGE

We're talking hip and happening at this quaint shopping area chock-a-block with shops, boutiques, restaurants, and artsy-crafty outlets. It's especially fun on the first Thursday after Thanksgiving, when all the establishments turn on the holiday cheer complete with food, drink, carolers, musicians, and even Santa himself. Shops include Encore Books, Inge's Fashions, antiques galleries, Harmony Works, and another 100 or so outlets.
♦ Follow S Catalina Ave, one block east of the beach, to the southwest corner of Redondo Beach between Palos Verdes Blvd and Ave 1. www.rivieravillage.org

18 PALOS VERDES INN

$$$ This 108-room hotel is only three blocks from the beach. The newly decorated guest rooms are attractive and simple in shades of blue, sandy yellow, and beige; some feature four-poster beds and a Southwestern motif. There's also a restaurant (which offers room service from 8AM to 11PM), an enclosed outdoor pool and spa, complimentary bike rentals, and passes to a nearby fitness center. ♦ 1700 S Pacific Coast Hwy (at Palos Verdes Blvd), Redondo Beach. 310/316.4211, 800/421.9241 in the US; fax 310/316.4863. www.palosverdesinn.com

19 ALPINE VILLAGE

Quaff a stein of beer and down huge portions of German-Swiss food while listening to the band in the beer garden at this replica of an Alpine village. Twenty-four shops offer an array of goods. For Bavarian fun, go for Oktoberfest—an entire month of food and beer-guzzling activities. ♦ M-Th, 11AM–7PM; Sa, 10AM–8PM; Su, 11AM–8PM. Dancing: daily until midnight. 833 W Torrance Blvd (between Hamilton and S Vermont Aves). 310/327.2483, 310/323.6520. www.alpinevillage.com

Within Alpine Village:

ALPINE VILLAGE

★★$$ This restaurant serves a menu of German (sauerbraten, knockwurst) and American (half chicken, steak, catch of the day) fare. ♦ Daily, lunch and dinner.

PALOS VERDES PENINSULA

In 1913, New York banker Frank Vanderlip bought most of this hilly peninsula and planned to turn it into a millionaires' colony. Slightly less ambitious developments began in the 1920s, leading to the creation of a series of exclusive residential enclaves and modest commercial centers, all in very conservative taste. Ranch houses alternate with Spanish haciendas, horse trails, and lovely hiking paths amid forests of eucalyptus trees. The hills are a succession of 13 marine uplift terraces created by Palos Verdes's slow rise from the ocean floor. www.palosverdes.com

20 DEL AMO PLAZA

With more than 350 stores in 2.6 million square feet of space, this is one of the largest retail centers of its kind. There are several chain stores and independent fashion stores, more than 55 restaurants, and dramatic interior spaces. ♦ Daily. Bounded by Madrona Ave and Hawthorne Blvd, and Sepulveda Blvd and Fashion Way, Torrance. 310/542.8525. www.delamo.fashioncenter.com

21 CHEF SHAFER'S DEPOT

★★$$ With whitewashed brick walls, dark wood, classic tilework, and Moderne-style sconces, this popular eatery was carved out of a 1912 Red Car electric railway station. Chef Shafer's rather offbeat and adventurous menu includes items like crispy Thai dyed chicken (a chicken breast covered in a blend of sweet spices on a bed of pasta), mac and cheese with buttermilk chicken fingers, and bento boxes filled with sweet treats. ♦ California Eclectic

♦ M-F, lunch and dinner; Sa, dinner. Reservations recommended. 1250 Cabrillo Ave (at Torrance Blvd), Torrance. 310/787.7501. www.depotrestaurant.com

22 MALAGA COVE PLAZA

In their 1922 plan for Palos Verdes, Charles H. Cheney and the Olmsted brothers envisioned four area community centers. This was the only one built. Designed by **Webber, Staunton & Spaulding** in 1924, it is a Spanish Revival design of two-story shops in an arcade. The plaza has a picturesque brick bridge over Via Chico and a fountain inspired by the Fountain of Neptune in Bologna, Italy. ♦ 200 Palos Verdes Dr W (at Via Corta), Palos Verdes Estates

23 RESTAURANT CHRISTINE

★★$$ Chef/owner Christine Brown has beefed up this cheerful bistro with Tucson hues of red, green, and orange, and offers an eclectic mix of Mediterranean, Pacific Rim, and California fare. Signature dishes include grilled lobster mac and cheese, chopped Greek salad, rosemary chicken with garlic mashed potatoes, mushroom ravioli, and fresh fish from around the world (like Costa Rican red silk snapper and African Lake Victoria perch). ♦ International ♦ M-F, lunch and dinner; Sa, Su, dinner. Reservations recommended. 24530 Hawthorne Blvd (between Newton and W 244th St), Torrance. 310/373.1952. www.restaurantchristine.com

24 LOMITA RAILROAD MUSEUM

Housed in a replica of the 19th-century Greenwood Station in Wakefield, Massachusetts, this museum displays memorabilia from the steam era of railroading. An impeccably restored 1902 steam locomotive and a 1910 wooden caboose flank the station. Both are open to the public. The annex across the street offers picnic benches, a 1913 boxcar, and an oil tanker that can be rented for special events. ♦ Admission. Th-Su, 10AM–5PM. W 250th St and Woodward Ave, Lomita. 310/326.6255. www.lomita-rr.org

25 SOUTH COAST BOTANIC GARDENS

Until 1956 this site was a diatomaceous earth mine. When mining activity ceased, the trash dumping began—3.5 million tons were poured in. Starting in 1960, though, the Los Angeles Department of Arboreta and Botanic Gardens initiated a landscaping program, and today the beautiful 87-acre gardens are a model experiment in land reclamation,

---

Restaurants/Clubs: Red | Hotels: Purple | Shops: Orange | Outdoors/Parks: Green | Sights/Culture: Blue

containing mature specimens from all continents except Antarctica. There are also horticultural and botanical displays, a gift shop, gardening workshops offered throughout the year, and a picnic area. ◆ Admission. Daily. 26300 Crenshaw Blvd (between Rolling Hills Rd and Palos Verdes Dr N), Rolling Hills Estates. 310/544.6815. www.southcoastbotanicgardens.org

26 DRUM BARRACKS CIVIL WAR MUSEUM

This is the last remaining building of **Camp Drum,** a 7,000-soldier Union Army outpost that closed in 1871. Although California sympathized with the Confederacy during the Civil War, this large Union military presence kept the state in the blue ranks. The barracks have been refurbished as a museum of Civil War memorabilia. ◆ Admission. Tours: Tu-Sa. 1052 Banning Blvd (between E Opp and E L Sts). 310/548.7509

27 WAYFARER'S CHAPEL

Architect **Lloyd Wright**'s most visited building occupies a prominent hillside location overlooking the ocean. The 1946 chapel is the national monument to Emmanuel Swedenborg, a Swedish theologian and mystic. A redwood frame that blends nicely with the surrounding redwood grove supports the glass structure. ◆ Daily. Services: Su. 5755 Palos Verdes Dr S (between Narcissa Dr and Barkentine Rd), Rancho Palos Verdes. 310/377.1650

28 TRUMP NATIONAL GOLF COURSE

"The Donald" teed off many times here when it was known as Ocean Trails. And he's still playing the course, only now he owns it. Trump bought the property in 2002 and spent the next three years designing the 7,300-yard, par 71 (black tees), rather posh public course. Perched on a cluster of cliffs, the $250 million Donald J. Trump Signature Design greens is typical Trump—luxurious—with crushed white marble lining walls of massive bunkers, lakes, waterfalls, a practice range, a 45,000-square-foot clubhouse, and even food service available via a GPS system placed on every golf cart. There are also three restaurants on premises: **Trump's** ($$$), a fine dining room done in French Victorian style with 180-degree views of the Pacific Ocean and four miles of rugged California coastline, open for dinner only, W-Su (reservations a must); **Café Pacific** ($$), an upscale casual dining venue, also providing panoramic ocean views, with a unique frescoed ceiling and carved limestone fireplace, open daily for breakfast, lunch, and dinner, and Sunday brunch; and the **High Tide Bar & Lounge** ($$$), offering a casual atmosphere, golfer-targeted menu, and adult beverages in a room with a view as well as several flat-screen televisions, open daily for

three squares. The TV celebrity, real-estate mogul, entrepreneur man-about-town is also building 50 homes on the Estates at Trump National with price tags of $5.2 million to $15 million. Just in case you were thinking of relocating. ◆ Open to the public daily. Tee times may be booked 2 weeks in advance; carts are optional. Greens fees range from $165-$250 M-Th, $215-$375 Su and holidays, and include carts and driving range; call 310/303.3245, 310/303.3240, or 310/303.3241. 1 Ocean Trails Dr, Rancho Palos Verdes. 310/265.5000; fax 310/265.5522. www.trumpgolf.com

LOS ANGELES HARBOR

In 1876, the first railroad arrived in Los Angeles, but the city still lacked access to the sea. Despite its shallow, unprotected harbor, San Pedro (pronounced by locals as San *Pee*-dro) outmaneuvered Santa Monica for federal funding and became the main port of entry for the emerging metropolis. Work began in 1899 on a new breakwater and port expansion. In 1909, LA annexed San Pedro and Wilmington, creating the shoestring strip (at places only a half-mile wide) from downtown to the harbor, which provided for a seaport and transportation route within city limits. Today's harbor is the busiest import and export trade port in the nation, a hub of industry (notably oil refineries and aircraft plants), and the foremost port of call in Southern California for passenger vessels.

At the center of the harbor lies **Terminal Island,** linked to San Pedro by the Vincent Thomas Bridge and to Long Beach by the Gerald Desmond Bridge. The streets of downtown San Pedro retain much of the flavor of their colorful past as a seafarer's port town. The region's commercial fishing fleet employs many mariners of Portuguese, Greek, Serbian, and Croatian descent, resulting in an area rich in ethnically diverse shops and restaurants.

29 VINCENT THOMAS BRIDGE

Spanning the main channel between San Pedro and Terminal Island, this 6,500-foot-long turquoise suspension bridge clears the water by 185 feet so military planes can fly under it.

30 HOLIDAY INN

$$ You can't beat the rates at this pleasant 60-room European-style hotel. First of all there's free parking. All rooms have coffeemakers, refrigerators, work desks, Internet gadgets, and of course TVs. There's a fitness room, pool, and the Club 111 Restaurant. ◆ 111 S Gaffey St (between Second and First Sts). 310/514.1414, 800/248.3188. www.holidayinnsanpedro.com

31 PAPADAKIS TAVERNA

★$$ If the mood is right, the waiters will dance in this lively, popular restaurant.

◆ Greek ◆ Daily, dinner. Reservations required. 301 W Sixth St (at S Centre St). 310/548.1186

32 LOS ANGELES MARITIME MUSEUM

A nautical history collection is appropriately housed in an old ferry building, refurbished by Pulliam & Matthews. Much of the old ferry gear remains, giving visitors a sense of imminent departure. Museum collections include ship models, the most impressive of which is a 16-foot scale model of the *Titanic*, fashioned from cardboard and matchsticks by a 14-year-old boy. The Naval Deck is replete with Navy memorabilia, including the bridge of the *Los Angeles*. ◆ Free. Tu-Su. Sampson Way (just south of E Sixth St). 310/548.7618

33 PORTS O' CALL VILLAGE

Nineteenth-century New England, a Mediterranean fishing village, and early California live again in this shopping and eating complex. It's a fun way to spend a day wandering, browsing through boutiques and quaint shops, and there are plenty of benches on which to sit when you're tired out. Check out the **African American Gift Shop** (Berth 77 P-6, 310/521.0203) for souvenirs and colorful outfits, or **Arts 'N Music Micci Collection** (Berth 77 P-3, 310/519.7744, www.artsNmusic.com) for cool shades and laser crystal engraving and collectibles. The **Village Boat House** offers daily cruises of the harbor area, where visitors can see the inner harbor, yacht harbor, freighter operations, scrapping yards, and the Coast Guard base. ◆ Tour hours vary with the season; call for hours and information. Nagoya Way (between Timms and Sampson Ways). 310/831.0287

Within Ports O' Call Village:

SPIRIT CRUISES

This outfit offers dinner cruises (Prime Rib Dinner Cruise, BBQ Cruise, and Buffet Sunset/Moonlight Party Cruise), whale-watching excursions, and harbor tours as well as special-event voyages. ◆ 310/548.8080. www.spiritmarine.com

PORTS O'CALL RESTAURANT

★★★$$ This restaurant offers one of the best Sunday brunches in the South Bay. The buffet fare is delicious and the harbor view mesmerizing. But the food's good every day, especially the filet mignon salad made with fresh garden greens and tender beef. The barkeep makes a mean margarita, too. ◆ Daily, 11AM-10PM. Berth 76. 310/833.9280

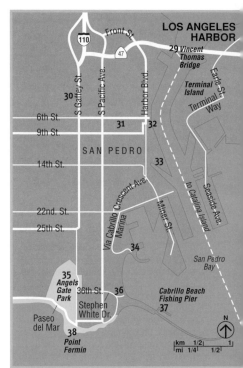

SAN PEDRO FISH MARKET

Pick up some freshly caught fish to cook at home from this little market, one of many within the complex. ◆ Daily, 11AM-8:30PM. 310/832.4251

BOARDWALK GRILL

★$ A cool place to stop for a bite. Have a burger, BBQ ribs and chicken, fish and chips, a sandwich or a salad, and relax. ◆ Daily, lunch and dinner. Berth 77 P-25, 310/519.751

34 MADEO RISTORANTE

★★$$$ A larger, more glamorous version of the Westside original, this restaurant serves great pasta, veal, and Florentine steak. ◆ Italian ◆ M-F, lunch and dinner; Sa, Su, dinner. Reservations recommended. 295 Whaler's Walk (east of Via Cabrillo Marina). 310/521.5333

35 FORT MCARTHUR RESERVATION AND ANGELS GATE PARK

The US Air Force still occupies part of this reservation (the fort dates back to 1888), but nearly 65 acres have been turned into a park and museum. The 20-acre park surrounding the **Korean Bell of Friendship** (a replica of a bronze bell made in AD 771, presented to the US by Korea during the 1976 Bicentennial celebration) offers picnic sites and a spectacular view of the Pacific and Point Fermin. A **military museum** preserves the workings (minus the guns) of the battery used as the biggest West Coast defense fortification during World War II, and also offers guided tours of the Port of Los Angeles control tower, by reservation. ♦ Free. Park: daily. Museum: Tu, Th, Sa, Su, noon-5PM. 3601 S Gaffey St (between Paseo del Mar and 30th St). 310/548.2631; e-mail: curator-ftmac@juno.com. www.ftmac.org

36 CABRILLO MARINE AQUARIUM

A multimillion-dollar renovation of this aquarium saw the addition of an **Exploration Center** tailored to children. The youngsters can observe nature, work on experiments, and even dress like scientists. An aquatic nursery provides a nurturing area for young sea animals: grunion, garibaldi, and white sea bass. Children will also love the imaginative displays of marine life in this museum, designed by **Frank Gehry** in 1981. To emphasize the spirit of fun, Gehry created a village-like cluster of small buildings housing an aquarium, classrooms, and a theater in a dramatically enclosed, child-friendly playground with chain-link fencing. Visitors also can handle tide-pool creatures in a "touch tank." For information on whale-watching tours (offered from late December through early April), call 562/832.4444. ♦ Free; parking fee. Tu-Su. 3720 Stephen White Dr (at Oliver Vickery Cir Way). 310/548.7562. www.cabrilloaq.org

37 CABRILLO BEACH FISHING PIER

🅟 A shop on the 1,500-foot-long publicly owned fishing pier sells equipment and live bait, but equipment rentals are not available. No license or fee is required to cast your fishing line. ♦ East of Oliver Vickery Cir Way

38 POINT FERMIN PARK

🅟 The 37 landscaped acres of this park along the palisades overlook the Pacific Ocean and Los Angeles Harbor. The lookout point has coin-operated telescopes, and the **whale-watching station** offers information on the California gray whales' annual winter migration to the Gulf of California. The Victorian Eastlake-style **lighthouse**, constructed in 1874 from bricks and lumber brought around Cape Horn by sailing ship, is not open to the public. The lighthouse used oil lamps approximating 2,100 candlepower until 1925, when electric power was installed. ♦ Free. Daily. Paseo del Mar and S Gaffey St. 310/548.7756

LONG BEACH

Situated east of the harbor, Long Beach, California's fifth-largest city, was founded in 1880 along five and a half miles of coastline. From the sandy strand south of the city, you can see the tropical camouflage of palm-clad islands created to conceal several still-producing offshore oil wells—each faux island covers 10 acres of sound-proofed wells. The **Long Beach Harbor,** which opened in 1911, is a major port for electric machinery and Alaskan crude oil, and a significant West Coast port of entry.

Devastated by the 1933 earthquake, Long Beach has been rediscovering its unique combination of rustic seaside charm and urban sophistication in recent years. A complete urban renewal has brought trendy restaurants, nightspots, and shops. Long Beach hasn't completely lost touch with its past, either: Several historic landmarks and districts still remain outside the city center.

A free Red Passport shuttle service takes passengers to the city's points of interest, and in the downtown area, guides (easy to spot in their khaki pants, red shirts, and caps) offer free advice about local attractions. ♦ The LA Rapid Transit District's Blue Line light rail runs from Long Beach's Transit Mall (W First St and Pacific Ave) to downtown LA daily from 5:30AM to 8PM; for more information, call 213/620.RAIL

39 RANCHO LOS CERRITOS

The romance of the old rancho days is recalled in this renovated 1844 Monterey-style adobe. Don Juan Temple built the two-story residence on part of the 1790 Nieto land grant. Although later expanded, the house remains furnished as it was between 1866 and 1881, when the Bixby family used it as headquarters for their ranching empire. In addition to the children's room, the foreman's bedroom, and a blacksmith's shop, a wing features memorabilia of rancho life and a research library on California history. Some of the original walks and trees planted in the mid-19th century remain in the restored five-acre garden. ♦ Free. W-Su; Tours: Sa, Su. 4600 Virginia Rd (north of E San Antonio Dr). 562/424.9423

40 BIXBY HOUSE

One of the few remaining examples of English architect **Ernest Coxhead**'s residential work, this 1895 house was built for a member of the Bixby family. The wood-shingle Victorian has Craftsman design elements. It's a private residence. ♦ 11 La Linda Dr (between E Bixby Rd and Long Beach Blvd)

41 LONG BEACH MUNICIPAL AIRPORT

This airport is served by American Airlines, Alaska Air, JetBlue, and America West Airlines. Private bus companies provide transportation to Long Beach, and to destinations within Los Angeles and Orange Counties. ♦ 4100 Donald

Douglas Dr (off Lakewood Blvd, between E Springs and Carson Sts). 562/570.2640

42 EL DORADO PARK

This 800-acre recreational facility is divided into two sections. **El Dorado East Regional Park** is an unstructured activity area containing meadows and several lakes (the largest rents paddleboats) where fishing is permitted, plus more than four miles of bicycle and roller-skating paths and an archery range. **El Dorado West City Park** offers an 18-hole golf course, night-lit tennis courts, roller-skate rentals, six baseball diamonds, a children's playground, a band shell, and a branch of the Long Beach Public Library. The **El Dorado Nature Center,** located in the east section, is an 80-acre bird sanctuary. ♦ Vehicle admission fee. Parks: daily. Nature Center: Tu-Su. 7550 E Spring St (between San Gabriel River Fwy and Studebaker Rd). Parks information 562/429.6310, Nature Center information 562/421.9431

43 DRAKE PARK

Almost every architectural style known is found in this Long Beach historic district. ♦ Daisy Ave and Loma Vista Dr

44 RANCHO LOS ALAMITOS

Another part of the original 1790 Nieto land grant, this rancho's adobe house has been enlarged several times since it was built in 1806. The interior is very much as it was when the Bixby family occupied it during the 1920s and 1930s. The grounds contain cow and horse barns, a blacksmith's shop, and a lush five-acre garden planted with native California cacti and succulents, herbs, and exquisite Chinese and Japanese wisteria. Visitors to the buildings must join docent-led tours. ♦ Free. W-Su. 6400 Bixby Hill Rd (just east of Palos Verdes Ave). 562/431.3541

45 BONO'S

★★★$$$ Sonny and Cher's famous daughter spearheads this hip and trendy California-style eatery. The décor is pure funk, with a glass-enclosed dining area, open ceiling with deep purple hues, and plenty of space between tables. As you might expect, the celebrity kid attracts her share of young Tinseltowners along with the usual complement of know-where-to-go stargazers. The food's good, too, and appeals to every appetite, with entrées ranging from BBQ shrimp to grilled ahi to New York steaks. ♦ California ♦ Daily, lunch and dinner. Reservations suggested. 4901 E Second St (two blocks from Corona Ave). 562/434.9501. www.bonoslongbeach.com

46 NAPLES

At the same time Abbot Kinney was creating his version of Venice in LA County, another American romantic, Arthur Parson, was dredging Alamitos Bay to create his own picture-perfect pastiche of Italy, building cottages on curving streets and along canals spanned by quaint footbridges. By the end of the 1920s, the community now known as Naples was complete. Today this residential neighborhood of Long Beach seems more American than Italian. The perimeter of the island is bordered by walkways that overlook the bay and a small beach. In the center, **Colonnade Park** is encircled by the Rivo Alto Canal. Although accessible by car, the island's true charm is seen only by the pedestrian.

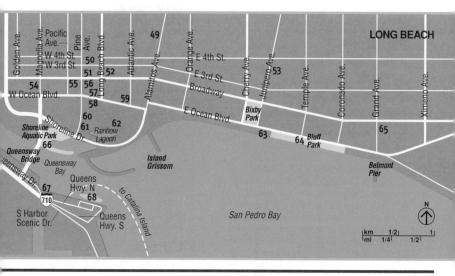

Restaurants/Clubs: Red | Hotels: Purple | Shops: Orange | Outdoors/Parks: Green | Sights/Culture: Blue

46 THE GONDOLA GETAWAY

Take a one-hour cruise on an authentic Venetian gondola—with costumed gondolier—threading through the canals of Naples. Reserve months in advance for December (Christmas lights) and February (Valentine's Day), and one month ahead in summer. ♦ 5437 E Ocean Blvd (between 55th and 54th Pls). 562/433.9595

47 MORRY'S OF NAPLES

This long-established wine and liquor store offers popular wine tastings, served with cheese and meat plates, Tuesdays through Saturdays. There are also winemaker samplings the last Saturday of every month. And you can drop by anytime to enjoy any of 36 wines by the glass. 5764 E Second St (between Campo Walk and Ravenna Dr). 562/433.0405

48 ALAMITOS BAY LANDING

On this finger of land surrounded by Long Beach Marina boat slips, several chain restaurants, including the **Crab Pot** (562/430.0272), **Buster's Beach House Restaurant and Long Board Bar** (562/598.9431), **Khoury's** (562/598.6800), and **Joe's Crab Shack** (562/594.6551), serve standard steak and fresh seafood fare. ♦ 182 Marina Dr (south of E Second St). 562/799.3870. Aqua-link water taxis are available to transport you anywhere around the harbor.

At Alamitos Bay Landing:

STAR PARTY CRUISES

Live reggae bands play on weekend cruises, and a Sunday champagne brunch features blues and jazz musicians aboard a 100-passenger boat. ♦ 140 Marina Dr (south of E Second St). 562/431.6833

49 MUSEUM OF LATIN AMERICAN ART (MoLAA)

Add a little salsa to your art appreciation at this thriving museum. Founded by Dr. Robert Gumbiner in November 1996, MoLAA is the only museum in the western US catering to contemporary Latin American art. Located in the **East Village Arts District,** in the former Balboa Amusement Producing Company building (where silent films were once shot), MoLAA houses both a permanent collection and traveling exhibitions. A high vaulted ceiling and wooden floors, left over from a time when the building was a Hippodrome for skaters, provides a fitting showcase for the exhibits. There's the perfunctory museum gift shop, as well as a welcoming restaurant that's open from 11AM to 3PM called **Viva** that dishes out Latin American fare. ♦ Tu-Su. Admission except on F. 628 Alamitos Ave (at Seventh St). 562/437.1680; fax 562/437.7043

50 LONG BEACH MURAL

This 1936 Federal Arts Project mosaic by Henry Nord was originally in the now-demolished Municipal Auditorium. It now sits at the south end of City Place. ♦ E Third St (between Long Beach Blvd and Pine Ave)

51 BLUE CAFE

How hip can you get? Blues bands, billiards, and a delightful café combine to make this an entertaining experience. ♦ Cover. Daily. 210 Promenade (between E Broadway and E Maple Way). 562/983.7111

52 ACRES OF BOOKS

Ray Bradbury acclaims this vast used-books emporium as a treasure. Nearly one million books line the miles of shelves in a 1922 Art Deco–style building. ♦ Tu-Sa. 240 Long Beach Blvd (between E Maple Way and E Third St). 562/437.6980

53 CARROLL PARK

The large houses here were built in the 1910s, and the bungalows in the 1920s. ♦ Bounded by Wisconsin and Junipero Aves, and E Third and E Fourth Sts

54 LONG BEACH HILTON

$$$ This 397-room mid-rise hotel in the World Trade Center offers a health club, an outdoor pool and Jacuzzi, 14 banquet rooms, a lobby bar, and a restaurant. Free LAX and Long Beach Municipal Airport shuttles are available. ♦ 2 World Trade Center (at W Ocean Blvd). 562/983.3400, 800/HILTONS; fax 562/983.1200

55 KING'S PINE AVENUE FISH HOUSE

★★$$ A classic grill ambience prevails in this corner restaurant, with rich wood textures and comfortable booths. The menu changes regularly but always includes a variety of well-prepared fish dishes in unique sauces like Hawaiian swordfish with papaya salsa and N'Awlins shrimp. A seasonal highlight is the Maryland soft-shell-crab piccata—blackened, deep fried. Also on the premises is the **King Crab Lounge,** an authentic New Orleans–style bar/oyster house, right down to the funky neon signs and Southern paraphernalia on the walls, offering six brands of microbrewery beers to accompany the seafood. ♦ Seafood/American ♦ M-F, lunch and dinner; Sa, Su, brunch, lunch, and dinner. Reservations recommended. 100 W Broadway (at N Pine Ave). 562/432.7463. www.kingsfishhouse.com

55 L'OPERA

★★★$$$ This handsome, cosmopolitan restaurant is located in a turn-of-the-20th-century bank building with heavy green marble pillars, original high recessed ceilings, and modern touches of lighting that give it some contemporary verve. The menu, too, mixes the old and the new, with wonderful Roman fare that is both classic and modern. The vegetarian lasagna and ravioli are excellent. ◆ Italian ◆ M-F, lunch and dinner; Sa, Su, dinner. Reservations recommended. 101 N Pine Ave (at W First St). 562/491.0066

56 SMOOTH'S SPORTS GRILLE

★★$$ Sports fans eat up this New York–style spot where athletic events are broadcast on 27 flat-screen monitors spread around the handsome room. The scene is lively, especially at night, when music on the rooftop terrace ignites the crowd to a fever pitch. The eclectic menu offers something for all tastes, from fish & chips to grilled rare ahi, burgers (beef, turkey, or vegan), wraps, sandwiches, salads, and burritos. Of course, there's a booming bar where serious sports enthusiasts congregate. ◆ Sports Bar/Grill ◆ Daily, lunch and dinner. Reservations not necessary. 144 Pine Ave (at E Broadway). 562/437.7700

57 RENAISSANCE HOTEL LONG BEACH

$$$ A longtime favorite of business travelers, this centrally located, 374-room hotel has everything you could ask for. Rooms are attractively appointed and equipped with the usual flat screens, high-speed Internet, 300-thread-count linens, and more. There's also a club level where for a few additional bucks you get a continental breakfast, hors d'oeuvres, and desserts. But the biggest draw is **Tracht's** (see below), created by Los Angeles super chef Suzanne Tracht (whose restaurant **Jar** is one of the best in Los Angeles). In addition to fine dining, the hotel sports a full business center, a pool, and a fitness center. FYI: This is a non-smoking facility. ◆ 111 East Ocean Blvd (at Pine Ave). 562/437.5900; fax 562/499.2509. www.renaissancehotellongbeach.com

Within the Renaissance Hotel Long Beach:

TRACHT'S

★★★$$ Part of a growing trend to gussy up hotel restaurants with high-profile chefs, bringing in chef Suzanne Tracht was pure brilliance. The diminutive culinary wizard has been pleasing palates at her fabulously popular **Jar** in LA. And now she thrills taste buds here with choices such as her signature deviled eggs, pot roast, char Sui pork chops, Kansas City steak, sirloin burger, meat loaf, and a huge delicious bowl of chocolate pudding. It's all good.

◆ California Comfort Food ◆ Daily, lunch and dinner. Reservations suggested. 562/499.2533. www.trachts.com

58 THE SKY ROOM RESTAURANT

★★★$$$ A 360-degree panoramic view of the downtown Long Beach skyline and the Pacific Ocean, combined with the historic Art Deco décor, superior service, and award-winning cuisine, makes this the perfect spot for special occasions. The menu satisfies all tastes with fresh fish, steaks, venison, lamb, and chicken entrées. Don't skip desserts here or you'll regret it. ◆ American ◆ Reservations suggested. M-Sa, dinner. 40 S Locust (at Ocean Blvd). 562/983.2703; e-mail: skyroom@earthlink.net. www.theskyroom.com

59 555 EAST STEAKHOUSE

★★★$$$ Looking for great steak? And perhaps some moody atmosphere? This is the place—dimly lit, with plush leather-upholstered banquettes, lots of marble and wood, and that wonderful aroma of sizzling beef. Dungeness crab cakes or fried calamari appetizers can be followed by juicy cuts of prime New York, porterhouse, and filet mignon, and a fine list of side dishes. ◆ American ◆ M-F, lunch and dinner; Sa, Su, dinner. Reservations recommended. 555 E Ocean Blvd (between Atlantic and N Linden Aves). 562/437.0626

60 LONG BEACH CONVENTION AND ENTERTAINMENT CENTER

The center is home to the acclaimed Long Beach Symphony Orchestra and International City Theater. The sports arena hosts rodeos, rock concerts, and other events. ◆ S Pine Ave (between E Shoreline Dr and W Seaside Way). Ticket information 562/436.3661; Ice Dogs 562/436.3661

61 HYATT REGENCY

$$$ This luxurious 502-room atrium hotel near the convention center offers 19 suites with scenic harbor views, two restaurants, an outdoor pool, a spa, and business and banquet facilities. ◆ 200 S Pine Ave (between E Shoreline Dr and E Seaside Way). 562/491.1234, 800/233.1234; fax 562/432.1972. www.hyatt.com

62 PLANET OCEAN

Life-size gray whales and dolphins are depicted on the walls of the Long Beach Arena in this 122,000-square-foot mural—the largest in the world, created by internationally acclaimed environmental marine artist Wyland. ◆ Rainbow Lagoon Park, E Shoreline Dr (between S Linden and S Pine Aves)

Restaurants/Clubs: Red | Hotels: Purple | Shops: Orange | Outdoors/Parks: Green | Sights/Culture: Blue

63 LONG BEACH MUSEUM OF ART

Located in a 1912 Craftsman-style house, this museum sponsors changing exhibitions that emphasize contemporary Southern California art. The permanent collection includes works by the Laguna Canyon School of the 1920s and 1930s as well as WPA-sponsored pieces. The carriage house has a bookstore, gift shop, café, and gallery. ◆ Admission (free the first of each month). W-Su. 2300 E Ocean Blvd (between 20th and 19th Pls). 562/439.2119

64 BLUFF PARK

This historic district contains diversified houses fronting Ocean Boulevard. ◆ Temple Ave and E Ocean Blvd

65 CHRISTY'S RISTORANTE

★★$$$ This uptown neighborhood trattoria is spread out in four dining areas offering good, sturdy Northern and Southern Italian fare. The specialty filet à la Gorgonzola is an interesting presentation of stuffed prime filet mignon. There are plenty of pastas and lots of salads, and an extensive wine list to complement it all. ◆ Italian ◆ Daily, dinner. Reservations a must. 3937 East Broadway at Termino Ave (between Mira Mar and Belmont). 562/433.7133. www.christysristorante.com

66 THE PIKE AT RAINBOW HARBOR

This 350,000-square-foot triplex of fun, food, and consumerism houses two pedestrian-friendly venues: Shoreline Village and the Pike at Rainbow Harbor. The area is chock-full of places to eat, shop, or play, all within easy walking distance or reachable by free Red Passport Bus. Adventurous souls can rent a Segway or participate in a 45-minute guided tour on one (how-to instructions are provided, should you not know how to work this popular contraption) at **Segway of Long Beach at Rainbow Harbor,** open daily (562/437.9348, 866/SEGWAY9, www.segwaylb.com). Video gamers and/or bowlers will be bowled over by Gameworks and **Pike Bowl,** with its amazing assortment of high-tech options and 10 lanes on which to toss the ball (562/308.7530, www.gameworks.com). There is also a multiplex cinema, several pizza places (including a California Pizza Kitchen), a branch of P.F. Chang's China Bistro, coffeehouses, a Laugh Factory, a Gladstone's 4 Fish, and other

The Beach Boys attended Hawthorne High, where Brian Wilson flunked a music class when he turned in the song that later became "Surfin' Safari."

The Academy Theatre (3100 Manchester Blvd, Inglewood) was built in 1939. Its distinctive pencil-like tower, crowned with a sunburst, rises 125 feet into the air.

spots to chow down. ◆ Between Queensway (around Shoreline Dr) and Pine Ave. 562/432.8325. www.thepikeatlongbeach.com

Within Rainbow Harbor:

MAI TAI BAR/RESTAURANT

★★$$ As the name suggests, mai tais are served here along with a fabulous view of the harbor, which you can enjoy indoors or on the verandah. A Hawaiian décor sets the scene for a fun menu of Asian fusion fare such as assorted tempuras, satay, Hoisin-glazed salmon, Asian pear chicken salad, and more. But most of the crowd goes for the drinks, especially at happy hour (8PM to 11PM), when prices for adult beverages are slashed ◆ Asian Fusion ◆ Daily, 11:30AM-2AM. Reservations not essential. 562/432.5777, cell: 415/425.9469. www.maitaibar.com

AULD DUBLINER IRISH PUB AND RESTAURANT

★$$ A replica of a rural pub, complete with furnishings shipped in from Ireland, this place oozes with ambience. The friendly owner and "publican," David Copley, a transplant from Limerick, Ireland, adds to the authenticity. A truly fun spot day or night, the food's good if you like boxtys (an old Irish country dish of potato crepes stuffed with various fillings such as corned beef, stew, or salmon), Guinness beef stew, shepherd's pie, and of course corned beef and cabbage. Its being an Irish pub, you'd expect a lively bar (where food is also served) and you get it here, amid lots of down-home frivolity. ◆ Irish Pub ◆ Daily, lunch and dinner; drinks and nightly entertainment until 2AM. No reservations accepted. 71 South Pine Ave. 562/437.8300

LONG BEACH AQUARIUM OF THE PACIFIC

This technologically advanced marine wonderland is recommended for kids of all ages. The $117 million facility offers up-close encounters with sharks, thousands of marine creatures representing 550 species, and myriad colorful fish. Waves crash overhead as visitors walk through the underwater tunnel of the seals' and sea lions' habitat. Throughout the complex, spectacular lighting and sound effects, touch tanks, hands-on wet labs, and multimedia activities make this a virtual walk through the Pacific. ◆ Admission. Daily. 100 Aquarium Way (south of W Shoreline Dr). 562/590.3100

SHORELINE VILLAGE

This ersatz historical waterfront shopping village features a few quaint tourist shops and popular restaurants (including two fish houses). A smaller reproduction of the 1906 Charles Looff **carousel** has replaced the original. For boat tours of Long Beach and Los Angeles Harbors and dinner cruises, call **Spirit Cruises** (562/495.5884) or **Shoreline Village Cruises** (562/495.5884). ♦ Daily. 407 E Shoreline Dr (between E Ocean Blvd and Queensway Dr). 562/590.8427

66 BELMONT PIER

This 1,300-foot municipal pier located about a mile from Rainbow Harbor is accessible via a 5½-mile beach bike path. There's a shop (with tackle rentals) and a snack bar. ♦ Bait shop: daily. 39th Pl and Allin St. 562/434.6781

On Belmont Pier:

DOCKSIDE BOAT & BED

$$$ Now here's a unique idea—bed-and-breakfast yacht rentals that allow you to spend the night, docked at the pier on one of four luxury crafts: a 38-foot Bayliner, a 40-foot Mainship Sedan Bridge motoryacht, or a 54-foot Stephens motoryacht. The idea appeals to honeymooners and other lovers, and it's a fun way to feel rich for the night. Each vessel has a galley, coffeemaker, microwave, television, DVD or CD player, and other amenities. ♦ Dock 5 at Rainbow Harbor. 562/436.3111. ww.boatandbed.com

67 WEST COAST LONG BEACH HOTEL

$$ This five-story, 200-room waterfront hotel boasts a swimming pool and courts for tennis, volleyball, and basketball. The menu at the hotel's **Oceana's Restaurant** includes everything from burgers and salads to steak and seafood. ♦ 700 Queensway Dr (between Queens Hwy N and S Harbor Scenic Dr). 562/435.7676, 800/255.3050; fax 562/437.0866. www.javhospitality.com

68 QUEEN MARY

This majestic 81,237-ton passenger liner is berthed permanently in Long Beach Harbor. Launched in 1934, the vessel epitomized Art Deco luxury when she and her crew of 1,200 cruised the North Atlantic. In 1964 she was retired from service; in 1967 she was purchased by the City of Long Beach and converted into a tourist attraction and luxury hotel with 365 cabins and three restaurants. If you're into nautical legend and lore, you'll find a treasure trove of maritime memorabilia. A variety of guided tours and exhibits help you explore everything from ghosts and myths to the behemoth ship's colorful history. By all means spend the night on board in one of the staterooms, each of which provides the feel of yesterday with its wood paneling, Art Deco

appointments, and portholes. Some suggest the presence of ghosts, so it could get a little eerie, but you'll get a good idea of what it must have been like to sail on this majestic Queen in her heyday. ♦ Queens Hwy N (between Windsor Way and S Harbor Scenic Dr). 562/435.3511, 800/437.2934; for stateroom reservations 562/432.6964. www.queenmary.com

Within the *Queen Mary*:

SIR WINSTON'S RESTAURANT

★★$$$$ Relive the glory of luxury sea voyages of old at this elegant dining room, where you can visualize the ghosts of women wrapped in boas, clutching long cigarette holders in their manicured hands, and men in tuxedos smoking cigars. A musty scent of the sea permeates the dark, handsome room. The food provides a fitting flashback to the grandeur of yesteryear's ocean liners with escargots, caviar, foie gras, chateaubriand for two, veal chops, and fish, all served under silver covers. Soufflés or raspberry mousse surrounded by white chocolate are best dessert bets. The waitstaff is exceptionally well trained. Be sure to request a table by the window for a great harbor view. ♦ Continental ♦ Daily, dinner. Reservations required. 562/499.1657

Adjacent to the *Queen Mary*:

POVODNAYA LODKA B-427

Code-named "Scorpion," this 3,000-ton Soviet-built submarine was commissioned in 1973—during the height of the Cold War—by the Soviet government and went on to ply the seas for 21 years before being decommissioned. Formerly berthed in Sydney, Australia, the sub will be on view to the public here until 2009. ♦ Admission. Information 562/435.3511

CARNIVAL CRUISE LINES LONG BEACH TERMINAL

Carnival Cruises welcomes its Fun Ships *Ecstasy* and *Pride* passengers in style at this technologically advanced 30,000-square-foot terminal situated next to the *Queen Mary*. Designed by BEA of Coral Gables, Florida, the $40 million facility features a 300-foot-long, 35-foot-high passenger gangway, a 1,450-vehicle parking garage, and convenient drop-off and pick-up areas. The best part is the Carnival check-in lounge aboard the *Queen Mary*, where passengers can relax or tour the ocean liner prior to embarkation. ♦ For additional information, call Carnival Cruise Lines at 800/CARNIVAL, or the *Queen Mary* at 562/432.6964. www.queenmary.com, www.carnival.com

---

Restaurants/Clubs: Red | Hotels: Purple | Shops: Orange | Outdoors/Parks: Green | Sights/Culture: Blue

CATALINA ISLAND

Twenty-six miles across the sea, Santa Catalina is waiting for ye . . .

A cheerful little island that bustles in spring and summer and snoozes in winter, Catalina sits just 26 miles across the sea from the mainland. As you arrive by air or sea, the awesome misty green peaks of a mountain range that rises from the ocean floor to form this and the other Channel Islands seem to greet you with a smile. Next, your eyes will focus on the gleaming buildings climbing the hillside above the Mediterranean-style port of **Avalon** and its legendary casino. Finally, you'll come into the thriving harbor, alive with pleasure boats and the occasional cruise ship. The picturesque, winding streets of the island are lined with red-tiled houses, boutiques, dive shops, quaint stores, and galleries. Alas, hotel rooms here are in short supply and are pricey during summer; many visitors simply take the ferry over for the day (it takes about an hour).

Catalina Island's resident population of 3,750 is far outnumbered by the influx of up to 12,000 visitors a day, and the town of Avalon, established in 1913, is straining at the seams. Fortunately, most of the island (21 miles long by 8 miles wide) has been preserved in its unspoiled natural state, and traffic is generally limited to golf carts and the buses that transport visitors along the back roads. (You can see even more of the island if you hike.)

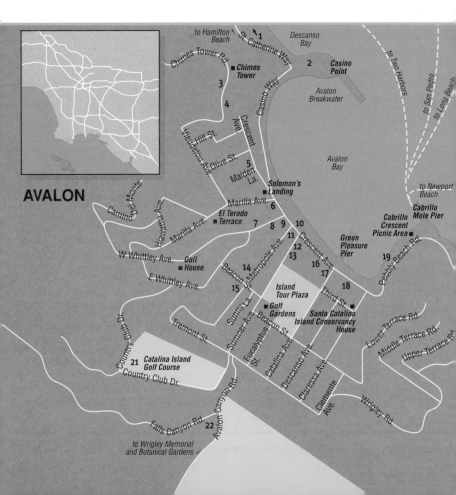

Most of the island has been privately owned since the native Indians were re-settled on the mainland in 1811. Avalon was named in 1888 by the sister of an early developer, George Shatto, after the island of Avalon in Tennyson's *Idylls of the King,* the refuge of blessed souls in Celtic mythology. In 1919, William Wrigley Jr., the chewing-gum scion, purchased the Santa Catalina Island Company, built a casino for ballroom dancing in Avalon and a mansion for himself, and established a spring-training camp for his baseball team, the Chicago Cubs. Avalon became a popular tourist spot during the 1930s, but most of the interior of the island and much of the coastline remained undeveloped. A nonprofit conservancy acquired the title to about 88 percent of the island in 1975 and now administers this unique open space in conjunction with the County of Los Angeles.

The native wildlife in Catalina's underdeveloped interior is extraordinary. It is home to more than 100 species of birds and 400 species of native plant life (including eight types found only on this island, such as the Catalina ironweed, wild tomato, and *dudleya hassei,* which translates to "live forever"). Herds of wild bison (left by a movie crew several decades ago) roam free over the back region of the island.

For more visitor information, call 310/510.1520 or check out the web site at www.catalina.com.

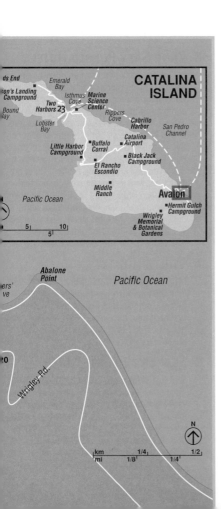

Getting to Catalina Island

BY BOAT

Your best bet is Catalina Express (310/519.1212, 800/622.2419, 800/315.3967; www.catalinaexpress.com), which operates three modern high-speed catamarans—the 300-passenger *Starship Express,* the 388-passenger *JetCat Express,* and the triple-deck, 360-passenger *Cat Express*—that make the trip to Avalon in less than an hour. Both sail round-trip from Long Beach, San Pedro, and Dana Point to Avalon daily year-round. For added comfort, pay a small extra fee for Commodore Lounge privileges, with which you get priority boarding, a free drink, a snack, and cushier seats. The company also operates four other vessels: a 56-passenger boat that takes campers to Two Harbors and three 150-passenger boats that arrive in Catalina in an hour from Long Beach or San Pedro and 90 minutes from Dana Point. The company also offers special hotel packages. The *Catalina Flyer* zips once a day from Balboa Pavilion Newport in 75 minutes flat. 800/830.7744.

Restrooms for the disabled can be found on the pier. Since most hotels and restaurants on the island were built before the California law mandating disabled access was put into effect, they are not necessarily wheelchair accessible. It's a good idea to ask when booking your room or making a restaurant reservation. For general visitor information, call 310/510.1520. www.catalinachamber.com

BY HELICOPTER

The fastest, most convenient access to Catalina is by helicopter, though charter flights from Long Beach are available. The ride takes about 14 minutes in fair weather. **Island Express** (310/510.2525) flies from San Pedro and from beside the *Queen Mary* in Long Beach.

Getting Around Catalina Island

BY RENTAL CAR

Cars are not allowed in the interior. If you have a friend with a car on the island, you may obtain a temporary card key from the **Santa Catalina Island Conservancy** (310/510.1421) to drive outside of Avalon.

HIKING

Permits are required to hike into the interior and may be obtained at the Santa Catalina Island Conservancy (310/510.2595) in Avalon or at **Two Harbors Enterprises Visitor Services** (PO Box 5086, Two Harbors, Catalina; 310/510.4205) at the Isthmus.

TOURS

There are many sightseeing tours on Catalina Island, from glass-bottom boat excursions to scenic drives and fly-fishing boat trips. **Discovery Tours** (310/510.8687, 800/322.3434) offers semisubmersible boat excursions that provide passengers with awesome underwater views of sea life through large windows on the sides of the vessel. The boat departs twice daily from the Green Pleasure Pier in Avalon. Other tour operators include **Catalina Adventure Tours** (310/510.2888, 877/510.2888, www.catalinaadventuretours.com), **Catalina Safari Bus** (310/510.2800), and **Island Navigation** (310/510.0409).

FYI

Vacation rentals can be arranged by calling 310/510.2276. Note that most hotels require a two-day or even a one-week minimum stay during the summer.

The **Chamber of Commerce information office** on the Green Pleasure Pier in Avalon is open daily. To receive brochures describing the trails at Black Jack or Little Harbor or to make camping arrangements, call 310/510.0688 Monday through Friday. Information is also available at www.catalinachamber.com and www.campingcatalinaisland.com.

Arrangements for camping at Little Fisherman's Cove (Two Harbors) must be made through **Catalina Cove and Camp Agency** (PO Box 5044, Two Harbors, CA 90704; 310/510.0303). All camping is by permit only and advance reservations are required. For additional information, call 310/510.3577 or check www.visitcatalinaisland.com.

1 DESCANSO BEACH CLUB

Sip your drink right on the sands at Avalon's only beachside restaurant/bar, where family cookouts are a popular event all year long—barbecue your own steaks or hamburgers, with salad and trimmings provided by the club. Descanso Beach Ocean Sports (310/510.1226), a private company on the premises, rents kayaks for exploring the ocean, guided or not. The beach is a short walk from the town of Avalon. The club is available for private parties. ♦ Call ahead for hours. Reservations required. St. Catherine Way (northwest of Casino Way). 310/510.7410. www.visitcatalinaisland.com

2 CASINO

The island's signature building, a circular Spanish Moderne structure designed by **Webber & Spaulding** in 1928, is situated on a rocky promontory at the north end of Avalon Bay. It houses a beautiful 1,100-seat movie theater with fanciful underwater murals and an organ that is sometimes played during silent films. (Each theater seat has a hat rack on the back.) The grand ballroom hosts big-band concerts and other special events; there's also a small museum/art gallery. Tours of the structure and evening showings of movies are offered daily. ♦ 1 Casino Way (at St. Catherine Way). Movie schedule 310/510.0179, private parties 310/510.7497

The
Zane Grey Pueblo Hotel

3 ZANE GREY PUEBLO HOTEL

$$ Tahitian teak beams in an open-beam ceiling, a hewn-plank door, a log mantel, and walls of mortar mixed with goat's milk are combined with blessed isolation and an extraordinary view of the ocean and the hills in this former home of the foremost writer of the American West. The pueblo was originally built for Zane Grey in 1929 as a haven for his literary labors and fishing desires. There are 17 rooms, and amenities include free taxi pickup, an outdoor pool, and, although there is no restaurant, complimentary tea and coffee all day. The rates decrease in winter. ♦ 199 Chimes Tower Rd (east of Vieudelou Ave). 310/510.0966, 800/3-PUEBLO

4 WOLFE HOUSE

In 1928, **Rudolph Schindler** created this icon of Modernism, comprising a stack of balconied floors that exploit the steep site and its panoramic views. It's a private residence. ♦ 124 Chimes Tower Rd (east of Vieudelou Ave)

5 SEAPORT VILLAGE INN

$$$ Just steps from the beach, this pretty 43-room hotel features a spa, studio suites with views, and off-season packages. Additional amenities include color TV with cable, private baths, fully furnished kitchens, and wet bars (but no restaurant). ♦ 119 Maiden La (west of Crescent Ave). 310/510.0344, 800/2CATALINA. www.catalinacatalina.com

LA STORY

Much has been written about the City of Angels—everything from fiction by such literary greats as F. Scott Fitzgerald to telltale historical accounts of Hollywood's rich and famous. If you'd like to brush up on the area before your trip, pick up any of these compelling and informative works:

Nonfiction

An Architectural Guidebook to Los Angeles by David Gebhard and Robert Winter (Gibbs Smith Books, 2003).

California Crazy and Beyond: Roadside Vernacular Architecture by Jim Heimann (Chronicle, 2001). Collection of amazing roadside architecture.

California Festivals by Carl and Katie Landau with Kathy Kincade (Landau Communications, 1989).

California People by Carol Dunlap (Peregrine Smith Books, 1982). Short biographies of men and women who made LA and the rest of the state what it is, from Earl C. Anthony to Frank Zappa.

The City Observed: Los Angeles, A Guide to its Architecture and Landscapes by Charles Moore, Peter Becker, and Regula Campbell (Vintage Books, 1984).

City of Quartz by Mike Davis (Vintage Books, 1990). A social history of LA, creatively researched and written with wit and irony.

East Los Angeles by Ricardo Romo (Texas, 1983). A history of the *barrio* from 1900 to 1930.

Ethnic LA by Zena Pearlstone (Hillcrest Press, 1990). Short histories of many of the city's ethnic groups, with statistical data from the 1980 census.

Golf in Hollywood: Where the Stars Come Out to Play by Robert Chew and Dave Pavoni (Angel City Press, 1998).

Inventing the Dream: California through the Progressive Era by Kevin Starr (Oxford University Press, 1985). Chapters on the growth of Southern California, Pasadena, and the movie industry, plus a thorough bibliography.

LA Freeway: An Appreciative Essay by David Brodsky (University of California, 1981).

LA Lost and Found by Sam Hall Kaplan (Crown, 1987). Photographs by Julius Schulman accompany an architectural history of the city.

Los Angeles: The Architecture of Four Ecologies by Reyner Banham (Penguin Books, 1971). An approving look at LA, years before it became fashionable, by a maverick English architectural historian.

Los Angeles: Biography of a City edited by John and LaRess Caughey (University of California, 1977). Brilliant anthology of writings on LA.

Raymond Chandler's Los Angeles by Elizabeth Ward and Alain Silver (Overlook, 1988). Quotations from LA's acerbic scribe juxtaposed with photos of real locations.

Southern California: An Island on the Land by Carey McWilliams (Peregrine Smith Books, 1973). An impassioned exposé of the dark side of the dream.

Fiction

Writers and journalists flocked to Hollywood with the coming of the talkies, and then bit the hand that fed them. Nathanael West's *Day of the Locust* (1939) is the classic put-down.

Budd Schulberg's *What Makes Sammy Run?* (1941) is a devastating portrait of greed and chicanery by a movie-industry insider.

F. Scott Fitzgerald's *The Last Tycoon* (published posthumously in 1941) is a romanticized portrait of Irving Thalberg, MGM's boy wonder.

Evelyn Waugh was invited by MGM to discuss a movie version of *Brideshead Revisited;* the visit yielded the funniest-ever poison-pen letter to LA, *The Loved One.*

John Fante created memorable portraits of Depression-era LA in *Dreams from Bunker Hill.*

F. Scott Fitzgerald, Henry Miller, and Raymond Chandler are just a few of several famed writers featured in John Miller's *Los Angeles Stories.*

Periodicals

Los Angeles Magazine is a hip, monthly city magazine that's heavy on celebrity, trends, and fashion, and is a good source for restaurants.

LA Weekly seems torn between compulsive consumerism and outspoken radicalism, but is valuable for its comprehensive listings of movies, concerts, and theater.

Valley Magazine is a fun, readable bi-monthly that concentrates on people, places, and things of the San Fernando Valley. Good restaurant reviews, a regular celebrity feature, and some savvy pieces make for enjoyable reading.

THE BEST

Dusty Fleming

Owner, Dusty Fleming beauty salon

Taking a drive up the **Pacific Coast Highway** for lunch in Malibu at **Geoffrey's** on the beach: the ride, beautiful and relaxing; the food, wonderful.

Treating myself to dinner at **The Ivy–LA Desserts.** It has the best food in all of Los Angeles—and probably the country for that matter.

Katsu 3rd has some of the freshest seafood in the city. Be it sushi or grilled tuna, Chef Katsu will prepare food with expertise.

For a quiet afternoon, sitting up on **Sunset Plaza,** sipping on a cappuccino at one of the many restaurants, is always a plus. It's a great place to do some people watching too!

For clothes shopping, **Maxfield** in West Hollywood has an incredible selection of top designer brands.

6 HOTEL VILLA PORTOFINO

$$$ Smack on the water's edge, this 43-room European-style hotel has two-bedroom units, a large inviting sun deck, and the ambitious **Ristorante Villa Portofino,** next door, offering fine Italian cuisine. A complimentary breakfast is included in the rate, and there's a coffeemaker and refrigerator in each room. ♦ 111 Crescent Ave (between Whittley and Marilla Aves). 310/510.0555, 800/346.2326. www.villaportofino.com

7 HOTEL CATALINA

$$ The allure and style of yesterday prevails in this renovated 32-room Victorian hotel, only half a block from the beach. There's no restaurant on premises, but plenty are within walking distance. ♦ 129 Whittley Ave (west of Crescent Ave). 310/510.0027, 800/540.0184; fax 310/510.1495. www.hotelcatalina.com

8 THE AVALON HOTEL

$$$ Even an island 22 miles across the sea from LA can't escape yuppie-fying, as evinced by this adorable 15-room boutique hotel, which has all the trimmings from 350-count-cotton linens and Supple Pedic mattresses to flat-screen TVs, CD/DVD players, high-speed Internet access, and Laura Ashley–like rooms with balconies or patios overlooking the harbor. The hotel was created out of the former Bayview Hotel, which was completely gutted by new owners and rebuilt with handcrafted hardwood floors and modernized bathrooms and public areas. The $2.5 million renovation retained a sense of Island history through paintings and photos by local artists, and the use of Catalina tiles. Rates include lavish continental breakfasts (yummy granola, bagels and cream cheese, fresh-baked pastries, and lots of fresh fruit), snacks available throughout the day in the lobby, wine and cheese in the evening, and pick-up at the dock. ♦ 124 Whittley Ave (west of Crescent Ave). 310/510.7070; fax 310/510.7210. www.theavalonhotel.com

9 CHANNEL HOUSE

$ The food's just passable, but the setting is spectacular. Go for lunch and order a salad or sandwich on the terrace, where you can gaze out over the bustling harbor. ♦ American ♦ Daily, lunch and dinner June-Oct; F-Su, Mar-June. 205 Crescent Ave (between Metropole and Whittley Aves). 310/510.1617

10 ARMSTRONG'S SEAFOOD RESTAURANT

★★$$ Specialties include mesquite-grilled swordfish, fresh lobster, and abalone. Check the chalkboard for the day's specials. ♦ Seafood ♦ Daily, lunch and dinner. Reservations recommended for large parties 300 Crescent Ave (at Metropole Ave). 310/510.0113

11 CHI-CHI CLUB

Live jazz and bluegrass tunes keep this club hopping. ♦ Cover charge on weekends during the summer. Call ahead for hours and programs. 107 Sumner Ave (just south of Crescent Ave). 310/510.2828

12 SNUG HARBOR INN

$$ Originally built in the late 1880s, the former Hotel Monterey was completely

Los Angeles is a city, a county, and a region. The city is 467 square miles; the county covers 4,083 square miles; and the five-county region (including Los Angeles, Riverside, Ventura, Orange, and San Bernardino Counties) is 34,149 square miles. Los Angeles County has 88 incorporated cities, of which the city of Los Angeles is the largest.

renovated and reopened in the fall of 1997 as this charming six-room inn. Each deluxe guest room features a private bath, bay views, terry-cloth slippers, goose-down comforters, custom-made rugs, a fireplace, and nightly milk and cookies to enjoy by the fire. They also throw in a free continental breakfast and an evening wine-and-cheese reception. ◆ 108 Sumner Ave (at Crescent Ave). 310/510.8400; fax 310/510.8418. www.snugharbor-inn.com

13 GLENMORE PLAZA HOTEL

$$$ This charming Victorian hostelry, built at the turn of the 20th century, offers 45 rooms with whirlpool tubs that include a continental breakfast, afternoon wine and cheese, and shuttle to the boat area. There's no restaurant. ◆ 120 Sumner Ave (between Beacon St and Crescent Ave). 310/510.0017, 800/422.8254; fax 310/510.2833. www.glenmorehotel.com

14 CASA MARIQUITA

$$ A quick jog from the beach, this precious hotel offers 22 cheerful guest rooms with king-size beds. Amenities include complimentary continental breakfast, shuttle service from the boat dock, cable TV, refrigerators, and a friendly staff. ◆ 229 Metropole Ave (between Beacon St and Crescent Ave). 800/545.1192, 310/510.1192. www.casamariquitahotel.com

15 HOTEL ST. LAUREN

$$$ Victorian décor and harbor views are two of the attractions of this charming42-room hotel, located three blocks from the water. Amenities include king-size beds, whirlpool tubs, oceanfront views, and continental breakfast. ◆ 231 Beacon St (at Metropole Ave). 310/510.2999, 800/645.2478; fax 310/510.1365. www.stlauren.com

16 AVALON BAY COMPANY

This little shop has the island's largest selection of women's clothing, shoes, and accessories. ◆ Daily. 407 Crescent Ave (between Catalina and Sumner ves). 310/510.0178. www.avalonbaycompany.com

17 HOTEL VISTA DEL MAR

$$$ Located smack on the beach overlooking Avalon Bay, each of this hotel's 15 rooms has a fireplace, refrigerator, wet bar, ocean view, balcony, and a Jacuzzi tub, and comes with a free continental breakfast. There's no restaurant on site, but there is room service. ◆ 417 Crescent Ave (at Catalina Ave). 310/510.1452; fax 310/510.2917. www.hotel-vistadelmar.com

18 PAVILION LODGE

$$ A large central courtyard, free cable TV, and group rates can all be enjoyed at this 73-room lodge, which is one of the island's more popular hotels. There's a free continental breakfast and special group rates available. No restaurant, however. ◆ 513 Crescent Ave (between Claressa and Catalina Aves), "14 steps from the beach." 310/510.2500, 800/322.3434. www.visitcatalinaisland.com

19 WET SPOT KAYAK RENTALS

Novice and experienced kayakers can explore the island's secluded coves and reefs on half- and full-day journeys (with guides on request). ◆ 120 Pebbly Beach Rd (northeast of Crescent Ave). 310/510.2229

20 INN ON MOUNT ADA

$$$$ The Wrigley Mansion has been converted into a luxurious bed-and-breakfast with just six guest rooms, all featuring ocean or harbor views. Guests enjoy all meals, wine, and hors d'oeuvres, a gas-powered golf cart, and a free shuttle to and from the hotel. ◆ 398 Wrigley Rd (east of Clemente Ave). 310/510.2030. www.innonmtada.com

21 CATALINA CANYON RESORT & SPA

$$ Nestled in the tranquil foothills above Avalon Bay, this Mediterranean-style resort offers 83 comfortable rooms with standard amenities: TVs, phones, king- or queen-size beds, and private baths. There's a full-service European spa, heated pool, restaurant, and courtesy shuttle. ◆ 888 Country Club Dr (between Tremont St and E Whittley Ave). 310/510.0325, 800/253.9361; fax 310/510.0900. www.catalinacanyonresort.com

22 THE SAND TRAP

$ This local favorite serves authentic Mexican fare. If you can stomach it, go for the menudo. ◆ Mexican ◆ Daily, breakfast and lunch; dinner during summer months only. Avalon Canyon Rd (south of Falls Canyon Rd). 310/510.1349

23 TWO HARBORS

Ⓟ Camping sites are available on this pretty stretch of beach reached by boat or Safari Bus (310/510.2800) from Avalon, 23 miles away. There's a general store, a snack bar, and a dive shop. ◆ Camping 310/510.2800. www.visittwoharbors.com

---

Restaurants/Clubs: Red | Hotels: Purple | Shops: Orange | Outdoors/Parks: Green | Sights/Culture: Blue

M-I-C-K-E-Y M-O-U-S-E...
Orange County, a sprawling, predominantly affluent metropolitan area, is now home to more than two and a half million people, but its development wasn't without some major growing pains. During the late 1980s, the county suffered a severe setback when mismanagement of county funds led to bankruptcy. The county is now safely back on its economic feet. The real financial history of the area started five decades ago, beginning with the 1955 opening of **Disneyland** in

Anaheim and followed in the 1970s by the development of **Irvine Ranch**. Orange County is a maze of separate communities that can be divided into two areas: the less-prosperous north, with its ethnic and blue-collar enclaves and huge entertainment parks centered on Anaheim, and the affluent south, with its luxurious houses, hotels and restaurants, and burgeoning cultural scene.

During the Spanish and Mexican periods, in the middle of the 19th century, ranchos were turned into Yankee farms and orchards. In 1857, a group of 50 Germans established an agriculture cooperative they later named Anaheim—a combination of the name of the **Santa Ana River** and the German word for home, *heim*. Originally part of Los Angeles County, the area's autonomy was mandated by the California legislature in 1889. For the first 50 years of the 20th century, Orange County seemed a land of milk and honey, where well-tended groves of Valencia orange trees perfumed the air with the fragrance of their blossoms. In the 1950s, land values began to skyrocket in response to a postwar generation eager for a suburban lifestyle. Soon, residential and commercial developments replaced the groves. Very soon the trees will be just a memory, immortalized in street and condominium names.

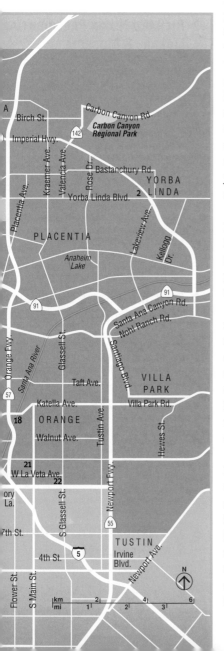

A $174 million program, completed in 2001, transformed the area southwest of **Interstate 5** between **Orangewood Avenue** and **Ball Road** into a more visually pleasing, pedestrian-friendly destination.

A $1.4 billion expansion of the **Disneyland Resort** culminated in 2001 with the opening of **Downtown Disney,** an eclectic assortment of adult-oriented shops, restaurants, and entertainment options; **Disney's Grand Californian Hotel;** and **Disney's California Adventure** theme park, which some critics say offers more commerce than theme.

More money in the area of $180 million went into remodeling the **Anaheim Convention Center** in 2003. The new design features $13 million worth of glass in a wave pattern that hugs the building—a worthy expenditure considering that 45 million people visited Anaheim/Orange County in 2004 and plunked down $8 billion while they were at it. The Center is now the largest of its kind on the West Coast. The bottom line is that five years and a total $5 billion investment later, Anaheim, California's tenth-largest city, has been totally reinvented as a major tourist mecca, with about 20,000 guest rooms in 150 hotels. There really is more to the city—which, by the way, is not part of Los Angeles—than Disneyland.

Getting Around Orange County

Public transportation here is erratic at best. An unusual way to reach the **Disneyland Resort** is by a brief (about 35 minutes) and delightful ride on the **Amtrak** local to Fullerton from Union Station (for schedules and information, call 800/872.7245). From the Fullerton train station, walk about one and a half blocks to Commonwealth Avenue and Harbor Boulevard. From there you can board **Orange County Transit Authority** (OCTA) bus no. 435 to get to the Disneyland Hotel, Disney's Paradise Pier Hotel, and Disney's Grand Californian Hotel. OCTA has service throughout the county, but allow a lot of time; on many routes the buses run only once an hour. Call 714/636.7433 for more information.

The **Southern California Rapid Transit District** has service from its main terminal at East Sixth and South Los Angeles Streets in LA to major locations in Orange County. **Greyhound** (800/231.2222) serves Anaheim and Santa Ana from LA, and also covers Newport Beach and Laguna Beach en route to San Diego. From the Westside, a convenient way to get to Orange County is the regularly scheduled **Airport Coach Service** (800/772.5299) from LAX. The coaches service the major hotels, Disneyland, and John Wayne Airport.

For local transportation, there's **Anaheim Yellow Cab** (714/535.2211), **Orange County Shuttle Service** (714/978.8855), and **West Coast TaxiCab** (714/547.8000). For even easier area navigating, **ART** (Anaheim Resort Transit) shuttles visitors to Disneyland, Disney's California Adventure, Downtown Disney, the Anaheim Convention Center, and throughout the 1,100-acre Anaheim Resort District. Tickets are available at hotels, ART kiosks, and visitor's centers. www.atnetwork.org. For extensive travel away from the major tourist sites, a car is the only practical option. For more information about transportation, special events, sightseeing services, or accommodations, the **Anaheim/Orange County Visitor and Convention Bureau** (714/765.8888) has an office at the **Anaheim Convention Center** (800 W Katella Ave, between S Harbor Blvd and S West St). Please note: The area code for Anaheim resort areas and some northern and central communities (Fullerton, Santa Ana, Huntington Beach) was in the process of being changed from 714 to 657 at press time.

1 CHILDREN'S MUSEUM AT LA HABRA

Railroad cars, hands-on displays (including a theater gallery with costumes and props),

and a hands-off beehive are housed in a restored 1923 Union Pacific depot. ♦ Admission. M-Sa. 301 S Euclid St (between W Olive and W First Aves), La Habra. 310/905.9793

2 RICHARD NIXON PRESIDENTIAL LIBRARY & MUSEUM

Admirers and detractors of the late thirty-seventh president should be equally rewarded by a visit to the Spanish-style museum designed by **Langdon & Wilson** in 1990 and built around Nixon's boyhood home. A treasure for political junkies, the museum provides background on the Watergate fiasco via plasma screens, verbal accounts, various White House tapes, scanned archives, and assorted footage of the famous hearings. One of the most popular items is the gun that Elvis Presley presented to Nixon in the Oval Office. The Nixon burial site rests here amid 1,300 rosebushes in a White House–style garden. ♦ Admission. Daily. 18001 Yorba Linda Blvd (at Eureka Ave), Yorba Linda. 714/993.5075, 714/993.3393, 800/872.8865. www.nixonfoundation.org

3 CALIFORNIA STATE UNIVERSITY AT FULLERTON

This 226-acre campus has 20 buildings and enrolls 25,000 students. It is a branch of the **California State University** system. ♦ 800 N State College Blvd (at Nutwood Ave), Fullerton. 714/773.2011

4 MUCKENTHALER CULTURAL CENTER

Located in a lovely 1923 Spanish Baroque house given to the city of Fullerton by the Muckenthaler family in 1965, the center is used for art exhibitions, classes, and receptions. ♦ Donation suggested. Daily. 1201 W Malvern Ave (at Buena Vista Dr), Fullerton. 714/738.6595

5 THE ART OF DENTISTRY/JIMMY Y. M. SHERN, D.M.D.

Even though there are dentists galore spread throughout the area, two dental clinics actually offer convenient weekend appointments. What's more, the specialized staff of dentists perform everything from teeth cleaning and whitening to oral surgery using the latest technology. ◆ Tu, Th, Sa. 1424 S Euclid St (at W Roberta Ave), Fullerton. 714/871.8333. Also at 3150 Colima Rd (in a minimall off Hacienda Heights Blvd), Suite A, Hacienda Heights. 626/369.9494. Open M-W, F, Su

6 MEDIEVAL TIMES

If you haven't overdosed on good cheer at the theme parks, end your day in a mock 11th-century castle that offers a tournament with knights on horseback, as costumed serfs and wenches serve your dinner—which you eat with your hands. ◆ Visits: M-F. Dinner shows: daily; call for times. 7662 Beach Blvd (between La Palma Ave and Artesia Fwy), Buena Park. 714/521.4740, 800/899.6600

7 KNOTT'S BERRY FARM

The nation's first theme park had its start in 1934 when Cordelia Knott began selling homemade chicken dinners to supplement income from the family's berry farm. Mrs. Knott's chicken kitchen survived the Depression and spawned a 150-acre entertainment facility that emphasizes the wholesome aspects of an idealized and simpler America. The six theme areas comprise 165 rides and attractions, live shows, restaurants, and stores. For thrill-seekers, there's a 30-story **Supreme Scream,** the tallest ride of its kind in the world, and **Ghost Rider,** the longest, fastest roller coaster known to man. Now imagine riding upside down, which is how you sit, harnessed in on **The Silver Bullet,** an inverted roller coaster that's about as screaming scary as it gets. Height and age restrictions apply on some rides. An admission ticket provides access to everything except Pan for Gold and the arcades. ◆ Admission. M-F, 10AM-6PM; Sa, 10AM-10PM; Su, 10AM-7PM, with extended hours during summer and seasonal periods. 8039 Beach Blvd (at La Palma Ave), Buena Park. General information 714/220.5200, recorded information 714/827.1776. www.knotts.com

Within Knott's Berry Farm:

CAMP SNOOPY

Six acres of fun with Snoopy and the *Peanuts* gang, with more than 30 rides including the unique spinning coaster Sierra Sidewinder—which is never the same twice.

GHOST TOWN

A replica of an 1880s Old West boomtown, complete with cowboys, cancan dancers, and gold panning, it includes several authentic buildings culled from real ghost towns. Old-time melodramas are presented in the **Birdcage Theatre.** The **Butterfield Stagecoach** tours the countryside, making riders bless the day that shock absorbers were invented. On the **Log Ride,** your log boat floats through sawmill and logging camps before splashing 42 feet in its final descent—plan on getting wet. A new multimedia laser extravaganza, **Edison International Electric Nights,** lights up the sky nightly. The swift **Ghost Rider** wooden roller coaster arrived in 1999.

THE BOARDWALK

This celebration of the California beach scene features Rip Tide, the HammerHead, the Boomerang, Supreme Scream, Perilous Plunge and Xcelerator, which takes you from 0 to 82 mph in 2.3 seconds—exciting rides not for the fainthearted. The **Charles Schulz Theatre** presents live ice skating shows seasonally with catchy tunes, elaborate costumes, and show-stopping special effects and choreography.

FIESTA VILLAGE

A tribute to California's Latino heritage, with piñatas, mariachis, a *mercado* (market), and a turn-of-the-century hand-carved merry-go-round within a lushly landscaped and tiled plaza. The 2,700-foot-long **Jaguar!** roller coaster thrills riders with swerves, circles, and 60-foot surges. One of the most popular rides is **Montezooma's Revenge,** a roller coaster with cars that spin through a 360-degree loop at 55mph and then shoot backward.

WILD WATER WILDERNESS

Turn-of-the-century California is featured here, with **Bigfoot Rapids,** a white-water river raft trip.

Within Wild Water Wilderness:

THUNDER FALLS

This mystical place has trees native to the Northwest Pacific coast, Native American artifacts and paintings, and a lake with four towering waterfalls. Its centerpiece is **Mystery Lodge,** one of the park's most technologically advanced projects. Inside this full-scale replica of a traditional tribal house, a storyteller sets the stage for a multisensory experience with special visual effects.

Restaurants/Clubs: Red | Hotels: Purple | Shops: Orange | Outdoors/Parks: Green | Sights/Culture: Blue

KNOTT'S CALIFORNIA MARKETPLACE

Just outside the park is a separate dining and shopping village where you can sample the chicken dinners and boysenberry pies that launched the farm; enjoy **Knott's Family Restaurant** (714/220.5067), the **Cable Car Kitchen** (714/220.5100), or a salad, burger, or barbecue.

INDIAN TRAILS

One of America's only live Native American interpretative centers educates and entertains visitors.

8 HANSEN HOUSE

Built in 1857, this white clapboard house with a narrow front porch was designed in the Greek Revival style. Also known as the Mother Colony House, it was the first house in Anaheim, built by George Hansen, founder of the Mother Colony, a group of Germans who left San Francisco to grow grapes in Southern California. Inside the restored structure is an interesting exhibition on Anaheim's history.
♦ Free. Tours usually held W mornings; call for an appointment. 414 N West St (between W Lincoln Ave and W Sycamore St), Anaheim. Library 714/254.1850

9 ANGELO'S

$ This classic drive-in, with pert carhops on roller skates and occasional rallies of vintage wheels, has a terrific neon sign.
♦ American ♦ Daily; Sa until 12:30AM. 511 S State College Blvd (between Chelsea Dr and E Santa Ana St), Anaheim. 714/533.1401

10 HOBBY CITY

This six-acre cluster of old-fashioned collectors' shops has 23 buildings, including a log cabin shop that carries Native American memorabilia. ♦ Daily. 1238 S Beach Blvd (between Starr St and W Ball Rd), Anaheim. 714/527.2323

11 MENAGE HOTEL

$ Billed as an "adult" hotel, this former Holiday Inn has an exotic new look with red lava lamps along the entrance and a gussied-up interior. All of the 248 loft-style rooms are done in hyper-hip with 41-inch plasma-screen TVs, oversized desks, leather-wrapped headboards behind king- or queen-size beds, cozy sitting rooms, and soothing tones. The recreational highlight is the one-acre pool area with a palapa bar, 42 speakers, and private cabanas. There's also the K'ya Restaurant, offering a casual setting for breakfast, lunch, and dinner.
♦ 1221 S Harbor Blvd (at W Ball Rd), Anaheim. 714/758.0900; fax 714/533.1804. www.hotelmenage.com

12 LOS ALAMITOS RACE COURSE

One of LA's top tracks features quarter-horse racing and harness racing; call ahead for racing dates. ♦ Admission. Post time: 7PM. 4961 Katella Ave (between Walker St and Portal Dr), Los Alamitos. 714/995.1234

13 DISNEYLAND HOTEL

$$$ Three towers surround the Peter Pan–inspired Never Land Kiddy swimming pool, complete with a pirate ship and 110-foot water slide, while the adult-friendly Cove Pool provides a tropical setting with tiki torch lights and a thatched-roof hut. The 990 rooms, 62 suites, and outrageously unique Mickey Mouse Penthouse (see below) are decorated in classic Disney. All have views of either the Never Land Pool or Disneyland, and some have balconies. There are also three other pools, a tropical beach, a shopping mall, and 11 restaurants and lounges, including a dedicated concierge lounge.
♦ 1150 W Magic Way (between Disneyland D and Walnut St), Anaheim. 714/956.6425; fax 714/956.6582. www.disneyland.com

Within the Disneyland Hotel:

THE MICKEY MOUSE PENTHOUSE

Are you ready for this? An ultra-deluxe VIP lodging, "designed for big cheeses of all ages," with floor-to-ceiling windows, techno gadgets, whimsical décor (you bet), and all things Mickey. The 1,600-square-foot posh play pen provides a magical Mickey Mouse aura with 3-D imagery, a giant impression of the celebrated rodent painted on the ceiling of the living room, glass tiles on the shower walls filled with yet more images of guess who, a Mickey Mouse built-in armoire, and a whole lot more, including flat-panel TVs, DVD players, and Jacuzzi tubs—all designed, according to Walt Disney Imagineering's Wing Chao, executive vice president, Master Planning, Architecture and Design, to make guests walk away saying, "This was a dream come true." M-I-C-K-E-Y.

13 DISNEY'S PARADISE PIER HOTEL

$$$ The hotel offers many guest rooms with views directly into the Paradise Pier section of Disney's California Adventure. It represents the ultimate beachfront amusement zone, featuring the unique boardwalks that used to line the California coast. Facilities include a pool with intimate poolside cabanas, two restaurants, and a coffee bar, fitness center, and retail shop. ♦ 1717 S Disneyland Dr (between Magic Way and Katella Ave), Anaheim. 714/956.6425. www.disneyland.com

13 DISNEY'S CALIFORNIA ADVENTURE PARK

Located next to the original Disneyland Park, Disney's California Adventure offers three themelands: Hollywood Pictures Backlot, Golden State, and Paradise Pier.
♦ 714/781.4000. www.disneyland.com

Within Disney's California Adventure Park:

HOLLYWOOD PICTURES BACKLOT

This themeland celebrates the magic of the movie business and the glamour, culture, fame, and celebrity atmosphere that surrounds it. Guests enter through the majestic studio gates and discover a place where reality blends seamlessly into illusion. Among the attractions featured are the **Hyperion Theater,** a 2,000-seat venue for Disney's Aladdin Musical Spectacular; **Jim Henson's Muppet Vision 3-D; "Turtle Talk With Crush,"** an adorable attraction featuring a 152-year-old animated sea turtle from *Finding Nemo* in his digital undersea habitat (the turtle talks, plays, and jokes with onlookers); and **Disney Animation,** where guests view test scenes from animation features that are still in production.

GOLDEN STATE

Golden State has six districts and is highlighted by the enormous bear-shaped mountain called **Grizzly Peak,** part of the **Grizzly River Run** white-water rafting ride that twirls guests 360 degrees as they drop down two waterfalls. The eight-acre mini-wilderness pays tribute to California's spectacular wilderness areas, featuring redwood trees, authentic Gold Country artifacts, and nature trails. The **Condor Flats** district celebrates California's aviation heritage in the design of the high desert airfields. **Soarin' Over California** suspends guests in their flying theater seats as they lift off, float, and soar in a thrilling flight over California's most spectacular scenic wonders. Celebrating the state's rich agricultural heritage is **A Bug's Land**, where guests can walk through areas growing with citrus, walnuts, avocados, and artichokes or sit in the Bug's Life Theater and watch *It's Tough to Be a Bug!*, a stunning and comical 3-D presentation. The theme park also has its taste of Napa Valley. The **Pacific Wharf** district of the Golden State is inspired by Monterey's Cannery Row and gives guests a firsthand look at sourdough bread baking at the Boudin Bakery and fresh tortilla making at the Mission Tortilla Factory. In **The Bay Area,** guests can experience *Golden Dreams,* a filmed theatrical celebration of California's cultural diversity. It's hosted by actress Whoopi Goldberg, who pays tribute to the people whose courage and creative spirit have made and continue to make California a dynamic and trendsetting state.

PARADISE PIER

The ultimate beachfront amusement zone, decked out in spectacular lighting and elegant graphics associated with the heyday of the great amusement park piers. One of the main attractions is **California Screamin',** a steel coaster disguised as a white wooden coaster, but with a Disney twist: Guests are looped upside-down around a Mickey Mouse silhouette! Another major attraction is the unique Ferris wheel, featuring a revolving sunburst. On this **Sun Wheel,** the carriages are on tracks that slide to the center of the wheel, adding an exciting gravity element to an already spectacular visual experience.

TOY STORY MANIA!

Disney Pixar characters appear in this new attraction that was designed and built simultaneously at the Disneyland Resort and at Walt Disney World.

GRAND CALIFORNIA HOTEL

$$$ This 745-room luxury hotel provides uptown accommodations for the more discerning Disney visitor. Still typically thematic with turn-of-the-20th-century designs created by Peter Dominick of the

An average of 150 productions are filmed daily on LA streets. The motion picture/TV production industry and related services generate more than $31 billion annually. The top 10 filming locations are located in:

Downtown

Griffith Park

Industrial East Side of Downtown Los Angeles

Ocean Front Walk

Hancock Park

Hollywood Boulevard

Pacific Palisades

Studio City

North Hollywood

Crenshaw/Adams Jefferson Park

Restaurants/Clubs: Red | Hotels: Purple | Shops: Orange | Outdoors/Parks: Green | Sights/Culture: Blue

CHILD'S PLAY

Seen enough of Disneyland, Knotts Berry Farm, Magic Mountain, and other amusement parks? There are plenty of other delightful, less time-consuming, and more affordable diversions for children visiting Los Angeles. Here are a few of the better ones.

Visit the **La Brea Tar Pits,** a rich deposit of Ice Age fossils. Okay, so they're not dinosaurs, but these mammals were larger than their modern counterparts. Nearby is the **Page Museum,** which displays fossils and models of the animals stuck in the ancient goo.

Soar 100 feet above the ocean on a Ferris wheel or ride an antique horse on the indoor carousel at the newly refurbished **Santa Monica Pier.** Touch sea stars at the **Cabrillo Marine Aquarium** in San Pedro.

Cruise the open Pacific on a **whale-watching tour.** Between December and April the big, beautiful mammals make their way along the LA coast in the company of dolphins, seals, and seabirds. Tours depart from Long Beach and San Pedro Harbors.

Learn about nature and model all kinds of wonderful costumes at the **Los Angeles County Museum of Natural History's Discovery Center.**

Laugh at a puppet show at the **Bob Baker Marionette Theater,** the oldest marionette theater in the US.

Climb aboard a vintage train, plane, or car at **Travel Town** in Griffith Park.

See the many endangered species at the **Los Angeles Zoo.**

Play with the fascinating, interactive nature exhibits at **Kidspace** in Pasadena.

Hear a story, read, and see some favorite illustrations from children's books at **Storyopolis.**

Urban Design Group of Denver, the décor attempts to capture California's ruggedly beautiful coastline while evoking memories of the Arroyo craftsmen. Rooms are equipped with pillow-top beds, flat-screen TVs, and other uptown amenities. The hotel provides 24-hour room service; a Mandara Spa offering signature treatments of the worldwide spa company, as well as steam, sauna, and massage rooms; two pools (one with a water slide); and lots of dining options. 714/635.2300

Within the Grand California Hotel:

THE NAPA ROSE RESTAURANT

★★$$$$ This uncharacteristically fine dining spot stars chef Andrew Sutton (formerly of Napa Valley's deluxe Auberge du Soleil), who creates magical menus served in a typically Disneyesque room where waiters wear vests with little roses embroidered on them and colors clash under a 20-foot-high vaulted ceiling. Floor-to-ceiling windows provide a view of California Adventure's Grizzly Peak. Adding to the mood is a display kitchen, lounge, and a vast wine cellar. Sutton's menu includes good seared rock scallops in a lemon lobster sauce, a creative Portobello mushroom cappuccino with a thyme froth, prime rib of pork, and a mean mustard-crusted rack of lamb. Best desserts are the Meyer lemon mousse brûlée served with a blood orange sorbet and the goat cheese flan with fresh fruit. ◆ California ◆ Daily, dinner. Reservations suggested. 714/300.7170 or dial *86 on any resort pay phone. Valet parking available

14 THE DISNEYLAND RESORT

A $1.4 billion expansion, completed in 2001, transformed the world-famous amusement park into one mega-theme resort with the addition of **Downtown Disney, Disney's California Adventure,** and two new hotels (see above). **Disneyland Park, The Happiest Place on Earth** is Walt Disney's original theme park, with eight themelands that showcase classic Disney characters, favorite attractions, and lots of live entertainment. Showcased on Friday, Saturday, and Sunday evenings is FANTASMIC!, a unique extravaganza of music, live performers, and sensational special effects, starring Mickey Mouse and his imagination, conjuring up fanciful images from a variety of Disney classics.

Included in the admission price is access to all rides and shows. Some rides have height and age minimums. Guided tours are available. ◆ Admission. For hours and show schedules, call 714/781.4565. S Harbor Blvd (between W Katella Ave and Santa Ana Fwy), Anaheim. 714/999.4000. www.disneyland.com

Within Disneyland Park:

MAIN STREET USA

This idealized turn-of-the-20th-century town is close to the entrance to the park. Small shops, with wooden floors that resound under your feet and glass display cases at precisely the right height for children's noses, sell a variety of nostalgic merchandise.

ADVENTURELAND

The **Indiana Jones Adventure** takes you deep into the jungles to the Temple of the Forbidden Eye. Watch out for snakes, insects, rats, fire, poison darts, and the deadly rolling rock. The **Jungle Cruise** takes you in a safari boat down simulated Nile, Congo, and Amazon Rivers, with lots of audio-animatronic magic.

NEW ORLEANS SQUARE

On the **Rivers of America,** filigreed balconies overlook winding streets ablaze with flowers and lined with quaint shops. Take a ride with the **Pirates of the Caribbean** on flat-bottomed boats that explore a haunted grotto hung with Spanish moss, and glide into a seaport for pillage and plunder. Ghosts inhabit the **Haunted Mansion,** which uses holography-like imagery to bring many of the 999 residents to wonderfully disembodied life.

CRITTER COUNTRY

Adventures of Winnie the Pooh takes toddlers on a gentle ride through the Hundred-Acre Wood to see Pooh as he dreams of Heffalumps and honey. We said it was for kids. **Davy Crockett's Explorer Canoes** let you paddle along the Rivers of America. Another attraction is **Splash Mountain,** a spectacular log flume adventure.

FRONTIERLAND

This area has battles, a blazing fort, and, through the swinging doors of a western saloon, the **Golden Horseshoe Jamboree,** complete with cancan dancers. The Rivers of America run along the shore and are plied by an amazing assortment of vessels such as the **Mark Twain Riverboat** and the sailing ship *Columbia.* **Big Thunder Mountain Railroad** is a roller-coaster ride through a deserted mine enhanced by special effects (an earthquake, a swarm of bats, and so on).

FANTASYLAND

Enter this magical land through the **Sleeping Beauty Castle.** Over the drawbridge and through the stone halls is the world of familiar storybook characters. The **Casey Jr. Circus Train** chugs past Cinderella's castle, Pinocchio's village, and the home of the Three Little Pigs. The whirling teacups of the **Mad Tea Party** will leave your head spinning. Boats glide through **It's a Small World,** filled with scenes of animated children from many lands all singing the same tune in their native tongues. The most popular ride in Fantasyland is the **Matterhorn,** a 14-story replica of the Swiss mountain built for white-knuckle fun. The **Fantasyland Theatre** hosts Disney's Princess Fantasy Faire.

MICKEY'S TOONTOWN

Cute is the operative word for this attraction, which features houses that belong to Mickey and Minnie and a whole toon-inspired town. The big draw, though, is the **Roger Rabbit Car Toon Spin,** the longest black-light ride in Disneyland history.

TOMORROWLAND

Sporting a futuristic look, complete with giant gardens of edible plants, this land of sci-fi now features an exciting 3-D experience, **Honey, I Shrunk the Audience.** The whimsical show combines 3-D techniques with zany antics by Rick Moranis, reprising his role in the similarly titled Disney films. Also on the bill are **Innoventions,** an interactive technology pavilion; **Space Mountain,** a superspeedy interstellar rocket ride amped up with special effects, rocket vehicles, and a custom sound track; and the 64-foot-high **Astro Orbitor,** where self-piloted spaceships soar and plunge through an animated system of planets and constellations. Be sure to catch Honda's ASIMO robot—the world's most advanced humanoid robot—that walks, turns, twists, climbs stairs, and has amazing capabilities. To further excite your senses, hop on the **Finding Nemo Submarine Voyage,** an underwater adventure offered on eight subs from which you can view an active undersea volcano, fish, and of course Nemo and company. To fill that black hole in your stomach, the food court at **Redd Rockett's Pizza Port** offers everything from salads to pasta and pizza.

15 ANAHEIM CONVENTION CENTER

Across the street from Disneyland Park, this huge convention center—the most successful on the West Coast—is used for events ranging from concerts to conventions. ◆ 800 W Katella Ave (between S Harbor Blvd and S West St), Anaheim. 714/765.8888; e-mail: mail@anaheimoc.org. www.anaheimoc.org

15 DOWNTOWN DISNEY

Just when you think you've had enough Disney already, enter Downtown Disney, a new public pedestrian esplanade that connects the two theme parks—Disney's California Adventure and Disneyland—together with the Disneyland Resort hotels. The complex of commerce hosts

---

Restaurants/Clubs: Red | Hotels: Purple | Shops: Orange | Outdoors/Parks: Green | Sights/Culture: Blue

a plethora of entertainment and dining venues such as a 21-screen megaplex theater with 3,000 stadium-like seats; a branch of West Hollywood's **House of Blues;** a Rainforest Café; a New Orleans branch of **Ralph Brennan's Jazz Kitchen,** offering spicy food and hot jazz; branches of the popular La Brea Bakery, Wetzel's Pretzels, and Häagen-Dazs ice cream shops, and more. ♦ 714.781.DINE. www.disneyland.com

Within Downtown Disney:

CATAL RESTAURANT AND UVA BAR

★★$$ Yet another Patina Group/Joachim Splichal venture, this one a dual-concept restaurant offering two different dining experiences. Uva, a part of Catal, is a casual indoor/outdoor affair with a large menu of tapas and 40 wines by the glass. Catal, on the upper level, features Mediterranean cuisine. ♦ Spanish/Mediterranean ♦ Tu-Sa, lunch and dinner. Reservations suggested. 714/774.4442

15 JW's STEAKHOUSE

★★★$$$ A carnivore's delight of New York steaks, porterhouses, and filet mignons served in a romantic, library-like dining room in the Anaheim Marriott. Specialties might include rack of lamb with garlic sauce, veal medallions with mushrooms, and Grand Marnier soufflé. ♦ International ♦ M-Sa, dinner. Reservations recommended. 700 Convention Way (between S Harbor Blvd and S West St), Anaheim. 714/750.8000

15 SHERATON PARK HOTEL AT THE ANAHEIM RESORT

$$$ A $40 million renovation transformed this 490-room, 14-story hotel into a special oasis. Situated adjacent to the convention center and across the street from the **Disneyland Resort,** the property features contemporary flourishes, highlighted by pastel colors. Attractively appointed rooms offer copious amenities such as signature Sweet Sleeper beds, coffeemakers, Wi-Fi, refrigerators, and balconies overlooking the landscaped pool and patio area or the Disneyland Resort. There are two restaurants, the Southwestern Bar and Grill and Molly's Kitchen; a swimming pool with a sundeck; and a club floor with special privileges, such as entry to a lush lounge offering complimentary food and beverages, and free local phone calls and Internet service. The 1,400-square-foot fitness center next to the pool sports state-of-the-art fitness tools. ♦ 1855 S Harbor Blvd (between Convention Way and W Katella Ave), Anaheim. 714/750.1811, 800/421.6662; fax 714/971.3626 ♿. www.coasthotels.com

16 DOLL CITY USA

Claiming to be the largest of its kind, this 7,700-square-foot specialty store has thousands of dolls, buggies, and related books. ♦ M-Sa. 2080 S Harbor Blvd (at W Orangewood Ave), Anaheim. 714/750.3585, 800/954.3655

17 ANGEL STADIUM OF ANAHEIM

This spectator-friendly home of the Los Angeles Angels of Anaheim comfortably seats 45,000. The ballpark underwent a complete overhaul that added terraced bullpens in the outfield, more concessions, modern club-level and dugout-level suites, a youth-oriented interactive game area, and three full-service restaurants. The stadium is a dedicated baseball-only sports venue. ♦ 2000 Gene Autry Way (between E Orangewood and E Katella Aves), Anaheim. Stadium 714/254.3000, Angels information 714/634.2000. www.angelsbaseball.com

18 HONDA CENTER

The National Hockey League's Mighty Ducks push the puck around at this 17,250-seat facility across the freeway from Anaheim Stadium. ♦ 2965 E Katella Ave (between Struck Ave and Orange Fwy), Anaheim. 714/704.2500. www.hondacenter.com

19 HYATT REGENCY ORANGE COUNTY

$$$ The flamingos, pools, and 60-foot palms in the glass atrium of this 17-story, 654-room hotel provide a resortlike ambience. The hotel is spiffier than ever after a $52 million face-lift that included upgrades of all public areas and guest rooms (which now boast Hyatt "Grand Beds"). There's tennis, a spa, three restaurants, and stylish décor. ♦ 100 Plaza Alicante (at Harbor Blvd and Chapman Ave), Garden Grove. 714/750.1234, 800/972.2929; fax 714/740.0460. www.hyatt.com

20 CRYSTAL CATHEDRAL

Hailed as the most spectacular place of worship on earth, this architectural marvel is just a few blocks from Disneyland Park but light-years away. Made of 10,000 panes of tempered silver glass covering a translucent, weblike frame of white steel trusses set in the shape of a four-pointed star, this cathedral of the Garden Grove Community Church was designed by **Johnson & Burgee** and dedicated in 1980. Seating 2,736, it's a shimmering extravaganza, 415 feet long, 207 feet wide, and 128 feet high. The 236-foot Crean Tower, built in 1990 of highly polished stainless-steel prisms, has a 52-bell carillon.

Architect Richard Neutra designed the church's previous center in 1961. The International Style steel-and-glass church was first used for drive-in services (passengers in 1,400 cars could congregate without ever leaving their autos). Today it hosts Sunday evening services complete with a cast of live animals, flying angels, and dynamic special effects, as well as weddings, meetings, and the annual "Glory of Christmas" and "Glory of Easter" pageants. Neutra's son Dion designed the adjacent 15-story Tower of Hope for the expanding church administration in 1967. Yet another architectural wonder opened in 2003: a cylindrical $20 million Hospitality Center. The **Richard Meier**-designed geometric gem houses a café, bookstore, auditorium, and exhibition rooms. ♦ Tours: M-Sa, 9AM-3:30PM every half hour. Services: Su, 8:30AM (Chapel), 9:30AM, 11AM, 12:30PM (Spanish), 6:30PM. 12141 Lewis St (between Dawn and Chapman Aves), Garden Grove. 714/971.4000. www.crystalcathedral.org

21 LA BRASSERIE RESTAURANT

★$$ This intimate and relaxed bistro specializes in home-style soups, well-prepared fish, and veal. The library dining room is appealing. ♦ French ♦ M-F, lunch and dinner; Sa, dinner. 202 S Main St (between W Palmyra and W Almond Aves), Orange. 714/978.6161

22 YEN CHING

★★$$ Wonderful food is served in a cool, modern setting; the unusually friendly service makes this place a consistent favorite. Specialties include Mandarin and Szechuan-style crispy duck, pot stickers, and whole fish with garlic sauce. ♦ Chinese ♦ Daily, lunch and dinner. 574 S Glassell St (between Garden Grove Fwy and W La Veta Ave), Orange. 714/997.3300

Restaurants/Clubs: Red | Hotels: Purple | Shops: Orange | Outdoors/Parks: Green | Sights/Culture: Blue

ORANGE COUNTY SOUTH

Money, money, and mo' money...
   This gilded area has blossomed into one of the priciest, ritziest sections of Southern California. Home prices are through the ceiling. There's so much money in the till that even teenagers own BMWs, while their parents ride Hummers, Porsches, Mercedes, Vipers, and Aston Martins—one thing's for sure, you won't spot a clunker

on the streets of OC. You will, however, see a preponderance of tall, blond trophy wives with little to do but shop, spa, and lunch; privileged children with lots of discretionary income; and tanned, golf-playing captains of industry.

The **California Gold Coast** is an earthly paradise devoted to boating, golf, and tennis, with a temperate climate, sandy beaches, rocky promontories, green canyons, and rolling hills. Beaches boast distinctive personalities: **Huntington Beach** is a surfer's paradise, **Newport Beach** and **Balboa** are havens for the yachting crowd, **Corona del Mar** is a quiet beachside community, **Laguna Beach** has an artsy-crafty aura combined with a sun-and-surf mentality, **Dana Point** life centers around a large marina, while **San Juan Capistrano** and **San Clemente** are made up of massive estates.

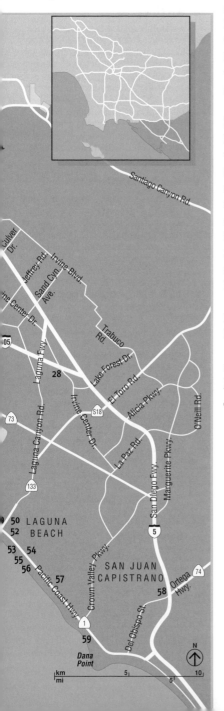

Trademarked "Surf City USA," in honor of the area's dedication to the sport, Huntington Beach boasts 8.5 miles of white sand along the ocean on which to sunbathe, stroll, or frolic in the sea. Like many coastal cities, it has become a boom town, aided by a multimillion-dollar renovation of the area south of the pier that includes a 31-acre oceanfront development called **Pacific City**. Scheduled for completion in 2009, the area will also boast a 178-room boutique resort and a 191,000-square-foot retail promenade. For more information about Huntington Beach, visit www.surfcityusa.com.

For everything you want to know about Newport Beach, go to www.newport beach-cvb.com or call 800/94 COAST.

1 WESTFIELD MAIN PLACE

The Jerde Partnership remodeled this 1958 indoor mall in 1987 in **Jon Jerde**'s trademark style, with colorful tiles, neon, and whimsical signs. The cramped, two-story, skylit center includes **Nordstrom, Macy's,** six movie screens, and 190 specialty shops. ♦ Daily. 2800 N Main St (between Santa Ana and Garden Grove Fwys), Santa Ana. 714/547.7800, 714/547.7000. www.westfield.com

2 THE HACIENDA

★★★$ This side-street restaurant, with a shaded flagstone courtyard and authentic Mexican artifacts, is such a popular wedding spot that the owners sell wedding dresses in

247

the back. Try the best margarita in the county, blue-corn chicken enchiladas, and a chile relleno made strictly with chilies grown in New Mexico's Sandia Valley. Everything comes with homemade *sopapillas* (sweet bread). ◆ Southwestern ◆ W-F, lunch; Th, dinner; Su, brunch. Call ahead, as it is often closed for weddings. Reservations recommended for large parties. 1725 N College Ave (between W 17th and W 19th Sts), Santa Ana. 714/558.1304. www.the-hacienda.com

3 SEAFOOD PARADISE

★★$$ Three dozen varieties of dim sum for connoisseurs are served daily for lunch. The regular Cantonese menu includes such treats as drunken chicken, roast duck, shredded jellyfish, and five-flavor beef. ◆ Chinese ◆ Daily, lunch and dinner; dim sum served daily, 10AM-3PM. 8602 Westminster Ave (between Shirley and Newland Sts), Westminster. 714/893.6066

4 PAGOLAC

★$ A great place to grab a bite while browsing through Little Saigon, this one offers seven-course meals of beef—delicate tender morsels that melt in your mouth, charbroiled or rolled in rice paper and served with lettuce, mint, and cilantro. ◆ Vietnamese ◆ Daily, 11AM-9:30PM. 14580 Brookhurst St (between Bolsa and Hazard Aves), Westminster. 714/531.4740

5 ZOV'S BISTRO & BAKERY

★★$$ It's located in a drab shopping center, but this little award-winning restaurant has the feel of a European bistro. Chef/owner Zov Karamardian's menu offers delicious Armenian pizza, fresh fish (try the salmon), rack of lamb, and mouthwatering desserts. The servers are sometimes curt, but meeter-and-greeter Gary Karamardian is always there with warmth and a handshake. ◆ Eastern Mediterranean ◆ M-Sa, breakfast, lunch, and dinner. 17440 17th St (between Enderle Center Dr and Yorba St), Tustin. 714/838.8855. www.zovs.com

6 PHO 79

★$ This Vietnamese eatery, situated in the heart of Little Saigon, is not suited to all tastes, but it's about as authentic as it gets with its noodles, soups, barbecue shrimp, and adventuresome meals in a bowl. ◆ Vietnamese ◆ Daily, lunch and dinner. No credit cards accepted, or reservations. 9200 Bolsa Ave (between Bushard and Magnolia Sts), Westminster. 714/893.1883 &

7 BOLSA CHICA ECOLOGICAL RESERVE

This wildlife sanctuary is the largest salt marsh preserve in the Los Angeles/Orange County metropolitan area. Its 300 acres provide an oasis for shorebirds and millions of transiting birds that migrate between the Arctic and South America along the Pacific Flyway. There are guides handy to take you on hikes and tours. ◆ Free. Daily. Pacific Coast Hwy (between Golden West St and Warner Ave). 714/846.1114. www.coastalconservancy.ca.gov

8 ANTONELLO

★★$$ This splashy spot is where OC's powerful politicos, social leaders, and businesspeople congregate. Owner Antonio Cagnolo is your typical friendly Italian host, who will happily suggest menu options such as a divine veal chop with porcini mushrooms and truffles or outstanding pasta. There's also an exceptional wine list. ◆ Italian ◆ M-F, lunch and dinner; Sa, dinner. 1611 Sunflower Ave (between Bristol St and Plaza Dr), Santa Ana. 714/751.7153. www.antonello.com

9 SOUTH COAST PLAZA

This upscale shopper's heaven has more than 270 stores on the main landscaped plaza and the adjoining Crystal, Carousel, and Jewel Courts, including department stores such as **Nordstrom, Saks Fifth Avenue,** and **Sears.** In between is a selection of designer boutiques to rival those in Beverly Hills: Gucci, Cartier, Chanel, Tiffany, Emporio Armani, Fendi, Escada, Hermès, Liz Claiborne, La Perla, Laundry by Shelli Segal, Book Soup, Brookstone, Jaeger, Louis Vuitton, and Godiva Chocolatier, to name a few. You can also pamper yourself with spa treatments at Aveda, Georgette Klinger, or **The Spa.** To fuel shoppers there are dozens of eateries, including **Pinot Provence, Morton's of Chicago, Royal Kyber,** and **Darya.** Shuttle service is available from area hotels for about $8 round-trip. This ranks as the busiest retail center in Southern California, with more than 18 million visitors a year (as many as any theme park). ◆ Daily. 3333 Bristol St (at San Diego Fwy), Costa Mesa. 800/782.8888, 714/435.2000, 714/435.2034. www.southcoastplaza.com

10 ORANGE COUNTY PERFORMING ARTS CENTER

From the **Kirov Ballet** and the **American Ballet Theatre** to *Cats*, this performing arts center has rivaled LA's Music Center since it opened in 1986. The auditorium is named for developer Henry T. Segerstrom, who spearheaded the effort to make it a center for the arts. Concerts and opera are also regularly featured. ◆ M-Sa. 600 Town Center Dr (at Ave of the Arts), Costa Mesa. 714/556.2787. www.ocpac.org

11 WESTIN SOUTH COAST PLAZA HOTEL

$$$$ The weekend specials are a good value at this 17-story, 390-room hotel, which features tennis and volleyball courts, a pool, 24-hour room service, and the **Garden Court Cafe.** ♦ 686 Anton Blvd (at Bristol St), Costa Mesa. 714/540.2500, 800/228.3000; fax 714/662.6695; e-mail: south@westin.com. www.westin.com

12 SOUTH COAST REPERTORY THEATRE

The Mainstage and Second Stage present a diversified program of live comedy and drama from September through June. ♦ Box office: daily. 655 Town Center Dr (between Ave of the Arts and Bristol St), Costa Mesa. 714/957.4033. www.scr.org

13 PLAZA TOWER

The curved façade and stainless-steel panels of this 1991 **Cesar Pelli** office building gleam in the light and capture the color of the sunset. The sophisticated structure has a formal front, a double grid of round-edged horizontal and vertical ribs, and double loggias and setbacks at the 17th and 21st floors. ♦ 600 Anton Blvd (at Ave of the Arts), Costa Mesa

14 CALIFORNIA SCENARIO

Artworks are scattered throughout **South Coast Plaza,** but the real treasure (worth the drive from LA) is Isamu Noguchi's 1.6-acre sculpture garden. Framed by reflective glass towers and the blank white walls of parking structures, this oasis is often overlooked by visitors. Noguchi created a contemporary version of a traditional Japanese garden in which natural rocks, sandstone structures and paving, trees, cacti, and running water symbolize different aspects of the state of California. ♦ Free. Daily. 611 Anton Blvd (between Ave of the Arts and Park Center Dr), Costa Mesa

15 AGORA CHURRASCARIA

★★$$ Similar to **Fogo de Chao** in Beverly Hills (see page 96), complete with really adorable, charming and handsome gaucho-wearing waiters who carve a variety of meats at your table, this carnivore's paradise specializes in the *Rodizio* style of cooking, which I guess you have be Brazilian to understand. Like at Fogo, there's a price-fixed menu that includes all the meat, hot food bar, and salad bar items you can swallow. There are seafood items available for non–meat eaters, but meat rules here, 101 varieties: filet mignon, sausage, chicken, top sirloin, tri tip, lamb chops, pork tenderloin, beef skirt steak, *pichana* (top sirloin cap), and *coraçao* (chicken heart, which may be hard to stomach for some). Specialty drinks such as Brazilian cosmos, mojitos, the Girl from Ipanema, and batida are big here. Agora's investors Choon Cho and Dan Kim operate a Korean fashion company, Seoul, and developed a taste for Brazilian food after living in São Paulo, where they also ran restaurants. The pair designed a dramatic interior to showcase the fare with rustic river-rock-lined walls, a 25-foot peaked cathedral ceiling with massive cedar beams, neutral earth tones, and skylights. ♦ Brazilian Steak House ♦ Daily, lunch and dinner. Reservations recommended. 1830 Main St (at MacArthur Blvd), Irvine. 949.222.9910; fax 949/222.9965. www.agorachurrascaria.com and www.agoranow.com

16 JOHN WAYNE/ORANGE COUNTY AIRPORT

Ten commercial and two commuter carriers serve this busy alternative to LAX, providing direct flights to 19 domestic destinations. In 1990, **Leason Pomeroy Associates** and **Gensler & Associates** designed an award-winning terminal, taking inspiration from the shape of an airplane fuselage. The rounded, bronze-tinted roofs of its three long, sleek, parallel vaults run perpendicular to the San Diego Freeway. The facility has been greatly upgraded with Wi-Fi outlets in all terminals and the addition of a third terminal (C). For ground transportation to LAX, call 949/252.5171. ♦ 3151 Airway Ave (at Paularino Ave), Costa Mesa. 714/252.5200. www.ocair.com

17 BISTANGO

★★$$ This modern restaurant, housed in the award-winning Atrium Building in Irvine, is highlighted by a granite bar, rough slate floor, chic Italian furniture, and nearly a hundred contemporary gallery artworks (they're for sale). A power-lunch meeting place by day and a jazz hot spot at night, outstanding menu choices include designer pizzas, New Zealand lamb, grilled filet mignon, grilled swordfish, mushroom-crusted Alaskan halibut, and a poached pear tart with vanilla ice cream and caramel sauce to swoon over. There's also a super three-course tasting menu. There's nightly entertainment and dancing. ♦ New American Cuisine ♦ M-F, lunch and dinner; daily, dinner. Reservations recommended. Atrium

Building, 19100 Von Karman Ave (between Campus and Dupont Drs), Irvine. 949/752.5222. www.bistango.com

18 PARK PLACE

Developed by Fluor Corporation, this complex of futuristic glass-clad structures along the San Diego Freeway has become an Orange County landmark. It's best viewed from the road. It was designed by **Welton Becket & Associates** and completed in 1976. ◆ 3333 Michelson Dr (between Harvard Ave and Jamboree Blvd), Irvine

19 FAIRMONT NEWPORT BEACH

$$$ The gorgeous-looking 440-room, 54-suite property, designed by architect Doug Lee of Irvine's Lee & Sakahara, integrates the sleek modern exterior originally created by Los Angeles Airport designer **Gin Won** with an airy, warm interior. The lively lobby features three handsome, gentlemen's club–like rooms for relaxing or watching TV; a wide-open restaurant open for breakfast, lunch, and dinner; and a bustling bar. Fairmont Hotel's signature **Willow Stream Spa** creates a warm atmosphere in which to enjoy penultimate pampering and treatments (a man's Recovery massage was rated a 10 by one partaker, and this writer's a 1^1/$_2$-hour sports massage, performed by Greg, went outside the rating box it was so good). The spa is blessed with a thoughtful staff who add to its charm. There are comfortable relaxation rooms, and locker areas with steam bath and showers. Guest rooms lean toward the masculine, with lots of rich woods and a textured natural palette of rye, chocolate, gold, and cayenne accented with tumbled granite, woven cane, and British Colonial woods. Pillow-top Simmons mattresses cover the beds, flat-screen televisions and DVD players provide in-room enjoyment, and wireless Internet hookups keep you in cyberspace. You might want to consider popping a few extra bucks for Executive Club privileges such as admission to a private lounge, just off the lobby, where a pretty lavish breakfast is served (eggs Benedict, pancakes, crepes, scrambled eggs, lox and bagels, and other specialties are offered along with an extensive array of starches, fruit, and juices). Luscious hors d'oeuvres are served before dinner and desserts are set out late at night. All soft drinks are also included, but adult beverages are extra. In addition to lounge amenities you get private check-out, shuttle service to/from local airports, free local calls, and room upgrades. The property also sports a small but well-used swimming pool. ◆ 4500 MacArthur Blvd (at Birch St), Newport Beach. 949/476.2001, 800/441.1414; fax 949/476.0153. www.fairmont.com

Within the Fairmont Newport Beach:

BAMBU RESTAURANT

★★★$$ No, we didn't misspell it; the "b" is lower-cased at this charming lobbyside restaurant, which seems to do its biggest business at breakfast and lunch with business travelers in a rush to grab a quick bite. But it would be a shame to miss dinner, as it's very good. A Caesar salad and halibut dinner proved exceptional, and so were the steak and desserts. There's a great Sunday brunch, too. ◆ California Cuisine ◆ Daily, breakfast, lunch, and dinner; Su, brunch. Reservations suggested for dinner. 949/476.2001

20 PASCAL

★★$$$ Superb seafood is served here, with a hint of Provence in the bold colors and seasonings. Mussels steamed with saffron, bass with thyme, and chicken with olives are among the signature dishes. ◆ French ◆ M-F, lunch and dinner; Sa, dinner. Reservations recommended. 1000 N Bristol St (at Jamboree Rd), Newport Beach. 949/752.0107

21 HUNTINGTON PIER

🄿 The first surfing contests were held at Huntington Beach, and today it remains a destination for surfers from around the world. This pier is the best place to watch the year-round action. There's a whole lot of shaking going on around the pier. For starters, a 157-room boutique hotel, Joie de Vivre, is going up on The Strand—a 3^1/$_2$-acre project overlooking the pier, just north of Main Street, that also includes upscale retailers (Abercrombie & Fitch, Urban Outfitters), a pedestrian plaza, and a link to Main Street restaurants. ◆ Pacific Coast Hwy and Main St, Huntington Beach

On and around Huntington Pier:

RUBY'S DINER

★$ Smack at the end of the pier, this member of the retro-style Ruby's chain is ideal for shakes, burgers, and fries. ◆ American ◆ Daily, breakfast, lunch, dinner, and takeout. 714/969.7829. www.rubys.com

DUKE'S HUNTINGTON BEACH

★$$ Adjacent to the pier on the south side, this restaurant, named for modern-day surfing pioneer Duke Kahanamoku, serves seafood with an Asian/Hawaiian flavor and fun drinks at its Barefoot Bar (but shoes are required). ◆ American ◆ Daily, lunch and dinner. 714/374.6446. www.dukeshuntington.com

CHIMAYO AT THE BEACH

★★$$ Downstairs from Duke's, Chimayo provides a cool South Seas–style spot to chill under the yellow umbrella-covered bar or on the outside dining patio. Chimayo specializes in premium aged steak, seafood, and barbecue. The baby back ribs are amazing, and so's the Maine lobster and cornmeal-crusted calamari. When you're jonesing for a refreshing adult beverage, you can create your own margarita from any of a number of top tequilas or order the ever-popular Chimayo mango martini made from fresh fruit. ◆ American ◆ Daily, lunch and dinner. 714/374.7274. www.culinaryadventures.com. Party animals, take note: Both Duke's and Chimayo turn into hot spots Thursday and Friday nights. Owned by one of Surf City's first women surfers, the kitchen turns out groovy plates of crisp bacon, eggs cooked to order, heavenly pancakes, and other morning jump-starters. A table on the patio is well worth the wait.

Sugar Shack

Surfers burn bodacious calories, so many begin the day by fueling up with hearty breakfasts at this place, just a short stroll from the pier. It's the perfect place to hobnob with surfing legends and other "ho daddies." The food's as American as it gets, the scene surf city. The rumor is that you can't call yourself a surfer until you've put in time at the Sugar Shack. ◆ American ◆ 213 Main St. 714/536.0355

Pete's Mexican Café

★$ A few blocks away, this is another boarder haven, where *huevos rancheros* headline the menu. ◆ Mexican ◆ 213 Fifth St. 714/960.8797

22 Hyatt Regency Huntington Beach Resort & Spa

$$$ Luxury personified best describes this four-story, 517-room resort with its sweeping views of the Pacific Ocean and tasteful Andalusian décor. Three restaurants, two lounges, a mega shopping plaza, a pool, tennis courts, a fitness center, and a 20,000-square-foot Pacific Waters Spa provide the guest diversions. Each room and suite is stocked with robes, a coffeemaker, a refrigerator, data ports and Wi-Fi Internet access, an oversized desk, down comforters, and a private balcony or patio. There's even shuttle service to Disneyland and environs. ◆ 21500 Pacific Coast Hwy (at Beach Blvd). 714/698.1234, 800/233.1234. www.hyatthuntingtonbeach.com

23 Crab Cooker

★$$ This popular, crowded fish restaurant doesn't accept reservations—not even, as one story has it, from the late President Richard Nixon, who wanted to circumvent the line. The Manhattan clam chowder is a big seller, but the specialty is any mesquite-broiled seafood, and if you like lobster, well, it's the best. The adjacent fish market opens at 10AM. ◆ Seafood ◆ M-Sa, lunch and dinner; Su, dinner. 2200 Newport Blvd (at 22nd St), Costa Mesa. 949/673.0100

24 Kitayama

★★★$$ This *kaiseki* restaurant (serving multicourse sushi, sashimi, noodle, and tempura meals in tatami rooms with kimono-clad waitresses) is so authentic you might want to bring a Japanese friend along to translate the menu—or you could always have a seat at the more accessible and likewise excellent sushi bar. The fixed-price *omakase kaiseki* (chef's choice) is your best bet if you don't want to spend time figuring out the menu. Other good choices are the beef shabu shabu that you cook at the table, buckwheat soba, and sukiyaki. Finish with red-bean ice cream, then take a walk through the pretty bonsai garden. ◆ Japanese ◆ M-F, lunch and dinner; Sa, dinner. Reservations recommended. 101 Bayview Pl (at Bristol St), Newport Beach. 949/725.0777. www.japaneserestaurantnavi.com/kitayama.html

25 Golden Truffle

★★$$ Chef/owner Alan Greeley continues to please the crowd that gathers nightly at this convivial neighborhood eatery. Much of the clientele are regulars who have eaten here for more than two decades. They bring wines by the bottle (corkage is charged) or order from his extensive list, and spend hours savoring such dishes as duck tacos, fillet of carpaccio with Genoa tuna sauce, Golden Truffle ground chuck cheeseburger, duck confit, prime beef Bourguignon, or a fish special of the day. On the other hand, many simply sit back and let the chef "surprise" them with his off-the-menu prix-fixe dinner. There's even a spa menu for waist watchers. ◆ French Continental ◆ Tu-Sa, lunch and dinner. Reservations recommended. 1767 Newport Blvd (at W 18th St), Costa Mesa. 949/645.9858. www.goldentruffle.com

25 The Yard House Restaurant

★★★$$$$ This massive 10,000-square-foot eating emporium with its exhibition kitchen and signature Oval Bar serves lobster tails like no other in clarified butter and blanched garlic, finishing with lemongrass beurre blanc and tomato oil. Executive chef Carlito Jocson does a kick-ass job with grilled New

---

Zealand chops, too, wrapping the tender meat around an herb crust and lathering on sweet balsamic syrup. Other great choices include a spinach salad with grilled Portobello mushrooms and Gouda cheese, and pan-roasted Chilean sea bass with bok choy and a miso glaze. To wash it down, there's the world's largest selection of draft beers (about 180) and a super wine list, served by the glass or bottle. And then there are desserts: warm chocolate soufflé cake with vanilla-bean ice cream, macadamia nut cheesecake with warm caramel sauce, warm lemon soufflé cake with raspberry sauce, and more. ◆ American Fusion ◆ Daily, dinner; Sa, Su, lunch. Reservations suggested. Valet parking. 1875 Newport Blvd (at Harbor Blvd), Costa Mesa, 949/642.0090. Also at 401 Shoreline Dr (in Shoreline Village), Long Beach. 562/628.0455; 71 Fortune Dr (at Irvine Spectrum), Irvine. 949/585.9477. www.yardhouse.com

26 UPPER NEWPORT BAY

Surrounded by the bluffs of Newport Bay, this remarkable and idyllic 741-acre spot is a preserve for ducks, geese, and other avian users of the Pacific Flyway. Paths along the far reaches of the estuary are wonderful for quiet early-morning walks. ◆ Backbay Dr, Newport Beach. 949/640.6746

27 UNIVERSITY OF CALIFORNIA AT IRVINE

UC Irvine was founded in 1965 on a thousand acres donated by the Irvine Company. Twenty-five buildings house five major schools and a number of interdisciplinary and graduate departments. Full-time enrollment is about 17,000. The campus was laid out as an arboretum; more than 11,000 trees from all over the world form a green grove in the center of the tan hills of the **Irvine Ranch.** A self-guided tree-tour brochure is available at the Administration Building. Rare exceptions to the prevailing architectural mediocrity of UC campuses are the **Information Computer Sciences and Engineering Research Facility**—a splendid complex of buildings by **Frank Gehry** located on the southeast edge of the inner ring—and works by **Morphosis** and other cutting-edge architects. The free **School of the Arts Gallery** sponsors exhibitions of 20th-century art and is open Tuesday through Sunday. Theatrical performances are held in the **Fine Arts Village Theatre,** the **Concert Hall,** and **Crawford Hall.** ◆ Campus Dr (between Culver and University Drs). 949/824.5011

28 WILD RIVERS

A water park with 40 rides and attractions is set on a lush tropical site formerly occupied by Lion Country Safari. You can shoot the rapids on an inner tube, be fired over water on the **Wipeout,** or simply lie back and work on your tan. Paddling pools keep the smallest children happy. Refreshments are available, as are group picnic sites by advance reservation. ◆ Admission. Daily, June-Oct; some weekends off-season. 8770 Irvine Center Dr (between Lake Forest Dr and San Diego Fwy), Irvine. 949/768.9453

29 BALBOA BAY CLUB & RESORT

$$$$ Catering to a prototypical country-club clientele who inhabit the multimillion-dollar manses of the surrounding area, this 132-room beauty is the only full-service waterfront hotel in Newport. Designed by Barry Design Associates of Los Angeles, the décor harbors an understated elegance orchestrated by soft classical columns, cream and gold stone floors, natural rattan furnishings, and tropical touches. Accommodations are spacious and attractively furnished with colorful drapes over plantation shutters, dark woods pitted with apricot, and rust-colored fabrics. Rooms are equipped with coffeemakers and the usual but upscale amenities. The makeup mirrors are about the best we've encountered. Bay-front rooms are choice, with views of multimillion-dollar boats and pricey town houses and homes across the narrow arm of Newport Bay on Lido Island. There's a large, inviting pool, a well-equipped, compact fitness room, and optional fee activities, such as use of the spiffy spa (an utter pamper emporium offering head-to-toe services) and the gym (a large, bustling body-buffing facility) at the **Balboa Bay Racquet Club.** There are also nearby boat rentals and golf. The culinary highlight is chef Josef Lageder's creative California cuisine served in the **First Cabin** (★★★$$$) dining room. Room service is available whenever and well worth it. In the evening, Duke's Place dishes out drinks and entertainment. Complimentary transportation to and from Orange County Airport provides a pleasant extra. ◆ 1221 W Coast Hwy (between Dover Dr and Tustin Ave), Newport Beach. 888/445.7153, 949/645.5000. www.balboabayclub.com

30 NEWPORT DUNES

This upscale aquatic RV park on a 15-acre lagoon has been called the "Ritz of Recreational Vehicle Facilities." Not your normal parking ground, this one offers Friday barbecues, crafts classes to kids, a laundry room, and Wi-Fi hookups, among other things. And it's not only for campers; visitors may rent all sorts of sports equipment, from paddleboats to sailboats, kayaks, windsurfers, boogie boards, roller skates, and bicycles. There are also rental cottages for those without RVs, meeting facilities, a

launching ramp, and dressing rooms.
♦ 1131 Backbay Dr (just west of Jamboree Rd), Newport Beach. General information 949/729.3863, resort watersports 949/729.3863, 949/729.1155, 800/765.1155. www.newportdunes.com

31 HYATT REGENCY NEWPORT BEACH

$$$ Located on **Upper Newport Bay,** this 26-acre resort has 405 rooms and four three-bedroom villas with private pools. The sporting options here include a nine-hole golf course, tennis, and swimming, and there's a spa with Jacuzzis for post-workout fun. **Duke's,** an English pub filled with John Wayne memorabilia (he used to frequent the resort, and started the tennis club), offers live entertainment Wednesday through Saturday. Summer concerts are held Friday evenings in an outdoor amphitheater.
♦ 1107 Jamboree Rd (just east of Backbay Dr), Newport Beach. 949/729.1234, 800/233.1234; fax 949/644.1552; e-mail: info@hyattnewportbeach.com. www.hyattnewportbeach.com

32 ORANGE COUNTY MUSEUM OF ART

Changing exhibitions of contemporary art and a permanent collection of 20th-century art emphasizing works by California artists are presented in this internationally famous museum. The **Sculpture Garden Cafe** offers light meals and snacks; the gift shop sells catalogs and books. ♦ Admission. Tu–Su. 850 San Clemente Dr (between Santa Cruz and Santa Barbara Drs), Newport Beach. 949/759.1122

33 ISLAND HOTEL

$$$$ This hotel feels good from the minute you walk into the lavish lobby, scented by huge arrangements of tropical flowers. You walk up to the front desk, where a pleasant receptionist greets you with a big welcoming smile. And it just keeps on getting better. The Island attracts business travelers during the week and a predominantly leisure crowd—who go to shop at nearby Fashion Island—weekends. It's all good at this 20-story, 295-room urban oasis, where accommodations are elegant but simply appointed with soothing shades of yellow, peach, melon, aqua, and touches of sage and terra-cotta. European furnishings in dark mink, rattan, cherry wood, and iron, lavish marble bathrooms stocked with upscale amenities, plush terry robes, 410-thread-count bed linens, high-speed Internet access,

coffemakers, and safes make up the long list of creature comforts. All rooms have balconies with either a water or garden view. There are 54 Executive suites and 29 Luxury suites that cater to big spenders. Additional services include a business center, concierge, 24-hour room service, daily newspaper delivery, valet parking, and transportation by town car to and from the airport. Feel like swimming laps? Pull up a chaise, or book a private cabana, next to the inviting 3,000-square-foot swimming pool—a lush oasis surrounded by palm trees and tropical foliage. Enhance your visit with some Balinese-style pampering at the stunning 4,000-square-foot Island Spa. The Island Boreh Remedy—two hours of pure bliss—will make you think you died and went to heaven; we're not kidding. Gender-specific treatments are equally fabulous: A Gentlemen's Face Therapy got rave reviews, and there are also metrosexual male manicures, pedicures, and massages. The fitness center is one of the best we've found in a hotel, with lots of modern-day equipment and plenty of space to move around. There are also two lighted outdoor tennis courts. Golfers qualify for preferred tee times and special rates available at Oak Creek Golf Club, a gorgeous 18-hole Tom Fazio–designed course. There are three dining choices: the pricey **Palm Terrace** (see below), a more casual lounge/café, and a poolside eatery open in season.
♦ 690 Newport Center Dr (at Santa Cruz Dr), Newport Beach. 949/759.0808, toll free 888/321.4752; fax 949/760.8073. www.theislandhotel.com

Within the Island Hotel:

PALM TERRACE

★★$$$$ The bright and cheerful room, created by Los Angeles–based Darrell Schmidt Design Associates, boasts a tropical oasis décor in which to savor the innovative cuisine of chef Bill Bracken, who spent nearly a dozen years at the Peninsula Hotel in Beverly Hills before jumping kitchens. Bracken's mouth-watering menus are filled with delectable choices, such as truffle-scented macaroni and cheese, potato-crusted Chilean sea bass, fish stew, bone-in Kansas City steak, and Kobe short ribs. A really nice touch is the "small bites" option, where you can order tastes of Bracken's dishes like "just one scallop," a taste of mac and cheese, a couple of slices of 30-hour short ribs, or a small bite of tuna tartare. Check out the four floor-to-ceiling wine cabinets stocked with more than 1,000 bottles. For a special treat, ask for a table out on the terrace—which is heated when necessary. ♦ American-style Cuisine ♦ M-F, breakfast, lunch, and dinner; Sa, dinner; Su, brunch and dinner. Reservations recommended. 949/760.4920

THE GRILL AT PELICAN HILL

★★★$$$ This charming Mission-style restaurant, with its beamed white ceiling, whitewash exterior, and hand-painted tiles, overlooks the eighteenth hole of the Tom Fazio–designed Pelican Hill Golf Course. The food's great too. ♦ American. ♦ Daily, lunch and dinner; Sa, Su, brunch. Reservations required for dinner. 949/717.6000

34 THE RITZ RESTAURANT & GARDEN

★★★$$$$ Don't confuse it with the **Ritz-Carlton** hotel down the coast, even though it draws the same well-heeled crowd. Its bouillabaisse has been acclaimed as the best west of the Mississippi, and the carousel appetizer (with fresh foie gras, sweet smoked trout, and gravlax), the liver with crispy onion sticks, and the classic osso buco have also won devoted fans. This place is kind of dressy, so don your best duds. ♦ Continental ♦ M-F, lunch and dinner; Sa, Su, dinner. Reservations recommended. 880 Newport Center Dr (between Farallon and Santa Barbara Drs), Newport Beach. 949/720.1800. www.theritz.com

35 FASHION ISLAND

This spiffy 1960s' mall serves as both a marketplace and gathering spot —especially for tall, blond OC trophy wives, often with two kids in tow. Anchored by **Neiman Marcus** and **Bloomingdale's,** the center houses 200 stores; 40-plus eateries including **Roy's Hawaiian Fusion Cuisine** (949/640.7697), **Blue Coral Seafood & Spirits** (949/856.2583), **Cafe R&D** (949/219.0555), and **California Pizza Kitchen** (949/759.5543); two food courts; and a farmers' market. The Mediterranean-themed parklike complex is so popular that families come just to stroll through the plazas and catch views of the Pacific. To make it even more enticing, the mall provides free wheelchairs and strollers, a play area for tots, and concierge services. For the hip shopper there's a **Juicy Couture, Lucky Jeans, Kate Spade,** and **Hugo Boss.** Located in the 75-acre **Newport Center** complex, the mall is 20 minutes south of Anaheim. Shuttle service is available from area hotels. ♦ Daily. Newport Center Dr (north of E Coast Hwy), Newport Beach. 949/721.2000. www.shopfashionisland.com

36 THE CANNERY

★★$$ This chimerical landmark restaurant, festooned with jellyfish lights, provides an animated, fun setting with excellent service and good food. There's seating outside on a balcony overlooking the bay and in an informal upstairs bar, lounge, and dining area with hardwood floors under an exposed-beam ceiling. The place, which actually was a real cannery circa 1921, called Western Canners, bustles day and night. The fresh fish dishes, like the halibut, Chilean sea bass, or king salmon, are excellent. Go early and join the crowd for drinks. ♦ Seafood ♦ Daily, lunch and dinner. 3010 Lafayette Ave (near 32nd St), Newport Beach. 949/566.0060. www.cannerynewport.com

37 BAYSIDE

★★★$$$ There's a pleasant uptown style to this restaurant by the bay on Balboa Island. The food is quite good, but the service can be spotty. You can dine inside or out on a pretty porch. As at so many seaside eateries, the fish is the best choice here. ♦ Seafood ♦ Daily, dinner. Reservations required. 900 Bayside Dr (between Balboa and Harbor Islands), Newport Beach. 949/721.1222. www.BaysideRestaurant.com

38 DORYMAN'S OCEANFRONT INN

$$$ This 10-room bed-and-breakfast inn offers ocean views and Victorian décor in a converted 1891 commercial building—the first in the city. Each charming room glows under fern-filled skylights while Italian marble sunken tubs, French etched-glass fixtures, and cozy fireplaces enhance the ambience. ♦ 2102 W Ocean Front (between McFadden and 21st Pls), Newport Beach. 949/675.7300. www.dorymans.com

39 LOVELL BEACH HOUSE

One of the great monuments of modern architecture, this 1926 beach house was designed by **Rudolph Schindler** for the same progressive doctor who was to commission a house by Richard Neutra in Los Feliz a few years later. It is a fine example of Schindler's early Constructivist style, combining grace, lightness, and strength in a design far ahead of its time. It's a private residence. ♦ 1242 W Ocean Front (at 13th St), Newport Beach

40 NEWPORT HARBOR

There are 10 yacht clubs and 10,000 boats in this aquatic playground. The bay surrounds Lido Isle, Linda Isle, Harbor Island, Bay Isle, and Balboa Island. Boat slips or moorings can be rented through the county sheriff's **Harbor Division** (949/723.1002). **Hornblower Yachts** (800/950.1920) offers brunch and dinner/ dancing cruises. ♦ Lower Newport Bay, Newport Beach

41 BALBOA FERRY

Three tiny auto ferries take pedestrians and bikers between the Balboa Peninsula and Balboa Island. ◆ Daily, 24 hours. Palm St (just north of E Bay Ave), Newport Beach

42 BALBOA PAVILION

Built as a Victorian bathhouse and electric Red Car terminal in 1906, this was a trendy destination for fashionably dressed bathers from the greater LA area. It is now the most visible point on the bay, outlined by twinkling lights at night, with a harbor-view bar and restaurant. It is the Newport Terminal for **Catalina Island tours, whale-watching expeditions,** and cruises aboard the *Pavilion Queen,* which last 45 to 90 minutes and take you around Newport Harbor. ◆ 400 Main St (just north of E Bay Ave), Newport Beach. General information 949/673.5245, sport fishing and skiff rentals 949/673.1423

43 RUBY'S

★$ The lovingly re-created Streamline diner helped launch a trend—and a growing chain, now in more than 30 locations—toward white Formica, red vinyl, and quilted stainless steel. Cuddle up in a booth for a feast on omelettes, mountains of fries, big salads, hot dogs, hamburgers (and really good veggie burgers), and milk shakes. There are also great views of the Pacific Ocean, which is just across the street. ◆ American ◆ Daily, breakfast, lunch, and dinner. Balboa Pier, Newport Beach. 949/673.7829

44 SHERMAN LIBRARY AND GARDENS

This jewel of a botanical garden and library specializes in the horticulture of the Pacific Southwest. The well-maintained grounds are vibrant with unusual flowers and hanging baskets. The tea garden serves pastries and coffee, while a gift shop sells horticultural items. ◆ Admission. Gardens: daily. Library: Tu, Th, 9AM-4:30PM. 2647 E Coast Hwy (between Fernleaf and Dahlia Aves), Newport Beach. 949/673.2261

45 CARMELO'S

★★$$ The well-rounded menu, friendly service, and live music draw crowds to this unpretentious trattoria. Entrées to try include pasta Sorrentina (with fresh porcini mushrooms and zucchini flowers), pumpkin-flavored gnocchi, and Dover sole Milanese. ◆ Italian ◆ Daily, dinner (music and dancing until 1AM). Reservations recommended. 3520 E Coast Hwy (between Orchid and Narcissus Aves), Newport Beach. 949/675.1922

46 FIVE CROWNS

★★$$$$ Fine food, professional service, and a charming ambience account for the popularity of this improved version of England's oldest inn (Ye Old Bell at Hurley, opened in 1135). Herb-roasted free-range chicken, roast duckling with apple-prune compote, and prime rib are dependable choices. ◆ Continental ◆ M-Sa, dinner; Su, brunch and dinner. Reservations recommended. 3801 E Coast Hwy (at Poppy Ave), Corona del Mar. 949/760.0331

47 THE RESORT AT PELICAN HILL

$$$$ Since it was still under construction at press time, we were only able to fantasize about this amazing 504-acre cliffside complex perched above the Pacific Ocean 10 minutes from Orange County's John Wayne Airport. An acropolis of indulgence, the resort offers everything from lavish villas (128) and bungalows (204) to a 20,000-square-foot spa, a wedding chapel, a Coliseum pool (136 feet in diameter with an amphitheater of terraced decks equipped with private cabanas), restaurants, and naturally, golf on the world-famous Pelican Hill Course. ◆ 22701 Pelican Hill Road S, Newport Coast. 949/467.6800. www.pelicanhill.com

48 CRYSTAL COVE

You really need to check out this sizzling seaside spot. Although it's been there a long time, young OC surfers, swimmers, and sun worshippers just recently began flocking to this pristine area adjacent to **Crystal Cove State Park,** off Pacific Coast Highway between Corona del Mar and Laguna Beach. Pristine, with awesome cliffs peering down over tide pools, quaint cottages, and a strip of beautiful beach, and part commercial with upscale offices and shops, it's definitely worth visiting if only to observe a slice of Orange County life. Start just south of the intersection where Los Trancos (east) and Crystal Cove (west) go west cross East Coast Highway, and stop for one of the best milk shakes you ever drunk at the **Shake Shack** (7703 E Coast Hwy, 949/464.0100); take your drink out to the cliffside patio, where you can peer down at the action on the beach below. Okay, after you've downed your shake, walk it off on the beach—drive

---

Restaurants/Clubs: Red | Hotels: Purple | Shops: Orange | Outdoors/Parks: Green | Sights/Culture: Blue

north to Crystal Cove and make a left down to the ocean. Then, when you're hungry again, head over to **The Beachcomber at Crystal Cove** ($$★★★), but expect a long wait for a table. First come, first served, it's California/OC personified. This funky little cottage has become one of the hottest joints in town. Super casual—you wear flip-flops, shorts, and tank tops—there's something for every appetite. For breakfast there's yummy macadamia nut pancakes; for lunch, Portuguese sausage and vegetable soup or Dungeness crab cakes; for drinks, you have Kahlúa coladas, mojitos, or margaritas; and at dinner time there's steak, roasted chicken, salmon with wild rice, and other options. ♦ American ♦ Daily, breakfast, lunch, and dinner. 15 Crystal Cove. 949/376.6900. www.thebeachcombercafe.com.

Or make a reservation for dinner at **Mastro's Ocean Club Fish House** ($$$★★★), another hot spot, popular with the area's brat pack, where the fish and ambience rule. ♦ Fish House ♦ Daily, lunch and dinner. Reservations suggested. 8112 E Coast Hwy, Newport Beach. 949/376.6990. For a fancier fare, sample **Sage on the Coast** (★★★$$$), a gorgeous spot to enjoy an unforgettable meal. Start out with the tortilla soup, spicy ahi spring rolls, or Sage's antipasto plate, and continue with seared sea scallops, grilled prime flatiron steak, panko-crusted striped bass, or a double-cut pork chop, then finish with a fantastic dessert and perhaps a stroll on the nearby beach. Or frolic around nearby Crystal Cove State Park, which offers lots of recreational options. Spread out along a three-mile strip of coastline with wooded canyons, open bluffs, and an underwater park. The park provides an enjoyable venue for camping (albeit at pretty primitive spots: Moro Ridge and Deer Canyon), dirt road biking, diving, kayaking, fishing, and surfing. You can even horseback ride if you bring your own horse, or hike through 2,000 acres of undeveloped woodland (park at Moro Canyon parking lot behind the school and get a map at the ranger station).

49 HORTENSE MILLER GARDEN

Docents lead two-hour tours through this spectacular two-acre private garden, overgrown with native flora and exotic plants. More than 1,200 species are represented. Reservations are required two weeks in advance. ♦ Admission. Tours: W, Sa, and occasionally Tu. 22511 Allview Terr (north of High Dr), Laguna Beach. 949/497.0716

50 FESTIVAL OF ARTS/PAGEANT OF THE MASTERS

Showbiz and technical wizardry are combined to simulate great works of art, such as *The Last Supper*, using live models. Artists apply innovative makeup to the models, who must remain motionless for up to a minute and a half during the performance. For seven or eight (it changes slightly) weeks each year, some 600 volunteers and a small staff of trained professionals draw oohs and aahs from thousands of wide-eyed spectators. Book well ahead for the July and August performances. ♦ Admission. 650 Laguna Canyon Rd (north of Forest Ave), Laguna Beach. 949.494.1145, 800/487.3378. www.foapom.org

51 LAGUNA BEACH

So beautiful it can take your breath away. So peaceful it could melt Rambo. Add to that a Mediterranean climate combined with a three-mile beach and an artsy atmosphere and you will understand why even Angelenos flock here for summer weekends or rent seaside cottages for weeks or months at a time. To maintain its pristine environment, the city strictly prohibits neon signs, T-shirt vendors, and buildings higher than three stories. The village bustles year-round with locals and visitors browsing through boutiques (this is where to find nifty bikinis), shopping for art or antiques, eating at sidewalk cafés, and playing beach volleyball till they literally drop on the soft sand beach. This is where John Steinbeck lived while penning *Tortilla Flat*, and Bette Davis made her home during the 1940s. For adventurers, explorers, or just plain sybarites, Laguna's South Coast Wilderness—a 17,000-acre greenbelt—offers an opportunity to commune with nature. You can snorkel, dive, go mountain biking, hiking, horseback riding or camping, or take guided tours. Nature lovers can catch glimpses of rare monkey flowers and bush lupine, while explorers will discover hidden caves and coves. It's easy to spend days trekking through this eco-friendly area that includes **Aliso and Wood Canyons Wilderness Park**, 28373 Alicia Parkway (949/923.2200); **Crystal Cove State Park**, 8471 Pacific Coast Highway (949/494/3539); **Laguna Coast Wilderness Park**, 20102 Laguna Canyon Road (949/923.2235); and **Laguna Beach Open Space and Marine Sanctuaries**, Mouton Meadows Park at Del Mar and Balboa Avenues (949/497.0716). Beyond recreation and tourist services, the community also supports a thriving cottage industry of boutiques, art galleries, artisan shops, and antiques dealers. For visitor information, call 800/877.1115 or see www.lagunabeachinfo.org. Although the town's filled with great dining spots, should you just want to eat in or take a picnic, call **Restaurants on the Run** (949/951.2500, fax 949/951.7700; www.ontherun.com) and they'll deliver food from any restaurant in the area, 11AM-2PM and 5:30-9PM daily

51 LAS BRISAS–SEAFOODS OF MEXICO

★★★$$$ This landmark 1938 restaurant, perched on a seaside cliff, fills up with locals, tourists, and folks who drive several hours for the great margaritas and spectacular view of Laguna Beach and the Pacific Ocean. The food is good, too, especially the fresh seafood and Mexican specialties. ♦ Mexican ♦ Daily, dinner; M-Sa, breakfast and lunch; Su, brunch. Reservations recommended. 361 Cliff Dr (between N Coast Hwy and Jasmine St), Laguna Beach. 949/497.5434. www.lasbrisaslagunabeach.com

52 CAFE ZINC MARKET

★★★$ A quiet sidewalk patio fronts this gourmet food market and vegetarian restaurant, where patrons line up to wrap their hands around a tall, hot mug of the county's best cappuccino. Enjoy bread from **La Brea Bakery,** along with  homemade granola, plate-size gourmet pizzettes, sandwiches, and salads. ♦ Vegetarian ♦ M, breakfast; Tu-Su, breakfast and lunch. Market: Daily. 350 Ocean Ave (between Beach St and Forest Ave), Laguna Beach. 949/494.6302

52 POMODORO

★★$$ This restaurant is quite the little charmer, where the scent of garlic and Italian spices lures you in from the sidewalk. And it doesn't disappoint, from the delightful Italian waitstaff to the cuisine. Best bets are the pan-roasted breast of chicken with Portobello mushrooms, spinach, and baked polenta; spaghetti *ai frutti di mare*, with mussels, clams, shrimp, and calamari; rigatoni or penne, and the baby spinach salad. The dessert star is the tiramisù. There's a good, reasonably priced wine list by the glass or bottle. ♦ Italian ♦ Daily, lunch and dinner. Reservations suggested for dinner. 234 Forest Ave (between S Coast Hwy and Beach St), Laguna Beach. 949/497.8222; e-mail: lagunabeach@pastap.com. www.Pastapomodoro.com

52 FIVE FEET (5'-0")

★★★$$$$ East meets West in this modern, arty restaurant, where chef/owner Michael Kang surprises and delights with such dishes as *kung pao* calamari (in a caramelized sauce of soy, Thai red chilies, peanuts, and scallions), a whole catfish with a variety of sauces, pot stickers, and even a yummy veal chop. Expect to wait for your table, as this is one popular spot. ♦ Chinese/European/California ♦ Daily, dinner. Reservations recommended. 328 Glenneyre St (between Mermaid St and Forest Ave), Laguna Beach. 949/497.4955. Also at Fashion Island, Newport Center Dr (north of E Coast Hwy), Newport Beach. 949/497.4955

52 SUNDRIED TOMATO

★★$$ This is a nifty spot to stop for a bite, especially on the cheery outdoor patio. The food is remarkably good and there's a large list of wines by the glass, draft beer, and oodles of ambience—what more could you want? Like the name implies, sun-dried tomatoes are featured on the menu (the sun-dried tomato soup is yummy). There's a good lamb burger, Asian-style short ribs, and a variety of pastas, salads, and fish. ♦ California with an Asian touch ♦ Daily, lunch and dinner. Reservations suggested. 361 Forest Ave (between S Coast Hwy and Beach St),Laguna Beach. 949/494.3312. www.thesundriedtomatocafe.com

53 VACATION VILLAGE

$$ This beachfront resort is a relative bargain, particularly in late September and October, when the rates drop but the weather is ideal. Accommodations include apartments with kitchenettes, studios, and 130 rooms (50 with ocean views). Among the amenities are two pools, a whirlpool and sauna, and a kids' game room. The delightful **Beach House Restaurant** (949/494.9707), on site but under separate ownership, serves California cuisine. At press time there was speculation that a major renovation was on the horizon; no details were available. ♦ 647 S Coast Hwy (between Cleo St and Sleepy Hollow La), Laguna Beach. 949/494.8566; 800/843.6895; fax 949/494.1386. www.vacationvillage.com

53 EILER'S INN

$$ Warm European hospitality is dished out at this charming bed-and-breakfast by the sea. There are 11 rooms and one suite with a kitchen and fireplace. The morning repast is a gourmet treat worth leaping out of bed for. ♦ 741 S Coast Hwy (between St. Ann's Dr and Cleo St), Laguna Beach. 949/494.3004; fax 949/497.2215

54 THE CARRIAGE HOUSE

$$ This charming New Orleans–style bed-and-breakfast (yet another in the area) has six suites with private entrances, and five

with kitchens. There's a pretty garden, a friendly dining room, and it's just a three-minute walk from the beach. ♦ 1322 Catalina St (between Mountain Rd and Cress St), Laguna Beach. 949/494.8945. www.carriagehouse.com

55 LA CASA DEL CAMINO

$$ This charming Mediterranean-style bed-and-breakfast, built in 1927, features 41 units and eight mini-suites with whirlpool tubs, all adorably decorated with antiques and pretty pieces and most with ocean views. Although refurbished, the décor retains some wonderful holdovers from the 1920s and 1950s. A 2,500-square-foot rooftop deck offers moderately priced snacks (Thai chicken wings, beef ribs, cheese plates, salads) and drinks along with panoramic views of the Pacific. You also get a lavish (really lavish) complimentary continental breakfast served daily in a lovely Italiante courtyard. On cool nights, the lobby lounge offers a cozy retreat where guests can relax beside a wood-burning fireplace. And there's free parking, high-speed Internet access, and beach towels and chairs, and pets are welcome—what more could you ask for? Maybe a massage, and that's doable for a fee. They'll even negotiate rates over the phone. ♦ 1289 S Coast Hwy (between Cress and Brooks Sts), Laguna Beach. 949/497.2446, 888/367.5232; fax 949/494.5581; e-mail: casacamino@aol.com. www.casacamino.com

Within La Casa del Camino:

K'YA

★★★$$ You must eat here whether you're staying at the hotel or not. Not only is the food great, but the bar, manned by a witty, wacky, crusty mixologist named Gerry, is a hoot (and he pours a mean drink). The menu covers the spectrum from ahi tuna poke and grilled spicy garlic and herb shrimp appetizers to hibachi salmon, seared sea scallops, pastas, Kobe beef burgers, and beyond. The mascarpone cheesecake and the chocolate torte rock. There's also a fairly priced wine list and a dizzying array of specialty cocktails. ♦ Asia-California Fusion ♦ Daily, breakfast (free for in-house guests) and dinner. Reservations suggested for dinner

56 SURF & SAND HOTEL

$$$$ Beach buffs, grab your boogie boards, surfing equipment, and other nautical gear and head on over to this fun seaside resort where the Pacific Ocean is just 20 feet from your door. Each of its 165 rooms offers the necessary comforts, like 42-inch plasma TVs, Internet access, mega-count cotton linens, marble bathrooms, and views of the Pacific Ocean. However, if air conditioning is important, be sure to request it, as it's available in only a few rooms. There's a casual (even shorts and flip-flops are acceptable), three-meal-a-day restaurant called **Splashes** (★$$$) that serves a mix of Mediterranean and California cuisine with an ocean view (714/497.4477), and meeting facilities and an outdoor pool. The botanical/ocean/earth-themed **AquaTerra Spa** provides a cozy seafront sanctuary for myriad salubrious treatments done with special elixirs and oils. 949/376.2SPA ♦ 1555 S Coast Hwy (between Bluebird Canyon Dr and Calliope St), Laguna Beach. 949/497.4477, 888/869.9299; fax 949/494.2897. www.surfandsandresort.com

57 DIZZ'S AS IS

★$$ Kind of funky, with a typical Laguna Beach bohemian crowd that dresses to please themselves, this eclectic Art Deco joint is designed for serious eating. The food's great, the menu changes daily, and the plates don't match. Cioppino and filet mignon are standouts. ♦ International ♦ Tu-Su, dinner. 2794 S Coast Hwy (between Nyes Pl and Highland Rd), Laguna Beach. 949/494.5250

57 MONTAGE RESORT & SPA LAGUNA BEACH

$$$$ What can we say? This is the most magnificent beachfront hotel in Southern California, where a devout regard for nature permeates with individually crafted designs through pottery and ceramic tiles, woodwork, and outstanding metalwork, all done by local artisans. Once known as Treasure Island, named for the Robert Louis Stevenson novel that was shot there in 1934, the 30 acres of grounds are indeed a treasure. Each of the 262 spacious (the smallest is 500 square feet) ocean-view rooms and suites is dynamite. Designed by Wilson & Associates of Dallas, Texas, each is done in dark woods and light fabrics. High beds are covered in feather tops and down. Televisions feature flat screens with DVD players and state-of-the-art sound systems. Bathrooms are big with lots of marble, shaving mirrors in the showers, and lavish tubs adorned with three candles to enhance the soaking experience. There are 51 spectacular suites and 37 equally extravagant bungalows. In-room amenities include the usual Internet accessories, iron and ironing

The first Jewish religious services took place in predominantly Catholic LA in 1854, and the first Protestant church was built 10 years later.

PLACE YOUR BETS ON THE SPRINGS

Much to the consternation of many, gambling came to Palm Springs in the late 1990s. Although full-scale gaming is prohibited in California, a federal law and a Supreme Court ruling allow Native American tribes to offer on their reservations any type of gaming. Inveterate gamblers can now try their luck at a number of casinos that operate 24 hours a day year-round. In addition to the usual card games, the following casinos offer video blackjack and poker, bingo, and off-track betting: **Spa Casino** (inside the historic Spa Resort Casino in downtown Palm Springs;

800/258.2WIN) is operated by the Agua Caliente band of Cahuilla Indians; **Fantasy Springs Casino** (located north of Interstate 10 near Indio; 800/827.2WIN) is operated by the Cabazon band of Mission Indians and includes a Las Vegas–style show; **Casino Morongo** (west of Palm Springs off Interstate 10; 800/252.4499) is run by the Morongo band of Mission Indians; **Spotlight 29 Casino** (located on Interstate 10 east of Fantasy Springs; 619/775.5566) is owned by the Twenty-Nine Palms band of Mission Indians.

---

board, and all the comforts of a luxury resort. And, ah, the spa—the only five-star award-winnng spa in the US, with cushy outdoor lounges set by a large Jacuzzi and cold-plunge pool, is so inviting, once you're inside you'll want to spend the day. No expense was spared doing the fitness center, either. Fully equipped, it's one of the best around, with ocean views, a private lap pool, plenty of bottled water, and a TV at each piece of machinery. However, it would be a shame to spend too much time in the room, since the outdoors is what this resort is all about, with a long stretch of sandy beach providing opportunity for a variety of water sports. There are three large, very inviting pools on premises. Room service, available around the clock, is always efficient and well done. There are three restaurants, **The Loft** (★★$$), a casual bistro offering three meals daily; the **Mosaic Bar and Grille** (★★$$), situated bluff-style, for California beach fare, open for breakfast and lunch on Sunday and dinner Friday and Saturday; and **Studio** (see below). ◆ 30801 S Coast Hwy (between Nyes Pl and Wesley St). 866/271.6953. www.montagelagunabeach.com Within Montage:

STUDIO

★★★★$$$$ Be prepared for an extraordinary dining experience in this charming bluffside bungalow with its 280-degree views of the Pacific Ocean through large open-air windows. The décor combines the resort's light and airy motif with a 20-foot-high raised ceiling of rustic, stained wood beams, two custom-built Paul Wyatt wine vaults perched in the entry, and walls filled with early California art. The food on the seasonally changing menu is as good as it gets. Go for the tasting menu or sink your teeth into a plate of Maine diver sea scallops or Alaskan halibut. And don't miss dessert. ◆ French ◆ Tu-F, dinner; Sa, Su, lunch and dinner. Reservations a must. 949/715.6420

58 MISSION SAN JUAN CAPISTRANO

Founded in 1776 by Father Junípero Serra, this simple adobe is one of the oldest churches in California. In 1796, Indian laborers under the charge of a Mexican stonemason began a grand stone church that was completed in 1806, only to be destroyed by earthquake six years later. The monumental structure was not rebuilt, and services resumed in an older adobe church. In the 1890s, the Landmarks Club saved this church from destruction, and in the 1920s it underwent major restoration. The famous swallows that return to Capistrano each 19 March, St. Joseph's Day, are cliff swallows that build their gourdlike nests in the broken arches of the ruins of the stone church. ◆ Admission. Daily. Camino Capistrano and Ortega Hwy, San Juan Capistrano. 949/248.2049

58 SAN JUAN CAPISTRANO LIBRARY

The harmonious but slightly tongue-in-cheek use of anachronism is a hallmark of celebrity Postmodern architect **Michael Graves,** who

---

The population of the five-county region of Los Angeles is larger than any state in the nation except California, New York, and Texas.

Restaurants/Clubs: Red | Hotels: Purple | Shops: Orange | Outdoors/Parks: Green | Sights/Culture: Blue

designed this 1983 library. The buildings are arranged around an arcaded courtyard, a lovely fountain, and gazebos for reading and resting, and the polychrome interior echoes the nearby Spanish mission. ♦ M-Th, Sa. 31495 El Camino Real (between El Horno St and Don Juan Ave), San Juan Capistrano. 949/493.1752

59 RITZ-CARLTON LAGUNA NIGUEL

$$$$ Knock-down gorgeous, with views to match, this crème de la crème of super-luxury beachfront resort hotels unites East Coast style and West Coast atmosphere on its perch atop a dramatic 150-foot-high bluff overlooking the Pacific Ocean. The architecture appropriately echoes the beachfront location with bright colors, triple-layered glass panels that add a nautical atmosphere, and lighter hues of blue and sand tones and silver. The décor is minimalist. All 394 rooms are furnished with mirrored minibars, and 42-inch flat-screen TVs hang on the wall in front of each oversized bed. Fitness fanatics will find all the essentials at the fetching two-story oceanfront fitness center, where you can witness sweeping views of the Pacific Ocean while working out on contemporary apparatus—each machine is equipped with a flat-screen monitor. There's the usual assortment of free weights, fitness balls, and other body-toning power tools as well as organized exercise classes (Pilates, yoga, power walks). A gorgeous spa, specializing in exotic treatments (the Botorelax facial has similar results to Botox, but is less invasive), sits just across the hall. There's a stiff fee to avail yourself of the facility ($30), but it's waived if you book a treatment. There are two swimming pools, four tennis courts, and

access by foot or shuttle to a startling two-mile-long beach below the bluff. The concierge can arrange sailing accommodations at nearby Dana Point, hikes in Wood Canyon Wilderness Park, visits to the Mission San Juan Capistrano, and more. Dining venues include The Club Grill & Ball, **Restaurant 161'** (see below), and a lobby lounge where you can enjoy a light breakfast, lunch, or dinner, dessert, or drinks. The library, with its floor-to-ceiling bookshelves, is the perfect place to sip high tea while looking out at spectacular ocean views. ENO, an upscale tasting room, provides a haven for wine lovers with more than 500 varieties ready to pour with 50 different cheese and chocolate choices from around the world. There's a well-trained sommelier on hand to help with your selections. Do expect to pay premium bucks per bottle or glass. Suites are knockouts (one even has its own Steinway), especially on the Club Floor, accessible by a special elevator key and available at an extra charge, which includes access to a posh lounge where you can enjoy complimentary breakfast, gourmet snacks, drinks, hors d'oeuvres, and more. ♦ Ritz Carlton Dr and Pacific Coast Hwy, Dana Point. 949/240.2000, 800/241.3333; fax 949/240.1061. www.ritzcarlton.com ♿

Within the Ritz-Carlton Laguna Niguel:

RESTAURANT 161'

★★★$$$$ A daring dining venture for Ritz-Carlton, 161' encompasses an area that spreads from an enclosed room, through shuttered doors that open wide, to a sort of indoor terrace area where tables face windows with ocean views. The interior room sports a chimerical ceiling, adorned with a strange array of dangling silver metal and crystal drop sculptures made from abstracted California poppies. Three Swarovski crystal chandeliers designed like tree branches complete the overhead leitmotif. The design incorporates dark

wood furnishings accented by cream and ice blue with an inset patterned wood floor. The cuisine is superbly prepared and presented. We loved the perfectly spiced Hawaiian tuna tartare, grilled Maine lobster with a hint of truffles, crispy duck breast with corn fondue, and seared Alaskan halibut almost as much as we did the sinfully rich warm chocolate cake, meringue white coffee cheesecake with warm amaretto chocolate sauce, and Chocolate Fondue for Two (we had to try it all in the name of research).
♦ Asian-Continental-California Fusion
♦ Daily, breakfast, lunch, and dinner. Reservations required for dinner.

59 St. Regis Monarch Beach Resort & Spa

$$$$ Perched just across Pacific Highway and up the road about a half mile, this 400-room Tuscan-style gem looks like it stepped out of a Renaissance painting with its tall palms, gracious fountains and courtyards, mosaic tiles, European stone, marble floors, oversized crystal chandeliers, and sweeping stairways. Walls are adorned with a one-of-a-kind art collection featuring original Picassos and Chagalls that sit among four Dale Chihuly glass pieces. When it opened in 2001, the hotel fast became a getaway for the Hollywood crowd, attracting Sarah Michelle Gellar, Selma Blair, and other Tinseltown types. The mood is genial and relaxed. And sometimes so is the service. Rooms are amazing, especially suites. All sport balconies or terraces and come equipped with high-tech tools like plasma televisions, digital sound, high-speed Internet access, and other techno gadgets. Attention to detail prevails, with gorgeous Filido Italian bed linens, goose-down comforters, Lissedell Irish terry towels, and Lady Primrose bath products. Even the hair dryers are top-of-the-line. Outdoor play areas include three pools, two Jacuzzis, tennis courts, jogging trails, nearby golf, and access to a 6.1-acre stretch of beach. The spa and fitness center are lavish affairs, offering head-to-toe treatments and every workout option known to fitness buffs. Here's an amenity you wouldn't expect: "surf butlers." You read it right. Not to be outdone, the St. Regis now has highly trained personnel who provide personalized surfboarding instructions, or for the less daring, bodyboarding. Available only to hotel guests, butlers are all skilled in lifeguarding, CPR, and first aid and available for a fee (which at last look was $85 an hour). There are plenty of dining choices, including **Motif** (★★$$$), specializing in small-plate cuisine with an international flair, the **Pool Bar & Grill** ($$), for casual light American fare, and super chef Michael Mina's Stonehill Tavern (★★★★$$$$), a chic urban bistro where signature dishes such as Berkshire pig, Tasmanian ocean trout, short ribs, and butterscotch pudding are served in an elegant setting. ♦ 1 Monarch Beach Resort Dr (just up from Pacific Coast Hwy; turn left at Starbucks and Ritz Carlton Dr), Dana Point. 800/772.1543, 949/234.3200. www.stregismb.com

---

Restaurants/Clubs: Red | Hotels: Purple | Shops: Orange | Outdoors/Parks: Green | Sights/Culture: Blue

GAY LOS ANGELES

Jonesing for an electric night on the town, chic boutiques, world-famous restaurants, homey coffeehouses, and trendy nightclubs packed with bronzed, buffed revelers? Join the crowd in **West Hollywood** (commonly called "WeHo"), the epicenter of Los Angeles gay heaven and the home of sexy, sizzling **Sunset Strip**, sandwiched between flashy Hollywood and haughty Beverly Hills. If the rough-and-tumble biker crowd is more your speed, vroom over to sizzling **Silverlake**. Or maybe you want to slip into something a bit more suburban? Then steer your mojo over the **Hollywood Hills** and down to the **San Fernando Valley**, where country-western clubs, cozy neighbor-hood haunts, and cabarets like the Queen Mary, catering to drag divas and their admirers, await your pleasure. For a seaside escapade, hit the beach—just throw on a tank top and spend a golden afternoon or cool evening in **Santa Monica, Venice, Long Beach**, or artsy/crafty **Laguna Beach**. In case you didn't know, image and style are everything in this burg—the right car, the right pecs, the right coffee beans, knowledge of wine, shopping choices, cool clothes (labels, of course; however, bespoke is mo' better).

The gay dollar speaks loud and proud in LA, too. While there's a multitude of unique homo-owned and/or -operated establishments, most mainstream shops, restaurants, and clubs are respectful of the community and its influence. Many predominantly straight venues, such as the **House of Blues**, the **Hollywood Palladium**, and even Anaheim's family-oriented **Disneyland**, often open their doors to gay and lesbian events, and most locals won't bat an eye should you decide to take your same-sex squeeze for a hand-in-hand stroll through Santa Monica or along sandy **Malibu Beach.**

With economic clout comes a measure of political power. In West Hollywood, at least half the city council members at any given time are gay, and the mayor (who serves a one-year term) often is as well. The local unified school system of Greater LA offers same-sex domestic partner benefits.

Much of this city's magic stems from the notion that wild things occur here. Harrison Ford, for instance, was discovered while working construction; it could happen to you. But if it doesn't, and you go home no more famous than before, don't worry; you'll still have memories of this singular city and its dynamic queer community to last a lifetime. The West Hollywood Convention & Visitors Bureau provides excellent service to visitors and locals. Call 800/368.6020 or 310/289.2525, or go to www.visitwesthollywood.com or GoGayWestHollywood.com. The Bureau has also teamed up with LA's Westside (www.visitwestlacom) to bring awareness to WeHo, Beverly Hills, Marina de Rey, and Santa Monica, and with Southern

California (www.gogaysocal.com) to encourage tourism in Palm Springs and San Diego.

Area code 310 unless otherwise noted.

Symbols

♂ predominantly/exclusively gay-male-oriented

♀ predominantly/exclusively lesbian-oriented

♂♀ predominantly/exclusively gay-oriented, with a male and female clientele

1 CLUB FUEL

♂ This big, spiffy spot is the place to cruise for cute, young Valley Boys, who rock the dance floor to the latest dance tunes under laser lights and music from six plasma screens playing dance music. Wallflowers can shoot pool or darts, play video games, or just ogle the buff bartenders; an adjacent patio offers a break from the noise inside. On Mondays there's karaoke; Tuesdays usher in singing competitions, where winners take home $1,000; Wednesday's theme is "Underwear"(for guys only); and on Thursdays it's "Club Nur," welcoming Middle Eastern gays, straights, and bi's for an evening of ribald fun. ♦ Cover. Daily, 4PM-2AM. 11608 Ventura Blvd (at Blue Canyon Dr). 818/506.0404. www.clubfuel.us ♿

1 OIL CAN HARRY'S

♂♀ A friendly mix of urban cowpersons calls this retro disco Valley country-western bar home, where classic and new country tunes and videos keep the Stetson- and Wrangler-clad crowd boot scootin' on the huge central dance floor, which is sandwiched between two bars. Tuesdays are bargain nights with cheap drinks, on Thursdays you can have free dance lessons, and on Fridays the cover charge is waived. ♦ Cover. Tu, Th, 7:30PM-2AM; F, Sa, 9PM-2AM. 11502 Ventura Blvd (at Berry Dr). 818/760.9749

2 MUSEUM OF CONTEMPORARY ART (MOCA)

Works by such homosexual heavyweights as Jasper Johns, David Hockney, and Félix González-Torres are included among the permanent pieces in this huge museum, the first major US building designed by **Arata Isozaki,** Japan's leading architect. Built in 1986, a sequence of luminous galleries with exposed vaults opens off a sunken courtyard; Isozaki has even incorporated his fascination with Marilyn Monroe in the sensuous curve of the parapet overlooking the courtyard. It's here you'll find a well-stocked shop and the elegant **MOCA Café,** along with a bar, free hors d'oeuvres, and, in summer, live entertainment. Below the galleries is a 162-seat auditorium used for film, video, and performing arts. Artists, critics, and curators give informative tours of current exhibitions. Parking is available at First and Grand Avenues (Lot 16) and at the nearby **Music Center;** the **DASH** shuttle will also get you there. ♦ Admission; free Th, 5-8PM. Tu, W, F-Su, 10AM-6PM; Th, 11AM-8PM. 250 S Grand Ave (between W Fifth and W First Sts). 213/621.2766, 213/626.6222

3 AKBAR

★★$ This location was once a watering hole-in-the-wall for the down and out, but now offers one of the hippest bars for trendy Hollywood gays and lesbians. The early evening starts with eclectic songs from the jukebox and then segues into nightly DJs spinning next to the front door, entertaining a closely packed crowd of the young and retro. The bartenders are among the most talented of any in town, able to fix any fun concoction you can think of, and then some. The décor is '40s Hollywood-style, with pictures of Ratpackers from way back mingling with other memorabilia. ♦ Daily, 6PM-2AM. 4356 Sunset Blvd (at Fountain). 323/665.6810

4 HIGHWAYS

Founded in 1989 by writer Linda Frye Burnham and gay performance artist Tim Miller, this is Southern California's center for cutting-edge talent, highlighting works from LA's diverse creative worlds—including the gay and lesbian HIV/AIDS communities. Featured here are prominent and emerging artists, with some 200 programs by solo performers, small theater ensembles, and dance companies, including appearances by gay artists such as Sir Ian McKellen, Marga Gomez, and Michael Kearns. In addition, the performance space sponsors a variety of annual festivals, such as "Ecce Lesbo/Ecce Homo," featuring eclectic works by performers from across the nation. ♦ 1651 18th St (between Olympic Blvd and Colorado Ave), Santa Monica. 453.1755; ticket information 660.8587

Restaurants/Clubs: **Red** | Hotels: **Purple** | Shops: **Orange** | Outdoors/Parks: **Green** | Sights/Culture: **Blue**

5 ROOSTERFISH

♂ ★★ After 10PM, the crew at this laid-back Venice bar is an interesting hodgepodge of handsome beach boys, low-attitude WeHo types, and young collegiates. The front provides an airy space to lounge and play pinball or darts, while the back area is more cruisy and houses a CD jukebox playing everything from R.E.M. to Cher; a small back patio offers a bit of fresh air and weekend barbecues. Friday nights are most popular here, when the crowd is wall-to-wall and looking for Mr. Right (or Mr. Right Now). ◆ Daily, 11AM–2AM. 1302 Abbot Kinney Blvd (at Santa Clara Ave). 392.2123 ♿

6 L.A. GAY AND LESBIAN COMMUNITY SERVICES CENTER

♂♀ Besides an abundance of health, legal, and youth-oriented services, this pillar of the community (since 1971) offers plenty of activities of interest to visitors, including lectures, exhibitions, parties, and movies. You also can catch meetings of groups such as Bears L.A., the Coalition of Older Lesbians, and even the Gay & Lesbian Postal Employees Network. *And* the center's got its own line of merchandise. ◆ M-Sa, 9AM–9PM. 1625 N Hudson Ave (between Selma Ave and Hollywood Blvd). 323/993.7400; fax 323/993.7699. www.gay-lesbian-center.org

7 HOLLYWOOD SPA

♂ This large private club/bathhouse provides a sanctuary for gay men with fully equipped gym, sauna, steam room, Jacuzzi, café, and a live DJ—plus three floors of lads in white towels looking for a quick, uncomplicated date. Whatever your taste, you'll find him here—from fey boys to rock-hard gym types to hairy bears and beyond. Evenings and weekends, not surprisingly, are busiest, and gym cards get admission discounts on Wednesdays. ◆ Admission. Daily, 24 hours. 1650 Ivar Ave (between Selma Ave and Hollywood Blvd). 323/463.5169

8 HOUSE OF BLUES

$$ This usually straight venue electrifies with once-a-month all-male bashes that draw LA's prettiest hotties. Popular dance and Top-40 tunes keep the floor sweaty and packed while buff go-go dudes shake it up on the main stage. Aside from the hot crowd, the big club space is a sight to behold, and the back patio provides a breathtaking view of the city. Partly owned by actor Dan Aykroyd and the band Aerosmith, the two-level club/restaurant re-creates the ambience of a Southern Delta home, with juke-joint décor and folk art by Delta-based black artists; the corrugated gray metal exterior was salvaged from a shack in Louisiana. Call to check for special events.

◆ Cover. Su, 9PM–2AM. 8430 Sunset Blvd (between Olive Dr and N La Cienega Blvd), West Hollywood. 323/650.0247 ♿

9 HOLLOWAY MOTEL

$ This gay-run affair in the thick of it all is styled like a little villa with 20 clean, no-frills rooms. Suites with small kitchens are also available. Don't be surprised if a (presumably off-duty) porn star is staying just down the hall. There's no restaurant. ◆ 8465 Santa Monica Blvd (between Hacienda Pl and N La Cienega Blvd), West Hollywood. 323/654.2454; fax 323/848.7161 ♿

10 MARIX TEX MEX

★$$ Undoubtedly WeHo's most popular cantina, this loud and lively spot off Santa Monica Boulevard is always packed with an eclectic mix of gays and straights. This is especially true on Friday and Saturday nights, when all the party *muchachos* and *muchachas* pile in for drinks or a spicy late dinner of fajitas and blue-corn tortillas before hitting the clubs. A tiny side patio offers respite from the throngs squeezed in near the back of the house, waiting their turn for a table. The fare's above average, the atmosphere electric, the humongo margaritas near-legendary, and the crowd is classic WeHo: drop-dead gorgeous. ◆ Tex-Mex ◆ Daily, lunch and dinner. 1108 N Flores St (between Santa Monica Blvd and Fountain Ave), West Hollywood. 323/656.8800 ♿

11 EAT WELL

★★★$ One of WeHo's hottest eating spots is a hip, homey little diner with a cool coffeehouse-ish atmosphere and great—yet cheap—eats. Burgers, omelettes, and the rest of the simple but extensive menu draw a young, good-looking, and surprisingly low-attitude bunch of people. A 15- to 20-minute wait is practically guaranteed on weekends, but the sociable, cruisy types waiting with you help pass the time. The staff is also incredibly easy on the eyes. ◆ American ◆ Daily, breakfast, lunch, and dinner. 8252 Santa Monica Blvd (between N La Jolla and N Harper Aves), West Hollywood. 323/656.1383 ♿

It started in Los Angeles:

1967—*The Advocate,* the US's oldest continuing national gay and lesbian periodical.

1969—The Metropolitan Community Church, the nation's largest gay and lesbian Christian denomination.

1972—Beth Chayim Chadashim, America's first gay synagogue.

1988—Lambda Delta Lambda, UCLA, the country's first lesbian sorority.

12 GOLD COAST

♂ This neighborhood spot attracts mostly men in their late thirties and older. Managed by Melissa Etheridge's uncle Carl, it's laid-back yet cruisy, with dance tunes spun by a DJ but no dance floor. Others may prefer the notoriously active parking lot out back, where some hang out in the alley, others sit in their cars, and still others circle and circle around the block. Busy, busy, busy . . . ♦ M-F, 11AM-2AM; Sa, Su, 10AM-2AM. 8228 Santa Monica Blvd (between Havenhurst Dr and N La Jolla Ave), West Hollywood. 323/656.4879 &

13 FRENCH QUARTER MARKET

★★$ For a campy experience, visit this expansive New Orleans–themed restaurant, considered the epicenter of gay and lesbian LA since the mid-1970s. An indoor terrace, fountains filled with live fish, patio tables with green-and-white canopies, and ubiquitous hanging plants lend a quirky charm. The reasonably priced, eclectic menu (from pancakes to baked orange roughy) makes the place popular with a varied crowd, from the WeHo gym boys to Silverlake bikedykes to straights. On weekend afternoons there's always a 15- to 20-minute wait for patio tables, but since the crowd is always friendly and the scene is always cruisy, no one minds a bit. ♦ Eclectic ♦ Daily, breakfast, lunch, and dinner. 7985 Santa Monica Blvd (between N Hayworth and N Laurel Aves), West Hollywood. 323/654.0898 &

14 THE PLEASURE CHEST

Whatever your pleasure—tame to tawdry, mild to wild—this clean and bright sex supermarket has it all. Domination buffs will be drawn to the first floor, home to a vast array of whips, chains, handcuffs, and bondage and leather gear, while the upstairs holds an extensive selection of gay, lesbian, bi, and straight porn vids, just across from a huge stock of sex toys. Safe-sex supplies abound (including virtually every shape, size, flavor, and color of condom), and the staff's knowledgeable and reasonably friendly, too. ♦ M-Th, Su, 10AM-midnight; F, Sa, 10AM-1AM. 7733 Santa Monica Blvd (at N Genesee Ave), West Hollywood. 323/650.1022

15 TOMKAT THEATRE

♂ For those into adult movie houses, here's a seedy specimen that should do the trick. It screens the latest gay porn releases on its wide screen and is open practically around-the-clock. Don't be surprised to see some of the patrons "acting out." ♦ Admission. Daily, 10AM-2:30AM. 7734 Santa Monica Blvd (between N Spaulding and N Genesee Aves), West Hollywood. 323/650.9551 &

16 YUKON MINING COMPANY

★$ More popular for its scene than for its greasy diner vittles, this gay landmark is packed with club kids and drag divas every weekend after the clubs let out and the Ecstasy wears off. The Gold Rush–themed dining room is dark, rustic, and especially easy on bloodshot eyes. There's also a side patio where smokers can light up. The rest of the week finds the all-night dining room frequented by locals who stop by for a quick omelette in the morning or fried chicken for dinner. ♦ Diner ♦ Daily, 24 hours. 7328 Santa Monica Blvd (between N Poinsettia Pl and N Fuller Ave), West Hollywood. 323/851.8833 &

17 CELEBRATION THEATRE

♂♀ A 64-seat venue catering to gay and lesbian theatergoers, this house specializes in comic productions on the order of *Naked Boys Singing*. High drama it isn't, but fun it is—and you can also catch more serious-minded dramaturgy here, too, such as the Lesbian Playwrights Festival. ♦ 7051B Santa Monica Blvd (between N Sycamore and N La Brea Aves). 323/957.1884, tickets 323/289.2999

18 THE ZONE

♂ Lots of hot-looking, seemingly unapproach-able WeHomos end up at this private sex club at one time or another, especially from early Friday evening until the small hours of Sunday night, when the joint is packed with shirtless jarheads, pretty boys, and average Joes cruising the dim maze of halls. There are tiny rooms with door locks and glory holes, a video room, and a back room with a sling in near-total darkness. The dress code (such as it is) is heavy on T-shirts, Levi's, or leather, and a loud industrial rock soundtrack makes conversation all but impossible—but so what? ♦ Cover. Daily, 8PM-dawn. 1037 N Sycamore St. 323/464.8881 &

19 CIRCUS DISCO

Located in a rather seedy part of Hollywood and modeled after a big-top arena, this huge and usually straight dance club heads south on Tuesday and Friday nights, turning into a hot spot for gay Latinos and their admirers. A *calientito* mix of disco, hi-energy, hip-hop, and house keeps the *machos* and salsa queens grooving on four separate dance floors. ♦ Cover after 10PM. Tu, 9PM-2AM; F, Sa, 9PM-4AM. 6655 Santa Monica Blvd (between Seward St and N Las Palmas Ave). 323/462.1291

Restaurants/Clubs: Red | Hotels: Purple | Shops: Orange | Outdoors/Parks: Green | Sights/Culture: Blue

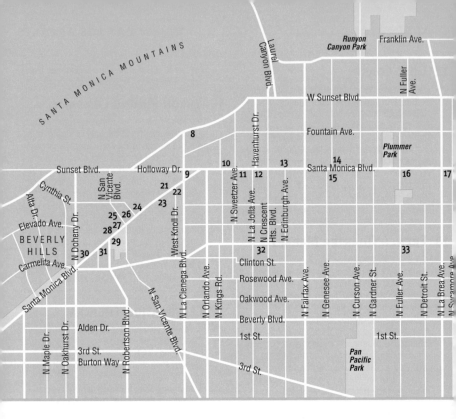

20 HOLLYWOOD MEMORIAL CEMETERY

A galaxy of top stars has found final refuge from its fans in this 65-acre oasis. Tinseltown biggies who were in the closet, out of it, or somewhere in between while aboveground include **Tyrone Power** and **Rudolph Valentino** (in wall crypt no. 1205); sadly, the lady in black who used to bring flowers on the anniversary of the latter's death comes no more. Also here are gravesites of the likes of **Douglas Fairbanks** (whose memorial is the most elaborate) and **Cecil B. DeMille** (who helped establish Paramount Studios, located just over the garden wall). ◆ Daily. 6000 Santa Monica Blvd (between N Van Ness Ave and N Gower St). 323/469.1181

21 RAMADA WEST HOLLYWOOD

$$ Designer Peter Shire's colorful metal flowers greet guests at this white-stucco Deco hotel right in the heart of WeHo. Its bright interior is also adorned with Warholesque portraits of Cher, Elvis, Janis Joplin, and other such famous mugs. The 135 rooms and 40 suites offer everything you'd expect from this worldwide chain; the back patio, though, is much more interesting, with lounge chairs, shaded tables, and a small, sparkling pool usually filled with studly sun worshippers. There's also a large health club across the street,

24-hour room service, a **Starbucks** (which has become the major gathering spot for the buff and beautiful), and the **Café Panini**, which is open for breakfast, lunch, and dinner; for lesbians, the popular club **The Palms** (see page 266) is directly across the street. ◆ 8585 Santa Monica Blvd (between West Knoll and Westmount Drs), West Hollywood. 323/652.6400, 800/228.2828; fax 323/652.2135

21 THE CHAMBERLAIN

$$ Tucked away in a residential neighborhood, these 112 upscale gay- and lesbian-friendly suites in the former Summerfield Suites Hotel—equipped with 250-count cotton sheets, down comforters, fireplaces, flat-panel TVs, and Carrera marble bathrooms stocked with Italian robes and luxury hair and body products—provide a peaceful escape just steps from bustling Santa Monica Boulevard. Amenities are many, including a nice fitness room, rooftop swimming pool and Jacuzzi, and a yummy American bistro tucked off the lobby. ◆ 1000 Westmount Dr (at West Knoll Dr), West Hollywood. 310/657.7400; 800/201.9652. www.chamberlainwesthollywood.com ⅃

22 ALTA CIENEGA MOTEL

$ Once a popular stay for up-and-coming rock stars on the order of Jim Morrison, Deborah Harry, and the Pretenders' Chrissie Hynde, this unassuming motel offers 21

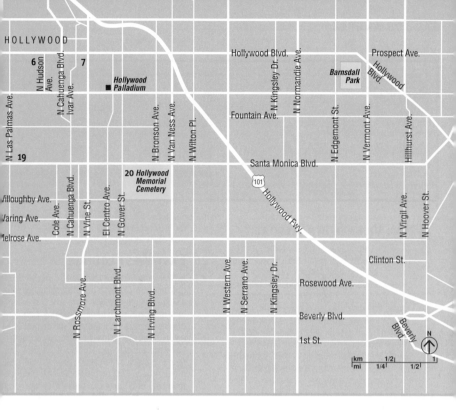

bargain rooms in the heart of WeHo. There is no restaurant, swimming pool, or other luxuries to speak of, but the basic rooms are clean and comfortable. Light sleepers take note: The loud traffic noise may bug you. ♦ No credit cards accepted. 1005 N La Cienega Blvd (at Santa Monica Blvd), West Hollywood. 652.5797 ♿

23 24-HOUR FITNESS SPORT

♂♀ When it was the Sports Connection years ago, many called it the "Sports Erection," due to the friskiness of the men's steam room, sauna, showers, and Jacuzzi. The four-story complex sports two aerobics rooms, large cardio and weight-training areas, and a sundeck, Jacuzzi, and lap pool outdoors. Despite attempts to attract more straight men and women and keep the wet-area shenanigans under control, the beat goes on. ♦ M-F, 6AM-11PM; Sa, Su, 8AM-8PM. 8612 Santa Monica Blvd (between West Knoll and Westbourne Drs), West Hollywood. 652.7440

23 THE PALMS

♀ On weekends, long lines of the butch and the beautiful await entry to this way popular lesbian bar. Inside, it's a tad dark, but mirrors, a verdant wall mural, and *Baywatch*-quality barmaids help liven things up. When the DJ isn't spinning the latest dance tunes or a live band isn't doing its thing, a CD jukebox keeps the house hopping with rock and Top 40—the large dance floor and billiards tables are always in use. Wednesday dollar drink nights and Sunday beer blasts are major events. Men are admitted, but might get a stare or two. ♦ Cover. M-F, 1PM-2AM; Sa, Su, noon-2AM. 8572 Santa Monica Blvd (between West Knoll and Westbourne Drs), West Hollywood. 652.6188 ♿

24 TANGO GRILL

★★$ If you could take your eyes off the foxy gym bunnies that frequent this Argentine-style bistro, you might notice that the service is quick and friendly and the no-nonsense skinless chicken and steak dishes are reasonably priced. A high ceiling, a brick and blond-wood interior, and pop and dance tunes give this hip eatery a festive, airy atmosphere; it's the perfect place to bring a date. Smokers can enjoy their dinner on the sidewalk patio, which is most advantageous for people watching. Inside or out, the place is always packed, but the wait for a table is rarely longer than 15 minutes. Reservations recommended. ♦ Argentine ♦ Daily, lunch and dinner. 8807 Santa Monica Blvd (between Palm Ave and Larrabee St), West Hollywood. 659.3663 ♿

Restaurants/Clubs: Red | Hotels: Purple | Shops: Orange | Outdoors/Parks: Green | Sights/Culture: Blue

25 SAN VICENTE INN/RESORT

♂ $$ Within stumbling distance of the hottest nightlife, Rocky Farren and Terry Snyman run one of LA's best-kept secrets: WeHo's only gay guesthouse. Arranged around a sparkling pool and Jacuzzi, 30 spacious, immaculate rooms and three garden cottages offer cable TV with VCR and private phone with answering machine; half have private baths. The pastel yellow and white exterior recalls Miami's South Beach, and the cruisy crowd sunbathing in the altogether might make you think you've found your way to heaven. There's also an in-house library, but no restaurant on the premises. ♦ 845 N San Vicente Blvd (between Santa Monica Blvd and Cynthia St), West Hollywood. 854.6915; fax 289.5929 &

26 MICKEY'S

♂ This roomy video/dance bar appeases its youthful crowd with pinball, sugary-sweet dance tunes, sweaty go-go boys, and studly (usually shirtless) barkeeps. A side lounge provides an overview of the crowd, and the sidewalk patio is good for cruising fellow bar patrons and passersby alike. It tends to attract the same "new clone"/twinkie crowd as the nearby **Rage;** of the WeHo clubs it's also the most popular with Hispanics, Asians, and blacks. Check local gay papers for theme parties and 18-and-over nights. The **Sidewalk** patio has become a haven for smokers. ♦ Daily, noon-2AM. 8857 Santa Monica Blvd (between Larrabee St and N San Vicente Blvd), West Hollywood. 657.1176 &

26 A DIFFERENT LIGHT

♀ Everyone has a grand old time browsing through aisles and aisles of gay and lesbian books, magazines, and CDs at this bookshop. There's also a jolly miscellany of items ranging from calendars and magnets to address books. The cruisy back of the store, meanwhile, is more suited to connoisseurs of "adult-oriented" periodicals. Check the signs in the window for open readings, book signings, and concerts, and don't forget to pick up a free copy of the local gay and lesbian magazines on your way out. ♦ Daily, 10AM-midnight. 8853 Santa Monica Blvd (between Larrabee St and N San Vicente Blvd), West Hollywood. 854.6601, 800/343.4002

26 EAST/WEST LOUNGE

♂ A WeHo staple since 1981 in various forms, this formerly laid-back bar is smoking hot with a well-heeled crowd who go for the upscale ambience and snob appeal. The posh lounge provides a cozy setting where you can relax on comfy sofas and actually carry on a conversation sans ear-deafening music. It's a great spot to go with a friend or a group. Insiders tag it the upscale joint on the Boulevard. There's a members-only lounge for those seeking anonymity. ♦ Cover, F-Sa after 9:30PM, holidays, and special events. M-F, 4PM-2AM; Sa, Su, 2PM-2AM. 8851 Santa Monica Blvd (at Larrabee St), West Hollywood. 360.6181 &

27 RAGE

♂ This still-trendy video/dance bar's famous red neon logo lit up Santa Monica Boulevard through the '80s, packing a hot mix of locals and tourists—mostly of the tanned-and-toned twinkie variety—into a drab black-lit interior virtually every night. The large dance floor literally throbs; an overhead lounge offers seating and an observation deck, but here, too, conversation usually loses out to blaring amps. Pinup-quality studs in tank tops always man the huge bars, and Monday "Alternative Music Nights" draw a rugged early-twenties to mid-thirties grunge crowd. There's also a weekly talent show and occasional drag events. ♦ Cover. Daily, 2PM-2AM. 8911 Santa Monica Blvd (between N San Vicente Blvd and Hilldale Ave), West Hollywood. 652.7055 &

28 CAFE D'ETOILE

★★$ Soft lighting, mellow music, and cozy booths make for an intimate, casual setting popular with a sophisticated thirty- to forty-something public that appreciates the solid, well-executed pasta, chicken, and seafood. The bar stretching along one wall is nearly always packed, and Sunday brunch is a big draw. ♦ American/International ♦ M-Sa, lunch and dinner; Su, brunch and dinner. 8941½ Santa Monica Blvd (between Hilldale Ave and N Robertson Blvd), West Hollywood. 278.1011 &

The Best

Lisa Phillips

Police Officer/Liaison to the Gay and Lesbian Community for the Los Angeles Police Department

Drive through the hills of **Silverlake** and take in the wonderfully different architecture of the houses, many of which overlook the **Silver Lake Reservoir**. Lots of

gay-owned homes, which is evident by the many rainbow flags hanging in the doorways. You will want to move here.

Go to the **"dog park"** (the animal!!) and mingle with the almost exclusively gay pet owners! Very, very fun and a great place to meet people and mix with the locals. The park is located right next to the Silver Lake Reservoir. Very pretty area!!!

29 THE ABBEY

★$ By far WeHo's hottest alternative to the club scene, this bustling spot reinvented itself into an attractive gathering spot. Most of the movement takes place on the outdoor patio beside a glorious oversized fireplace, where java junkies gather for conversation or to take in a game of chess or backgammon over great coffee and desserts (including killer lemon squares) amid plants and cement sculptures. There's a full dining menu along with light fare like salads and sandwiches (try the chicken on focaccia) and of course a well-stocked bar. The back patio sports private cabanas in which to hide out, as well as a special VIP area. It's definitely one of the hot spots in town. ◆ Coffeehouse/bar & lounge ◆ M-Th, 7AM-2AM; F, Sa, 7AM-3AM; Su, 8AM-2AM. 692 N Robertson Blvd (between Melrose Ave and Santa Monica Blvd), West Hollywood. 289.8410 ♿

29 HERE LOUNGE

♂ One of WeHo's trendiest clubs, this place—formerly The Firehouse—rocks with a cool dance area in the back with hunky strippers strutting their stuff. Every night is cool here, but Sundays are the best, when promoter Tom Whitman stages his weekly Player Night with jock-rocking big-name DJs and studly strippers. There are front and back patios for further mingling. The place is jam-packed weekly. ◆ Cover. M-F, 5PM-2AM; Sa, Su, 3PM-2AM. 696 N Robertson Blvd (between Melrose Ave and Santa Monica Blvd), West Hollywood. 310/360.85455 ♿

29 MOTHER LODE

♂ This popular imbibing den with its rustic wood interior may sit right in the heart of WeHo on Santa Monica Boulevard, but it has a friendly, neighborhoody feel. Dance, pop, and alt-rock tunes cater to the jeans and T-shirt crowd in its two bars, packed to the rafters on weekends and especially during Sunday afternoon beer busts, when it's too jammed to take advantage of the arcade games or pool table (not that you'll care, with everything else there is to

do . . .). ◆ Daily, noon-2AM. 8944 Santa Monica Blvd (between N San Vicente and N Robertson Blvds), West Hollywood. 659.9700 ♿

29 DRAKE'S

♂ Brightly lit, cheery, and friendly, this adult novelty shop takes the awkwardness out of shopping for the latest gay and bi erotic videos, lube, or condoms. The store also sells T-shirts sporting gay-positive slogans, posters, postcards, magnets, stickers, and nifty doohickeys, so it's worth the trip just for a browse. ◆ Daily, 10AM-2AM. 8932 Santa Monica Blvd (between N San Vicente and N Robertson Blvds), West Hollywood. 289.8932. Also at 7566 Melrose Ave (between N Sierra Bonita and N Curson Aves), open 24 hours. 323/651.5600 ♿

30 MURANO

★★★$$$$ Gay power agents mingle with buff gym boys on padded leather banquettes at this gay haven, highlighted by red lamps, white linens, and striking Murano chandeliers. House-made pastas, short ribs, and fresh seafood fuel the hungry crowd, while tipplers satisfy their thirst at the mirrored bar. ◆ Franco-Italian ◆ Tu-Su, dinner. Reservations advised. 9010 Melrose Ave (at N Doheny Dr), West Hollywood. 310/246.9185

31 BOSSA NOVA

★★$ Just across the street from **The Abbey** (page 267), this hip eatery's jam-packed covered patio gives some refuge from the hustle and bustle of "the scene," allowing you to watch the boys go by at a peaceful distance. Its vivid canary-yellow interior mixes well with the colorful crowd and spicy fare, which combines sandwiches, pastas, and grilled meats with Brazilian touches like *croquetes de camarão* (shrimp and cheese, breaded and deep-fried). Don't be surprised to find yourself sitting next to your favorite porn star or even one of the Red Hot Chili Peppers. ◆ Brazilian/International ◆ Daily, lunch and dinner. 685 N Robertson Blvd (between Melrose Ave and Santa Monica Blvd), West Hollywood. 657.5070 ♿

Restaurants/Clubs: Red | Hotels: Purple | Shops: Orange | Outdoors/Parks: Green | Sights/Culture: Blue

GONE TO LAGUNA

Gay and lesbian Angelenos flee the city, especially in spring and summer, for the sandy shores and cultural offerings of Laguna Beach, 60 miles south of LA on the scenic Pacific Coast Highway. In the tradition of other arts colonies turned gay, the arrival here in 1903 of painter Norman St. Claire started this hamlet of rocky cliffs and eucalyptus trees on the road to becoming a vibrant, upscale town of 25,000, a haven for artsy types, Hollywood celebs, and a large but fairly discreet homo population of both sexes. Yes, it's in Bob Dornan/John Birch Society territory, but there are enough progressive types around that Laguna Beach actually had a gay mayor, Bob Gentry, as far back as the early 1980s.

Laguna's hottest spot—and a favorite with the WeHo set—is the **Boom Boom Room,** a four-bar nightclub inside the Coast Inn ($; 1401 S Pacific Coast Hwy, at Mountain Rd; 949/494.7588, 800/653.2697; fax 949/494.1735). For more than three decades, this beachside complex has also been feeding the boys in its **Coast Inn Cafe** (★★$) and putting them up in 24 rooms with sundecks, fireplaces, a heated pool, and ocean views. (By the way, if taking a moonlit stroll along the beach below the inn, keep your wits about you: Gay bashings are a rare but occasional problem here.) Up the road a ways, the gay-and-lesbian-welcoming **Casa Laguna Inn** ($$; 2510 S Pacific Coast Hwy, between Solana Way and Upland Rd; 949/494.2996, 800/233.0449; fax 949/494.5009) offers 21 charming rooms, plus a pool, lovely grounds, and great views.

About halfway between Laguna Beach and WeHo, the **Ozz Supper Club** (★★★$; 6231 Manchester Blvd, at Western Ave, Buena Park; 714/522.1542), popular with a youngish gay male crowd (and with some lesbians and straights), serves hearty steak, seafood, and pasta dishes.

For something sweet, head over to Laguna's gay-owned and homo-popular coffeehouse **Cafe Zinc** (★$; 350 Ocean Ave, between Beach St and Forest Ave; 949/494.6302).

Shopping's a blast in this town, with its many galleries and boutiques, including **Gaymart** (168 Mountain Rd, at S Pacific Coast Hwy; 949/497.9108); **Jewelry by Poncé** (1417 S Pacific Coast Hwy, between Calliope St and Mountain Rd; 800/969.7464), specializing in commitment rings; and the local lesbigay bookstore **Different Drummer Books** (1294 S Pacific Coast Hwy, at Cress St; 949/497.6699). The main attraction, however, is naturally the beach. There's a gay section below the Coast Inn, but the queerest male stretch of sand in town is farther south, at **West Street Beach.**

Gay and lesbian Laguna Beach is covered by the biweekly *Orange County Blade,* available free at homo-popular venues. More information is available from the Laguna Beach Chamber of Commerce (357 Glenneyre Ave, Laguna Beach, CA 92652; 949/494.1018, 800/877.1115, www.lagunabeachinfo.org), or the Gay and Lesbian Community Center of Orange County (12752 Garden Grove Blvd, Laguna Beach, CA 92843, 949/534.0961,714/534.0862, fax 714/534.5491, www.thecenter.org). For accommodations information, contact California Riviera 800 (714/376.0305, 800/621.0500).

32 FRED SEGAL

A favorite of hip "industry" types (like queer REM front man Michael Stipe, supermodel Rachel Hunter, and crooner Rod Stewart), this block-wide gay-popular complex of stores hawks everything from pricey designer duds by Prada, Gucci, and Armani to funky, relatively inexpensive T-shirts, accessories, and gadgets in a fun, youthful atmosphere. Bargains can be found, and the late-September sale fills every parking spot for six blocks around. The patio and coffee shop offer copacetic settings for watching celebs while sipping frosty mochaccinos. ◆ M-Sa; Su, noon-6PM. 8100 Melrose Ave (at N Crescent Heights Blvd). 213/651.4129 ᵴ

33 CONDOMANIA

It's latex-o-rama: colored condoms, lollipop condoms, scented condoms, glow-in-the-dark condoms, and every other variety you could possibly imagine. Inventive safe sex is the message, and browsing through this funky outlet is almost as much fun as the main event. ◆ Daily; F, Sa until 10PM. 7306 Melrose Ave (at N Poinsettia Pl). 323/933.7865 ᵴ

34 CUFFS

♂ A mostly older and fairly fierce bunch of pierced fetishists and bewhiskered leather daddies give character to what's basically a one-room shack, so dim that its few shards of décor barely register. The joint's busiest on weekends, when curious WeHo boys mix with the regulars in a scene that can get raunchy, with plenty of groping (and sometimes more) going on in the rear; even the bathrooms, set up just right for voyeurs, offer no escape. You have been warned. ◆ Cover. M-Th, 4PM-2AM; F, 4PM-4AM; Sa, 2PM-4AM; Su, 2PM-2AM. 1941 Hyperion Ave (between De Longpre and Lyric Aves). 323/660.2649 ᵴ

GAY OUTINGS IN WEHO & BEYOND THE FRINGE

Looking for exotic adult toys? Head over to the **Pleasure Chest** (7733 Santa Monica Blvd, 323/650.1022). Need leather? **665 Leather** (8222 Santa Monica Blvd, 310/854.7276) suits all dungeon needs. Slip into something sexy at **CoCo de Mer** (8618 Melrose Ave, 310/652.0311), the answer for any occasion with high-end lingerie, accessories, massage oils, and an erotic library for browsing.

For gay porn, take in a show at **Studs at the Pussy Cat Theatre** (7724 Santa Monica Blvd, West Hollywood, 323/656.6392). Enjoy gay and lesbian performances at the **Celebration Theater** (7501 Santa Monica Blvd, 323/957.1884)—a positive outlet for progressive gay and lesbian voices.

For gay gym wear, sexy underwear, tight jeans, and trendy tops, go to **In2Male** (7974 Santa Monica Blvd, 323/650.2340)—man, you'll look cool.

For Fido or other pets, check out the **Beverly Hills Dog Club**, which is actually in WeHo, offering day and overnight villas as well as gourmet food for your four-legged friends (www.theclub-beverlyhills.com).

For the ultimate spa experience, succumb to the decadent gay-oriented treatments at **The Gendarmerie** (9069 Nemo St, West Hollywood, 310/858.9009, www.thegendarmerie.com). Housed in a cheery yellow bungalow, hidden away on a residential road, offerings include facials, manicures, pedicures, massages, and hair styling.

Gays can party hard at **MJ's** in Los Feliz (2810 Hyperion Ave, 323/660.1503), a swinging urban-style bar, or enjoy sensual bathhouse amenities at **Hollywood Spa** (1650 Ivar Ave, Hollywood, 323/463.5169).

35 EAGLE LA

♂ ★★★★$$$ There's lots of leather, buff bods, chains, and exotic entertainment going on at this sizzling, sexy Silverlake spot. It roars, it rocks; if you don't believe us, check out the web site. ♦ M-F, 4PM-3AM; Sa, Su, 3PM-3AM. 4219 Santa Monica Blvd (at N Hoover St), Silverlake. 323/669.9472. www.eaglela.com

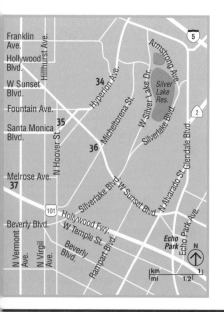

36 MILLIE'S

★★$ Tiny and trendy, the main attraction at this no-frills Silverlake diner is certainly not the standard burgers, sandwiches, and omelets, or the tacky vinyl tablecloths. It's the entertaining crowd—especially the waiters and waitresses, mostly struggling musicians with more piercings than Pinhead. Famous and not-yet-famous rockers are also among the patrons; don't be surprised to see some of them on MTV one day. ♦ Diner ♦ Daily, breakfast and lunch. 3524 W Sunset Blvd (between Golden Gate and Maltman Aves). 323/664.0404 ℅

37 FAULTLINE

♂ Located in a seedy area where Silverlake and Hollywood meet, this smoking-hot denim-and-leather joint has a large indoor bar, a huge outdoor patio with a stage, and a shop hawking everything from T-shirts to leather whips and masks. As in most Silverlake bars, inside it's dim and black, and posters of hunky NFL players and leathermen pass for décor. The masculine, often cigar-smoking crowd is fairly tame, but can get carried away at once-a-month events such as a night for bears or a watersports soirée. Faultline is an orgy of hard rock and homocore that draws a bevy of pierced and tattooed grungemeisters, and Sunday's beer bust is popular with local leather dudes. ♦ Cover. Tu-F, 4PM-2AM; Sa, Su, 2PM-2AM. 4216 Melrose Ave (between N Vermont and N New Hampshire Aves). 323/660.0889. www.faultlinebar.com ℅

Restaurants/Clubs: Red | Hotels: Purple | Shops: Orange | Outdoors/Parks: Green | Sights/Culture: Blue

DESERT AREAS

Macho Macho Man . . .

The area called The High Desert attracts an adventurous, sometimes extreme crowd who ride their dirt bikes and dune buggies or perform daredevil hijinks on the tall sand mounds of Lancaster at the mouth of **Antelope Valley**. Other recreation seekers go for the bungee jumping and hot-air ballooning offered in **Perris Valley** near **Riverside**. Tamer types simply wander through the many natural splendors of the unusually varied terrain. The most popular getaway destination, **Palm Springs**, buzzes during spring break, when hordes of sun-worshipping collegians converge for wild antics. It is also a year-round haven for golfers, tennis players, and senior citizens who prefer a warm, dry climate. The mid-1990s might be called the new "Gay 90s," because that's about the time the homosexual community began flocking to the Springs, buying up tear-downs and remodeling them into ultra-lavish weekend and winter getaways. Vacationing non-property-owning gays have plenty of places to stay, with dozens of gay-friendly inns in areas such as Warm Sands, San Lorenzo Road, and along Palm Canyon Drive. An additional three are for lesbians. The hub of the gay social scene, known as the **Castro district**, houses a variety of bars, coffeehouses shops, and a live theater. The Palm Springs Bureau of Tourism offers a dedicated toll free number to assist members of the gay community (888/866.2744) as well as a *Gay Visitor's Guide,* available by calling 800/347.7746 or online at www.palm-springs.org/

Palm Springs provides an ideal getaway for people of all persuasions. If golf's your bag, you've got more than 100 impeccably landscaped courses to choose from throughout the lower desert. There's also plenty of tennis, hiking, or communing with nature—all just a couple of hours' drive from LA.

ANTELOPE VALLEY

This arid region north of LA County was a more peaceful place until a major building explosion erupted, bringing with it new homes, urban blight, drugs, crime, and gangs. The air is still smog-free, but there's a bit of an edge.

1 EDWARDS AIR FORCE BASE

See the space shuttle land on the dry surface of Rogers Lake. There's also the **Air Force Flight Center Museum,** where you can see exhibits on aircraft hardware, rocket engines, ancient lake-bed formations, early homesteading, the very first military uses of Edwards, and the story of Glen Edwards. Daily tours of Edwards Air Force Base are offered except on federal holidays and during shuttle operation. ♦ Free. You must call ahead for sponsorship (661/277.8050). There is also an open-house and air show held each October. Rosamond Blvd (east of Sierra Hwy). 661/277.3510. www.edwards.af.mil/index-static.html

2 WILLOW SPRINGS INTERNATIONAL RACEWAY

This "fastest road in the west" is one of the best tracks in the country for watching top car and motorcycle racing year-round, with weekend races that last all day. Light refreshments are available. There's also a new **Racer School** that is open from 7AM to 5PM when there are WSMC weekend events. ♦ Admission. Call ahead for hours. Rosamond Blvd (between 60th St W and 90th St W). 661.256.1234; fax 661.256.1583. www.race-wsmc.com

3 ANTELOPE VALLEY CALIFORNIA POPPY RESERVE

Two thousand acres have been set aside for the preservation of the golden poppy, the California state flower. During springtime, the reserve is carpeted with a solid covering of flowers. ♦ Daily, Mar-May. Lancaster Rd (between 120th St W and 160th St W)

4 SADDLEBACK BUTTE STATE PARK

Native chaparral can be seen on a sandstone bluff here. There is also a magnificent stand of Joshua trees, bizarrely shaped plants that are, improbably, members of the lily family. ♦ Admission. Daily, 24 hours. 170th St E and E Ave J. 661/942.0662

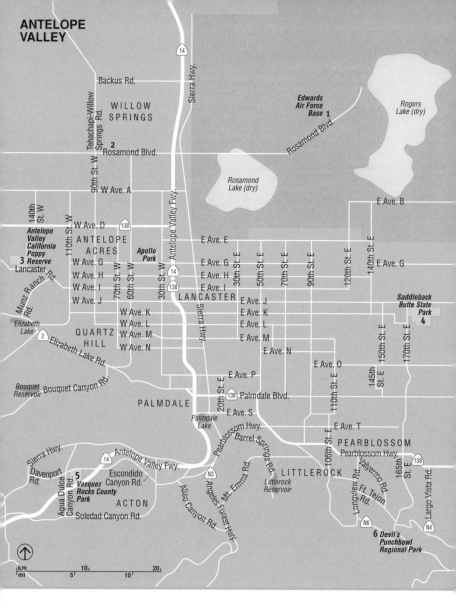

ANTELOPE VALLEY

5 VASQUEZ ROCKS COUNTY PARK

The surrealistic tumble of lacy sandstone rocks, some several hundred feet high, is great for climbing. The area is named for Tiburcio Vasquez, a 19th-century bandit who used it as one of his numerous hideouts.
♦ Escondido Canyon Rd (between Antelope Valley Fwy and Agua Dulce Canyon Rd)

6 DEVIL'S PUNCHBOWL REGIONAL PARK

Located in the high desert area near Pearblossom, the rocky landscape of this 1,310-acre county park is rich in native plants and includes a number of hiking trails. The park also has a lovely stream (the size of which varies greatly with the season) ringed with willows and other water-loving plants. The **Punchbowl** is a natural depression in a slope of tumbled boulders.
♦ 2800 Devil's Punchbowl Rd (southeast of Tumbleweed Rd). 661/944.2743

LAKE ARROWHEAD

This bucolic lakeside community, 90 miles east of Los Angeles and a half-hour drive from San Bernardino, is perfect for a weekend escape, especially since the

Restaurants/Clubs: Red | Hotels: Purple | Shops: Orange | Outdoors/Parks: Green | Sights/Culture: Blue

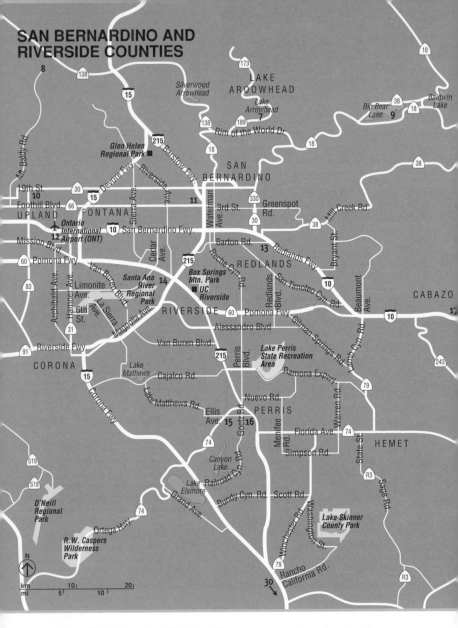

SAN BERNARDINO AND RIVERSIDE COUNTIES

opening of the spiffy **Lake Arrowhead Resort and Spa** (see below). There is also a variety of alternate lodgings around the area, from cabins and bed-and-breakfast rooms to rental homes. Perched at an altitude of 5,106 feet, the 782-acre alpine lake offers an aquatic playground for jet skiers, boaters, and anglers (but it's not too swimmer-friendly), and provides a pastoral setting for multimillion-dollar vacation homes (many of which are occupied only on weekends). The commercial center is an attractive village lined with boutiques, outlet shops, art galleries, and restaurants. There are also free weekend concerts, live entertainment, a weekly farmers' market, an arcade, an amusement park, and a children's museum. The weather can be quite hot in summer and cold enough to snow in winter. For more information, go to www.lakearrowhead.net or call 909/337.3715.

7 LAKE ARROWHEAD RESORT AND SPA

$$ Carved out of a formerly funky hotel, this spiffy facility offers 173 mountain lodge–like guest rooms and 10 lavish suites. Nice

to Twentynine
Palms
→

JOSHUA
TREE

Joshua Tree
National Park
19

hitewater
Canyon
18

Pierson Blvd.
DESERT
HOT SPRINGS

Dillon Rd.

N. Palm Cyn. Dr.
Indian Canyon Dr.
Palm Dr.

Palm Springs
International
Airport

20

Varner Rd.

22
21 ✈
23 Ramon
Rd.
Washington
St.

Date Palm Dr.

Mount
Jacinto
,084 ft.
PALM
SPRINGS

24

Monterey Ave.

Country
Club Dr. **25**

S Palm
Canyon Dr.

DYLLWILD

27
Indian
Canyons

(111)

28
Living
Desert
Reserve

50th
Ave.

Eisenhower Dr.

29
Lake
Cahuilla

(74)

(74)

uilla Rd. (371)

rby
Rd.

Terwilliger Rd.

include free use of two high-speed Internet-connected computers, a help concierge, and special privileges at Lake Arrowhead Country Club's private 6,232-yard, 18-hole golf course. **BIN189** (★★★$$$) serves breakfast, lunch, and dinner daily—start your day with yummy multi-grain pancakes with pure maple syrup, have the chopped chicken salad or juicy hamburger for lunch, and at night opt for a Caesar salad, tuna tartare, and one of the fresh fish dishes. As the name implies, there's also a super wine list. The most romantic accommodations are the scenic lake-front suites—perfect for enjoying meals or cocktails served on your balcony. A variety of spa and family packages are available. ◆ 17984 Hwy 189, Lake Arrowhead. 909/336.1511, 800/800.6792; fax 909/744.3088. www.laresort.com

SAN BERNARDINO AND RIVERSIDE COUNTIES

Just an hour from desert, beach, or mountains, San Bernardino is ideally located for beaching, biking, hiking, or just soaking in the view of often snowcapped mountains. While its relatively affordable land has attracted some of the ugliest developments in the state—and while it does often have the worst smog in the country—there are a number of things well worth seeing and doing here.

8 MOUNT BALDY

Ⓟ Ski this mountain in winter or hike it in summer. By lift or on foot, it's more than 10,000 feet to the top and worth it for the view. ◆ Mt. Baldy Rd (north of Mountain Ave). 909/982.2829, 818/335.1251

9 BIG BEAR LAKE

Ⓟ At 9,000 feet and surrounded by forests, this lake has a tranquility sadly lacking in Lake Arrowhead to the west. You can stay at **Gold Mountain Manor** (909/585.6997; www/bigbear.com/goldmtn), a historic 1938 log mansion where Clark Gable and Carole Lombard honeymooned, replete with wood-burning fireplaces and antiques; at the historic **Knickerbocker Mansion** (909/866.8221; www.knickerbockermansion.com), a restored 1920 log mansion and carriage house; or at any of a number of unique mountain hideaways. There are great places to eat, like **Bistro at the Mansion** (909/878.9190), which serves a mean five-course menu on Saturday nights; **Nottingham's Restaurant** (909/866.4644), for California cooking; **Grizzly Manor Café** (909/866.6226), a good ole American-style eatery; **Mandoline**

touches include in-room ice makers (suites only), coffeemakers, press pots (beans and a grinder are also included), flat-screen TVs, fireplaces, free local calls, robes, balconies overlooking the lake, and fine linens and toiletries. The adorable 11,000-square-foot spa is the main attraction with steams, saunas, whirlpool baths, indoor/outdoor relaxation areas, and the gamut of treatments (massages rule here; ask for Linda). There's also a small but well-equipped fitness room and an outdoor pool. The resort offers Champagne and hors d'oeuvre cruises around the lake at sunset (for a fee). Nice touches

Bistro (909/866.4200), serving continental fare; and **Cowboy Express Steak House** (909/866.1486), for big, juicy cuts of beef cooked just right. ♦ Rtes 18 and 38. Information 800/4.BIG.BEAR; fax 909/866.5671. www.bigbearinfo.com

10 SYCAMORE INN

★$$ Built on the site of a historic stage-coach stop, this restaurant continues an old tradition of warm hospitality and service. Prime rib steaks, chops, and 20 wines by the glass plus a huge stone fireplace and wing-back chairs warm the atmosphere. ♦ American ♦ M-F, lunch and dinner; Sa, Su, dinner. 8318 Foothill Blvd (between Carnelian St and Red Hill Country Club Dr), Rancho Cucamonga. 909/982.1104. www.thesycamoreinn.com

11 SAN BERNARDINO

There's a **City Hall** (300 N D St) designed by **Cesar Pelli,** and to the west on the old Route 66, a marvelous folly: the **Wigwam Village Highway Hotel** (2728 W Foothill Blvd; 909/875.0241). www.sanbernardino.org

Within San Bernardino:

BOBBY RAY'S TEXAS BBQ

★$ Ribs, chicken, and links are slowly cooked in a smoky oven and served with a zesty sauce. ♦ American ♦ W-Sa, lunch and dinner. 1657 W Baseline St (at Medical Center Dr). 909/885.9177

12 ONTARIO INTERNATIONAL AIRPORT

This features lots of glass, bright surfaces, and $1.6 million in art exhibits. It is also a very attractive alternative to LAX, offering 12 major passenger carriers. Designed by the architectural firm of **Daniel, Mann, Johnson & Mendenhall,** the passenger-friendly twin terminals offer a choice of 14 restaurants and 21 retail shops. The airport is about 35 miles east of LA and 20 miles west of San Bernardino, northwest of Riverside, between the Pomona and San Bernardino Freeways. Long-term and short-term parking are available, as is parking in several privately operated lots outside the airport. Public transportation to the surrounding areas is limited, although local hotels operate free shuttles to and from the airport. Information kiosks on local hotel pickups, car rentals, and shuttle services, including **Inland Express** (909/626.6599) and **SuperShuttle** (800/258.3826, 714/517.6600), can be found in the baggage-claim areas. ♦ Archibald Avenue, just off exit I-10 of the San Bernardino Fwy, Ontario. 909/937.2700. www.lawa.org/ont.com

13 REDLANDS

An architectural gem created during the early citrus-farming period, this city is notable for the Tuscan-style loggia of the **Santa Fe Railroad Station** (Orange St, between Redlands Blvd and Redlands Fwy); the picturebook 1890 **Morey Mansion** (190 Terracina Blvd, 909/793.7970), a bed-and-breakfast inn that may be toured on Sundays; and the grand Victorian mansions along **Olive Street.**

Within Redlands:

KIMBERLY CREST HOUSE AND GARDENS

℗ The flamboyant 1897 château features Tiffany glass, formal gardens, lily ponds, and citrus groves recalling the city's heyday. ♦ Admission. Tours: Th-Su, 1-4PM every half hour. 1325 Prospect Dr (off Highland Ave, between Cajon St and Ramona Dr). 909/792.2111

14 MISSION INN

$$$ The centerpiece of Riverside's historic downtown, this 232-room (including 32 suites) architectural treasure began life in 1876 as a 13-room adobe house, and was opened as a hotel by town father Frank Miller in 1902. The design incorporates an eclectic ensemble of Mission Revival, Victorian, and Beaux Arts architectural styles inspired by Miller, who had a penchant for travel and collecting. Over the years the hotel has hosted a celebrated guest registry, from aviation pioneers Amelia Earhart and Charles Lindbergh to industry barons Andrew Carnegie and Henry Ford. But the inn rapidly declined after Miller's death in 1935, and was dangerously close to demolition until rescued by the Riverside Redevelopment Agency. Further protection was guaranteed when the inn entered the National Register of Historic Places in 1977. ELS/Elbasani & Logan led the painstaking renovation process, which involved extensive seismic upgrading and interior restoration. Several unique architectural elements, including domed ceilings, wrought-iron balconies, tile floors, and leaded-glass windows, characterize the guest rooms. One of the two wedding chapels (the Nixons were married here) features a 17th-century altar.

The inn has an Olympic-size swimming pool (heated year-round), a Jacuzzi, and **Kelly's Spa,** a 6,000-square-foot Tuscan-style facility with villas, a nail salon, and attractive treatment rooms in which to enjoy body scrubs, massages, facials, and other salubrious therapies done with herbs and oils from Italy. There are six places to eat: a Mexican cantina called **Las Campanas; Bella Trattoria**, specializing in Italian food;

the charming **Duane's Prime Steak Restaurant,** also known for its seafood dishes, a Spanish-tiled room with outdoor patio dining; **The Mission Inn Restaurant,** which features vaulted ceilings, colorful tiles, ornate wall sconces, and marble accents; and the **Spanish Patio,** offering alfresco dining amid lush plants and a graceful fountain. ♦ 3649 Mission Inn Ave (between Orange and Main Sts), Riverside. 951/784.0300, 800/843.7755; fax 951/784.5525. www.missioninn.com

14 RIVERSIDE MUNICIPAL MUSEUM

This Renaissance-Revival building contains several exhibits on local and natural history, including a variety of flora and fauna, birds, and a gallery devoted to the city's citrus industry. ♦ Free. Tu-Su. 3720 Orange St (between University and Mission Inn Aves), Riverside. 951/782.5273

14 RIVERSIDE ART MUSEUM

The gallery spaces in this 1929 **Julia Morgan**–designed structure showcase a full range of artwork, from historical exhibits to works of contemporary Southern California artists. Located within the museum's courtyard is **A Moveable Feast,** a charming café serving light fare for lunch. There's also a gift shop. ♦ Admission. Tu-Sa. 3425 Mission Inn Ave (between Lime and Lemon Sts), Riverside. 951/684.7111

14 CALIFORNIA MUSEUM OF PHOTOGRAPHY

Stanley Saitowitz remodeled a downtown Kress store in 1990 to house this photography collection, which rivals those of Eastman House and the Smithsonian. Director Jonathan Green presents a lively program of exhibitions and events. Researchers may use the study center. ♦ Admission; free on Wednesday. W-Su. 3824 Main St (between Ninth St and University Ave), Riverside. Recording 951/784.3686, office 951/787.4787

PERRIS

n 1882, real estate and railway development helped establish the town of Perris, named after Fred T. Perris, he chief engineer of the California Southern Railroad ine, which stretched from San Diego to Riverside. The ity prospered with the wool trade, but fortunes leclined in the 1890s when the water system failed to keep up with demand and many residents fled westward toward Riverside.

15 ORANGE EMPIRE RAILWAY MUSEUM

This museum displays more than 150 rail vehicles, including steam, diesel, and electric locomotives and streetcars. You can ride several of these on the property. For special events the museum allows locomotives to make trips into town, where there's a fine surviving train station. ♦ Free, except for some special events. Daily. 2201 S A St (between Mapes Rd and Ellis Ave). Recording 909/657.2605, office 909/943.3020

16 PERRIS VALLEY AIRPORT

You won't find any commercial airlines landing on the runways here, just gliders, hot-air balloons, ultralight planes, and parachuters. ♦ 2091 Goetz Rd (between Mapes Rd and Ellis Ave). 909/657.3904

PALM SPRINGS

A smartly casual resort at the base of Mount San Jacinto, the **Palm Springs Desert Resorts** has become the generic name for a thriving group of resort and residential areas spread out around the Coachella Valley: Desert Hot Springs, Cathedral City, Rancho Mirage, Palm Desert, Indian Wells, La Quinta, and Indio. At the beginning of the 1980s, Palm Springs was a prime tourist destination, boasting more than 7,000 hotel rooms. As the decade ended, though, American companies began tightening their belts, reducing the business and convention travel that had fueled the area's economy. As a result, some hotels folded, real estate values plummeted, and residents started moving away. Palm Springs was definitely on the skids.

But the region has rebounded, thanks to some aggressive promotion on the part of the Palm Springs Desert Resorts Convention and Visitors Authority, not to mention a few boosts from its late mayor and congressman, Sonny Bono. Many also credit the gay population, which turned deteriorating houses into palatial estates and added a je ne sais quoi aura to the area. It still rules as the golf capital of the world, with more than 100 golf courses spread throughout the 150-square-mile valley. And the sublime climate remains the primary draw, with light-as-a-feather air quality, low humidity and rainfall (an average of 5.39 inches annually), and an average daytime temperature of 88°F (though it can easily reach a broiling 120°F in summer or a freezing 20°F on winter nights). Gay couples and singles account for a major portion of the winter and weekend population. College kids take over Palm Springs at spring break. The numerous hot springs attract a health-conscious crowd that goes to "take the waters."

Many celebrities keep second homes in Palm Springs. Throughout the city are some remarkable modern desert

---

Restaurants/Clubs: Red | Hotels: Purple | Shops: Orange | Outdoors/Parks: Green | Sights/Culture: Blue

houses designed by **Richard Neutra** and **John Lautner.** And speaking of celebrities, Celebrity Tours provides a peek into the lavish lifestyles of 70 famous people with escorted excursions to their homes. You can't go in, but you'll get a good picture of what it's like living *la dolce vita.* The trip also includes a ride on the Aerial Tramway and lunch atop Mt. San Jacinto, as well as dessert and drinks at Palm Springs VillageFest. The half-century-old company offers a variety of tailored treks through the area. Call 760/770.2700, or check the web site at www.celebrity.com. For information on hotels, restaurants, and other attractions in the greater Palm Springs area, call 800/34.RELAX or 760/770.9000, or try the Palm Springs web site at www.palmspringsusa.com.

17 DESERT HILLS PREMIUM OUTLETS

More than 120 factory outlet stores here offer designer men's and women's apparel, footwear, home furnishings, toys, and leather goods. If the kids get bored, treat them to nearby **Dinosaur Gardens** (see below). ♦ Daily. 48400 Seminole Dr (at Millard Pass), Cabazon. 909/849.6641

17 DINOSAUR GARDENS

Claude Bell designed and built the 150-foot-long brontosaurus and matching Tyrannosaurus rex that occupy a garden in the San Gorgonio Pass, 18 miles northwest of Palm Springs. ♦ Nominal admission; children under 10 free. Hours vary; call ahead. 5800 Seminole Dr (at Main St), Cabazon. 909/849.8309

18 WHITEWATER CANYON

The canyon offers interesting scenery and a trout farm. Tackle and bait are available to rent, and those who get lucky can cook their catch on grills in the picnic area. ♦ Whitewater Canyon Rd (north of Whitewater Cutoff), Whitewater

19 JOSHUA TREE NATIONAL PARK

A natural wonder just two and a half hours from LA, this park is 874 square miles of beautiful mountain and desert flora, the highlight of which is the unusual Joshua tree, a member of the lily family whose crooked limbs can grow to 50 feet long, producing clusters of greenish-white flowers. Mormon settlers, who thought it resembled the prophet Joshua showing them the way, named the tree and the park. **Keys View** has the best sampling of Joshua trees. More than 80 percent of the park is designated wilderness area, and it is a haven for rock climbers. Over thousands of years, the elements have formed the granite monoliths of the **Wonderland of Rocks** in Hidden Valley into bizarre shapes that challenge the skills of climbers. A trail from the Oasis Visitors Center leads to the **Oasis of Mara,** one of the world's most popular climbing sites. The park has plenty to offer those who enjoy remote desert hiking; experienced hikers should stop at a visitors' center for a map and to learn the rules and regulations before beginning their trek, and should carry at least a gallon of water per person per day. More than 500 campsites are available; all are filled on a first-come, first-served basis, except for Black Rock (for reservations, call MISTIX at 800/365.2267, ext 5674). ♦ Oasis (main) Visitors Center: Utah Tr (south of Rte 62), Twentynine Palms. 760/367.7511. Cottonwood Visitors Center: Cottonwood Spring Rd (north of I-10). Black Rock Visitors Center: Quail Springs Rd (south of Rte 62), Joshua Tree

20 PALM SPRINGS AERIAL TRAMWAY

A spectacular tram ride—the largest vertical cable rise in the US—climbs to an altitude of 8,516 feet on Mount San Jacinto for a fantastic view of the surrounding area. In October 2000, spiffy, roomier 80-passenger Rotair tramcars from Switzerland finally replaced the original cars, which were installed in 1963. At the top is a bar, restaurant, shops, and 54 miles of hiking trails. The cars run every 30 minutes. There's camping (by permit only) at **Mount San Jacinto State Park and Wilderness;** reservations required. ♦ Daily. Tramway Rd (west of N Palm Canyon Dr). Recording 760/325.1391, office 760/325.1449, camping information and reservations 909/659.2607. www.pstramway.com

21 PALM SPRINGS INTERNATIONAL AIRPORT

This commercial airport has become one of the busiest in Southern California, with jet service offered by Alaska, America West, American, Continental, Delta, Horizon, Sun Country, Westjet, and United Airlines. ♦ 300 E Tahquitz Canyon Way. 760/318.3800. www.palmspringsairport.com

Adjacent to Palm Springs International Airport:

PALM SPRINGS CONVENTION CENTER

Greatly expanded to meet the needs of hordes of conventioneers who hit this town annually, the $34 million facility offers 120,000 square feet of exhibit space. Designed by Fentress Bradburn Architects, Ltd., an award-winning Denver-based firm best known for its design of Denver International Airport's passenger terminal complex, the center features an 18,000-square-foot contemporary lobby with sweeping mountain views, an outdoor function area, and high-speed Internet access throughout.

WYNDHAM HOTEL

$$$ Ideal for convention groups, this 410-room hotel comes with all the necessities for both business and leisure travelers, although most of the amenities are geared to the former. There's a preponderance of meeting spaces, while guest rooms come equipped with oversized desks, Internet hookups, and other essential tools of the trade. For rest and recreation there's a pool, a fitness center, spa services, and nearby golf (which in Palm Springs is never far away). The hotel also provides free transportation to the airport. ♦ 888 East Tahquitz Canyon Way, Palm Springs. 760/322.6000, 800/996.3426. www.wyndhamhotels.com

22 THE COLONY PALMS HOTEL

$$$ Chic gone wild describes the vintage glamour of this 56-room hotel, of which 10 rooms are casitas and three are suites with private entrances. Built in 1936 by Purple Gang mob member Al Werheimer, the hotel's checkered past seems to permeate its walls. Rooms are decked out with Turkish Suzani headboards, Italian linens, robes, and minibars stocked with goodies from Dean & Deluca, along with the perfunctory Wi-Fi, high-def flat-panel TVs, and other contemporary necessities. There's a pool, gym, hot tub, Moroccan spa, serene courtyards for lounging, a fine dining restaurant (see below), and spectacular mountain views from every angle. ♦ 572 N Indian Canyon Dr (at E Via Colusa), Palm Springs. 760/969.1800, 800/557.2185. www.colonypalmshotel.com

Within The Colony Palms Hotel:

THE PURPLE PALM

★★$$$ Designed by Martyn Lawrence-Bullard to reflect the hotel's glam appeal, the stylized room is a showcase for chef Jim Shiebler's Mediterranean cuisine, with walls covered in photographs of palm trees silhouetted against a purple sunset (in recognition of Purple gangster Werheimer), colonial-style furnishings, and antique tile floor. Best menu bets are forks down the prime filet mignon, roasted Chilean sea bass, and Maine lobster. And for the grand finale, go for the mango tarte tatin, crème brûlée, or chocolate soufflé. ♦ Contemporary Mediterranean ♦ Daily, breakfast, lunch, and dinner. Reservations suggested for dinner

23 PALM SPRINGS ART MUSEUM

This 100,000-square-foot cultural center houses the **Steve Chase Art Wing and Education Center,** where more than 120 of the interior designer's large-scale contemporary works are on display. Also here are changing exhibitions of contemporary and historical art, including a fine collection of more than 1,300 American Indian artifacts. ♦ Admission. Tu-Su. 101 Museum Dr (at W Tahquitz Canyon Way). 760/325.7186; fax 760/327.5069. www.psmuseum.org

23 INGLESIDE INN

$$$ The most nostalgic and historic hostelry in Palm Springs, this is a place where you wish walls could talk. Originally built as a private residence in 1925, it was converted into a hotel in 1935 and fast became an exclusive playground/hideaway for big-name celebrities of the era (Garbo, Gable, Lombard, Marilyn Monroe, Frank Sinatra, and Ava Gardner were regulars). Somewhere along the line the hotel went to seed until local luminary raconteur Mel Haber (Melvyn of **Melvin's Restaurant,** below) bought, renovated, and brought the place back to life in 1975. The catalyst of its success was Mel's appearance on 60 Minutes, where he expounded on the virtues of Palm Springs and his hotel to millions of viewers, emphasizing that his inn attracted Hollywood's most elite. Over the years Cher, Marlon Brando, Bob Hope, George Hamilton, John Travolta, Larry King, Jerry Lewis, Mickey Rooney, Barry Manilow, Liza Minnelli, presidents, directors, and writers have slept at the Inn. Today the hotel is a loveable combination of vintage glitzy glamour with a hint of Las Vegas and a touch of class. The 30 accommodations include suites, mini-suites, and villas. Each features a distinct décor. Some recall yesterday with Louis XV furnishings; others indulge you in florals, neutral tones, or tropical or American Indian themes. All have terraces, fireplaces, minibars stocked with complimentary snacks, fruit and cold drinks, and oodles of charm. A few rooms have showers that convert to steam baths and private Jacuzzis. Ideally located close to town and hiking trails, the Inn is ideal for walkers. It is not, however, recommended for children. ♦ 200 West Ramon Rd (between S Palm Canyon Dr and Belardo Rd). 760/325.0046, 800/772.6655; fax 760/325.0710. www.inglesideinn.com

23 MELVYN'S RESTAURANT

★★★$$$ This is forks-down one of the best restaurants in the area. The food is always reliable, and the romantic room, with its overhead mirror and chandelier, antiques, rows of photographs of Mel with his celeb pals, and gorgeous restored 1895 carved oak and mahogany bar, oozes with appeal.

Restaurants/Clubs: Red | Hotels: Purple | Shops: Orange | Outdoors/Parks: Green | Sights/Culture: Blue

The saloonkeeper pours one of the best martinis, shaken not stirred, while the chef turns out memorable meals. The menu is a throwback to another era, with a Caesar salad tossed at your table, a Cobb salad, flaming steak Diane, veal Ingleside, and other classics combined with outstanding fresh fish dishes and a cheesecake that goes outside your diet. After dinner you can enjoy musical entertainment and dancing in the lounge or curl up by your fireplace with a cognac. If you want to spot a star, keep a lookout for Mel. It's easy to recognize him from the pictures plastered on the wall. He's the slim, nattily dressed dapper Dan with the longish gray hair, working the room so his VIP guests feel welcome. Actually, everybody who walks in Melvyn's feels welcome. ♦ American/Continental ♦ M-F, lunch; daily, dinner. Reservations advised. 200 W Ramon Rd (between S Palm Canyon Dr and Belardo Rd). 760/325.0046, 800/772.6655; fax 760/325.0710. www.inglesideinn.com

23 VICEROY PALM SPRINGS

$$$ Looking for a special spot to get away from it all? This stylish, upscale celebrity hideaway is just the ticket. Book a Dorrington or Sovereign Villa and entrench yourself amid pristine white walls. Enjoy a blazing fireplace (in winter), flat-screen TV viewing, a private patio, a big comfortable bed with Italian linens and down comforters, and plush terry robes to wear during your stay. For additional comfort, reserve one of the spiffy bungalows that come with kitchens featuring full-size appliances, a dining room, a large living room, and high-tech equipment for Internet access and phone service. Our favorite amenities are the French-pressed coffee and tea makers placed in every room—so civilized. Stay fit in the well-equipped gym. Take a steam bath and enjoy a massage or facial at the jaunty, well-run Estrella Spa. Then swim night and day in one of two adult-only pools and one for families, relax in the outdoor whirlpool baths, or take the short stroll into town. At night join locals and other hotel guests at the bustling bar, then enjoy a fantastic dinner in the attractive indoor/outdoor restaurant. 415 S Belardo Rd (at Ramon Rd). 800/237.3687. www.viceroypalmsprings.com

Within Viceroy Palm Springs:

CITRON

★★★$$$ Revelers from nearby and out of town swarm into this stylish restaurant nightly. A chic combination of black and white with splashes of vibrant yellow swathes the walls and furnishings. Gaiety prevails, with a noise level to match. Still, the mood can prove intimate if you sit off to the side. The food is so special you don't want the evening to end. Everything on the menu will delight. For a starter order the lobster and fingerling potato salad, then enjoy an entrée of Day Boat scallops, and end with banana curd and coconut French beignets. Citron ranks as a major celebrity hangout, so keep your eyes peeled, but please act judiciously. ♦ California/French ♦ Daily, breakfast, lunch, and dinner. Reservations for dinner are essential

23 THE FALLS

★★★$$$ If you like your steaks large and your drinks big and potent, this is the place. Every selection (porterhouse, rib-eye, or New York) is served to order. The beef is some of the tenderest and best you can get. The clientele is high energy, and the waitstaff are fast on their feet and eager to please. There are all sorts of sides to go with your meat, and plenty of dessert choices. On a warm night, opt to sit out on the balcony so you can view all the action on the busy promenade below. ♦ Steak House ♦ Daily, dinner. Reservations suggested. 155 Palm Canyon Dr (between Arenas and Tahquitz Canyon). 714/416.8656. www.thefallsprimesteakhouse.com

23 RUBY'S DINER

★$ There's great grub at this nationwide chain like malts, shakes, fries, burgers, and salads. ♦ Daily, breakfast, lunch, and dinner. 155 S Palm Canyon Dr, Mercado Plaza, just downstairs from The Falls.

24 PARKER PALM SPRINGS

$$ Talk about quirky! "Sweet" best describes this idiosyncratic 131-room hideaway with its eccentric décor of furs, armored knights, and whimsical artwork, including a DSL (LSD spelled backwards), a naked woman arising from a Baby Ruth candy bar, and some Andy Warhol knockoffs. Everything about this fanciful place brings a smile to your face. Laid-back, wry, witty, humorous, it's so welcoming you'll never want to leave the premises. A friendly, folksy staff treats you more like an invited guest or family friend than a customer. All the rooms are works of art. We especially like the 12 roomy villas, where you can really spread out. Each comes with plasma televisions, entertainment centers, private patios, wet bar, mini fridge, big bathrooms, living room, and separate bedrooms. The rest of the accommodations are also nifty, large and comfortable. Most have patios and all come with large bathrooms and chimerical artwork and furnishings. Bathrobes, upscale toiletries, DVD players, televisions, high-speed Internet, and complimentary coffee with morning wake-up calls are standard in all rooms. There are four pools, including two indoors located in the spa, one on the men's side, the other on the women's, and both clothing optional. Each pool contains saline water as opposed

to chlorine, which is a pleasant feature. The largest pool, located near the villas, provides the most esthetic setting for sunbathing, swimming, enjoying drinks, or just relaxing in a covered lounging area. Four well-groomed clay tennis courts are complimentary for guests. There are two restaurants: **Norma's** (★★$$$), serving breakfast, lunch, and dinner, and **Mister Parker's** (★$$$), open for dinner only. Morning meals at Norma's are the culinary highlight, with extensive options such as lemon pancakes, smoothies, egg-white frittatas, French toast, quesadillas, *huevos rancheros*, and more, and all our meals there were real treats. Recent dinners at Mister Parker's proved unexciting. The pamper-centric 22,000-square-foot spa *PSYC*, which management whimsically translates as the **Palm Springs Yacht Club**—although there is a distinct absence of a marina—sports his and hers facilities equipped with the aforementioned indoor pools, Jacuzzi, steam, sauna, and treatment rooms. Designed by New York potter and interior decorator Jonathan Adler, the spa supports the hotel's eccentric décor with its sailor's-knot carpeting, white and blue nautical-themed walls and furnishings, and a big ceramic monkey centerpiece set in the lobby. Unlike most pampering spots, this one encourages conversation among guests, the livelier the better, and promotes participation in physical activities. The unique philosophy it fosters is more about making you feel great than providing any life-changing experiences or spiritual awakenings. In so many words, it's just plain honest, down-home pampering. In addition to the usual treatments, therapists perform various cutting-edge rituals and techniques with the use of assorted elixirs such as wheat grass to drink along with—get this—a shot of whiskey, and gold and thermal sea mud and minerals to massage over the body. All the therapists are top-notch, and many have worked at the hotel for years. There's a well-equipped fitness center for staying in shape, petanque, croquet, and lots of hiking and biking trails. ◆ 4200 E Palm Canyon Dr (between S Cherokee Way and S Gene Autry Tr). 760/770.5000, 888/450.9488. www.theparkerpalmsprings.com

25 SALTON SEA

Not quite the pristine spot it once was, this 38-mile-long inland sea, which lies 235 feet below sea level, has been plagued with dead fish washing up on its shores. However, there's still a **National Wildlife Refuge,** located at the southern end, and a **Visitors Center** that offers wildlife exhibitions and tourist information. ◆ Rte 111 (southeast of Mecca). West Shores Chamber of Commerce 760/394.4112

26 IDYLLWILD

A community nestled in mile-high mountains, Idyllwild has tall pines, a tumbled rock formation for climbing, and trails for hiking in summer and cross-country skiing in winter. Drive-in campgrounds for overnight stays are located within Idyllwild and **Stone Creek Park.** ◆ Rte 243 (north of Rte 74). Reservations 800/444.7275 (ask for C6161 for Idyllwild camp; C6162 for Stone Creek camp)

27 INDIAN CANYONS

Andreas, Murray, and Palm Canyons offer large and unusual rock formations, good hiking trails, and a stand of majestic Washingtonian palms believed to be almost 2,000 years old. ◆ S Palm Canyon Dr (south of Canyon Heights Dr)

28 LIVING DESERT RESERVE

This 1,200-acre endangered species habitat houses the rare cheetah—the fastest land animal on earth—and presents "Wildlife Wonders," a show featuring exotic creatures such as the South African serval and the fennec fox, as well as birds of prey like the red-tailed hawk and the barn owl. **African Savanna** houses the tallest giraffes and the largest ostriches in a virtual two-acre setting that is also inhabited by lions, baboons, rhinoceros, and Nile crocodiles. There are also nature trails, a botanical garden, a visitor center, the **Meerkat Cafe,** and a gift shop/bookshop. Group tours are available. ◆ Admission. Daily, Sept to mid-June. 47900 Portola Ave (between Mariposa and W Vintage Drs), Palm Desert. 760/346.5694; fax 760/568.9685. www.livingdesert.org

29 LAKE CAHUILLA

Twenty-five miles southeast of Palm Springs, this lake is great for fishing, swimming, boating, and picnicking. ◆ Daily. Keller Pit Rd (just southwest of Ave 58), La Quinta. 760/564.4712

30 ANZA BORREGO DESERT

This 470,000-acre state park is a well-maintained desert preserve with unusual varieties of flora and fauna. The striking geological formations resemble a miniature Grand Canyon. ◆ Free. Visitors Center: Rte S22 (between Rtes S3 and 79). 760/767.4205, park information 760/767.5311

BEACH AND MOUNTAIN TOURS

Over the mountains and to the sea . . .

Only in Southern California can you journey from sun-drenched beaches to snow-capped mountains in one day. Of course it's best to allow more time to soak in the sites, enjoy a picnic in the park, horseback ride, or hike the carefully, chaparral-carved trails winding through the mountains. So hop in your car, Jeep, or SUV or if you prefer, book a guided tour and go explore the natural wonders that lie ahead.

PACIFIC COAST HIGHWAY

Area: A drive up and down the Pacific Coast Highway past some of the loveliest beaches in Los Angeles County

Mileage: 53 miles round-trip from the intersection of the Santa Monica Freeway (I-10) and Route 1

Take the **Santa Monica Freeway** to its end at **Santa Monica,** where it will merge with **Route 1.** Continue north on this road for the tour. Although much of the beachfront is free and open to the public, you will see private homes, many of which are elaborate residences belonging to the rich and famous. You may have to pay for parking in the adjoining lots. Getting across the Pacific Coast Highway on foot or turning your car around is dangerous; extreme caution is advised.

The first major public beach is **(1) Will Rogers Beach State Park,** a 187-acre natural playground named after the famous humorist/writer/entertainer who lived there from 1924 to 1935. Rogers's original home still stands and is open to the public; weekend matches take place year round on what once was his private polo field. This beach stretches for several miles along the Pacific Coast Highway and offers ample parking, facilities, and picnic and volleyball areas. Surfers congregate in the area opposite **Sunset Boulevard.**

You may want to detour up Sunset Boulevard to visit the **(2) Self-Realization Fellowship Lake Shrine** or **(3) Will Rogers State Historic Park.**

At the corner of Coastline Drive is the **(4) Getty Villa.**

At Topanga Canyon Boulevard, a right turn will take you to the semirural community of **(5) Topanga,** to **Topanga State Park** (see page 153), or on a drive to the **(6) San Fernando Valley** through a winding and scenic canyon. For more information, see the "San Fernando Valley" chapter on page 158.

The seaside community of **(7) Malibu** is as famous for its residents as for its scenery. The area on the right side of the Pacific Coast Highway is subject to landslides; note retaining walls holding back the earth. Much of the beach is walled off by "cottages" owned by celebrity types, but there are about 10 public-access paths, with parking, posted on the highway. You also can walk down from the pier.

The **(8) Malibu Pier,** located about 10 miles along this route, is open to the public.

Just east of **(9) Malibu Point** is **Surfrider State Beach,** a favorite with surfers. About 12 miles out, you may take a detour right onto Malibu Canyon Road,

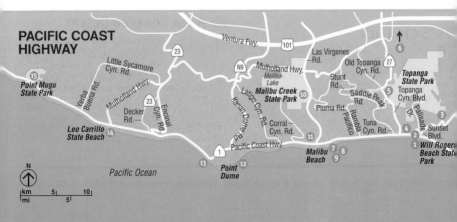

PACIFIC COAST HIGHWAY

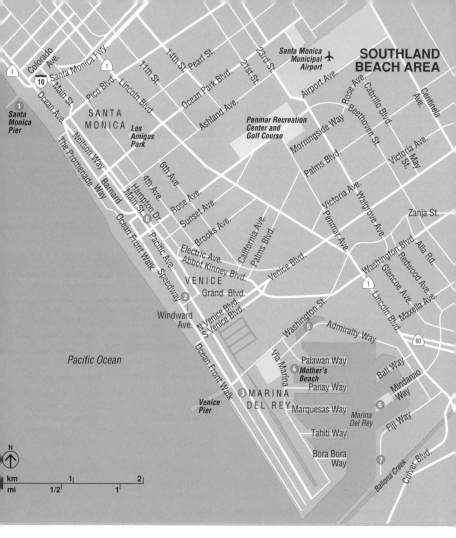

Las Virgenes Road, which traverses the **Santa Monica Mountains** to the San Fernando Valley, following the edge of a colorful and rugged canyon. **(10) Malibu Creek State Park** is located beside this road. **(11) Pepperdine University** is just west of Malibu Canyon Road on the Pacific Coast Highway.

(12) Paradise Cove is just east of **Point Dume,** approximately 16 miles along this route. It is a sheltered beach with white sand, tumbled sandstone cliffs, and fishing and boat-launching facilities. Admission is charged.

(13) Zuma Beach, on the west side of Point Dume, is a broad, flat beach offering volleyball, picnic facilities, easy parking, miles of smooth sand, and good body- and board-surfing.

Beautiful and secluded **(14) Leo Carrillo State Beach** is located in a wide cove that is slightly sheltered by rocks at either end. The northern portion of the beach is very popular with surfers. Swimmers should go to the center of the cove to avoid underwater rocks.

Across the Pacific Coast Highway, approximately 26 miles from the start of this tour, is **(15) Point Mugu**

State Park. For more information on this park and other sites mentioned above, see the "Malibu/The Canyons" chapter on page 148.

To return, retrace your route on the Pacific Coast Highway to the Santa Monica Freeway.

SOUTHLAND BEACH AREA

Area: Santa Monica, Venice, and Marina del Rey, the most popular and colorful of the Southland beach areas

Mileage: Four miles round-trip from the Santa Monica Pier

Santa Monica/Marina del Rey is a compact area navigable by foot or bicycle. (The use of a car is preferable only to get from neighborhood to neighborhood.) The bike path begins at the **Santa**

Monica Pier and parallels the beach south to **Torrance,** a distance of some 18 miles. A short ride through the marina to **Playa del Rey** is highly recommended. The best walking and skating sites are on **The Promenade** and **Ocean Front Walk,** between the Santa Monica Pier and **Venice Pier,** and along **Main Street.**

To get into the proper playful mood for the tour, you might want to begin with a carousel ride at the **(1) Santa Monica Pier** at the end of Colorado Avenue in Santa Monica. Take Ocean Avenue south to the intersection with Pico Boulevard, where the road forks, then follow the right-hand fork that parallels the ocean; this is **Barnard Way.** Stay on Barnard around to the left until it hits **Neilson Way.** Turn right at Neilson and continue. The street becomes Pacific Avenue in the next block as you enter **Venice.**

Continue down Pacific past the corner of **(2) Windward Avenue,** whose beachfront is a frenetic mixture of skaters, cyclists, joggers, entertainers, and assorted eccentrics. At Washington Street, a short stroll takes you to the **Venice Pier** for views, fishing, people watching, and snacks. Continue down Pacific. You are now entering **(3) Marina del Rey,** about three miles from the Santa Monica Pier. The marina section of Pacific takes you past frayed relics of old Venice: canals, bridges, and a few disguised oil wells.

At the end of Pacific, where it abuts **Via Marina,** a small promenade area and jetty look out over the Marina del Rey entrance channel. This is a fine place to stop and watch the sailboats glide by. Via Marina curves around the entrance channel and enters a densely built area of apartments and condominiums until it reaches **Admiralty Way.**

At the corner of Admiralty Way and Via Marina is **(4) Mother's Beach,** with a children's swimming area and picnic facilities.

Turn right onto Admiralty. After about half a mile you will pass the **(5) Bird Sanctuary** on the left and the **Marina City Towers** on the right.

Follow Admiralty to **Mindanao Way** and turn right. Continue to the end of the street, where you will find the entrance to **(6) Burton Chace Park.** The well-maintained park has picnic areas, barbecues, soft grassy knolls, rest rooms, and a tower you can climb to watch the boats in the marina.

Return to Admiralty and turn right to the next peninsula, **Fiji Way.** Go right again to **(7) Fisherman's Village,** a place for shopping, eating, and strolling.

Follow Fiji back to Admiralty and veer left. At the corner of Admiralty and Via Marina, turn right. Go to **Washington Street** and turn left. Continue a few blocks to Pacific and turn right. At **Rose Avenue,** turn right, go one block to Main Street, and turn left.

(8) Main Street, beginning near Marine Street and continuing almost to Pico Boulevard, is a booming shopping and dining area. Many of the restaurants along this street have rear patios that face the Pacific Ocean. Park in the city lots west of Main Street. To return to downtown LA on the **Santa Monica Freeway,** follow Main

Street to Pico, turn right, and at **Lincoln Boulevard,** turn left. The freeway intersects Lincoln in two blocks.

SOUTHERN BEACHES

Area: The Gold Coast beaches of Orange County from Newport Beach to Laguna Beach, and the planned community of Irvine; an alternate route leads to Mission San Juan Capistrano

Mileage: 150 miles round-trip from the downtown LA Civic Center

Take the **Santa Ana Freeway (I-5)** south from the Civic Center; an alternate route is the **San Diego Freeway (I-405).** At 34 miles, take the **Newport Freeway (Route 55)** south. At the end of the freeway it becomes Newport Boulevard, a four- to six-lane street. Continue through Costa Mesa into **(1) Newport Beach.** For more information, see the "Orange County South" chapter on page 246.

At 44 miles, get into the left lane and go over the bridge onto the **(2) Newport Peninsula.**

You'll notice the yacht anchorage in the **Lido Channel** on your left as you pass over the bridge. Continue on Newport Boulevard, which curves to the left as it follows the peninsula. Opposite the **(3) Newport Pier,** Newport Boulevard becomes **Balboa Boulevard.**

At Palm Street, turn into the parking lot for a visit to the **(4) Balboa Pier** to enjoy the ocean view. You can also rent roller skates here.

Walk across Balboa Boulevard into the **Fun Zone** for some snacks and a visit to the **(5) Balboa Pavilion.**

To get to the ferry to **(6) Balboa Island,** follow the signs from the parking lot to the crossing. The three-minute cruise across the Main Channel can be made aboard the *Admiral, Commodore,* or *Captain.* When you disembark at Agate Avenue, continue straight for one block to **Park Avenue.** Go left on Marine, through the center of the business district, and over **Back Bay Channel** on a little bridge. Continue straight a short distance to Bayside Drive, veer left, and continue up the hill to the Coast Highway. Go right, past the **(7) Fashion Island** shopping center.

For a detour, turn left at Newport Center Drive and visit the **(8) Orange County Museum of Art.**

Continue straight on the Coast Highway, past the **(9) Sherman Gardens,** and turn right on Marguerite Avenue. Go through the beautifully manicured residential streets to Ocean Boulevard. Turn left and park near the knoll that tops **(10) Corona del Mar State Beach.** This beautiful seaside area is rocky on the south and sandy on the north, and boasts a superb view. There is excellent swimming in the northern waters, which are protected by the east jetty of the Newport Harbor entrance.

Follow Ocean to Poppy Avenue and turn left, back to the Coast Highway. Turn right onto **Coast Highway** and continue south. The stretch between Poppy and Laguna Beach has rolling hills coming down to meet the undeveloped beach, giving a glimpse of what the coast was like prior to the 20th century. **(11) Crystal Cove,** just north of Laguna Beach, is a breathtaking scene, with a rock promontory and emerald-green water.

At approximately 55 miles, you enter **(12) Laguna Beach,** an area known for its beautiful scenery and painters devoted to capturing that scenery on canvas. Go left at Forest Avenue. Find a parking spot and stroll down pleasant shop-lined streets, or cross the Coast Highway to follow the Pacific Ocean along the boardwalk. For more information, see the "Orange County South" chapter on page 246.

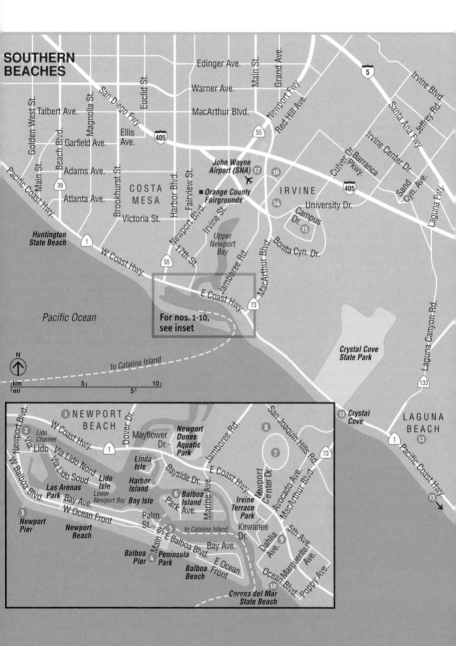

THE BEST

Felice Richter

Director of Communications, Simon Wiesenthal Center/Museum of Tolerance.

For jazz aficionados, **St. Mark's** in Venice is a happening spot.

I can quote the menu from **Remi** by heart. My friends all know that if the dinner reservations are up to me, we'll be dining at Remi and after dinner strolling along the **Promenade** in Santa Monica, where you'll find an assortment of shops, each with its own eclectic taste (and always something that you *must* have!).

I am fortunate that most of my driving around Los Angeles takes me through some of the most beautiful canyons in the West. From the **Hollywood Hills,** where you can visit **Lake Hollywood,** to the funky architecture of the houses of **Beverly Glen,** a drive through these canyons shows a side of Los Angeles that most visitors don't know about or get to see.

About one hour north of Los Angeles on I-5, you can find hiking trails up to **Mt. Pinos** that are easy on the novice hiker. The upper levels are closed during the winter months, but that only means February here! And if you are interested in snow, the town of **Frazier Park** is quaint and accommodating—and surprisingly warm considering you're in the snow!

For a bit of Los Angeles history, the **Richard J. Riordan Library** houses four levels of books, interactive computers, storytelling hours, and more. After you've exhausted yourself learning, you can step out the front entrance to the **Cafe Pinot** for delicious food and wine in the outdoor sculpture garden, designed by artist Jud Fine.

The **Museum of Tolerance** addresses today's issues of racism, prejudice, and anti-Semitism. It's definitely a one-of-a-kind experience that must not be missed!

To return to LA from this point, go north a short distance on the Coast Highway to Broadway. Go right to Laguna Canyon Road (Route 133), and then to the San Diego Freeway (I-405).

At this point, hardy souls with unflagging energy may wish to continue south to **(13) Mission San Juan Capistrano,** where the famous cliff swallows return annually to this Spanish adobe church. Follow the Coast Highway down to **Del Obispo Street,** which is just past Dana Point. Go left to **Ortega Highway (Route 74),** then left to the mission at the intersection of Ortega Highway and Camino Capistrano. To return to LA from San Juan Capistrano, take the San Diego Freeway (I-5) north from its intersection with Ortega Highway.

To continue back up to **(14) Irvine** from Laguna Beach, return north on the Coast Highway to MacArthur Boulevard (Route 73). Turn right.

Lovers of trees, education, and/or architecture may wish to detour to the **(15) University of California at Irvine.** From MacArthur, go right on University Drive to Campus Drive. Go right on Campus to Bridge Road. Go right on Bridge to North Circle View Drive, then turn left. The **Administration Building** and **Visitor Center** are located on the right-hand side of North Circle View Drive.

Meanwhile, the future takes shape in the **(16) Irvine Industrial Park,** located on both sides of MacArthur Boulevard. The simple, monolithic shapes of these structures contain businesses whose products vary from computer software to advanced technological hardware.

(17) John Wayne Airport, located on the left side of MacArthur Boulevard, is a busy commercial and small-craft airport. The terminal, designed by Leason Pomeroy Associates and Gensler & Associates in 1990, takes its shape from an airplane fuselage: three sleek vaults with rounded metal roofs.

To return to LA, go to the **San Diego Freeway (I-405)** off MacArthur Boulevard and head north.

COASTAL MOUNTAINS

Area: Some of the most scenic but easily driven coastal routes showing rugged mountains and beautiful ocean views

Mileage: Minimum of 47 miles round-trip from Ocean Avenue and Route 1 in Santa Monica; maximum of 100 miles round-trip with alternate routes from Ocean Avenue and Route 1

Begin at **Route 1** where the Santa Monica Freeway (I-10) ends near the **Santa Monica Pier.** Follow Route 1 north for five and a half miles to **Topanga Canyon Boulevard;** turn right. The highway winds past a sycamore-shaded creek. The 10,000-acre **Topanga State Park**—which by the time you read this may have become part of a massive conservation effort to preserve the entire sweep of land from Pacific Coast Highway, relocate business and homes, and turn it into an even larger state park (see Topanga Canyon, page 153)—features 18 miles of bicycle trails and 32 miles of hiking trails. Camping is permitted through special reservations; call 818/880.0350.

About two miles north of Topanga State Park is the hub of the rustic community of **(1) Topanga.** The

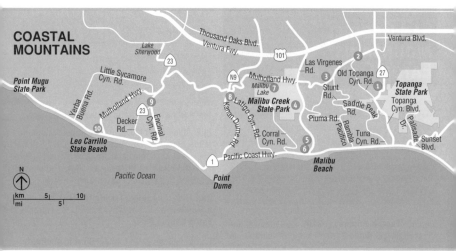

arrowness of this winding road sometimes slows traffic, particularly on the weekends.

At 15.2 miles, the road descends to a panoramic view of the **San Fernando Valley,** the **Simi Hills,** and the **Santa Susana Mountains.** This is a good place to stop and appreciate the huge expanse of the valley.

At 16.9 miles, turn left on **(2) Mulholland Drive.** A great deal of housing construction (mostly multimillion-dollar super-sizers) is going on in this once rural area.

At this point, those who wish to make only a short trip can continue straight on Topanga Canyon Boulevard to the **Ventura Freeway (Highway 101),** which takes you back to LA.

For those who wish to continue this tour, at 17.5 miles make a left near the Woodland Plaza Shopping Center onto **Mulholland Highway.** The road widens to four lanes near Daguerre Avenue but narrows back to two soon afterward.

At about 19 miles, the intersection of **Old Topanga Canyon Road** and Mulholland Highway is confusing, but continue driving straight ahead and soon a sign will appear confirming that you are indeed on **(3) Mulholland Highway.** Steep rock, jagged hills, and abrupt terrain become an interesting backdrop for the road at around 23.7 miles. Breathtakingly beautiful scenery and rock formations with all the drama of an old western movie begin at around 25.5 miles.

At 27 miles is a stoplight intersection for **Las Virgenes Road.** Turn left. The two-lane highway passes rugged, wide-open vistas of classic western scenery and horseback-riding trails. Coming up soon on the right is 7,000-acre **Malibu Creek State Park,** with more than 15 miles of hiking and equestrian trails; for information, call 818/880.0350.

At 28.7 miles is **(4) Tapia Park,** a wilderness park near Malibu Creek with great hiking paths. This is an ideal place for picnicking and relaxing.

Just south of Tapia Park the highway's name changes to **Malibu Canyon Road.** At about 30 miles, a series of gorges and steep valley formations begins. Many turnouts provide opportunities to stop and examine the intricate stratification of rock layers, all tilted upward.

At 32.5 miles, several palm trees announce the **(5) Hughes Research Laboratories,** where the first practical laser was built. The lab is at the peak of a hill, and just at the other side is a spectacular ocean view.

The road to **(6) Pepperdine University** soon appears. The intersection of the Pacific Coast Highway and Malibu Canyon Road is at 33.4 miles. Turn left to return to Santa Monica.

Alternate routes: At the intersection of Las Virgenes and Mulholland Highway, continue straight on Mulholland and go west past **(7) Malibu Lake.**

At the intersection of **Kanan Dume Road (Route N9)** and Mulholland Highway, a detour can be made through the rugged scenery of Latigo Canyon by going south (left) for a short while on N9 and then turning left on **(8) Latigo Canyon Road.**

Mulholland Highway (Route 23) loses its state highway designation to **(9) Decker Road.** You can follow Decker south to the ocean from the intersection, or continue west on Mulholland, skirting the Ventura County line until Mulholland takes you onto the **(10) Pacific Coast Highway** at Leo Carrillo State Beach.

Follow the Pacific Coast Highway back south to Santa Monica. For information, call the **National Park Service** (818/597.9192, www.nps.gov/state/ca) or the **Santa Monica Mountains National Recreation Area** (818/597.9192).

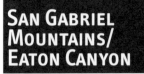

SAN GABRIEL MOUNTAINS/ EATON CANYON

Area: A vigorous driving and hiking expedition that traverses the San Gabriels from La Cañada–Flintridge to the Antelope Valley, with a hiking stop at the Arroyo Seco Cascades

Mileage: 60 miles by car from the intersection of Interstate 210 and Route 2 to the intersection of Route 14 and Interstate 5, and a four-mile hike

From the **Foothill Freeway (I-210)**, take the **Angeles Crest Highway (Route 2)** north into the mountains for 10.5 miles. At approximately a half-mile past the intersection of **Route 2** and the **Angeles Forest Highway (Route N3)**, turn right off Route 2 at the **Switzer Trail Camp.** (For information, call the **Clear Creek Station** at 818/797.9959.) The foot trail then crosses the **Arroyo Seco,** whose waters abruptly drop off into a 50-foot fall. Follow the trail uphill to a fork. Take the left branch of the fork into the gorge beneath the falls. To return, retrace your steps. Drive back to the intersection of Route 2 and the Angeles Forest Highway (Route N3). Go right for 30 minutes to the intersection with the **Antelope Valley Freeway (Route 14).** Go west to the **Golden State Freeway (I-5),** a distance of 20 miles.

Area: Hikes within Eaton Canyon, ranging from a short hike to Eaton Falls to a 16-mile jaunt to Mount Wilson; for information, call 818/398.5420 and see the map above

Mileage: 30 miles by car round-trip from the Foothill Freeway (I-210), and a half-mile to 16-mile hike

The starting point may be reached by car or bus.

Bus: Take **No. 79** north on Olive Street in downtown LA to the intersection of Huntington Drive and San Gabriel Boulevard, then transfer to **No. 264.** Get off at **New York** and **Altadena Drives** and walk one block north on Altadena to the gate of **Eaton Canyon Park.**

Car: From the **Foothill Freeway (I-210),** turn on Altadena Drive to No. 1750, which is the entrance to **Eaton Canyon Park.**

Go through the gates to the **Robert M. McCurdy Nature Center,** a quarter-mile down the path. The center has brochures for the self-guided **Arroyo Nature Trail,** as well as information on the other trails in the park and canyon. Among the possibilities are a half-mile hike to **Eaton Falls;** a three-mile climb to the **Henninger Flat Campground and Ranger Station;** a three-mile excursion to the natural stone pools in **Upper Eaton Canyon;** and a 16-mile overnighter to **Mount Wilson.**

The **San Gabriel Mountains** tower above the city to the north. A century ago, naturalist John Muir described them as among the "most rigidly inaccessible" mountains he had ever trod. Today,

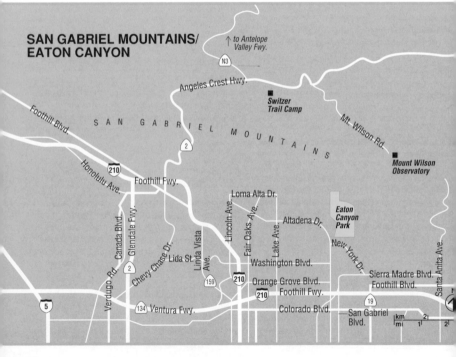

SAN GABRIEL MOUNTAINS/ EATON CANYON

these guardians are laced with trails and roads. The visitor who tours by car will see spectacular vistas from **Angeles Crest Highway (Route 2)** and **Angeles Forest Highway (Route N3),** but the serenity and majesty of the range is revealed only to those who explore it on foot. Information and maps are available from the **Angeles National Forest San Gabriel Canyon** entrance station (Route 39; 818/969.1012) or from the **National Park Service** (30401 Agoura Rd, No. 100, Agoura Hills, CA 91301; 305/370.2310, www.nps.gov/state/ca). Hikers are not required to have entry permits but are strongly urged to advise friends of their itinerary in case of an accident. All visitors should bring water and take special precautions during the fire season (from June through December).

Don't touch the shiny clusters of trilobed serrated leaves; they are poison oak. And the rattlesnakes that live in this wilderness strike only to protect themselves, so if you leave them alone, they will leave you alone.

ARCHITECTURAL TOURS

L os Angeles boasts a vast architectural heritage which, while doable on your own, is easiest explored through guided tours offered by a plethora of knowledgeable companies. The following itineraries provide roadmaps for a self-guided wide-

ranging pilgrimage to some of LA's most distinctive landmarks. The tours are color-coded. Occasionally you'll drive by a featured site that's in a color different from that of the tour you're following. Relax. Enjoy. As you'll soon find out, LA has many surprising charms. If you'd prefer to let someone else do the navigating, contact **Architours** (323/294.5821, fax 323/294.5825; info@architours.com; www.architours.com). The company offers a series of day and overnight tours that includes "Rediscovering the Southland," plus downtown walking tours, art and architecture tours, and others designed for individuals or groups.

Our **ACCESS guided tour** will delight those who prefer a modicum of walking—in typical LA fashion, you hardly have to leave your car to make this 46-mile excursion. Plan on driving about five hours. And please bear in mind that the private residences should be viewed only from the street.

THE MOSTLY ORANGE TOUR

For this tour follow the orange numbers on the map opposite. Set out from **Pasadena,** an area rich in fine turn-of-the-20th-century domestic architecture. Slightly north of the interchange of the Foothill (I-210) and Ventura (Route 134) Freeways, or north from the Orange Grove Avenue exit of the Pasadena Freeway (Route 110), is the **(1) Gamble House** (4 Westmoreland Pl; open Thursday through Sunday; admission charge), a large vacation bungalow designed in 1908 by Pasadena Craftsman architects **Charles and Henry Greene.** Other houses by the Greenes can be seen all along **(1) Arroyo Terrace,** to the west of the Gamble House.

Take Orange Grove Boulevard south to the **Pasadena Freeway.** Head south on the freeway, stay to the right, and connect with the **Hollywood Freeway (Hwy 101)** going north. Exit at Echo Park–Glendale Boulevard and turn right at the end of the exit onto Bellevue Avenue. Turn left (north) on Edgeware Road East and left again on Carroll Avenue. The 1300 block of Carroll is the **(2) Carroll Avenue Historic District.**

Take Edgeware south to Temple Street, turn left (east), continue into downtown, and turn right on Broadway. At Third Street on the left is the **(3) Bradbury Building,** which you must see from the inside in order to appreciate its interior court. Saturday tours of the lobby are conducted by the LA Conservancy (admission charge); for more information, call 213/623.2489. To continue the tour, take a right on Third, drive through the tunnel, turn right on Flower Street, and stay left at the fork. The structure on the right is the architectural wonder **(3) Walt Disney Concert Hall** designed by **Frank Gehry**. Take a right on First Street and a right on Grand Avenue. On your left at 250 Grand Avenue is the **(3) Museum of Contemporary Art (MOCA),** by internationally renowned Japanese architect **Arata Isozaki.** Continue to Fifth Street, and on your left is the **(3) Gas Company Tower** (555 W Fifth St), designed in

1991 by **Skidmore, Owings & Merrill/R. Keating, Designer.** On your right at the southwest corner is the 1926 Beaux Arts landmark **(3) Richard J. Riordan Central Library** by Bertram Goodhue and **Carleton Winslow Sr.** Turn left on Sixth Street and left on Olive Street. On your right is **(3) Pershing Square,** renovated at a cost of $14 million by Ricardo Legorreta and Hanna Olin. On your left is the restored Italianate Beaux Arts **(3) Millennium Biltmore Hotel,** designed by **Schultze & Weaver** in 1923.

Turn left onto Fifth Street and on your right is the tallest building in LA, the 73-story **(3) First Interstate World Center** (633 W Fifth St), designed in 1990 by **Pei Cobb Freed & Partners Associates/ Harold Fredenburg.** Next door are **Lawrence Halprin's** 1990 **Bunker Hill Steps.** Continue west and on your right you will see the cylindrical towers of the **(3) Westin Bonaventure Hotel** (404 S Figueroa St), designed by **John Portman** in 1976. Turn left (south) on Flower Street, right (west) on Eighth Street, and right on Figueroa. Ahead on your left you'll find the **(4) Sanwa Bank Plaza,** designed in 1991 by **AC Martin Partners.** Turn left (west) on Wilshire to see some Modernist commercial buildings. Visible at a distance is the tan terra-cotta and green-copper-trimmed tower of the **(5) I. Magnin Wilshire** building (3050 Wilshire Blvd), which was designed by **John and Donald Parkinson** in 1929. Farther west is the **(6) Wiltern Center** (3790 Wilshire Blvd), a zigzag Modernist complex of turquoise terra-cotta designed in 1931 by **Morgan, Walls & Clements.**

Turn right (north) on Western Avenue and then right (east) at Hollywood Boulevard. Enter **Barnsdall Park** on the right, before the intersection with Vermont Avenue. Here is **Frank Lloyd Wright's** first Los Angeles project, the **(7) Hollyhock House,** which was completed in 1920. Tours are offered Tuesday through Sunday (nominal admission charge); for more information, call 213/662.7272. Return to Hollywood going right (east) and turn left at Vermont Avenue. Turn right (east) on Franklin Avenue. Between Myra Avenue and St. George Street is the **Shakespeare Bridge,** a handsome open spandrel with long Gothic arches. Turn back in a westbound direction on

Franklin and turn right at Vermont Avenue. Cross Los Feliz Boulevard, and where Vermont forks, go to the left on Glendower Avenue. In a spectacular setting in the hills at 2607 Glendower Avenue is **Frank Lloyd Wright**'s stunning concrete **(8) Ennis-Brown House,** designed in 1924.

Return to Vermont and at Franklin Avenue, turn right (west). On the right is the dramatic **(9) Sowden House** (5121 Franklin Ave) by **Lloyd Wright,** Frank Lloyd Wright's son. Continue on Franklin. Three blocks past Highland, turn left (south) on Orange Drive and come up the back way to **Meyer & Holler**'s extravagant **(10) Mann's Chinese Theatre** (designed in 1927), at 6925 Hollywood Boulevard.

Turn right (south) onto Highland and left (east) onto Sunset Boulevard. At 6671 Sunset Boulevard is the **(11) Crossroads of the World,** a group of international theme shops designed by **Robert Derrah** in 1936 as a tourist attraction. Turn right (south) on Cahuenga Boulevard and right again (west) on Santa Monica Boulevard. Continue on to San Vicente Boulevard and turn left (south). The large blue-and-green glass structure at the corner of San Vicente and Melrose Avenue is the **(12) Pacific Design Center,** designed in 1975 by **Cesar Pelli** for Gruen Associates.

Backtrack on San Vicente to Sunset and turn left (west). Continue on Sunset past the **University of California, Los Angeles (UCLA),** and turn left at Veteran Avenue. At the first street, Cashmere, turn right, then right again on Greenfield Avenue. **Rudolph Schindler**'s **(13) Tischler House** (designed in 1949) is at 175 Greenfield Avenue. Take Greenfield to the end of the block and turn left (west) on Sunset. At Bundy Drive turn left (south) and at Montana Avenue turn right. Turn left on 22nd Street. At Washington Avenue and 22nd is **Frank Gehry**'s dramatic **(14) Gehry House,** a 1977-78 remodeling of an older house, using corrugated steel, wood, and glass. Go east on Washington Avenue to 26th Street and turn right. At Broadway turn right and at Ocean Avenue turn left.

To conclude the tour, drive past the white cubistic **(15) Horatio West Court Apartments** (140 Hollister Avenue) designed in 1919 by **Irving Gill,** one of California's leading Modernist architects. To get back to the Santa Monica Freeway, take Neilson Way north to Pico Boulevard and turn right. At Lincoln Boulevard turn left and you will see signs for the Santa Monica Freeway, which heads toward downtown.

THE MOSTLY GREEN TOUR

LA living has been established in style by trend-setting architects. The second tour is a sampling of the finest houses designed by modern architects (with the addition of a few excellent Revival-style homes) from Silverlake west through Hollywood to Santa Monica. For this tour, follow the green numbers on the map (on page 290).

The tour is approximately 37 miles long and takes at least three hours. The following sites are all private residences and should be viewed only from the street. Begin in **Silverlake.** The Silverlake area cannot be entered directly from Sunset. To get there, turn south on Reno Street from Sunset Boulevard, then onto Silverlake Boulevard. Follow Silverlake to the right around the reservoir. At 2300 Silverlake Boulevard is the **(16) Neutra House,** an International Style structure designed in 1933 and rebuilt in 1963 by Viennese immigrant **Richard Neutra.** Down the street are other houses by the architect: **nos. 2250, 2242, 2240, 2238, 2226, 2218, 2210,** and **2200.**

Continue north on Silverlake and turn left at its end onto Glendale Boulevard. At the fork, go left on Rowena Avenue, and at Los Feliz Boulevard turn left. Two blocks farther, at Commonwealth Avenue, turn right (north). Turn left at the third block on Dundee Drive. At the end of the street is Neutra's **(17) Lovell House** (No. 4616), designed in 1929. Return to Los Feliz and turn right (west). At Vermont Avenue turn right and veer to the left to Glendower Avenue. Winding up the hill you will reach **Frank Lloyd Wright**'s spectacular 1924 **(8) Ennis-Brown House** at 2607 Glendower Avenue.

Return to Vermont and turn right at Hollywood Boulevard. On the left is **Barnsdall Park.** See **Frank Lloyd Wright**'s first Los Angeles project, the **(7) Hollyhock House,** designed in 1917-20. Tours are held Tuesday through Sunday (admission charge); for more information, call 213/485.4581.

Return to Hollywood and turn left. At Normandie Avenue turn right (north), and at Franklin Avenue turn left (west). **Lloyd Wright**'s dramatic 1926 **(9) Sowden House** is at 5121 Franklin Avenue. Continue on Franklin and turn right (north) on Western Avenue. Take Western to its end where it veers right, connecting with Los Feliz. Get in the left lane in preparation to turn left at the first street, Ferndell Drive. Turn left again on Black Oak Drive. Turn left on Live Oak Drive East and right on Verde Oak Drive. Veer to the left on Valley Oak Drive to see **Lloyd Wright**'s copper-trimmed **(18) Samuels-Navarro House** (no. 5609), built in 1922-24.

Retrace back to Los Feliz, and at Western turn left (south). At Franklin, turn right and continue past the jog to the left at Highland Avenue. Three blocks past Highland, turn right on Sycamore Avenue and drive up to **(19) Yamashiro's Restaurant** at 1999 North Sycamore Avenue, designed as an authentic Chinese palace by **Franklin Small** in 1913.

Return to Franklin, turn right (west), then left on Sierra Bonita and right on Hollywood, which turns into Laurel Canyon Boulevard. Follow it up to Mulholland Drive and turn right (east). At Torreyson Place turn right again. From here you can see the **(20) Malin House,** also known as the **Chemosphere House,** a residence designed by **John Lautner** in 1960.

Return to Mulholland and turn left (south) on Laurel Canyon. When you reach Sunset, turn right (west). At the intersection of Cory Avenue and Sunset, take the small street to the right on Sunset Boulevard, going straight onto Doheny Road. In **Greystone Park,** the English Tudor **(21) Greystone Mansion** (501 Doheny Rd; open daily; no admission charge) was designed by **Gordon Kaufman** in 1923 for oil millionaire Edward Doheny, and today is owned by the city of Beverly Hills. For more information, call 310/550.4654.

Return to Loma Vista and head south. At Mountain Drive, veer left and turn right (west) at Sunset Boulevard. Continue on Sunset and pass the **University of California, Los Angeles (UCLA).** Turn left on Veteran Avenue and then right at Cashmere Street. Turn right on Greenfield Avenue and see Viennese immigrant architect **Rudolph Schindler**'s ingenious **(13) Tischler House** (175 Greenfield Ave), designed in 1949. Continue north on the street to return to Sunset and turn left (west). Just west of Bundy Drive turn right onto Kenter, and at the second block on the right (Skyewiay Road), turn right to see **Frank Lloyd Wright**'s redwood-and-stucco 1939 **(22) Sturgis House** at no. 449.

Return to Sunset and turn right (west). One block past Mandeville Canyon, turn right at Riviera Ranch Road. Here and on Old Oak Road are architect **Cliff May**'s original ranch houses, a style popularized throughout America during the 1940s and 1950s. Return to Sunset and turn left (east). Turn right at Rockingham Avenue. Across 26th Street, Rockingham becomes La Mesa Drive. From 26th to 19th Streets, La Mesa is draped by huge Moreton Bay fig trees, and in the 2100 to 1900 block of La Mesa are a number of **(23) Spanish Colonial Revival homes** by **John Byers** from the 1920s to 1930s. They are **nos. 2153, 2101, 2034,** and **1923.**

At the end of the road is San Vicente Boulevard. Take it to the left one block and turn right on 20th Street, jogging left at Montana Avenue. Turn left on Washington Avenue. At 1002 22nd Street, you will see the dramatic **(14) Gehry House,** a Dutch Colonial structure remodeled in 1977-78 by architect **Frank Gehry** using corrugated metal, wood, and glass. The tour concluded, you can return to the Santa Monica Freeway by heading west on Washington. At 20th, turn left to connect with the freeway.

THE MOSTLY BLUE TOUR

The next tour views a number of Spanish Colonial, Mexican, and Mission Revival buildings. It also concentrates on the Craftsman movement from the turn of the century. For this tour, follow the blue numbers on the map (on page 290).

The Pasadena area abounds in fine architecture of many styles, but the English-based Arts and Crafts movement found one of its strongest American outlets here. This tour is approximately 19 miles long and takes at least four hours. Private residences should be viewed only from the street. Begin at a location adjacent to the Pasadena Freeway (Route 110). On the west side of the freeway at the Avenue 43 exit is the **(24) Lummis House** (built between 1898 and 1910) at 200 East Avenue 43. The boulder home was built by **Charles F. Lummis,** enthusiast of the Spanish, Mexican, and Indian heritage of Southern California (tours are held on Saturday and Sunday; admission charge). Across the freeway, **(25) Heritage Square** is a bright cluster of Victorian mansions in various stages of renovation.

Now take Avenue 43 left (west) to Figueroa Street and turn left. At Marmion Way, turn right. On the corner of Marmion and Museum Drive is the **Southwest Museum,** which was designed in 1912 by **Sumner Hunt** and Silas Burns and houses an impressive collection of Southwest Indian art. A monument to the Mission style, it is embellished with architectural references to the Alhambra in Spain. Return to Figueroa and turn left. At 4603 Figueroa Street is the **(26) Casa de Adobe,** a 1917 reconstruction of a Mexican adobe house by **Theodore Eisen.** Continue on Figueroa going northeast to Arroyo Glen Street and turn right. At 6211 Arroyo Glen is the **(27) San Encino Abbey** (built between 1909 and 1925), a private residence designed by **Clyde Brown** in a combination of Spanish Mission and European Gothic styles.

Return to Figueroa and turn right, continuing northeast. At York Boulevard, turn right (east). The turn-of-the-19th-century **(27) Judson Studios** (200 S Avenue 66) are famous for their Craftsman glass and mosaic work. Return to York and turn right. Continue on as the road becomes Pasadena Avenue and then Monterey Road. At Huntington Drive, jog left and turn right (south) on San Marino, and at a fork in the road, go to the right onto Santa Anita Street. At the corner of Santa Anita and Mission Drive is the **(28) Mission Playhouse** (320 S Mission Dr), designed in 1927 by **Arthur Benton** to appear similar to the Mission San Antonio in Monterey County. Go east one block to visit the **(28) Mission San Gabriel Archangel** at 537 West Mission Drive, the fourth mission established by Father Junípero Serra. The mission was built between 1791 and 1805 and is open daily; there's an admission charge.

Now head north on Serra Drive and turn left on San Marino Avenue. Turn left on **(29) Lombardy Road** and notice the Spanish Revival homes, all private residences, in the 1700 to 2000 blocks, especially **no. 1750** by architect **Roland E. Coate; no. 1779** by **George Washington Smith,** at the corner of Allen

THE BEST

Tom LaBonge

Los Angeles City Council member

Some of my favorite things in Southern California:

1. Hiking to the top of **Mt. Hollywood**, to watch the sun rise over Los Angeles at an elevation of 1,621 feet, in **Griffith Park**

2. Chatting with the regulars sitting at the counter at **Nick's Café** near the Cornfields in downtown Los Angeles while enjoying a short stack

3. Showing off our magnificent restored **City Hall** to visitors, especially the Tom Bradley Room at the top with its 360-degree view of downtown Los Angeles

4. Taking my children to play on the trains at the **Travel Town Museum** and Live Steamers train in Griffith Park or to ride on the merry-go-round where Walt Disney took his daughter and daydreamed about building the amusement park that later became Disneyland

5. Cycling the length of the **Los Angeles River Bikeway** and envisioning how wonderful it will be when it connects all the way from the San Fernando Valley to the Pacific Ocean

6. Enjoying a patty melt and malt with constituents at **Eatz Restaurant** in **Los Feliz** or walking through the **Farmers Market** at **3rd and Fairfax** to visit with old and newer merchants, but always settling for lunch at Stall #177, the **China Depot**

7. Visiting the historical map and photography collections at the **Los Angeles Central Library**, where there's always some new discovery from the archives that piques my interest

8. Indulging in my love of photography by shooting rolls and rolls of film, especially on those rare superclear Los Angeles days from the top of **Silver Lake**, my home for nearly 50 years, looking toward the Hollywood Sign, the San Gabriel Mountains, or downtown Los Angeles

9. Crossing the landmark **6th Street Bridge** to **Boyle Heights** in the afternoon for a Foster's Freeze cone and a quick run by **Mariachi Square**

10. Joining honorees and Hollywood's Honorary Mayor Johnny Grant for a star ceremony on the **Hollywood Walk of Fame**, followed by lunch at **Musso and Frank Grill** on Hollywood Boulevard

11. Taking my family to the **Hollywood Bowl** or **Symphony in the Glen** in Griffith Park for a picnic dinner and evening concert of music

---

Avenue; **665 Allen Avenue,** another Smith house; and two **Wallace Neff** houses at **nos. 1861** and **2035 Lombardy.** Turn right (north) on Hill Avenue and go one block to California Boulevard. Across California is the campus of the **(30) California Institute of Technology.** The oldest buildings, from the 1930s, were designed by **Gordon Kaufman** in the Spanish Renaissance and Spanish Baroque styles. Note especially the **(30) Atheneum Club** facing Hill Avenue and the adjacent dorms seen as you turn left (west) onto California Boulevard. Continue on California to El Molino Avenue and turn right (north).

At 37 South El Molino Avenue is the Spanish Colonial **(31) Pasadena Playhouse,** designed in 1924-25 by architect **Elmer Grey.** Turn left at the corner of Colorado Boulevard heading west and at Fair Oaks Avenue turn left again. One block away is Green Street. Turn left and then right at Raymond Avenue. You will be in front of the large turretted Spanish Colonial **(32) Hotel Green & Castle Green Apartments,** designed in 1890-99 by architect **Frederick Roehrig.** Head north on Raymond and at Colorado Boulevard turn left (west). Turn right on Orange Grove Boulevard. Just past Walnut Street, you will see a small street flanking Orange Grove Boulevard on the left. This is Westmoreland Place. At no. 4 is the **(1) Gamble House,** built in 1908 by famous Pasadena Craftsman architects **Charles and Henry Greene** (open Thursday through Sunday; admission charge; call 818/793.3334 in advance for tours). To the west of the house is **(1) Arroyo Terrace,**

which has a number of houses designed by the Greenes. All are private residences. Pay particular attention to **nos. 368, 370, 400, 408, 424,** and **440,** which were built between 1902 and 1913.

Return to Orange Grove Boulevard and turn right. At Holly Street, one block away, turn right on Linda Vista Avenue. Turn left and then go one block to **(33) El Circulo Drive,** then turn left. At **95 El Circulo** and **825 Las Palmas Road** are two rural Spanish Revival homes designed by amateur architect **Edward Fowler** in 1927. Backtrack to Linda Vista Avenue. Turn right (north) on Holly Street and then right (east). At Orange Grove Boulevard turn right (south). Turn right at California Boulevard and note the **(34) E.-J. Cheesewright House** at 686 West California Boulevard, a 1910 Craftsman house that looks like an English snuggery with its thatch roof. At Arroyo Boulevard turn left (south). See the **(34) Batchelder House** (626 S Arroyo Blvd), built in 1909 by **Ernest Batchelder,** Pasadena craftsman and renowned tilemaker. Conclude this tour with the finest example of a Spanish Monterey–style house, the home at **(34) 850 South Arroyo Boulevard,** designed by **Donald McMurray** in 1927.

To return to the Pasadena or Ventura Freeways, turn left at Grand Avenue and right on Bellefontaine Street to get to Orange Grove. From Orange Grove you can connect with the Pasadena Freeway (Route 110) by turning right and heading south, and with the Ventura Freeway (Route 134) by turning left.

THE MOSTLY PURPLE TOUR

The next tour is a sampling of some of LA's fantastic architecture, from the serious to the whimsical. For this tour, follow the purple numbers on the map (on page 290).

A bit of fantasy abounds on almost every street of LA, so along the way you might note additional structures that have adopted the styles of other areas and other cultures, or buildings that are straightforwardly indulgent and delight in commercialism, futurism, and personal eccentricities. This route leads you around the city in an extremely broad sweep from downtown to Watts, and north to Glendale, ending in Beverly Hills.

The tour is approximately 52 miles long and takes at least four hours. Please keep in mind that the private residences should be viewed only from the street. In downtown LA the shimmering futuristic apparition at 404 S Figueroa Street is the **(3) Westin Bonaventure Hotel** by architect **John Portman.** Take Flower Street south to Olympic Boulevard and turn left. At Hill Street turn right to see the former **(35) Mayan Theater,** now the Mayan Nightclub, at 1038 South Hill Street. The pre-Columbian façade was designed by **Morgan, Walls & Clements** in 1927. Continue on Hill to Pico Boulevard and turn left (east). At the end of Pico you will come to Central Avenue and the shiplike **(36) Coca-Cola Building** (1334 S Central Ave), designed in 1935-37 by **Robert Derrah** with enormous Coke bottles at the entrance to the plant. Turn right onto Central and follow the signs on the right to enter the Santa Monica Freeway (I-10) going west (to Santa Monica). After a short distance, connect with the Harbor Freeway (I-110) south (toward San Pedro).

Turn off at the Manchester Avenue exit and go left (east). Manchester turns into Firestone Boulevard. At Elm Street turn right (Elm turns into Wilmington Avenue), and at the intersection of 107th Street, turn right again. At 1765 E 107th Street you will see the unique, monumental **(37) Watts Towers,** a personal vision fashioned of broken tile, glass, and debris between 1921 and 1954 by Italian immigrant tile-layer **Sam Rodia.** The three-tower structure was completely renovated in 2001.

Retrace your way back to the **Harbor Freeway (I-110).** Go north on the freeway (toward Pasadena) and connect with the Hollywood Freeway (Highway 101). Take the Hollywood Freeway west and get off after a short distance at the Echo Park exit. Proceed north on Echo Park Avenue to Baxter Street and turn right. At

Avon Street turn left (driving the streets around here is like riding a roller coaster). You will want to park and walk on the right (east) side of Avon, to Avon Park Terrace. There you will see what looks like an authentic Indian pueblo, the **(38) Atwater Bungalows** at 1431-33 Avon Park Terrace, built in 1931 by **Robert Stacy-Judd.**

Return to your car and at Baxter turn right. At Alvarado Street turn left and at Glendale turn right. Proceed north to Rowena Avenue and turn left. Glendale continues at the right; take it to San Fernando Road and turn left. At Grandview Avenue turn right and take it to its end.

At the intersection of Mountain Street and Grandview you will enter the **(39) Brand Library,** formerly the Brand House (built in 1902), an exotic East Indian and Moorish mansion that is now a public library. Return to Grandview and at San Fernando turn left. At Los Feliz Road turn right. Turn left at Vermont Avenue and right onto Sunset Boulevard, and you will pass the Indian **(40) Self-Realization Temple** at 4860 Sunset Boulevard and the **(11) Crossroads of the World** at 6671 Sunset Boulevard. The latter, a 1935 tourist attraction, presents a ship sailing into a courtyard of shops representing various European countries. At Highland Avenue turn right and at Hollywood Boulevard turn left. At 6925 Hollywood Boulevard you will see **(10) Mann's Chinese Theatre** (formerly **Grauman's**), an extravagant and exotic Chinese design dating from 1927.

Continue west on Hollywood and at La Brea turn left. At Santa Monica Boulevard turn right and at San Vicente Boulevard turn left (south). On the right, just north of Beverly Boulevard, is the **(41) Tail-o'-the-Pup** hot dog stand, at 329 North San Vicente Boulevard. There is also a large digital billboard displaying the diminishing number of the world's rain-forest acreage and the alarming rise in the global population.

Turn right on La Cienega Boulevard, right again on Wilshire Boulevard, and continue west into Beverly Hills. Right after the intersection of Wilshire and Santa Monica, turn right on Carmelita Avenue. At the corner of Walden Drive and Carmelita is the **(42) Spadena House** (516 Walden Dr), a 1921 Hansel-and-Gretel cottage that was originally a combined movie set and production office. From Wilshire going west, you can connect with the San Diego Freeway (I-405) to the Santa Monica Freeway (I-10).

This tour by no means covers all the fantasy architecture in Southern California. Interested viewers should also make a point to see the **(43) Avalon Casino, (44) Queen Mary, (45) Crystal Cathedral, (45) Disneyland, (46) Drive-thru Donut,** and **(47) Hollywood Sign.**

HISTORY

1771 Founding of **Mission San Gabriel.**

1781 On 4 September, Los Angeles is officially incorporated as a city. A plan for its initial settlement and layout is unveiled by Felipe de Neve, California's first governor. The population is 44 people, primarily a mix of Spanish, Mexican, Indian, and black farmers.

1818 **Avila Adobe** is built by Don Francisco Avila, mayor of the pueblo, as his town house. It later serves as the headquarters for Commodore Robert Stockton during the Mexican-American War.

1822 **La Iglesia de Nuestra Señora La Reina de Los Angeles** (Church of Our Lady of the Queen of the Angels), the city's first Catholic church, is dedicated.

1825 California becomes a territory of Mexico.

1826 The **Biscailuz Building** is constructed to house the headquarters of the United Methodist Church. It is named after Eugene Biscailuz, a Los Angeles County sheriff who helped protect the area.

1842 Gold is discovered in California near the **San Fernando Mission,** six years before the discovery at Sutters Mill.

1848 The Treaty of Guadalupe Hidalgo is signed, ending the Mexican-American War. California officially becomes part of the United States.

1850 California becomes a state.

1853 Don Matteo Keeler plants the state's first orange trees. Within a decade, Southern California becomes the top orange producer in the United States.

1869 Pio Pico, California's last Mexican governor, builds the **Pico House.**

1872 In an attempt to promote train travel to the area, the Southern Pacific Railroad hires Charles Nordhoff to write the first guidebook to Southern California. The book, *California: For Health, Pleasure, and Residence,* is a tremendous success, bringing hundreds of visitors to the state.

Biddy Mason, a former slave who became one of the richest women in the city, organizes the **First African Methodist Church** in her home.

1876 The first transcontinental railroad—the **Southern Pacific**—arrives in Los Angeles, followed shortly by the **Santa Fe Railroad** in 1885.

1880 The **University of Southern California** is founded. It has 12 teachers and 53 students.

1881 The *Los Angeles Times* publishes its first issue. (It also features home delivery—by horse-drawn carriage.)

1884 The *Los Angeles Times* begins a carrier pigeon service to and from **Catalina Island.** The birds bring information between the summer vacation colony and the mainland. The service lasts until 1887.

1892 Edward Doheny discovers oil in what is now downtown Los Angeles.

Palisades Park, encompassing more than 26 acres overlooking the Pacific Ocean, is dedicated.

1893 The **Bradbury Building** is erected. It's now the city's oldest commercial building.

1896 Welsh newspaperman Griffith J. Griffith donates 4,400 acres to the city. It becomes **Griffith Park,** one of the nation's largest urban parks.

1900 Los Angeles's population increases tenfold in 20 years (from 10,000 in 1880 to 100,000 in 1900).

1902 The **Electric Theatre,** the world's first movie house, opens on Main Street.

1904 The first Buddhist temple in the United States opens in Los Angeles.

1906 The first **Rose Bowl** football game is played.

1907 **Hollywood** becomes an incorporated city.

1909 The **Santa Monica Pier** is erected.

1910 The **Beverly Hills Hotel** is built, luring movie industry people to Beverly Hills from Hollywood.

Hollywood is annexed to the City of Los Angeles.

1911 The Nestor Company rents the old **Blondeau Tavern and Barn** at Sunset Boulevard and Gower Street and begins making movies.

1912 The first gas station in the country opens at the corner of Grand Avenue and Washington Boulevard.

1913 **Cecil B. DeMille** makes the industry's first full-length film, *The Squaw Man,* in a barn near Selma Avenue and Vine Street. (Declared a state monument, the barn has been moved and now houses the **Hollywood Studio Museum.**)

William Mulholland, head of the Los Angeles Water Department, spearheads efforts to install an aqueduct that brings water to Los Angeles and to the San Fernando Valley from some 233 miles away in the Owens Valley.

The nation's first public defender, Walton J. Wood, begins his practice on 13 June.

1914 Carl Laemmle opens **Universal Studios Hollywood,** operating on the concept that filmmaking itself is an attraction.

The first air-conditioned railroad cars begin service between Los Angeles and Chicago aboard the Atchison, Topeka, and Santa Fe Railroad's *California Limited.*

1915   D.W. Griffith produces *The Birth of a Nation.* It paves the way for the great movie palaces that were soon to take over Los Angeles and the rest of the country. Eventually, the film drew controversy over its favorable portrayal of the Ku Klux Klan.

1916   The Watts district sends the first black man, **Frederick Roberts,** to the California State Assembly.

1917   **Mary Pickford** is the first movie star to sign a million-dollar contract with a studio.

1919   William Wrigley Jr. purchases **Santa Catalina Island.**

1920   Douglas Fairbanks builds the **Pickfair mansion** in Beverly Hills for his young bride, Mary Pickford.

1923   The nation's first chinchilla farm opens in Los Angeles.

A 50-foot-high sign reading **"Hollywoodland"** is built to advertise a real estate development. In 1949, the Hollywood Chamber of Commerce buys the sign, removes the "land," and a civic symbol is born.

1927   Grauman's Chinese Theatre (now Mann's) opens. Norma Talmadge makes cement imprints of her hands and feet in the sidewalk out front, and a tradition is born.

On New Year's Eve, the **Beverly Wilshire Hotel** celebrates its grand opening.

The **Academy of Motion Picture Arts & Sciences** is officially incorporated. During the celebratory dinner at the Biltmore Hotel's Crystal Ballroom, plans for the first award ceremonies are laid, and the first sketch of the trophy is scrawled on a linen napkin by Cedric Gibbons.

1928   Los Angeles's first airport, **Mines Field,** opens on the current site of LAX. It's a single dirt strip.

1929   The airship *Graf Zeppelin* completes the first trans-Pacific flight, from Japan to Los Angeles.

1930   The **Polo Lounge** is added to the **Beverly Hills Hotel,** creating a hub for Hollywood deals and the social elite.

1931   The **California Edison Building,** the first all-electric structure, opens for business.

1932   The **Summer Olympics** take place in Los Angeles. Automatic timing and the photo-finish camera are introduced during the games.

1935   The **Griffith Observatory** is built, the legacy of a trust fund left by Griffith J. Griffith.

1939   **Union Station** is built in downtown Los Angeles. The historic landmark is one of the finer examples of California Mission-style architecture.

1940   The six-mile stretch of the new **Arroyo Seco Parkway** (later known as the Pasadena Freeway) opens for traffic. It's the first freeway in Los Angeles.

1942   New Year's Day brings an unprecedented one inch of snowfall in Los Angeles.

1945   The **Mattel company** is founded in Hawthorne. Boosted by skyrocketing sales of Barbie, it would become the world's largest toy manufacturer.

1947   The **Hollywood Freeway** opens, linking Los Angeles with the San Fernando Valley.

KTLA, the first TV station west of the Mississippi, begins broadcasting.

The **Rams,** a professional football team, come to Los Angeles from Cleveland, Ohio.

Howard Hughes designs and builds the largest wooden plane in the world, the *Spruce Goose,* and takes it out on a taxi run in the **Long Beach Harbor.** At the last minute, Hughes takes off and flies for about a mile, surprising even the flight crew.

1949   The **Pantages Theatre** in Hollywood begins hosting the Academy Awards ceremony. It will do so until 1960.

1955   **Disneyland** opens in Anaheim.

1956   The **Capitol Records Tower,** the nation's first circular office building, opens. The architectural concept is the brainchild of Capitol recording stars Nat King Cole and Johnnie Mercer.

1957   Walter O'Malley, owner of the **Brooklyn Dodgers,** moves the team west to Los Angeles.

The next year, the team plays its first games at the **Coliseum**—a doubleheader, defeating the New York Yankees and the San Francisco Giants.

1960   **John F. Kennedy** is named the Democratic presidential candidate at the party's national convention, held in Los Angeles.

The **Lakers** basketball team comes to Los Angeles from Minneapolis.

1961   Hollywood's **Walk of Fame,** which honors the leading names in entertainment, is started by the Hollywood Chamber of Commerce.

1962   **Dodger Stadium** is built on land purchased by team owner Walter O'Malley.

1964   Beatlemania comes to Los Angeles as the Fab Four perform in what will be remembered as a legendary concert at the **Hollywood Bowl.**

1966   The new **Los Angeles Zoo** opens with 1,000 animals. It will become one of the world's major collections of rare and endangered species.

1967   The *Queen Mary* docks permanently at Long Beach.

1973   Thomas Bradley, LA's first African-American mayor, is elected.

1980   According to the US census, the population of the Los Angeles/Orange County area is 10 million. Since 1880, the region has changed from a small, rural town to a world-class metropolis.

1984   The **Summer Olympic Games** are held again in LA. It is the first Games to make a profit for the Olympic Committee.

1986   The **Museum of Contemporary Art (MOCA),** designed by Arata Isozaki, is unveiled as a showplace for contemporary California artists.

1988   The **Gene Autry Western Heritage Museum,** an institution dedicated to western movie stars and the country's rodeo heritage, opens.

1990   The 62-story **First Interstate Tower,** designed by I.M. Pei, opens. As the tallest building west of Chicago, it changes the formerly low-rise skyline.

LA begins construction on its first subway system. The **Metro Rail**'s **Blue Line** opens, connecting downtown Los Angeles with Long Beach.

1991   **Malibu** becomes a separate city.

1993   The newly expanded **Los Angeles Convention Center** reopens. It's now the largest meeting facility on the West Coast.

1994   The **World Cup soccer finals** take place at the Rose Bowl.

1995   The trial of **O.J. Simpson** for the murder of ex-wife Nicole Brown Simpson and Ronald Goldman focuses the world's attention on Los Angeles for most of the year. In the end, Simpson is acquitted in a jury decision that ignites controversy throughout the country.

1997   The **Getty Center,** a 110-acre expansion of the J. Paul Getty Museum, opens in Bel Air.

1999   The **Staples Center,** lavish home of four pro sports franchises, opens its doors with a concert by Bruce Springsteen.

The **Democratic National Convention** takes LA by storm, costing the city more than they bargained for.

The **Hollywood and Highland Development Project,** a $567 million revitalization of the area between Highland Boulvard east along Hollywood Boulevard, heralds the opening of a massive retail/entertainment complex that includes the **Kodak Theater,** the new home for the annual Academy Awards spectacular.

The Archdiocese of Los Angeles **Cathedral of Our Lady of Angels** opens between Grand Avenue and Hill Street in downtown LA. The $163 million house of worship, which acts as the mother church for the Archdiocese of LA, was designed by Spanish architect José Rafael Moneo and features a 20,000- square-foot plaza, with Mission-style colonnades.

2002   The **Kodak Theater,** touted as the central landmark at the heart of TrizecHahn's **Hollywood & Highland** entertainment complex, opens. The theater seats 3,500 audience members and is the official home of the Academy Awards ceremonies, movie premieres, entertainment events, and other major celebrations.

The Frank Gehry–designed **Walt Disney Concert Hall** finally reaches completion. Located in downtown LA, the 2,290-seat home of the LA Philharmonic and Los Angeles Master Chorale features an outdoor park, restaurant, café, bookstore, and gift shop.

2003   California Governor Gray Davis is recalled in an unprecedented election that puts Hollywood's "Terminator," Arnold Schwarzenegger, in the state's driver's seat. Stay tuned, folks.

2005   LA elects **Antonio Villaraigosa** as its first Latino Mayor in 133 years.

2006   A rather uneventful year for Los Angeles, save for some celebrity trials and the beginning of one of the longest droughts in history.

2007   Not much happened this year either, save for brat pack diva Paris Hilton's celebrated incarceration and yet another celebrity murder trial (the music industry's Phil Spector). Oh yeah, O.J. was back in the news, but this time it happened in Las Vegas.

INDEX

RESTAURANTS

Only restaurants with star ratings are listed below. All restaurants are listed alphabetically in the main (preceding) index. Always call in advance to ensure a restaurant has not closed, changed its hours, or booked its tables for a private party. The restaurant price ratings are based on the average cost of an entrée for one person, excluding tax and tip.

★★★★ An Extraordinary Experience
★★★ Excellent
★★ Very Good
★ Good

$$$$ Big Bucks ($105 and up)
$$$ Expensive ($75–$100)
$$ Reasonable ($40–$70)
$ The Price is Right (less than $35)

★★★★

★★★

HOTELS

The hotels listed below are grouped according to their price ratings; they are also listed in the main index. The hotel price ratings reflect the base price of a standard room for two people for one night during the peak season.

$$$$ Big Bucks ($500 and up)
$$$ Expensive ($250–$495)
$$ Reasonable ($130–$248)
$ The Price is Right (less than $125)

$$$$

$$$